GREAT BATTLES
OF THE CIVIL WAR

GREAT BATTLES OF THE CIVIL WAR

BY THE EDITORS OF
CIVIL WAR TIMES ILLUSTRATED

Introduction by William C. Davis

GALLERY BOOKS
An Imprint of W. H. Smith Publishers Inc.
112 Madison Avenue
New York City 10016

Published by Gallery Books, an imprint of W. H. Smith, Inc., 112 Madision Avenue, New York, New York 10016.

1 2 3 4 5 6

CONTENTS

INTRODUCTION

For four painful years the young manhood of America marched and fought and bled across the landscape. They fought for principle, for glory, sometimes for plunder, and often just for the adventure of it. Whatever their cause, they fought with a ferocity never yet witnessed in this hemisphere, and never seen again since.

The battles, campaigns, skirmishes and sieges, in which they participated, have become a part of the American character. Placenames like Gettysburg, Atlanta, Manassas, Vicksburg, have come in our collective national memory to stand for the best that is in us, for heroism, endurance—and occasionally savagery—and many of the other traits that make us as a people what we are.

GREAT BATTLES OF THE CIVIL WAR offers a look backward at those men and their deeds, and "look" is perhaps the salient feature of this book, for here are not just endless lines of narrative. Here, in the old portraits, the battlefield photographs, the illustrations from the newspapers of the day, is the real "look" of America at war. Culled from public and private archives, supplemented with some of the finest battle maps ever produced for the Civil War, these pictures and the texts they illustrate offer a vivid overview of a whole continent in ferment. They present as close a look to actually being there that twentieth century mortals can hope to achieve.

These battle accounts originally appeared in the magazine CIVIL WAR

TIMES ILLUSTRATED, for twenty-five years the leading magazine in the nation covering the war between the states. Once each year an entire issue has been devoted to a single major battle or campaign. Here, now, in GREAT BATTLES OF THE CIVIL WAR, these battles are gathered together in a comprehensive illustrated account of all the major actions of that four-year drama. Some of the finest historians and writers of our time are represented in these pages, ample testimony to the eternal appeal that the Civil War wields in drawing to it not only our interest, but also our finest people of arts and letters.

It was a hard time for America. Its echoes are still heard. Even some of its pain still is felt. But most of all, its greatness is fondly remembered by a people who look back to a seemingly simpler time, when issues and decisions were perhaps more clear to the people making them, though no less painful. They were the days of a young America struggling to define itself, in a struggle that erupted onto the beautiful fields and hills of a verdant land that had not wanted war. But once war came, Americans—as usual—would not do something by halves. It was a unique conflict that has captured the interest and attention of all the world ever since. GREAT BATTLES OF THE CIVIL WAR offers ample evidence of just why that is, and why we will never lose interest as long as names like Shilo, Chickamauga, and Antietam, continue to stir our blood.

William C. Davis

FORT SUMTER

Text by Albert Castel
Designed by Frederic Ray

IN 1846 Congressman Jefferson Davis of Mississippi presented to the House of Representatives a resolution calling for the replacement of Federal troops in all coastal forts by state militia. The proposal died in committee, and shortly thereafter Davis resigned from Congress to lead the red-shirted 1st Mississippi Rifles to war and glory in Mexico.

Now it was the morning of April 10, 1861, and Davis was President of the newly proclaimed Confederate States of America. As he met with his cabinet in a Montgomery, Alabama hotel room he had good reason to regret the failure of that resolution fifteen years earlier. For had it passed, he would not have had to make the decision he was about to make: Order Brigadier General P.G.T. Beauregard, commander of Confederate forces at Charleston, South Carolina to demand the surrender of the Federal garrison on Fort Sumter in Charleston Harbor.

But before Davis made this decision, other men had made other decisions—a fateful trail of decisions leading to that Montgomery hotel room on the morning of April 10, 1861.

IN A SENSE the first of those decisions went back to 1829 when the War Department dumped tons of granite rubble brought from New England on a sandspit at the mouth of Charleston Harbor. On the foundation so formed a fort named after the South Carolina Revolutionary War hero, Thomas Sumter, was built.

Fort Sumter as it appeared before the outbreak of hostilities. Painting by Seth Eastman.

10

However, it was built very slowly, as Congress appropriated the needed money in driblets. Thirty-one years later it was over 80 percent complete, though without a garrison and with most of its cannons unmounted. Even so, potentially it was quite formidable. Surrounded by the sea, its five-sided brick walls stood 50 feet high and varied in thickness from 12 feet at the base to 8½ feet at the top. Adequately manned, gunned, and supplied, it could—and in fact eventually would—resist the most powerful assaults.

THREE AND A THIRD MILES to the northwest across the harbor lay Charleston. Here on December 20, 1860 a state convention voted unanimously that "the union now subsisting between South Carolina and other States, under the name of 'The United States of America,' is hereby dissolved." During the rest of that day and all through the night jubilant crowds celebrated.

To South Carolinians the election of the "Black Republican" Abraham Lincoln to the presidency in November had been tantamount to a declaration of war by the North on the South. They had responded by secession, the doctrine so long advocated by their great leader John C. Calhoun, now lying in Charleston's St. Philip's churchyard beneath a marble monument. Soon, they were confident, the other slave states would join them in forming a glorious Southern Confederacy.

Secession Hall, Charleston, South Carolina, scene of the passage of the Ordinance of Secession. Drawing from a photograph.

CHARLESTON
MERCURY
EXTRA:

Passed unanimously at 1.15 o'clock, P. M., December 20th, 1860.

AN ORDINANCE

To dissolve the Union between the State of South Carolina and other States united with her under the compact entitled "The Constitution of the United States of America."

We, the People of the State of South Carolina, in Convention assembled, do declare and ordain, and it is hereby declared and ordained,

That the Ordinance adopted by us in Convention, on the twenty-third day of May, in the year of our Lord one thousand seven hundred and eighty-eight, whereby the Constitution of the United States of America was ratified, and also, all Acts and parts of Acts of the General Assembly of this State, ratifying amendments of the said Constitution, are hereby repealed; and that the union now subsisting between South Carolina and other States, under the name of "The United States of America," is hereby dissolved.

THE
UNION
IS
DISSOLVED!

Notice of adoption of South Carolina's Ordinance of Secession.

Jefferson Davis, President of the Confederacy, made the fateful decision that began the war with the firing on Fort Sumter.

11

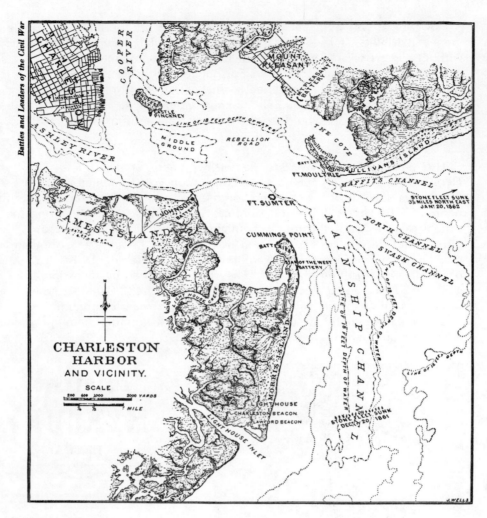

Fiery Governor Francis W. Pickens of South Carolina urged immediate seizure of Fort Sumter after the Ordinance of Secession.

Map of Charleston Harbor and vicinity, showing the strategic position of Fort Sumter at the mouth of the harbor.

Secretary of War John B. Floyd selected Major Anderson to command the garrison at Fort Moultrie, possibly hoping that Anderson would favor the secessionists.

Meanwhile South Carolina would be a nation among nations. For that reason the continued presence of "foreign" United States troops in the forts which controlled Charleston's harbor was more than irritating—it was intolerable. They must go!

Hopefully the Federal Government would pull them out. To that end Governor Francis Pickens of South Carolina appointed three commissioners to go to Washington and negotiate the evacuation of the forts. But if the troops did not leave voluntarily, they would have to be removed.

That did not appear difficult to accomplish. Hundreds of militia, Citadel cadets, and freelance volunteers were gathering in Charleston, spoiling for a fight. In contrast the United States soldiers numbered a scant eighty-five— nine officers and seventy-six enlisted men, of whom eight of the latter were musicians. Furthermore, nearly all of these troops were stationed in Fort Moultrie on Sullivan's Island. Designed to repel sea attack, this fort was practically defenseless on its land side: Overlooking it were high sand dunes from which riflemen could slaughter the garrison.

IN 1780 Major Richard Anderson gallantly but unsuccessfully defended the original Fort Moultrie against British assault. Eighty years later his son, Major Robert Anderson of the 1st United States Artillery, arrived at the new Fort Moultrie and took command of the Federal troops stationed at Charleston.

Secretary of War John B. Floyd of the lame-duck Buchanan Administration personally selected him for the post in November 1860. Fifty-five, a West Pointer, and twice promoted for bravery in battle, he was an experienced and competent officer—exactly what was needed at Charleston. Moreover, his background should have been reassuring to the Carolinians. As a Kentuckian he qualified as a Southerner, he had owned slaves, and his wife came from an aristocratic Georgia family. Indeed, it is just possible that Floyd, a Virginian, hoped that the major would do what he himself was already doing: support secession.

If so, Floyd had picked the wrong man. Anderson may have been a Southerner but he was dedicated to "Duty, Honor, Country." Above all he was resolved to do everything in his power consistent with those principles to avoid a clash at Charleston that might plunge the nation into civil war.

That is why Fort Moultrie's vulnerability alarmed him. As early as November 23 he reported to the War Department that the Carolinians have "a settled determination . . . to obtain possession of this work." Since then they had made their determination even more evident. Should they attack, duty would compel him, despite the odds, to resist. And that meant war.

Hence he decided to transfer his troops to Fort Sumter. There they would be much more secure and so would peace. For on being confronted with a target less tempting than Moultrie, presumably the Carolinians would be less bellicose.

To be sure, Floyd had instructed him on December 11 to "avoid every act which would needlessly tend to provoke" the Carolinians. But Floyd had

Major Robert Anderson (later Major General), unhappy defender of Fort Sumter.

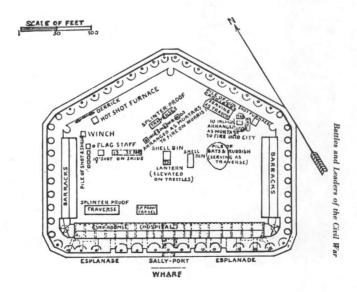

The ground plan of Fort Sumter, based on an official drawing.

13

Evacuation of Fort Moultrie by Major Anderson on the night of December 26-27, 1860.

Colonel J. Johnston Pettigrew, Pickens' messenger to the fort, later became an able general in the Army of Northern Virginia.

14

also authorized him to move his command to either of the other two forts in Charleston Harbor should he have "tangible evidence of a design to proceed to a hostile act." He ignored a "confidential" letter from Floyd, received December 23, which in effect urged him to surrender the forts rather than "make a vain and useless sacrifice of your life and the lives of the men under your command, upon a mere point of honor." Also he was unaware that on December 10 President Buchanan had informally promised a group of South Carolina congressmen that no change would be made in the military status quo at Charleston.

The transfer to Fort Sumter took place December 26-27. Private John Thompson described how it was managed in a letter to his father in Ireland:

> Our Commander set about fortifying himself in Moultrie, with such unparalelled [sic] vigor that our opponents soon became thoroughly convinced that he intended to make a desperate stand in the position he then held, and the duty of watching us was performed with a laxity corresponding to the strength of their conviction. So completely did our Commander keep his own counsel, that none in the garrison[,] officer or soldier[,] even dreamed that he contemplated a move . . .
>
> On the night of the 26th Dec. shortly after sun down, we were formed in heavy marching order and quietly marched out of Moultrie leaving only a few men behind on Guard, and embarking on board a number of small boats . . . were safely landed in Sumter.

Several schooners carrying food, munitions, medical supplies, and forty-five army wives and children followed the soldiers. In the morning the rear guard also made the crossing after spiking Moultrie's cannons and setting fire to their carriages.

THE COLUMN of smoke which rose from Moultrie merely confirmed what had been reported in Charleston by the crew of a harbor patrol boat: The Federals had slipped away to Sumter. The Carolinians fumed with anger and chagrin, and Governor Pickens promptly sent Colonel J. Johnston Pettigrew to the fort.

Pettigrew accused Anderson of breaking Buchanan's December 10 promise to maintain the existing military situation at Charleston. Anderson replied, truthfully enough, that he knew of no such promise, that he had every

right to move to Sumter, and that he had done so to protect his men and prevent bloodshed. "In this controversy between the North and South," he added, "my sympathies are entirely with the South"—but his duty came first.

"Well, sir," said Pettigrew with a bow, "however that may be, the Governor of the State directs me to say to you, courteously but peremptorily, to return to Fort Moultrie."

"I cannot and will not go back," answered Anderson.

Pettigrew left. Soon afterward, at noon, Anderson assembled his troops on Sumter's parade ground. Chaplain Matthias Harris delivered a prayer of thanksgiving; then to the accompaniment of the band playing "Hail Columbia" Anderson personally raised the United States flag that he had brought from Moultrie to the top of a pole, where it waved above the fort.

In Charleston Pickens, on learning that Anderson refused to return to Moultrie, ordered the state troops to seize that fort, Castle Pinckney, and the Federal arsenal, treasury, customhouse, and post office. He believed that he was carrying out justified retaliation against aggression. Instead he committed a bad blunder.

Harper's Weekly, January 12, 1861

Major Anderson's command enters Fort Sumter on the night of December 26, 1860 in the transfer from Fort Moultrie.

Harper's Weekly, January 12, 1861

Occupation of Castle Pinckney by the Charleston militia, December 27, 1860, in retaliation for Anderson's move to Fort Sumter from Fort Moultrie.

BUCHANAN would retain the constitutional powers of the presidency until March 4, 1861. However, he no longer possessed its moral and political authority, he was old and tired, and his overriding desire was to finish out his term in peace—and with the nation still at peace.

To that end he sought to appease the South and thus prevent war. The North, he declared, was to blame for the sectional crisis. Secession, he announced, was unconstitutional—but so would be any attempt of the Federal Government to resist it by "coercion." He refused to reinforce the tiny garrison at Charleston and even ordered it to return muskets and ammunition it had drawn from its own arsenal. This was in keeping with his December 10 promise to the South Carolina congressmen which, along with the instructions sent Anderson, he hoped would keep the Charleston powder keg from exploding.

On December 26 the three commissioners appointed by Pickens to negotiate the evacuation of the Charleston forts arrived in Washington. William Trescot, a South Carolinian who was acting as an intermediary, informed Buchanan of their arrival and purpose. Buchanan replied that he would see them "as private gentlemen" and that he would submit to Congress their proposal that the forts and other Federal facilities in Charleston be turned over to South Carolina in exchange for a fair monetary compensation.

Residence of the South Carolina commissioners in Washington, D.C.

President James Buchanan and his cabinet. Left to right seated: Secretary of Interior Jacob Thompson, Secretary of War John B. Floyd, Secretary of Navy Isaac Toucey, Attorney General Jeremiah Black. Standing: Secretary of State Lewis Cass, President Buchanan, Secretary of Treasury Howell Cobb, Postmaster General Joseph Holt.

Senator Louis T. Wigfall of Texas received Anderson's surrender of Fort Sumter. A Brady photograph.

Edwin McM. Stanton, Black's replacement as Attorney General, strongly advised against ordering Anderson to return to Fort Moultrie.

The following morning the commissioners were discussing matters in the mansion Trescot had rented for them when a burly, bearded man came slamming through the door. He was Senator Louis T. Wigfall of Texas, a native South Carolinian and fanatical secessionist. A telegram, he announced, had just arrived from Charleston: Anderson had spiked his guns at Moultrie and moved his troops to Sumter.

The commissioners refused to believe it. So did Secretary of War Floyd, who also showed up. Then came another telegram from Charleston confirming the first.

Trescot, accompanied by two top Southern leaders, Senators Jefferson Davis of Mississippi and Robert M.T. Hunter of Virginia, hastened to the White House. Davis told the President the news from Charleston. Buchanan was dumbfounded. "I call God to witness," he exclaimed, "this is not only without but against my orders. It is against my policy."

The Southerners urged him to order Anderson back to Moultrie. Otherwise, they warned, South Carolina almost surely would seize the other forts, attack Sumter, and begin civil war. But he refused to do so until he had consulted with his cabinet.

At the cabinet meeting Floyd charged that Anderson had disobeyed orders. Secretary of State Jeremiah S. Black, a Pennsylvanian, disagreed. To settle the issue, Buchanan and his secretaries examined a copy of Anderson's December 11 instructions. There it was, the authorization to leave Moultrie "whenever you have tangible evidence of a design to proceed to a hostile act." Obviously what constituted "tangible evidence" had to be determined by Anderson—and he had so determined.

Nevertheless, Floyd (who had been asked several days previously by Buchanan to resign for having misappropriated $870,000 of government funds) insisted that Anderson be ordered back to Moultrie. Unless this was done, he argued, Buchanan would be guilty of breaking his "pledge" to the South Carolina congressmen.

Attorney General Edwin Stanton, backed by the other Northern cabinet members, took a different view. "A President of the United States who would make such an order," he asserted, "would be guilty of treason."

"Oh, no! not so bad as that, my friend!" cried Buchanan in dismay. "Not so bad as that!"

The cabinet meeting ended without a decision. Several days later Floyd finally resigned. Eventually as commander of Confederate forces at Fort Donelson he would render great service—to the Union cause.

On December 28 the South Carolina commissioners visited the White House. They demanded that Anderson's troops be removed from Charleston Harbor, "as they are a standing menace which renders negotiations impossible and threatens a bloody issue." They also pressed for an immediate reply to this ultimatum.

Again Buchanan refused to commit himself: "You don't give me time to consider; you don't give me time to say my prayers. I always say my prayers when required to act upon any great State affair."

As Trescot shrewdly noted, Buchanan had "a fixed purpose to be undecided." Yet he could not avoid making a decision much longer. What would it be?

His impulse was to grant the Carolinians their demand: Anything to forestall war. But he felt countervailing pressures. The North cheered Anderson's action and hailed the pro-Southern major as a hero. To repudiate what he had done by ordering him to evacuate Sumter would raise a storm that might result in impeachment. Moreover, Black, a close friend, declared that he would resign if the Sumter garrison was pulled out—and undoubtedly the other Northern cabinet members would follow suit.

Harper's Weekly, January 26, 1861

Left: Guns and gun carriages dismantled by Major Anderson at Fort Moultrie prior to his move to Fort Sumter.

Harper's Weekly, January 26, 1861

Right: Confederate battery at Fort Moultrie, its guns bearing on Fort Sumter. Note South Carolina's Palmetto Flag.

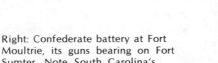

What tipped the balance, however, was Pickens' seizure of Moultrie, Pinckney, and the other Federal installations in Charleston. This was, Black pointed out, an act of aggression which could not be justified. It was also something which could not be ignored by a President of the United States without violating his oath of office.

Hence on December 30 Buchanan sent a reply, drafted by Black, to the South Carolina commissioners. After referring to the "armed action" taken by South Carolina against Federal property in Charleston, Buchanan stated: "It is under . . . these circumstances that I am urged immediately to withdraw the troops from the harbor of Charleston, and am informed that without this, negotiation is impossible. This I cannot do: This I will not do." Instead, Sumter would be defended, and "I do not perceive how such a defense can be construed into a menace of the city of Charleston."

Having thus decided, Buchanan next gave the commanding general of the army, Winfield Scott, the go-ahead on a plan proposed by him earlier: To send the warship *Brooklyn* with supplies and 250 troops from Fort Monroe in Virginia to reinforce Sumter.

AT SUMTER Anderson's soldiers and a number of loyal civilian workers busily prepared to resist attack, which they expected at any time. They had a lot to do. Although the fort contained sixty-six cannons, only fifteen had been mounted prior to their arrival. Forty-one unfinished embrasures resulted in as many eight-foot square holes in the ramparts. There was plenty of powder and shot, but it lay scattered about the parade ground amidst piles of bricks and sand. Means for repelling a landing on the wharf, which lay outside the wooden gate on the south or gorge wall, were practically nonexistent.

Kean Archives

Lieutenant General Winfield Scott, military adviser to President Buchanan, was not optimistic about reinforcing Fort Sumter.

Fortunately for the garrison, the Carolinians thought the fort impregnable. "Twenty-five well-drilled men could hold it against all Charleston," warned the Charleston *Courier* on December 31. "Its batteries could level Fort Moultrie with the ground in a few hours, and shell the city effectively. . . ." Besides, the South Carolinians were confident that Buchanan would evacuate the fort, thus making an attack unnecessary.

Hence they concentrated on building up their own defenses. They removed the soft iron nails with which the Federals, for lack of anything better, had spiked Moultrie's cannons, then remounted the big guns on new carriages. At the same time they constructed a battery on the east shore of Morris Island parallel to Charleston Harbor's main channel. Hundreds of black slaves and white volunteers did the work. Among the latter was 67-year-old Edmund Ruffin of Virginia. For years he had dreamed and preached secession. Now he had come to Charleston to "commit a little treason."

While the Carolinians labored, so did the garrison. By early January Anderson was able to report to the War Department that he could "hold this fort against any force which can be brought against me," and that therefore the government could reinforce him "at its leisure."

This was exactly what the government was doing. First Buchanan postponed sending the *Brooklyn* to Sumter until the South Carolina commissioners replied to his rejection of their ultimatum. Then General Scott had some second thoughts—he feared that the deep-draft *Brooklyn* would have trouble crossing the bar of Charleston Harbor and that Virginia secessionists might seize Fort Monroe if its garrison was reduced. So with Buchanan's approval he arranged to charter the unarmed paddle wheeler *Star of the West*

Rabid secessionist Edmund Ruffin fired the first shot from the Iron Battery against Fort Sumter.

Officers at Fort Sumter, 1861. Left to right, seated: Abner Doubleday, Major Robert Anderson, Samuel W. Crawford, J.G. Foster. Standing: G. Seymour, G.W. Snyder, Jefferson C. Davis, R.K. Mead, T. Talbot.

at New York, where several days were consumed loading her with supplies and 200 troops. He and Buchanan also hoped that a vessel of this type would be less provocative to the Carolinians than a warship.

Because of this shilly-shallying the relief expedition did not set forth until January 5. Worse, not until that date did the War Department get around to dispatching a letter to Anderson informing him that the *Star of the West* was on the way with reinforcements and instructing him to aid the ship if she was attacked. Furthermore, instead of sending this vital message by special courier, it entrusted it to the regular mail, apparently oblivious to the possibility that the South Carolina authorities might be intercepting all letters to Sumter—which in fact they had been doing for a week.

Consequently Anderson and his men remained unaware that a relief expedition was on the way. In fact, they were about the only ones in the Charleston area who did not know. Despite efforts by Buchanan and Scott to keep the *Star of the West*'s voyage secret, Southern sympathizers in Washington and New York provided ample advance warning. Panic gripped Charleston, and the South Carolina forces frantically prepared to beat back the Yankee ship when it appeared. However, their commander openly doubted that his ill-trained artillerists could hit a fast-moving steamer and predicted that Sumter's guns would blast Moultrie off the face of the earth.

At dawn January 9 the *Star of the West*, with 200 soldiers below deck, entered Charleston's main channel. When she was two miles from Sumter the Morris Island battery, which had been alerted by a patrol boat, opened fire. George Haynesworth, a Citadel cadet, touched off the first cannon. He missed. So did most of the other rounds from the battery's two cannons. Soon the *Star of the West* passed by, having suffered only minor damage.

From the ramparts of Sumter, Anderson watched the approaching ship through a spyglass. The normally calm major appeared "excited and uncertain what to do." He could see that the Carolinians were shooting at an unarmed

Firing on the *Star of the West* from the South Carolina battery on Morris Island, January 10, 1861.

Harper's Weekly, January 26, 1861

The Soldier in Our Civil War

vessel flying the United States flag, and only the day before he had read in the Charleston *Mercury* that the *Star of the West* was heading for Sumter with reinforcements. However, that rabidly secessionist paper was notoriously unreliable, and in any event he had no official information or instructions concerning the ship. Besides, the Morris Island battery was beyond the reach of Sumter's guns.

Then the *Star of the West* came within range of Fort Moultrie, which opened up on her. Anderson's gunners eagerly expected his order to return the fire. However, one of his officers, Lieutenant Richard K. Meade of Virginia, pleaded with him not to give the order: "It will bring civil war on us." In contrast, Captain Abner Doubleday, the New York-born "inventor of baseball," stamped his feet in frustration, and a soldier's wife attempted by herself to fire a cannon aimed at Moultrie!

Meanwhile, shot and shell rained about the *Star of the West* and an armed schooner approached her. Concluding that he could expect no assistance from Sumter, and fearful of sinking or capture, the *Star of the West*'s captain turned his ship about and headed back to sea.

On seeing the ship retreat, Anderson decided not to fire on Moultrie. Instinct and training urged him to do so, but while there remained the slightest chance of peace he would not strike the blow that could lead only to war.

BY ALL PRECEDENTS of law and history the Federal Government would have been justified in employing the full power of its armed forces against South Carolina for having fired on the *Star of the West*. It did nothing of the kind, nor did Buchanan even consider such action. First of all the armed forces of the United States were not very powerful. To be sure, the navy probably could have bombarded Charleston in retaliation, but the bulk of the army was scattered throughout the West, barely holding its own against the Indians.

More importantly, the free states were not ready for a showdown over secession. Most Northerners hoped for, even expected, another great sectional compromise like the ones in 1820, 1833, and 1850. Many of them believed that South Carolina was merely "throwing a tantrum," that the talk of a Southern Confederacy was simply a bluff designed to extract concessions. Others.

The *Star of the West,* with supplies for Major Anderson, is fired on from Fort Moultrie and the Morris Island batteries as she approaches Fort Sumter.

Benson Lossing, Civil War in America

The old Custom House in Charleston.

Harper's Weekly, January 26, 1861

BROAD STREET. "MERCURY" OFFICE. CUSTOM HOUSE. CASTLE PINCKNEY. FORT MOULTRIE. FORT SUMTER. MORRIS ISLAND.

Wartime Charleston, South Carolina, looking toward Fort Sumter.

Battles and Leaders of the Civil War

Lieutenant Adam J. Slemmer, aggressive defender of Fort Pickens.

mainly Democrats, sympathized with the Southerners, whom they viewed as defending themselves against Republican radicalism. Thus Democratic Congressman John Logan of Illinois compared the Dixie secessionists to the patriots of the Revolution. At the opposite ideological extreme, such prominent abolitionists as William Lloyd Garrison, Wendell Phillips, Charles Sumner, and Horace Greeley expressed a willingness to "let the erring sisters go in peace." That way the United States would rid itself of the sin of slavery!

Hence, as George T. Strong, a disgusted New Yorker who favored retaliation against South Carolina, wrote in his diary, "The nation pockets this insult to the national flag, a calm, dishonorable, vile submission."

THE ATTEMPT to reinforce Sumter incensed the Southern secessionists, who saw it as coercion. At the same time the repulse of the *Star of the West* and the failure of the North to react to it made them all the more confident that the money-grubbing Yankees would not dare fight to keep the South in the Union. Senator Judah P. Benjamin of Louisiana sneered that the Federal Government in effect had relinquished all claim to sovereignty. Jefferson Davis met with other Cotton State senators in Washington to plan a convention at Montgomery, Alabama for the establishment of an independent confederacy. During January Georgía, Florida, Alabama, Mississippi, and Louisiana seceded and Texas prepared to do the same.

As these states pulled out, their militia took over Federal arsenals, forts, customhouses, and post offices. Nowhere did they encounter resistance. Thus on January 12 semi-senile Commodore James Armstrong surrendered the Pensacola Navy Yard to Florida and Alabama troops. However, two days

Front view of Fort Pickens, Pensacola, showing the sally port and glacis.

Harper's Weekly, March 9, 1861

before 1st Lieutenant Adam Slemmer, anticipating such an eventuality, had transferred forty-six soldiers and thirty sailors from nearby Fort Barrancas to powerful Fort Pickens on Santa Rosa Island in Pensacola Bay.

Following the seizure of the naval yard, representatives of the governors of Florida and Alabama demanded the surrender of Fort Pickens (named after the grandfather of the South Carolina governor). Slemmer replied, "I am here by authority of the President of the United States, and I do not recognize the authority of any governor to demand the surrender of United States property,—a governor is nobody here."

Thanks to Slemmer's initiative, the Federal Government now held another fort off the coast of a seceded state. Like Sumter it was too strong for the secessionists to seize immediately, but unlike the Charleston fort its location made reinforcement easy.

Confederate "water battery" at Pensacola, 1861.

National Archives

ANDERSON had refrained from blasting Fort Moultrie. Nevertheless, he was angered by the firing on the United States flag. As soon as the *Star of the West* steamed out of sight he dispatched a note to Governor Pickens. In it he threatened to close Charleston Harbor—which he could readily do—unless Pickens disavowed the attack on the ship as having been made without his "sanction or authority."

Pickens answered that the attempt to reinforce Sumter was a deliberate act of hostility, and that to close the harbor would be to impose on South Carolina "the condition of a conquered province"—something it would resist. In effect he countered Anderson's threat with a threat of his own: all-out war.

Since this is what Anderson hoped to avoid, he agreed in subsequent negotiations to a de facto truce while one of his officers, Lieutenant Theodore Talbot, went to Washington for instructions. For his part Pickens allowed mail to enter Sumter and the women and children to leave. Moreover, the garrison could purchase bread, meat, and vegetables (but not flour) in Charleston, and a South Carolina officer sent over several cases of claret.

Notwithstanding these friendly gestures, Pickens was anxious to attack Sumter. Two factors restrained him. First, a number of other Southern leaders cautioned him that precipitate action at Charleston might produce war before a confederacy could be organized. Thus Jefferson Davis wrote him on January 20 that the "little garrison" at Sumter "presses on nothing but a point of pride . . . you can well aford [*sic*] to stand still . . . and if things continue as they are for a month, we shall then be in a condition to speak with a voice that all must hear and heed. . . ."

The other and more basic factor was that Pickens lacked the means to assault Sumter successfully. Time was needed to furnish these means, the truce supplied the time, and the governor made the most of it. At his orders four hulks crammed with stones were sunk in the main channel in order to block future relief ships (though the tide soon swept the sunken hulks away). Working day and night, militiamen and slaves added more guns to Moultrie, strengthened the "Star of the West Battery," established an "Iron Battery" on Cumming's Point due south of Sumter, built batteries at Fort Johnson on James Island, implanted additional cannons at various other places, and constructed an ironclad "Floating Battery."

Battles and Leaders of the Civil War

The garrison watched as the "enemy" surrounded Sumter with a circle of fire. Captain Doubleday, who was second in command, proposed to Anderson that he tell the Carolinians to cease work, and that if they refused, to level their still-vulnerable fortifications. But the major rejected his advice. Even had he been willing personally to accept it, he could not. His orders from the new Secretary of War, Joseph Holt, echoed those from Floyd: He was to "act strictly on the defensive."

Furthermore, the Carolinians represented no immediate or direct danger to the fort. By January 21 the garrison had fifty-one guns in position, among them two 10-inchers planted in the parade ground as mortars. Also the soldiers and the forty-three remaining civilian workers had closed the open embrasures and prepared a variety of devices calculated to inflict ghastly casualties on storming parties. Some cannoneers, experimenting with one of the 10-inchers, discovered that Charleston itself could be bombarded: Using only a small powder charge, they splashed a cannonball near the city's waterfront.

What worried Anderson—and all of his men—was the long-range prospect. Despite purchases in Charleston, food stocks were dwindling steadily. At the same time the ever-increasing strength of the Carolina batteries, Anderson notified the War Department, "will make it impossible for any [relief expedition] other than a large and well-equipped one, to enter this harbor. . . ." In short, unless relieved or evacuated soon, the garrison would starve.

View of Fort Johnson from
Fort Sumter.

Harper's Weekly, March 2, 1861

BUCHANAN realized Anderson's predicament. But after the *Star of the West* fiasco he returned to his basic policy of appeasing the South—which probably was for the best, given the fragmented and fluctuating state of public opinion in the North.

Hence when Lieutenant Talbot returned from Washington to Sumter on January 19, he brought instructions from Secretary of War Holt which boiled down to this: The government did not "at present" intend to reinforce or supply the fort. An "attempt to do so would, no doubt, be attended by a collision of arms and the effusion of blood—a national calamity which the President is most anxious, if possible, to avoid. . . ." But if Anderson decided he needed more troops and supplies, he was to inform the War Department at once, "and a prompt and vigorous effort will be made to forward them."

In other words, the peace-seeking major was asked to decide whether there would be war. It was a decision that he was not prepared to make.

AT ABOUT THE SAME TIME that Talbot reported back to Sumter, Buchanan agreed to let General Scott send the *Brooklyn* with a company of Regulars to Fort Pickens. As already noted, the Florida fort differed from Sumter in that there was no way the secessionists could block access to it, thus there was little risk of an armed clash. Meanwhile three other United States warships took stations in Pensacola Bay.

Former United States Senator Stephen R. Mallory of Florida, soon to be the highly competent Confederate Secretary of the Navy, assessed the situation at Pensacola and found it inauspicious. Therefore, through Washington intermediaries, he proposed a deal: If the Federal Government promised not to reinforce Fort Pickens or try to retake the naval yard, he pledged that no attack would be made on Slemmer's garrison. Buchanan agreed to this de facto truce, even though it meant that the government was refraining from doing what it could do easily, whereas the secessionists merely promised not to do what they were incapable of doing successfully. When the *Brooklyn* arrived February 9, it landed supplies but not troops at Fort Pickens, then joined the other Federal ships nearby. As for the secessionists, they stepped up their preparations for an attack on the fort.

USS *Brooklyn,* relief ship for Fort Pickens.

Harper's Weekly, March 9, 1861

Inauguration of Confederacy's President
Jefferson Davis at Montgomery,
Alabama, February 18, 1861.

ON FEBRUARY 18, 1861 the sun shone brightly over Montgomery, Alabama.
Jefferson Davis, standing on the portico of the state capitol, took the oath
of office as the first President of the Confederate States of America.

So far, however, the Confederacy consisted of only seven states, all from
the Lower South. The Upper South (Virginia, North Carolina, Tennessee,
and Arkansas) and the slaveholding Border States (Delaware, Maryland,
Kentucky, and Missouri) remained outside the fold. Even worse, a foreign flag,
that of the United States, waved over forts in two of the Confederacy's main
ports, flouting its claim to independence.

Davis pondered the situation, decided what had to be done, then did it.
Late in February he dispatched three commissioners—Martin J. Crawford,
John Forsyth, and A.B. Roman—to Washington. He instructed them to
seek recognition of the Confederate States by the United States and to settle
"all questions of disagreement between the two governments"—that is, induce
the Federal Government to evacuate Sumter and Pickens.

Next, early in March he sent Brigadier General P.G.T. Beauregard to
Charleston and Brigadier General Braxton Bragg to Pensacola. Both had the
same orders: As rapidly as possible make all preparations necessary to take,
respectively, Fort Sumter and Fort Pickens.

Davis hoped that Crawford, Forsyth, and Roman would succeed in persuading
Washington to let the South and the two forts go in peace. But if they failed,

Battles and Leaders of the Civil War

Brigadier General Braxton Bragg.

time would have been gained for the Confederacy to acquire the means to assert its independence and take the forts by war. Either way, peace or war, the result would be the same: the establishment of a great new nation embracing all of the slave states.

MARCH 4, 1861 was dreary and chilly in Washington, D.C. Standing on a wooden platform in front of the domeless Capitol, Abraham Lincoln donned his steel-rimmed spectacles and began reading his inaugural address. The crowd listened intently. Since his election nearly five months earlier he had not given the slightest public clue as to what he proposed to do about secession in general and Forts Sumter and Pickens in particular. Now, surely, he would announce his decision on these matters.

He did so. Secession, he said in essence, was unconstitutional and unjustifiable. The seceded states remained in the Union. He would not send troops into any state nor interfere with slavery. But he would "hold, occupy, and possess" those places in the South still under Federal control—e.g., Sumter and Pickens. Should they be attacked, they would be defended.

"In your hands, my dissatisfied fellow countrymen, and not in mine, is the momentous issue of civil war. The Government will not assail *you*. You can have no conflict without being yourselves the aggressors. *You* have no oath registered in Heaven to destroy the government, while *I* shall have the most solemn one to 'preserve, protect, and defend' it."

Lincoln thereupon took that oath.

28   Inauguration of Abraham Lincoln, March 4, 1861.

President Abraham Lincoln in a thoughtful pose.

Postmaster General Joseph Holt.

THE NEXT MORNING Joseph Holt, who was remaining on as Secretary of War until Simon Cameron arrived in Washington to take over, handed Lincoln a letter from Major Anderson which had arrived on Inauguration Day. It stated that the Sumter garrison had only forty days' food left and that the Confederate batteries at Charleston were now so formidable that to reinforce and supply the fort would require "twenty thousand good and disciplined men" in order to succeed.

Lincoln was dismayed. His declared intention to "hold, occupy, and possess" the forts was threatened with becoming so many hollow words, at least as it applied to the most important fort of all. Anderson's communication also implied strongly that he believed that his garrison should be evacuated— that indeed there was no alternative.

Did Holt, asked Lincoln anxiously, have any reasons to suspect Anderson's loyalty? None, replied Holt. Had there been any previous indication from the major that he was in such a precarious plight? Again Holt said no—which was not quite accurate. During February Anderson had kept the War

29

Department fully informed about the increasing power of the Confederate armaments at Charleston and the decreasing level of his food reserves. What he had not done was to state explicitly, in accordance with his January 19 instructions from Holt, that he *needed* supplies and reinforcements. He knew that to do so would result in another relief expedition which in turn would lead to war.

Faced with this unexpected crisis on his first day in office, Lincoln asked General Scott's advice. That night Scott gave it: "I see no alternative but a surrender, in some weeks." He also informed Lincoln of the Buchanan-Mallory "truce" with respect to Fort Pickens—another disturbing bit of news.

Though Scott's opinions on military matters carried great weight, Lincoln, the one-time militia captain, was unwilling to give up on Sumter without further consideration. Therefore he directed Scott to make a thorough study of the problem of relieving the fort.

On March 11 "Old Fuss and Feathers" reported: To "supply and re-enforce" Sumter would require such a large force of warships, transports, and troops that it would take six to eight months to assemble it. Thus, "As a practical military question the time for succoring Sumter . . . passed away nearly a month ago. Since then a surrender under assault or from starvation has been merely a question of time."

But even this did not convince Lincoln that Sumter was doomed. There *must* be some way of relieving it, or at least some alternative to meek surrender. In any case, there was one thing that could be done to affirm his determination to retain possession of the surviving Federal outposts in the seceded states: Reinforce Fort Pickens. To be sure, there was the Buchanan-Mallory truce, but he did not consider himself bound by it, and obviously the Confederates were taking advantage of it to prepare an attack on the fort. So he instructed Scott to order the commander of the troops aboard the *Brooklyn,* Captain Israel Vogdes, to land them as soon as possible and hold Pickens at any cost. Scott sent the order to Vogdes the following day, March 12.

Reinforcement of Fort Pickens.

Harper's Magazine, November 1866

WILLIAM HENRY SEWARD was the new Secretary of State. He believed he should be President. As a senator from New York he had been playing a leading role in national affairs while Lincoln was just a country lawyer in Illinois. Only bad luck had prevented him from getting what he thought should have been his: the Republican nomination in 1860.

But if he could not be President in name he proposed to be so in fact. Twice before he had been the power behind the White House throne—first with William Henry Harrison, then with Zachary Taylor. There should be no difficulty in establishing the same sort of domination over Lincoln. Already the Illinoisan was revealing his inexperience and incompetence by his hesitation over what to do about Sumter.

Seward knew what to do: Evacuate the fort immediately. Indeed, do everything possible to avoid an armed showdown with the secessionists. For he was convinced—utterly convinced—that the majority of Southerners remained in their hearts loyal to the Union, and that sooner or later their latent patriotism would assert itself, thereby setting the stage for North-South reconciliation. On the other hand, for the Federal Government to employ force against the Confederates, or even threaten to do so, would only intensify and spread the secessionist distemper and result ultimately in civil war.

From the vantage point of historical hindsight it is easy to condemn Seward for underestimating Lincoln and overestimating Southern Unionism. But it should be remembered that few people sensed Lincoln's greatness in the spring of 1861, and that Seward himself was among the first to recognize it. Also it should be pointed out that some of the seven original Confederate states approved secession by very narrow margins, that the other slave states either rejected it or refused even to consider it prior to the actual outbreak of hostilities, and that many knowledgeable people in the South as well as the North shared Seward's belief that the secessionist fever would ultimately burn itself out. Indeed Lincoln himself hoped that the South's love of Union would prevail over its hatred of the North, and had sought to appeal to this in his inaugural address.

William H. Seward, Secretary of State under Lincoln.

Nevertheless, the fact remains that Seward's unrealistic view of Lincoln's ability and of Southern attitudes caused him to pursue a course that was morally dubious and nearly disastrous for the Union cause.

First, via pro-Southern ex-Senator William Gwin of California, he assured Confederate commissioner Crawford, now in Washington, that Lincoln's announced intention to "hold, occupy, and possess" the forts actually meant only "so far as practicable." Next he implied to Crawford and another of the commissioners (again through Gwin) that the evacuation of Sumter was being delayed only by "the difficulties and confusion incident to a new administration." At the same time he told his good friend James Harvey, Washington correspondent of the New York *Tribune*, that the government had decided to withdraw Anderson. As he no doubt anticipated, Harvey, a native of South Carolina, telegraphed this intelligence to Charleston on March 11—the same day that Scott, who also had close personal ties with Seward, reported to Lincoln that it was impossible to relieve Sumter.

Seward said and did these things without Lincoln's knowledge, much less approval. But he believed that sooner or later the President would abandon Sumter. He would have no other choice.

BUT THERE WAS another choice, declared Postmaster General Montgomery Blair. When on March 11 Lincoln informed him and the other cabinet members that Scott had stated that Sumter could not be relieved and so must be evacuated, he telegraphed his brother-in-law Gustavus Vasa Fox in Massachusetts to come to Washington immediately.

Lincoln's Postmaster General Montgomery Blair.

31

Blair was more than just a Postmaster General—the lowest ranking cabinet post. His father, Frank, had been Andrew Jackson's right-hand man; his brother Frank, Jr. was a congressman from Missouri. Together the three Blairs constituted the most politically influential family in America.

Nor was Gustavus Fox an ordinary brother-in-law. Thirty-nine and an Annapolis graduate, he had served with distinction in the navy before entering the textile business. Back in February he had submitted to Scott a scheme for relieving Sumter. Now on the morning of March 13 he arrived at the White House, accompanied by Montgomery Blair, to present his plan to Lincoln.

Organize, he said, an expedition of two warships, a transport, and three tugboats. When it arrives outside Charleston Harbor, transfer troops and supplies from the transport to the tugs, then at night run the tugs in to Sumter. Darkness would protect them from the Confederate shore batteries and the warships from naval attack. It all could be done within a few days and Fox would be proud to command the operation.

Here was an alternative to the impossibly large force of ships and soldiers deemed necessary by Anderson and Scott. But would it work? And would it not put the Federal Government in the role of the aggressor? As Lincoln had declared in his inaugural, if war came, it would have to be by an act of the South.

On March 14 Lincoln informed his cabinet of Fox's plan, then the following day asked each member to give a written answer to the question: "Assuming it to be possible to now provision Fort Sumter, under all the circumstances is it wise to attempt it?"

Later in the day Seward promised Supreme Court Justice John A. Campbell, a Virginian who had replaced Gwin as his go-between with the Confederate commissioners, that Sumter would be evacuated in three days. Exactly three days later the cabinet members submitted their replies to Lincoln's question. Five of them—Seward, Secretary of War Cameron, Secretary of the Navy Gideon Welles, Secretary of the Interior Caleb Smith, and Attorney General Edward Bates—advised withdrawing the garrison. Only Blair and Secretary of the Treasury Salmon P. Chase favored making an effort to maintain it—and the latter did so with many qualifications.

Obviously Seward had expected this outcome—hence his promise to Campbell. But to his dismay Lincoln still refused to order an evacuation. Instead he adopted a suggestion from Blair and sent Fox to Sumter for an on-the-spot investigation. He also had two of his Illinois friends, Stephen Hurlbut and Ward Hill Lamon, go to South Carolina to sound out Unionist sentiment.

Harper's Weekly, January 26, 1861

Interior of Fort Sumter, as viewed from the parapet.

Below, left to right: Secretary of Navy Gideon Welles, Attorney General Edward Bates, and Secretary of War Simon Cameron.

While Lincoln's three agents were away, Davis' three commissioners repeatedly asked Seward (via Campbell) when the promised evacuation of Sumter would occur. Seward repeatedly assured them that it was just a matter of time. The commissioners hoped, but did not fully believe, that what he said would prove true. In any case, for the time being it did not make much difference. Davis had instructed them to "play with Seward"—that is, hint to him that the seceded states would voluntarily return to the Union if the Federal Government gave certain guarantees regarding slavery. That way additional time would be gained for the Confederacy to arm.

On March 25 Fox returned to Washington and reported to Lincoln. During a quick visit to Sumter Anderson had told him that relief from the sea was impossible. However, after studying the situation himself he was more confident than ever that his plan was feasible. Anderson had also stated that by putting his men on short rations he could hold out longer than previously estimated. Possibly because he distrusted the major's loyalty, he made no arrangements with Anderson for supplying or reinforcing the fort, nor did he reveal his plan for doing so.

Two days later Lamon and Hurlbut likewise came back from Charleston. The former had accomplished worse than nothing. Having been led by Seward to believe that Lincoln intended to evacuate Sumter, he had not only told Governor Pickens, but also Anderson. Hurlbut, on the other hand, brought valuable information. A native of South Carolina, he had talked with many intelligent and informed people there. All agreed that Unionism in the Lower South was as good as dead. Furthermore, even "moderates" in South Carolina would approve resisting any attempt to provision Sumter.

THROUGHOUT THE NIGHT of March 28 Lincoln lay in bed sleepless, his mind churning. A decision on Sumter could not be postponed any longer—in two, at most three weeks, the garrison would be starving. But what should it be? An attempt to supply the fort would certainly result in war and probably the secession of most, perhaps all, of the slave states still in the Union. On the other hand, evacuation would discredit him, undermine the already sagging authority of the Federal Government, demoralize the North, and increase the prestige and strength of the Confederacy. Moreover, it would not settle anything. The crisis would merely be transferred to Fort Pickens or to some other issue.

Harper's Weekly, February 23, 1861

Officers' quarters at Fort Sumter.

When Lincoln got up in the morning he felt depressed—but he had made his decision. That afternoon he proposed it to his cabinet: a relief expedition to Sumter. Governor Pickens would be informed that it was on the way and that if it met no resistance, supplies only would be landed. Otherwise, troops as well as provisions would be sent into the fort under cover of cannon fire.

Every member of the cabinet approved except Seward. And even he based his opposition on the grounds that it would be better to have the war start at Pickens than Sumter. His stated reasons for so contending were deficient both in logic and sincerity.

HAVING MADE his decision, Lincoln proceeded to implement it. He ordered the Navy Department to assemble ships and the War Department 300 troops and supplies at New York, then sent Fox there to take charge.

Seward, however, was far from abandoning his effort to impose his leadership and policy on Lincoln. On the evening of March 29 he went to the White House, accompanied by Captain Montgomery C. Meigs of the Army Corps of Engineers, for the purpose of discussing the situation at Fort Pickens. Two days earlier Lincoln had learned from a newspaper report that the *Brooklyn*, which he had sent to reinforce Pickens early in March, had appeared at Key West (which the Union also retained) with troops still aboard. Obviously, as Lincoln put it, the Pickens expedition had "fizzled out." Would Meigs, he asked, prepare a plan for relieving and holding the fort?

Meigs said he would and left to do so. Seward was pleased. He was hopeful now that Lincoln would call off the Sumter expedition in order to concentrate on holding Pickens. In addition, Seward had influenced certain New York businessmen to withhold the assistance needed by Fox to acquire ships and supplies.

On March 31 Meigs presented his Pickens plan to Lincoln, who approved it and instructed Scott that "he wished this thing done and not to let it fail." He adopted this peremptory tone toward the ancient general because several days before Scott had shocked him with a proposal to evacuate the Florida fort as well as Sumter.

Captain (later Major General) Montgomery C. Meigs.

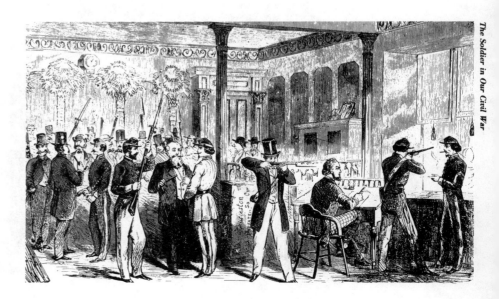

Southern bluebloods sharpen their marksmanship at the Ordnance Bureau, Charleston.

Lieutenant (later Admiral) David Dixon Porter.

On **APRIL 1** confirmation that the order to reinforce Pickens had not been executed reached Lincoln in a letter from Captain Vogdes, commander of the troops on the *Brooklyn.* Vogdes neglected to explain this failure, but did speak of "uncertain" communications with Washington and warned that the Confederates might attack Pickens "without a moment's notice."

This alarming news hastened preparations for the Pickens expedition. All through the day Meigs and Navy Lieutenant David D. Porter sat in a White House office drawing up orders for Lincoln to sign. Seward, who in a sense was sponsoring the expedition, personally handed many of the orders to Lincoln. One of them was a telegram to the New York Naval Yard to "Fit out *Powhatan* to go to sea at the earliest possible moment." Meigs and Porter planned to use this warship to support the landing of men and stores at Pickens.

Pickens, however, was not the only thing on Seward's mind that day. There was still Sumter. On March 30 he had promised Justice Campbell that on April 1 he would give him definite word about the government's intentions concerning that fort to pass on to the Confederate commissioners. Now Campbell came to Seward for that word.

Seward excused himself, visited Lincoln, then returned and wrote a message to be delivered in Campbell's name to the commissioners: "I am satisfied the government will not undertake to supply Fort Sumter without giving notice to Governor Pickens."

Campbell protested that this was a betrayal of Seward's oft-repeated promises, which Campbell had personally guaranteed, that Sumter would be evacuated. Seward, however, somehow persuaded him that this was not so, with the incredible result that Campbell reported to the commissioners that Seward's promise still held good.

But the commissioners themselves were not so easily fooled. They telegraphed Robert Toombs, the Confederate Secretary of State, that Lincoln would not issue an order to evacuate Sumter because he feared the North's reaction. Instead, they reported, he intended to "shift responsibility upon Major Anderson by suffering him to be starved out."

Meanwhile, on this same eventful April Fool's Day Seward, during one of his frequent calls at the White House, handed Lincoln the most remarkable memorandum ever submitted by a cabinet member to a President. Entitled "Some Thoughts for the President's Consideration," it stated that the government was "without a policy either domestic or foreign." Regarding the former, it proposed abandoning Sumter but defending Pickens. This, for reasons unexplained, would "change the question before the Public from one upon Slavery . . . for a question upon Union or Disunion." As for foreign policy, let the government initiate war with France (which was meddling in Mexican affairs), or with Spain (which had occupied Santo Domingo), or with both. Then, faced with a common alien foe, the people of North and South would forget their differences and the Union would be restored.

Seward concluded the memorandum by declaring that "whatever policy we adopt, there must be an energetic prosecution of it. . . . I neither seek to evade nor assume responsibility."

In brief, Seward offered to take command.

Lincoln would have been perfectly justified in demanding his resignation both for insubordination and incompetency. Instead, later in the day he sent a reply to Seward which calmly, tactfully, and firmly said: No.

Confederate Secretary of State Robert Toombs.

SEWARD now realized that he could not dominate Lincoln. But he still hoped to influence him—and to head off the Sumter expedition.

The President, he knew, was especially anxious to keep Virginia in the Union, for should she pull out, the rest of the Upper South soon would follow.

Therefore on the morning of April 4 he brought to the White House John B. Baldwin, a leading Unionist member of the Virginia Convention, which had been called to consider secession. His object was to arrange a deal whereby Lincoln would agree to evacuate Sumter in exchange for the adjournment of the Virginia Convention.

Lincoln and Baldwin conversed long and earnestly—but to no avail. Baldwin somehow got the impression that Lincoln was simply asking for the disbandment of the convention. Lincoln, on the other hand, concluded that Baldwin had contemptuously rejected his offer to give up Sumter in return for the non-secession of Virginia. Following the interview he denounced Virginia Unionists as nothing but "white crows." Again Seward experienced frustration.

That afternoon Lincoln and Fox, who had returned to Washington, made final preparations for the Sumter expedition. Despite the Seward-inspired obstacles he had encountered in New York, Fox had obtained the passenger steamer *Baltic* and three tugboats. In addition he had authority to employ the warships *Pawnee* and *Pocahontas* and the revenue cutter *Harriet Lane*. Lincoln instructed him to rendezvous this flotilla outside Charleston Harbor, then to send an unarmed supply boat toward Sumter. If the Confederates opened fire, the boat was to turn back at once, and Fox would endeavor to land troops and provisions at Sumter by means of tugboats covered by the cannons of his warships and of the fort.

In order to make sure that *this time* the fort's cannons would fire, Lincoln also had Secretary of War Cameron send Anderson a letter (by regular mail) notifying him of the relief expedition and urging him to hold out, "if possible," until it arrived. However, should surrender become a necessity, he was "authorized to make it."

Before returning to New York, Fox asked Secretary of the Navy Gideon Welles for another and more powerful warship for use in repelling Confederate

Assistant Secretary of Navy Gustavus V. Fox.

General view of the city and harbor, Charleston, South Carolina.

Commodore Andrew H. Foote.

naval attack and transporting 300 sailors, with howitzers and landing boats. Welles, who had been kept totally in the dark about the Pickens expedition, promptly sent orders to Captain Samuel Mercer to take command of the *Powhatan* as part of the Sumter expedition.

The result was a farce. On April 5 Captain Meigs and Captain Mercer both showed up at the New York Naval Yard, where the *Powhatan* was berthed. Meigs insisted that his authority to assume control of the ship took precedence because it was signed by the President. No, maintained Mercer — his order from Welles bore a later date. Finally Meigs telegraphed Seward asking him to settle the dispute.

Feeling rather embarrassed, Seward notified Welles of the mix-up. Welles, understandably enough, was angry over not being informed of the Pickens expedition. Together he and Seward hastened to the White House, arriving shortly before midnight.

Lincoln apologized to Welles, explaining that he had confused the *Powhatan* with the *Pocahontas*! Welles asked him to confirm his order assigning the *Powhatan* to Mercer. Seward, however, insisted that the ship go to Meigs — possibly he hoped even yet to thwart the Sumter expedition by denying it the means for success.

In any case, Lincoln supported Welles; Sumter was more urgent and important than Pickens. He instructed Seward to telegraph the New York Naval Yard to deliver the *Powhatan* to Mercer. Seward did so, but (perhaps deliberately) signed the message "Seward," not "Lincoln" as he should have.

As a consequence the officer in charge of the New York Naval Yard, Commander Andrew H. Foote (whose gunboat operations on the Tennessee and Cumberland rivers soon would make his a household name), decided to turn over the ship to Meigs's colleague Captain Porter (who also would become a Union naval hero). After all, the President's authority was supreme.

And so it was that on the afternoon of April 6 the *Powhatan*, unknown to Lincoln and against his desire, left New York as part of the Pickens' expedition. By the same token, two days later Fox, confident that the *Powhatan* soon would do the same, headed for Charleston aboard the *Baltic*, which carried 200 troops, sixteen launches, and supplies. The three tugboats were to follow him, and he expected to meet the *Pawnee, Pocahontas,* and *Harriet Lane* outside Charleston Harbor. Strangely, no one thought to inform him that the *Powhatan* had been turned over to Porter, nor did he bother to check on the ship despite the fact that she and her landing boats and sailors were now a key element in his plan to relieve Sumter.

As FOX steamed out of New York, Lincoln dispatched Robert Chew, a State Department clerk, to Charleston with the following unaddressed and unsigned message to Governor Pickens:

> I am directed by the President of the United States to notify you to expect an attempt will be made to supply Fort Sumter with provisions only, and that if such attempt be not resisted, no effort to throw in men, arms or ammunition, will be made, without further notice, or in case of an attack upon the Fort.

By thus giving advance notice of his intention to supply Sumter, Lincoln created a situation in which there was at least a chance that the Confederates would decide to withhold their fire. If they so decided, fine—Sumter would be relieved and United States sovereignty upheld. But if not, then they would have been maneuvered into firing the first shot.

View of Charleston, a wartime photograph.

LINCOLN did not know it and many historians have failed to realize it, but Jefferson Davis already had decided to shoot first.

His reasons were a mirror image of Lincoln's motives for sending the relief expedition to Charleston. As long as the United States flag flew over Sumter and Pickens, the Confederacy's claim to independence was a self-evident fiction. Unless that flag came down the authority of the Confederate Government would melt away with the coming of the hot Southern summer. On the other hand, by forcing the Federal Government to relinquish the forts the Confederacy not only would establish itself but grow in power as the other slave states flocked to join it.

So the question was when and where to use force. By April "when" could be soon, for the preceeding weeks had been put to good use in raising, organizing, equipping, and deploying troops. As for the "where," on April 3

Gorge and sally port at Fort Sumter.

Harper's Weekly, January 26, 1861

Brigadier General Pierre G.T. Beauregard, commander of Confederate forces in Charleston.

Davis addressed an "unofficial" letter to General Bragg at Pensacola: Was he ready yet to take Fort Pickens? If so, he was to take it.

On April 8 Bragg's reply arrived. If ordered, he would attack Pickens. Unfortunately, however, he could not guarantee success—and casualties would be severe.

That same day another message reached Davis. It came from Governor Pickens. Chew had delivered Lincoln's message. A relief expedition was heading for Sumter.

Now Davis had an answer to "where." It would be at Charleston. Immediately he had his Secretary of War, Leroy P. Walker, telegraph Beauregard: "Under no circumstances are you to allow provisions to be sent to Fort Sumter."

THE PREVIOUS DAY, April 7, Davis' commissioners had demanded, through Campbell, that Seward make good on his assurances that Sumter would be evacuated. On April 8 Seward replied: "Faith as to Sumter fully kept; wait and see. . . ." Even now he was unwilling to admit that he had promised what was not his to promise. But later in the day he followed this message with an official memorandum, delivered to Campbell at the State Department, in which he flatly denied Confederate independence and refused to negotiate with the commissioners. The game he had been playing with them, and they with him, had ended.

The commissioners, who meanwhile had learned of Lincoln's note to Governor Pickens, were incensed by what they deemed to be Seward's duplicity. On April 9 they addressed to him a letter which asserted that Lincoln's announced intention of supplying Sumter "could only be received as a declaration of war." They also telegraphed Davis that the Federal Government "declines to recognize our official character or the power we represent."

39

Davis, on reading this message, perceived that there was no longer the slightest possibility of establishing Confederate independence by negotiation. It would have to be done by war. And so it was that late on the morning of April 10 Davis laid before his cabinet a proposal that Beauregard be instructed to demand the surrender of Fort Sumter and to attack it if the demand was rejected. Citing in support a telegram just received from Beauregard himself, Davis declared that Sumter had to be taken before the Federal relief expedition arrived, for once supplied and reinforced the fort would be practically impregnable.

All the cabinet concurred except Secretary of State Toombs: "The firing upon the fort will inaugurate a civil war greater than any the world has yet seen. . . ."

Davis realized that this probably would be the consequence. Yet it would have to be risked. He saw no alternative if the Confederacy was to survive. Consequently he had Secretary of War Walker telegraph Beauregard to demand Sumter's evacuation, "and if this is refused proceed . . . to reduce it."

Above: Captain (later Lieutenant General) Stephen D. Lee. Below: Colonel (later Brigadier General) James Chesnut.

AT 3:30 P.M. on the afternoon of April 11 a small boat flying a white flag tied up to the wharf of Fort Sumter. Three men climbed out—Captain Stephen D. Lee, Lieutenant Colonel A.R. Chisholm, and Colonel James Chesnut, an ex-U.S. Senator from South Carolina. All were members of Beauregard's staff.

They handed Anderson a letter from Beauregard demanding the surrender of the fort. In it Beauregard, who as a cadet had studied artillery tactics at West Point under Anderson, stated that means would be provided for the removal of the garrison, and that "The flag which you have upheld so long and with so much fortitude . . . may be saluted by you on taking it down."

Anderson had been awaiting—and dreading—such an ultimatum since April 7. On that date he had received Cameron's message that Fox's expedition was on the way and that he was to hold out as long as possible. Until then he had both expected and hoped for an order to evacuate: Expected it not only because of Lamon's assurance but also because he considered it impossible to relieve the fort; hoped for it because he believed it was the only way to avert the calamity of civil war, his prime objective from the start. Consequently, in the words of one of his officers, Cameron's letter "deeply affected" him.

However, in responding to it he wrote: "We shall strive to do our duty, though I frankly say that my heart is not in the war which I see is to be thus commenced." And in keeping with that statement he gave Beauregard's aides a reply which read:

> General: I have the honor to acknowledge the receipt of your communication demanding the evacuation of this fort, and to say, in reply thereto, that it is a demand with which I regret that my sense of honor, and of my obligations to my Government, prevent my compliance.

The aides, without a word, headed for the wharf. Anderson accompanied them. As he did so, he suddenly thought of something which might even yet stop civil war from beginning at Fort Sumter. For the past week the Confederates had not permitted the garrison to purchase fresh food in Charleston. The fort had only a few barrels of salt pork remaining.

"Will General Beauregard," he called to the aides, "open his batteries without further notice to me?"

"No, I can say to you that he will not," replied Chesnut after some hesitation.

"Gentlemen," said Anderson, "if you do not batter the fort to pieces about us, we shall be starved out in a few days."

Surprised by this important admission, Chesnut asked if he might repeat it to Beauregard. Anderson gave him permission to do so. In effect he was telling the Confederates: Wait a few days—if the relief expedition does not show up, Sumter will be yours without a shot.

40

Col. Chesnut and Capt. Lee will
for a reasonable time await your answer.
I, am, Sir,
Very respectfully
Your obdt servt.
G. T. Beauregard
Brig. Gen. Comdg

Major Robert Anderson
Commanding at Fort Sumter
Charleston Harbour
So. Ca.

Facsimile of part of Beauregard's letter to Anderson.

LESS **THAN AN HOUR LATER** Beauregard sent a telegram to Montgomery in which he described Anderson's remark and asked for further instructions. Davis pondered, then had Walker telegraph Beauregard:

> Do not desire needlessly to bombard Fort Sumter. If Major Anderson will state the time at which, as indicated by him, he will evacuate, and agree that in the meantime he will not use his guns against us, unless ours should be employed against Fort Sumter, you are authorized thus to avoid the effusion of blood. If this, or its equivalent, be refused, reduce the fort as your judgment decides to be most practicable.

This meant that unless Anderson agreed to a prompt surrender he was to be attacked at once. Davis did not intend to risk the relief of Sumter. One way or another it must be occupied before Fox's expedition arrived. And above all, he was determined to assert the power and independence of the Confederacy.

Confederates mounting cannon on Morris Island, preparatory to attack on Fort Sumter. Wash drawing by William Waud.

FORTY-FIVE **MINUTES** past midnight, April 12, Chesnut, Chisholm, and Lee again docked at Fort Sumter. Remaining in their boat was Colonel Roger Pryor, an ex-congressman from Virginia and ardent secessionist, also a member of Beauregard's staff. Anderson read the message they brought from Beauregard: "If you will state the time at which you will evacuate Fort Sumter we will abstain from opening fire upon you."

While the three Confederates waited with growing impatience, Anderson conferred with his officers for over two hours. All of them rejected immediate surrender—even Lieutenant Meade of Virginia, who later joined the Confederate Army. However, in two more days, April 14, the garrison's food supply would be exhausted. Accordingly Anderson wrote a letter to Beauregard stating that he would "evacuate Fort Sumter by noon on the 15th instant . . . should I not receive prior to that time controlling instructions from my Government or additional supplies."

Beauregard's aides, who had been authorized by him to determine whether or not Anderson met the terms of his ultimatum, read the reply. Chesnut pronounced it "manifestly futile." Then, standing in a casemate, Captain Lee (who was 27 and destined to become the youngest lieutenant general in the Confederate Army) wrote the following, which both he and Chesnut signed before giving it to Anderson:

> Fort Sumter, S. C., April 12, 1861, 3:20 A. M.—Sir: By authority of Brigadier-General Beauregard, commanding the Provisional Forces of the Confederate States, we have the honor to notify you that he will open the fire of his batteries on Fort Sumter in one hour from this time.

41

Anderson read these words, displaying great emotion as he did. Then he escorted the Confederates to the wharf where he shook hands with them and said, "If we never meet in this world again, God grant that we may meet in the next."

INSTEAD of proceeding directly to Beauregard's headquarters in Charleston, Chesnut's party went to Fort Johnson. There, at 4 a.m., Chesnut ordered the fort's commander, Captain George S. James, to fire the gun which would signal the other batteries trained on Sumter to open up. Chesnut acted under authority previously given him by Beauregard and obviously felt no need to check with the general. The prospect of civil war did not unduly disturb him. Back in November he had declared, "The man most averse to blood might safely drink every drop shed in establishing a Southern Confederacy."

Captain James offered Colonel Pryor, the Virginian, the "honor of firing the first gun of the war." But Pryor, who two days before had made a speech

Fort Sumter and vicinity, from the painting by Albert Bierstadt. Fort Johnson appears in left foreground. Directly above, on horizon, is Fort Moultrie. Fort Sumter is seen in center of painting; Cumming's Point is in right distant background.

urging the Charlestonians to "strike a blow," declined. "I could not fire the first gun of the war," he said huskily.

Chesnut and his companions thereupon returned to their boat and continued across the bay toward Charleston. At 4:30 they heard James's cannon boom. They turned and saw a shell burst one hundred feet directly above the fort.

The Civil War had begun.

SOON nearly all of the Confederate batteries were blazing away. According to many historical accounts, the elderly Virginia secessionist Edmund Ruffin, now an honorary member of the Palmetto Guard, fired the first shot directed at the fort and struck it. Support for this contention comes from his own diary, in which he wrote:

> The night before, when expecting to engage, Capt. [George B.] Cuthbert had notified me that his company [the Palmetto Guard] requested of me to discharge the first cannon to be fired, which was their 64 lb. Columbiad, loaded with shell. By order of Gen. Beauregard, made known the afternoon of the 11th, the attack was to be commenced by the first shot at the fort being fired by the Palmetto Guard, & from the Iron Battery. In accepting & acting upon this highly appreciated compliment, that company had made me its instrument. . . . Of course I was highly gratified by the compliment, & delighted to perform the service—which I did. The shell struck the fort, at the north-east angle of the parapet.

However, it seems in fact that Ruffin merely fired the first shot from the Iron Battery on Cumming's Point, and that he did not do so until after other batteries had opened up. In his official report of April 17, 1861 Captain Cuthbert stated:

> The mortar battery at Cummings Point opened fire on Fort Sumter in its turn, after the signal shell from Fort Johnson, having been preceded by the mortar batteries on Sullivan's Island and the mortar battery of the Marion Artillery. . . . At the dawn of day the Iron battery commenced its work of demolition. The first shell from columbiad No. 1, fired by the venerable Edmund Ruffin, of Virginia, burst directly upon the parapet of the southwest angle of the fort [a more likely place for it to strike than the northeast angle referred to by Ruffin].

Other Confederate accounts, official and unofficial, confirm Cuthbert's statement.

If the signal shell from Fort Johnson be considered the opening shot of the Civil War, as it should, then Lieutenant Henry S. Farley fired it. He commanded the mortar which lobbed the shell over Sumter and according to his own testimony, which is supported by two eyewitnesses, he personally yanked the lanyard.

Beauregard's guns—thirty cannons and seventeen mortars—pounded the fort during the rest of the night and on into the dawn. Thousands of Charlestonians—men, women, and children, many in nightclothes—crowded the Battery, rooftops, and wharves to watch the pyrotechnics. In her excitement Mary Chesnut, wife of the colonel, sat down on a chimney atop the Mills House with the result that her dress caught fire! Friends beat out the flames before much more than her dignity was damaged.

Sumter's cannons remained silent. This disappointed the spectators and caused some of the Confederate soldiers to feel like bullies hitting a man who will not fight back. Ruffin was "fearful that Major Anderson, relying on the security of his men in the covered casemates . . . did not intend to fire at all. It would have cheapened our conquest of the fort, if effected, if no hostile defence had been made—& still more increased the disgrace of failure."

Ruffin need not have worried. Anderson intended to fire back—but not until daylight. His guns lacked breech sights, and although Captain Doubleday and another officer had devised notched sticks as imperfect substitutes, they could not be aimed accurately in the dark. Moreover, he had a stockpile of only 700 powder bags (the cartridges used to discharge the cannons), which his men had made out of sheets and shirts. It would be foolish to squander them in nocturnal pot shots.

At 6 a.m., their regular time, the soldiers assembled in the bombproofs for reveille, ate a quick breakfast of pork and water, and then manned the

Doubleday prepares to fire first gun in Fort Sumter.

44

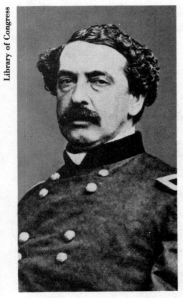

Captain (later Major General)
Abner Doubleday.

Bombardment of Fort Sumter,
as sketched from Morris Island.

guns on the lower tier. To the irritation of many of them, Anderson previously had decided not to operate the pieces on the more exposed upper tier (the parapet) because he feared excessive casualties to the small garrison which would leave it with insufficient strength to repel a landing attempt (something, however, which the Confederates did not plan, as they considered it a hopeless enterprise). It is possible, too, that he wished to save these guns to cover Fox's relief expedition.

Anderson offered Doubleday, his second-in-command, the honor of firing (at least in the figurative sense) the first Union shot of the war. The New Yorker gladly accepted it. As far as he was concerned the war was "simply a contest, politically speaking, as whether virtue or vice should rule" in America.

Shortly before 7 a.m. Doubleday aimed a 32-pounder at the Iron Battery, then stepped back and shouted "Fire!" The gunner (apparently his name has gone unrecorded) yanked the lanyard and the cannon belched forth an iron ball which whizzed across the bay and bounced off the slanting roof of the Iron Battery.

Following this shot the other gun crews went into action. At first they concentrated their fire on the Iron Battery and the Floating Battery, which had been anchored off the western tip of Sullivan's Island. The musicians and most of the workmen assisted by carrying ammunition to the casemates. Also some of the latter sewed up more powder bags, handicapped because only six needles were available! Owing to the lack of manpower and powder bags, the garrison after a while employed but six cannons. On at least one occasion a group of workers took the place of the soldiers in serving a piece.

When it became apparent that no damage was being done to the Floating Battery, Anderson authorized a shift of fire to Fort Moultrie. However, most of the projectiles directed against it merely buried themselves harmlessly in piles of sandbags. Equally futile were the few shots aimed at the mortars on James Island. As for the Iron Battery, a Union cannon ball put one of its guns out of action by jamming the steel shutter protecting its embrasure, but the Confederates soon repaired the shutter.

The Federals' fire would have been more effective, especially against Moultrie, had they been able to use shells, but they lacked the fuses necessary to explode the shells, and an attempt to improvise them failed. Likewise the 8-inch and 10-inch columbiads on the parapet almost certainly would have made things rougher on the Confederates. Not only did they shoot projectiles weighing 65 and 128 pounds, but their angle of fire was superior. Frustrated by the ineffectiveness of the 32-pounders that were being used, Private John Carmody ignored orders and went to the top parapet where he single-handedly fired a number of the big guns which already were loaded and trained on Moultrie. In addition, two sergeants managed to get off a couple of shots from a 10-inch columbiad aimed at the Iron Battery. No one, however, attempted to drop a cannonball on Charleston from one of the guns mounted as mortars in the parade ground.

INITIALLY the Confederates tended to fire too high. But with daylight they soon got the range, with the result that numerous mortar shells exploded inside the fort and solid shot riddled the walls. On three different occasions the supposedly fireproof barracks began burning. The first two times parties of workmen headed by Peter Hart, an ex-sergeant serving as Anderson's personal aide, put out the flames. The third time, however, only the coming of an evening rainstorm completely doused the blaze.

Despite the hurricane of shot and shell, none of the garrison was seriously injured. The same held true of Sumter itself. Although the parapet and gorge wall were badly battered, its defensive capacity remained substantially unimpaired. On the other hand, the closest the Confederates came to suffering some casualties was when Doubleday put a couple of 42-pound balls through the roof of the Moultrie House, a resort hotel located near Fort Moultrie. These, a Charleston newspaper reported, caused the men inside to scatter "miscellaneously." Doubleday's excuse for firing on the hotel

A 10-inch columbiad, mounted as a mortar in Fort Sumter.

Harper's Weekly, February 16, 1861

was that prior to the bombardment it flew a secessionist flag. As a joke, he told a Confederate officer that once he had received poor service there.

At nightfall Anderson ordered firing ceased in order to conserve the fast-dwindling supply of powder bags. The Confederates for their part slackened off to an occasional shot designed to prevent the garrison from resting. However, most of the weary Federals could have echoed Private Thompson, who wrote "I for one slept all night as sound as ever I did in my life."

April 13 dawned bright and sunny, and some people in Charleston witnessed what they hailed as an omen of victory: A gamecock alighted on the tomb of Calhoun, flapped its wings, and crowed! Beauregard's batteries resumed a heavy barrage; the fort resonded sporadically. At midmorning flames again engulfed the barracks. Desperate efforts to extinguish them proved futile. Moreover, they threatened to reach the powder magazine, which as a result of very bad planning was located on the ground floor of one of the buildings. Falling embers prevented the removal of more than a small portion of the powder.

By noon, wrote Doubleday later, "The roaring and crackling of the flames, the dense masses of whirling smoke, the bursting of the enemy's shells, and our own which were exploding in the burning rooms, the crashing of the shot, and the sound of masonry falling in every direction, made the fort a pandemonium." According to Private Thompson, the "only way to breathe was to lay flat on the ground and keep your face covered with a wet handkerchief." Yet Anderson's gunners still managed occasionally to fire a cannon as a token of continued resistance. Each time they did so the Confederates gave forth with a cheer in admiration of the garrison's gallantry.

Since early afternoon on April 12 both the garrison and the Confederates had observed ships lying off the bar of the harbor. They were Fox's. At 3 a.m. on April 12 he had arrived in the *Baltic*, having been delayed by gales. He found the *Harriet Lane* waiting for him, and three hours later the *Pawnee* showed up. None of the three tugboats appeared. A storm had driven one into Wilmington, North Carolina and chased another past Charleston to Savannah, and the owner of the third had refused to let it leave New York.

The "floating battery" firing on Fort Sumter.

During the rest of the day Fox waited, then searched for the *Pocahontas* and the all-important *Powhatan*. Not until the morning of April 13 did he learn from the commander of the *Pawnee* that the *Powhatan* had been detached from the expedition. Without the tugs and without the *Powhatan*'s supplies, launches, and 300 sailors, his whole plan for relieving Anderson fell through.

Frustrated but undaunted, Fox then considered trying to reach Sumter in longboats from the *Baltic*, but the heavy sea forced him to reject this idea. Next he proposed to use a commandeered ice schooner to make a run for the fort at night, even though he realized that such a venture would be suicidal: "I should certainly have gone in, and as certainly been knocked to pieces," he subsequently reported. Fortunately, however, he did not have an opportunity to make the attempt.

At 12:48 p.m. a shell cut Sumter's flagstaff. Peter Hart, assisted by several others, quickly replaced it and the banner it bore. But not long after he did so Louis Wigfall of Texas, now (like seemingly all Southern politicians) a colonel on Beauregard's staff, appeared outside one of the fort's embrasures waving a sword with a white handkerchief tied to its point. Having seen the flag go down, on his own initiative he had crossed the harbor to Sumter in a small boat to demand that Anderson surrender.

Anderson agreed to do so on the same terms Beauregard previously had offered. Flames were raging out of control through the fort. At any time the magazine might blow up. Nearly all the powder bags—including two dozen pairs of Anderson's socks—had been expended. The main gate had been blasted away and the fort lay open to a storming party. Above all it appeared obvious that no help could be expected from Fox. Hence there was no point in subjecting his hungry, exhausted, and half-suffocated men to further pounding. They had done their duty. So had he.

The flames in the fort burned down before blowing up the magazine. On the afternoon of April 14, a Sunday, the garrison marched out with drums playing "Yankee Doodle" and boarded a Confederate boat which transferred it on the following day to one of Fox's ships. That morning Anderson's soldiers, who had made additional powder bags out of scraps of blanket and even paper, had begun firing what he intended to be a hundred-gun salute to the flag before lowering it. However, midway in the ceremony a cartridge exploded prematurely. Five cannoneers were wounded, one mortally, and another killed outright. His name was Daniel Hough. He was the first soldier to die in the Civil War. Four years and some weeks and days later, over 600,000 others would be dead also.

Sergeant Hart nailing the colors to the flagstaff. Painting by Gilbert Gaul.

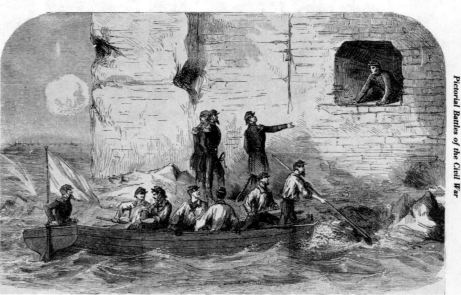

Anderson's interview with Colonel Wigfall through the porthole at Fort Sumter.

ON APRIL 15 Lincoln issued a call for 75,000 volunteers to put down the Southern rebellion. Promptly Virginia, North Carolina, Tennessee, and Arkansas seceded, and Maryland, Kentucky, and Missouri threatened to do likewise. At the same time the vast majority of Southerners rallied enthusiastically behind the Confederacy, confident of victory and independence. Davis' decision to force a showdown at Sumter appeared justified by the outcome.

But the attack on the fort had outraged the North. There, too, men flocked to the colors and crowds cheered them as they marched off to do battle for the Union. On May 1, 1861 Lincoln was able to state quite accurately in a letter to Fox consoling him for the failure of his expedition: "You and I both anticipated that the cause of the country would be advanced by making the attempt to provision Fort Sumter, even if it should fail; and it is no small consolation now to feel that our anticipation is justified by the result."

In years to come historians would debate the question: Who caused the Civil War to begin at Fort Sumter—Lincoln or Davis?

The answer is simple: Both.

Lincoln as President of the United States had a duty to preserve a nation. Davis as President of the Confederacy had a mission to create one. Each decided to do what had to be done. The difference is that Lincoln's decision ultimately led to the success of his cause.

THE FIRING on Fort Sumter decided that war would determine whether the North and South would be two or one. In the war itself the fort did not play a decisive part. Yet its role was prominent. To both Federals and Confederates

Explosion of the gun while saluting the flag at the surrender of Fort Sumter.

South Carolina's Palmetto Flag.

49

it symbolized the Confederacy. Hence the former resolved to take it, the latter to keep it.

On April 7, 1863 nine Union ironclad ships tried to blast their way into Charleston Harbor. Sumter's cannons helped repulse them. In August 1863 the Federals opened on the fort with dozens of huge siege guns implanted on Morris Island. Their navy joined in. By September Sumter was a ruin, its cannons silenced. Yet when on the 9th 500 sailors and Marines tried to storm it, 320 Confederate defenders drove them back with heavy losses.

In December a second "Big Bombardment" took place. This, combined with an explosion in the powder magazine, reduced Sumter to a "volcanic pile." Nonetheless the gray garrison held on, crouching in bombproofs, its musicians defiantly playing "Dixie" whenever there was a lull in the shelling.

In July 1864 the Federals made a third and last attempt to pulverize Sumter into submission. It was no more successful than the first two. In fact, the fort emerged stronger than ever. As a later generation of American soldiers were to learn at Monte Cassino, rubble makes good defense.

Sumter did not fall into Northern hands until February 1865, when the approach of Sherman's army forced the Confederates to evacuate Charleston. By then the "Cradle of Secession" was a ruin, a "city of ashes." First there had been a devastating accidental fire in December 1861 — the anniversary of secession. Then during 1863 and 1864 shellfire smashed and burned what was left. Even Calhoun's tomb was empty; the Charlestonians had reburied the coffin in an unmarked grave to prevent the Yankees from getting hold of it.

Shortly before noon, April 14, 1865, a Good Friday, Robert Anderson, now a general on the inactive list, returned to Fort Sumter. With him were his 6-year-old son and Peter Hart. The latter carried the same flag which had been hauled down there four bloody years before. A large crowd stood around a newly erected flagpole; many other people watched from boats in the harbor.

Hart attached the flag to the halyards of the pole; Anderson made a short speech, then seized the halyards and pulled the flag to the top of the pole. Sumter no longer was the symbol of the Confederacy. It now was the symbol of the victorious Union.

That night in Washington, D.C. the last important shot of the Civil War was fired. It came from a derringer aimed at the back of Abraham Lincoln's head.

Fort Sumter, a mass of rubble at the end of the war.

50

THE BULL RUN CAMPAIGN: FIRST MANASSAS

Text by V. C. Jones
Designed by Frederic Ray

Capitol at Washington. Lincoln's inauguration, March 4, 1861. Note unfinished dome on which work was continued during the war.

When a hot, relentless sun rose on Sunday, July 21, 1861, Bull Run and Manassas were names that meant virtually nothing throughout the world. By nightfall they were on their way to immortality.

That morning, the casual observer casting his eyes over the sweep from Centreville Ridge on the east to the hazy-blue Bull Run Mountains ten miles to the west would see nothing to indicate that over a part of that area within the next few hours would be fought one of the great battles of modern history and the first major conflict of the Civil War, America's internecine struggle between the North and South.

Here lay deceiving country. Pastoral in appearance, with rolling, gentle hills a mile or so apart, it was wooded mostly, but here and there occasional cleared acreage marked moderately prosperous farms. Scattered about, too, were houses of varying proportions and construction, some far apart, some close, but none closer than the pair separated by only a few hundred yards on the brow of Henry Hill, where the crux of the battle would occur. This hill, six miles from the little railroad junction of Manassas, meeting point of the Orange & Alexandria and Manassas Gap lines, overlooked Bull Run, a meandering stream. With Cub

Run and Rocky Run to the east, it was the largest of the three, all parallel. The first two would play proportionately important roles in the forthcoming conflict, one of the bloodiest of all time.

Other factors would come into play. On a thirty-odd-foot tower near Manassas a signal officer would stand with binoculars, meticulously scanning the countryside and bringing to warfare a new mode of communication. He would wigwag Boy Scout fashion an important message. And miles to the west, onto the dirty, smoke-blackened cars of the little Manassas Gap Railroad running from Manassas to Strasburg over in the Shenandoah Valley, soldiers under Joseph E. Johnston would clamber by the thousands, en route to a union of forces that would turn out to be one of the major coups of the day.

The man on the tower, Captain E. P. Alexander, later a prominent Confederate general, and many others like him, of little fame at the time, would rise into prominence like shooting stars. By the close of day, records and actions would be shaping up names for the history books—Beauregard, Burnside, Jubal Early, Ewell, Hampton, A. P. Hill, Jackson, Longstreet, Sherman, Stuart, and many more—a bevy of "greats" whose names would ring on the tongues of succeeding generations without respect to the side on which they fought. But at least two of those who participated—George A. Custer and John S. Mosby—would have to wait until a later day for the chroniclers to find them.

On the Northern front there was a frantic impatience for troops to march upon the Confederate Capital. "On to Richmond!" was the cry. The United States Congress had gone into extraordinary session on July 4 in Washington, D. C., the Federal Capital. Early on the agenda was a message from President Abraham

Lincoln reviewing hostilities that had gone on in the seceded states since the preceding fall and urging steps to save the Union.

On Tuesday, July 16, troops started marching out of Washington. They were clad in a heterogeneous mixture of uniforms, few of which gave definite indication of the allegiance of the men who wore them. Their leader was a physically powerful man named Irvin McDowell, 43, only two months a brigadier general. He had been educated in France and at the United States Military Academy, and had distinguished himself in the Mexican War. He was looked upon as an officer well informed outside and inside of his profession. Though inexperienced as a leader and no military genius, he knew the 30,000 troops under his command were mostly untrained and ill-equipped for the assignment ahead of them. But the word was "Go!"

Behind, he was leaving Winfield Scott, General in Chief, on whose staff he had served. Scott, actually a year older than the Federal Constitution and a hero of the War of 1812 and the Mexican War, was too decrepit to take the field. From his desk near the White House, however, he would play a part in the unfolding drama.

Not all the urgency for battle action rested with the North. The Southerners had their notion about when fighting should begin, too.

At Richmond, an officer who would take his place with Alexander the Great and Napoleon as one of the military leaders of all time surveyed the terrain in the vicinity of Washington. He was Robert E. Lee, newly resigned from the United States Army to defend his native state of Virginia and serving at the moment as adviser to the Confederacy's President, Jefferson Davis.

Lee's eyes focused on Bull Run, flowing southeast from the Bull Run Mountains and only thirty miles from the Union Capital. This narrow, crooked stream,

Confederate Capitol at Richmond, from photograph taken in April 1865 after evacuation. Observe the broken windows.

with alternately precipitous and marshy banks, seemed to him to be a good base line for the protection of the railroads at Manassas and possibly for offensive operations against the enemy.

On May 8, Brigadier General Philip St. George Cocke, West Point graduate and well-to-do Virginia and Mississippi plantation owner, was stationed at the junction with four companies of infantry and cavalry. This force was soon increased to a dozen companies, and camps of instruction sprang up. Before the month was out, Brigadier General M. L. Bonham, Indian fighter, Mexican War veteran, and ex-United States Congressman, arrived with a brigade, and on June 1 Brigadier General Pierre Gustave Toutant Beauregard took over as commander of all the Confederate forces in northeastern Virginia, bundled together as the Army of the Potomac. This last officer, a West Point-trained, Mexican War veteran who had served on General Scott's staff, had more recently been superintendent of the Military Academy and still more recently toasted as the hero of Fort Sumter, where he was in command of the Confederate attack. He was a military engineer, more curbed by personality than lack of ability.

53

General Pierre Gustave Toutant Beauregard. Portrait by B. F. Reinhardt, painted December 19, 1861.

54 **General Joseph Eggleston Johnston, whose reinforcements to Beauregard turned the tide of battle.**

Beauregard began early to think of offensive action, but it was July 14 before he was well enough along with his plans to express them to others. They revolved around General Johnston and his army of 12,000 men facing an army of 18,000 under Brevet Brigadier General Robert Patterson over in the Shenandoah Valley. Here was a veteran of the regular service confronting a leader who had received his training through the Pennsylvania militia. Johnston was a West Pointer, Indian fighter, and Mexican War veteran who had personally led the storming column at Chapultepec. He had been wounded numerous times. While Patterson had served with the militia in the War of 1812 and also the Mexican War, he had no such extensive battle experience as Johnston.

On July 14, Beauregard sent his plan to Richmond via Colonel James Chesnut, a South Carolina lawyer who had served in the United States Senate with Jefferson Davis. It was briefly this:

General Johnston should leave from 3,000 to 5,000 men in the passes of the Blue Ridge Mountains to hold Patterson in check, while with the bulk of his army he should move by the Manassas Gap Railroad to join forces with Beauregard. The two of them would advance rapidly on Fairfax Court House, establishing themselves between the lines of Union troops around Falls Church and Alexandria and attacking them separately with large forces, exterminating them or driving them into the Potomac River. Johnston would then, with a part of Beauregard's troops and those left in the passes, attack and destroy Patterson at Winchester or wherever he might be. The attack would next be on Washington, Johnston moving from the Maryland side and Beauregard from Virginia. There must be no delay.

At least one part of this plan had been under consideration since the Confederates first started fortifying at Manassas. As early as May 15, General Cocke, in a dispatch to Lee, had pointed out the importance of the Manassas Gap line, which would enable troops to be moved from the Valley to Manassas, or vice versa.

But Beauregard's grandiose plan to take the offensive never materialized, for at 3 o'clock on the afternoon of July 16 the vanguard of the Federal army started from Washington. Experienced officers and men of distinction were at the head of the units involved, as follows:

1st Division—Commanded by Brigadier General Daniel Tyler, West Pointer and authority on artillery maneuvers. The division consisted of the 1st Brigade, under Colonel Erasmus D. Keyes, West Point graduate and instructor, Indian fighter, and specialist in coastal defense; 2d Brigade, Brigadier General Robert C. Schenck, former U.S. Congressman and minister to

Brazil; 3d Brigade, Colonel William T. Sherman, West Pointer and Mexican War veteran; and 4th Brigade, Colonel Isaac B. Richardson, West Pointer and Indian fighter, known as "Fighting Dick" because of his record in the Mexican War.

2d Division—Under Colonel David Hunter, West Pointer and Mexican War veteran. His command included: 1st Brigade, Colonel David Porter, West Pointer and Mexican War veteran; and 2d Brigade, Colonel Ambrose E. Burnside, West Pointer, Mexican War veteran, and firearms manufacturer, distinguished also by his unusual growth of side whiskers.

3d Division — Led by Colonel Samuel P. Heintzelman, West Pointer, Indian fighter, and Mexican War veteran. His brigades were: 1st Brigade, Colonel William B. Franklin, West Point graduate and instructor and Mexican War veteran; 2d Brigade, Colonel Orlando Bolivar Willcox, West Pointer, Indian fighter, and Mexican War veteran; and 3d Brigade, Colonel Oliver O. Howard, West Point graduate and instructor and Indian fighter.

4th Division—Under militia Brigadier General Theodore Runyon, left seven miles from the battle area to guard communications.

5th Division — Commanded by Colonel Dixon S. Miles, West Pointer whose first assignment had been at Fort Leavenworth, Kansas. His division: 1st Brigade, Colonel Lewis Blenker, German officer who had served with the Bavarian Legion; and 2d Brigade, Colonel Thomas A. Davies, West Pointer and Indian fighter.

That night, most of the men reached Annandale, about ten miles to the west, and went into camp. Their movement was not unknown to General Beauregard. He had employed espionage to learn what the Federals were doing. A former clerk in one of the government departments in Washington volunteered to go into the city and bring back the latest information on the happenings there. Below Alexandria, just across the Potomac from the Capital, this man crossed by boat, carrying a small scrap of paper bearing the

National Archives

Later Major General Irvin McDowell, unfortunate Union commander at Bull Run.

words "Trust bearer." In the early morning he handed this to Rose O'Neal Greenhow, Southern sympathizer and a society leader who was able to move about with ease in political circles. She reacted promptly, and the agent was soon on his way back to Beauregard with this message: "Order issued to McDowell to march upon Manassas tonight."

Other things were happening on this important July 16. Over in the Shenandoah Valley, Colonel J. E. B. Stuart, another West Pointer and Indian fighter, commanding a regiment of Confederate cavalry, reported that General Patterson had moved from Martinsburg and halted at Bunker Hill, nine miles from Winchester, where the Confederates lay. This gave Johnston the impression that the Union leader was creating a diversion to keep him occupied while Beauregard was being attacked at Manassas.

On July 17, the Federal troops pushed on to Fairfax Court House, another ten miles from Washington. There they began to encounter the Confederates, who departed hastily leaving behind camp equipage and forage. The Northerners paraded through town four abreast, with bands playing and flags waving.

That day Colonel Chesnut returned from Richmond. He had found Davis sick in bed, but the President received him "with great kindness and cordiality." Later the emissary unfolded Beauregard's plan of action at the Spotswood Hotel in a meeting with Davis, Lee, Inspector General Samuel Coper and Colonel John S. Preston, successful planter and brother-in-law of Wade Hampton. The scheme was considered "brillant and comprehensive," yet Davis and Lee found two faults with it: 1) Johnston's army was not strong enough to allow the withdrawal of enough troops to effect the object and keep Patterson from coming down on Beauregard's left; and (2)—this mainly—the Federals were still so close to cover that they could fall back upon their intrenchments or be reinforced by their reserves. Later, when the lines were longer, the plan could work, they advised, but not now.

Failure of the plan to get approval from Richmond actually made little difference. Already the Federals were clogging the roads west out of Washington, and by the 18th they were gathering along the heights of Centreville. Beauregard, in the meantime, completed the withdrawal of his troops behind Bull Run, General Bonham's 1st Brigade barely getting across unscathed after midnight. If unable to get reinforcements from the Valley, Beauregard still had hopes of support from the Aquia District of the Department of Northern Virginia below Fredericksburg. It was commanded by Brigadier General Theophilus H. Holmes, veteran of the Seminole and Mexican Wars and a West Point classmate of Jefferson Davis.

The Confederate forces lay along an eight-mile stretch of Bull Run, concentrating at or near seven crossing points—six fords and a bridge—with reserve units in supporting distance. In the array, as in the case of the North's high command, were fighting strength and talent. The defense stations from east to west were:

Union Mills Ford, near the railroad—three regiments of infantry, four 12-pounder howitzers, and three companies of cavalry, under Colonel Richard S. Ewell, Mexican War veteran and Indian fighter.

McLean's Ford—three regiments, two brass 6-

Post-war photograph of signal tower similar to the one used by the Confederates in detecting McDowell's flank march against the Confederate left.

pounders, and one company of cavalry, under Brigadier General D. R. Jones, West Pointer, Indian fighter, Mexican War veteran, and chief of staff during the bombardment of Fort Sumter.

Blackburn's Ford—three regiments and two 6-pounder guns, under Brigadier General James Longstreet, West Pointer, Indian fighter, and Mexican War veteran.

Mitchell's Ford, in the center—four regiments, two batteries of artillery, and six companies of cavalry, under General Bonham, closing out his second month of service at Manassas.

Ball's and Lewis' Fords, three miles farther west and near Stone Bridge—three regiments, one battery, and one company of cavalry, under General Cocke, first commander on duty in the area.

Stone Bridge—one regiment and a battalion of infantry, four 6-pounder guns, and two companies of cavalry, under Colonel Nathan G. "Shanks" Evans, West Pointer and Indian fighter.

During the 17th, Beauregard sent a message to Richmond by telegraph, a system of communication then in use for only seventeen years. This would be its first use in a war. The message read:

"The enemy has assaulted my outposts in heavy force. I have fallen back on the Bull Run, and will make a stand at Mitchell's Ford. If his force is overwhelming I shall retire to the Rappahannock Rail-

Above: Scene at Manassas Junction, Union-held in 1864. Box cars are considerably smaller than those now in use. Below: Post-war photograph of the famous Stone Bridge over Bull Run.

road Bridge, saving my command for defense there and future operations. Please inform Johnston of this, via Staunton, and also Holmes. Send forward any re-inforcements at the earliest possible instant and to every possible means."

At 1 o'clock on the morning of July 18, General Johnston received a telegram from Inspector General Cooper at Richmond that indicated Beauregard's plan of action had not been ignored altogether. It stated: "General Beauregard is attacked. To strike the enemy a decisive blow a junction of all your effective force will be needed. If practicable, make the movement, sending your sick and baggage to Culpeper Court House either by railroad or by Warrenton. In all the arrangements exercise your discretion."

Johnston was a man of action, and the telegram from Richmond got immediate attention. "The best service which the Army of the Shenandoah could render was to prevent the defeat of that of the Po-tomac," he later wrote. His decision was to elude Patterson, a speedier course than trying to defeat him. Quickly he made dispositions of the advance guard to bring about the evasion, provided for his sick at Winchester, and started moving his army through Ashby's Gap to Piedmont, a station on the Manassas Gap line. What he was doing would bring Patterson's dismissal from the Federal Army in a matter of days.

Meanwhile, pursuing his advance, McDowell moved with confidence. He had been assured by Scott that

Patterson would prevent Johnston from reinforcing Beauregard. At 8:15 a.m. July 18, he sent a message ahead to General Tyler, commanding the 1st Division and in the advance:

"I have information which leads me to believe you will find no force at Centreville, and will meet with no resistance in getting there. Observe the roads to Bull Run and Warrenton. Do not bring on an engagement, but keep up the impression that we are moving on Manassas."

At 9 a.m., the 4th Brigade of Tyler's division, under "Fighting Dick" Richardson, moved into Centreville. It found the enemy had indeed gone, so it turned along the road to Manassas and halted to obtain water. Tyler came up and, despite his instructions not to bring on an engagement, took a squadron of cavalry and two light companies from the brigade and, with Richardson, went to make a reconnaissance.

"We soon found ourselves overlooking the strong position of the enemy situated at Blackburn's Ford, on Bull Run," he reported. "A moment's observation discovered a battery on the opposite bank, but no great body of troops, although the usual pickets and small detachments showed themselves on the left of the position.

"Suspecting from the natural strength which I saw the position to possess that the enemy must be in force, and desiring to ascertain the extent of that force and the position of his batteries, I ordered up the two rifled guns, Ayres' battery, and Richardson's entire brigade, and subsequently Sherman's brigade in reserve, to be ready for any contingency. As soon as the rifled guns came up I ordered them into battery on the crest of the hill, nearly a mile from a single battery which we could see placed on the opposite side of the run. Ten or a dozen shots were fired, one of them seeming to take effect on a large body of cavalry who evidently thought themselves out of range."

But the Confederates refused to satisfy Tyler's curiosity. They threw a few shells and sent out a few skirmishers, after which they remained in the woods. Tyler made more advances and sent out a section of a battery supported by a squadron of cavalry. Suddenly the Southerners came alive "with volleys which showed that the whole bottom was filled with troops."

Two Federal officers watching the action from a hill in the rear became alarmed at this new turn of affairs. They were Major J. G. Barnard of the U. S. Corps of Engineers, a Mexican War veteran who had served as superintendent of the Military Academy and more recently as Chief Engineer of Washington, D. C., and Captain J. B. Fry, Assistant Adjutant General, West Point graduate and artillery teacher, and Mexican

War veteran. They sent a messenger to remind Tyler that McDowell had advised against bringing on an engagement. This seemed to have its effect. Anyway, Tyler had learned all he wanted to know: "This attack . . . showed that the enemy was in force and disclosed the position of his batteries."

It was Tyler's intention to withdraw in orderly fashion, but something went wrong. Some of the men left the scene in confusion, especially a regiment of New Yorkers, who panicked and ran a mile and a half before they could be rallied.

"The fire which the regiment encountered was severe, but no excuse for the disorganization it produced," Tyler reported. Longstreet, commanding the Confederates on the other side of the stream, dismissed the incident with the observation that the presence of his regiments "probaby intimidated the enemy as much as the fire of the troops that met him."

The action had begun about noon and continued with an exchange of gunfire until 4 o'clock in the afternoon. The Confederates answered the Federals gun for gun, but discontinued the moment Tyler ordered a halt. There were casualties on both sides.

Union soldiers pose exuberantly on the roof of Fairfax Court House.

have a look the next day and try to bring in more information.

The 19th was spent in contemplating the best way to get around the Confederate left. McDowell's engineers had information that there was a ford about three miles above Stone Bridge at a place listed on the maps as "Sudley Springs." They were reliably informed—some of the details came from Mathias C. Mitchell, a local resident who represented himself as a Union man and was secured as a guide—that Bull Run was passable at this point even for wheeled vehicles. Moreover, maps indicated a farm ford between Sudley and Stone Bridge that was also said to be good, though little used. They were further advised that a road branched off in the direction of Sudley a short distance after passing over Cub Run, which was spanned by a suspension bridge.

As promised, Major Barnard went out on reconnaissance. With him rode Captain Daniel Phineas Woodbury, of the engineers, who had had experience in constructing roads on the east coast and even on the frontier, and Governor William Sprague of Rhode Island, commanding a regiment of militia and a battery of light horse artillery from his state. A company of cavalry escorted them. They passed over Cub Run and, truly enough, found a road that seemed to lead to Sudley. It was a tortuous, narrow trace of a rarely used byway, much of its course lying through a dense

That night McDowell called a council of some of his officers to discuss plans. He had made some reconnaissance during the day and had reached a definite decision. Originally it was planned to make a sweep to the left of Manassas, from Fairfax Court House and Centreville to Fairfax Station and on to Wolf Run Shoals, but he had had a look and so had some of his Engineers, and they had determined that the country in that direction was unfit for the operations of a large army. Therefore the movement must be by the right, turning the enemy's left. This would mean that their advance would be along the Warrenton turnpike out of Centreville, instead of along the road toward Blackburn's Ford, where Tyler's men had been repulsed.

But there would be time to see, he advised. The provision trains were just beginning to come in, and the troops would require at least another day to cook their provisions for the continued march, which would afford opportunity to examine the country more carefully. Major Barnard, who was present, promised to

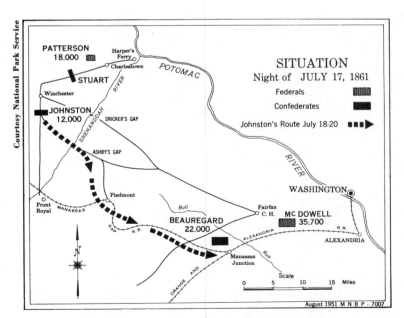

On July 17, with McDowell's army of more than 35,000 men advancing from Washington, Confederate forces were divided between Winchester and Manassas. By means of the Manassas Gap Railroad, Johnston's force was transferred to Manassas in time to reinforce Beauregard.

Uniforms of Federal units which fought at Bull Run. Left to right: 2d Ohio, Blenker's 8th New York, 1st Massachusetts.

woods. For some distance they followed it, opening gates and passing through private grounds, but stopped when they encountered enemy patrols. To go farther would be dangerous, not so much for fear of their personal safety, but because they did not wish to attract attention to their designs in this quarter.

Captain Woodbury suggested that he make a reconnaissance at night with a few Michigan woodsmen, but this later turned out to be a failure. There were too many Confederates wandering around through the woods.

While the Federals were having their troubles on the 19th in deciding what to do, so was Beauregard at Manassas. During the day this telegram came in from Inspector General Cooper:

"We have no intelligence from General Johnston. If the enemy in front of you has abandoned an immediate attack, and General Johnston has not moved, you had better withdraw your call upon him, so that he may be left to his full direction. All the troops arriving at Lynchburg are ordered to join you. From

this place we will send as fast as transportation permits. The enemy is advised at Washington of the projected movement of Generals Johnston and Holmes, and may vary his plans in conformity thereto."

Beauregard did not consider the telegram an order in terms, but rather an "urgency" from Richmond that left him technically free to decide his further course. He determined to make every effort to bring about the prompt arrival of the Shenandoah forces and, should they come before McDowell attacked, to take the offensive himself. Fortunately for him, the Union commander was delaying, partly because of lack of rations and partly due to the need for more information.

Centreville is an old village; in the early days it was a stage stop on the route from Washington to Winchester and a busy crossroads with an inn known far and wide as Newgate Tavern. The village had been incorporated in 1798, lots and streets laid off, and plans made for a considerable community. To some of the Union soldiers who halted there on the march to Bull Run it did indeed seem a thriving community,

Left to right: Garibaldi Guards, 14th New York, 11th New York (Fire Zouaves).

although they noticed only a few houses, and most of these on the west side of the ridge running north and south.

July 20 of 1861 also found it busy. Troops seemed everywhere, although most of them were quartered along the eastern slope of the ridge, the road to Blackburn's Ford, and Braddock Road, coming into the village from the southeast. This latter route was an old one from Williamsburg built by Braddock's army during its advance on Fort Duquesne in 1755.

Even though almost within cannon range of the Confederates, the bivouacs of the Union soldiers swarmed with visitors during both the 19th and 20th. Some were official and some unofficial, but they all moved about without military restraint, passing to and fro among the troops as they pleased. Many of them had come out from Washington in carriages and had brought their own supplies. Some of the women had even packed along their best finery, for it was common knowledge that there would be dancing at Fairfax Court House after the Northerners had driven the Southerners back to Richmond. Surveying the scene,

Fry was impressed that it had the "appearance of a monster military picnic." Two factors detracted from the jolly atmosphere: the heat and the dust. Clouds of the latter were stirred from the clayey soil by even the slightest movement.

Throughout the 20th campfires burned everywhere. Soldiers were cooking the rations sent out by wagon train from Washington. They had received orders that they must have at least two or three days' supply in their haversacks when the march was resumed. The daily ration consisted of a pound of hardtack, three quarters of a pound of pork or bacon or a pound and a quarter of fresh or salt beef, an ounce and a half of coffee, twenty-four ounces of sugar, and a small quantity of salt.

McDowell had definitely made up his mind that the swing must be to the right along the Warrenton turnpike. The affair at Blackburn's Ford had convinced him that the enemy position was too strong at that point for passage to be forced without great loss. As for the movement to the right, Stone Bridge was the problem. He had information that it was

61

Confederate troops en route to Manassas. Allen C. Redwood sketch.

mined, defended by a battery in position, and further fortified by heavy abatis. But this point could be avoided by making only a feint there and swinging the bulk of his troops across Bull Run at Sudley Springs. Then they would go on to break the Manassas Gap line and prevent Johnston from joining Beauregard.

It was his intention to move the several columns out on the road a few miles on the evening of the 20th, so they would have a shorter march in the morning and thus be fresher for whatever fighting might be in store. But his officers gave him some bad advice. They urged starting in the early dawn and making only one move. McDowell consented, thus giving the Southerners more time in which to bring up reinforcements.

McDowell summoned his brigade commanders to headquarters for a final meeting as night closed in. Each was told what he was to do. Most of the troops would move off at 2:30 a.m. and head down the Warrenton turnpike, but the 5th Division under Colonel Miles, along with the 4th Brigade, 1st Divi-

sion, commanded by Colonel Richardson, would remain behind and guard Blackburn's Ford to make sure the Confederates did not execute a turning movement from that direction while the Union thrust was being made to the right. As soon as cannon fire was heard from upstream around Stone Bridge, Richardson, nearest to the ford, was to open with his guns for the purpose of making a diversion.

A few other matters were on McDowell's mind. He was anxious over the inability of his troops to make their rations last as long as they should, and he was especially bothered by the fact that the term of service of some of them was expiring. This had been one of the reasons for the impatience in the North. The men had signed up for three months, and the three-month period was drawing to a close for some of them. Even that day it had ended for the 4th Pennsylvania and the 8th New York Militia, and these regiments turned a deaf ear to pleas that they remain a few days longer. On the morrow they would move to the rear "to the sound of the enemy's cannon." The Union commander, expecting within the next few days to lose thousands of the best troops in the army for this reason, ironically noted that every day made the enemy's force stronger and his weaker. He believed that the repulse at Blackburn's Ford on the 18th was largely to blame for the attitude of the retiring units.

Still other things were bothering him. He had word from a man who said he had just come from the Valley that Patterson was falling back. And there were rumors that Johnston had actually joined Beauregard.

At Manassas during the 20th, the biggest development was the arrival of the vanguard of troops from the Shenandoah Valley, confirming the rumor at Centreville. In came the 7th and 8th Georgia regiments, and then the 1st Brigade under Brigadier General Thomas J. Jackson, consisting of the 2d, 4th, 5th, 27th, and 33d Virginia regiments. About noon, in chugged a train bringing General Johnston and, with him, Brigadier General Barnard E. Bee, with Alabama and Mississippi troops. For the first time in history, steam-propelled locomotives had been used for the rapid movement of troops.

The Manassas Gap line was young and poorly equipped, with little rolling stock of its own. Some of the engines in use had been run out of Alexandria before that city was occupied by the Federals. Many of the cars were captured in May when the Confederacy took over more than 100 miles of the Baltimore & Ohio's main line and transported them, as well as locomotives, over the turnpikes by animal power to railroads farther south.

Battles and Leaders of the Civil War

"Listening for the first gun at Manassas." A. C. Redwood sketch.

Johnston was in an optimistic mood when he stepped off the train at Manassas. The president of the railroad had assured him that the remainder of his troops should arrive during the day. His cavalry and artillery were coming by turnpike, and he knew they were well on their way. Moreover, he had eluded Patterson without trouble, although he suspected the Union commander would follow as soon as he learned the size of the force confronting him. This might be as early as the 22d.

Sherman's battery of light artillery, engaged at First Bull Run.

Harper's Weekly, June 8, 1861

Without delay, Johnston rode to look over the field and found Beauregard's position so extensive and the ground so densely wooded that he knew it would be virtually impossible for him to gain knowledge of it and the enemy's position in the brief time at his disposal, so he informed Beauregard that he would rely upon his judgment, having full confidence in it.

Beauregard also was feeling good about developments. Johnston was bringing 8,340 men and twenty guns from the Valley, and General Holmes already had arrived with 1,265 rank and file, with six pieces of artillery, from Aquia. The latter force, with the 6th Brigade of the Army of the Potomac under Colonel Jubal A. Early, at forty-five a profane, tobacco-chewing Indian fighter, Mexican War veteran, and lawyer, would be placed back of the fords on the right as a reserve. The others would be stationed so as to strengthen the left center and left, the latter being particularly weak owing to lack of available troops.

Little sleeping went on in the Federal camp at Centreville the night of the 20th. The men had their canteens filled and their haversacks packed. But many of them, untrained and unaccustomed to the physical effort that had been involved in the march from Washington, were already fatigued almost to the point of exhaustion, not to mention the trouble they were having with sore feet and the suffering from the heat. Much of the latter was due to the heavy uniforms they were wearing, certainly not the light material necessary for mid-July weather in Virginia.

From the start there was delay as the troops were aroused from their billets before the hour set by McDowell for the start of the march. The artillery was ready on schedule, but the infantry was not, and there was nearly an hour of waiting before Tyler's division took to the road. Three of his brigades were to go straight down the turnpike to Stone Bridge and had to clear the turnoff point beyond Cub Run so that Hunter's and Heintzelman's divisions could turn to the right and cross Sudley Ford at least by 7 a.m. The movement had been scheduled so as to avoid the burning heat that would come as the day advanced.

It was about two miles to the turnoff, but it took hours to cover that distance. March was route step and, despite their aches and pains, the soldiers were in a light mood. Most of them knew nothing about the horrors of war. They sang and they joked in the dark, knowing that the eyes of the North were upon them. The vocal press and the even more highly vocal element exempt from military service had assured them that it should be no problem to drive the Confederates toward whom they were marching back to the rebellious homes whence they had come.

The road from Centreville was not winding. It was downhill half a mile or so, then it curved slightly to the left and climbed gently uphill, the last rise before the descent to the suspension bridge over Cub Run. But it was dusty, and this slowed the marchers as they choked and fell out of line to catch their breath. Then, as the dawn began to break, they made out blackberry bushes in the fields on each side, and this was an irresistible lure. They fell out, picked handfuls of the ripened berries, and then sauntered back to their lines.

Another delaying factor was a 30-pounder Parrott gun attached to Tyler's division. It was to open the

firing at Stone Bridge and might even turn out to be the deciding factor, for it was looked upon as a mighty weapon. Thus it had the green flag for the advance, but its nineteen-horse team found difficulty in moving it along the narrow and sometimes rough road. A cloud of dust hovered over it whenever it was moved. And when it arrived at Cub Run there was considerable delay, while the men in charge made up their minds to gamble that the suspension bridge would not collapse under the gun's considerable weight. As it turned out, the span was equal to the test, and the Parrott rolled on toward Stone Bridge.

The progress of Tyler's division was so slow that Hunter's and Heintzelman's columns found it took them two to three hours to cover the distance from Centreville, something a fast-walking man could do in half an hour easily. It was far past the scheduled time before they were able to turn off on the road toward Sudley—this had been set for early daylight or about 4 a.m.—and then they gradually realized something they had not expected. The route was much longer than information gathered by the Engineers had indicated. Fry put it at twelve miles instead of six; both figures were exaggerations, but toiling over a little-

The 30-pounder Parrott of Carlisle's battery fires the first shot at Bull Run.

used trail in dust and oppressive heat distorted the best of estimates.

Some time after daylight the first shot was fired from the 30-pounder Parrott. The exact time of this action and the exact person who pulled the lanyard have been lost to history. The gun was attached to the battery of Captain J. Howard Carlisle, commanding Company E of the 2d Artillery, and was under the direction of Lieutenant Peter C. Hains of the U.S. Artillery Corps.

McDowell recorded: "General Tyler commenced with his artillery at 6:30 a.m." From Tyler came this report: "After examining the position and posting Sherman's and Schenck's brigades and the artillery, I fired the first gun at 6:30 a.m., as agreed upon, to show that we were in position." Lieutenant John M. Wilson of the 2d Artillery stated: "At 5 a.m. exactly the first gun was fired by Captain Carlisle. . . ." Lieutenant Stephen C. Lyford, 1st U.S. Dragoons, attached to Schenck's brigade, wrote: "We arrived in view of the enemy's position about 5 a.m., and immediately opened fire with the 30-pounder rifled gun attached to our battery. . . ."

The Confederates also gave their version as to the actual time. Colonel Evans, at whose forces the gun was aimed, recorded: "The enemy made his appearance in line of battle on the east side of the bridge

. . . and opened fire with rifled cannon at 5:15 a.m." Beauregard differed with him, reporting: "About half-past 5 o'clock, the peal of a heavy rifled gun was heard in front of the Stone Bridge."

Lieutenant Hains, who, in view of his assigned responsibility for the gun, would seem to have been the individual who fired the first shot of the first major engagement of the war, apparently left no record.

Regardless of when the shot was fired and who fired it, two others followed in quickly succession. One of these went through the tent of Signal Officer Alexander, but it did not harm him, for he was off on the tower at Manassas scanning the countryside. The Confederate artillery made no reply.

Almost immediately after the three shots were heard, Richardson's guns opened at Blackburn's Ford. Confederates watching from across Bull Run at that point saw Federals moving about in force, maneuvering as though they were about to launch a major attack.

At 6:30 a.m. Beauregard, directing action with Johnston's approval, received a message from Evans. It announced that some 1,200 men were deployed in his front.

This news brought about an immediate change of plans at Confederate headquarters. Only two hours

66

earlier Johnston had given his approval in writing to an offensive plan of action prepared by Beauregard. Now both leaders knew that the Union had taken the initiative away from them. The Federal movement from Centreville definitely put them on the defensive. Beauregard ordered Evans and also Cocke (the latter commanding at adjacent Ball's and Lewis' Fords) if attacked, to maintain their positions to the last extremity.

"In my opinion," wrote Beauregard later, "the most effective method of relieving that flank [his weak left] was by a rapid, determined attack with my right wing and center on the enemy's flank and rear at Centreville, with due precautions against the advance of his reserve from the direction of Washington. By such a movement I confidently expected to achieve a complete victory for my country by 12 m."

After sending off the message to Evans, Beauregard ordered Jackson's brigade to take up such position along Bull Run that, in case of need, he could sup-port Bonham on his right, at Mitchell's Ford, or Cocke on his left. With him were to move the battery of Captain John D. Imboden, Virginia lawyer turned soldier, and five pieces of the battery of Major J. B. Walton of the Washington Artillery, crack outfit with thirteen guns. The parts of Bee's and Georgia Colonel F. S. Bartow's brigades that had arrived from the Valley—about 2,800 men—were sent forward to the support of Evans at Stone Bridge.

Tyler had deployed his troops on each side of the road leading to the bridge, Schenck's brigade below and Keyes's and Sherman's brigades above it. The demonstration they made was not vigorous, for the main drive was to come farther upstream at Sudley. A moderate fire from a battery of rifled pieces was maintained. It was directed for a while against the bridge and then was turned farther downstream toward Cocke's position. Skirmishers moved forward from both sides and kept up a brisk fire for about an hour.

Confederates could be seen in groups beyond the bridge, some out of range in the edge of the woods,

Harper's Weekly, Aug 3, 1861

"Colonel Hunter's attack at the Battle of Bull's Run."

Photograph of the Stone House, at the junction of the Sudley-Manassas road and the Warrenton turnpike taken long after the war. Utility poles and outbuildings have since been removed.

but maintaining their silence. The silence bothered McDowell, now making his way with Hunter's and Heintzelman's columns toward Sudley. Did it mean the Confederates were not in any force in his front? Did they intend themselves to make an attack—and at Blackburn's Ford? As time passed, this seemed to the Union commander to be more and more a possibility. He gave orders for one of Heintzelman's brigades to be held in reserve, in case it should be necessary to send troops back to reinforce Miles. His anxiety would have been relieved had he known that the Southerners were silent because their guns were smoothbores, too short-ranged to shell the Federal line effectively.

Around 8:30 a.m., Evans began to wonder. The Federal attack did not increase in boldness and vigor. He could see dust clouds in the distance toward Centreville, indicating that troops were on the move, and wisps seemed to be rising in places off to the left.

They were vapory at first, and then increased in density as marching feet ground the dry earth into powder.

Suddenly a signal officer—one of the occupants of that tent through which Tyler's shell from the Parrott had passed—uttered an exclamation and focused his binoculars anew. From the tower on Signal Hill beyond Manassas Alexander was signalling, for he had seen the sun glittering on bayonets and brass cannon up toward Sudley Ford. The officer repeated the message as it was wigwagged to him:

"Look out for your left! You are turned!"

Evans stared with increased interest at the dust clouds gathering off to his left. Forces definitely were moving toward Sudley Ford, a passage he did not have enough troops to guard.

He sent Cocke word of the enemy's movement and of his own plans to meet it. Leaving four companies under cover at Stone Bridge, he hurriedly marched upstream three quarters of a mile with the remainder of his force, about 1,100 men—six companies of the

Liberia house, General Beauregard's headquarters.

4th South Carolina and five companies of Louisiana Zouaves under the colorful Major Chatham Roberdeau Wheat, prominent criminal lawyer and preacher's son, an adventurous man who had fought in the Mexican War, in Latin America, and with Garibaldi in Italy.

They moved across the valley of Young's Branch, Bull Run tributary coursing from the west, and went toward Sudley, taking along two 6-pounder howitzers. Most of the concentration of troops in the beginning had centered around the point at which the road from Sudley to Manassas crossed the road from Centreville to Warrenton. Near this crossroad, in the northeastern angle, sat a stone farmhouse already in use as a hospital. After this day, history would call it the Stone House; shells would damage but not destroy it.

From the other side of Bull Run, the Parrott gun occasionally sent off a shot to let the Confederates know the Federals meant business. A high tree had been found that could be used as an observatory for

Tyler's forces, and a lookout was maintained from its topmost branches.

Reaching high ground on a shoulder of Matthews' Hill above the Stone House and about 400 yards in rear of "Pittsylvania," the home of the Carter family, Evans formed a battle line at right angles to his former position. His left rested on the road running past the Carter mansion, with troops distributed on each side of a small copse where they could take advantage of such cover as the ground afforded. They lay facing open fields, with woods beyond, along which the Federals must advance. A howitzer was placed at each end of the line. Later, discovering that the road along which they waited was a branch of the main highway from Sudley, he swung his force farther to the left onto Matthews' Hill and stationed some of his men in a shallow ravine. Union officer Fry later wrote in admiration: "Evans' action was probably one of the best pieces of soldiership on either side during the campaign."

69

Evans had not long to wait. The march of Hunter's and Heintzelman's columns had been anything but a success from the standpoint of timing. It was not 7 a.m. but at least two hours later before the leading brigade, Burnside's, reached Sudley. Some of the delay had been caused by Tyler's slow advance during the dark hours of morning, but most of it was due to the circuitous route the engineers serving as guides had followed in an effort to conceal their movement from the enemy.

When McDowell reached Sudley Ford, he found that a part of Burnside's brigade had crossed, but the men following were slow in getting over. The scene about them was not altogether one of war. Picnickers in groups had accompanied the column and engaged the soldiers in conversation. Across the way stood the Sudley Church, later to be used as a hospital, and about its lawn stood a crowd of worshippers, waiting for the Sunday sermon that would not be preached.

Burnside's men were hot, sweaty, dusty, and thirsty, and they stopped to drink and fill their canteens. The water they gulped was mostly from Bull Run, but some managed to take advantage of the cooling flow from Sudley Springs, the center of a swarming, shouting horde of desperately dry men. The Union commander urged them to hurry. He could see clouds of dust rising from the direction of Manassas and feared that the Confederates might come down on the head of his column and scatter it before it could be reinforced.

Orders were hurried back to urge the commanders of regiments in the rear to break from the column and come forward separately as fast as possible. McDowell also sent word to the reserve brigade of Heintzelman's division to come by a nearer road across the field, and sent an aide-de-camp to tell Tyler to press forward his attack, as large bodies of the enemy were passing in his front to head off the force at Sudley. This was a sharp change of plans. It had been hoped the defenses of Stone Bridge could be taken in rear and that it could be passed without force.

When they finally broke away from the refreshing coolness at Sudley Ford, Burnside's men moved southward along the road toward Matthews' Hill. Evans' troops had orders to open fire as soon as the enemy approached. This they did at 9:15 a.m., causing the first of the Federals who came in sight to halt in confusion and then fall back. A vigorous burst of fire from the Southerners followed, and Wheat charged with his battalion, later falling severely wounded in both lungs.

Hunter came up. Major Barnard of the Engineers was with him and suggested confining operations to the left flank, so as to drive the Southerners from the immediate vicinity of Bull Run and form a junction with Tyler at Stone Bridge. Hunter moved forward to judge better how to direct the attack. As he advanced, a fragment of shell struck him and took him out of action.

Shortly thereafter, as he left the field, Hunter met Burnside and asked him to take charge. It was 9:45 a.m.

Burnside immediately began debouching troops from the woods into the open fields. He threw forward skirmishers, and they became engaged with Wheat's command. Up came the 2d Rhode Island, with its vaunted battery of six 13-pounder rifled guns. More Union troops were crossing at Sudley and on the way.

For about an hour Evans maintained his position on Matthews' Hill, but at the end of that period he began to waver, for the Federals were coming up rapidly. Acting on McDowell's order to press his attack, Tyler directed Sherman's and Keyes's brigades to cross Bull Run at the farm ford shown by the maps about 800 yards above Stone Bridge and go to the aid of Hunter's column. Before Keyes's troops could get fully under way, an enemy battery on the other side of the stream threw twenty-five or thirty rounds of shot and shell upon the 1st and 2d Regiments of Connecticut Volunteers, causing temporary confusion and wounding several men.

More Union artillery was crossing at Sudley and

Colonel Burnside's Rhode Island brigade and the 71st New York open the flank attack at Bull Run. Pencil and wash drawing by A. R. Waud.

pushing on toward the battle action. Soon there would be five batteries—Griffin's, Ricketts', Arnold's, the Rhode Island, and the 71st regiment—twenty-four pieces. Their shells would add further to the pressure now building up, especially on the Confederate right toward which Barnard had suggested the attack be aimed.

Shortly after McDowell arrived at the front, Burnside rode up to him and said his brigade had borne the brunt of the battle and was out of ammunition; he asked permission to withdraw and refit. In the excitement of the moment, the commander gave consent. The brigade marched to the rear, stacked arms, and took no further part in the fight.

Long believed a photo of Confederate dead on Matthews Hill, this was a shot posed by Federals.

As directed earlier in the morning, General Bee, the South Carolinian, moved his column nearer Stone Bridge and brought it to a halt on Henry Hill overlooking Young's Branch, some distance to the rear of where Evans' troops were fighting. From there, Imboden's batteries were able to drop shells with telling effect upon the oncoming Federals. It was Bee's hope to get Evans to fall back to this hill, a superior position, he felt, but Evans insisted on continuing the battle near the Matthews house and urged the other officer to join him. Finally Bee gave in and moved forward, taking with him the 7th and 8th Georgia, 4th Alabama, 2d Mississippi, two companies of the 11th Mississippi, and Imboden's battery.

The morning advanced. Meanwhile, the sound of firing convinced General Johnston, waiting with Beauregard near Mitchell's Ford, that a major battle was under way and that the enemy's great effort was to be made with his right. They had been expecting for some time to hear action that would indicate the turning movement against the Union left was taking place. This did not come, for orders had failed to reach some of the officers involved. So the plan was abandoned, and dispositions were made to meet the enemy's drive instead of giving him some of his own medicine.

Accordingly, orders were sent to General Holmes and Colonel Early, waiting in reserve back of the fords to the east, to move with all speed to the scene of action. Generals Ewell, Jones, Longstreet, and Bonham were instructed to make demonstrations on their respective fronts. The two commanding officers then left headquarters and galloped off toward Stone Bridge, having four or five miles to cover.

When Heintzelman reached Sudley Ford after 11 a.m., one brigade of Hunter's division was still on the eastern side of the run. Smoke was rising from two points on the left, indicating the battle front. McDowell had already gone forward, and soon he sent word for two regiments to be hurried forward. Heintzelman accompanied one of them, leaving orders for the remainder of his division to follow.

As noon approached, the Confederates, with Bee in over-all command, fell back. The pressure upon them was too great. Porter's Union column, and then the brigades of Franklin and Willcox, arrived to extend the Union right across the fields to the Warrenton turnpike west of the stone house at the crossroads. Threatened with disaster, and despite the efforts of Bee and Bartow and Evans to rally them, the demoralized Southerners retreated across Young's Branch and back toward Henry Hill where Jackson waited with his brigade, as stolid and calm as the nickname he was about to receive.

The rebuilt Henry house, showing the Union monument of the first battle. From an 1884 photograph.

72

The open, level top of this hill is more than 200 yards across. On the western brow sat the home of the bedridden widow, Judith Carter Henry, born in 1777 at "Pittsylvania," near where the fighting had raged. She was a direct descendant of Colonel Robert "King" Carter, a man greatly responsible for the settlement of this portion of Virginia. Her two semi-invalid sons had managed to get her out of the house on a mattress and had started toward a neighbor's. But as the fighting in the distance grew hotter, she insisted on being returned to what she considered the safety of her bedroom, where she now lay cared for by a young Negro woman named Rosa Stokes. Only a few hundred yards away at the northeastern end of the plateau stood the modest home of James Robinson, a free Negro.

Carried back with the tide of his retreating regiments, Bee reached the brow of the hill and spied Jackson, standing with his men in line of battle in the edge of a pine thicket from which their fire could sweep the plateau. Whether in praise or derogation—there are two schools of thought—he shouted to the panicky men around him:

"Look! There stands Jackson like a stone wall! Rally behind the Virginians!"

It was that sudden. A nickname that would live forever—"Stonewall"—had been given a man who would prove during the next two years that he deserved it.

Even in the beginning, it inspired soldiers who heard it. They steadied and began to form a solid line, while off to the right around the Robinson house the Hampton Legion, 600 strong and just arrived after twenty hours on the train from Richmond, carried on some desperate, confused fighting to check the Union pursuit. This gallant outfit had been organized by the wealthy and aristocratic South Carolina planter, Colonel Wade Hampton, a man renowned for his intellect and physical strength.

Some time after noon, Johnston and Beauregard reached Henry Hill. The fighting was still in progress, though not at its previous rapid pace. Finding that most of the field officers of the 4th Alabama had been disabled, Johnston led it forward, the regimental flag at his side. The sight among them of this veteran who had been wounded so many times in previous wars brought new spirit to the Confederates on the field, and they cheered as loudly as their dusty and parched throats would allow.

For some unexplained reason, a lull settled over the battle area between 1 and 2 o'clock. It was like a lunch break for the heat-exhausted men on both sides. Firing almost completely died out, and the only real activity for a time was in the background of each line, where more troops were coming up. Among those on the Federal side was Willcox' brigade, consisting of the 1st Michigan, 11th New York (Fire Zouaves), 38th New York, and Arnold's battery. And for the Confederates, just off the train at Manassas were 1,700 infantrymen

Above: Troops of Bee, Bartow, and Evans rally behind the Robinson house. From painting by Thure de Thulstrup. Below: J. E. Taylor painting of Jackson at Bull Run. But unlike this painting, Jackson was dressed in his old Mexican War uniform.

Federal attack up the slope of Henry Hill to recapture the guns of Griffin's battery. Drawing by Walton Taber.

from the Shenandoah Valley led by Brigadier General Kirby Smith, Indian fighter, Mexican War veteran, and ex-mathematics professor at West Point. Their arrival was a triumphant accomplishment for the Manassas Gap line. It had been having troubles—confusion in shunting trains back and forth on a single track, one collision, and overworked crews.

latest arrivals among the Federals were taking position. As soon as this was completed, Beauregard urged Johnston to leave the conduct of the field to him and to retire to "Portici," the nearby home of the Francis W. Lewis family at the rear, from which he could direct reinforcements to the front and have a better look at the entire Confederate line. Johnston reluctantly agreed.

This break in the fighting was a welcome development for soldiers on each side. Some of them had been awake since before 2 a.m. and fighting since shortly after 9 a.m. Their uniforms were wringing wet with sweat, their bodies and their clothes coated with dust. Water was an urgent necessity, especially at this season of the year; food was scarcely considered in the excitement.

With the two Southern commanders on the field, the line of battle was rearranged slightly and some troops were moved to strengthen it on the left, toward the Sudley road and toward the west where the

The Henry house from Jackson's position.

Wartime photograph of the Matthews house.

McDowell had at hand the brigades of Franklin, Willcox, Sherman, and Porter, as well as a battalion of Regular cavalry. Howard's brigade was in reserve. Keyes's brigade, accompanied by Tyler, had become separated from Sherman and opened a gap in the line by marching down Young's Branch below Stone Bridge, entirely out of the battle. Close to the front were the crack batteries of Captain Charles Griffin, experienced soldier, Indian fighter, Mexican War veteran, and instructor in artillery at West Point—and Captain James B. Ricketts, veteran of the Mexican and Seminole Wars. But the Union commander had no equivalent officer like Johnston to look over the field from the rear and to forward reinforcements.

When McDowell's line again advanced, Sherman was on the left, Porter and Franklin in the center, and Willcox on the right.

Willcox' b r i g a d e had reached the front near the intersection of the Warrenton and Sudley roads. Troops on their left, in the vicinity of the Robinson house, the commanding officer noticed, were engaged in desultory firing. He posted the 38th New York in line and was moving up the Zouaves when he re-

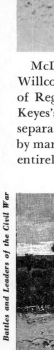

The Robinson house from Jackson's position.

Slaughter and rout of Ricketts' battery by the 33d Virginia. Painting by Sydney King, after drawing by A. R. Waud.

ceived an order to detach a regiment for the support of Rickett's battery on a hill a quarter of a mile or more to the right. The Zouaves were turned in that direction.

It was now 2 p.m., and the fighting was picking up in force all along the front. Whereas the Southerners had been retreating before 1 o'clock, they now stood fast—Bee's, Bartow's, and Evans' commands merged with Jackson's brigade of fresh troops, 6,500 men, with thirteen pieces of artillery and Stuart's cavalry.

Some time early in the renewed fighting, Imboden, who had been going from battery to battery on Jack-

76

son's orders to see that the guns were properly aimed, came up to ask permission to return to his own command. As "Stonewall" gave permission, his eyes shining, he characteristically extended the open palm of his left hand toward the artillery officer. Suddenly he jerked it down. Blood was streaming from it. "General, you are wounded!" exclaimed Imboden. Jackson drew a handkerchief from his breast pocket. "Only a scratch—a mere scratch," he said, galloping off.

Griffin's and Ricketts' batteries were soon ordered to cross the Sudley road and to move up Henry Hill, to within 330 yards of the opposing guns, a move that some military students have insisted was McDowell's blunder of the day. It is their contention that more would have been gained by sending one battery forward and leaving the other where it could enfilade

Stuart's 1st Virginia Cavalry charge and rout the New York Fire Zouaves supporting Ricketts' and Griffin's batteries on Henry Hill.

the hilltop. At any rate, the guns soon became engaged in a hot duel with Imboden's and other Confederate batteries.

As the tempo of the battle increased, the action became dramatic—and tragic. The infantry moved back and forth, first one side and then the other occupying the plateau. Suddenly Confederate snipers began firing at Ricketts' and Griffin's batteries from the Henry house, or from the cover of it. At last, in desperation, some of the Union guns were turned upon the building. Several shots passed through it, scattering shingles and boards and splinters over a wide area. Inside, the aged widow was struck by five fragments; she died before sundown. Her maid, Rosa Stokes, was wounded in the heel, an injury that would lame her for life.

The Confederate fire concentrated upon the two batteries. Stuart's 1st Virginia Cavalry, guarding Jackson's left, charged down upon the protecting Zouaves and routed them. Then Jackson's 33d Virginia came over a rise on Griffin's right. As the Parrott rifles prepared to open upon it with canister, Major William F. Barry, Chief of Artillery, assured Griffin it was a regiment that had been sent to their support by Heintzelman. Uniforms worn by the advancing regiment gave no clue, and a fatal mistake was made. The Southerners came to within sixty or seventy yards and delivered a deadly volley, killing and wounding fifty-four officers and men and 104 horses. Griffin was among the wounded.

Another wounded was Adelbert Ames of East Thomaston, Maine, commanding a section of Griffin's battery. He refused to leave the field until he was so weak he was unable to sit on the caisson on which he had been placed by his men. Thirty-three years later, on June 22, 1894, he would be presented the Congressional Medal of Honor, an award originated during the Civil War. Ames established a record as the first to earn the honor, though he was not the first to receive it. In 1933, he would die as the oldest living graduate of the U.S. Military Academy.

The eleven guns in Griffin's and Ricketts' batteries were put out of action and temporarily lost. Soon there was a countercharge and they were regained, but remained unmanned and silent on the field. This was repeated two or three times as contending infantry surged around the stilled pieces, sitting amid the heaps of dead men and horses.

The over-all battle was just as changeable. Five assaults were made by the Federals, driving the Confederates from the plateau. Each time the Southerners would rally and drive the Northern troops back.

Beauregard, leading some of the charges in person, was constantly moving about, trying to "infuse into the hearts of my officers and men the confidence and determined spirit of resistance to this wicked invasion of the homes of a free people which I felt." He reminded them that they were fighting for their homes, their firesides, and the independence of their country. And he promised them reinforcements.

It was while watching for this new support that he noticed something wrong about the flag they were carrying. In the brightness of the hot July sun, it could scarcely be distinguished from that of the enemy. Later he would report this, and design a new banner to take the place of the Stars and Bars.

The promised reinforcements arrived at 3 p.m. in the form of Kirby Smith and the last units from the Valley. But soon Smith was severely wounded by a ball in the left breast, and the command devolved upon Colonel Arnold Elzey, another Indian fighter and Mexican War veteran, who at West Point had dropped his last name, Jones.

Now the time was 3:30, and the heat on the bare, sun-baked hilltop was intolerable. The Federals formed a crescent-shaped line covering three sides of the plateau, on and behind which waited the Southerners. The last Union brigade, Howard's, took position in two lines of battle on the extreme right.

"It was a truly magnificent, though redoubtable, spectacle as they threw forward in fine style on the broad, general slopes of the ridge occupied by their main line a cloud of skirmishers, preparatory for another attack," remembered Beauregard.

The Confederates braced. Up came more reinforcements, these some that should have been there sooner. An order sent Colonel Early at noon had failed to reach him in his reserve position back of the fords at the far end of the line until 2 p.m. He brought his brigade hurriedly to the front, arriving just in time. Passing through the woods behind Elzey, he spread his men on the Confederate left, facing Howard.

The final assault came after 4 o'clock. Beauregard sensed that the Confederates had the advantage and did his utmost to whip them into a frenzy of resistance. Jackson advised his men that the situation called for use of the bayonet. All along the line the Rebel Yell rang out for the first time in battle.

The two armies surged forward. But, almost as suddenly as the first gun had blasted forth in the early dawn, men from Alabama and Georgia, North Carolina and Virginia, and seven other seceded states swept onward. The balance of power had shifted to the side of the Southerners. An accumulation of delays—that permitted by McDowell on the 20th, the

A Louisiana Zouave drummer boy.

79

slow march from Centreville, and the respite after Evans' troops had been driven back from Matthews' Hill—made it possible for the South to bring together enough reinforcements to bring victory to their banners. Brigades all along the crest of Henry Hill drove against the Northerners, down the slope of the plateau, across the valley of Young's Branch, northward and eastward, in a fan-shaped phalanx of yelling, screaming, maddened warriors who realized that they had at last gained what they had hoped for.

"Under this combined attack," wrote Beauregard, "the enemy soon was forced first over the narrow plateau in the southern angle made by the two roads so often mentioned into a patch of woods on its western slope, then back over Young's Branch . . . and rearward, in extreme disorder in all available directions towards Bull Run. The rout had become general and complete."

The Northerners ran over one another in a frantic effort to get away from the charging hordes coming down from the crest of Henry Hill, pushing in on Howard's brigade from the west, driving toward Stone Bridge. Some of the Union commands held temporarily and withdrew in order, but the vast majority ran away in a continuous trail of dust, most of them going back by Sudley Ford, the way they had come, instead of straight down the turnpike.

"The retreat soon became a rout, and this soon degenerated still further into a panic," wrote McDowell.

"Such a rout I never witnessed before," agreed Heintzelman. "No efforts could induce a single regiment to form after the retreat was commenced."

Heintzelman was particularly critical of troops from Minnesota, Michigan, and New York: "The want of discipline in these regiments was so great that most of the men would run from 50 to several hundred yards to the rear and continue the fire—fortunately for the braver ones, very high in the air—compelling those in front to retreat."

But he manifested some sympathy: "Much excuse can be made for those who fled, as few of the enemy could at any time be seen. Raw troops cannot be expected to stand long against an unseen enemy."

After the rout got under way, many of the Confederates dropped to the ground, utterly exhausted. But some of them managed to administer a final sting to the fleeing Federals.

A battery under the command of Captain Delaware

Kemper, Mexican War veteran, lawyer, and one day to be Virginia's governor, made its way across Bull Run near Stone Bridge and, on the opposite side, joined up with infantry and cavalry to hurry eastward along the turnpike. On topping the rise overlooking Cub Run, the Confederates looked down upon a fine target. Cannon, caissons, ambulances, wagons, and other vehicles, most of them abandoned by their drivers, were congregated in a confused mass around the turnoff to Sudley Ford. Civilians—men and women, including members of Congress—mingled with the mob.

Kemper unlimbered two guns. He signalled to a white-haired, 67-year-old, ardent secessionist who had ridden down from Stone Bridge astride the barrel of one of the weapons, a man who in 1865 would shoot himself to death rather than live under the U.S. Government. This volunteer was Edmund Ruffin, prominent agriculturist and writer, who had fired one of the first cannon aimed at Fort Sumter. Since morning he had been fighting. And now he pulled a lanyard that sent a shot into the center of the suspension bridge, overturning a wagon and completely blocking the span.

The confusion became greater than ever. Soldiers and teamsters fled. Some of them cut the horses from their traces, jumped upon their bare backs, and rode away, leaving behind fourteen artillery pieces, ammunition, forges, thirty wagons, and forty or fifty horses—and assorted Congressmen. Several persons were killed.

McDowell left the battlefield convinced that "could we have fought a day—yes, a few hours—sooner," the North would have won. He must have been among the first of the fleeing Federals to reach Centreville. At 5:45 p.m. he telegraphed Washington:

"We passed Bull Run. Engaged the enemy, who, it seems, had just been reinforced by General Johnston. We drove them for several miles, and finally routed them.

"They rallied and repulsed us, but only to give us

Union troops retreat in panic from the battlefield. Painting by Walter Russell.

Edmund Ruffin fired the last shot of the battle.

Ruins of the Stone Bridge in 1862 looking along the Warrenton turnpike toward the battlefield.

again the victory, which seemed complete. But our men, exhausted with fatigue and thirst and confused by firing into each other, were attacked by the enemy's reserves, and driven from the position we had gained, overlooking Manassas. After this the men could not be rallied, but slowly left the field. In the meantime the enemy outflanked Richardson at Blackburn's Ford, and we have now to hold Centreville till our men can get behind it. Miles's division is holding the town. It is reported Colonel Cameron is killed, Hunter and Heintzelman wounded, neither dangerously."

Cameron, brother of Secretary of War Simon Cameron, was dead, shot down while leading his men. So were Bee and Bartow and 844 others, Federal and Confederate. The wounded totaled 2,706—all shot in a matter of seven hours. This total of 3,553 killed and wounded would be compared nearly a century later with the casualties of later wars—3,178 at Tarawa in 4 days, 20,326 at Iwo Jima in 36 days.

The fleeing Federals hurried on past Centreville and through the night toward Washington, leaving the road behind them littered with guns, haversacks, blankets, canteens, camp equipage, clothing, and other property. They would arrive next morning in a pelting rain.

Back on the battlefield, Johnston and Beauregard made their separate ways toward their headquarters at Manassas. Awaiting them was Jefferson Davis. He had come by train during the afternoon and ridden hurriedly toward the sound of firing, arriving too late to witness the fighting.

Days would pass before the two Confederate leaders issued a congratulatory proclamation to their soldiers. It began with these two paragraphs:

"One week ago a countless host of men, organized into an army, with all the appointments which modern art and practical skill could devise, invaded the soil of Virginia. Their people sounded their approach with triumphant displays of anticipated victory. Their generals came in almost royal state; their great ministers, senators, and women came to witness the immolation of our army and the subjugation of our

81

people, and to celebrate the result with wild revelry.

"It is with the profoundest emotions of gratitude to an overruling God, whose hand is manifest in protecting our homes and our liberties, that we, your generals commanding, are enabled, in the name of our whole country, to thank you for that patriotic courage, that heroic gallantry, that devoted daring, exhibited by you in the actions of the 18th and 21st, by which the hosts of the enemy were scattered and a signal and glorious victory obtained."

The battle had been fought mainly by Johnston's troops. His men and officers made up two thirds of the killed and wounded.

No effort was made on the part of the Southerners to pursue the Federals into Washington. There were many reasons, chief of which was that the soldiers after their hard day of fighting, were exhausted. Furthermore, they had neither equipment nor supplies for such a pursuit.

The first battle of Bull Run ended with Edmund Ruffin's shot at the suspension bridge over Cub Run. Quite evenly matched in numbers were the two armies —30,000 Federals and 32,000 Confederates—but only about 18,000 on each side saw action.

Although a victory for the South, this battle would turn out to be a poor bargain. The North profited by its repulse, licked its wounds, and prepared for a long, relentless, and bloody war. The Southerners on the other hand were lulled into underestimating the fighting capacity of the forces they still had to defeat. Many who fought that day went home feeling the war was over and the South had won. They would not so readily take up arms again.

Comparative quiet settled down over the Manassas battlefield after July 21. But matters were not to remain that way. Little more than a year later, Stonewall Jackson would slip through Thoroughfare Gap in the Bull Run Mountains with his "foot cavalry" and drop down behind a railroad bed that had never had rails on it, an unfinished line that lay slightly to the west of where McDowell's men had marched from Sudley Ford. There he would wait to pounce upon the army of Union General John Pope, steadily marching eastward on the Warrenton turnpike and unaware that the Confederates were in force anywhere in their vicinity. For four days, August 29-September 1, 1862, there would be bloody fighting, with 19,514 killed and wounded.

But the Second Battle of Bull Run was the continuation of a war and not the beginning. It had not the "firsts" of the First Battle, and its centennial, unlike that of July 21, 1961, would pass almost unnoticed.

The Long Bridge, Washington. Retreating Union troops passed into the Capital over this bridge.

W.H. Shelton

SHILOH

Text by Wiley Sword
Designed by Frederic Ray

"**I**n numbers engaged, no such contest ever took place on this continent; in importance of results, but few such have taken place in the history of the world." The author of this terse assessment was a general destined to become one of the most famous of American soldiers—later Lieutenant General Ulysses S. Grant. The battle he referred to was the one he came to regard as "more persistently misunderstood than any other engagement between National and Confederate troops during the entire rebellion"—the terrible bloodbath of Shiloh.

Grant had good reason to regard Shiloh with unfeigned respect. It was a conflict that nearly cost him his reputation, his military career, and even his life. Feeling he had been "shockingly abused" by the press, he wrote to his wife shortly after the battle: "I am thinking seriously of going home . . ." Following the war General Grant continued to reflect upon the battle's bloody significance. "Shiloh was the severest battle fought at the West during the war, and but few in the East equalled it for hard, determined fighting," he asserted in his memoirs.

Yet Shiloh has suffered from a want of general understanding. Long accorded a controversial and complex status, the Battle of Pittsburg Landing, as the North referred to it, represents a paradox in American military history. Fought essentially to restore a disastrously lost war balance, the battle only compounded an already dire military situation in the South. But the conflict represented perhaps the Confederacy's greatest opportunity for a devastating victory in the West, one that might have altered the course of the war. By the narrowest of margins a disaster of the greatest magnitude was averted by the Federal army at Shiloh. Although, as Bruce Catton has written, the fact that this effort came close to being a dazzling victory did not offset the failure, the story of that miscarriage at Shiloh is as remarkable as it is fascinating, befitting one of the pivotal events in our nation's history.

Left: Map showing Forts Henry and Donelson, scene of Grant's campaign prior to his moving to Pittsburg Landing. Below: Then Major General Ulysses S. Grant, victor in the Henry-Donelson Campaign.

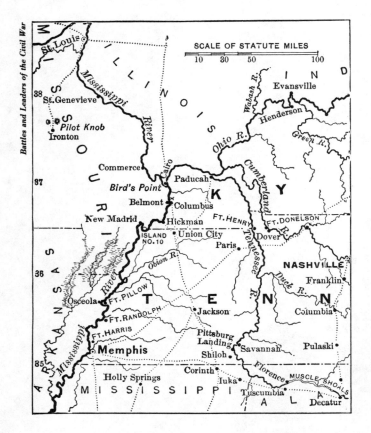

THE CAMPAIGN

The mastermind of the Federal Tennessee expedition was Henry Wager Halleck, the 47-year-old major general whose bulging eyes and receding hairline had earned him the nickname "Old Brains." As commander of the Department of the Missouri, Halleck had been constantly harassed by President Abraham Lincoln during the winter of 1861-1862 concerning the inactivity in the Western Theater. Confronted by a virtual stalemate in the military situation, with the Confederates occupying a vast defensive network stretching from Columbus to Bowling Green, Kentucky, Halleck sought an early opportunity to penetrate the Middle South.

In January 1862 a conference at his St. Louis headquarters with Brigadier Generals George W. Cullum, Halleck's chief of staff, and William T. Sherman, his friend and subordinate, produced a tentative plan that envisioned the Tennessee River as "the true line of operations."

To the rather obscure, middle-aged Illinois brigadier general who had led the combined Army and Navy expedition up the Tennessee against Fort Henry during the first week in February 1862, the operation afforded an outstanding opportunity at a minimum risk. Utilizing the Navy's gunboats almost exclusively, Ulysses S. Grant quickly reduced the two uncompleted works, Fort Heiman, on the west bank, and Fort Henry, on the eastern shore. Both Confederate forts had been erected on low ground near the river's edge for political rather than strategic considerations, and a climatic artillery duel on February 6 proved the vulnerability of Fort Henry. The fort surrendered after a bombardment of two hours and ten minutes, and Grant was thus provided with easy access to another major Confederate defensive bastion.

Fort Donelson, only twelve miles distant across a narrow neck of land, and guarding the Cumberland River approach to Nashville, was invested on February 12 by Grant's army. Following some horrendous generalship on the part of Confederate Generals John Floyd and Gideon J. Pillow—including an attack against the Federal army's right flank that became so bungled as to lead ultimately to the loss of vital entrenchments which had been vacated for that purpose—it was decided to surrender the fort and garrison. On February 16 about 9,000 prisoners, thirteen heavy cannon, and nearly 15,000 small arms were turned over to Grant's troops. Famous almost overnight, Grant was promoted to major general, and Halleck was granted his ardent wish—command of several consolidated departments which made him virtual commander west of Knoxville, Tennessee.

Union gunboats at Fort Donelson, February 14, 1862. The land attack in the distance. Sketch by Rear Admiral Walke.

Major General Henry Wager Halleck.

85

Recognizing the enormous importance of having breached the Confederates' outer line of defense, Halleck immediately prepared to capitalize on the opportunity. Using the Tennessee and Cumberland rivers as broad avenues of access, Halleck sent Federal gunboats deep into the Middle South's interior.

On the Tennessee, Union vessels cruised as far south as Florence, Alabama, wrecking bridges, breaking up numerous militia camps, and destroying Rebel shipping. Then, in late February, following the fall of Nashville, a major invasion column was organized, again under Grant's command. His orders were to conduct the "decisive movement" that would probably end the war.

At this point several untoward incidents involving army high command occurred to retard the campaign. Perhaps sensing an emerging rival in the arena of popular esteem, Halleck in early March callously removed Grant from field command on the pretext of neglect and inefficiency. Alleging that Grant had returned to his former whiskey drinking habits which had reportedly caused him to resign from the Regular Army in 1854, Halleck attempted to justify his actions with the administration in Washington.

Within a week, however, Halleck learned that President Lincoln had become involved and that he would be required to provide specific information on his allegations against Grant. Halleck quickly backed down. Restoring Grant to active command of the Tennessee expedition on March 13, he attempted to cover his culpability in the affair by forwarding a copy of an exonerating letter to Fort Henry for Grant's perusal.

Then Brigadier General William Tecumseh Sherman.

Major General Don Carlos Buell.

Meanwhile, Brigadier General C.F. Smith, Grant's replacement, had led a column of sixty-three transports forward for the purpose of destroying the vital enemy railroad bridge over Bear Creek, near Eastport, Mississippi. This would sever the major east-west artery, the Memphis & Charleston Railroad, that provided interior mobility and crucial supplies to the Mississippi Valley region.

Numbering about 25,000 men, with twelve batteries of artillery, Smith's column approached Savannah, Tennessee on March 11. "The weather was soft and fine," an officer recorded, and from the long, winding column of transports flags fluttered and bands played. To one observer the grand and awesome column of boats made it seem "we had men enough . . . to clean out the Confederacy and half of Europe."

Savannah had been chosen as a base of operations, it seems, largely because of a planned rendezvous with Major General Don Carlos Buell's Army of the Ohio, then at Nashville.

Wasting little time to achieve his immediate objective of cutting the enemy's railroad communications, Smith ordered two successive raids by elements of his column on March 12. The first foray, led by the dapper Indiana Brigadier General Lew Wallace (later the author of *Ben Hur*), failed in its objective of seriously damaging a bridge on the north—south route of the Mobile & Ohio Railroad. Thereafter Wallace's troops remained concentrated on the southern bank of the Tennessee at Crump's Landing.

The second raid ordered by C.F. Smith was led by the irascible and controversial William Tecumseh Sherman, who had been relieved from command less than six months earlier as being temporarily "unfit for duty"; physically and mentally broken. Like Wallace's attempt, Sherman's venture resulted in little net gain, but became important in the rapidly unfolding scheme of events. Forced by inclement weather to return from Yellow Creek in northern Mississippi, Sherman had been unable to reach the Memphis & Charlestown Railroad, about nineteen miles inland.

Since the Tennessee had been rapidly and heavily swollen by a sustained torrential rain—the river had risen fifteen feet in less than twenty-four hours—Sherman returned upriver to the first landing site above water—Pittsburg Landing, Tennessee.

Brigadier General Lew Wallace, tardy reinforcer of Grant at Shiloh.

Wartime sketch of Pittsburg Landing.

Here on March 16, 1862, in conjunction with Brigadier General Stephen A. Hurlbut's division, which had also moved up to the landing site as support, Sherman disembarked his men to make another attempt on the Memphis & Charlestown Railroad east of Corinth. Following a minor skirmish Sherman concluded that he would not be able to strike the railroad from this site without a severe conflict since the enemy was watching all approaches too closely.

Sherman had been favorably impressed by the location as a major base of operations though. Pittsburg Landing not only provided a strategic position from which to strike the railroads, but it also afforded an "admirable camping ground for a hundred thousand men," and the terrain "admits of easy defense by a small command," said Sherman.

Ironically, the man who was to act upon Sherman's observations had only belatedly arrived upon the scene. "Sam" Grant, as his friends knew him, had at last been restored to field command by Halleck, and had hastened upriver from Fort Henry, arriving on the 17th. C.F. Smith, who had recently scraped his leg on boarding a small yawl and had been stricken with a tetanus infection, and Sherman were the only West Point officers commanding divisions in the expedition. Grant placed full confidence in both, and remembering Sherman's gallant gesture in offering to waive seniority during the Donelson Campaign, readily accepted Sherman's strong endorsement of Pittsburg Landing as a base. All troops remaining at Savannah, except later Major General John A. McClernand's division, were accordingly ordered forward nine miles to Pittsburg Landing.

By the last week in March most of Grant's command, later officially designated the Army of the Tennessee, had encamped within a three-mile perimeter of the nearly 100-foot-high bluffs at the landing. Only Lew Wallace's division remained detached at Crump's Landing, four miles north along the river. As the men observed, Pittsburg Landing and vicinity "excited nothing but disgust and ridicule." One officer described the area as "an uninteresting tract of country, cut up by rough ravines and ridges." Within a few weeks of its occupation by Grant's troops, however, the vast wilderness site had been transformed into a teeming quasi-city, cluttered with army tents, parked wagons, boxes of munitions, and dozens of steamboats vying for the limited landing access. "Men were everywhere," wrote an awed young private, and another volunteer noted that a person might "march for miles and . . . see nothing but the white tents of infantry, cavalry, and artillery. . . . The sound of drums and the blowing of trumpets," he observed, "fill my ears from morning to night."

The original purpose of the concentration at Pittsburg Landing, as a base from which to readily strike the enemy's railroads, had been substantially changed in light of recent strategic developments. Henry Halleck, at last endowed with the authority he had long courted— over-all command in the Western Theater—had ordered the concentration of Buell's 50,000-man army with Grant's troops along the Tennessee River. Buell, who acknowledged orders for a joint offensive on March 10, was allowed to march overland from Nashville rather than move by river transport. Accordingly, on March 16 Buell's leading division broke camp and began its direct march toward Savannah, the point of rendezvous. Although Buell had reckoned that he could "move in less time, in better condition, and with more security . . ." by marching overland than by river, he failed to consider the route. Ahead lay a 122-mile backwoods road, rutted and muddied by early spring rains, and inundated by several badly swollen rivers.

Confederate private with flintlock rifle and Bowie knife.

As Buell's troops laboriously trudged south in late March, Grant's men languished at Pittsburg Landing. Among more than 51,000 Union soldiers reported there and at Crump's Landing, the inevitable sickness and internal bickering over food and seniority undermined the troops' morale. Constant drill and inspections were tedious, and the monotony of camp life was boring in the extreme. "It will be two weeks tomorrow since I done anything but eat and lay around the encampment," wrote a disgruntled Illinois soldier.

With the advent of April the skies cleared and a warm sun dried the ground and brought forth a profusion of leaves and blossoms. It became so hot that it was uncomfortable in the daytime, thought one soldier, but the health and spirits of the troops improved rapidly with the weather. Regarding their encampment as a sort of martial picnic ground, the men roamed through the surrounding woods filled with "johnny-jump-ups" and other wild flowers. Delicate pink peach blossoms fluttered by the thousands in the breeze throughout the numerous orchards adjacent to their encampments, and one private observed that "the nights are delicious, just cool enough to sleep well."

General Pierre Gustave Toutant Beauregard.

General Albert Sidney Johnston.

THE COUNTER OFFENSIVE

A measure of the enormity of crisis in the Mississippi Valley region during March 1862 was suggested by the furor that arose within the Confederacy over the retention of General Albert Sidney Johnston as commander in the Western Theater. Following the loss of Forts Henry and Donelson, forcing the abandonment of much of Kentucky and Tennessee to the enemy, the Southern press, many congressmen, and even several of his high ranking subordinate generals openly criticized Johnston and demanded his removal.

Last autograph of Albert Sidney Johnston.

The son of a former New England doctor and his second wife, Sidney Johnston had grown up in Kentucky and become a dedicated soldier. After graduating from West Point in 1826, he took up an active military career that included service in the Texas Revolution of 1836 and the Mexican War. Despite several lackluster assignments, including duty as a paymaster on the Texas frontier during the 1850's, Johnston had been appointed colonel of the newly formed 2d U.S. Cavalry in 1855. Partly responsible for this good fortune had been Jefferson Davis, Secretary of War in the Franklin Pierce administration and Johnston's close friend and admirer since their college days at Transylvania University. A brigadier general commanding the Department of the Pacific in 1861 when war broke out, Johnston immediately resigned to cast his lot with the South. Jefferson Davis had amply rewarded Johnston by appointing him a full general with rank second only to Adjutant General Samuel Cooper, an administrative official. As commander of Confederate Department No. 2, Johnston was responsible for a huge area of the South, including all or portions of seven states stretching from the Appalachian Mountains to Indian Territory.

A group of Confederate artillerymen, typical of those who fought at Shiloh.

Johnston's tenure in this assignment had been anything but successful, however. In January 1862 a subordinate, Brigadier General Felix K. Zollicoffer, had been soundly defeated at Logan's Cross Roads, Kentucky, opening east Tennessee and the Cumberland Gap to enemy incursions. Following the loss of Forts Henry and Donelson, important sites such as Columbus, Kentucky and Nashville had been abandoned.

Though Johnston's subordinates had been generally responsible for these disasters, the department commander was bitterly criticized. One congressman, traveling with the army, wrote to Jefferson Davis that Johnston had committed inexcusable "errors of omission,

A squad of soldiers in the Western Union armies, possibly Ohio troops. From a tintype.

commission, and delay." Coupled with other vociferous protests, the pressure to remove Johnston was extensive; all but one of Tennessee's congressmen called on Davis to demand his removal. Davis' reply revealed his unshakable confidence in his close friend. If Sidney Johnston was "no general," he said, they had best give up the war, for they had no general.

Johnston, aided by another of the South's premier generals, P.G.T. Beauregard, rapidly determined on a bold plan to recoup lost Southern fortunes. Sent west in February 1862 following political difficulties with the Davis administration, the victor of Bull Run had tentatively suggested to Johnston in late February that he might wish to co-operate with or join the independent command then being gathered by Beauregard to defend the vital railroads about Corinth, Mississippi.

Sidney Johnston reached a decision almost immediately. Stating that defense of the Mississippi Valley was "of paramount importance," he would risk interception by Buell's Federal army to join with Beauregard. This "hazardious experiment," as Johnston termed it, was initiated in late February, and following a three-week combined march and journey by railroad, the vanguard of Johnston's army reached Corinth without mishap.

Including the troops from Columbus, Kentucky, and contingents from the Gulf states, Beauregard had managed to gather about 21,000 troops for defense of the railroads. To these were added about 10,000 men in mid-March from Major General Braxton Bragg's Department of Alabama and West Florida. Sidney Johnston's command further swelled the Confederate forces in and about Corinth to nearly 50,000 by the end of the month.

Reorganized as the Army of the Mississippi, this formidable gathering was to be further augmented by Major General Earl Van Dorn's Trans-Mississippi Army, ordered on March 22 to join at Corinth as soon as possible. Yet events along the Tennessee River had occurred so rapidly that Confederate plans soon became largely reactive in nature.

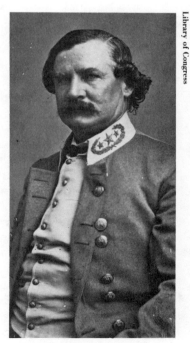

Brigadier General Benjamin F. Cheatham.

Shiloh Church.

Following the initial occupation of Pittsburg Landing by Sherman's troops on March 16, a growing apprehension had developed for the safety of the Memphis & Charleston, and Mobile & Ohio railroads, deemed "the vertebrae of the Confederacy" by one general. Various detachments had been posted at outlying locations along the railroads, and a series of false alarms soon began to wear upon the nerves of the Confederate generals. At Bethel Station, twenty-three miles northwest of Corinth on the Mobile & Ohio road, a strong force of infantry and cavalry under Brigadier General Benjamin F. Cheatham had been posted. Sent to this site to defend the region from an advance by Lew Wallace's Federal division, part of which was reported at nearby Adamsville, Cheatham was instructed to establish a strong outpost at Purdy, four miles distant in the direction of the enemy. While carrying out his instructions on April 2, Cheatham's movement was discovered by Federal scouts lurking in the vicinity.

Fearing that an attack was pending on his lone brigade stationed at Adamsville, Federal Colonel Charles R. Woods immediately sent word of a Confederate "advance" to Lew Wallace at Crump's Landing. The alarmed Wallace promptly started two brigades to Woods's relief, and before midnight stood with his entire division in line of battle, waiting for an attack that never came.

Cheatham's cavalry scouts, meanwhile, had observed Wallace's forced march to Adamsville. Compounding the error, they alarmed Cheatham, who sent an urgent telegram to Corinth about 10 p.m., warning of a Federal movement in force. Placed in Beauregard's hands, Cheatham's telegram precipitated a major crisis. Concluding that Wallace's aggressiveness suggested that a junction of Buell's and Grant's armies was near at hand, and that the enemy was preparing to advance in strength, Beauregard endorsed Cheatham's telegram: "Now is the moment to advance and strike the enemy at Pittsburg Landing." This message was entrusted to Adjutant General Thomas Jordan, who immediately carried it to General Johnston for final disposition.

Johnston was still awake and, being uncertain of the tactical implications, walked across the street to Bragg's quarters to confer with his chief of staff. Bragg, after being roused from bed, soon became involved in a critical discussion. Both Bragg and Jordan, speaking on

Union private of the 2d Minnesota Volunteers.

Beauregard's behalf, allegedly urged an immediate advance against the enemy. Johnston was said to be reluctant, but was influenced by several related developments. On the previous day, one of Johnston's staff officers, Lieutenant Thomas M. Jack, had returned from Richmond bringing important dispatches from Jefferson Davis and Robert E. Lee, the President's military adviser. Both letters urged Johnston to strike the enemy before the arrival of Buell's army, enroute from Nashville. Further, it is believed that during the evening of April 2 a report on the rapid approach of Buell's 30,000 troops was received from two detached companies of Louisiana cavalry, watching Buell's movement along the Duck River in middle Tennessee.

This coincidence of information served to support the theory that the junction of the two Federal armies was near at hand. Accordingly Johnston ordered preparations for an advance at 6 a.m. the following morning, drafting the orders in Bragg's bedchamber after midnight. Final plans and arrangements were written by Beauregard early in the morning of April 3, and somewhat belatedly, about midafternoon, the advance elements of the army cleared Corinth.

However, due to widespread confusion over the proper roads to take, the poor condition of the narrow backwoods wagon trails, and improper communications, the march was so protracted as to require three days to traverse the approximately twenty-three miles to Pittsburg Landing. A light rain began to fall during the afternoon of the 4th, miring the already soft roads. Thereafter the widely dispersed troops often found their way blocked by bogged wagons and artillery.

Though it had been intended to attack during the early morning of April 5, Johnston found this plan thwarted by a heavy rainstorm that lasted nearly three hours during the night. By dawn the roads were vast quagmires of mud and standing water, and the scattered corps were unable to move faster than a slow crawl. Although the front line, Hardee's Corps, was in position by 10 a.m. the second and third assault waves lagged far behind, creating huge gaps in the Confederate array.

The Confederate council of war before the opening of the Battle of Shiloh. Left to right are: Beauregard, Polk (sitting), Breckinridge, Johnston, Bragg, and Hardee.

Major General Braxton Bragg.

Major General William Joseph Hardee.

By late afternoon, when most of the troops were finally deployed, the nerves of the Confederate commanders were so frayed that several wanted to call off the entire operation. Braxton Bragg, in a surly mood and commenting unfavorably on the troops' lack of secrecy and their insufficient provisions, urged a withdrawal. Even Beauregard, who had initiated the movement and planned much of the attack, also proposed a retreat. The noise of the inexperienced troops and the delay, said Beauregard, had alerted the enemy, and they would be found "entrenched to the eyes."

Sidney Johnston was astounded. Supported by Leonidas Polk, commander of the I Corps, Johnston declared, "Gentlemen, we shall attack at daylight tomorrow." The enemy, he reasoned, could present no greater front than the Confederates, and thus he would "fight them if they were a million."

That night the Confederate army slept within two miles of Shiloh Church, which marked the outer perimeter of Grant's army. Although it had been originally intended to attack corps abreast, Beauregard had earlier decreed a battle formation modeled after "Napoleon's order for the Battle of Waterloo." Thus, succeeding waves of infantry, with corps in tandem aligned across the entire front, were ordered deployed. The basic premise, advised a staff officer, was that "no force the enemy could [amass] could cut through three double lines of Confederates." In the heavily wooded terrain, with scattered enemy encampments throughout affording natural pockets of resistance, Beauregard's plan presented a fatal flaw.

Johnston, who had determined to trust in the "iron dice of battle," by now was more intent on the tactical objectives of the attack. By turning the enemy's left flank, the Federal army's line of retreat to the Tennessee River might be cut off, and the opposing troops forced back against deep Owl Creek, "where [they] will be obliged to surrender," said Johnston.

Mindful of his recent assertion: "The test of merit in my profession with the people is success. It is a hard rule, but I think it right,"

Major General Leonidas Polk.

Men of the 9th Mississippi in camp before the Battle of Shiloh.

Sidney Johnston's terse battle orders urged resolution, discipline, and valor. "The eyes and hopes of eight millions of people" were resting upon them, Johnston told his soldiers. They were to fire at the feet of the enemy to avoid overshooting, and soldiers would not be permitted to break ranks "to strip or rob the dead." Anyone running away on any pretext would be "shot on the spot."

Oblivious of the dire implication of these words, Johnston's soldiers prepared for the morrow's fight with considerable, if ill-judged, enthusiasm. Campfires, although forbidden by orders, were ablaze in a wide perimeter throughout the Confederate lines. Shouts, bugle calls, and drum rolls echoed through the forests. "I have a great anxiety to see and be in a great battle," wrote one Confederate before the fight, and another talked of his "breathless anxiety" as Beauregard had ridden past on the 5th, saying, "Fire low, boys, fire low." In all, the campaign was largely looked upon as a grand adventure by the many soldiers who would soon be involved in their first combat. Unfortunately for many, it would also be their very last experience.

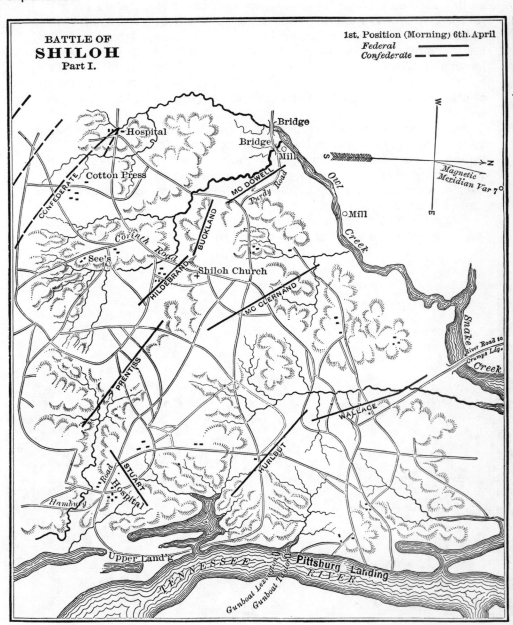

Battle of Shiloh: Positions on morning of April 6.

THE SURPRISE

To William Tecumseh Sherman, the events of the first week in April reflected the dire inexperience of his untried division. Since most of his men were recruits unfamiliar with army life, he had ordered daily drill and instruction. On April 3 Colonel Ralph Buckland's brigade had marched three miles out the Corinth road to perform this routine duty. Actually, the men of the 70th Ohio remembered the jaunt as "a kind of picnic excursion." After marching a few miles the men stacked arms for dinner, sending out a small picket detachment. These pickets were advancing to their posts when they were suddenly fired on by Confederates.

According to one private, a hasty retreat by the pickets was followed by a short council among the officers, and they decided to withdraw promptly to their Shiloh Church encampment. When later informed of the affair, Sherman regarded it as so minor that he made no report to army headquarters.

On the following day, April 4, another of Buckland's regiments, the 72d Ohio Infantry, was drilling in the open fields near their outpost pickets. About 2:30 p.m. sharp firing in the nearby woods resulted in a further advance by a few companies of the regiment. They soon learned that an entire outpost consisting of a lieutenant and six men had been captured by Confederate cavalry. When two of the 72d's companies sent into the woods as flankers failed to return, a strong 150-man detachment of the 5th Ohio Cavalry was sent by Sherman to investigate.

Guided by the sporadic sound of firing, the cavalrymen soon came up with Buckland's missing companies, then engaged with a larger force of enemy cavalry. The Ohio cavalrymen burst on the scene with a shout and chased the scattering Confederates for nearly a quarter-mile, capturing about thirty prisoners.

Atop a nearby knoll the pursuers suddenly came face to face with a Confederate battle line of infantry supported by artillery. Surprised by the blast of musketry and three cannon shots, the Ohioans fled the scene, losing most of their prisoners in the confusion. Unknowingly, Sherman's cavalrymen had uncovered the advance elements of Hardee's Corps, marching to their assigned position as spearhead of the planned assault on the Federal camps.

When the retreating Federals returned to the line of outposts, they found Sherman present, and in a surly mood. Angrily upbraiding Buckland for nearly drawing the whole army into battle, Sherman further chided his officers for their "irregular proceedings." Even the commander of the Ohio cavalry, Major Elbridge Ricker, was scoffed at by Sherman for his alarmist report of having encountered a strong enemy force. "Oh!—tut, tut. You militia officers get scared too easily," remarked Sherman.

After returning with his men to their Shiloh camps, Sherman sent a routine report to Grant estimating that the Confederates occupied the village of Monterey in considerable force, and inferred that Buckland had perhaps encountered a brigade making a reconnaissance in force.

Since he was informally the camp commander, despite the presence at Pittsburg Landing of Major General John A. McClernand, who ranked him, Sherman was responsible only to Grant, who was then quartered at Savannah awaiting Buell's arrival. Alerted by several preliminary reports of an attack on the army's outposts, Grant hastened

Private William Graul, 32d Indiana Volunteers, who fought at Shiloh.

Private Abraham W. Shively, 5th Ohio Light Artillery, who fought at Shiloh.

to Pittsburg Landing late that night. He arrived in the midst of a driving rainstorm and was unable to reach Sherman's camps at Shiloh Church. In the darkness and slippery footing Grant's mount fell heavily, pinning the major general's leg. Although the soft ground prevented a fracture, Grant's ankle became so swollen that his boot had to be cut off. During the next several days Grant was unable to walk without crutches.

Several of Grant's staff officers had reported all quiet along Sherman's front, however, and thereafter the skirmish of the 4th was largely disregarded. The following day, Saturday, April 5, Sherman sent word to Grant: "I have no doubt that nothing will occur today more than some picket firing. The enemy is saucy, but got the worst of it yesterday, and will not press our pickets far. I will not be drawn out far unless with certainty of advantage, and I do not apprehend anything like an attack on our position."

Major General John A. McClernand.

Brigadier General Benjamin M. Prentiss.

Sherman, as suggested by the evidence, was deeply embarrassed by the affair of the 4th. Disdainful of his officers and men, he wrote that they had "as much idea of war as children." The officers, in particular, he thought were "afraid of the men," and extremely careless. "I will do all I can with my division, but regret I have not better discipline and more reliable men," he confided.

Orders that served as a demeaning critique were soon issued to his division. In case of alarm regiments were to await orders before going to the front. Brigade commanders were to go no farther than the advanced pickets without Sherman's order. Detachments adjacent to the flank of a marching column were absolutely prohibited—on and on read the lengthy orders.

Thereafter, Sherman was particularly harsh in dealing with his alarmist officers. On April 5, when the colonel of the 53d Ohio Infantry formed his men following an exchange of shots between pickets, Sherman sent over a staff officer with a caustic comment: "General Sherman says: 'Take your damned regiment [back] to Ohio,'" announced the staff officer, "'There is no enemy nearer than Corinth.'"

Yet if Sherman remained indifferent in his attitude, his resulting lack of vigilance was shared by others, including the man who later came to be regarded as one of the heroes of the battle.

Brigadier General Benjamin M. Prentiss was a curious addition to Grant's command. A quarrelsome Illinois politician who had feuded with Grant over seniority during service in Missouri in 1861, Prentiss was also on unfriendly terms with several of his subordinates. As commander of the newly created 6th Division, Prentiss was allocated ten recently arrived regiments, only one of which had been in battle. The commander of this unit, the 25th Missouri Infantry, was Colonel Everett Peabody, a highly competent if headstrong former railroad engineer known for his outspoken manner. Peabody had been wounded and captured during the siege of Lexington, Missouri by Price's Confederates in September 1861. Upon his exchange his old unit had been quickly reorganized and sent east into Tennessee. As an experienced senior colonel, Peabody, upon assuming a brigade commander's responsibility, objected to the "kind of loose" camp life permitted in the division. During the evening of April 5 Peabody had gone to Prentiss with a suggestion that the division be put in a condition to resist an attack, and that at least one battery of artillery be deployed to protect the outer line.

Prentiss, undoubtedly regarding Sherman's adjacent camp at Shiloh Church as the outer portion of the army most exposed to any enemy buildup, is said to have "hooted" at Peabody's suggestions.

Although forming a portion of the army's outer periphery, since it was on the immediate left of Sherman's camps, Prentiss' pickets were stationed only about 300 yards in front. Several officers who reported about a dozen "butternuts" observing a review of the 6th Division from the underbrush on the afternoon of the 5th had felt uneasy enough to urge Prentiss to make a reconnaissance patrol late that afternoon. Routinely obliging these officers, Prentiss had allowed five companies under Colonel David Moore of the 21st Missouri to march into the brush to search out the offending Confederates. Moore had returned after dark and reported no contact of any sort. Apparently, Moore marched only about a mile diagonally across Sherman's front to an "old cottonfield," where several Negroes said they had seen a few Rebel cavalry that afternoon.

Consequently, Prentiss was convinced, like Sherman, that his men were unduly alarmed, and that few enemy were nearby.

After listening to taunts from the handful of Confederates captured during the skirmish of the 4th—"If you ain't mighty careful, they'll [Confederates] run you into hell or the [Tennessee] river before tomorrow night," said one prisoner—an undercurrent of apprehension had, indeed, run through the Federal ranks. One rather dismayed lieutenant colonel of an Illinois regiment had gone bathing at a nearby creek along the front and found no Federal pickets guarding the approaches. The army must have some "queer generals" he surmised in his diary.

Yet, almost at the very last possible moment, events occurring on the evening of April 5 were to result in a crucial detection of the Confederates, in time to provide a narrow margin of survival for perhaps the entire army.

About 8:30 that evening an officer of the outer picket guard, Captain Gilbert D. Johnson of the 12th Michigan Infantry, returned to camp and reported to the officer of the day that "he could see long lines of camp fires" and "hear bugle sounds and drums." Fully concerned, the officer of the day, Lieutenant Colonel W.H. Graves, promptly went to see Prentiss with this information.

Johnny Clem, the "Drummer Boy of Shiloh." Unofficial drummer of the 22d Michigan, he was probably, at 10, the youngest participant in the battle. In later years he became a major general; he died in 1937 and was buried in Arlington Cemetery.

Federal private.

The river landing at Savannah, Tennessee, nine miles north of Pittsburg Landing. General Grant's headquarters were in the Cherry mansion on the right.

Prentiss, however, had recently received Moore's negative report, and merely told Graves to withdraw Johnson's company, saying the cause of concern was only an enemy patrol. When Johnson dutifully returned to camp with his men about 10 p.m., however, he had been further alarmed by the continuous noise in the woods. Again Graves went to see Prentiss, this time taking Johnson with him. But the Illinois brigadier rather abruptly told them not to be alarmed, that everything was "all right."

Frustrated by Prentiss' lack of concern, they went to the tent of their brigade commander, Everett Peabody, and told him of the recent events. Although it was then about midnight, Peabody pondered the alternatives. At last, saying he would not be taken by surprise, he ordered out upon his sole responsibility a reconnaissance patrol consisting of three companies of the 25th Missouri and two companies of the 12th Michigan regiments. Under the command of a veteran Regular Army officer, Major James E. Powell, the patrol was hastily organized and marched from camp about 3 a.m.

Working their way forward about a mile to an obscure cotton field known as Fraley's Field, Powell's men approached the open spot cautiously, just as the first streaks of light gathered on the horizon. Three warning shots rang out in the semi-darkness, but Powell pressed forward into the clearing, his men deployed in a long skirmish line.

Ahead, the advanced pickets of Brigadier General S.A.M. Wood's Confederate brigade were surprised to see the approaching Federals. Following an exchange of shots between Powell's men and a few forward vedettes, Wood's outpost pickets, 280 men under Major A.B. Hardcastle, opened fire with a volley. A second lieutenant of the 25th Missouri was here struck down, becoming the first of what was soon to be a dreadful butcher's bill of casualties.

The first fire had occurred at about 4:55 a.m., and doggedly Powell's and Hardcastle's units continued firing, both sides losing an increasing number of men. A half-hour passed before word came from Wood's headquarters for Hardcastle to hold his ground until the general advance

Brigadier General Charles F. Smith.

could begin. Yet another half-hour went by, and still the Federals stubbornly refused to yield in front.

Acting under Peabody's orders to "drive in the guard, and . . . develop the force," holding the ground as long as possible, Powell also had anxiously awaited his own reinforcements. About 6:30 a.m., however, a long battleline of men in butternut uniforms emerged from the woods and swept into Fraley's Field, their muskets glimmering in the soft morning sunlight. A portion of Hardee's corps, which comprised the first of three successive Confederate battlelines, this frontal assault column numbered more than twenty-two regiments, in all about 9,000 effective troops. The awesome sight was enough to convince Powell of his danger, and a hasty withdrawal was initiated by a bugler sounding retreat. Chased by the skirmishers of two Arkansas infantry units, Powell's men disappeared into the woods at a run, heading for camp along the same route by which they had earlier advanced.

Confederate private "armed to the teeth."

At Savannah, Ulysses Grant was asleep in his headquarters at the Cherry house, having been up "to a very late hour" the previous evening while socializing with his officers aboard the steamboat *Tigress.* The advance elements of Buell's army, William Nelson's division, had arrived only yesterday following a forced march. Grant had no boats to transport these troops upriver, however, and he had assured one of Buell's officers, "I will send boats for you Monday or Tuesday, or sometime early in the week. There will be no fight at Pittsburg Landing; we will have to go to Corinth, where the Rebels are fortified."

At Pittsburg Landing the normal camp routine was already underway. With the usual Sunday morning inspection in the offing, many of the men in Hurlbut's and Sherman's divisions were cleaning their equipment. Breakfast was being prepared in many of Prentiss' camps, and one 20-year-old Wisconsin private, having just returned from all-night picket duty, was so exhausted that he told his sergeant he was "going to sleep today, even if Abe Lincoln comes." Another soldier, a newly appointed brigadier general, was at breakfast, unaware that his wife had just arrived at the landing for a surprise visit and even now, dressed in her Sunday finery, was preparing to go to him.

Even the crusty, bedridden brigadier, C.F. Smith, was in fine spirits that morning, laughing and joking with several visiting officers. Only yesterday Smith had offhandedly commented on the army's current welcome respite. The enemy, he said, are "all back in Corinth, and, when our transportation arrives, we have got to go there and draw them out, as you would draw a badger out of his hole."

Federal artillery going into action.

Confederate charge upon Prentiss' camp on Sunday morning. Drawing by A.C. Redwood.

THE ONSLAUGHT

Albert Sidney Johnston had risen early, and was discussing the general plan of attack with General Beauregard that morning when they heard the sound of gunfire. Mounting his thoroughbred bay, Fire-eater, Johnston appeared to be in fine spirits, and told his staff, "Tonight we will water our horses in the Tennessee River."

As the advancing lines hurried forward, it seemed to Beauregard, who remained in the rear forwarding reserves, that the dense columns were as irresistible as "an Alpine avalanche." The weather had cleared and a bright sun was now rising in a cloudless sky, prompting an officer to remark that it must be another "sun of Austerlitz."

But in the rough terrain south of Shiloh Church, brigades and regiments were already experiencing difficulty in maintaining an intact battleline. Gaps appeared and widened as much of Hardee's line veered northeast toward Prentiss' camps. Consequently, frequent delays occurred as troops were realigned or moved forward into the void.

At a small clearing near Fraley's Field, Shaver's Arkansas brigade belatedly encountered a regiment of Federals, sent by Peabody to reinforce Powell's patrol, which was known to be in difficulty by the trickle of wounded returning to their camp. Expecting to meet only a skirmishing party, the reinforcements had joined Powell's retreating men, but their commander insisted on pressing forward into the open field. Colonel

Moore, who had returned to the scene of his earlier reconnaissance, was almost immediately shot down by a heavy volley from behind a fence row. Although his men promptly fell back, taking position along a timbered knoll fronting a small ravine south of their camp, they were soon assaulted by overwhelming numbers of Confederate infantry, and scattered in confusion.

In Prentiss' camp about 7 a.m. the sharp volleys issuing from the nearby woods had caused Colonel Peabody to order a drummer to sound the "long roll," calling the division to arms. As the men were forming, down the line galloped their irate general. Prentiss reined in his horse in front of Peabody, and angrily demanded to know if the colonel had provoked an attack by sending out a force without orders. Peabody attempted to explain, but the general cut him short by shouting, "Colonel Peabody, I will hold you personally responsible for bringing on this engagement."

The two men glared at one another. With obvious contempt, Peabody remarked that he was personally responsible for all of his actions, then mounted his horse and rode away. In Prentiss' official report, his lingering anger was manifested by omitting all mention of his senior colonel, except listing him as a brigade commander.

Advancing toward the sound of the nearby firing, Peabody soon encountered the fugitives from Shaver's attack. The sun was already two hours high, and Peabody rapidly deployed his brigade along a prominent oak ridge south of camp. Seventy-five yards away the onrushing Confederates swept over the crest of an opposite ridge. To one Federal private it was the "grandest scene" he had ever witnessed. A seemingly endless line of men covered the ground in front.

Yet miraculously Peabody's deadly volleys of musketry soon brought the Rebel line to a halt, and even caused a few units to break and run away on the enemy's left flank. Soon the Confederates returned to the fray, however, and about 8:15 a.m. a peculiar, high-pitched cry rang from the woods in front, followed by the appearance of a massive column of brown-clad infantry with fixed bayonets.

To Private Henry Morton Stanley, one of Shaver's men, it was the first time he had heard the bloodcurdling Rebel yell. According to Stanley it "drove all sanity and order" from them, and inspired the men with the wildest enthusiasm.

Attacked by nearly two full brigades of Confederate infantry, Peabody's line was overlapped and enveloped in what seemed like an instant. As rapidly as they could go, the remnants of Peabody's line began streaming back through their camp, losing in the process much of their organization and discipline.

Everett Peabody, bleeding from four wounds—in the hand, thigh, neck, and body—vainly attempted to reform his men. Unable to find Prentiss, he galloped among the tents urging his frightened soldiers to "stand to it yet!" Perhaps cursing Prentiss for refusing to allow artillery to be parked in front of his brigade camps the night before, Peabody was still mounted on his big horse, gesturing and shouting amid the swirling smoke. Having earlier believed he would be killed, he had shaken hands that morning with his officers and bid them good-bye. Now he was struck by a fifth missile, which entered his upper lip and passed out the back of his head, killing him instantly. His terrified mount bolted away, and the colonel's body was tossed limply against a log. Not yet 32, Everett Peabody's premonition of death had been fulfilled.

For Peabody's men, the next few minutes became utter chaos. Unable to reform in sufficient strength to stabilize a defensive line, they rapidly melted away in the face of the approaching enemy. One youthful Wisconsin lieutenant, realizing that their camp would soon be lost, ran to his tent to retrieve a tintype of his fiancée. Emerging just in time to avoid capture, he raced away down the company street, a hail of musket balls whizzing close about his ears.

By 8:45 a.m. all of Peabody's camps were in Confederate hands, and the mass exodus toward the river landing had begun, most of the Federal units being so scattered that they ceased to exist as regiments during the remainder of the battle. While many men joined with other regiments and continued to fight, others simply clogged the roads and wandered about aimlessly. Said one private with unabashed candor, ". . . [by now] everybody was running, . . . so I ran too." Inevitably these fugitives were joined by the remainder of Prentiss' division, including their sorely pressed commander.

Sherman's troops hurrying to meet the Confederate attack. Shiloh Church on the left. Drawing by Henry Lovie.

Prentiss' remaining brigade, led by Colonel Madison Miller of Missouri, had earlier formed in a small parade ground clearing known as Spain Field. Attacked by Brigadier General Adley H. Gladden's brigade, Miller's men, assisted by two batteries of 6-pounder guns, had handily beaten off the first assault. Indeed, Gladden had been mortally wounded by a Federal shell, and nearly an hour was lost in attempting to re-form and reinforce the Confederate line at this point. Then, with Peabody's camps lost, the Confederates had renewed their assault on Miller. The brigades of Chalmers and Gladden, the latter now commanded by Colonel Daniel W. Adams, pressed forward so rapidly that several of Prentiss' cannon were overrun before they could be withdrawn.

One of Miller's regiments just off the boat, the 15th Michigan, had marched from the landing that morning to join their new command. En route, they had passed several idle camps where some of the 15th's men had inquired about the firing heard ahead. The unconcerned soldiers told these greenhorns that some of the pickets were likely "shooting squirrels." Farther on, the regiment encountered several wounded men. When asked about the pickets shooting squirrels, one soldier held up a bloody hand and said they were the "funniest squirrels" he ever saw.

Once on the firing line, the 15th was rushed into position in time to confront Gladden's Confederates. Yet, somehow, the regiment had marched to the front without ammunition, and they now stood with empty Austrian rifles, unable to return the enemy's fire. The regiment was soon withdrawn and marched to the rear; they were unable to draw ammunition and fight until much later in the day.

As the order to fall back spread through Prentiss' remaining regiments, so many men had already abandoned the fight that only an estimated 150 men of an original 862 were present in one Wisconsin regiment.

In the chaos and confusion of Miller's retreat, the scene became "perfectly awful," according to one officer. Sick and wounded soldiers were running in all directions, some dressed only in underclothes. A young lieutenant of artillery who had witnessed the loss of his section and the virtual annihilation of the battery, was found crying like a child.

Prentiss' shattered division was by now nearly a total wreck. Of the approximately 5,000 fighting men, only two or three regiments retained enough effective strength to continue functioning as units. Much of their artillery, many small arms, and all of their camps and equipment with seven stands of colors were already in Confederate hands. To add to the misery, a portion of the abandoned camps caught fire, utterly destroying their former occupants' possessions. One of Prentiss' privates, having run in full flight for a half-mile, was convinced that they were forever disgraced. "What will they say about this at home?" he pondered in utter frustration.

Brigadier General James Abram Garfield fought under Buell on the second day at Shiloh. He later became 20th President of the United States.

Scene at Pittsburg Landing April 6. Routed Federals flee to the river bank as reinforcements land. Drawing by Henry Lovie.

105

SHERMAN'S PLIGHT

Reacting with obvious alarm to the sound of nearby firing, the most advanced of Sherman's regiments, the 53d Ohio Volunteers, had formed on their color line about 6 a.m. When word of this was sent to Sherman's headquarters, an officer rode over and told the colonel, "General Sherman says you must be badly scared over there."

Yet before 7 a.m. the advancing columns of the enemy could be detected in the timber by the bright flash of their gun barrels glinting through the green leaves.

Riding a magnificent "sorrel race mare" captured from the enemy several weeks earlier, William Tecumseh Sherman rode into Rhea Field in front of the 53d Ohio's camp shortly after 7 a.m. His attention was caught by a body of troops marching across the distant end of the field, and he uncased his telescope to study their movements.

Screened by brush bordering a small stream about fifty yards to the right, the skirmishers of Cleburne's brigade now emerged into the field and discovered a mounted party of Federals diagonally in their front. Raising their muskets, they prepared to fire at what was obviously an important officer. At the last instant, one of the 53d Ohio's officers gasped a warning. "General, look to your right!"

Sherman dropped his telescope and whirled about, just as the skirmishers fired. "My God, we are attacked!" he blurted out, and threw up his hand as if to ward off the bullets. Close by his side Private Thomas D. Holliday, his orderly, was struck and immediately killed. Too, Sherman at this point was probably struck in the hand by a single buckshot (part of a "buck and ball" cartridge containing a ball and three buckshot, commonly used in .69 caliber smoothbore muskets). Immediately dashing to safety, Sherman merely shouted to the astonished Ohioans to hold their position, he would bring them support.

Advancing at the time onto Rhea Field was one of the most aggressive fighters in all the Confederacy, Brigadier General Patrick Ronayne Cleburne. A 34-year-old Irishman with daredevil courage, Cleburne had

Brigadier General Patrick Ronayne Cleburne.

First position of Waterhouse's battery. From a sketch made shortly after the battle.

experienced bad luck that morning. His brigade had been split apart by "an almost impassable morass," and now he faced the 53d Ohio's position with only two small regiments present. Immediately attacking, his men were surprised and cut down by cannon fire from a strategically placed Federal battery atop a nearby hill. Waterhouse's Illinois battery had been prepared for inspection when the alarm sounded that morning, hence these guns were harnessed and ready for action almost immediately. Waterhouse's rifled cannon continued to fire downhill with shell and canister, even as another attempt was made by Cleburne to get past the 53d Ohio's camp.

Charging unsupported by artillery or their companion regiment, which was too broken to re-form in time, the 6th Mississippi moved alone through Rhea Field. A small regiment, 425 men strong before the fighting began, the Mississippians again endured a terrific storm of fire. Although their attack caused the 53d Ohio to flee the field when their colonel, his nerves at the breaking point, called out, "Retreat and save yourselves," the Confederates were driven back in disorder. In less than a half hour these Mississippians had sustained a loss of 300 men, representing the fourth highest loss during the entire war by any Southern regiment in a single battle.

Unable to press the Federals further in this sector until reinforcements arrived about 8 a.m., Cleburne galloped around the intervening swamp to see to his remaining regiments. Here on the left he found four of them, in all about 1,500 men, attacking a strong Federal brigade posted in their front. Here Buckland's brigade of Sherman's division had not only more men, but also a favorable field of fire from behind heavy timber. Again Cleburne's units met a bloody repulse.

At last, the advance elements of Braxton Bragg's second Confederate battleline made their appearance about 8:30 a.m. But due to the colossal mistake of arranging each corps in tandem across a wide front, Bragg's units had already become so intermixed and retarded by the rough terrain that effective deployment was almost impossible. Bragg's leading brigade, James Patton Anderson's, had advanced only a mile in two and one-half hours, and being unsupported, had had to wait until one of Polk's brigades, Russell's, appeared. Part of the third Confederate battleline, by marching along the main Corinth road this brigade had made faster progress than most of Bragg's units.

Together, Russell and Anderson attempted to assail Waterhouse's deadly guns, posted on the knoll beyond the 53d Ohio's camp. They quickly became entangled in the same morass that Cleburne had found impenetrable, however. Regiments and companies were separated in the heavy going, and when these units emerged in piecemeal fashion, they were taken in flank by Barrett's Federal battery, posted opposite Shiloh Church. The result was a bloody repulse that further mixed and confused the survivors. When another trailing brigade, Bushrod Johnson's, came up, this unit was jumbled and intermixed with Russell's and Anderson's men, creating an unwieldy mass. So many Confederates were soon found advancing, however, prodded on by an angry Braxton Bragg, that the 57th Ohio, one of two remaining regiments supporting Waterhouse's guns, broke and ran away.

Waterhouse's cannoneers next limbered up and started for the rear, only to have one of Sherman's staff officers halt and redeploy the battery, thinking their retreat was too hasty. Here one of Russell's regiments, the 13th Tennessee, swung around to the east and approached from the flank, taking the battery unawares. The hard-charging Con-

Brigadier General Bushrod Rust Johnson.

107

Battery of 24-pounder siege guns that formed a part of the "Last Line" above the landing, April 6. Photograph taken a few days after the battle, before they had been moved from their battle position.

federates were within fifty yards before any attempt was made to bring off the guns. In the smoke and confusion three cannon were wheeled away, but the remainder of the equipment was lost. Disgustedly, a nearby Federal officer watched the enemy claim the cannon that had cost the Confederates so many lives. "They swarmed around them like bees," he said. "They jumped upon the guns, and on the hay bales in the battery camp, and yelled like crazy men."

Alone on the extreme left flank of Sherman's line stood the 77th Ohio, doggedly fighting near Shiloh Church. Although this unit promptly changed front, attempting to compensate for the loss of Waterhouse's battery and the other two Ohio regiments, the Rebels began working around their flank, causing the regiment to gradually break up. Then three

of Bushrod Johnson's regiments, separated by the swamp, pushed directly toward Shiloh Church from the south. The pressure was too great for the 77th Ohio, and "they ran like sheep," said an officer of Barrett's battery. Left alone to confront the attacking Confederates, Barrett's unsupported guns put out such a devastating fire that the enemy regiments in front ultimately broke and withdrew in disorder. In front of the smoking cannon, the Confederates lay in windrows. Devastated by effective Federal artillery fire, and wasted in piecemeal attacks lacking counter-battery support and proper brigade co-ordination, the Confederates had suffered a severe reverse at the hands of a Federal brigade half their strength.

Yet, ironically, the vicious fighting and stout defense of the Federal artillery went for naught. Although the fighting momentarily abated in Barrett's front, it was quickly understood that Sherman's left flank had been turned. The enemy could be seen in the rear, advancing at almost right angles to Barrett's guns, and Sherman sent word for the plucky cannoneers to fall back.

Sherman, despite the close call that morning in Rhea Field, had refused to believe the attack was anything more than a foray against his own camp until the appearance of Bragg's men—"a beautiful and dreadful sight," he observed. Embroiled in the fighting near Shiloh Church, a grimly determined Sherman had endured such a withering fire that staff officers when approaching were seen to bend low in their saddles, as if in the midst of a driving rainstorm. At least three horses had been killed under Sherman that morning, including his "sorrel race mare." All about him were astounded by his imperturbable demeanor, and an aide said his cool conduct "instilled . . . a feeling that it was grand to be there with him." Calmly smoking a cigar, his short, scraggly red beard masking a stern expression, Sherman gave the impression that ice water ran through his veins.

Once again Sherman was called upon to handle a burgeoning crisis, which had its beginning in the chaos that developed upon his initial withdrawal from the Shiloh Church area. At ten minutes past ten, following nearly three hours of fighting, the order to fall back to the Purdy-Hamburg road, about 500 yards in the rear, was passed along Sherman's line.

All of Buckland's nearby regiments, and Colonel John A. McDowell's right flank brigade, were ordered to fall back to join with the remnant of the Shiloh Church defenders at this location. After both brigades withdrew and re-formed in the middle of the Purdy road, they created an opportunity for disaster. Captain Frederick Behr's 6th Indiana battery, ordered from McDowell's right flank to replace Barrett's guns, now low on ammunition, soon came dashing down the Purdy road at a full gallop. Because of the heavy brush on each side of the road, Buckland's men still jammed the right of way, and were abruptly shoved out of the road by the wildly careening guns and caissons. In the resulting confusion a mass of fugitives running up the road from the opposite direction added to the disorder. Then the onrushing Confederates, following in the tracks of the retreating Federals, burst upon the scene. Behr's battery, attempting to unlimber near the crossroads, here took a point-blank volley which felled their captain. Sherman later recalled that the men then became panic-stricken and abandoned their guns without so much as firing a shot.

Sherman's Purdy road line now shuddered in total disorder. When the Confederates again charged, the line gave way almost completely. Only McDowell's brigade, farther up the road, remained intact. Still,

109

Sherman's desperate stand had counted for much. The division's lengthy ordeal had bought sufficient time for the more distant divisions to form a strong defensive line. With the rapidly growing confusion of intermixed units in the belatedly victorious enemy impeding their rapid pursuit, additional time, soon to be a key element, was afforded.

To Sherman, his shirt collar twisted askew, his hand bloodied, and his uniform torn and besmudged by the grime of battle, the events of that morning involved the essence of effective battlefield leadership. His personal example continued to fire his men's souls. It inspired bravery and steadied their nerves. Sherman's genius was never more evident than in the fiery crisis of battle. On an occasion when he, more than others, had reason to fear the result, Sherman appeared to one admiring officer to be "the coolest man I saw that day."

Capture of McClernand's head-quarters, McAllister's and Schwartz's artillery, and Dresser's battery, April 6. Sketch by Henry Lovie.

A RUDE AWAKENING

Frank Leslie's Illustrated Newspaper

Ulysses Grant had been eating breakfast that morning at his Cherry House headquarters in Savannah when an orderly came in to report the sound of firing coming from the direction of Pittsburg Landing. Leaving his breakfast unfinished, Grant walked outside, heard the distant gunfire, and immediately boarded the *Tigress*. While steam was being generated Grant dictated several messages to the advanced elements of Buell's army that had only yesterday arrived at Savannah, asking them to proceed to Pittsburg.

Then, about 8:00 a.m., Grant hastened upriver to Crump's Landing, not knowing if that point was under attack. Finding Lew Wallace there aboard a transport, Grant merely told him to hold his troops in readiness to march, then sped ahead to Pittsburg Landing.

Grant arrived on the field of battle at about 9:30 a.m. Convinced for the first time that his Pittsburg Landing camps were the true object of the enemy's attack, he sent word by a staff officer to Lew Wallace to "come up" to Pittsburg Landing. By the time Captain A.S. Baxter had proceeded with the *Tigress* to Crump's Landing and met Wallace some distance inland it was about 11:30 a.m.

Wallace had his troops concentrated at Stoney Lonesome, a point midway on the road to Purdy, since he was uncertain if the enemy might approach from that direction. Deciding to utilize an interior road that led to Sherman's camps at Shiloh Church, rather than the so-called river road direct to the landing area, Wallace was confident that this was the shorter of the two routes.

Actually, Wallace was courting disaster. The road he had chosen was not only about three miles longer, but it also led to what was now the rear of the Confederate army, where his entire division might be cut off or even captured. Following a half-hour delay for "dinner," Wallace's troops marched briskly toward the sound of the raging conflict, heedless of their danger.

At Savannah, Buell's commanders had desperately sought a means to get to Pittsburg Landing, but without success. The roads along the river were swampy at best and were now inundated by water. No transports were then at Savannah to provide river transportation. With difficulty, about noon a local doctor was found who knew a backwoods route estimated at eight miles, five of which were through a "black mud swamp." Thus, about 1:30 p.m., Colonel Jacob Ammen's brigade began their arduous journey, not knowing if they could get through at all.

At Pittsburg Landing, Grant, dressed in his full major general's uniform complete with sword and sash, was soon in the midst of the heaviest fighting. Concerned by the rapidly deteriorating military situation, Grant dispatched another note to Lew Wallace to "hurry forward" with all speed.

Then, following a brief chat with Sherman, he attempted to return to the small log cabin on the hilltop at Pittsburg Landing designated as his headquarters. With his staff officers at his side, Grant galloped across the northern fringe of Duncan Field in order to reach the Pittsburg-Corinth road.

In the opposite fringe of timber a Mississippi battery had just unlimbered and rapidly trained its guns on what appeared to be an important group of Federal officers. At the discharge of these guns Grant said, "the shells and balls whistled about our ears very fast...." A staff officer's horse was killed, and following a rapid dash for cover, Grant discovered that his sword had been struck just below the hilt, the missile striking with such force it had broken his scabbard and blade nearly in two.

Soon returning to Pittsburg Landing, Grant was later found on board the *Tigress* by General Buell, who had commandeered a passing steamboat at Savannah. Buell said of Grant at the time that he looked much worried and certainly lacked "that masterly confidence" which was a highly publicized character trait.

Grant had obvious cause to be greatly concerned. Already a milling crowd of fugitive soldiers, estimated in the thousands, had gathered at the riverbank by the landing. As was discovered by nearly all who attempted to rally these men, they for the most part were so frightened and panic-stricken as to be insensible to entreaty or threats.

A CRUCIAL MISTAKE

Albert Sidney Johnston had confidently advanced with the front line that had swept through Prentiss' camps about midmorning. In the camp of the 18th Wisconsin Johnston had picked up a little tin cup, saying that such would be his share of the spoils today. Here he detached his personal physician, Dr. D.W. Yandell, to look after the many wounded Federals until other medical officers could be found.

It was at this point that a critical turn in the battle occurred, without so much as involving an exchange of shots.

On the extreme Federal left was an isolated brigade attached to Sherman's division, originally assigned to watch the bridge crossing Lick Creek from the direction of Hamburg. This minimal command of 2,811 men was led by a Chicago lawyer turned soldier, Colonel David Stuart, who by midmorning was thoroughly alarmed by his isolated position. Stuart had formed his three regiments about 8 a.m., and as the morning hours continued he shifted his men from location to location, not knowing from what direction an enemy attack might come.

This constant shuffling and defensive activity resulted in one of the battle's major mistakes. Captain S.H. Lockett of Braxton Bragg's staff, and the assistant chief engineer of the army, had been sent by Bragg to scout the critical sector nearest the Tennessee River early that morning. Taking with him Lieutenant S.M. Steel, an engineer who had surveyed the region before the war, Lockett proceeded to the Lick Creek area and observed Stuart's camp. Following the opening of the battle on the distant left, Lockett and Steel saw "alarming" activity among these Federal troops. Mistakenly interpreting this force to be a "division," Lockett sent a report to headquarters expressing fear that these troops would "swing around and take ours in flank, as it was manifest that the Federal line extended farther in that direction than ours."

Johnston ultimately received Lockett's report, following the collapse of Prentiss' line. Since the Confederate right flank was the most critical sector, requiring the overwhelming of all Federal resistance at this point so as to roll the enemy army back against Owl Creek, Johnston acted promptly in accordance with the master plan. Staff officers were sent to bring then Brigadier General John C. Breckinridge's Reserve Corps forward to the extreme right. Further, two frontline brigades that had helped in overrunning Prentiss' camps, Chalmers' and Jackson's, were pulled out of line and sent on a roundabout circuit over two miles to reach a point not even a half mile distant by direct line. The ultimate consequence was a delay of several hours in engaging these withdrawn brigades, and the depletion of the Confederate front line at a most inopportune time.

112

Mass.—MOLLUS Collection

Federal transports at Pittsburg Landing a few days after the battle. The second steamer from the right is Grant's headquarters boat, the *Tigress*.

THE HORNETS' NEST

Benjamin Prentiss, following the loss of his camps and the virtual breakup of his division, had been surprised to see two brigades of Stephen A. Hurlbut's division hastening to his support about 9 a.m. Approaching from the rear, Hurlbut soon deployed his nearly 5,400 men about a half mile behind Prentiss' camps, since it was apparent that the Federal troops along the outer perimeter had been routed.

Although without Colonel James C. Veatch's brigade, which had been sent to Sherman's support, Hurlbut occupied a strong position, fronting moderately open ground. Many of his troops were behind an old split rail fence, with a peach orchard, fragrant with delicate pink blossoms, in their front. A minimum of 300 yards of mostly cleared ground lay between Hurlbut's line and any approaching Confederates, providing a favorable field of fire. To support this line Hurlbut had three well-equipped batteries of artillery deployed at the critical angles.

113

Although Chalmers', Jackson's, and Adams' (Gladden's) Confederate brigades had observed Hurlbut's deployment, and were preparing to attack, two of these units had been pulled out of line and sent to the right by Johnston's order just as their skirmishers were becoming engaged. Since Wood's and Shaver's brigades had gone to the left to help in the struggle against Sherman, Gladden's brigade, commanded by Colonel Daniel Adams, remained alone in front of Hurlbut. But Adams reported his regiment nearly out of ammunition, and soon withdrew a short distance pending reinforcement.

While a rather desultory artillery duel occurred between opposing batteries in this sector, Sidney Johnston sat patiently astride his horse, awaiting the appearance of Breckinridge's troops. He had nearly two hours to wait. The protracted delay on Hurlbut's front was to become one of the decisive factors in the battle.

When the Confederates failed to pursue their advantage, Hurlbut allowed the remnant of Prentiss' division to form as an extension of his right flank. Among these men were what remained of two of Peabody's regiments, including Major James E. Powell with a fragment of the 25th Missouri. When another Missouri unit came up—the 23d Infantry, fresh off a transport at Pittsburg Landing—Prentiss' command was more than doubled in size and now numbered perhaps 1,000 men. The position they took, in a sunken road worn by many years' use as a wagon trail, was further strengthened by eight field guns that remained from Prentiss' artillery.

Ironically, Prentiss' improvised command was to occupy one of the critical sections of the field, being the means of linking another large segment of the makeshift Federal perimeter then forming.

Brigadier General W.H.L. Wallace, still ignorant of his wife's presence at the river landing, had gone forward on the main Corinth road with his two remaining brigades shortly after Hurlbut's advance along the Hamburg-Savannah road. Taking position about 10 a.m. along the

Then Brigadier General John Cabell Breckinridge.

114

northern fringe of Duncan Field, Wallace's men were appalled by the stream of fugitives going to the rear. Among these stragglers was a wagon containing a few Confederate prisoners. When one of the captured enemy taunted an Iowa regiment, calling them "damned Yankees," and cursing them heartily, one soldier said he "never felt more like shooting a Rebel."

With about 5,800 men in line, W.H.L. Wallace anchored the right flank of what had become a great convex battle formation, stretching more than a half-mile along the wagon road ridge. Although loosely tied together the two main segments, Hurlbut's and W.H.L. Wallace's, were linked by Prentiss' command at the apex of the arc. In all, more than 11,000 men supported by seven batteries of artillery totaling thirty-eight field guns now confronted the advancing Confederates. Instead of attacking highly vulnerable and fragmented enemy defenses, the protracted delay in pursuit now compelled the Confederates to dislodge a formidable Union battleline.

Oddly, the first troops to advance against this Federal stronghold were from the third Confederate line, Polk's Corps. Braxton Bragg, who, like his fellow corps commanders, was exasperated at the confusion and delays occasioned by the tandem battle formation being utilized, already had been compelled to improvise a makeshift arrangement. The three primary Confederate lines had become so intermixed by midmorning that Bragg had agreed to control all troops in the center if Polk and Hardee would go to the left and direct operations there.

Unfortunately for the South, Braxton Bragg was one of the worst combat tacticians in the army. A supremely adept organizer and disciplinarian, Bragg was more suited for the role of chief of staff than active battle command. The sector in which he had chosen to exercise control was the middle of the battlefield, directly in front of the Hurlbut-Prentiss-W.H.L. Wallace line.

Brigadier General W.H.L. Wallace, mortally wounded in the Union retreat from the Hornets' Nest.

Below, left: Prentiss' troops, supported by Hickenlooper's battery, repulse Hardee's attacking Confederates at the Hornets' Nest. Below, right: Gibson's brigade charging Hurlbut's troops in the Hornets' Nest.

Brigadier General Benjamin F. Cheatham, leading the mostly Tennessee brigade of Colonel William H. Stephens, had been ordered into the fight by Colonel Thomas Jordan, Beauregard's roving adjutant general. Appearing in front of the left of W.H.L. Wallace's line defending Duncan Field about 11 a.m., Cheatham attacked unsupported, his three regiments going up against portions of three Federal divisions.

Caught in a terrible crossfire, Cheatham's men were slaughtered in the open field, only their right flank regiment closing to within ten yards of the Federal line in heavy brush. A half-hour after the attack was launched the Confederate dead "literally covered" the ground in front of one of Colonel Jacob Lauman's Indiana regiments, and Cheatham's soldiers were so bloodied that they withdrew from the fighting.

Next, a lone brigade under Colonel Randall Lee Gibson was found standing idle nearby, and Bragg personally ordered an attack on the Federal stronghold. Leading his four regiments forward at noon, the dapper Yale graduate Gibson marched straight for the sunken road perimeter. Like Cheatham's men they were murdered at short range, being unable to see far ahead in the thick undergrowth there. Terming this ground a "valley of death" the Confederates broke and ran back after suffering grievous losses.

Bragg, who had remained nearby, was incensed at what he regarded as Gibson's premature withdrawal, and sent a staff officer to rally these men and order another attack. Directed to attack this same position without the aid of other infantry or even artillery support, Gibson protested, yet complied with Bragg's orders. Again this sadly depleted Louisiana and Arkansas brigade rushed forward, screaming the high-pitched, eerie Rebel yell.

Prentiss' soldiers, supported by a fresh regiment detached from W.H.L. Wallace's line, braced for the attack by lying prone in the sunken road. With their covering artillery firing charges of double canister into the Confederates the din was terrific. Despite obviously severe losses Gibson's men pressed grimly on. Then, when the onrushing gray line was about twenty yards distant the Federal infantry jumped to their feet and delivered a point-blank volley. So many Confederates were shot down that a private later described the scene as a "slaughter pen." Yet the remaining enemy rushed up to the very muzzles of the Federal cannon. In hand-to-hand fighting the Confederates were finally overwhelmed and driven off.

As the thick cloud of gunsmoke gradually cleared, the Federal defenders looked out on a scene of complete devastation. The enemy bodies lay in piles observed an Indiana colonel. The brush had been so cut to pieces that, said another eyewitness, it had "the appearance of a Southern corn field that had been topped." To the survivors among Gibson's brigade the storm of enemy missiles had seemed like facing a swarm of hornets, and they appropriately named the Federal stronghold "the Hornets' Nest." Incredibly, Gibson's men were again required to attack this formidable line unsupported. Bragg, further enraged by what he regarded as a repulse due to enemy "sharpshooters occupying the thick cover," sent orders for still another frontal attack.

Colonel Henry W. Allen of the 4th Louisiana, a bullet hole through each cheek, seized his colors from Bragg's staff officer, and bitterly led the remnant of the brigade forward. In a few minutes they stumbled back repulsed in another, the fourth, forlorn attack on this front. By now it was nearly 3 p.m., and important action was occurring on the opposite, or left flank of the Federal perimeter.

Brigadier General John A. McArthur.

A FATAL WOUND

Following a wait of nearly two hours the extreme left of Grant's army had at last been engaged by Brigadier General James R. Chalmers' and Brigadier General John K. Jackson's brigades. The Federals in their front by this time numbered two brigades; a three-regiment unit commanded by the colorful Scotsman Brigadier General John A. McArthur had been detached earlier by W.H.L. Wallace and sent to help Stuart.

Commencing at about eleven o'clock, the action on the Stuart-McArthur front had been desultory until about noon. Fighting "like Indians," behind trees and logs in heavily timbered terrain cut by huge ravines, the blue coated soldiers had been able to hold their ground. Yet with a dwindling supply of ammunition and the prospect of added pressure being applied by approaching Confederate reinforcements, Stuart began to consider a retreat. Unknowingly, these two Federal brigades, seemingly fighting an isolated battle on the outer periphery, were anchoring the entire left flank of Grant's army. Should they retreat, an entire corridor direct to Pittsburg Landing would be open.

Although Chalmers and Jackson had been bolstered by the arrival of Breckinridge's Reserve Corps about noon, the more than 8,000 infantry with four batteries of artillery had been unable to break the Federal line. Beyond cautiously maneuvering in McArthur's front, the Confederates had wasted considerable time in attempting to mount a coordinated attack in the rugged terrain.

Sidney Johnston, riding Fire-eater, had gone with Brigadier General John S. Bowen's brigade of Breckinridge's Corps. Meanwhile, Statham's brigade, farther to the west, had encountered the extreme left flank of Hurlbut's peach orchard line. Hearing of confusion among Tennessee troops here, Johnston had sent his volunteer aide Governor Isham G. Harris to rally this line, and also ordered a bayonet attack by Statham's men.

Breckinridge presently confronted Johnston, saying he could not get the brigade to charge. Johnston then personally came up and addressed the men. Apparently on the spur of the moment, he determined to

Brigadier General James R. Chalmers.

lead the attack. Passing along the line and touching their bayonets with the little tin cup taken earlier that morning, Johnston cried, "I will lead you."

Word was passed to Bowen's brigade on the right and to Stephens' bloodied brigade on the left, recovered from their initial assault on the Hornets' Nest. This entire line was to go forward in a coordinated effort to break the Federal left flank.

An officer pulled off his cap, placed it on the point of his sword, and raised it high in the air. It was approximately 2 p.m. as the long line swept forward with a loud shout.

First to break under this tremendous pressure was McArthur's thin line of fewer than 2,000 men. Bowen, joined by several of Jackson's regiments, enveloped the Federal flank, bypassed Stuart, and chased McArthur's crumbling line nearly a quarter of a mile.

On Bowen's immediate left, Johnston's bayonet attack was aimed directly at the Peach Orchard line defended by Hurlbut. Although an entire Federal brigade quickly fell back, their artillery continued firing until the last moment. After clearing the orchard, Johnston's men, however, encountered severe resistance along the wooded ridge that led to the sunken road.

Having sustained heavy casualties crossing the generally open ground, the Confederates here took cover and returned the fire. Stephens' brigade, in fact had been repulsed. Caught in an old open cottonfield, they had lost so many men that their dead "looked like a line of troops laying down to receive our fire," thought a Federal infantryman.

Brigadier General John Stevens Bowen.

In the rear of Statham's line Sidney Johnston sat for nearly a half-hour, issuing orders and preparing to renew the attack. Amazingly, no one noticed that he was then desperately wounded. During the attack on the Peach Orchard Johnston had been struck perhaps four times. Only one projectile had broken the skin, however. A minie ball, nearly spent, had entered his right leg behind the knee joint and cut the large artery. Judging from the location of the wound, it is possible that one of his own men had accidently launched the fatal missile. The blood flowed into Johnston's high boot, and no one noticed the wound, even when he collapsed in the saddle.

Albert Sidney Johnston receives his mortal wound.

Moved to a ravine nearby, his staff desperately tore off his shirt looking for the wound, and poured brandy down his throat. No physician was nearby, Johnston having ordered Dr. Yandell to remain with the Federal wounded at Prentiss' camps. In Johnston's pocket was a field tourniquet that might have staunched the flow. Johnston never regained consciousness. About 2:30 p.m. the awful truth dawned on those present. The highest ranking field general in the Confederacy was dead from an acute loss of blood, the fatal wound not being discovered until it was too late. Hastily, a note advising Beauregard that he was now in command was sent to the rear, yet little was done to alter the lull that now occurred in the battle.

THE LOST OPPORTUNITY

Although, as noted above, Stuart had been bypassed by Chalmers, this last remaining segment of the Federal left was ordered to retreat about 2:15 p.m. Fired into by the pursuing Confederates and confused by the rugged terrain, Stuart's men ultimately fled all the way to Pittsburg Landing.

A huge gap of nearly three-quarters of a mile now existed all the way to the vital core of the Federal army, Pittsburg Landing, only a mile and a half distant. Yet Sidney Johnston was dead and no one seemed to be in control in this vital sector. Moreover, instead of advancing due north to envelop the entire Federal army, most Confederate commanders, following Beauregard's earlier instructions to march toward the sound of the heaviest fighting, soon turned in a wide arc toward the Hornets' Nest line. To complicate matters, Bragg ultimately arrived upon the scene, still intent on reducing the deadly Federal stronghold by frontal assault.

A MASS SURRENDER

Stephen A. Hurlbut, observing the debacle on his left flank involving Stuart's and McArthur's troops, acted promptly to protect his exposed left flank. Pulling Lauman's entire brigade out of line, he rushed these troops to a ten-acre clearing known as Wicker Field. Lauman was just in time to meet the mass of Confederates pursuing McArthur. In a stubborn firefight Lauman's men temporarily held Chalmers' brigade at bay. About 3:30 p.m., however, Hurlbut saw that the enemy was working around his left flank and he ordered a general retreat. Although he hoped to make another stand near his line of encampments, in the confusion of the movement Hurlbut's division was virtually fragmented and only one regiment stood to cover their withdrawal.

Moreover Hurlbut's withdrawal exposed the remnant of the original Hornets' Nest line under Prentiss and W.H.L. Wallace. His line now bent back in the shape of an elongated U, Prentiss sought to cover the void, convinced he could still hold his ground. Although Bragg hurled the remnant of Gladden's brigade against the center of this line—only to be beaten off—and had directed another forlorn attack by Shaver's brigade against W.H.L. Wallace's troops, the buildup on all sides of Prentiss convinced him that he was surrounded. Still he refused to retreat, believing, so he said, that Lew Wallace's division might yet come up.

To add to the Federal woes at this point, Confederate Brigadier General Daniel Ruggles had brought up and organized the largest concentration of artillery yet seen on the North American continent—

Brigadier General Stephen Augustus Hurlbut.

119

eleven batteries and one section, a total of sixty-two field guns. In all, two separate concentrations had developed, fronting the sunken road and Duncan Field perimeters. About 4 p.m. these cannon unleashed a devastating fire that sounded to one Federal lieutenant "like a mighty hurricane." The brush and trees around the position were so blasted by this fire that it seemed a relief to a Federal captain when he observed the Confederate infantry advancing upon them.

Soon one of W.H.L. Wallace's brigades, depleted by detachments to more hotly contested parts of the Hornets' Nest, began to break up. Colonel Thomas W. Sweeny, the one-armed Irishman who led this brigade, had taken another wound—in his good arm. Here his two Illinois regiments observed massed Confederate troops maneuvering beyond their extreme right flank.

These Confederates, Polk's troops, were pursuing the remnant of McClernand's division, which had shored up Sherman's battered line, and were already north of the Hornets' Nest defenders. The commanders of Sweeny's two regiments ran their men out to the northeast, precipitating the breakup of W.H.L. Wallace's entire command.

Tree under which Prentiss surrendered to Polk.

Following a sustained fight of nearly six hours, W.H.L. Wallace at last realized that his position was untenable. After hastily issuing orders for a retreat, Wallace and his staff tried to gallop past the encircling Confederates. Several advancing Rebel skirmishers drew a bead on the fleeing party, and Wallace went down with a mortal head wound.

In the confusion of the precipitate retreat all discipline was lost, and the withdrawal quickly became a "mad race" to escape to the landing. When it was found that the Confederates were on all sides, having "marched to the sound of the heaviest fighting," white handkerchiefs began fluttering throughout the thicket in token of surrender. Only one of W.H.L. Wallace's regiments, the 7th Illinois, escaped without serious loss.

The only remaining defenders of the Hornets' Nest line, Prentiss' improvised command, by now had realized that they were caught in a deadly trap. Pushed back by a spirited cavalry charge led by Colonel (later Lieutenant General) Nathan Bedford Forrest, Prentiss' line numbered eight regiments, nearly 2,000 men, although only about 300 men remained of his original division.

Attacked on three sides about 5 p.m., Prentiss finally gave the order to retire. But it was too late. A small ravine behind the Hornets' Nest was found to be a valley of death as bullets crisscrossed from several directions.

Those few who escaped the ravine ran straight into Polk's infantry blocking escape to the north. In one of Hurlbut's abandoned encampments several Tennessee soldiers charged to find Prentiss "holding aloft the white flag." In the space of a half-hour about 2,000 Federals surrendered; it was the largest capture yet made by the Confederacy. Although the jubilant Southerners demonstrated their joy by tearing up the 8th Iowa's cotton flag for souvenirs, and numerous Confederate officers were observed laden with bundles of the surrendered swords of their Federal counterparts, the Hornets' Nest defenders could well be proud of their accomplishments. Their stubborn defense had taken a tremendous toll among the enemy. Many of the Federals had been armed with Enfield rifles, and the fire of these deadly accurate weapons had been so effective that nearly a dozen separate charges were repulsed. Indeed, never in the history of warfare had the efficacy of rifled arms been so apparent.

Brigadier General Daniel Ruggles.

120

ON THE BRINK OF DISASTER

Brigadier General Alexander Peter Stewart.

The scene of a great army verging on collapse was "humiliating in the extreme," wrote a Federal eyewitness. Thousands of men, routed and weaponless, were milling about the landing area, some so panic-stricken that they rushed aboard and nearly swamped several transports laden with wounded in their effort to escape the mounting danger.

Adding to the chaos at the landing were many of Sherman's and McClernand's troops, present at this spot since midday. McClernand's division had originally supported Sherman's line along the main Corinth road, a quarter-mile in the rear. Here McClernand had been attacked by many of Hardee's, Polk's, and Bragg's troops, fresh from their victory over Sherman.

Despite such mistakes as allowing a Confederate unit to approach unopposed, thinking their state flag was a Federal banner, McClernand's units fought hard, but were quickly overwhelmed. The division had been all but broken up by 11 a.m., and only the presence of a lone brigade sent by Hurlbut, Colonel James C. Veatch's, had prevented a rout.

Yet the Confederates were so weakened by the losses sustained against Sherman and McClernand that they stalled in effective pursuit. By the time ammunition was replenished and the Southerners had rested, Sherman and McClernand were able to piece together a defensive line amid McClernand's camps.

The effort to break this patchwork Federal right flank had involved nearly five additional hours of fighting by often isolated Confederate units. Finally gaining some cohesion with the appearance of Trabue's brigade of Breckinridge's Reserve Corps, the Confederates about 5 p.m. forced Sherman's and McClernand's remnants back to within a quarter-mile of the landing.

BATTLE OF SHILOH Part II.

2d. Position (Noon) 6th. April
Federal ———
Confederate ─ ─ ─ ─

Battle of Shiloh: Positions at noon, April 6.

121

So many Southern brigades had already either retired for want of ammunition or had gone toward the center to participate in the assault on the Hornets' Nest line, however, that it was readily perceived that the danger was greatest on the Federal flank nearest the river.

Precisely at 2:50 p.m. the wooden gunboat USS *Tyler*, responding to an urgent plea from Hurlbut for help, had begun firing her 8-inch naval shells in the direction of the Confederates. Although these shells overshot the mark, generally falling in the extreme enemy rear, the deafening noise from the bursts added to the dismal battle scene. A massive pall of smoke rose from the fought-over ground, making the day seem like night, a Federal officer thought.

With the routed blue soldiers streaming in broken clusters back to the high ground about the landing, "all appeared lost," wrote an exhausted private, who considered that "it was Bull Run over again."

As the afternoon wore on, U.S. Grant anticipated that the enemy would make a "desperate effort" to capture the landing. Accordingly, plans were made to defend the high bluffs in a final stand. Grant's chief of staff, Colonel Joseph D. Webster, had been busy moving a battery of heavy siege cannon into position a quarter-mile from the river. Intended for use in besieging Corinth, the chance presence of these five monster 24-pounder guns enabled Grant to form a stout defensive line. As other artillery units came back they formed an elongation of this original line. By 6 p.m. this Federal artillery concentration consisting of at least ten batteries extended nearly a half-mile. Yet infantry supports were seriously lacking. The remnants of Hurlbut's and W.H.L. Wallace's divisions were in line fronting south, with McClernand and Sherman bent back along the "river road" to the north. In all, Grant's last line covered a perimeter barely more than a mile in length, all that remained of a fighting force that had numbered more than 40,000 men that morning.

To make the dismal situation even worse, it was learned that Lew Wallace's division would not arrive in time to be of help. Several of Grant's staff officers, sent to hurry this division forward, had found Wallace about 2 p.m. on the "wrong road." Belatedly convinced of his error, Wallace was persuaded to countermarch, but he was so cautious and dilatory as to double his leading brigade back through the entire line, rather than to face about and reverse his line of march. Too, Wallace first refused to leave behind his artillery, which marched behind his advance brigade, and insisted on ordering halts to keep his column "closed up." In all, said an irate staff officer, Wallace's march seemed more like a cautious reconnaissance than a forced march to relieve a hard-pressed army. Near sundown Lew Wallace's men had still not crossed Snake Creek, although they could hear the terrific crashes from the heavy artillery in the distance, warning that the last line of the army was engaged.

Braxton Bragg, in company with Generals Breckinridge and Polk, had been active in organizing a final assault in the last hour of daylight remaining. Gathering all available troops they pushed forward toward a deep chasm known as Dill Branch. On the opposite ridge they could see Grant's line of heavy artillery, largely unprotected by infantry. It was about 6 p.m. as Chalmers' and Jackson's brigades pushed forward, their massed lines resembling some "huge monster clothed in folds of flashing steel," said an eyewitness.

The sight of these attacking Confederates was spectacular in the extreme, a Michigan private later remembered. The sun hung as a huge fireball, slowly falling out of sight, and the gleaming bayonets of the enemy sparkled in its waning rays.

122

Confederate private.

Across the river from Pittsburg Landing the vanguard of Buell's army had appeared about 4:30 p.m. Belatedly, several steamboats had been appropriated to ferry the men of Jacob Ammen's brigade across. Touching shore about 5:20 p.m. Buell's advance contingent hastened up the bluff, shouting "Buell" to encourage the mob of disheartened troops milling about—now estimated at between 7,000 and 10,000 men "frantic with fright and utterly demoralized."

With only the 36th Indiana and a portion of the 6th Ohio in line, Grant's army braced for the oncoming attack, directed at the extreme flank nearest the river. The roar from the great guns and the supporting infantry created a noise "not exceeded by anything I . . . heard afterward," said a staff officer. Chalmers' brigade advanced into Dill Branch ravine but was beaten back by the storm of fire, and Jackson's men, on their left, lay down behind the crest of a ridge to escape the deadly missiles. Bragg and others, however, were bringing up reinforcements when Jackson's brigade suddenly pulled back.

Unknown to many of the Confederate generals present one of Beauregard's staff officers, Major Numa Augustin, had ordered a halt to the fighting and a withdrawal by the front line to the captured enemy camps. Beauregard, in the rear near Shiloh Church, had been persuaded to put an end to the fighting because of the widespread disorder in the Confederate rear, and a belief that the victory was sufficiently complete for the day. Years later he confided that he believed his men "demoralized by the flush of victory," and that he had Grant "just where I wanted him, and could finish him up in the morning." This opinion of disarray was undoubtedly enhanced by the bursts of the gunboat shells in the rear, spreading confusion, plus the widespread looting and pillaging observed in the captured camps.

Being thus distant from the scene of the fighting, Beauregard had made what Bragg later termed one of the great mistakes of the war on the basis of other than first hand information. "One more charge, my men," Bragg had previously told his troops, "and we shall capture them all."

Battle of Shiloh: positions at sunset, April 6.

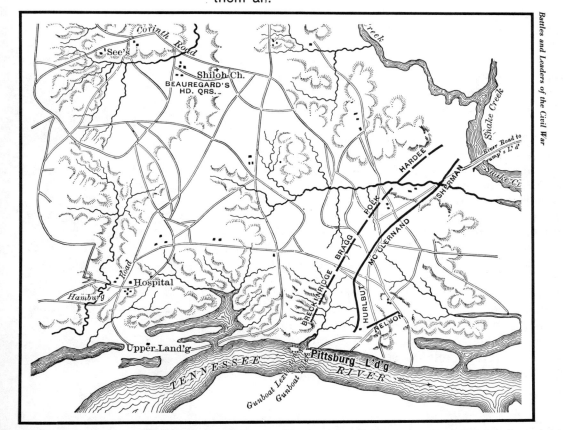

NIGHT OF MISERY

When darkness finally put an end to the sporadic fighting, there was an immense sense of relief within the Federal army. Although driven to the brink of disaster, Grant's men could now anticipate more favorable prospects for the morrow. Indeed, throughout the night Buell's advanced troops were ferried across the river, while others were brought up from Savannah by transports. By daylight about 7,500 men of Buell's army were present, including most of two divisions, Brigadier Generals William Nelson's and Thomas Crittenden's. A third division, McCook's, was ashore by early morning on the 7th, expanding Buell's force to nearly 15,000 men. Buell, in fact, had already contemplated a counteroffensive, and issued orders for an attack by his men at daylight. Almost contemptuous of Grant for what he regarded as the disgraceful rout of his army, Buell considered his army independent, and merely "presumed" Grant would be in accord with his plans.

Grant, preoccupied with getting Lew Wallace's division up, did not meet with Buell that night. With Wallace finally present along the river road beginning about 7:15 p.m., Grant also anticipated an advance on the 7th, though he issued no specific orders that night. Lew Wallace's more than 7,000 troops represented the means to achieve "a great moral advantage" by becoming the attacking party, said Grant, and he planned accordingly.

Unable to sleep under a towering oak because of a raging thunderstorm that began about midnight, Grant went to the little log cabin near the landing, now being used as a hospital. Again he was unable to sleep in the presence of the grisly amputations being carried on continuously during the night. His injured ankle paining him severely, he then hobbled back to his "tree in the rain," thoroughly exhausted.

The night of April 6, later wrote one of Buell's soldiers, "was the worst night of our entire three years service." The cold driving rain continued until after 3 a.m., and the hungry, beaten Federal soldiers huddled in dire misery. "It seemed like the Lord was rubbing it in," wrote an Ohio youth. One private, unable to find a dry spot, put his blanket over his shoulders, stuck his bayoneted musket into the ground, placed his chin on the butt, and slept standing up. To add to the misery, about 9 p.m. the Federal gunboat *Tyler*, acting under instructions from General Nelson, began firing 8-inch naval shells in the enemy's direction at ten minute intervals. Taken up by the USS *Lexington* about 1 a.m., the

Then Colonel Nathan Bedford Forrest.

124

fire continued throughout the night, the deafening concussions doing little damage, but keeping men on both sides awake.

For the Confederates the night of April 6 represented a further crucial breakdown in communications. Sent by Nathan Bedford Forrest to spy on the enemy's activities that night, a detachment of scouts discovered Buell's troops debarking and returned to Forrest with this vital information. Forrest quickly informed Hardee and Breckinridge, but was directed to find Beauregard. Unable to locate the commanding general's headquarters after a lengthy search, Forrest returned to see Hardee, who told him merely to return to his regiment and report all hostile movements. Beauregard, ensconced in Sherman's captured tent near Shiloh Church, apparently had not left word where he could be found. On the afternoon of the 6th, Beauregard had received a telegram from a colonel near Florence, Alabama reporting elements of Buell's army marching toward Decatur, Alabama. Thus within the span of twenty-four hours the circumstances had been substantially reversed. It would be the Confederates who were to be surprised on April 7.

REVERSED FORTUNES

The fighting on April 7 began with a few lingering Confederates being driven from Lew Wallace's front by artillery fire at daylight. Although Wallace began his attack about 6:30 a.m., his advance was so cautious in the face of minimal opposition that he had advanced only to the main Corinth road by midday.

Most of the initial action during the morning occurred on the Federal left flank, where Buell's troops confronted the large concentration of Southern infantry remaining from the Hornets' Nest fight of Sunday. However, since many of these units had withdrawn to the captured camps of Sherman's and Prentiss' divisions, the Confederates allowed more than a mile of hard-won ground to be occupied by Buell's troops before they offered serious resistance.

About 10 o'clock Hardee, who seemed to be the "master spirit" on this front, ordered a counterattack in the vicinity of the much fought over Peach Orchard. Shouting taunts of "Bull Run! Bull Run!" at Buell's advancing men, several Confederate regiments swept into the underbrush, and were soon fighting hand-to-hand with their blue enemies. Soon discovering that they were outnumbered, the Confederates broke and ran back. One overly ambitious Federal brigade, Colonel William B. Hazen's, which pursued too closely was in turn routed by some reserve Louisiana troops, and became scattered.

Federal troops bivouac in the rain on Sunday night on the battlefield.

Battles and Leaders of the Civil War

125

Yet Hardee, his magnificent black horse having been shot from under him and his coat torn by several rifle balls, was unable to prevent the Confederate line from falling back under a heavy artillery fire. Several brief counterattacks stabilized the line, however, and by noon a general stalemate existed. Amid a burgeoning artillery duel, the men on both sides lay down to rest as best they could. One Federal private, exhausted by the events of the past two days, was found fast asleep under a tree despite the storm of shot and shell that raged about him.

In the center of the battlefield Crittenden's division and some of Bragg's troops had struggled for possession of thickets in the vicinity of the Hornets' Nest. Again Bragg had insisted on hurling fragmented and often isolated units against the Federal line in piecemeal assaults. One Kentucky regiment, marching into action singing the "Kentucky Battle Song," had been fearfully decimated in halting a Federal advance. Here the Confederate provisional governor of Kentucky, serving in the ranks, was mortally wounded.

Slowly driven back to the vicinity of Sherman's former headquarters in heavy fighting, by 1 p.m. the middle of the Confederate line verged on collapse. Several batteries had been lost, and many of the men were so demoralized that an officer, found cowering under a tree with some of his men, refused to re-form his command. He didn't give a damn what any general might call him, said the officer, he was not going back into the fighting. By now stragglers in a steady stream were making their way to the rear, while a critical shortage of ammunition compounded the growing difficulties.

Beauregard, at last aware of Buell's reinforcements, refused to panic, however. To a Louisiana regiment he seemed cool and collected, and told the men, "The day is ours—you are fighting a whipped army, fire low and be deliberate."

Yet, as his staff surmised about midday, many of the troops were beyond further effort. While several officers were sent to gather all the arms and ammunition about the camps and load them into wagons to be taken to the rear, Beauregard organized his remaining troops for one last attempt to achieve an overwhelming victory.

Since noon a raging conflict had been underway in the vicinity of Water Oaks Pond, near the main Corinth road. Here Lew Wallace's troops, aided by the remnant of Grant's army, had advanced and then retreated in what one Federal general termed "one of the severest conflicts" of the two days of fighting. Pat Cleburne had attacked here, ordered by Bragg to make an assault without support. Though Cleburne protested what were obviously foolish tactics, he had led the remnant of his brigade, reduced from 2,700 men to about 800, in a forlorn charge.

About 2 p.m. Beauregard in person brought Colonel Preston Pond's relatively fresh brigade forward in a final effort to break the Federal line. Supported by several other random regiments the tattered grey line sprang forward and fell on some of Buell's troops, McCook's division, only recently arrived on the field. "The fires from the contending ranks were two continuous sheets of flame," observed Alexander McCook, and his men were pushed back to a point near McClernand's camps. Still, the Federal artillery punished the attackers severely, and a reserve unit, Lauman's brigade, was brought into action with decisive results.

About 3:30 p.m. the Confederate infantry began streaming to the rear and Beauregard ordered a general retreat.

Slowly and ponderously the jaded Confederate army trudged away from the smoldering battlefield. Several of the Federal camps were on fire,

Brigadier General Thomas L. Crittenden.

and the windrows of dead bodies, already swollen by the heat, presented a gruesome sight. Some of the retreating men were so fatigued that they could not move rapidly. "I never was exhausted so completely in my life," said one Southern soldier.

Grant's men made little effort to pursue the retreating enemy, however. "I was without cavalry," lamented Grant, who also noted that his men were scattered and had no knowledge of the various country roads. Buell likewise was content to let the Confederates go, even believing that defensive preparations should be made "for tomorrow's fight." Shocked by the carnage they found in the recaptured camps, the men bedded down for an uneasy sleep. Thousands of wounded had to be attended to; the confusion and disorder was extreme following what was then the bloodiest battle in the nation's history.

A steady, cold rain fell throughout most of the night, adding further misery to the terrible ordeal. One Confederate private, unable to walk farther, stood under a tree for shelter but fell asleep standing up. When he awoke he lay down and slept in a pool of water, content to lie there all night.

Despite an abortive pursuit by Sherman's division on April 8, which involved a fight with Nathan Bedford Forrest's cavalry at Fallen Timbers, the Battle of Shiloh had ended by mutual consent.

Recapture of artillery at Pittsburg Landing by the 1st Ohio under Rousseau, Monday, April 7. Drawing by Henry Lovie.

Although both sides claimed a victory, the newspapers were subsequently filled with controversial and indignant accounts citing the many mistakes and lost opportunities. What was largely overlooked in the tremendous publicity that ensued, however, was what was most evident to those who had fought at Shiloh. "It is time our people were getting rid of the idea that the courage is all on our side," wrote an enlightened Federal captain, "It is a mistake. The enemy seemed to fight determinedly and I know they fell back steadily when forced to, contesting every step of the way." It was a sentiment equally appropriate for both sides.

Shiloh witnessed the metamorphosis of the American soldier. Beyond the aspects of territory won or lost, of initiative gained or squandered, of new technology implemented, or unspeakable horror viewed, it produced a radical change in the attitude of fighting men both North and South. The hardening of perspective and the heightening of dedication that ultimately resulted in such bloody trials as Stone's River, Vicksburg, Chickamauga, and on through the Atlanta and Carolinas campaigns, was first manifested and nurtured at Shiloh.

William Tecumseh Sherman saw this vital aspect clearly when he stated after the war: "That victory [Shiloh] was one of the most important which has ever occurred on this continent. I have always estimated the victories . . . at Fort Donelson and Shiloh the most valuable of all, because of their moral effect. They gave our men confidence in themselves. . . ."

The true significance of the battle lay in its vital personal influence. From the cauldron of Shiloh sprang the tenacity of a Grant, the icy, calculating nerve of a Sherman, and the furious combative ardor of a Forrest and a Cleburne. If an enigma, the indelible impression Shiloh produced on the soldiers who fought there would never be effaced in the subsequent course of the war. That, perhaps, may serve as an explanation for the battle's fascination, even to this day.

FORT DONELSON

Text by Stephen E. Ambrose
Designed by Frederic Ray

Fort Donelson

"The blow was most disastrous and almost without remedy." So Albert Sidney Johnston described the loss of Fort Donelson and nearly fifteen thousand men. His powers as a prophet exceeded his abilities as a general. The Confederacy spent the three years in the West after February 1862, trying without success to recover from the blow.

It may be that the Confederacy was never strong enough to hold onto its vast western empire, that it just did not have the manpower to defend Tennessee, southern Missouri, Mississippi, Arkansas, Alabama, Texas, Louisiana, and southern Kentucky. Certainly the Confederate strategy of trying to protect everything was futile, and nearly all military historians today agree that Jefferson Davis should have concentrated his forces. Still, when the South did concentrate, as at Donelson and later at Vicksburg, the result was the capture of more men. In both cases, however, the Northern victory was primarily the result of timid Southern generalship.

The Donelson Campaign, like the Vicksburg Campaign a year and a half later, offered the Confederacy a glittering opportunity to surround and capture or destroy the most important Union army in the West. That the South let the opportunities pass was, in both cases, due to the lack of imagination and the cautious approach of two generals named Johnston. Neither seemed to realize that the Confederacy had to take chances to win. At Donelson, it was Albert Sidney Johnston who failed, and the failure was especially bitter because many, including President Davis, considered him the finest soldier in North America.

To be sure, Johnston's task was not easy. With a total force of less than seventy-five thousand men he was supposed to defend the entire area from the Appalachian Mountains to the Mississippi River. The Union had nearly two hundred thousand men in the vicinity, half under Don Carlos Buell in central Kentucky and half under Henry Halleck, with headquarters in St. Louis. Johnston had stationed his troops along a concave line that began at Columbus, Kentucky, on the Mississippi River, ran southeast to Forts Henry and Donelson, and then northeast to Bowling Green, Kentucky. He had a railroad for lateral communications, but the rivers were against him, as they ran perpendicular to his lines. The Cumberland and Tennessee Rivers offered natural highways to the Yankees, and the Union had river gunboats—Johnston did not. To seal off the rivers he had two forts, Henry on the Tennessee and Donelson on the Cumberland, ten miles apart at that point. Neither were good natural defenses nor did Johnston have them strongly garrisoned. He should have moved either forward or back to a better defensive line, but lack of troops forbade the one and states-rights politics the other.

Johnston's troops were raw recruits, untested in battle, led by untried junior officers, poorly armed and inadequately supplied. A Belgian who traveled across Kentucky that first winter of the war thought the Confederate men fantastic. What they wore for uniforms beggared description; he could not tell officers from privates nor soldiers from civilians, their weapons were often antiques, and he shuddered at the unshaven men who brandished "their frightful knives." They all looked dangerous, for "their determination is truly extraordinary, and their hatred against the North terrible to look upon, there is something savage in it." These Southerners would, someday, be among the world's finest fighting men, but it would take time.

The Yankees had problems, too. Their troops were better armed, supplied, and disciplined, but not necessarily better led. They had to take the offensive in an inhospitable territory plagued by bad weather and served by atrocious roads. They had no unity of command—Halleck and Buell were equals who reported to General-in-Chief McClellan, who in turn usually ignored them both. Worse, neither trusted the other nor the subordinate facing the Confederate forts, U.S. Grant.

But President Lincoln wanted action and Grant, at Cairo, Illinois, was anxious to move against Fort Henry, which he thought he could capture with two gunboats. Halleck still hesitated, but when on January 29, 1862, he heard that General P.G.T. Beauregard was coming west with fifteen regiments to reinforce the forts—a false rumor—Halleck gave Grant permission to seize Henry.

Grant began his movement early in February. By the sixth he had come up to the fort. The Confederate commander, Lloyd Tilghman, sent most of his men eastward to Fort Donelson before Grant's troops got close to his lines. Tilghman himself stayed in Henry to help a handful of men work the guns in an attempt to beat off the Yankee gunboats. They did a good job, disabling one of Flag Officer Andrew H. Foote's boats, but Foote's big guns soon broke down the Confederate parapets, dismantled some guns, and dismembered a few of the gunners. Early in the afternoon Tilghman hauled down his flag.

Johnston believed that the brief engagement had changed the entire situation in the West. His line was broken, the Tennessee River was open to the invaders (Foote sent a couple of gunboats tearing south on the river to spread panic throughout west Tennessee and northern Alabama), and his army was demoralized without ever having fought a battle. The bulk of Foote's gunboats had started back down the Tennessee—they were obviously going to swing east on the Ohio and then south on the Cumberland to attack Fort Donelson. Johnston thought the situation was approaching disaster; he met it with half-hearted measures. Instead of falling back to a new defensive line or, more appropriately, concentrating everything he had against Grant, Johnston

*General Ulysses S. Grant on horseback at the battleline at Fort
Donelson. Detail from a painting by Paul Philippoteaux. (LC)*

sent half his men into Fort Donelson. He evidently hoped they could hold Grant. With the other half of his force he retreated, falling back from Bowling Green towards Nashville.

Johnston had put too few men into Fort Donelson to hold Grant, but more than he could afford to lose. He compounded the error by his selection of commanders at the fort. All the decisions Johnston made that winter can be, and have been, defended, save this one. Nothing a theater commander does is more important than his choice of subordinates, and here Johnston's failure was unmitigated. The man in charge at the fort was John B. Floyd, a one-time United States secretary of war who had no military experience, no leadership ability, no sense of responsibility, and whose sole concern was with his personal safety. Second to him was Gideon J. Pillow, formerly James K. Polk's law partner, a veteran of the Mexican War and the only Confederate toward whom Grant ever expressed outspoken contempt. His sense of responsibility about equalled Floyd's. The only real soldier in the fort was Simon Bolivar Buckner, and he was third in command. (Buckner was a year behind Grant at West Point and the two were close friends. In 1854, when Grant showed up broke in New York after resigning from the Army, Buckner had given him a life-sustaining loan.) Buckner was a professional who knew his business, but Floyd and Pillow saw to it that he never had a chance to show it. After the battle Buckner told Grant that if he had been in command the Yankees would not have invested the fort as easily as they did. Grant replied that if Buckner had been in command, "I should not have tried in the way I did."

Grant's great genius as a soldier, the characteristic in which he outdid every opponent he ever faced, was that he did not worry about what the enemy might do to him, but concentrated on what he might do to the enemy. Grant showed this trait at Donelson. Here he was, in midwinter in hostile territory with scarcely seventeen thousand men, dependent on a single river for supplies and reinforcements, surrounded by Confederates. From one point of view (Halleck saw it this way) he was a reckless subordinate in the heart of the enemy's territory with nothing to hold to in case of disaster. In effect, he was in a bag, with the enemy to the northeast, northwest, and directly in his front. If Johnston saw his opportunity and pulled the strings, Grant would be trapped. Most of Foote's gunboats and the transports that had carried his men up to Henry were gone. If Johnston had seen the situation as Halleck did, he might have changed the course of the war in the West. But he did not.

Neither did Grant. He figured that the Confederates were demoralized and panicky and that one more push would drive them out of middle and west Tennessee. He determined to cut loose from Fort Henry and march overland to Donelson. Bad weather held him up for a few days; he started on February 11.

Fort Donelson was built in the early winter of '61 on a ridge just west of Dover, Tennessee. Its purpose was to deny the Yankees the use of the Cumberland River, and the batteries placed in the fort were well suited to the task. The fort itself consisted of little more than a series of shallow earthen entrenchments that extended in a semicircle around the batteries and just south of Dover. Hickman's Creek, to the north, and Indian Creek, to the south, gave additional protection to the flanks. The entire area was hilly and heavily forested, with only a few poor roads running through it. The most important of these was the Wynn's Ferry Road, running southwest from Dover.

Grant's forces were well up to the fort by February 13. He had a total of twenty-four infantry regiments, seven batteries of artillery, and several mounted units; Floyd had twenty-seven regiments of infantry and additional supporting troops. As Grant had expected, the enemy made no attempt to contest his advance. He later wrote that "I had known General Pillow in Mexico, and judged that with any force, no matter how small, I could march up to within gunshot of any intrenchments he was given to hold." Grant's forces were divided into two divisions: the 1st, under John A. McClernand on the right, or eastern end of the line, and the 2nd, under Charles F. Smith, on the left. McClernand was an Illinois politician whose military experience consisted of a few marches in the Black Hawk War. He was ambitious, untactful, hated West Pointers, and had little ability. By contrast,

Smith was Regular Army and an outstanding soldier. Lew Wallace described him: "He was a person of superb physique, very tall, perfectly proportioned, straight, square-shouldered, ruddy-faced, with eyes of perfect blue, and long snow-white mustaches." When reviewing troops, Smith had the bearing of a marshal of France. Rumor had it that he knew the Army regulations by heart. He was the only general officer in the Union Army who could ride along a line of volunteers in regulation uniform, plume chapeau, epaulets and all, without exciting laughter.

The infantry on both sides had a miserable day on the fourteenth. Grant had received some reinforcements, Lew Wallace's 3d Division, which had come up the Cumberland on transports behind Foote's gunboats. Wallace, a newspaper reporter, lawyer, politician, and veteran of the Mexican War, put his men into line between McClernand on the right and Smith on the left. There had been a blizzard the previous night, and as the troops could not have camp fires they had been cold, wet, and unhappy. A few wounded men froze to death.

Most regiments had a special company composed of their best marksmen, and during the investment of the fort they went out as individuals. The captain usually checked with them at first light. "Canteens full? Biscuits for all day? All right; hunt your holes, boys." They dispersed and like Indians sought cover behind rocks, stumps, or in hollows. Some dug holes, others climbed into trees. Once in a good spot they stayed there all day, shooting at anything in the enemy breastworks that moved. It was dangerous to show a head and impossible to start campfires. Both sides contented themselves with hardtack.

Grant's plan was to keep the Confederate infantrymen pinned within their lines while the gunboats attacked the batteries at close range. Both he and Foote thought that the boats would reduce the opposition at Donelson just as they had at Henry. When the batteries were destroyed and the fleet controlled the river, while Grant's men blocked the exits, the Confederates would have to surrender.

All of this depended on Foote, and was with his approbation. A Regular Navy man, he had had wide and varied experience. In the 'fifties, when the navy had been called upon to take certain Chinese forts, he had led a storming party across rice fields under heavy fire, holding an umbrella over his head for protection from the oppressive Oriental sun. On his ships sailors practiced total abstinence, refrained from profane swearing, and strictly observed the Sabbath; by the force of his personality Foote had maintained these rules without precipitating a mutiny.

133

Gunboats attack the water batteries at Fort Donelson.

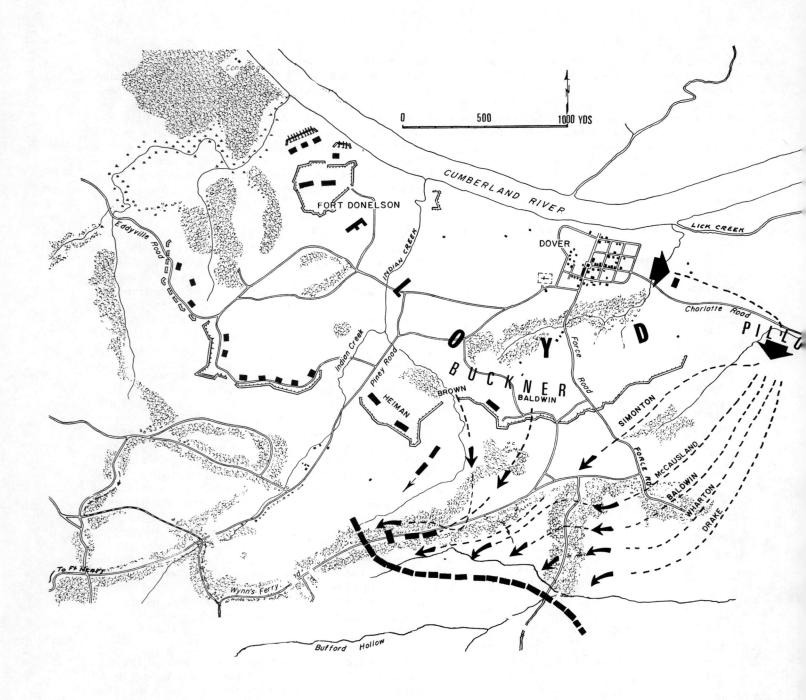

A simplified version of a map at Fort Donelson National Military Park by Edwin C. Bearss portrays the Confederate attempt to break out of Fort Donelson defenses from about 12:15 p.m. to 1 p.m. on February 15, 1862. In the sweep against the Union right flank, Pillow's command included Simonton's and Drake's brigades of Bushrod Johnson's division, Wharton's and McCausland's brigades of Floyd's division, and part of Baldwin's brigade of Buckner's division. Buckner, in the center, had Brown's and part of Baldwin's brigades of his own division. Confederate troops remaining in the trenches were Heiman's brigade of Johnson's division, the 30th Tennessee under Colonel J. W. Head, and in the fort itself two other Tennessee regiments under Colonel J. E. Bailey. Later in the afternoon the fort proper was commanded by Colonel C. A. Sugg. The gunboat attack of the 14th is shown at the top of the map. Small rectangles on the map represent regiments—Confederates in black, Federals in brown.

He was a little skeptical about this attack. He knew that the Donelson guns were stronger than those at Henry; but Grant urged speed, and so at mid-afternoon of the fourteenth he came up the river with his four ironclads, *Pittsburg, St. Louis, Carondelet,* and *Louisville.* Two unarmored gunboats, *Tyler* and *Conestoga,* followed. *St. Louis* was Foote's flagship.

Foote opened fire at about a mile's range. His shells fell short and he moved in closer—he had won at Henry by coming in close, and he was determined to do the same at Donelson. Slowly the distance lessened—three quarters of a mile, half a mile, a quarter of a mile. In the Crimean War the French and English fleets, composed of much larger ships than Foote's, had engaged the Russian shore batteries, which were little if any stronger than those of the Confederates at Donelson, from a maximum distance of eighteen hundred yards to a minimum of eight hundred yards. Still Foote moved in until he was only four hundred yards away. All the ironclads were taking hits, the decks were slippery with blood, the surgeons were absorbed in tending to the wounded, and the carpenters were busy making repairs. *St. Louis* alone took forty-nine hits. But the men cheered, for the fire from shore seemed to slacken and lookouts reported that the enemy was running.

Foote moved in, too closely this time. At 380 yards a solid shot tore through the pilot-house of *St. Louis.* It carried away the wheel, mortally wounding the pilot and injuring Foote. At the same instant the tiller ropes of *Louisville* were disabled. Both vessels were unmanageable and began to float down the current, whirling round in the eddies like logs. *Pittsburg* and *Carondelet* closed in to cover them. Foote was compelled to retreat, and the fleet backed up with the best grace and most speed it could manage. Any victory won at Fort Donelson would have to be won by the army.

Grant was disappointed at Foote's failure, but he did not panic. He knew that the Confederates could not get significant reinforcements into the fort nor bring supplies to the besieged men. He was fairly certain Johnston was not going to mount an attack on his rear. He was willing to wait for starvation to bring him victory.

The Confederates decided not to wait. That night Floyd held a council of war and all present agreed with his plan to attack the Union right wing and force a breakout. The Southerners spent the night of February 14 preparing for the

This engraving of a gun explosion on the Carondelet *during the attack on Fort Donelson was based on a sketch by Rear Admiral Walke. (BL)*

attack. Most of the troops left their rifle pits and massed over on the left. They made every effort to keep silent, but heavy gun carriages just could not be moved without making some noise. Yet, because of high winds from the tail of the blizzard, the Yankees did not hear them.

At dawn, when the woods were ringing with reveille and the numbed Union soldiers were rising from their icy beds and shaking off the snow, the Confederates struck. Pillow led the attack on the left, Buckner in the center. The general direction was along Wynn's Ferry Road. After the first confused moments, with shots and shouts ringing out in the cold air, McClernand's brigade commanders got their units formed into line and began to return the Confederates' fire. Both sides slugged away for the better part of the morning, spreading a lurid red over the snow, toppling limbs from trees, and sending up a continuous roar. The Yankees held.

About noon officers from various regiments road up to the Union brigade commander on the right, Richard J. Oglesby, with news that their men were running out of ammunition. They asked where they could get more, but he could only weakly reply, "Take it from the dead and wounded." Actually, there was plenty of ammunition all around him, but at that early stage of the war junior officers were not very good at their distribution functions. Before the officers could even get back to their men, Oglesby's right-hand companies began to give way, the men holding up their empty cartridge boxes as they retreated to prove that they were not cowards.

Seeing them, the Southerners gave a whoop and swept around Oglesby's flank, quickly appearing in his rear. Sick at heart, he gave the order to retire.

The commander of the next brigade to the left, W.H.L. Wallace, looked to his right and saw the crumbling line. Coming towards his own unprotected flank was Bedford Forrest and the Confederate cavalry. Wallace's men were also out of ammunition, and he quietly told them to join the by now general retreat. The Confederates had control of the Forge Road; the road to the southeast and Nashville was open to them.

The time had come to begin the retreat to the south. There can be no doubt that had the Confederates started out at noon they would have made it safely to Nashville. The Union force probably would not have even mounted an effective pursuit, since Grant was not on the scene to direct it. He had left before daybreak to consult with Foote, and was in the middle of the Cumberland River on the *St. Louis*. But Pillow, the hero of the morning, now proceeded to make himself ludicrous. He convinced himself that Grant's whole army was fleeing in rout for Fort Henry. Ignoring Floyd, he rode over to Buckner and accused him of cowardice. Napoleon, he exclaimed, followed up his victories, and the Confederates would do no less. Pointing to a road that ran up a gorge in front of Buckner, he ordered an attack. Then he sent an

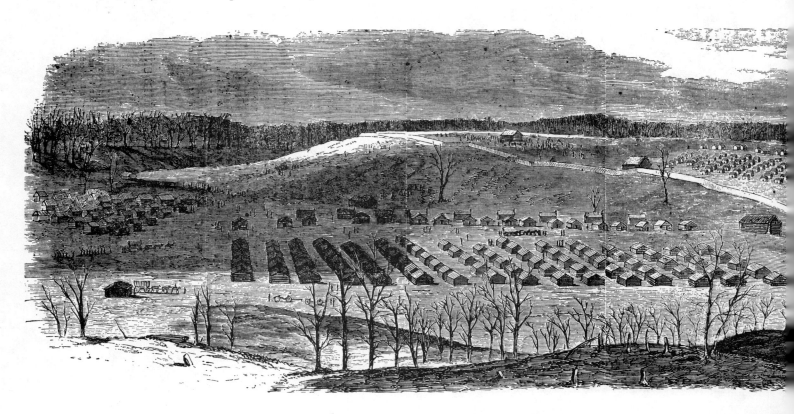

aide to the nearest telegraph station with a dispatch for Johnston, asserting on his honor as a soldier that the day was his. His head swimming with his own glories, Pillow abandoned all thought of a Confederate retreat to Nashville.

McClernand's division had retreated to Bufford's Hollow south of Wynn's Ferry Road, and Wallace had sent two brigades of his division over to the right to help out. Buckner's men were coming along the road, anxious to pour more minie [rifle] balls into McClernand's ammunition-less men. Wallace, riding over, saw a Union officer gallop by, shouting, "All's lost! Save yourselves." Behind him, riding at a walk, with one leg thrown over his saddle horn, and looking for all the world like a farmer coming home from a hard day's plowing, came W.H.L. Wallace and what was left of his brigade.

"Good morning," Lew Wallace said.

"Good morning," W.H.L. Wallace replied.

"Are they pursuing you?" "Yes." "How far are they behind?" W.H.L. Wallace calculated, then said, "You will have about time to form line of battle right here." "Thank you. Good-day." "Good-day."

Lew Wallace looked behind him and saw Battery A, 1st Illinois Light Artillery, and Colonel John M. Thayer's six-regiment brigade coming up. He placed the artillery across the road, with the infantry on either side and in reserve. The Confederates hit the roadblock at full speed and rebounded like a rubber ball. For the next ten minutes they tried to break through, finally decided it was impossible, and stopped to catch their breath. A lull settled over the field.

Just then Grant rode up. He had ridden the entire length of his line, and was satisfied with what he saw on the left and in the center. On the right, however, "I saw the men standing in knots talking in the most excited manner. No officer seemed to be giving any directions. The soldiers had their muskets, but no ammunition, while there were tons of it close at hand."

It probably never occurred to Grant that he should have panicked, that he should have begun riding this way and that, shouting orders, making threats, beating enlisted men with the flat of his sword. Most officers would have reacted in this way. Not Grant. His solidity and basic common sense were never in better evidence than here at this, one of the most decisive moments of his career.

Noticing the full knapsacks on the Confederate dead, Grant immediately realized that Floyd and Pillow were trying to cut their way out. He began walking his horse along the line, calling out to the men, "Fill your cartridge boxes, quick, and get into line; the enemy is trying to escape and he must not be permitted to do so." It worked. The men cheered, set to work, and quickly re-established the line on the right.

Grant then decided to launch an attack of his own. He was sure that Floyd must have stripped his entrenchments to make the attack, so he rode over to Smith's headquarters and told that general to attack.

The position was a mean one, uphill and criss-crossed with felled trees. Smith, in what Grant called "an incredibly short time," got his men into line and began the movement. Smith himself went to the front and center of the line to keep his men from firing while they worked their way through the abatis. From time to time he turned in his saddle to make sure the alignment was kept. He looked as if he were on review; one private remarked, "I was nearly scared to death, but I saw the old man's white mustache over his shoulder, and went on." Confederate fire began to increase, men began to fall. Smith's line hesitated. The general put his cap on the point of his sword, held it aloft, and called out, "No flinching now, my lads! Here—this is the way! Come on!" Most of his men followed him, broke through the abatis, and scattered the Confederates.

Grant now held an important section of the Southern entrenchments. Lew Wallace and McClernand meanwhile had reorganized their men and launched their own attacks, driving Pillow's and Buckner's men back into their entrenchments. The Confederate attempt to break out had failed.

The interior of Fort Donelson as depicted in Harper's Weekly.

That night, as both sides gathered their wounded, Floyd and Pillow argued about ways of extricating the army from its embarrassing position. Unable to reach an agreement, at one a.m. they called a meeting of all general officers and regimental and brigade commanders. When most of the leaders had asembled, Floyd began to speak. His scouts had just discovered that Grant had five regiments of reinforcements coming to join his army. Floyd wanted to get out before Grant's reinforcements arrived, and he ordered his officers to have their men ready to march by four a.m. The brigade and regimental commanders left to make their preparations; Floyd, Pillow, and Buckner remained in Dover at Pillow's headquarters. Buckner argued that Floyd's orders were as unrealistic as Pillow's actions had been the preceding morning. The troops had fought all day and were exhausted. There had been no regular issue of rations for days, the ammunition was nearly expended, Grant had four times as many men and half of his were fresh. It would be madness to try to fight their way through. If he persisted, Floyd would lose three-quarters of his men, and Buckner said he "did not think any general had the right to make such a sacrifice of human life." Pillow argued that they ought to hold on and wait for transports to carry them across the river; then they could make their escape by way of Clarksville, and "thus save the army." Buckner pointed out that Smith had already

gained their entrenchments—the Yankees would overrun them the next day.

Pillow stood up and declared, "Gentlemen, if we cannot cut our way out nor fight on there is no alternative left us but capitulation, and I am determined that I will never surrender the command nor will I ever surrender myself a prisoner." Floyd chimed in, "Nor will I; I cannot and will not surrender." Pillow added that he thought "there were no two persons in the Confederacy whom the Yankees would prefer to capture than himself and General Floyd." He then asked Floyd if he could scurry off with him. Floyd replied, "It was a question for every man to decide for himself."

At this point Forrest entered the room, looked at the gloomy faces, and demanded to know if they intended to surrender. Someone nodded. Forrest stomped out of the room, assembled his officers, and announced, "Boys, these people are talking about surrendering, and I am going out of this place before they do or bust hell wide open." He got his troops together and marched them through the icy streams and creeks to safety—most of the eastern end of the line was unguarded.

After Forrest left, the comic opera at headquarters reached its climax. Floyd started the last act. "General Buckner," he said, "I place you in command; will you permit me to draw

Right: *Confederate infantry escaping from Fort Donelson. Drawing by W. A. Rogers.* (*HW*)

out my brigade?"

"Yes, provided you do so before the enemy act upon my communications," Buckner replied.

Turning to Pillow, Floyd said, "General Pillow, I turn over my command."

Pillow exclaimed, "I pass it."

Buckner grimly declared, "I assume it; bring on a bugler, pen, ink, and paper." While Buckner began his bitter duty, Floyd and Pillow dashed out and got down to the river, where they were expecting a steamboat. Just before dawn the boats arrived. Floyd and his Virginia troops got on and sailed away. Pillow and his staff crossed the river on a flatboat and later rejoined Floyd.

Johnston, now in Nashville, knew nothing of these proceedings, and did nothing to change the situation at Donelson.

Buckner, who held to his old-fashioned belief that a general's responsibility extended to going into captivity with his men, composed his note to Grant, asking for terms of capitulation. Grant received it just before daylight. His reply was terse: "No terms except unconditional and immediate surrender can be accepted. I propose to move immediately upon your works."

Buckner was shocked. He had not slept in over thirty hours, had spent most of the previous day engaged in hard fighting, and was disgusted with his superiors. He did not quite know what Grant meant by "unconditional surrender," as the term was a new one, and he did not like to think about the implication of it. Perhaps he allowed himself a fleeting thought of further resistance. But he had a role to play, and he was determined to play it out to the end, with dignity. So he wearily wrote his reply to Grant. "The distribution of the forces under my command incident to an unexpected change of commanders and the overwhelming force under your command compel me, notwithstanding the brilliant success of the Confederate arms yesterday, to accept the ungenerous and unchivalrous terms which you propose." So Donelson was gone, and with it all of western Kentucky and Tennessee.

The Confederates had run the gamut from glittering opportunity through brilliant victory to buffoonery and finally bitter defeat. All three senior officers had blundered, or worse. Only Buckner emerged untarnished, and he at least managed to restore some dignity to the last act.

Later that morning Grant rode into Buckner's headquarters. The two commanders made final practical arrangements—the prisoners went north on Yankee transports, Buckner went with them—and gave each other cigars. At the conclusion of the meeting, when Buckner was walking off, Grant stopped him and said, "Buckner, you are, I know, separated from your people, and perhaps you need funds; my purse is at your disposal." Buckner declined, then thanked him for the offer. It was a strange war.

Dover Tavern, General Buckner's headquarters and the scene of the surrender, as it appeared in 1884. (BL)

Fort Henry

Mound City were 175 feet long, 51½ feet wide, and mounted six thirty-two-pounders, three VIII-inch Navies, and four forty-two-pounder Army rifles.

Eads was also given a contract by the quartermaster general to convert the giant salvage boat *Submarine No. 7* into a powerful ironclad to be known as *Benton*. The steamboat *New Era* was converted into the ironclad *Essex* by a St. Louis contractor. *Benton*, when commissioned, was the most powerful ironclad on the western waters.

Three weeks after the Civil War began, Lieutenant General Winfield Scott suggested that the Union Army establish a chain of fortified positions along the Ohio and Mississippi Rivers from Louisville, Kentucky through Paducah, Memphis, Vicksburg, and New Orleans to the Gulf of Mexico. Such a river blockade, "in connection with the strict blockade of the seaboard" already begun by the Navy would, said Scott, "envelop the insurgent States and bring them to terms with less bloodshed than any other plan." Although Scott's *Anaconda Plan* was loudly derided by those who thought, as Horace Greeley did, that the Confederate states could be brought to terms by a quick thrust at Richmond, its merits were so obvious that it was immediately adopted by the government.

As one means of carrying out Scott's plan the War Department quickly took steps to organize a flotilla of gunboats for service on the western rivers. On May 16, 1861, the Navy Department sent Commander John Rodgers to Cincinnati in response to the War Department's request for advice and assistance in connection with this novel undertaking.

Rodgers found that steamers of the kind available in the West were poorly suited for use as fighting craft because, as he put it in an official report, they had "their high pressure boilers on deck with all their steam connections entirely exposed [to damage by gunfire], and with three-story houses of thin white-pine plank erected on their hulls." But, driven by the same necessity that caused the Navy to use ferryboats, excursion steamers, merchantmen, and the like to blockade the coast, he bought *Conestoga, Lexington,* and *A.O. Tyler.* A Cincinnati contractor converted these craft into gunboats of sorts by dropping their boilers below their main decks, lowering their steam pipes as much as possible, covering the thin walls of their deckhouses with oak planking five inches thick, and arming them with a number of thirty-two-pounder smoothbores, VIII-inch Navies, and VIII-inch Dahlgrens.

The War Department had contracted with James B. Eads to build seven ironclad gunboats big enough to carry heavy batteries and broad enough to provide steady gun platforms. *Cairo* and her sisters *Cincinnati, St. Louis* (later renamed *Baron deKalb*), *Carondelet, Pittsburg, Louisville,* and

While the North was building these gunboats the South occupied a defense line which extended from Columbus, Kentucky, on the Mississippi River, through Forts Henry and Donelson, Tennessee, to Bowling Green, Kentucky, then southeastward to Cumberland Gap. Long before the movement into Kentucky, the state of Tennessee had started work on Forts Henry and Donelson to guard the Tennessee and Cumberland rivers about seventy miles south of (upstream from) their confluences with the Ohio River. In mid-November 1861 these posts and the country between them were placed under the command of Brigadier General Lloyd Tilghman, a soldierly looking man with piercing black eyes and a resolute countenance. He had graduated from West Point in 1836, then resigned the same year to become a civil engineer with the Baltimore & Susquehanna Railroad. At the outbreak of the Mexican War he rejoined the army, serving on General Twiggs's staff and as a captain in a battalion of volunteers. After the war he was an engineer with several railroads until he entered the Confederate service.

On inspecting his new command Tilghman found Fort Henry to be a well-designed, five-bastioned earthwork situated just above a bend in the Tennessee where it could command a straight reach of river about three miles long. It was on low ground, however, liable to be flooded by spring freshets, and overlooked by hills on both sides of the river. As an artilleryman Tilghman immediately recognized that these hills could present the same sort of threat to Fort Henry that Dorchester Heights did to the British in Boston when General Washington occupied them. To offset this danger Tilghman ordered a work named Fort Heiman to be built on a bluff across the river almost opposite Fort Henry. The fact that Fort Heiman had not been completed by the beginning of February 1862 had an effect on future events.

When Tilghman took command of the area, Fort Henry mounted two twelve-pounders, one six-pounder, and six thirty-two-pounder smoothbore cannons. At his insistence its armament was increased to ten thirty-two-pounders, two forty-two-pounders, two twelve-pounders, one twenty-four-pounder, a ten-inch columbiad, and a rifled twenty-four-pounder (originally a smoothbore that had been rebored to take a sixty-two-pound conical projectile banded at the breech). Thus he had, all told, seventeen guns. As one of the

Above: General Lloyd Tilghman, the Confederate commander of Fort Henry. Below: Commodore Andrew H. Foote, whose gunboats hammered Fort Henry into submission.

officers said, however, the twelve-pounders were so much like pot metal that they were test-fired, whereupon they burst.

Because the Confederates were kept well informed by Northern newspapers of the Union's gunboat building program, eleven of Fort Henry's heavy guns, including the columbiad and the twenty-four-pounder rifle, were placed on the river front where they could command the main channel east of Panther Island.

As was true of most Confederate installations throughout the war, Fort Henry had gunpowder of poor quality. Captain Jesse Taylor said that the fort's ammunition was so bad that "it was deemed necessary to add to each charge a proportion of quick-burning powder." Until this was done it was impossible to reach a target more than a mile distant.

During this fall of 1861 several Union Army and Navy officers told their superiors that they believed Fort Henry could be attacked without too much risk, and overcome without too much difficulty either by a couple of gunboats or by some troops assisted by gunboats. Flag Officer Andrew H. Foote, who had succeeded Rodgers as senior naval officer assigned to the Western Flotilla, and Brigadier General U.S. Grant were among the most ardent advocates of a joint movement.

At the beginning of the third week of January 1862, soon after the Eads gunboats were commissioned, Grant proposed such a movement to his department commander, Major General Henry W. Halleck. "Old Brains" curtly told Grant that the plan was preposterous. Halleck was then well known for his accomplishments in military and civilian life, whereas what little was known of Grant did not inspire confidence in him.

On January 28, 1862, perhaps at Foote's instigation, Grant again applied to Halleck for permission to move against Fort Henry. Foote helped by writing to Halleck: "General Grant and myself are of the opinion that Fort Henry...can be carried with four ironclad gunboats and troops, and be permanently occupied. Have we your authority to move for that purpose when ready?"

This concurrence of a navy man with Grant's opinion seems to have impressed Halleck, as well it might in view of Foote's record. In 1856, while Foote was commanding the USS *Plymouth* during a Sino-British war, a fort at Canton fired upon his vessel. He obtained permission from his superior to demand an apology. When this was refused he attacked the forts, four in number, employing the *Plymouth* and another sloop, the *Levant*. After breaching the walls of the largest fort he carried it by storm, with a loss of only forty men to four hundred for the Chinese.

141

Whatever his reasons may have been, Halleck telegraphed to Grant and Foote on Wednesday, January 29, that he would decide about their proposed movement as soon as he could receive a report on the condition of the road from Smithland, Kentucky to Fort Henry. Foote, who had become aware of Halleck's tendency to procrastinate, replied: "I have just received your telegram in relation to Fort Henry and will be ready with four ironclad boats early on Saturday. . . . As the Tennessee will soon fall, the movement up that river is desirable early next week (Monday), or, in fact, as soon as possible."

At or about the time these messages were being exchanged, Halleck heard, from what he supposed was a reliable source, that General Pierre G.T. Beauregard had been ordered from Virginia to the West with a large body of Confederate troops. Although this report was not entirely correct—Beauregard was being sent west, but without troops—it forced Halleck's hand. On January 30 he ordered Grant and Foote to move against Fort Henry.

Halleck's message reached Foote and Grant on the same day. By February 2 they had assembled a fleet of transports large enough to carry half of Grant's troops, and the gunboats *Conestoga, Tyler, Lexington, Carondelet, St. Louis, Cincinnati,* and *Essex.*

The *Essex* was commanded by William (Dirty Bill) D.

Porter. Since no one ever seems to have suggested that Porter was physically unclean, he probably earned his sobriquet by his methods of seeking professional advancement.

The plans for the movement against Fort Henry were kept a far better secret than was the case with most Civil War expeditions. Consequently the Confederates were taken completely by surprise when, to quote one of them, "countless transports" appeared below Fort Henry on February fourth.

Because it had been raining heavily for several days the Tennessee was at flood stage and its current was so rapid that the ironclads had to ride to double anchors and keep their engines running at full speed ahead while they were waiting for the transports to bring up the rest of the troops. A number of torpedoes (cylindrical mines about 5½ feet long, containing about seventy pounds of gunpowder), torn loose from their moorings by driftwood borne on the swift current, floated past the anchored boats. Foote had one of them fished out for examination. While he and Grant were watching the *Cincinnati*'s armorer dismantle it, a sudden hissing sound caused everybody to vacate the fantail. Foote, although the elder by sixteen years, beat Grant up the nearest ladder to the top of the casement. Reaching the top, and

The gundeck of a gunboat engaged in the attack on Fort Henry, as depicted in Harper's Weekly.

realizing that the danger, if any, had passed, Foote turned around to Grant, who was displaying more energy than grace, and said, "General, why the haste?"

"That the Navy may not get ahead of us," responded the general.

When the noise died down the armorer finished what he had been doing.

Late on the afternoon of February 5 the rest of the troops reached the rendezvous, some four miles below Fort Henry. Grant, on the fourth, had asked to have the *Essex* run him upstream close enough to the fort to permit him to have a good look at it. The *Essex,* accompanied by two other gunboats, stood cautiously up river. As the vessels chugged along, they shelled the woods on either side to see if they could flush any masked batteries. Passing up the main channel to the east of Panther Island, the gunboats took position near the mouth of Panther Creek. Having gained a point within one mile of Fort Henry, the vessels opened a deliberate fire on the Rebel works. Several of the gunboat's shells were seen to fall into the fort. The Confederates replied with their ten-inch columbiad and twenty-four-pounder rifle. Being inexperienced in handling the big guns, they had difficulty registering.

Grant having seen what he wanted, the gunboats started to turn around. A projectile from the rifled twenty-four-pounder screamed over the spar-deck of *Essex,* narrowly missing Grant and Porter, and struck the officers' quarters. After ripping through the cabin, captain's pantry, and steerage, the shell erupted from the stern, and dropped hissing into the river.

Foote and Grant met late on the fifth to draft final plans for a joint attack on Fort Henry. The soldiers were to advance up both sides of the river against Forts Heiman and Henry, while the gunboats were bombarding Fort Henry. (Fort Heiman did not seem important enough to warrant the gunboats' attention.) Originally Foote had supposed that the boats would have to use the main channel, which would permit the fort to bring them under fire at the extreme range of its guns—about three miles. His subordinates told him that high water would enable the boats to navigate a chute to the west of Panther Island, where they would be screened by dense woods until they were within a mile and a quarter of the fort. He gladly took advantage of this piece of good luck.

On February 6 Grant and Foote were ready to make their attack. The weather was ideal. A thunderstorm ended at daybreak, the temperature became comfortably mild, and there was enough wind to clear smoke away—an important consideration in the days of black powder. At 10:30

a.m., the flagship *Cincinnati* signalled "prepare for action." Thirty minutes later the gunboats got underway in line ahead. They cleared the upper end of Panther Island about 12:30 p.m., and formed in line abreast, with the *Essex* on the extreme right, the *Cincinnati, Carondolet,* and *St. Louis* to the left; the three wooden gunboats formed another line abreast about one-half mile astern of the ironclads and fired over them.

Opening fire at a range of seventeen hundred yards, the ironclads gradually closed to six hundred yards. As they neared the fort the fuses were cut from fifteen to ten to five seconds and the elevation of the guns was reduced from seven degrees to six, five, four and finally to three degrees.

Before the battle Foote had warned his gunners that every shot or shell they fired would cost the government eight dollars, so he wanted none of them wasted. To the grim amusement of the gunners of the other boats the *Cincinnati's* first salvo completely missed the fort. The boats seldom missed again and, as a Confederate officer remarked, their "shot and shell penetrated the earthworks as readily as a ball from a Navy Colt would pierce a pine board." This gunfire drove the Confederate gunners from their pieces and dismounted many of the cannon. Two thirty-two-pounders were hit, one of them squarely on the muzzle, almost at the same instant.

The Confederates' gunnery at first was as good as that of the gunboats. Seven hits were made on the *St. Louis* and nine or ten on the *Carondolet,* but neither of them was much damaged and neither suffered any casualties. The other ironclads were less fortunate. The *Cincinnati* was hit thirty-two times; two of her guns were disabled, her chimneys, main cabin, and small boats were badly damaged, one man was killed and eight were wounded. A shot that pierced the *Essex*'s forward casement just above the port gunport killed one of Porter's officers, Acting Master's Mate Samuel B. Britton, Jr., in its flight; then it struck the middle boiler. Escaping steam and hot water killed ten and wounded twenty-three. Five men, who leaped overboard to escape being scalded, were never seen again. When it became possible to pass forward of the boiler room Pilot James McBride was found dead at his post, with one hand on the steering wheel, the other holding the engine room bell rope; James Coffey, a member of No. 2 gun crew, was found dead on his knees in the act of taking a shell from the box to be passed to the loader.

The Confederates suffered nearly as much from bad luck as they did from the Union bombardment. The fort's best gun, the rifled twenty-four-pounder, burst (perhaps because it was partly loaded with quick burning powder), killing one of its crew and wounding the rest. A few minutes later a priming wire jammed in the vent of the columbiad, putting it out of action. A premature discharge of a thirty-two-

143

pounder (again possibly caused by quick burning powder) killed two men and disabled the piece.

As a consequence of these misfortunes and of the gunboats' accurate shooting, only four of Fort Henry's guns remained usable after seventy minutes. They were kept in action long enough to enable most of the garrison to escape to Fort Donelson. Fort Henry was then surrendered to Foote before Grant's troops, delayed by muddy roads, were in position to carry out their mission.

As time passed and bigger battles were fought, the engagement at Fort Henry came to be regarded as of only minor importance. But by their capture of Fort Henry, the Federals had driven a wedge into the Confederate defense line guarding the heartland of the Confederacy. The left flank of this line had been anchored at Columbus, and the right on Cumberland Gap, and with the loss of Fort Donelson, this line was hopelessly shattered. To make matters worse, the Confederates had lost a powerful field army and an immense amount of war material.

The fruits of the victory at Fort Henry were quickly apparent. As early as February 8, two days after its fall, and in the face of the threat to Fort Donelson, General Albert Sidney Johnston had notified Secretary of War Judah P. Benjamin that he was giving up his position at Bowling Green and was retiring on Nashville. When Fort Donelson fell, Nashville was uncovered, and it was expected that Federal gunboats would ascend the Cumberland, compelling the Confederates to give up Nashville, a vital industrial and transportation complex. On February 17 and 18, Johnston evacuated the city and moved the main body of his Central Army of Kentucky to Murfreesboro. The Confederate rear guard left Nashville on the night of the twenty-third, and the vanguard of Brigadier General Don Carlos Buell's Army of the Ohio appeared the next morning on the right bank of the Cumberland, opposite the city.

At the same time, Columbus, the Confederate bastion on the Mississippi River, was rendered untenable. Major General Leonidas Polk was forced to order the evacuation of "The Gibraltar of the West." This was carried out on the night of March 2. The Union troops occupied Columbus the next day. Thus, by the capture of Forts Henry and Donelson and the destruction of the defending army, the Federals at one stroke had forced the Confederates to give up southern Kentucky, and virtually all of middle and west Tennessee. Falling back, the Confederates began to concentrate their troops for a new stand on Corinth in northeast Mississippi.

With the fall of Forts Henry and Donelson, the entire picture of the war in the West was changed almost overnight. Grant had seized the initiative and, despite temporary set-

backs, he was never to lose it. The deep wedge driven into the South by the fall of Forts Henry and Donelson would eventually split the Confederacy. Just over the horizon lay Shiloh, Corinth, Memphis and, seventeen months later, Vicksburg.

Abroad, the effects of the loss of these forts were quickly felt by the Confederate diplomatic agents who were seeking to persuade Great Britain and France to recognize their government and to denounce the Union blockade as ineffective. In March 1862 James Mason, writing from London, somewhat euphemistically said, "The late reverses at Fort Henry and Fort Donelson have had an unfortunate effect upon the minds of our friends here." And John Slidell, mincing no words, wrote from Paris that, if these defeats were not soon counterbalanced by some substantial victories, the Confederate government would not only have to give up hope for early recognition but must also expect that the declaration of the inefficiency of the blockade, which he had confidently expected at no distant date, would be indefinitely postponed. These defeats were not counterbalanced and the Confederate states never stemmed the tide that began to flow against them when Fort Henry fell.

Attack on Fort Henry. Operations from noon to midnight, February 6, 1862.

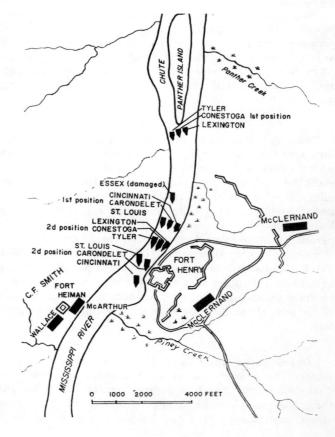

144

STONEWALL IN THE SHENANDOAH

Text by James I. Robertson, Jr.
Designed by Frederic Ray

One of the most famous campaigns in the annals of military history, it lasted barely three months. It began with the withdrawal of a small Confederate army of 4,600 ill-equipped soldiers; it ended with three Federal armies totaling 64,000 men in full retreat. For embattled Virginia at that time (to alter a phrase by Winston Churchill): "Never have so few done so much for so many."

A few words are necessary about the stage and the leading actor in this drama.

The Shenandoah Valley is one of the most beautifully contoured and deeply fertile regions in the world. It lies between the two easternmost ranges of the Alleghdeny Mountains. Its eastern boundary is the famed Blue Ridge, with the Alleghenies proper to the west. An average of 30 miles wide, the Shenandoah stretches 165 miles from Lexington northward to Harpers Ferry, where the Baltimore & Ohio Railroad—the main line of transportation between Washington and the West—crossed the Potomac, and where the Shenandoah flows into the great river. The Valley loses altitude as it stretches northward. Hence, and in contrast to general terminology, one journeys northward *down* the Valley and southward *up* the Valley.

The Shenandoah region was a veritable breadbasket, first for Virginia and then for the Confederacy. Grain of all kinds, orchards, large herds of livestock, all were in great abundance. The Upper South's very existence depended in great part on the harvests of the Shenandoah. Moreover, the Valley was of primary military importance. It was a natural avenue into both North and South. Any army in the Eastern Theater that launched an invasion had of necessity to have control of the Valley. Otherwise, it left itself dangerously vulnerable to flank attack and/or counter-invasion. In short, the Valley was the key to military movements, if not military supremacy, in the East.

Jackson's camp, near Harrisonburg, from a sketch by Frank Vizetelly. The sketch was intended for the *Illustrated London News* but was intercepted by the Federal blockading fleet off Charleston, South Carolina.

By early 1862, this important area was under the command of an eccentric, ingenuous man now regarded nationally as almost a legend.

His name was Thomas Jonathan Jackson. History remembers him as "Stonewall." His men called him "Old Jack" or "Old Blue Light"; and cadets at the Virginia Military Institute (where Jackson had been a professor of military science before the war) dubbed him "Tom Fool" because of his consistently odd behavior.

Jackson was a large man, strong of build and close to six feet in height. Deep-set blue eyes stared directly ahead. His hair and beard were brown and slightly curly. A partial deafness in one ear sometimes made it difficult for him to detect distant artillery fire or to determine the direction from which it came. His uniform customarily was a single-breasted, threadbare coat that he had worn in the Mexican War, a battered kepi which he wore with the broken visor pulled far down over his eyes, and an outsize pair of flop-top boots that covered feet estimated at size fourteen.

Correspondent George Bagby of the New Orleans *Crescent* interviewed Jackson in February 1862, and wrote that he was "a spare man, above the medium stature with dark hair and eyes, a sallow complexion, and a habit of holding his head back so that he never

Harper's Weekly, 1862

T. J. Jackson

Lieutenant General Thomas J. Jackson.

147

looks at the ground. He is as brave and cool as a human being can be; a Presbyterian who carries the doctrine of predestination to the borders of positive fatalism . . . . Silent and uncommunicative, exceedingly polite, yet short and prompt in his speech, he has but little to do with the commanders under him, but is devoted in his attention to the men. . . ."

He was a plain man who put on no airs. He was also a man of few words; and on those rare occasions when he laughed, he threw back his head, opened his mouth widely—and emitted no sound whatsoever. He lived simply, required little sleep, arose early, worked hard, and considered *duty* as the primary responsibility of a soldier.

Jackson could aptly be termed a religious fanatic. A staunch, unyielding Calvinist, he prayed regularly, attributed everything to God's will, and sometimes interrupted his soldiers at their poker by strolling through camp and passing out Sunday School pamphlets. His men came in time to believe that he was in direct communication with the Almighty. Many of his men hoped so, for Jackson took them places, and ordered them to perform deeds, that seemed beyond human accomplishment.

Even his marching pace was a test of endurance: fifty minutes of each hour at a jog, then ten minutes for rest. A one-hour lunch period was the only respite from a marching day that usually lasted seventeen hours.

Little Sorrel (later Old Sorrel), Jackson's favorite horse. Ridden through all Jackson's campaigns, he was never wounded and died in 1886 at the age of 36.

148

Most Civil War units were lucky to make eighteen miles a day. Jackson expected his men to do twenty-five or thirty miles—and then fight a battle, if necessary. He tolerated no excuse for soldiers breaking ranks. To him, a sick soldier and a straggler were but two of a kind. One of his officers observed that Jackson "classed all who were weak and weary, who fainted by the wayside, as men wanting in patriotism. If a man's face was as white as cotton and his pulse so low you could scarcely feel it, he looked upon him merely as an inefficient soldier and rode off impatiently."

Jackson's diet was as odd as his behavior. To ease the pain of dyspepsia, he subsisted on cornbread, milk, and butter—supplemented by lemons, dozens of lemons which he sucked feverishly. He refused to use seasoning on his food. Pepper, he claimed, made his left leg ache.

On the march, "Old Jack" was easily recognizable. A begrimed man who slumped awkwardly in the saddle, he rode a small tanglefoot named Little Sorrel. The horse's gait bore a resemblance to the rhythm of St. Vitus' Dance; and as the little beast loped down the road, Jackson's big feet were always dangerously close to the ground. The rider and his mount had little likeness to a champion on his charger, but together they would alter the course of modern warfare.

Jackson had been given command of the Valley in November 1861; and in the three months that followed—quiet months broken only by Jackson's trying winter campaign against Romney, the Confederate general concentrated on the fundamentals of drill and discipline. His headquarters was Winchester, twenty-six miles southwest of Harpers Ferry. Winchester guarded all of the mountain passes in the lower Shenandoah and, hence, was the key to that entire area. Jackson's force consisted of 3,600 infantry, 600 cavalry and 6 batteries of 27 guns. All of the men were Virginians save for a small battalion of Irish "navvies." Most of the troops were from the Valley. As such, they were familiar with the mountainous countryside and accustomed to outdoor life.

Late in February 1862 a Federal force began inching into the Valley. It numbered 38,000 men (including 2,000 cavalry and 80 guns). Like their Confederate opponents, these troops were mostly farm boys; products of the hardy life in Ohio, Indiana, Wisconsin, and western Virginia. The commander of this army, and of the newly created Department of the Shenandoah, was 56-year-old Major General Nathaniel P. Banks.

Tall, thin, and heavily mustached, Banks had risen from a laborer in a cotton mill to a political power in Massachusetts. He had served ten terms in Congress, gained national prestige as Speaker of the House of Representatives, was governor of Massachusetts, and a principal organizer of the Republican party. He

Major General Nathaniel P. Banks.

"If this Valley is lost, Virginia is lost."

owed his general's stars to the unrealistic custom in the Civil War of granting field command to men of political prominence. Banks had an air "of one used to command"; even captured Confederates remarked that they "never saw a more faultless-looking soldier." Yet in the words of his chief biographer, Banks "had courage but was short on talent and experience." He proved to be a devoted servant who gave the military everything he had. The weakness was that, by both training and intuition, Banks had very little to give.

In the face of Banks's army, Jackson's tasks remained the same as they had been since he took command of the Valley. He had to protect the left flank of the Confederate army at Manassas, guard Virginia's breadbasket against all intrusions, and carry out these two duties with no expectation of reinforcements. (The closest body of Confederate troops was at Culpeper, sixty miles away on the other side of the formidable Blue Ridge Mountains.) If Jackson was upset over this seemingly superhuman assignment, he made no display of it. However, his determination was strongly evident in a letter he wrote at this time to a congressional friend: "If this Valley is lost," Jackson stated, "Virginia is lost."

Jackson's little army was no match for the hordes that Banks was concentrating. A Federal move on Winchester late in February left Jackson no choice but to abandon the city. On the night of March 11, the Confederates slowly withdrew from the area and marched southward up the Shenandoah. The citizens of Winchester hardly greeted Banks's men with open arms. A New York cavalryman characterized the town as being "as rebellious and aristocratic as it was beautiful. Thoroughly loyal Union families were there, but they were like angels' visits, 'few and far between.'"

attended to final details for the surprise assault.

When Jackson returned to the army a few hours later, he learned that, through some misunderstanding, the wagons had gone to Kernstown and Newtown, from three to eight miles distant, and that the Stonewall Brigade was already en route to those points to obtain rations. The men would have to march hard in the darkness for ten miles in order to strike Banks. Jackson's face blazed with anger. In calling off the proposed attack, he snarled: "That is the last council of war I will ever hold!" It was.

The Confederates then fell back to Strasburg, eighteen miles south of Winchester. When Banks dispatched another political appointee, Brigadier General James Shields and his division of 11,000 men and 27 guns toward that village, Jackson withdrew 25 miles southward to Mount Jackson. The Confederate general hoped that the Federals would continue in pursuit so that he could pull them farther from their Winchester base. Yet by then Banks had learned Jackson's true strength, and for the time being he regarded Jackson more as a nuisance than as a threat.

Several Federal officers did not share Banks's feelings. Colonel George H. Gordon, a Massachusetts soldier of proven ability, later wrote: "Much dissatisfaction was expressed by the troops that Jackson was permitted to get away from Winchester without a fight, and but little heed was paid to my assurances that this chieftain would be apt, before the war closed, to give us an entertainment up to the outmost of our aspirations."

Meanwhile, Major General George B. McClellan began moving a massive Federal army toward the Virginia peninsula for a campaign against Richmond.

"That is the last council of war I will ever hold!"

A few miles south of Winchester, Jackson halted his columns. He had no intention of relinquishing Winchester without some sort of demonstration. On the night of March 12, the Confederate general summoned a council of war composed chiefly of regimental commanders from the Stonewall Brigade. Jackson came quickly to the point: He wanted to launch a night attack on the Federal army. Banks's men were inexperienced, Jackson stated; Confederate morale was high; and the confusion of a night attack might possibly send the Federals scurrying back across the Potomac. On these premises, orders were issued. Jackson directed the wagon trains to be parked immediately south of Winchester. He then made a social call while his lieutenants

McClellan, who had a penchant for drawing reinforcements from all sectors, wanted another Federal army to swoop down on Richmond from the north in a simultaneous assault. He thus ordered two of Banks's three divisions to leave the Valley and proceed to Fredericksburg. Banks complied routinely with the order, at the same time directing Shields to fall back to the more secure ground around Winchester.

Shields's division contained some devoted elements, but his command had early acquired a reputation for rowdiness and mismanagement. A New York *Times* reporter described a regiment of Germans in the division as being "as lawless [a] set as ever pillaged hen roosts or robbed dairy-maids of milk and butter." An

Ohio captain summarized the general inefficiency prevailing with the comment: "When a supply of nails finally arrived, they came consigned to the medical director. The difficulty with which they were rescued from his clutches would lead one to suppose that the surgeon thought them a newly invented tonic intended to promote the digestion of our country's defenders."

On a dark, sleety March 21, Shields's men abandoned Strasburg and started slowly down the Valley toward Winchester. Jackson learned of the withdrawal that evening. The news came to him from his ever-alert cavalry chief, Brigadier General Turner Ashby. One of the South's most romantic idols, Ashby was a dark-skinned, dark-haired, militarily untutored officer who hated Yankees passionately because of the murder of his younger brother in the war's first months. Ashby was a born leader: a gentle and soft-spoken man off the field, but daring and impetuous in battle. That Jackson trusted him implicitly was a high testimonial in itself. Jackson immediately realized the implications of Shields's withdrawal and resolved to stop Banks's army from uniting with McClellan. The fate of Richmond could depend on what now happened in the Valley.

Battles and Leaders of the Civil War

Brigadier General James Shields.

Harper's New Monthly Magazine, 1867

Brigadier General Turner Ashby, a caricature by "Porte Crayon," Federal Colonel David H. Strother.

Jackson had his men on the road early the next morning, March 22. Ashby's 280 troopers rode hard and struck Shields's picket line a mile south of Winchester. In the skirmish that followed, fragments from a shell fractured Shields's arm and removed him from the battle that followed. Jackson's infantry covered twenty-five miles that day and tramped an additional sixteen miles the next day—a cold, raw Sunday—before arriving at Kernstown, two miles south of Winchester, at 2 p.m.

The Confederate army defending the Valley now numbered no more than 3,000 men, for Jackson's fast pace had left 1,500 stragglers scattered along the road from Mount Jackson. Nevertheless, when Ashby reported that only four regiments of Shields's division were blocking the way, Jackson decided to attack and, by winning, to contain Shields in the Valley.

Two factors gave Jackson pause for consideration. He himself had made no reconnaissance of the Kernstown situation; and—more disquieting to Jackson—that day was the Sabbath. Jackson normally refused even to write a letter on the Lord's Day. To do battle on Sunday might be tempting the power of Satan. Yet every military exigency demanded prompt action. If Jackson were to continue to do the Lord's work, no time could be wasted. His brigades were quickly deployed in attack formation.

At 3 p.m. (only an hour before Jackson struck), Banks confidently went to Harpers Ferry. He was totally unaware that an attack was pending. Thus, with Banks gone and Shields hospitalized, command of the Federal forces at Kernstown fell to Colonel Nathan Kimball. Born in southern Indiana in 1822, Kimball was a physician by profession. However, he had served as a captain in the Mexican War and, prior to Kernstown, had proven his worth in the Cheat Mountain campaign. His troops referred to him affectionately as "that stout old fighter."

The late afternoon sun glistened off a countryside made spongy from constant rain. Jackson's troops could

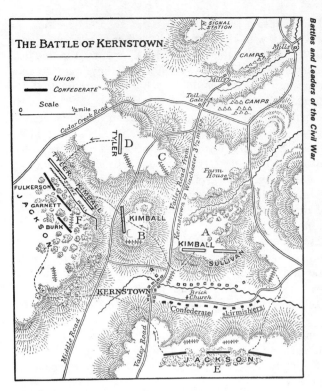

Map of the Battle of Kernstown, Virginia, March 23, 1862, by Major Jed. Hotchkiss, Jackson's topographical engineer.

Battlefield of Kernstown. From a photograph taken in 1885. Jackson formed his line of battle on this side of the stone wall.

Brigadier General Richard B. Garnett.

Brigadier General Turner Ashby.

Brevet Major General Nathan Kimball.

clearly see Federals in the distance, but everyone was of the opinion that only a thin rearguard of Shields's division blocked the way. The Union line extended on both sides of the Valley pike, with the heaviest concentration appearing to be east of the road. To the west of the pike was a sparsely wooded knoll called Pritchard's Hill. A Federal picket line was visible at the base, and two Union batteries stood posted on the summit.

Jackson made hasty plans to turn the apparently weak Federal right, which would then give him control of the commanding ridge overlooking the entire area. Ashby's cavalry would cover the turnpike while two Confederate infantry brigades and Carpenter's battery swung westward from the pike to assail what every Southerner was convinced was only a weak screen of troops.

At 4 p.m. the battle opened explosively. Federal cannon began a bombardment from a mile away and received an answer from Carpenter's guns, posted along the turnpike. Some 2,000 Confederate infantrymen moved quickly under the artillery duel and, in twenty minutes, seized Pritchard's Hill. The 5th Virginia then took a supporting position in the rear. The remainder of the Stonewall Brigade, reinforced by the 21st Virginia and three battalions, drove forward along the ridge. Jackson's battle plan was working perfectly.

Suddenly and unexpectedly, from the woods to the north, came a loud, long roar of musketry. Too late Confederates realized that Shields's entire division was in battle position! The 27th Virginia was the lead element of Jackson's advance, and it reeled from a point-blank volley of Federal rifle fire. The Confederates faltered momentarily, then drove ahead and overran two Federal skirmish lines. On the far left, the 37th Virginia in Colonel Samuel Fulkerson's brigade was advancing into an open field when it saw Federal troops entering the field from woods at the opposite end. A stone fence bisected the clearing. Blue and gray troops made a simultaneous dash for this cover. The Virginians arrived first and delivered a heavy volley of musketry that shattered a Pennsylvania regiment only a few yards away. The remaining Federals retired to the cover of the trees.

The whole battle line now became a flaming stalemate. For two hours soldiers fired muskets that often became red-hot. A Massachusetts infantryman was convinced that "there was not an interval of a second between the firing of the musketry." A lieutenant in the 5th Ohio observed that "a perfect whirlwind of balls was flying, as if the air was filled with hissing snakes." Five times his regimental flag fell to the ground as one colorbearer after another was hit. A reserve unit, the 14th Indiana,

153

rushed into action; and in the smoke, confusion, and excitement of battle, the Hoosiers fired precipitately into the rear of the 5th Ohio, inflicting several casualties. George L. Wood of the 7th Ohio commented: "The roar of musketry was now deafening. The dying and the dead were lying thick upon the hillside, but neither army seemed to waver. The confusion attending the getting of troops into action ceased. The great 'dance of death' seemed to be going forward without a motion. The only evidence of life on that gory field was the vomiting forth of flame and smoke from thousands of well-aimed muskets."

Kimball now had his entire Union division in action. Union fire maintained a destructive volume, and the Confederates began running low on ammunition. Slowly the Federal line surged forward on the Southern flanks. In the center of Jackson's line, Brigadier General Richard B. Garnett saw his Stonewall Brigade in real danger of being totally overwhelmed. No time existed to await orders. Garnett instructed his regiments to withdraw. On his left, Fulkerson's men had no choice but to follow suit in order to protect their flank. The whole Confederate line fell back, Southerners fighting and firing as they gave ground. An astonished Jackson rode up and attempted to rally the broken line. But it was no use. His army was in disorganized retreat.

The 5th and 42d Virginia made a gallant stand against hordes of oncoming Federals. The 84th Pennsylvania charged three times and withdrew only after its colonel fell dead. As night descended, the final elements of Jackson's army abandoned the field. The Confederates fell back to the wagon trains at Newtown, four miles south.

Harper's New Monthly Magazine, 1867

Dead at Kernstown, Jackson's only defeat, by "Porte Crayon."

thick woods, there were at least thirty of the enemy lying just as they fell; they were sheltered by a ledge of rocks, and most of them were shot through the head and had fallen directly backwards, lying flat on their backs with their arms stretched out in an easy, natural manner over their heads."

Federal losses at Kernstown were 568 men; Jackson's casualties numbered 455 men, in addition to 263 soldiers missing and presumed captured.

Jackson retired unmolested up the Valley. Banks termed the Confederate withdrawal a "flight" and commented that Jackson was now "not in condition to attack, neither to make strong resistance."

Kernstown was tactically a stunning defeat for Jackson. Yet the question persists whether Kernstown was a strategic setback. To be sure, Jackson was driven from the field and suffered the higher losses. General James Shields never let the world forget that. An Irish

"I never felt so tired and broke down in my life."

Jackson's men were exhausted after three hours of intense battle against heavy odds. One of Jackson's staff officers wrote: "In the fence corners, under the trees, and around the wagons [at Newtown] they threw themselves down, many too weary to eat, and forgot, in profound slumber, the trials, the dangers, and the disappointments of the day." A member of the 21st Virginia verified this statement by stating: "I never felt so tired and broke down in my life."

Shields's division bivouacked that night on the field it had successfully held. "All night long," one Federal soldier reported, the wounded "were brought in by the wagon load, every empty house and room in town was filled with them." Early the following day, a member of the 2d Massachusetts walked over the battlefield. "The hardest fighting," he noted, "was along a ridge which the enemy attempted to hold. Along it for nearly a mile, the bodies of our soldiers and those of the enemy were scattered thick. . . . In one little piece of

soldier in his fifties, Shields had served in the U.S. Senate from both Illinois and Minnesota. He was a lean, combative man who had once challenged Abraham Lincoln to a duel. He now tried hard to take all the credit for the Kernstown victory, even though he was miles from the field throughout the engagement. Nevertheless, he boasted thereafter that Jackson was afraid of him—a statement Jackson was to refute abruptly and painfully.

Many Federal soldiers openly and derisively referred to Shields as "Dirty Dick." Major George Wood of the 7th Ohio spoke for his compatriots when he wrote of Kernstown: "Colonel Kimball was mainly instrumental in achieving the victory. The skillful manner in which the troops were managed was entirely due to him; and the authorities regarded it in that light, for he was immediately made a brigadier general. . . ."

In a number of respects, however, Kernstown can be regarded as a Confederate victory in disguise. Jackson's small army had given Shields's division a rough treatment. Jackson was not boasting when he stated that "night and an indisposition of the enemy to press further terminated the battle." Moreover, Lincoln promptly stopped the transfer of Shields's division from the Valley. Banks was detached from McClellan's command and, with Williams' division, ordered back into the Valley. It was hoped that his 16,000 men, plus an additional 9,000 troops transferred from Major General John C. Frémont's forces would enable Banks to drive Jackson up the Valley.

The Union army now outnumbered Jackson by no less than 6 to 1. Although McClellan ordered Banks to "push Jackson hard," the Federal general made a casual and cautious pursuit. He established outposts at Tom's Creek, seventeen miles south of Kernstown, and was content thereafter to leave the Confederates alone. In reality, Banks fell victim to a host of imagined dangers and minor obstacles. He considered his men weary and short on supplies. The weather was not to his liking. Part of his army needed shoes. He was always in fear of an exposed flank. "Jackson and Ashby are clever men," one of Banks's officers moaned. "We are slow-w-w!"

In the meantime, Jackson was sternly reorganizing his army. Here he demonstrated how iron-willed he could be. He cashiered one of his best generals, Richard B. Garnett, for withdrawing the Stonewall Brigade prematurely from battle. Granted, the brigade was out of ammunition, badly outnumbered, and in danger of being flanked on both sides. A withdrawal was but common sense. Yet in this instance common sense ran counter to duty. Anyhow, Jackson snorted, the men could have held their position by using the bayonet—an instrument that no one but Jackson admired.

"an army of the living God"

This stigma on Garnett's reputation proved fatal: the following year, the young brigadier in quest of vindication threw himself into the jaws of death at Gettysburg. Yet the episode of Garnett's removal had a memorable effect on the soldiers, as well as on all other generals who served under Jackson.

In those post-Kernstown weeks, Jackson's foot soldiers slowly acquired a new faith in their commander. Perhaps grudgingly, they came to understand his careful attention to details, his devotion to Virginia, and his sense of urgency about the war. He searched the countryside for food and clothing for the soldiers, and he personally molded his tattered, beaten force into a new army with an indomitable will of its own. On April 17, Jackson optimistically wrote his wife: "Our gallant little army is increasing in numbers, and my prayer is that it may be an army of the living God as well as of its country."

Jackson's "foot cavalry," from the drawing by Allen C. Redwood.

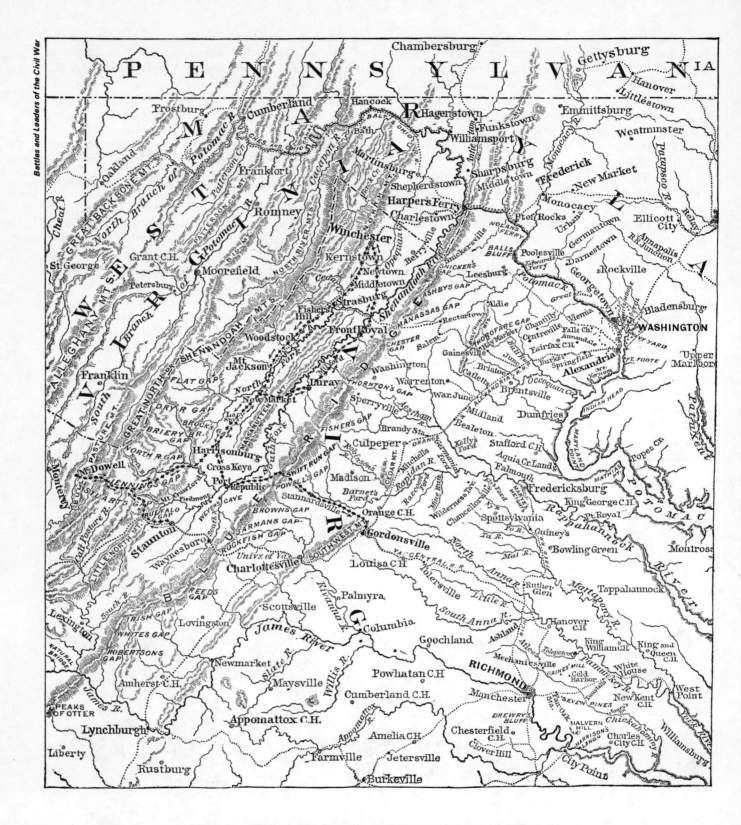

Jackson's campaign in the Shenandoah. The crosses and arrows indicate his
movements from Staunton, on May 6, to McDowell two days later, to
Front Royal, Newton and Winchester on May 23d, 24th, and 25th, then to
Cross Keys on June 8, and finally Port Republic the next day, June 9.

It was also during this inactive period that Jackson and General Robert E. Lee (then President Jefferson Davis' military adviser) worked out a plan so daring as by its sheer audacity, to have a chance for success. What Jackson wanted to do was to pin down all Federal forces west of the Blue Ridge firmly to the Valley theater, thereby preventing any of them from concentrating with McClellan against Richmond. Then, if Jackson could keep them separated one from the other, he could assault and defeat each one individually. This would take a degree of luck; but since Jackson defined luck as "the assistance of an ever kind Providence," he was confident of the outcome.

Both Lee and Jackson were painfully aware of the odds they faced. By April, the lower end of the Shenandoah was literally swarming with Union forces. Banks's large army was solidifying near Winchester. To the west, beyond the Alleghenies, was another Federal army under Frémont. Handsome and magnetic, a general who "gave at the same time an impression of wise maturity and buoyant youth," Frémont was a champion of the abolitionists and a hero to every Republican.

Major General Richard S. Ewell.

"The Pathfinder" had a reputation both exalted and overblown; in reality, his military activities—like himself—proved to be "showy and futile."

Jackson's trick, simple but at the same time dangerously complicated, was to keep the forces of Frémont and Banks from uniting. Jackson concluded that he could accomplish this through a combination of speed, deception and, most of all, desperate marching. Any other factors involved, Jackson was content to entrust to God's keeping.

Jackson and his chief engineer, Jedediah Hotchkiss, now made a careful study of the lower Valley. Winchester was the northern key to the Shenandoah. Moving southward up the Valley, one passed Strasburg (with Front Royal a few miles due east), then New Market, Harrisonburg, and Staunton. From Harrisonburg to the Front Royal-Strasburg area, however, there are actually *two* valleys. The reason for this is an imposing eminence, known as Massanutten Mountain, that is situated in the middle of the Valley floor. A tree-covered, uninhabited range that runs some fifty miles down the Valley, the Massanutten contains a lone pass at New Market. Otherwise, it splits the lower Valley into separate halves. Movements in one sector cannot be perceived in the other. Jackson carefully memorized these details.

In mid-April, Jackson received the only reinforcements he was to get: 8,500 infantry and 500 cavalry under Major General Richard S. Ewell. This eccentric, spry bachelor was a short man in his mid-forties—a tough old soldier who spoke awesome profanity with a sort of twittering lisp and who subsisted on a diet of cracked wheat in order to calm the pain of dyspepsia. Ewell had a sharp nose and bald head, which he frequently let droop toward one shoulder. Bulging eyes and prominent mouth added to an appearance that some people regarded as similar to that of an eagle. Others thought the likeness more akin to a buzzard. Ewell was a West Pointer who had spent too many years on the frontier. He always regarded his command—whether brigade, division, or corps—as of regimental size. Once, when his 8,000 men complained of a shortage of beef, Ewell left camp and returned triumphantly with a solitary, aged bull in tow.

Jackson effected a union with Ewell's division by moving to secure Swift Run Gap, a strategic pass that would give him a link with Ewell's troops on the upper Rappahannock. On April 18, after a leisurely march of fifty miles, Jackson reached the gap. With Ewell's division and 2,800 men under Brigadier General Edward Johnson in western Virginia, Jackson's force had now swelled to 16,000 troops and forty-eight guns.

157

"following a mirage into the desert."

Meanwhile, morale in the Federal armies was deteriorating badly. From "Camp Misery," two miles south of New Market, a Massachusetts soldier wrote on April 21: "The regiment has been here for three days without tents, on a bare field, with no other shelter than what the men could rig up out of rails and straw. The rain has been pouring down, in torrents most of the time, making the whole surface of the ground a perfect mire. We are lying around, like pigs, in straw, with wet blankets, wet feet, wet everything, and a fair prospect of nothing for dinner. We have had some pretty tough times lately, but this knocks everything else higher than a kite!"

Major Wilder Dwight of the 2d Massachusetts stated the Union case more succinctly: "Here we are, eighty miles from our supplies, all our wagons on the road, our tents and baggage behind, our rations precarious, and following a mirage into the desert."

Jackson now went into action with a zeal that had become customary, and with tactics that always seemed incredible. Leaving Ewell's men at Conrad's Store to check Banks, Jackson on April 30 began withdrawing his own brigades southward up the Valley. The march was a nightmare: rain poured incessantly, and the mud became ankle-deep. Soon Jackson turned left, and the column headed eastward. Confederate soldiers muttered dejectedly as Banks happily reported that Jackson was abandoning the Valley and marching toward Richmond.

A few miles down the road, however, Jackson halted his men at a rail junction. Trains soon appeared; the soldiers boarded cars; and, to the surprise of the Southerners, the trains left the station moving westward. The cars rumbled through Staunton without stopping and proceeded several miles beyond. Jackson's men detrained and found themselves uniting with Johnson's command of just under 3,000 men. On May 7, this combined Confederate force marched sixteen miles westward, overran a Federal picket, and continued up the Staunton-Monterey turnpike to within two miles of the hamlet of McDowell. That village had been occupied two days earlier by 3,700 Federals under Brigadier General Robert H. Milroy. "The War Eagle," as this Indiana-born officer was known, was a proven soldier of great energy and courage. His McDowell command consisted of the 3d West Virginia, 32d and 75th Ohio, Hyman's battery and detachment of cavalry. At Jackson's approach, Milroy rapidly concentrated his forces and sent an urgent call for reinforcements to his superior, Frémont. Recent snowstorms and heavy rains would delay the arrival of Federal troops in strength.

Early on Thursday morning, May 8, Jackson put his army in motion. Johnson's brigade of six regiments took the advance; Brigadier General William Taliaferro's small brigade of three regiments followed; Colonel John A. Campbell's three regiments came next; and Brigadier General Charles S. Winder's Stonewall Brigade brought up the rear. The numerical superiority of the Southern army forced Milroy back into Mc-Dowell. Jackson's forces immediately occupied Bull Pasture Mountain, which lay to the north of the turnpike and overlooked the McDowell valley.

The Confederates wasted no time in fortifying the broken, hilly summit of Bull Pasture Mountain. From an eminence one and a half miles away, Hyman's Federal battery unleashed several salvos in a vain attempt to dislodge the Confederates from their commanding position.

Frank Leslie's Illustrated Newspaper, July 5, 1862

"Army of Gen. Frémont and part of McDowel[l]

158

Near 10 a.m., the Federal brigade of Brigadier General Robert C. Schenck arrived from Franklin after a tortuous march of thirty-four miles in twenty-three hours. Milroy then dispatched a strong skirmishing party to clear a section of Bull Pasture Mountain known as Sitlington's Hill. Yet the 52d Virginia, comprising Jackson's left, easily repulsed this Federal stab. The situation for Milroy was becoming increasingly critical. As Captain E. R. Monfort of the 75th Ohio stated, Milroy's little army "was in a position of great peril, for, should the Confederates succeed in planting a battery on Sitlington's Hill, they could, with a plunging fire, clear the valley very soon."

Hence, Milroy took the offensive. "His restless nature and love of conflict prevailing," he sent the 25th and 75th Ohio across Bull Pasture Mountain and up Sitlington's Hill in a heavy assault on Jackson's left. The attacking column was under the command of Colonel Nathaniel C. McLean of the 75th Ohio. Captain Monfort later stated: "McLean formed his men quickly for the charge, which was made up the precipitous mountain-side. Suddenly the whole mountain seemed ablaze with the flashes of rebel guns that thundered and vomited forth showers of leaden hail. The rocks, and crags, and trees seemed clothed in the wild sublimity of the glory of a natural storm, as when mountain-tops salute each other with heaven's artillery."

The 12th Georgia was in the center of the Confederate line that caught McLean's attack. When the Union ranks swept up the hillside, the Georgians displayed more valor than judgment by standing up to shoot down at their enemy rather than withdrawing behind the hill. Silhouetted against the sky, they were ideal targets for Federal soldiers. All too soon, the Georgia regiment sustained losses of 19 officers and 156 men.

The Ohioans gained the mountaintop. Completely un-

...ps, in pursuit of Jackson's Rebel army, marching through the rain." From a sketch by Edwin Forbes.

Battle of McDOWELL.
May 8, 1862.

Camp McDowell

HALLS RIDGE

SCALE OF MILES

Map of the Battle of McDowell, by Major Jed. Hotchkiss.

Federal cavalry conducts reconnaissance of Confederate position at Strasburg, previous to occupation by Frémont.

supported, they nevertheless withstood Confederate assaults for four and one half hours. Meanwhile, Milroy had rushed the 32d and 82d Ohio, plus the 3d West Virginia, to turn Jackson's unengaged right flank. This assault was initially successful; but Jackson swiftly ordered in the 25th and 31st Virginia regiments to support the 44th Virginia, which had borne the brunt of the Union onslaught.

A curious battle developed in one small sector. Members of the 3d West Virginia suddenly discovered that they were fighting neighbors serving in the 25th Virginia. Both regiments had been formed in the same western Virginia counties. The fighting here was particularly vicious. Yet at times, when men on opposite sides recognized one another, they exchanged greetings.

With the Confederate left now stabilized, Jackson dispatched the 21st Virginia to turn the attacking column on his right. Neither side would give ground, and for several hours the battle raged without interruption. Many of the soldiers later remembered a large Newfoundland dog that was a mascot in Milroy's brigade. The animal ran back and forth along the battle line, "barking and snapping at the flying missiles, but before the fight was over he fell, pierced by a score of balls."

At 8:30 p.m., with darkness settling over the field, the Battle of McDowell ended. The Federal regiments had

Shenandoah River.   Union Prisoners.

been repulsed at every point, and nothing was left for them to do but to retire in order from the field. Jackson could organize no counterattack because of approaching nightfall, the confusion on the field, and the rugged terrain where the conflict had been waged. Jackson had suffered 498 casualties, while Milroy had lost but 256 men. Yet the Federal position at McDowell was now untenable. That night Milroy withdrew his forces toward the west and the mountains. Whereupon Jackson contemptuously turned his back on Frémont's menacing army, closed off the mountain passes, sent a cryptic battle report to Richmond ("God blessed our arms with victory at McDowell"), and returned to more serious business in the Valley.

The South by then was desperately in need of a victory, for those spring days of 1862 had been beset with disaster. Early in April, General Albert Sidney Johnston had lost a battle and his life at Shiloh; the vital port of New Orleans had surrendered three weeks later; McClellan had a toehold on the Virginia peninsula and was pushing westward toward Richmond with an army three times in size what General Joseph E. Johnston could bring to bear in defense. The capital city of Richmond was already preparing for evacuation.

Jackson was cognizant of these setbacks, but now, with his left flank protected after the success at McDowell, he was ready to concentrate against Banks. This Federal general had a measure of bravery born of ignorance.

Major General William B. Taliaferro.

Brigadier General Charles S. Winder.

Major General Robert C. Schenck.

sburg.   Rebel Cavalry and Infantry.   Fortifications.

161

He was firmly convinced that the size of his army would more than compensate for any thrust that Jackson might be so foolish as to make. Indeed, Banks considered his position in the lower Valley so secure that he again made preparations for transferring Shields's division to McClellan. Such an action substantiated the belief of many of Bank's officers that he had never learned to reconnoiter well or to utilize all components of his army.

In mid-May, Shields's 11,000 men began departing the Valley. Banks was left with only 8,000 soldiers to guard the main passage northward. To protect himself, Banks fell back from New Market to Strasburg.

His men by then were unhappy and dispirited. One Federal soldier commented that every dooryard on the retreat was full of "jeering men and sneering women"; others added that secessionist-minded roosters perched on fenceposts and crowed derisively as the Union columns passed. A Federal brigadier was apprehensive that "if the amount of swearing that has been done" in

Frank Leslie's Illustrated Newspaper, April 26, 1862

162   **View of Strasburg in the Shenandoah Valley during occupation by Federals under Banks. Sketch by Edwin Forbes.**

the ranks of the Union army "is recorded against us in Heaven, I fear we have an account that can never be settled." Despondent Federals then plodded into Strasburg, which a Massachusetts chaplain characterized as the "dirtiest, nastiest, meanest, poorest, most shiftless town I have yet seen in all the shiftless, poor, mean, nasty, dirty towns of this beautiful valley." Obviously, morale in Banks's army was sagging.

While this slow retreat was taking place, Jackson

A straggler, as depicted by Confederate veteran Allen C. Redwood. When General Richard Taylor's brigade came out of the Keezletown Road on the evening of May 20, 1862 after a 26-mile march, the bands were playing and every man was in his place in line. Jackson said to Taylor, "You seem to have no stragglers." "Never allow straggling," replied Taylor. "You must teach my people," Jackson commented. "They straggle badly."

Signal Station

Harper's New Monthly Magazine, 1867

"The peaked mountain from New Market," by "Porte Crayon."

was on the move. He drove his men rapidly down the Valley. On May 20, Ewell's division joined Jackson at New Market. Jackson now found himself in a blissful situation: For the first time in his career, he had an army that could do full battle. Small wonder that the first glimpse many of Ewell's soldiers had of Jackson was a man contentedly sitting on a rail fence and sucking a lemon as he watched the gray lines pass. In the gray light of dawn, May 22, Jackson's army marched northward from New Market. Soon the column turned right and advanced toward the pass through the Massanutten. None of the soldiers knew their destination, and Jackson made no effort to erase their bewilderment. Only he knew that the army was headed into the Luray Valley—that portion of the Shenandoah east of the mountain, and an area completely screened from Federal view.

In Washington, Northern optimism was at its height. The national Capital was regarded as so secure that recruiting offices had been closed. President Lincoln and Secretary of War Edwin Stanton were preparing to leave for Fredericksburg in anticipation of the imminent fall of Richmond.

Had Banks been more sharply alert to topography and reconnaissance, he might have avoided disaster. He was correct in regarding his position at Strasburg as "dangerously exposed." Yet he took no action to have a clear road for possible retreat; he retained his supplies, and his sick and wounded, with him rather than release these burdens to the safety of Winchester; and he gave little or no heed to possible dangers from the Luray Valley.

Thus, when Jackson's 16,000 troops entered the Luray, they stood squarely between Banks and eastern Virginia. The Massanutten Mountain would effectively hide any movements they made. More dangerously, Jackson now had an almost unobstructed route to Front Royal, the flank of the Federal army. Once Front Royal was seized, the Confederates would then have a straight shot at Winchester, Banks's major supply base. When Jackson's men realized the opportunities that lay ahead, not even persistent rain and occasional hail could deter their march northward.

Jackson, unlike Banks, knew that the Luray Valley's key city of Front Royal was completely indefensible. High ground looked down on it from almost every side. In addition, the small Federal garrison stationed there

Federal camp at Front Royal, from an Edwin Forbes sketch.

Battles and Leaders of the Civil War

164

Brigadier General John R. Kenly.

Major General Irvin McDowell

Brigadier General John D. Imboden

consisted principally of Colonel John R. Kenly's 1st Maryland (U.S.) Infantry. Jackson's plan was to seize Front Royal with such speed as to gobble up Kenly's men and prevent any warning from reaching Banks.

Friday, May 23, was clear and intensely hot. Late in the morning, Kenly's Marylanders were seeking cool relief from the sun's rays when suddenly from the forests emerged long gray lines of men and a deadly explosion of musketry. George W. Clarke, an army correspondent of the New York *Herald,* was staying in the Front Royal home of the aunt of the famous Confederate spy, Belle Boyd. When gunfire erupted, Clarke bounded down the stairs and shouted: "Great Heavens! What is the matter?"

"Nothing to speak of," Miss Boyd replied coolly. "Only the rebels are coming, and you had best prepare yourself for a visit to Libby Prison."

Clarke was en route to prison that night.

Kenly tried desperately to put up a fight against the hordes of Confederate soldiers swarming against his lines. Soon word reached him that Southern cavalry were galloping around his right flank. Kenly ordered his men—many of whom were grappling fiercely with their Southern counterpart, the 1st Maryland (C.S.) Infantry—to fall back. The Federals made a short stand at Guard Hill, an eminence north of Front Royal; but again Confederate numbers drove them from their positions. Kenly's troops then retired to the hamlet of Cedarville, three miles farther. They had barely

165

formed a line when Jackson's "foot cavalry" seemingly struck from every direction.

The small Federal force disintegrated. When Kenly fell, desperately wounded, most of his men laid down their arms. Barely an hour after Jackson had struck, the fight for Front Royal was done. Jackson had inflicted 904 casualties (including 600 prisoners), and had captured a wagon train—all at a cost of fewer than 50 men. Moreover, he was now in a clear position to isolate Banks from the Federal supply base at Winchester.

smashed remains of vehicles that had collided in the mad excitement. Frightened horses were stampeding, army teamsters had deserted their stations. The baggage train stood still, and it looked as though Banks's army would crack up before it met the enemy."

A wild race for Winchester now ensued, with Banks hurrying down the macadamized Valley Turnpike from the south and Jackson lunging through the mud from the southeast. Despite his inward despair, Banks presented an outward appearance of calm and confidence. One Federal trooper stated: "General Banks (God bless

"By God, sir, I will not retreat!"

A courier carried news of the Front Royal disaster to Banks at Strasburg. "By God, sir," Banks shouted, "I will not retreat!" He was initially inclined to dismiss the Front Royal incident as a Confederate raid. At the same time, the adverse effect on his political standing in the North if he did retreat created in Banks an obstinate expediency. "We have more to fear from the opinion of our friends," he remarked to a fellow officer, "than from the bayonets of our enemies."

Through the night of May 23-24, Banks refused to consider withdrawal. Not until 3 a.m. did the despondent general finally agree to dispatch his sick and wounded to Winchester. Only at midmorning of the 24th did the division begin the march to Winchester. By then, Jackson's troops were closing fast from the east. An air of panic filled the Federal ranks. One writer observed: "A few soldiers had lost all sense of discipline. Steadier troops were hampered by the tangle of bewildered fugitives and by the crush of military wagons. Ambulances packed with the disabled were blocked by the

him!) was here, there, everywhere, urging the men on, and determined to fight the cruel foe until the last."

Midway through the afternoon of May 24, Jackson's foot cavalry struck the Valley pike and collided with the rear third of Banks's retreating columns. A Confederate soldier observed: "The rout of Banks surpassed in many respects anything of the kind I saw during the war. It beggared description. Pell-mell, helter-skelter, without check, without any effort to rally or form, the retreating mass of men, horses, artillery and wagons rushed down the Valley Turnpike, everything going at breakneck speed. . . ." Discarded Federal wagons and equipment littered the road for a full six miles, as Banks literally raced for his life.

Banks momentarily escaped from the panic gripping his army and began to display a real talent for retreat. He bought precious time by discarding wagons and supplies that he knew would prove a tempting distraction to Jackson's hungry soldiers. The ploy worked.

Harper's New Monthly Magazine, 1867

Rebel troopers at breakfast, by "Porte Crayon."

Jackson at Winchester, from the painting by William Washington.

To Jackson's chagrin, Ashby's cavalry stopped their forceful pursuit of Banks's columns in order to plunder. Moreover, Colonel George H. Gordon, in charge of Banks's rearguard, used ambuscades and other devices to blunt Jackson's advance. Such tactics enabled most of the Federal army to reach Winchester ahead of Jackson's forces.

Banks considered Winchester "the key to the valley, and for us the position of safety." He was confident that Jackson would not dare attack him there. Comforted by this rationale, Banks sent a reassuring telegram to Washington and then went to his rooms for a leisurely bath. Yet the bluecoats desperately strengthening the earthworks south of town did not share their general's optimism. The sound of small arms fire continued to come closer as the nighttime hours passed. By midnight, even Banks realized that Jackson was not stopping the pursuit. Banks thereupon ordered his military train to start toward the Potomac. The wagons were still moving slowly through the city streets when dawn came—and with it Jackson's onslaught.

The indefatigable Confederate general subjected his men to a test of endurance that night of May 24-25. Most of the Southern troops had marched at least eighteen miles on the 24th; many of them were actively engaged in heavy skirmishes with Federals; and none of the Confederates had eaten since dawn. They were, in short, jaded by nightfall. But Jackson sensed a smashing victory; and at such a time, personal feelings were of little importance. On through the night he pushed his men. The few rest periods were of the briefest duration. In the end, Jackson achieved his objective: Sunlight of the 25th found the Confederate army massed in battle array on the southern outskirts of Winchester.

Losses at Front Royal and on the retreat had reduced Banks's force to no more than 6,500 men. Jackson was bringing to bear against him more than twice that number. Jackson's battle plan was simple: Ewell would assail the Federal left; and, while a portion of Jackson's command held the Federal center in check, the remaining Confederate regiments would turn the Federal right and dash for Winchester.

167

"Stop, men! Don't you love your country?"

A mist hung over the rolling hills when, at 5 a.m., the Confederates struck. Jackson's skirmishers brushed aside the Federal pickets and made contact with Banks's weak lines. Skirmishing gave way to an artillery duel, and soon intense musketry drowned out the noise of cannon. Federals manning the left met Ewell's initial advance with "murderous" volleys that ripped one Confederate regiment to shreds and left Ewell's forces (according to one Union soldier) "fumbling in the fog." On the Federal right, however, Jackson's men pushed forward in such heavy numbers that Banks's men were hard-pressed to maintain their position.

For three hours the Federals managed to hold fast. Then Jackson dispatched eleven regiments to turn the enemy's flank. This turning movement broke Banks's right into fragments, and it came just at the moment when Ewell's determined soldiers curled around the Federal left. Banks, on the field, now saw that he had been flanked for half a mile on either side. His order to retreat was not heard, for the remaining elements of his army had already broken from the lines. Across the way, Jackson was riding among his own soldiers and shouting: "Order forward the whole line! The battle is won!"

When the entire Confederate line surged forward in triumph, Banks watched horrified as his army disintegrated. Outflanked, beaten, and bewildered, the Federals lost all semblance of order. Blueclad soldiers streamed into Winchester "like a muddy torrent with the sunlight glittering on its turbid waves." Once in town, all remaining discipline vanished, for dozens of local residents began taking shots at soldiers in the crowded streets. A member of the 10th Maine, which was guarding the downtown, observed: "Nothing that day was more trying than standing there in the streets of Winchester, with that panic-stricken mob rushing past our front, from left to right, every one telling a different tale, but all saying, 'They're coming!'— 'Right on you!'—'Hurry up or you'll be lost!' . . ."

Banks himself tried desperately to halt the tide. He encountered the 3d Wisconsin in headlong flight. "Stop, men!" he shouted. "Don't you love your country?"

One soldier looked back over his shoulder and replied: "Yes, by God, and I'm trying to get back to it just as fast as I can!"

Hundreds of Federal soldiers discarded their weapons in the frantic dash northward. Fear-crazed troops commandeered horses, wagons, carriages—even cattle —to speed the trip to safety. Every effort by Banks to reorganize and restore order failed. Sheer exhaustion brought a brief halt at Martinsburg; at sundown the retreat resumed and did not stop again until the army reached Williamsport, Maryland. Federal soldiers had raced thirty-five miles in fourteen hours. "All of us," a New England soldier confessed, "had our feet blistered, some having more blisters than natural skin, but to describe the thousand aches and cramps we felt cannot be done." Yet even Banks admitted that "there were never more grateful hearts . . . than when at midday on the 26th we stood on the opposite shore [of the Potomac]."

Jackson was disappointed that the bulk of the Federal army escaped his clutches. Only the tardiness of the Confederate cavalry in going into action north of Winchester, he felt, saved Banks from total disaster. Yet the harvests of victory were enormous. In three days of fighting, Banks lost 3,030 of 8,500 men. Jackson's casualties were fewer than 400. The Confederates had bagged 9,300 new muskets, two cannon, and veritable storehouses of medical supplies and military equipment. The Southern soldiers had handled Banks with such ease, and were consuming his supplies with such regularity, that he became known as "Old Jack's Commissary General." Of greater import, Jackson's thrust had cancelled Federal Major General Irvin McDowell's intended advance from Fredericksburg to Richmond. And, for the moment, the Valley was clear of Federal forces.

Authorities in Washington were abruptly awakened to the awesome realization that the Shenandoah Valley was like a loaded musket aimed at the heart of the North—with Stonewall Jackson fingering the trigger. The Washington *Star* snorted editorially that Jackson was "popping around" in the Valley "like a quill of quicksilver in a hot shovel." Such popping

"Yes, by God, and I'm trying to get back to it just as fast as I can!"

had created terror in the national Capital and waves of panic throughout the North.

Lincoln thereupon interceded and made hasty but concrete plans to destroy Jackson once and for all. This would have the added dividend of giving the North control of the Shenandoah. Lincoln's strategy called for a giant pincer movement. A reinforced Banks would push southward straight up the Valley; Frémont would close in from the west; Shields would retrace his steps and come in from the east. Together, these three Federal armies (totalling 64,000 men) would trap Jackson somewhere between Winchester and Strasburg. Then, with Banks, they would strike Jackson from three directions—with each Federal army at least as large as Jackson's force of 16,000 men.

It was a daring and desperate counterattack, and it came within a hair of succeeding. Jackson, comfortably quartered at Winchester, and with the Stonewall Brigade in the van thirty-six miles farther north at Harpers Ferry, did not realize what was taking place until almost the last moment. Then, on the night of May 30, Jackson ordered his scattered command to fall back toward Strasburg. The retreat began on the morning of the 31st. Federal prisoners, escorted by the 21st Virginia, led the way. Jackson's infantry and wagon trains followed. The Confederate column, a full seven miles long, moved slowly southward.

Meanwhile, Frémont was closing fast on Strasburg; and Shields, by occupying Front Royal, locked the door to the Luray Valley. A few more hours, and the single remaining escape route for Jackson would be blocked.

Thereafter, for the North, occurred a series of errors. Banks was still so battle-scarred that his "forceful advance" up the Valley did not begin in earnest until June 10—the day after the campaign ended. No communication existed between Frémont and Shields, for Jackson held the country between those two Federal armies. Yet this point was probably academic. With the destruction of Jackson within their grasp, Shields and Frémont both failed to exercise the speed and determination necessary for success.

Shields tardily left Front Royal and led his men westward to the cutoff point at Strasburg. An Ohio officer summarized caustically what then happened: "It was late in the afternoon before Shields got ready to move, and then owing to some blunder never clearly explained, he took the road to Winchester." By the time the mistake was discovered, it was nightfall. Shields lost fully half a day as his men angrily retraced their steps.

Frémont's conduct is even more inexplicable, if not inexcusable. To Frémont, Lincoln sent a number of telegrams emphasizing the need for prompt movement. "Put the utmost speed into it," the President wired. "Do not lose a minute." Yet Frémont mysteriously chose to take a different route into the Valley from the one that Lincoln had ordered. As a result, it took

View from Banks's fort, near Strasburg, across to Fisher's Hill. From a photograph taken in 1885.

169

Near Strasburg, Virginia—On June 1, 1862 Frémont arrived from West Virginia to intercept Jackson, who was moving south in the Valley. This is a view of Frémont's advance party sighting the tail end of Jackson's train which, escorted by troops in the background, is about to clear Strasburg. It shows how closely Jackson calculated his time-and-place factors. Sketch by Edwin Forbes.

Frémont's army eight days to cover seventy miles—at a time when Jackson's "foot cavalry" were marching fifty miles in two days. Nevertheless, Frémont's men reached the top of the Allegheny Mountains in ample time to deliver a smashing blow. Clearly visible below to Frémont was Jackson's army, strung out along the Valley floor, with flanks unprotected and burdened by seemingly endless wagon trains.

The Federal opportunity to wreak destruction, however, came to naught. Instead of attacking, Frémont began constructing defenses on the mountains six miles west of Strasburg. After a painful delay, he dispatched a timid probe into the Valley. Jackson countered by sending Ewell's division westward in full battle array. Ewell's advance so paralyzed Frémont that a Confederate officer stated contemptuously: "Sheep would have made as much resistance as we met."

Jackson then spent several hours waiting for the Stonewall Brigade and his cavalry to rejoin the army.

The men in Jackson's brigade never forgot the living hell of that dash for survival. They had been at Harpers Ferry when the orders came to fall back rapidly. In thirty-six hours, through driving rain and bottomless mud, and with neither food nor rest, those men trudged forty-five miles. On reaching the safety of Jackson's army, many of the infantrymen collapsed in the road where they stood and fell asleep half-buried in the mire. Fatigue was so all-engulfing that few of the men knew where they were.

Their general was never content merely to be safe. Jackson's army was intact, but his beloved Valley was still in the grip of heavy Federal pressure—and his primary responsibility remained the security of that region. Early in June, the hunted became the hunter.

By then, rains had turned the countryside into mud. A series of cavalry engagements marked those first days of June as Ashby's troopers contested first Shields and then Frémont. The Confederate cavalrymen also burned all bridges between the two Federal hosts so as to keep them from uniting. Jackson's plan was to allow Frémont and Shields to converge upon him, and then to strike each before the two could merge into a superior force.

Frémont's army in those first days of June displayed an alacrity that its commander had never before shown. His cavalry galloped rapidly up the Valley and began closing on the Confederates. On the afternoon of June 6, Ashby's horsemen repulsed a force of 800 Federal cavalry some three miles from Harrisonburg. Frémont quickly dispatched heavy reinforcements. In the fierce fighting that ensued, the Confederates began to give ground. Ashby then rode up and called on his men to charge. Suddenly his horse collapsed from a fatal bullet wound. Ashby leaped to his feet and shouted: "Charge, men! For God's sake, charge!" The gray ranks swept out into the open and sent the Federals into general retreat. Yet on the field lay Ashby, "the idol of his troopers," dead from a musket ball through the head.

"Poor Ashby is dead."

Several weeks earlier, a New England officer had written of Ashby: "He is light, active, skillful, and we are tormented by him like a bull with a gad-fly." A New York cavalryman echoed these sentiments by observing: "His exploits had been so daring, quick, and so generally successful, that he had made himself a great name, and become a terror to our forces."

For Jackson, Ashby's loss was a personal tragedy. Jackson viewed the remains in a room at Port Republic and stated: "Poor Ashby is dead. He fell gloriously— one of the noblest men and soldiers in the Confederate army."

By now, Shields was bursting with confidence. Referring to Jackson's army as "a broken, retreating enemy," he urged Frémont on June 7 to push hard against "the demoralised rebels." Shields was convinced that if Frémont would launch an attack, Shields's own forces could then come "thundering down on Jackson's rear."

What Shields incredibly overlooked was that muddy roads, swollen streams, and the strangeness of the terrain had converted his army into a disconnected series of brigades scattered almost the length of the Luray Valley.

Jackson was well aware of that fact. His army waited quietly at the point where the two main roads of the Federal advances converged. His main body was at Port Republic, with Ewell's division four miles northwest at Cross Keys. Jackson was not immediately concerned about Shields, since his division was strung out twenty-five miles down the Luray Valley. Frémont's army was closer and more concentrated. Jackson's main attention, therefore, was given to it.

On Sunday, June 8, Frémont's army moved out of Harrisonburg. Federal skirmishers and Ewell's pickets became engaged at 8:30 a.m. Ewell had at hand about 6,000 infantry and 500 cavalry; Frémont's army numbered 10,000 infantry, 2,000 cavalry, and twelve batteries of artillery. The Federal superiority in num-

Frank Leslie's Illustrated Newspaper, July 5, 1862

"Gen. Frémont's division marching through the woods to attack the Rebels." From a sketch by Edwin Forbes.

Officers of Brigadier General Louis Blenker's division. Blenker is right center, hand on belt. At his left is Prince Felix Salm-Salm; at his right is (then) Brigadier General Julius Stahel.

"Mount Jackson, the headquarters of Gen. Frémont, on his advance to Harrisonburg." Edwin Forbes sketch.

bers could have been used to decisive advantage. Yet, as one historian has stated, "Frémont was more afraid of losing the battle than anxious to win it." He therefore "sought refuge in half-measures, the most damaging course of all."

Of twenty-four regiments at his disposal, Frémont gingerly dispatched five into action. This was the German brigade of Brigadier General Louis Blenker, which attacked the Confederate right. The Federals got to within sixty yards of Ewell's position when a concentrated volley of musketry rolled down the Southern lines. The German regiments broke and fell back in disorder. For a short while the field was quiet. Brigadier General Isaac Trimble, commanding the right of Ewell's line, then received permission to make a counterattack against Frémont's left. This onslaught caught the Federals by surprise. Frémont's left crumpled back a mile from its original position.

Trimble's attack came just as Frémont was probing other sectors of the Confederate works. A line of bluecoated skirmishers tested the Confederate center and found it too strong to break. On the Federal right, Milroy and Schenck advanced on their own, drove in the Confederate skirmishers, and were making satisfactory progress when Frémont ordered them back to protect his shattered left. Under Frémont's prodding, his troops frantically constructed earthworks; and from their strong positions, they warily watched the Confederates for the remainder of the day.

The battle of Cross Keys was a relatively minor affair. Frémont's casualties were 684 men, as compared to 288 Confederate losses. The 8th New York in Blenker's brigade was "almost annihilated."

An Ohio officer aptly described Jackson's subsequent strategy: "Jackson's plan for the next day

View of the Battle of Cross Keys, from the Union position, looking east. From a sketch made at the time.

Map of the Battle of Cross Keys, by Major Jed. Hotchkiss.

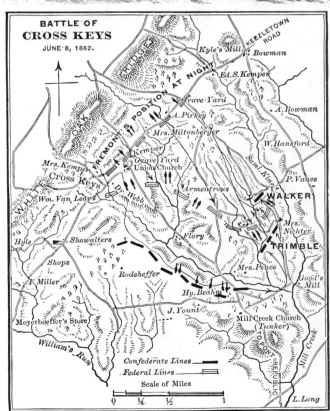

[June 9] was to leave a brigade to amuse Frémont, for whose enterprise and military talents he seems to have entertained a profound and not ill-founded contempt; to throw the remainder of his troops across the river and polish us [Shields's division] off in short order; then to return and put a quietus on Frémont."

At 5 a.m. on Monday, the Stonewall Brigade opened the battle of Port Republic by advancing across an open expanse against a strong Federal position. Shields again was absent from the field. He remained at Conrad's Store throughout the day. Command of the Federal forces fell to Brigadier General Erastus B. Tyler, who had at his disposal two brigades of 4,000 men plus sixteen guns. The remainder of Shields's division was strung out far to the rear. However, most of the regiments under Tyler's command had been at Kernstown and had witnessed the rare spectacle of Jackson being defeated. Small wonder that the Fed-

173

erals had a measure of confidence as they prepared to meet Jackson's attacks.

Winder's Stonewall Brigade struck hard at the Federal right but soon was forced back by intense fire from Tyler's lines. As the Valley brigade launched another assault, Brigadier General Richard Taylor's Louisianians swept around the Federal left and, after severe fighting, seized a key Federal battery near an abandoned coaling station. The Federals were now hard pressed, but they maintained their position with grim determination and continued to inflict casualties on Jackson's army. Near 10 a.m., the lead elements of Ewell's forces reached the field. The 44th and 58th Virginia reinforced the Stonewall and Louisiana brigades in a third assault that shattered Tyler's lines. Defeated Federals streamed down the Luray Valley in unbroken columns. Jackson's men gave pursuit for nine miles before falling back to Port Republic.

This battle was the most costly engagement of the Valley Campaign. Jackson lost over 800 of 5,900 engaged, while Tyler's casualties constituted one fourth of his command. The fighting at Port Republic was second to none in the Shenandoah. The outcome might have been different had Frémont advanced on Jackson's left flank. Yet Frémont steered clear of making further contact with the Southern army, and his apathy proved costly. By nightfall of June 9, both Frémont and Shields were in retreat. Banks was warily approaching Winchester, with no intention of venturing farther. The great Valley Campaign was over.

Major General Edward Johnson.

Brigadier General George H. Steuart

Brigadier General Arnold Elzey.

SECOND BATTLE OF MANASSAS

Text by Dennis Kelly
Designed by Frederic Ray

The year 1862 was half over. It had begun as a year of promise for the Union, a year promising extermination for the Confederacy. Kentucky, Missouri, and western Virginia were in Union hands. Tennessee had been pierced by Union armies, New Orleans captured, and the Atlantic coastline overrun. With the Federals' Army of the Potomac advancing up the Virginia Peninsula on Richmond, President Abraham Lincoln's sometimes impulsive Secretary of War, Edwin M. Stanton, became so confident no more soldiers would be needed, that the end of war was so close at hand, in April he closed down army recruiting stations. Confederates, by contrast, resorted to conscription to keep manpower in the ranks.

Then, just as the Union war wagon seemed to be rolling smoothly, its wheels came off. That elusive Confederate, Major General Thomas J. "Stonewall" Jackson, appeared and disappeared in the

Confederate General Robert E. Lee. His Army of Northern Virginia had pushed the enemy from Richmond to the outskirts of Washington in three months.

Virginia countryside with his troops, defeating Major General John C. Frémont in the mountains west of the Shenandoah Valley. Stanton, from piles of contradictory reports, concluded Jackson was withdrawing from the valley. Major General Irvin McDowell believed he might surface on his front at Fredericksburg. With speed unimagined by the Federals, Jackson doubled back from the mountains and struck at Front Royal, then again two days later at Winchester, defeating Major General Nathaniel P. Banks and sending his soldiers fleeing across the upper Potomac River.

Jackson's whereabouts and intentions now seemed assured—he was advancing on Washington! From Baltimore, Maryland and Washington, D.C. every available fighting man rushed to where he was figured to surface next, Harpers Ferry, Virginia. Appeals for help were telegraphed to the Northern states; militia and home guard regiments were hurried to rescue the capital.

It was all for nothing. Jackson had already accomplished his objective; any threat to the capital was a ruse. He was withdrawing back up the valley. McDowell's corps, which had been ordered to advance on Richmond and reinforce Major General George B. McClellan, simply dispersed, de-

feated without having fought. The president and his war secretary had hoped to intercept and destroy the impudent Jackson by squeezing him between Frémont, marching from the west, and McDowell, moving from the east. But Jackson's fast-marching infantry had slipped between the two, defeated Frémont at Cross Keys, then beat McDowell's leading division at Port Republic before entraining to join the main Confederate army in front of Richmond.

Far away in St. Louis, a 40-year-old major general named John Pope, temporarily on leave of absence from his command in Mississippi, received an urgent telegram from the War Department ordering him to Washington immediately. The president, with whom Pope was on friendly terms, was absent at West Point, New York. So on arrival in the capital Pope reported to the War Department asking after his orders. There he met Secretary Stanton, a man who seemed to have "lost much sleep and was tired in both body and mind." The armies of Frémont, Banks, and McDowell needed to be united, declared the war secretary in his usual curt, dictatorial manner. Together they should threaten Rebel railroad communications at Gordonsville and Charlottesville. That would draw off some enemy forces confronting McClellan, making it easier for him to storm Richmond.

Stanton was not merely musing. He held the general's new assignment. A new army, christened the Army of Virginia, was officially brought into being and Pope placed in command on June 26, 1862. Ironically, this was the very day that Confederate General Robert E. Lee — not McClellan — initiated the battles for Richmond: Mechanicsville, Gaines' Mill, Savage's Station, Frayser's Farm, Malvern Hill. And each blood-spattered place was a little farther away from the Confederate capital than the one preceding.

To Richmond and the South, these fights, the Seven Days' Battles, signified redemption. An enemy on the verge of victory was turned away. Not since the Battle of Manassas, nearly a year past, had there been a cause for Southern celebration. Confederate President Jefferson Davis looked and felt relieved. In seven days, Robert E. Lee had made himself the South's foremost soldier.

To McClellan, the sacrificial week was not a retreat, but a change in the base of operations. He believed his move from the Pamunkey to the James River was accomplished through masterful strategy. To him the Seven Days was a salvation of a different sort. Incompetent spies had deluded McClellan into believing the Confederates had twice the men he had. McClellan felt he and the Army of the Potomac had been deliberately placed in jeopardy, nearly sacrificed by scheming Washington politicians. He was irrationally bitter at the civil administration for not supplying reinforcements he demanded in impossible numbers. His army shared this belief. Now camped twenty-five miles from Richmond at Harrison's Landing, he felt he too had turned back an enemy intent on destroying him.

For the Lincoln Administration and the Union cause, the week of retreat amounted to a disaster. Jackson's raid in the valley had created local alarm, but the failure on the Virginia Peninsula bred deep gloom, national gloom, a feeling that crept over the Northern states like a sickness. Recruiting offices reopened, and the president issued a call for 300,000 more soldiers. The response was feeble.

The Confederacy was rejuvenated, ascending its pyramid of military power in the summer of 1862. The Union was despondent, its enthusiasm sapped, its strategic initiative stolen, its leadership quarreling among itself, the very purpose of its cause in question. Thus the campaign which culminated in the Second Battle of Manassas began not at a geographic location, with generals pointing at their maps deciding this or that northern Virginia railroad intersection was strategically important. It began at a point in time.

New Leaders and New Plans

The president had grown dissatisfied with the management of the war. He returned to Washington from the crowded, unhealthy camps at Harrison's Landing, hardly reassured by McClellan. The general had repeated what he had so often written: if an advance on Richmond were to be resumed, he would need heavy reinforcements. He still firmly believed the Confederates greatly outnumbered him.

Despite his misconceived situation, McClellan found time to write his president a long letter, purely political in substance, advising military force not be used as an instrument to upset "the relations of servitude." He believed Americans would rally to the cause of reuniting the nation, but not to freedom for the Negro. If slavery were tampered with, he warned, "our cause will be lost." Lincoln, pondering the necessity of emancipation for some time, replied he was much obliged, and put the document in his pocket.

Soon Lincoln would have two Union armies in Virginia, McClellan's and Pope's, widely separated with the Confederates between them. What should be done with them? Should McClellan be withdrawn to reinforce Pope, or could the two perhaps cooperate and attack Richmond from two directions at once?

The president and Stanton took to reading military manuals. But Lincoln at last concluded strategy was something more than a pair of industrious lawyers could easily master by borrowing primers from the Library of Congress. Expert military judgment was needed. On July 11, Major General Henry Wager Halleck was called from the western theater to Washington to direct all Union forces. John Pope tarried in the capital at the president's request, acting as an unofficial adviser before Halleck arrived.

Lincoln was well acquainted with the Pope family; the general was connected to Mary Todd Lincoln's family by marriage. His father was a Federal judge, and his uncle was a United States senator from Kentucky. He was a West Point graduate, class of 1842, and a Mexican War veteran. And Pope was the polished type of officer, one who preferred staff duty with the topographical engineers to frontier posts and chasing marauding Indians.

At White House dinners he told stories to Lincoln, and Lincoln liked stories. Pope always tried to say the right thing to the right Republican. To an abolitionist like Treasury Secretary Salmon P. Chase, he appropriately mentioned that slavery must perish. To others he spoke forcefully of vigorously prosecuting the war. Among McClellan's many political enemies, when the subject was brought up, he criticized his generalship and endorsed McClellan's removal from army command. He liked telling of his own relatively bloodless victories at New Madrid, Missouri and Island No. 10 on the Mississippi River earlier on the year. And it was duly noted that what John Pope especially liked to talk about was John Pope.

Pope made a good first impression in his uniform, maintained good eye contact, and had a stiff, rectangular

177

Native German Franz Sigel commanded the Army of Virginia's I Corps at Second Manassas.

U.S. Army Military History Institute

beard. Nevertheless, he did not always impress everyone the way he intended. He was known as the "bag of wind" to his fellow officers in the Regular army. Presidential adviser Postmaster General Montgomery Blair told Lincoln the general's father, Judge Pope, was "a flatterer, a deceiver, a liar, and a trickster; and all the Popes are so." Lincoln admitted Pope's many faults, but credited him with "great cunning."

The general of "great cunning" remained in Washington for several weeks. There he conferred with dignitaries, devised plans, defined procedures and policies, and took stock of his scattered command. He drafted a series of general orders designed to deter any hostile activities behind his troops' Virginia lines, orders which would go harshly on the noncombatant populace of the state. Guerrilla warfare would not be tolerated; guerrillas and anyone who aided them would be shot. Virginians would either take an oath of allegiance to the United States or relocate beyond Union lines. If they violated their oath or returned, they would be treated as spies and shot. No commander was to furnish guards for private property; he was to confiscate whatever horses, forage, or other supplies he needed.

The most severe parts of these orders were not enforced—probably no one was shot. But civilians were outraged, and for good reasons. Many a plantation, farm house, or log cabin in the path of Pope's far flung Army of Virginia suffered pillage at the hands of renegade bands of Union soldiers. "General Pope's orders," they cracked to defenseless families being robbed.* Even Pope was appalled when he learned how his orders were being misapplied, and he threeneed severe punishment to miscreants.

The Army of Virginia consisted of three corps, all formerly the forces of three military departments headed by Major Generals Frémont, Banks, and McDowell. Frémont, insulted because he was Pope's senior in rank, resigned his command the day after he learned the general was to be his new commander. About 11,500 men, the Army of Virginia's I Corps, was the new command of Frémont's successor, Major General Franz Sigel. Sigel was enthusiastically received by the corps' predominantely German-American regiments. He was a German-born exile, a veteran of Europe's 1848 insurrections, and he had fought with some distinction in the Civil War's early western battles in Missouri and Arkansas. His personal popularity was such that "I fights mit Sigel" became almost a watchword among the abolitionist German immigrants that swarmed to fill his ranks. This gave his corps a decidedly ethnic tang. Within his three divisions were leaders with names like Schenck, Steinwehr, Shurz, Bohlen, Schimmelfennig, and Kryzanowski. But enthusiasm had its limits. Not long after taking command the corps, encamped in the lower Shenandoah Valley at Middletown, was "in very bad condition in regard to discipline, organization, equipment, and to a great extent, demoralized," Sigel reported to Pope.

Not far from Sigel was the II Corps, commanded by Major General Nathaniel Prentiss Banks, sometimes called "the Bobbin Boy of Massachusetts" because his start came from his father's Bay State cotton mill. Banks was a "political" soldier, which was close to saying he was no soldier at all. He had been Speaker of the House of Representatives in 1856, and was governor of Massachusetts at the outbreak of the war when Lincoln appointed him general because he strongly advocated the Union cause. He was brave and energetic, but Stonewall Jackson's Rebels had captured so much of his foodstuffs that they derisively called him "Old Jack's Commissary General." His two divisions numbered only 8,800 men, hailing mainly from New England, Ohio, New York, and Pennsylvania.

Commanding the III Corps was Major General Irvin McDowell, a luckless general who magnified his own misfortunes. He could be rude, ill-tempered, pompous; he was obese and renowned for his indulgence. "While he drank neither wine nor spirits, he fairly gobbled the larger portion of every dish within reach," wrote an officer who once dined with McDowell. That evening he had finished his meal "with an entire watermelon, which he said was 'monstrous fine!'"

His soldiers hated him, and for some irrational reason they believed McDowell was a traitor in league with the enemy. It was McDowell who had commanded in the Union disaster at Manassas the previous summer, and the stigma of failure still lingered. His two divisions were huge, totalling 18,500. One was located at the old battleground, Manassas, the other at Fredericksburg. The corps was predominantely made up of New Yorkers and Pennsylvanians. In this corps was also a conspicuous brigade of westerners from Wisconsin and Indiana.

Completing the compliment of troops was a small reserve corps under Brigadier General Samuel D. Sturgis that had been assigned to Pope but was undergoing organization at Alexandria and not yet available. Together with some 5,000 run-down cavalry divided into two brigades, the Army of Virginia totalled 43,800 men.

Pope's mission had undergone only slight modification since he first reported to Stanton. He was to protect Washington; secondly, secure and guard the Shenandoah Valley (now free of Confederates since Jackson departed for Richmond) and, last, help McClellan by operating against enemy communication lines at Gordonsville and Charlottesville.

---

*Later in the war such policies would be considered routine, but at the time Pope became notorious as a moral monster.

Even as McClellan was "changing his base" on the Peninsula, Pope issued orders to concentrate his forces along the upper Rappahannock River. Sigel was to move up the Shenandoah Valley to Luray, cross the Blue Ridge at Thornton's Gap, and post himself at Sperryville. Banks was to march across the mountains at Chester Gap and proceed to Little Washington. Brigadier General James B. Ricketts' division of McDowell's corps was to move from Manassas to Waterloo Bridge on the Rappahannock.

The march was slow and disjointed, quickly using up Pope's scant supply of patience. Instead of prompt compliance with his orders, Pope encountered procrastination, excuses, and questions. Instead of pressing forward, subordinates inquired about designated routes of retreat, or what should be done if the enemy were encountered.

"Do?!" roared Pope, "Fight 'em, damn 'em, fight 'em!"

Pope felt his command needed inspiration; it needed to be infused with fresh enthusiasm. "Let us understand each other. I have come to you from the West, where we have always seen the backs of our enemies . . ." He said he assumed he was called to Virginia "to pursue the same system." He was tired of hearing from subordinates who worried about lines of retreat and their bases of supplies. "Let us study the probable lines of retreat of our opponents, and let our own take care of themselves. Success and glory are in the advance," he closed, "disaster and shame lurk in the rear."

An egoist's attempt to get tough and "create a cheerful spirit," Pope's address was a flat failure. Worse, it backfired. His men, many of them good soldiers, were humiliated by their recent defeats, sensitive to criticism, resentful of any of his comparisons to Westerners. Pope's tactlessness made him the object of scorn and ridicule in three armies—his own, McClellan's Army of the Potomac, and Robert E. Lee's Army of Northern Virginia.

As if this *faux pas* was not bad enough, Pope was said to have told a newspaper reporter that his headquarters would be located "in the saddle." Everybody everywhere howled, saying this general did not know his headquarters from his hindquarters.

Halleck, the eagerly awaited Western expert, reported to Washington in mid-July and immediately departed for Harrison's Landing to confer with McClellan. He, like Pope, had come out of the West with an aura of prestige, based on victories won by his subordinates. Halleck was a West Pointer, author of a book on military science, and a successful San Francisco businessman and lawyer. No one could have foreseen it, but Halleck was not a man on the rise; he had already passed his zenith. Called "Old Brains," he was little more than a scholarly bureaucrat, an officer whose hand was better fitted to the pen than the sword.

When the two generals sat down, McClellan, who recently held the post of general-in-chief and regarded Halleck's appointment "as a slap in the face," told Halleck his 101,000 troops were outnumbered by Lee two to one. Halleck pointed out Pope was making threatening gestures southward and it was necessary for McClellan's army to do likewise. McClellan said he could attack only if he had 30,000 more men. Halleck responded that the government would be strained to come up with 20,000. McClellan promised he would try if given those reinforcements.

The two men also briefly touched on the idea of removing the Army of the Potomac to northern Virginia and uniting it with Pope's; Halleck created the impression McClellan would command the force. McClellan maintained this would be a bad idea; the true shield to Washington, he argued, was with his continued presence on the Peninsula.

No sooner had Halleck returned to Washington than McClellan telegraphed, crying he would require no less than 35,000 more men to advance to Richmond. This time, his routine reinforcement demands and overassessments of enemy strength finally caught up with him. Rubbing his elbows while pondering the matter (an irritating and distracting mannerism displayed whenever he was engrossed in thought), Halleck reflected on the estimated size of the Confederate army and reasoned it would be unsound strategy to approach the enemy capital with divided forces. McClellan's and Pope's armies must be united as quickly as possible. On August 3, the Army of the Potomac got its orders: Board transport vessels in the James River and proceed by convoy for the Chesapeake Bay and up the Potomac River to Aquia Creek near Fredericksburg. This would be the army's new base of operations. There, it would be situated to defend Washington, support

Major General Nathaniel P. Banks, nicknamed "Old Jack's Commissary" for the beating he took from "Stonewall" Jackson in the Shenandoah Valley, again set his sights on Jackson at Second Manassas.

Pope, and begin a fresh overland campaign against Richmond. Also, Major General Ambrose E. Burnside's IX Corps, returning from a successful expedition to North Carolina, and now aboard transports at anchor off Fort Monroe, was to sail for the same base.

Burnside moved promptly. McClellan, seething with resentment, did not. If his army were recalled then the long, painful trek to Richmond and back would have led to nothing and McClellan would be a failure. He protested as strenuously as he could. The order was a week old when he requested permission to advance on Richmond, but the administration was adamant. Despite repeated messages from Halleck to speed things up, eleven days passed before McClellan got the hated movement underway. Even then he moved with deliberate slowness.

While the Federals made changes, Robert E. Lee rested, refitted, reor-

179

Lee Had Been Moved To The Depths Of His Knightly Soul By Pope's Threats. . . . "I Want Pope Suppressed"

Major General John Pope. Called the "bag of wind" by his fellow officers, Pope failed miserably at Second Manassas. Shown here as a brigadier, when he took command of the Army of Virginia he managed to alienate himself from his entire command; he was tactless and egotistical. But the citizens of Virginia hated him even more.

180

Library of Congress

ganized, and reinforced his Army of Northern Virginia. Its successful defense of the Confederate capital established Richmond as *the* symbol of the Confederacy, much as Washington was the symbol of the Union. So between drills, Confederate soldiers spent a great deal of time digging earthworks around it, a precaution that would make it easier for Lee to make detachments for field operations elsewhere. Meanwhile, the hero of the Shenandoah Valley, Stonewall Jackson, was chafing to take an offensive, one that would extend to an outright invasion of the enemy's country. Jackson would get his chance soon enough.

On July 12 the Confederates received information that part of Pope's forces had entered Culpeper, Virginia. That meant they were just twenty-seven miles above Gordonsville, a community on a northerly bend of the Virginia Central Railroad. This was ominous. Any threat to that railroad, the lone vital rail supply link between Richmond and the Shenandoah Valley, had to be countered whatever the risk, whatever the cost. The Shenandoah produced food the army and much of the northern Confederacy needed. The very next day Lee ordered Jackson with his own division and Major General Richard S. Ewell's division, to board trains for central Virginia.

For two weeks nothing happened. At Gordonsville, Jackson was unable to learn much about Pope's strength or movements. Pope, commanding from Washington, was still concentrating his army along the upper Rappahannock. Only an advance brigade was at Culpeper. McClellan remained idle on the Peninsula, whining for more men.

Lee next dispatched Major General Ambrose Powell Hill's Light Division to reinforce Jackson, bringing Stonewall's strength to 24,000. He retained only 56,000 in the Richmond earthworks to resist a possible advance by McClellan.

Lee had been moved to the depths of his knightly soul by Pope's threats and live-off-the-country measures against his fellow Virginians. For no other opponent did he ever possess the personal dislike he developed for John Pope. "I want Pope suppressed," he told the departing Hill. And Pope "ought to be suppressed, if possible," he wrote his Confederate president. Now with Hill, Jackson might have enough men to suppress Pope and, if necessary, still return to deal with McClellan.

While Jackson waited for an opening, he set up camps in the lovely Virginia Piedmont country, with its lush crops, good water, grassy fields, and groves of timber, far away from the old camps and unhealthy swamps of the Peninsula and the fights for Richmond. For Stonewall it, was a new beginning. His performance in the Seven Days had been disappointing, at best. But Lee never expressed one word of dissatisfaction over it. He believed in this general. Formerly a mediocre professor at the Virginia Military Institute, Jackson was a reclusive eccentric with a somewhat unkempt appearance who was profoundly, if not fanatically, religious. His field library consisted of just three books: the *Holy Bible*, *Webster's Dictionary*, and Napoleon's *Maxims of War*. With a fresh start, in the days ahead he would need all three.

Temporarily in command of Jackson's old division was Brigadier General Charles S. Winder, who had a reputation as a tyrant. He had about thirty of Jackson's old troops, the Stonewall Brigade, "bucked"—a humiliating and painful form of punishment*—for straggling during the march to Gordonsville. Half of the punished deserted that night; the others swore revenge, threatening the next battle "would be the last for Winder." Beside the Stonewall Brigade was a Louisiana brigade, and another unit, three Virginia regiments brigaded with an untried pair from Alabama. Relatively weak, the division numbered only 4,000 soldiers.

Second in popularity to Stonewall or "Old Jack," was "Old Bald Head," Major General Richard S. Ewell, Jackson's premier subordinate in the Shenandoah. In peculiarities he was not unlike Jackson; both suffered from stomach ulcers and had unnatural sleeping habits. But Ewell was an ex-dragoon and Indian fighter who habitually cursed in a high-pitched lisp. The two of them got along famously. Ewell's division consisted of Virginians, Louisianans, and a heterogeneous brigade of one regiment each from Alabama, Georgia, and North Carolina. Together, they totalled 7,200 men.

Half of Jackson's infantry, 12,000 men, were in the six-brigade Light Division of A.P. Hill. Two brigades were from North Carolina, one each

*Each soldier was seated with his hands and feet tied. His knees were drawn up, and a rod inserted, horizontal to the ground, between the arms and the backs of the knees.

from South Carolina, Georgia, Virginia, and one predominated by Tennesseans. Hill was a hothead, a proud, sensitive sort with an explosive temper. In part, Lee sent this division away from Richmond to head off an impending duel between Hill and Major General James Longstreet. But after two weeks with Jackson, Hill was bickering again.

Under Brigadier General Beverly Robertson's command, with whom Jackson was displeased, were the 1,200 cavalry. "Where's the enemy?" Jackson had asked with a rare smile. "I don't know," replied Robertson. Jackson's face fell and without a further word to Robertson he wrote to Richmond calling for cavalry commander Major General J.E.B. Stuart.

Then came the news Jackson was awaiting. Scouts and spies returned reporting the Yankee army was converging on Culpeper, but only a portion of their force was there now. This was Banks' corps. Ricketts' division of McDowell's corps was also nearby, but a Union division led by Brigadier General Rufus King was far away at Fredericksburg protecting that place until Burnside arrived. Sigel's corps was strung out along the road between Culpeper and Sperryville, one of its divisions still loitering in camp at the base of the Blue Ridge. For some time Jackson had believed Pope would advance to Culpeper. With a swift march he might be able to crush the Federal vanguard before Pope could concentrate his troops or reinforce Banks.

Brigadier General Charles S. Winder. Jackson's tyrannical subordinate in the "Stonewall Brigade," Winder was barking orders to his artillerymen when an enemy shell knocked him backward and left him mortally wounded at Cedar Mountain.

This required a twenty-mile march to the hamlet of Orange. The hike went well on August 7, but the men did not march as tightly knit columns of disciplined troops. The temperature was in the sweltering 90s, and everybody was miserably hot. The army straggled badly. Several men keeled over and died from sun stroke. Only eight miles were covered the next day. Without informing Hill, the secretive Jackson changed the route of march, producing an exasperating mix up. Hill blamed Jackson, Jackson blamed Hill, and a bitter feud between the two began. When one of the staff asked Hill about their next destination, Hill glumly replied he supposed they would go to the top of the next hill, but that was all he knew. Jackson was irritated and gloomy; by now Federal cavalry had obviously reported his location. He decided to press on to Culpeper on August 9, anyway.

A Fight At Cedar Mountain

Major General Pope, who had at last joined his army on July 29, was developing a plan to threaten the Virginia Central Railroad at Charlottesville. He had heard Rebels were coming. But despite urgings from Halleck to be cautious until reinforced, Pope prepared for a fight. Banks' corps was to stop the Confederates, who, Pope decided, were making a reconnaissance in force, until the entire army could be brought up.

Banks' two divisions, under Brigadier Generals C.C. Auger and A.S. Williams, marched forward to support the advance brigade of Brigadier General Samuel Crawford. Crawford, in turn, was supporting a cavalry screen eight miles south of Culpeper along Cedar Run. Concealing Williams' division on the right flank was a thick woods northwest of the Culpeper Road. Three-quarters of it surrounded a large, rectangular wheat field. Southeast of the road were Auger's troops, hidden in rolling corn fields, his left reaching toward immense Cedar Mountain. It was also known ominously as Slaughter Mountain, after Dr. Slaughter the landholder who farmed its shoulder.

Banks, with 8,000 troops and several cannon, would be on his own. Ricketts' division of McDowell's corps was just three miles to his rear, but Ricketts would spend the day idle. He had no orders to participate. Nor would Sigel take part in the fight. Sigel halted his troops on the only road between Sperryville and

Jackson Galloped Past His Columns Of Puffing Men To Where He Found General Ewell, Amusing Himself...

Culpeper and stupidly inquired which route to take.

Again the temperature was climbing toward 100° in the late morning when Banks' cannon muzzles blazed fire and roared thunder over Cedar Run, bringing the Confederate vanguard to a halt. Jackson galloped past his columns of puffing men to where he found General Ewell, amusing himself, playing with some little chil-

Confederates galloped three field pieces to the front. Early had them unlimber in a grove of cedars, and a spirited duel began.

He detached one regiment on his right to partially cover the mile distance between him and Ewell, whose men were approaching the summit of Cedar Mountain. Then Winder's men neared the danger area along the road to Early's left. Four mangled corpses

Drawing by Dale Gallon

...Playing With Some Little Children On A Porch. Jackson Spread A Map And The Two Studied It

dren on a porch. Jackson spread a map and the two studied it. The obvious key terrain feature was Cedar Mountain. Jackson instructed Ewell to take two brigades and some artillery over its shoulder and turn the enemy's left flank. Ewell's remaining brigade, commanded by Brigadier General Jubal A. Early, was to sheer off and proceed straight ahead. Winder's small division was to support Early in echelon along the Culpeper Road. Hill's division would be the reserve. With 20,000 men within reach, Jackson held all the advantages.

A little past 2 p.m., Early's brigade easily drove away Federal cavalry. Then, as they hiked over a ridge, they were hit by Federal artillery fire.

lay victims of one cannon shot. "What is the matter?" a tuckered-out Confederate by the roadside was asked. "I don't want to fight" he replied. "I ain't mad with anybody."

Winder had been ill. Pale and sick, he pulled himself from an ambulance and hurried to the front on horseback, where he deployed Brigadier Generals Richard Garnett's and William Taliaferro's brigades along the road at right angles to Early, and withheld the Stonewall Brigade as reserves. Adjacent to their position were five cannon answering the Union artillery. Winder dismounted, removed his tunic and began to direct their aim. Far away on the mountain, Ewell was booming away with six guns placed in Dr. Slaughter's yard. Books from Slaughter's library were strewn around the cannon. Yankees had paid an earlier visit.

For two long hours under the smothering August sun the opposing artillerists rammed, primed, and fired at each other. Infantry, for the most part, kept out of sight.

Peculiar things were noticed. In Winder's artillery, every man hit was an officer; not a private was scratched. One officer was given a short ride by a low-flying projectile, but was otherwise unhurt. Some of the infantrymen pinned slips of paper to their jackets with their names and units on them for identification in case they were killed. And some darted from their marching columns to hide things under leaves by the roadside—decks of playing cards. It would be embarrassing to many to be found dead with the Devil's playthings in their pockets.

Gradually, Federal batteries gained the upper hand. Winder was considering a charge across Early's front to take them when the Union guns began shifting their positions. Shouting some inaudible orders to a nearby cannoneer, Winder put his hand to his mouth to repeat himself. A shell tore through him, causing a ghastly, mortal wound. He fell straight backwards. Brigadier Taliaferro, who knew virtually nothing of Jackson's or Winder's plans, was notified the division command had devolved upon him.

After five o'clock the artillery's exchange of iron slackened. Suddenly, Union infantry came swarming out of the woods, charged across the wheat field on the left, over a rise and through the corn in the center. All of Banks' two divisions, less one brigade, was in the assault.

Why Banks attacked later provoked heated controversy. That morning a staff officer from Pope delivered Banks' verbal orders; Banks had him commit them to paper. They read: "General Banks to move to the front immediately, assume command of all forces in the front, deploy his skirmishers if the enemy advances, and attack him immediately as he approaches, and be reinforced from here." Pope contended Banks knew full well he was only supposed to take a strong defensive position and hold it until help arrived. Banks flaunted the message, retorting the language gave him discretion to attack. Banks, "Old Jack's Commis-

sary," was probably looking for a chance to even the score with Jackson, and as soon as he thought he saw an opportunity, he seized it. Like Pope, he had no inkling Jackson's force outnumbered his by more than two to one.

Banks' attack dealt the Confederate army an unexpected and staggering blow. "I tell you they slaughtered our men," one Virginia officer wrote home. Crawford's Union brigade crossed the wheat stubble and struck Garnett's brigade in the flank, shattering it. The 1st Virginia Battalion was nearly destroyed. Union Brigadier General George H. Gordon's Brigade followed on the heels of Crawford's. Here, where it counted, there were more Federals than Confederates.

Taliaferro's men, aligned in the roadway shooting to their front, suddenly found Yankees coming from their left and rear. Their artillery limbered up quickly and cleared out. Brutal hand to hand fighting followed. "We were literally butchered," wept a Virginian. The 47th and 48th Alabama, new regiments, fled in panic—"ran like turkeys," commented another Virginian. "Raw men can't stand that kind of music."

The terrible tune spread to Early's brigade across the road. Brigadier General Edward L. Thomas' brigade had come up on Early 's right, and together the two were holding back Auger's Union division. Now out of the woods came Crawford's Federals and Early's left began to melt away. It looked as though Jackson's whole army was on the verge of a rout.

Stonewall Jackson spurred his horse into the smoking melee along the Culpeper Road. There armed men and their deadly missiles seemingly came from all directions at once. Witnesses said he was a transformed man, the "light of battle" was in his grim eyes. He was in danger; his army was teetering on the brink of disaster. He went for his sword, but it was stuck in its scabbard. Unfastening its clasps, he waved the cased sword. "Rally, brave men, and press forward! Your general will lead you," he cried. "Jackson will lead you. Follow me."

His presence was electric. The Southerners began to resist. "What officer is that, Captain?" a captured Federal lieutenant asked. When told, dazzled at being in the presence of a celebrity, he shouted, "Hurrah for General Jackson! Follow your general, boys." (His captors released him then and there.)

The Stonewall Brigade advanced from its reserve position. It was partly broken and driven back. Jackson galloped to the rear for A.P. Hill's division. He found the leading brigade in ranks and Brigadier General Lawrence O'Brian Branch exorting his North Carolinians with a speech. In few words Jackson ordered Branch to lead the counterattack. Brigadier Generals William D. Pender's and James Archer's brigades followed closely behind to his left.

Now the Federals were outnumbered and overwhelmed. Fresh masses of Rebels were coming up through the trees, and the exhausted Northerners broke ranks and tumbled out into the wheat field, the North Carolinians in hot pursuit. A Wisconsin field officer, conspicuously turning to rally his regiment, was felled by a volley that riddled him. Ewell had descended from the mountain and was turning the Federals' left. Early and Thomas had stopped Auger's attack and now began to push it back. "General," called one of Early's colonels, "my ammunition is nearly out; don't you think we had better charge them?"

Williams' and Auger's division were steadily forced back across Cedar Run, where they had started their attack an hour and a half before. The Yankees made one last thrust. A 164-horse battalion of the 1st Pennsylvania Cavalry came thundering down to blunt the Confederate attack and cover the artillery's withdrawal. Every able Southerner drew a bead and fired, sending riders and horses crashing to the ground. Only seventy-one men returned from the charge.

The fighting was all but over by 7:00 p.m.; Hill's division was pursuing Banks with fresh units. Jackson got a report that a second enemy corps, Sigel's, was not far away. He ordered the men to camp where they were.

Pope rode to the scene, inspected the damage and, after nearly getting himself captured, rode away again. He later pronounced the battle a Union victory. One of his suprised officers, more honest than Pope, wrote to his parents: "I'm sorry I can't twist the facts into a glorious victory. It was a glorious defeat if such an adjective can be used with a noun. A hotter fire than that endured by our men, I do not believe was ever poured upon soldiers, certainly not in this war." Banks' losses totalled 2,377, of whom 400 men and a brigadier

183

Artist Edwin Forbes recorded this charge of Union troops on the left flank of Jackson's army at Cedar Mountain. Forbes' copper-plate etchings were later purchased by William T. Sherman for the U.S. government.

general were prisoners. Some of the Southerners noted, however, the prisoners did not behave like beaten men. The Federals knew they had fought well and their jaunty, cocky attitudes reflected this.

Confederate casualties numbered 1,276. General Winder's death was mourned everywhere save the Stonewall Brigade. Because of his personal participation, certainly not because of his tactics, Jackson regarded Cedar Mountain the most successful of his exploits. He wrote to Lee: "God has blessed our army with victory."

Even so, he was six miles short of Culpeper and had failed to prevent Pope from concentrating his army. There was no fighting on August 10 or 11; the dead were buried and the wounded removed. The night of the Cedar Mountain fight, the Confederate army left its camp fires burning and by morning had fallen back behind the Rapidan River.

A Lost Hat, Lost Orders, Lost Chances

Pope's first impulse was to pursue (exactly what Jackson hoped for),

but he was held in check by General Halleck. The Battle of Cedar Mountain changed nothing strategically. Pope was to hold his position and prevent any Confederate advance while McClellan moved to join him. Pope believed when that happened, Halleck would come from Washington and assume field command; with Pope and McClellan as wing commanders, the combined armies would take care of Lee and Jackson.

Lee's desire to quickly dispose of Pope was increasing. Of course he was delighted with the victory, but he recognized Jackson did not have enough strength to exterminate Pope or eliminate the threat to the Virginia Central Railroad. On August 13 he started three divisions under Major General James Longstreet for Gordonsville, leaving scarcely 25,000 men to protect the capital. That same day rumors that McClellan's army was departing the Peninsula were confirmed; it was leaving, Lee concluded, to join Pope. Two days later Lee himself departed.

The race was on. If Lee could move quickly enough, using railroads and taking advantage of the shorter

route, he might be able to put an end to Pope's army before McClellan's arrived. Whoever won this race might win a great victory. On the other hand, whoever lost stood a chance of losing the war.

By August 15 Pope had about 52,000 soldiers under his command. Burnsides' IX Corps, 8,000 veterans under Major General Jesse Reno, had joined him from Fredericksburg, and Rufus King's division of McDowell's corps had arrived, too. Lee had about the same number, but he quickly divined Pope had his army in a potentially dangerous place.

They were camped in a horizontal "V" between the Rapidan and Rappahannock rivers, along the Rapidan's banks. The Orange & Alexandria Railroad, Pope's supply and communications line with Washington, ran back at a diagonal to the northeast. Studying his maps, Lee saw Clark's Mountain. If he could move his army undetected behind the mountain, throw it across the Rappahannock around Pope's left while cavalry demolished the Rappahannock railroad bridge, Pope would be helpless and might be destroyed. The opportunity

was there. Speed was essential. Lee planned to strike on August 18.

But the Confederates did not assemble quickly enough, and the cavalry blundered. J.E.B. Stuart, in charge of all Southern horsemen, ordered cavalry to rendezvous in back of Raccoon Ford prior to crossing the Rappahannock, but his orders did not stress the urgency involved. Riding up to the hamlet of Verdiersville, he found no one knew anything about the Confederate cavalry camp that was supposed to be nearby. An aide was dispatched to locate the missing brigade of Brigadier General Fitzhugh Lee, the commanding general's nephew, while a puzzled Stuart and the rest of his staff bedded down on a porch. About daybreak a cavalry column clattered up the road toward them. Stuart sent two men to investigate. Instead of a hearty welcome from Fitz Lee there came pistol shots. "Yankee cavalry!" was the warning. The staff scattered. Stuart was on his horse in an instant and jumped it over the garden fence.

Everyone escaped except the officer designated to locate Fitz Lee. Stuart, in his haste, left behind his cloak, plumed hat, and more serious, his haversack containing maps and orders. "Where's your hat?" greeted him for several days. Stuart was humiliated. "I intend to make the Yankees pay dearly for that hat," he wrote to his wife.

What happened was that Fitz Lee, utterly ignorant of the timetable, took a roundabout route and was a day late. At the same time a brigadier who had gone visiting pulled away two Georgia infantry regiments, supposedly guarding the ford road, and had them prepare rations. The unhindered Federal patrol came and departed with all the information they needed. Combined with the over-all unpreparedness of the army, the incident caused Lee to postpone the attack until the 20th. By then it was too late.

Halleck in Washington worried Lee might overwhelm the Army of Virginia before the sullen McClellan joined, and on the 16th telegraphed Pope to seek a more convenient position behind the Rappahannock. Pope, warned fully by both friends and foes, withdrew from the trap.

For the time being, all the advantages seemed to be with the defending Federals. Deployed along the higher Rappahannock north bank for seven or eight miles above Kelly's Ford, Pope had simply to guard the crossings, protect the railroad, and fend off Lee until the Army of the Potomac arrived. With each passing day, Lee's chances grew smaller. He could not afford to lose time or men forcing the Rappahannock. His strategy was to maneuver upstream and at the first opportunity swing the Army of Northern Virginia across the first undisputed ford and attack the Union right. For his part Stuart rode ahead of Jackson and Longstreet to probe the fords. But wherever the Confederates moved, there was Pope, alert and blocking their jabs.

Stuart for his part was still smarting over the loss of his hat and haversack. He proposed a cavalry raid to break the Orange & Alexandria Railroad. Lee approved.

On August 22 Stuart crossed the Rappahannock at Waterloo Bridge with about 1,500 troopers and two cannon. Quickly covering the seven

185

U.S. Army Military History Institute

miles around Pope's right he rode into Warrenton. So far so good. The excited residents said no Yankees had been around for days. But as the jangling column rode for Catlett's Station and the railroad bridge over Cub Run, massive dark clouds gathered. Late that afternoon they erupted into a violent Virginia summer thunderstorm.

Approaching Catlett's in the evening, Union sentinels were silently eliminated by Stuart's men and replaced by Confederates. A reconnaissance by Captain W.W. Blackford, Stuart's engineer officer, revealed "a vast assemblage of wagons and a city of tents, laid out in regular order and accompanied by the luxuriously equipped quartermasters and commissaries . . . but no appearance of any large organized body of troops." Captured Federal guards disclosed even more exciting news—this was Pope's headquarters! A contraband Negro, one freed from slavery by virtue of residing in Union occupied territory, was also captured and agreed to guide the raiders to the headquarters tent. Fitz Lee and Stuart selected one of Robert Lee's sons, Colonel W.H.F. "Rooney" Lee, and his 9th Virginia for that task. Two regiments were to hit the camps on the far side of the depot. Another led by Blackford the engineer would set fire to the railroad trestle. When the bugle sounded, everyone was to give a "Rebel Yell."

Union officers that day did not even bother to verify a report Confederate cavalry was on the move. Some were sitting on the verandah of a house, feet up on the railing, watching the rain. One was having some friends over for a drink. "Now this is something like comfort," said a guest,

U.S. Army Military History Institute

lifting his glass. "I hope Jeb Stuart won't disturb us tonight." Just then a bugle was heard—close, but the call was drowned out by 1,500 screaming Rebels and their running horses. "There he is, by God!"

Tables and tents were knocked over in the scramble. "I went in with the leading regiment," recalled Blackford later, "and the consternation as we charged down the main street, scattering our pistol balls promiscuously right and left, made men laugh until they could scarcely keep their saddles." Some Pennsylvania infantrymen grabbed rifles and returned the fire from the depot, but the Virginians vaulted their horses onto the platform and crashed into the freight room, ending resistance. A couple of raiders shinnied up telegraph poles, and with a few quick saber swipes the Union army was out of touch with its capital.

General Pope was out for the evening, but to Stuart's delight, his hat,

Top: Pope made his headquarters at Culpeper near the critical depot of the Orange & Alexandria Railroad. Above: Pope's Yankees set afire an Orange & Alexandria train to keep its cargo out of Confederate hands. Opposite: The Orange & Alexandria Bridge over Bull Run, Pope's only supply line from Washington.

cloak, and one of his dress uniforms were left behind. Most important, the Army of Virginia's headquarters dispatch book and a number of recent messages fell into Confederate hands. This in itself more than compensated for the raid's lack of total success.

The thunderstorm let up a while then broke out anew. Only lightning lit what Stuart called "the darkest night I ever knew." Gusting winds driving a deluge foiled attempts to burn the captured property or the trestle, and by now the recovering Federals were beginning to resist from across the stream. Stuart gave it up as hopeless.

Jackson Was To Take His 24,000 Men Up The Rappahannock... Around The Federal Rear And Seize The Orange & Alexandria Railroad... Longstreet's 28,000 Rifles Would Take Over Jackson's River Position

MOLLUS—Philadelphia, PA

With dawn approaching and rising streams a cause for worry, Stuart recalled his soaking, happy troopers. Hundreds of horses and mules, 300 prisoners and valuable military property, plus the Army of Virginia's money chests, were netted. Pope was broke. Unmolested, the Confederate caravan returned to the Rappahannock the way it came.

Stuart, as a prank, offered to trade Pope's coat back to him in exchange for his plumed hat. Receiving no reply, he sent the coat to Richmond, where it was put on public display. Pope's anger was surely aroused (in Culpeper he gave his lagging troops "a salutation of profanity . . . that would have graced a Mississippi stevedore much better than a major general of the United States Army"), but of that there is no official record. When the telegraph was repaired he told Halleck the damage was "trifling; only some officers' baggage destroyed."

The information gleaned from the raid proved a turning point in the campaign; Lee now knew the plans and strength of his opponents. The situation was grave. To fight now, with Pope and McClellan about to merge forces, would be too dangerous. If Lee could not attack, he could maneuver and force Pope to keep pace with him, all the while moving Pope away from McClellan's reinforcements. This, too, would remove the ravaging Yankees from the agricultural districts of central Virginia.

On Sunday, August 24, Lee rode to Jackson's headquarters at Jefferson-ton and conducted a conference outlining his strategy. Jackson was to take his 24,000 men up the Rappahannock and get around the Federal rear and seize the Orange & Alexandria Railroad. The Bull Run Mountains would screen a great part of his movement. Longstreet's 28,000 rifles

would take over Jackson's river position, deceive the Federals temporarily, and give him a good start. Speed and surprise were vital; risks were immense. If Pope discovered Confederates were dividing their forces, he could keep them separated, overwhelm one, then the other with superior numbers.

Jackson was excited and drew a rough diagram on the ground with his boot. Napoleon Bonaparte had used similar maneuvers many times in his campaigns, and no doubt Jackson was familiar with them. He made preparations immediately and began the great march before dawn the next morning, Monday, August 25.

Ewell's division took the lead, then A.P. Hill's Light Division, followed by Jackson's under Taliaferro. Only ordnance wagons and ambulances were taken, no extra baggage, and knapsacks were left behind. The regiments and batteries departed their

187

bivouac areas even before rations could be cooked. Many a soldier ate nothing but green apples and raw corn for several days. Covering twenty-six miles the first day, they went past Amissville, across a tributary of the Rappahannock called Hedgemen's River, to Orlean, then another dozen northward miles to Salem on the Manassas Gap Railroad. Villagers and rural folk along the way handed out biscuits, cold chicken, ham, and dippers of water, which were gratefully snatched up by the trudging columns. Homes were besieged by hungry soldiers looking for something to eat. "Please, ma'am," called one South Carolina joker to a lady, "give me a drink of water. I'm so hungry, I ain't got no place to sleep."

The march was continued on August 26, through White Plains toward the looming wall of the Bull Run Mountains. Having turned in an easterly direction now, the men knew their destination was the Union rear. Had Thoroughfare Gap been disputed, there might have been trouble, but not so much as an enemy outpost was encountered. True to his address, Pope was letting his rear take care of itself.

At Gainesville Stuart's cavalry screened the flank toward Warrenton. The last long leg of the journey was to Bristoe Station on the railroad, twenty miles behind Pope's army. Stuart's troopers jumped a small Union guard post there, and Pope's supply line belonged to the Confederates.

They just missed a northbound train, which rumbled through a hasty barricade before it was quite ready. The next two were not so fortunate. The first was derailed and riddled by small arms fire as it turned on its side and crashed down an embankment.* A second train rammed the rear cars of the first. It, too, plunged down the bank in a twisted wreck. The engineer of another train sensed danger, applied the brakes and chugged backward into the gathering darkness, eventually to warn Pope.

Jackson had moved an extraordinary fifty-four miles in forty hours. Not only was he on the enemy's supply line, but he learned their supply base was at Manassas Junction, only three more miles away. Brigadier General Isaac Trimble was asked to take his brigade and seize the junc-

*This train was pulled by the locomotive "President." To the Rebels' glee, Mr. Lincoln's portrait on the steam dome had a bullet hole through it.

188

I Reckon, Colonel, You Have Got In The Wrong Crowd

Drawing by Dale Gallon

tion. "I don't need my brigade," he said. "Just give me my two twenty-ones"—the 21st Georgia and 21st North Carolina.

Stuart's horsemen moved along a parallel road while Trimble's boys hiked the railroad tracks. At midnight they swept over a pair of earthen forts guarding the depot. A battery of artillery was captured, but not before it got off a few token shots.

"Give 'em another round, boys, it's only some damned guerillas." Having hollered that, the battery's officer felt a tap on his shoulder and a Georgia voice drawled from the darkness, "I reckon, colonel, you have got in the wrong crowd."

Maneuvering For Advantage

Pope, after a poor start, had handled his army well along the Rappahannock line. Halleck instructed him to hold on for two days and help would be with him. Pope put off Lee for the greater part of a week, throwing him back from the fords, dueling furiously

with artillery, keeping cavalrymen always in their saddles.

At last, nineteen days after the order to evacuate the Peninsula, installments from the Army of the Potomac began arriving. First came the Pennsylvania Reserve Division, about 4,700 men under a first-rate Pennsylvanian, Brigadier General John F. Reynolds. These were assigned to McDowell on the northern flank near Warrenton. Pope had become so dissatisfied with Sigel's mishandling of his corps that Sigel, too, was placed under McDowell's guidance. The two corps—McDowell's and Sigel's—and Reynold's division would constitute an informal wing. Pope himself directed the rest of the army from Warrenton Junction on the railroad.

Following Reynolds by several days, on the last leg of a leisurely march upstream from Aquia Creek, was the V Army Corps of Major General Fitz John Porter; two divisions of 10,000 men, one composed mainly of U.S. Regulars, the other of volunteer state troops. These were McClellan men; Porter and his troops had fought and won two of the Richmond battles almost on their own. Once Pope and Porter finally met, Pope noticed Porter's attitude seemed one of "listlessness and indifference not quite natural under the circumstances." If the two were not already enemies they quickly developed an intense mutual dislike for one another. Both orally and in writing, Porter freely expressed his discontent at being under Pope's orders. This would later have bitter and tragic consequences for him.

By rail, another pair of divisions came down, one by one, from the Potomac River wharves at Alexandria. This was the 15,000-man III Army Corps of Major General Samuel P. Heintzelman, a gruff, old Regular, suspected by Pope of being another McClellan supporter. His two divisions' commanders were outspokenly anti-McClellan, so Pope chose to deal directly with them. The first was Brigadier General Joseph Hooker, never one to get along with any of his superiors. Through a journalistic slip he had recently become known as "Fighting Joe Hooker," a nickname he never quite lived down nor up to. The other was one-armed Brigadier General Philip Kearny, a Mexican War veteran. A leader with dynamic qualities, he had also fought for the French in the Italian War of 1859, leading cavalry charges with the bridle reins clenched in his teeth. Kearny hated McClellan. He wrote to a friend up North, "McClellan is a dirty, sneaking traitor."

As fighting material, the reinforcements were excellent. Including a brigade from the mountains of western Virginia awaiting transportation, Pope now commanded more than 75,000 soldiers. Two additional corps of Peninsula veterans were due to disembark at Alexandria within a few days.

But if the movement to reinforce the Army of Virginia was slow, it was also nearly chaotic. Neither Heintzelman nor Porter had wagons or ambulances. Heintzelman's artillery was still en route; Porter had no reserve supply of artillery ammunition. One of Reynolds' brigades was on the verge of riot because it was being fed irregularly.

Their problems could never be solved as long as a communication chasm existed between the generals. Pope and McClellan had not been on speaking terms for six weeks and each dealt directly with Halleck, the

But If The Movement To Reinforce The Army Of Virginia Was Slow, It Was Also Nearly Chaotic. . . . One Of Reynolds' Brigades Was On The Verge Of Riot Because It Was Being Fed Irregularly

general-in-chief. Halleck in his War Department office was evading responsibilities and becoming irritable. Despite what Pope believed, he had no intention whatever of taking the field. When Pope complained he was in the dark about McClellan's forces, Halleck wired: "Just think of the immense amount of telegraphing I have to do and then say whether I can be expected to give you any details as to the movements of others, even when I know them."

To McClellan, now at Falmouth near Fredericksburg desiring information on the whereabouts of Pope, Halleck replied: "You ask for information I cannot give. I do not know either where General Pope is or where the enemy in force is. These are matters which I have all day been most anxious to ascertain." His orders were indefinite, he ignored pressing dispatches. In those last August days Halleck devoted three-quarters of his time to recruiting new troops and to matters far away in the West.

When the telegraph line to Washington went dead on the evening of August 26, Pope first believed Rebel cavalry had done him a favor. He chafed at being tied down to the Rappahannock line; there had been a great deal of marching and countermarching without accomplishing much. Jackson's flanking maneuver had been detected, and to Pope it seemed likely the Rebel army was heading back to the Shenandoah Valley. He wanted to conduct a reconnaissance in force and, if his guesses were correct, he planned to pitch into

their rear. But within twenty-four hours he recognized the situtation had taken a turn for the worse; something very wrong was going on in *his* rear.

On the morning of Wednesday, August 27, Pope sent word to Halleck through the Falmouth telegraph office; he believed the Confederate army was now at White Plains, northwest of the Bull Run Mountains. They had thrust "a strong column" to Manassas and destroyed the railroad bridges, he reported. "I think it possible they may attempt to keep us in check and throw considerable force across the Potomac in the direction of Leesburg."

This was Pope's appraisal: The enemy was making a large-scale raid and they would have to attempt an escape. For the next four days he would obstinately cling to his false belief. No amount of persuasion, no compilation of contradictory evidence, would shake his convictions.

To counter the Confederates, Pope about-faced his forces and had them march northeastward, creating a moving wall of Federal soldiers to penetrate the twenty-mile gap between the supposed raiders and the main army. McDowell, with Sigel's corps leading, and Reynolds' division, followed by his own corps, took the Warrenton Turnpike toward Gainesville. This would seal off the obvious Confederate retreat route to Thoroughfare Gap. Kearny's division and a corps commanded by one of Burnside's recent arrivals from the Carolinas, Major General Jesse L. Reno, moved toward Greenwich. (This put them about in the center, where they would be within supporting distance of McDowell.) Pope himself took command of the southern flank. Hooker's division was to go back up the tracks to Bristoe Station, followed by Porter's corps, just now arriving from Aquia Creek. Banks' beaten-up corps guarded the trains and brought up the rear.

Meanwhile, Jackson ordered Hill's and Taliaferro's divisions to join Trimble at Manassas Junction. Ewell remained behind at Bristoe to watch for approaching Federals; the cavalry patrolled the roads in all directions. Trimble's men guarded a small military city of tents and warehouses alongside two half-mile-long railroad trains, all filled with great quantities of quartermaster and commissary stores bound for their enemies. Trimble considered them Confederate property; Hill's hungry men saw

189

them as rewards and began helping themselves. Artillery booms signaled Yankees were coming. Officers hustled grumbling, hungry men to defensive positions on the east edge of the storage area.

Cautious, a Washington garrison outfit serving as infantry, the 2d New York Heavy Artillery, called "heavies," advanced from the Centreville area toward a large brick house called Liberia. It had been General P.G.T. Beauregard's headquarters the previous year during the Manassas battle. Near it long ranks of Hill's Confederate Light Division forming into battle array and bursting Rebel artillery shells confirmed the New Yorkers' suspicions. These were not guerrilla raiders. The heavies beat a hasty retreat.

Next, farther south, came Brigadier General George W. Taylor's four New Jersey regiments. This brigade, sent by train from Alexandria, jumped out east of Bull Run to disperse what Taylor had been told was Confederate cavalry. They blundered straight into a hornet's nest. Waving a handkerchief and calling them to surrender, Jackson actually tried to save the Jerseymen. One of them took a shot at him; it was their only response. They were beaten bloody. Taylor was mortally wounded, and his troops fled back across Bull Run.

Fitz Lee, returning from a reconnaissance to Fairfax, finished off what was left of them. It was all over before noon.

The remainder of Wednesday afternoon was spent plundering Manassas storehouses, a feast and frolic such as few of these Sons of the South ever attended. There were new shoes for the barefooted, new Union-blue clothes for the ragged, saddles for cavalrymen, medicines for surgeons, blankets, candles, toothbrushes, and soap for all. Best, of course, was the food. Hardtack and coffee were plentiful. There were sutler stores, luxury items even the average Union enlisted man rarely saw: lobster salad, fresh fruit, sardines, pickled oysters, cigars, canned meats, French mustard, white wine, and for the German Yankees, beer. Some men could not decide what to take, there was so much, while those who fought during the day griped that all the delicacies were consumed before they arrived, especially by Ewell's men.

Ewell got into a sharp fight at Bristoe with Hooker, each side losing nearly 300 men. Stonewall's instructions were to not risk a general engagement, so late in the afternoon, Ewell fell back across Broad Run to Manassas. There, his men sat down to eat. Since only a minute fraction of the captured goods could be hauled

away, the rest were put to the torch. To the relief of a Louisiana chaplain who feared temptation had overcome his rowdy Confederate flock, near dusk the men formed ranks and began to march away. They had to get away from Manassas quickly before Pope arrived with his whole army.

The first part of Jackson's mission was successfully completed. Federal supplies were interrupted, and Pope was rapidly moving away from the Rappahannock. Now Jackson had to safeguard his command until the two separated Confederate wings could be reunited. A disguised cavalryman brought word Lee and Longstreet had departed the Rappahannock on August 26, the previous evening. Good news, for sure, but they still had a long distance to travel. What Jackson felt he needed was a position near Thoroughfare Gap, a concealed place to hide, one strong enough defensively to hold a day or two. From there he could strike at Pope and prevent the Federal army from retreating any farther toward Washington.

He selected a long, partly wooded ridge about a mile northwest of the year-old Manassas battleground. This ridge roughly paralleled a stretch of the Warrenton to Alex-

Men of John Gibbon's Black Hat Brigade. Named for their special, non-regulation slouch hats, these Indiana and Wisconsin natives earned fame in some of the fiercest fighting of the war.

Below: Brigadier General David R. Jones. His division was responsible for taking the slopes on both sides of Thoroughfare Gap for the Confederates. Right: Brigadier General Cadmus Wilcox headed a division in Longstreet's Rebel command. Far right: Brigadier General Joseph "Fighting Joe" Hooker never really lived up to his nickname.

Southern Historical Collection, University of North Carolina at Chapel Hill

National Archives

CWTi Collection

andria turnpike, near a hamlet called Groveton. Taliaferro's division took the direct route, Sudley Springs Road, while Hill went to Centreville, and turned west. Ewell crossed Bull Run and sidled upstream toward Stone Bridge. (Actually, the march by three routes was a lucky blunder on Jackson's part, for it added to the confusion of an already confused John Pope.)

Just as Hooker's fight with Ewell was concluding, Pope rode to Bristoe and learned for the first time it was Stonewall Jackson confronting him. The thought of destroying the arch Rebel was intoxicating to Pope. He lost his head and forgot strategy. His scouting cavalry was worn worthless, so he relied on his intuition as a substitute for facts. He imagined he had surprised Jackson, who probably would fight.

Pope ordered his army to concentrate at Manassas on August 28. Por-

ter was to march at one a.m. to Hooker's support; Hooker's men were low on ammunition and Jackson might attack. (Pope's foot soldiers carried 100 rounds of ammunition, the Army of the Potomac men had only 40.) Reno's, Kearny's, and McDowell's wings were to "move at the very earliest blush of dawn." If everyone moved promptly and acted expeditiously, said Pope, "we shall bag the whole crowd."

But Porter did not move promptly. His corps started two hours late and reached Bristoe at 10:00 a.m. instead of daylight. While the Confederates marched through the night, Porter claimed it was too dark to see the road and a wagon train blocked his way.

McDowell did not move fast. Sigel was five hours late getting started. Then his wagons stalled one of McDowell's divisions led by Major General Rufus King. Next, instead of

keeping to the left of the Manassas Gap Railroad, he inclined to the right, explaining he thought the unnamed railroad in the order meant the Orange & Alexandria, seven miles farther south. Finally, McDowell entrusted a copy of Pope's marching order to a courier. Dispatched in the very direction the order stated the enemy was located, the courier was, of course, captured.

Still, McDowell had a much clearer idea of Lee's intent than Pope. The man Lincoln had called a general of "great cunning" had completely lost sight of the fact that most of the Confederate army was somewhere beyond the Bull Run Mountains. When he rode into the smoldering ruins of his supply base and questioned witnesses, Pope jumped to the conclusion Jackson was fleeing by way of Centreville. This was his reason for changing his orders and directing the army to concentrate there.

191

*Right: Special artist Edwin Forbes sat
on the Bald Hill, while he sketched
this battle scene for* Frank Leslie's Illustrated Newspaper. *Below: Brigadier
General James J. Archer led a brigade
in A.P. Hill's second column near
Sudley Springs Road.*

U.S. Army Military History Institute

McDowell had an efficient cavalryman on his left flank named Brigadier
General John Buford, and Buford reported to McDowell that Longstreet
was at White Plains. Far from believing Jackson was escaping to rejoin
Lee, McDowell correctly suspected
Lee was coming to join Jackson. To
hold Longstreet west of the mountain, McDowell detached Ricketts'
division to Thoroughfare Gap.

Sigel and Reynolds were to countermarch, King to continue ahead,
and the three to converge on Centreville.

Meanwhile, Lee was accomplishing
what McDowell feared. Two days ear-

lier he had set out with Longstreet's
wing to follow Jackson's tracks. One
division, Major General Richard
Heron Anderson's, was left behind to
watch the Rappahannock line for an
additional day.

Including Anderson, Longstreet's
command amounted to about 30,000
men, organized loosely into five divisions, usually of three brigades each.
Divisions were commanded by senior
brigadiers: D.R. Jones, Cadmus Wilcox, James L. Kemper, and John B.
Hood. None of them were particularly outstanding except for Hood.

By late afternoon Lee was approaching Thoroughfare Gap. Couriers had arrived with the welcome
news of Jackson's success at Manassas and his march to Groveton. The
two could unite the next day. Then
came the rolling, reverberating sound
of artillery fire in the mountain pass.
It boded ill. The Yankees might make
a stubborn stand. Longstreet might
be held off long enough for Pope to
demolish Jackson.

James B. Ricketts, usually a capable soldier, hardly put up a fight at
all. Lee got D.R. Jones' division to
push straight up the mountain on
either side of the pass, while some of
Hood's men found a trail leading
through a cleft in the rocks on the

left. Wilcox, three miles farther on,
tried Hopewell Gap. Ricketts sensed
he was being flanked, decided his
position was untenable, and withdrew toward Gainesville, the way he
came. The distant rumble of gunfire
coming from over his right shoulder
might also have influenced him.

Groveton Combat: "A Painfully Interesting Sight"

It was nearly 5 o'clock that August
28 afternoon, when Rufus King's division of McDowell's corps came plodding eastward along the Warrenton
Turnpike. For a while, a lone horseman appeared on a rise bordering the
road. He trotted back and forth, and
stopped several times to study the
Yankee column intently. Then he
turned toward the distant woods and
was gone.

"Here he comes, by God," exclaimed one of the gathered Confederate officers in the trees. Stonewall
Jackson, the line rider, reigned up,
touched his cap in salute and, without any trace of excitement said,
"Bring up your men, gentlemen."

The men, when they saw the group
of conferring officers break up, knew
what was about to happen. From the
woods one of them remembered there

192

arose "a hoarse roar, like that from cages of wild animals at the scent of blood." General Taliaferro, on the right, started his division forward. Ewell had two brigades on his left. Three batteries jangled to the front. General Trimble took his place at the head of his troops and in a voice so loud it echoed, bellowed, "Forward, guide center, *march*!"

Federal Brigadier General John Gibbon was trotting ahead of his brigade, the second in the passing Yankee column. He passed through a belt of timber to a knoll for a look around. Gibbon was a North Carolina Yankee who had three brothers fighting against him. He was a West Pointer and had been an artillerist before his promotion to lead a brigade of Westerners, men who stood out not only because of where they came from, but also because in the field they wore the U.S. Army's dress uniforms — knee length frock coats topped by black, high-crowned hats. They were nicknamed the "Black Hat Brigade." Except for the 2d Wisconsin, which ironically had fought nearby at Bull Run the year before, the outfit had never burnt powder.

Scanning the horizons, Gibbon noted that Union Brigadier John P. Hatch's brigade had already passed

the cluster of houses and haystacks at a crossroad called Groveton and was out of sight. In the other direction, through a vista, he made out several parallel lines of horsemen approaching, about a half-mile distant. As he began to speculate which army these cavalry belonged to, the horse columns veered simultaneously, and Gibbon's artillery experience told him that this was not cavalry at all, but field artillery going into battery.

Behind their general, the 6th Wisconsin regiment had just cleared the timber and one soldier was loudly complaining how they had been in the service for a year and not seen combat yet: "I tell you, this damned war will be over and we will never get into a battle." Then came six, rapid, distant booms, followed a second or two later by screaming shells exploding in the treetops. The neat column scattered for the road bank. The second round, closer, sent a horse tumbling over and over, smashing it against a rail fence.

At this point, Gibbon believed since Hatch's brigade had passed this way a half-hour before, no enemy infantry were around; the guns probably belonged to J.E.B. Stuart's roving cavalry. They needed to be chased off or, better yet, captured, so that

the march could continue. Gibbon called for his old battery, and soon up the roadway, kicking up a cloud of dust, came Battery B of the 4th U.S. Artillery, commanded by Captain J.B. Campbell. A rail fence was kicked over and six Napoleon guns unlimbered by Gibbon's side. While the general rode off to locate an infantry regiment to take the Rebels in flank, Battery B opened a well-aimed, destructive counter-battery fire. West of the woods, the 2d Wisconsin left-faced into a two rank fighting formation and started across a large broom-sedge field. The field sloped upward toward an orchard. There, silhouetted peacefully against the evening skyline, trees surrounded the log house rented by a farmer named John Brawner.

Rebel skirmishers suddenly rose from the grass and began firing. Then the Wisconsin men saw them: Confederate infantry, six brigades strong, advancing swiftly over the crest, crimson battle flags dancing over their heads.

At seventy-five yards the two lines halted, and the long tearing sound of musketry started. Seeing he needed more force, Gibbon ordered up the rest of his brigade and called on the division for support. The 19th Indiana and 7th Wisconsin rushed to their comrades in the 2d; the 6th Wisconsin, recovering from their initial shock, moved up on their right.

Advancing astride the woods created a massive gap in the Federal front. But with rapid blasts of cannister, Battery B kept the Rebels from penetrating it until two regiments from Brigadier General Abner Doubleday's brigade, untried like those of Gibbon, came over and sealed the dangerous hole.

For over an hour and a half the two battle lines stood locked in a deadly shooting contest. Part of the Stonewall Brigade got some protection from Brawner's house and orchard, and Doubleday's two Union regiments were deployed in the edge of the woods, but for the most part, soldiers stood upright loading and firing without cover of any sort. The Civil War rifle-musket, at 100 yards, could place its bullets within a 12-inch circle. Here the only hindering conditions were fading light and the hovering gray haze of gunsmoke. The effect of the gunfire in the open belies imagination.

Casualties accumulated at a frightful rate. General Taliaferro went down with three wounds. Colonel John E. Neff of the 33d Virginia was killed. Lawson Botts, once defense council for abolitionist raider John Brown, now a Confederate soldier, fell mortally wounded. Among the 200 dead from the Stonewall Brigade's ranks was Jackson's young hometown friend, Lexington, Virginia's 16-year-old Willie Preston. (It was said Jackson broke down and cried that evening when he learned of the boy's death.) General Ewell ventured too near the firing line and caught a bullet in his knee.*

On the Union side, 900 Black Hats were killed or wounded, and Doubleday's two regiments counted 350 more. Every field grade officer of the 7th Wisconsin was shot, including the distinguished Lieutenant Colonel Charles A. Hamilton, former Secretary of the Treasury Alexander Hamilton's grandson. Still they fought. "Don't mind us," called stricken Federal men to their friends leaving the ranks to aid them. "Whip 'em, whip 'em!"

The sky darkened, but this was a

fight nightfall did not stop. When the 6th Wisconsin moved a little to its left, Brigadier General Alexander Lawton's brigade charged to get around the Yankee flank; but Battery B stopped them cold by using Rebel muzzle flashes for targets. Jackson, to get a decision from the standoff, ordered twenty artillery pieces to the front. Only a few guns, however, successfully navigated the terrain. Captain John Pelham, cavalry commander Stuart's young artillery chief, managed to get two cannon within sixty yards of the 19th Indiana's flank, but the fire only caused the Federals to step over bodies and refuse their left.

At last, about 9 p.m., the firing subsided as the lines slowly drew apart. Returning to the pike, the 6th Wisconsin shouted three defiant cheers into the night. No reply came from the Rebels.

More than one-third of the Federals had been shot. The Confederates suffered about the same. Confederate engineer W.W. Blackford, when he inspected the human debris the next morning, found "a painfully interesting sight." The rival lines were marked by long ranks of prostrate bodies. "On each front the edge was sharply defined, while towards the rear it was less so, showing how men had staggered backward after receiving their death blow." A cow and a half-grown colt lay dead in Brawner's farmyard. And Confederate Private Ned Moore noticed a dead rabbit and a dead field lark.

While the Black Hats took their wounded to a cabin on the pike for treatment, their generals huddled around a camp fire across the road. McDowell was absent. Having left

*Not all wounds were fatal or so serious. Oddly, Private Ned Moore, a cannoneer, noticed that three-quarters of those Confederates passing to the rear with slight wounds had been hit in the left hand.

Captain John Pelham . . . Managed To Get Two Cannon Within Sixty Yards. . . . But The Fire Only Caused The Federals To Step Over Bodies And Refuse Their Left

his command that afternoon to seek General Pope at Manassas Junction, he had become lost in the woods somewhere. Next in command was Rufus King. He was an epileptic and had remained in Gainesville, missing the battle, "sick in body and mind." Their last orders were to proceed to Centreville, now a dubious proposition. Gibbon said if they did anything other than retire to Manassas, where the bulk of the army was thought to be, they would be annihilated at daylight.

After some discussion, that was what was decided. Sometime after midnight, the weary Federals stole off silently toward Manassas, relinquishing the battlefield to the Confederates. King notified Pope of his men's fight with Jackson, wildly overestimating the enemy force. And Ricketts, after his fight with Longstreet at Thoroughfare Gap, began withdraw-

ing to Bristoe.

Here was another serious Federal mistake. The route for Lee to unite with Jackson was entirely undefended. Of lesser importance, King's and Ricketts' movements were not what General Pope had wanted.

But at 10:00 p.m. Pope was elated and still poorly informed. He had learned of Gibbon's fight and believed McDowell's wing had run head-on into Jackson's retreat and stopped it. Presuming McDowell with 25,000 men blocked the turnpike west of the Rebels, and knowing he himself had an equal number around Centreville, Pope believed Jackson would be crushed between the two wings the next morning. Orders were dispatched for McDowell to hold his position at all cost; his men would serve as an anvil, Pope's would be a hammer, Jackson's would be smashed between them. At Cen-

treville, Kearny was to take the Warrenton Pike at 1:00 a.m., make contact as quickly as possible and attack at dawn. Hooker and Reno would be close behind. Fitz John Porter, the McClellan man at Manassas, was to move to Centreville and be the reserve.

Toward morning, however, Pope was not so cheerful: "God damn McDowell," he swore when he discovered his left wing was scattered over half of Prince William County. "He's never where I want him." Sigel's corps and Reynolds' division, which attempted to march toward Gibbon's battle before dark halted them, were bivouacked on the hills above the Stone House intersection, about midway between Groveton and Bull Run. Pope ordered these units "to attack the enemy vigorously as soon as it was light enough to see, and bring him to [a] stand if possible." Jackson must not be allowed to escape. Old General Sam Heintzelman was instructed to join the attack with Kearny and Hooker as soon as he reached the battlefield.

Far from fleeing, Jackson was ready to fight and waiting on Lee. After the bloody fight with Gibbon, he drew his men back to an interesting position, an abandoned railroad right-of-way. The independent line of the Manassas Gap Railroad was to have connected at Gainesville, and run to Alexandria. For five years after 1853, picks and shovels and barrels of black powder hacked out a roadbed, but no bridges or trestles were ever built, no track was ever laid. Financial difficulties in 1858 halted the project. What remained was a series of cuts and embankments which rendered ready-made trenches and breastworks along two miles of Confederate front. From Catharpin Run near Sudley Church on the left, the Confederate line ran along the base of Stoney Ridge southeastward to a point on the unfinished railroad north of Brawner's farm.

If the position had any weakness, it was on the left, where A.P. Hill oversaw the Sudley Springs Road, the Confederate escape route to Aldie Gap. There a thick forest blanketed the front for several hundred yards, offering good concealment, but shrinking the field of fire. Hill therefore arranged his brigades in two lines: Brigadiers Maxcy Gregg, Charles Field, and Colonel Edward Lloyd Thomas in the front line supported in depth by Lawrence Branch, William

Drawing by Dale Gallon

195

D. Pender, and James J. Archer close behind.

The center, where a lane between Sudley Church and Groveton crossed the railroad grade, was held by two brigades of Ewell's division. Ewell's knee wound required his leg's amputation during the night, so now his men were led by Brigadier Alexander Lawton. The other two brigades, detached under Jubal Early, guarded Jackson's right along the Warrenton Turnpike and watched for Longstreet's approach from Thoroughfare Gap.

On the right, where the fields of fire were unobstructed and the land more elevated, Jackson placed his own battered division, commanded by Brigadier General William E. Stark. Some regiments were virtually without officers and had been reduced to the size of companies. Totaled, Jackson had about 20,000 men to face Pope's Yankee hordes, more than double his number.

Forty Confederate cannon massed into 24-gun and 16-gun concentrations on Stoney Ridge overlooked the left and right flanks, positioned to

Brigadier General Robert C. Schenck. A shot to the arm disabled him permanently, but he fought admirably, commanding the 1st Division of Sigel's I Corps.

196

converge their fire on almost any avenue of approach. Stuart's cavalry secured the flanks. The positions and dispositions proved ideal. Not only defensively strong, they were strategically located where Lee, only a few hours' march away, could unite quickly with Stonewall's outreaching right. Jackson's immediate task now was to hold on and beat back Pope's attacks until Longstreet arrived and Lee took over.

The Second Battle Of Manassas

At 5:30 a.m. on Friday, August 29, following Pope's attack-at-dawn order, Sigel started his 9,000 Germans forward across a wide front. Brigadier General Carl Schurz with one division moved north toward the Rebel left. Brigadier General Robert Schenck with the other division headed west along the Warrenton Pike. Brigadier General Robert Milroy, with his Independent Brigade, advanced into the intervening vacuum. McDowell, who had at last surfaced from parts unknown, directed Reynolds' division to cooperate with Schenck and advance on his left.

Once across a stream called Young's Branch, Schurz, a scholarly-looking general, could see an expanse of open, rolling land ahead. There were a few scattered farms, and farther on in the long stretch of green forest, the enemy was supposed to be waiting. Schurz formed his division into regimental marching columns, Colonel Alexander Schimmelfennig on the right, Colonel Wladimir Krzyzanowski on the left, and skirmishers well ahead. All was quiet and still for an hour, until they entered the woods. Two shots, a silent pause, then a round of musketry, and the battle was on.

The Rebels seemed to give ground, but Schurz was unsure exactly what was happening because he could see so little in the smoky woods. Despite all the shouting and waving of swords by company officers trying to hold their units together, the tangled underbrush broke the men into irregular squads. After advancing for what seemed to Schurz about a half-mile, the sound of fire suddenly increased.

A.P. Hill's Light Division barred progress. The 1st and 12th South Carolina of Maxcy Gregg's brigade struck back in a bruising counterattack, knocking Schimmelfennig's brigade back on its heels. His and Krzyzanowski's brigades had drifted apart, struggling through the woods; another sortie first threw their center

into confusion, then threw it out of the woods.

By late morning, though his center and left had barely fought, Sigel decided his corps was outnumbered and had made its contribution. Milroy, with his brigade, advanced about a mile under a brisk shelling. But once near the enemy, Milroy got nervous, sent two regiments to help Schurz, feebly attacked with the remaining two and was easily repulsed. General Schenck, a reputed expert on the game of draw poker, did little more with his division. Not up for gambling, cautiously, slowly, he moved west along the turnpike past Groveton to about where Gibbon's fight took place the evening before. Confederate artillerists saw him coming and moved twelve guns down the ridge to meet him with fire, and Schenck stood pat. He dueled them with his artillery until it ran out of ammunition, called for more guns, then sent a brigade to help Milroy. By this time the Union's John Reynolds, using a circuitous southern route, came up beside Schenck's left and advanced a brigade north of the turnpike. Instead of attacking, the two generals took alarm when they discovered a great body of Confederates on their flank and beat a hasty retreat.

"It is Longstreet!" cried a courier. The general called "Old Pete" had arrived. After an eight-mile march, his long columns began filing off the pike

Major General Ambrose Powell Hill before the war. A native Virginian, his "Light" Division could have been the deciding factor in the Southern success at Cedar Mountain.

into battle position behind a screen of woods. Hinged on Jackson's three divisions, extending northeast along the unfinished railroad, Longstreet's line formed nearly southward, so that the Confederate front formed a great V of about 160°, facing a bit southeast.

The angled front was strongest at its apex, where Confederate John B. Hood's division and Major J.B. Walton's battalion of New Orleans' Washington Artillery connected with Jackson's right. Perpendicular to the pike, and behind Hood's left, was Brigadier General Cadmus Marcellus Wilcox's division, with Brigadier General James Lawson Kemper's division alongside his right. To the south, fresh from their service at Thoroughfare Gap, was D.R. Jones' division; its right sat on the Manassas Gap Railroad. The front was now nearly four miles long. When Richard Anderson's division arrived, expected late in the afternoon from its Rappahannock River guard duty, it would bring Lee's strength to 55,000 men, all he could expect to put into action.

His instinct was to launch an immediate attack, employing Longstreet's fresh troops, against the Union left.

Longstreet, however, was not satisfied. Never one to jump into anything too quickly, Old Pete wanted to examine the ground first and see if any Yankees were around his flank. Lee consented, and Longstreet rode to a hill for a long, careful look. When he returned he was most apprehensive. The Yankees were extended far south of the turnpike, he said, and he was not at all pleased with the terrain. To attack might expose his flank to any Federal force coming from the direction of Manassas.

Lee was disappointed but still favored an attack. While the two generals debated, a message from Stuart arrived saying a strong Yankee force was indeed approaching from Manassas; he was having his cavalrymen drag bundles of brush behind their horses to raise dust clouds and create an impression thousands of marching Confederates were moving

Major General James "Old Pete" Longstreet. His command would prove almost unstoppable at Second Manassas.

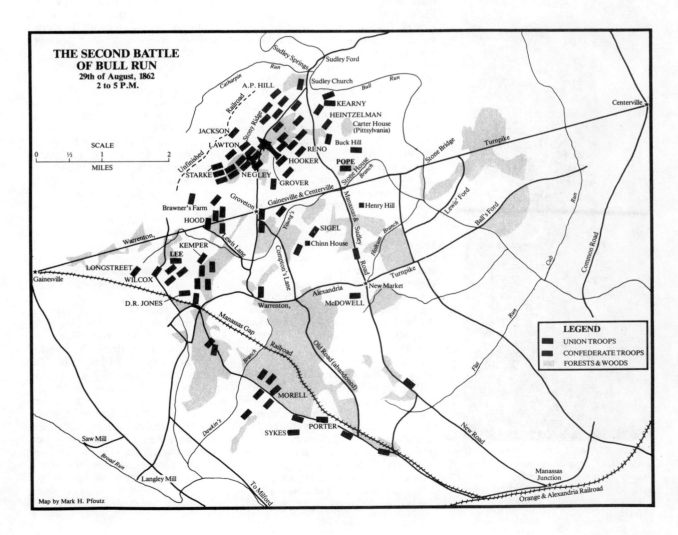

197

to meet them. If the high command wanted to hold the ground, they needed reinforcements immediately.

Wilcox's division started off to move to D.R. Jones' right, and Longstreet went with them to investigate.

As Lee studied the land in front of him, Stonewall Jackson rode up and briefed him on what had occurred since their meeting four days earlier. As they talked, Longstreet returned, still cautious. He reported that the force he saw was not dangerous, but there was dust behind them.

"Hadn't we better move our line forward?" Lee asked. "I think not," replied Longstreet; "we had better wait till we hear more from Stuart about the force he has reported moving aginst us from Manassas."

Jackson said nothing. The volume of gunfire from his sector was rapidly increasing and he quickly departed. Stuart arrived and confirmed what Longstreet observed, and he added the Yankees belonged to the corps of Fitz John Porter from McClellan's

Major General Irvin McDowell. Pope's III Corps commander, he was "rude, ill-tempered, and pompous." After the battle his own soldiers called him a scoundrel and a traitor.

198

U.S. Army Military History Institute

army. Lee, growing impatient, mounted his horse "Traveler" and rode to the right to look the situation over for himself.

Pope, meanwhile, had arrived on the battlefield from Centreville at about the same time as Lee (approximately noon) and established headquarters on Buck Hill behind the Stone House tavern there.

Believing Jackson's the only Confederate force before him, Pope's plan was for Sigel, Reno, and Heintzelman to attack in front, while McDowell and Porter came up from Manassas to deliver the crushing blow on Jackson's right flank and rear. It was a good plan in concept, but Pope possessed only sketchy knowledge about the lay of the land, where his own troops were, or for that matter, even where the enemy was.

He had about 33,000 men on the field by then. The Union front paralleled the unfinished railroad and overlapped Jackson's line slightly at either end. As Reno came up, Sigel dispersed the small corps to reinforce his own line; nevertheless Sigel reported to Pope that his line was weak, his divisions cut up, and he wanted permission to retire. Pope sternly replied no replacements were available and Sigel must hold his ground. McDowell and Porter would strike soon, he added.

From about 1:30 to 4:00 p.m. Federal brigades launched a series of disjointed, unsupported attacks against Stonewall Jackson's position. Hardly was there a time when an assault was not in progress. Most of the action fell on Confederate A.P. Hill.

Between the right of Maxcy Gregg and the left of Colonel Edward Thomas' Georgians a dangerous 150-yard interval had been left undefended. Schurz got a second attack going after his German boys crept silently into a railroad cut opposite the opening; they came out threatening to snap off Gregg's brigade from the rest of the Confederate army. The 14th South Carolina and 49th Georgia countercharged, exchanged blazing musket fire at a 10-yard range, forcing the Germans back and putting an end to the threat. Another Southern counterstroke broke three regiments holding the Germans' center and again sent them flying out of the woods. But Schurz had a battery and a regiment in reserve; pursuing Rebels entering the open fields were cut down in their tracks.

The Federals went back once more, reached the railroad grade and held

it, but Schurz was fought to a standstill. Hooker's and Reno's troops came forward, and relieved Schurz. Some Germans were indignant. "What battery is that?" laughed some of Hooker's soldiers. Sigel's artillery contained a pair of mountain howitzers—miniature-looking field pieces which could be disassembled and loaded on the backs of mules. "The shackass pattery, py Gott. Get out der way, or we plows your hets off."

Colonel Joseph B. Carr's brigade took over from Krzyzanowski and engaged in a hot skirmish fire, keeping the Rebels pinned in place. At 3:00 p.m. Union Brigadier General Cuvier Grover received orders to carry the embankment in front and hold the woods beyond.

"Where are my supporters?" asked Grover.

"They are coming," assured a staff officer. Grover's brigade got no help from anybody.

They were New England regiments, mostly: 1st, 11th, 16th Massachusetts, 2d New Hampshire, and 26th Pennsylvania. Grover rode the length of his line saying they would rely on the bayonet. Moving through the woods to the attack, they stepped over dead and wounded from Milroy's earlier effort.

A sudden explosion of Rebel musket fire was answered by a 1,500-man Yankee cheer; they went up to the top of a 10-foot embankment. Here a short, brutal hand-to-hand struggle occurred. The Virginians of Charles Field's brigade had already fired, and most of them got caught hugging the shelter of the bank, expecting a return volley that never came. Those who tried to fight were shot, bayoneted, or had their skulls crushed by musket butts; many threw up their hands and surrendered, some "played possum," feigned death. Others made a run for it and Grover's men were right behind.

The fragments of the first line stampeded into a supporting line, which the 2d New Hampshire also overpowered. A third Confederate line held. On the 2d's left, the 11th Massachusetts carried the embankment and got into a savage fight with the second Rebel line while artillery fire tore at its flank. Grover tried getting the 16th Massachusetts through the 2d's penetration, but the Rebels had recovered. It was the Yankees' turn to run. As they recrossed the embankment, they were exposed to a murderous crossfire. "To say nothing of the very bad language used by the

Rebels in calling us to stop," a survivor added. In twenty minutes the brigade lost 487 men. One thinned regiment had its flag torn away; its scattered men answered to the command "Rally 'Round The Pole."

Next came a brigade of Reno's corps, the men of Pittsburgh, Pennsylvania's Colonel James Negley. They had come up through the backwash of battle, heard all the discouraging remarks, watched men in bloodied blue uniforms being carried rearward to surgeons at the operating stations. Remembering it later, one of them wrote sagely: "Such sights were enough to make the stoutest and bravest man look pale." Their officers dismounted and the resting brigade got to its feet; it was time to go in.

Some of Pope's staff officers urged them on, bawling, "Porter is in their rear; you'll hear his guns in a minute. Fight sharp, boys, and you've got 'em sure!" Once they entered the woods, unseen Rebels peppered the air with bullets and Negley's soldiers fired and reloaded on the move. They hit Jackson's center about where a back country lane crossed the railroad grade. Across the deeply rutted lane they charged, leaping into a cut with bayonets level, up the other side and beyond. Then from underbrush on their left came a roar of gunfire. It cut into the flank of the 6th New Hampshire. Back to the cut, hollered the officers. Swearing it was their comrades of the 48th Pennsylvania shooting at them by mistake, the 6th's colorbearer angrily waved the Stars and Stripes.

The response was more bullets. Colonel Peter Starke's and Johnson's Confederate brigades wheeled around, and Negley's men abandoned their dead and wounded—nearly 50 percent their original number—and scrambled out of the woods into a field. The Confederates swept out into the open after them and hit General Nelson Taylor's unsuspecting Excelsior Brigade square in the flank, turning it's men into a disordered mob. The 14th Louisiana captured a cannon and merrily had it hauled back to their lines using downcast Yankee prisoners hitched up like draft horses.

Porter's Ruin — Longstreet's Position

In his official report of the battle, Pope dismissed the afternoon fighting in a single sentence, calling it "very severe skirmishes . . . at various points." What most concerned him

Drawing by Dale Gallon

The 14th Louisiana Captured A Cannon And Merrily Had It Hauled Back To Their Lines Using Downcast Yankee Prisoners Hitched Up Like Draft Horses

was the silence from the southwest. What had happened to McDowell and Porter?

Porter, an able general, but dedicated to McClellan, earlier received Pope's orders to countermarch and head northwest for Gainesville instead of Centreville. Rufus King was ill. His division, now commanded by Brigadier John P. Hatch, was also temporarily attached. About noon Porter received the so-called "Joint Order." It read: "HEADQUARTERS ARMY OF VIRGINIA, Centreville, August 29, 1862. Generals McDowell and Porter: You will please move forward with your joint commands toward Gainesville. I sent General Porter written orders to that effect an hour and a half ago. Heintzelman, Sigel, and Reno are moving on the Warrenton turnpike, and must now be not far from Gainesville. I desire that as soon as communication is established between this force and your own the whole command shall halt. It may be necessary to fall back behind Bull Run at Centreville tonight. I presume it will be so, on account of our supplies. . . .

"If any considerable advantages are to be gained by departing from this order it will not be strictly carried out. One thing must be had in view, that the troops must occupy a position from which they can reach Bull Run tonight or by morning. The indications are that the whole force of the enemy is moving in this direction at a pace that will bring them here by tomorrow night or the next day. My own headquarters will be for the present with Heintzelman's corps or at this place. Jno. Pope, Major-General, Commanding."

General George Morell's division, in the lead, halted short of a stream called Dawkin's Branch on the road out of Manassas heading for Gainesville to verify a report hostile troops blocked the way. When General McDowell arrived on the scene about noon, the two discussed Pope's instructions. (By any standard, the Joint Order was a dreadful piece of writing.) They rode northward for a distance and decided it was impractical to cut cross country to the battlefield, especially since dust columns raised by the ruse of Stuart's cavalry seemed to indicate Confederate troops were moving east toward Jackson. McDowell had a dispatch written at 9:30 a.m. by cavalry General John Buford stating he had observed seventeen enemy infantry regiments with artillery and cavalry pass through Gainesville. He showed it to Porter, but did not make an effort to forward it to General Pope. Obviously, the moving enemy troops belonged to Confederate General James Longstreet.

Neither McDowell, who was senior in grade, nor Porter seemed sure of what to do. McDowell then decided he should take Hatch's division and backtrack up the Sudley Springs Road and go to Pope.

Left with the Joint Order in his hands, Porter had several options. He could fight his way toward Gainesville, but McDowell had advised against that, saying his present position was "too far out." He could remain where he was. Or, since Pope said the whole army might fall back to Bull Run that night, he could probably retreat without disgrace. Pope's sentence about "considerable advan-

tages . . . gained by departing from this order" gave him a great deal of leeway.

Porter concluded to stay where he was. His couriers were apparently captured by Rebels so he had no contact with the main force. He listened to his skirmishers fire at the enemy, and debated whether the intermittent artillery fire he heard three miles beyond the trees indicated Pope was fighting a battle. Late in the afternoon the noise seemed to recede to the east. Porter wrote a dispatch to McDowell saying he was going to fall back to Manassas. Then he did not do it. Instead, he ordered a reconnaissance across Dawkin's Branch by Morell with four regiments.

At 6:00 p.m. Captain Douglas Pope, the general's aide and nephew, delivered another order: "HEADQUARTERS IN THE FIELD, August 29-4:30 p.m. Major General Porter: Your line of march brings you in on the enemy's right flank. I desire you to push forward into action at once on the enemy's flank, and, if possible,

on his rear, keeping your right in communication with General Reynolds. The enemy is massed in the woods in front of us, but can be shelled out as soon as you engage their flank. Keep heavy reserves and use your batteries, keeping well closed to your right all the time. In case you are obliged to fall back, do so to your right and rear, so as to keep you in close communication with the right wing. John Pope, Major-General, Commanding."

Porter urged Morell to hurry, but Morell was sick. He was worried about his flanks, the heavy odds he believed he faced, and the lateness of the day. Porter finally agreed it was too late and halted the moving lines before they became engaged. In the end, Porter had done nothing all day.

After the battle was lost and Pope removed from command, Porter was courtmartialed for disobedience of orders and misbehavior in the face of the enemy. Charges were preferred by Pope's inspector general, but it was no secret the actual accuser was Pope.

The court convened in November, in an atmosphere of gloom brought

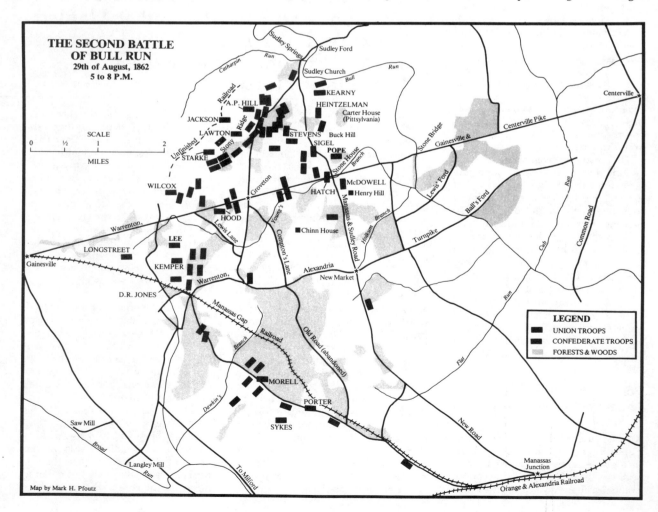

200

about by a season of Union defeats. The deck was stacked against Porter from the onset. The majority of court officers were Porter's juniors in rank, his defense council was a civilian who handled the case badly, and much of the prosecution's case was based on a distorted map showing incorrect troop positions for both Porter and the enemy. Pope testified Longstreet had not arrived; Jackson's flank was vulnerable all afternoon and Porter failed to attack it. In January 1863, the court found Porter guilty and sentenced him to be dismissed from the service.*

But all of that was in the future. On August 29, Porter's corps sat inert.

Back on the battlefield, Pope, believing Porter would attack any minute, ordered a fresh attack at five o'clock by Kearny and Reno against Jackson's depleted, but undefeated left. Kearny, filled with enthusiasm, his kepi tilted jauntily, took two brigades across the Sudley Springs Road and wheeled to the left so they would come down behind and along the length of the railroad grade. They wore a red patch on their caps, and when they were not called the "Red Diamond Division" they were called "Phil Kearny's thieves." Stevens' division of Reno's Corps added their weight to that of the "thieves" by attacking more frontally, to the Red Diamond Divison's left.

Facing them, A.P. Hill's men were desperately short of cartridges. "Good for you, boys! Give them the rocks and the bayonet," Hill encouraged. "Hold your position and I will soon have ammunition and reinforcements for you." Hill's staff filled their pockets and haversacks with cartridges for distribution while he rode to consult Jackson, reporting his men might not be able to stave off another onslaught. Jackson replied they must.

A loud crash of gunfire swept the field. "Here it comes," said Hill.

"I'll expect you to beat them," Jackson called after him.

Maxcy Gregg's South Carolinans began stepping backward under the pressure. General Gregg strode along the line waving his old Revolutionary War sword, saying, "Let us die here, my men, let us die here!" Officers

popped with their pistols. The Federals pressed so close some found they could save themselves by anticipating a shot from the other side. One soldier reflected on his experiences afterwards: "One may fight at long range as a patriot and a Christian, but I believe that no man can engage in one of those close struggles, where he can look into the eyes of his adversary and see his blood, but he becomes for the time, at least, a mere beast of prey."

Hill's line was forced to a position almost at a right angle with the railroad, his men fighting with all the strength left to them. Colonel Henry Forno's brigade of Ewell's division was thrown in on the left. Then, typical this day, the Federals lost some of their impetus and cohesion. Confederate reinforcements rushed to tip the balance. Jubal Early's brigade, returning from outpost duty after Longstreet arrived, charged toward the bending flank. With the 8th Louisiana and 13th Georgia picked up and added to either flank along the route, Early's Virginians surged over Gregg's prone troops and slammed into the fragmented Yankees. Once more thrown out of the woods, all the lost Confederate ground recovered, the Federals were forced back to where they launched their first attack that morning.

A courier rode to Stonewall Jackson announcing the good news. Jackson, with one of his rare smiles, answered: "I knew he would do it."

Kearny, furious at the setback, rode to Pope's headquarters for reinforcements. Pope replied none were to be had. For a moment Kearny showed his dismay, but only for a moment. "Look at that! Did you ever see the like of that? Isn't it beautiful?"

To the distant west a blood-red sun was setting behind enormous billowing clouds, brilliant hues above a landscape of dark forest green. Below the horizon, tiny blinking lights were visible, twinkling like fireflies. There was a battle going on along the Warrenton Turnpike, but it was all color. Not a sound could be heard. All the gathered Union officers and their staffs paused to admire the spectacle.

War could be admired by commanders at a distance, but up close for participants it was another outbreak of confusing, deadly violence.

McDowell had reported to Pope with Hatch's division at the height of Kearny's assault. Since the resounding noise indicated Kearny was win-

ning, and a fresh report said the enemy was moving troops to their right, presumably to confront Porter, McDowell was told to make an attack down the turnpike. He rode to the double-quicking 76th New York and yelled they were on the heels of a retreating foe. "Push 'em like hell!"

Lee, that afternoon, had encountered nearly the same difficulty as Pope: getting a subordinate to make an attack. He returned from a personal reconnaissance satisfied Longstreet's line was longer than the Federals', and it outnumbered theirs. For the third time he urged Longstreet to make an attack. Longstreet remained immobile. In his opinion it was too late; a full-scale advance might result in disaster. He preferred making a forced reconnaissance with General Hood. Lee, sometimes unwilling to force his will on a subordinate, finally acceded, Longstreet got his way. Cadmus Wilcox's division was ordered back to support Hood, if necessary.

And so two divisions collided along the highway in the twilight— Hood's coming from the west and Union General Hatch's from the east —in a battle Pope, Kearny, and the other commanders watched in awe from a distance. From the Federal vantage point on Buck Hill, the twinkling lights advancing from the west increased, those from the east grew weaker, receded, and finally sputtered out. Hood's line, longer, had come out of a dark wood on Hatch's left, crumpled it, and driven the Federals splashing across Young's Branch. A major in the 76th New York nearly made himself a prisoner of war when in the confusion he began to rally the 2d Mississippi. For the Federals, confusion had also been typical this day.

A Night Of Pain And A Morning Of Indecision

Evening turned to dark night and ended the terrible fighting of August 29. The atmosphere at Pope's headquarters mixed elation with frustration. The major general commanding optimistically appraised the day's bloody events and believed his army had fought successfully. Although he figured his army had lost between 6,000 and 8,000 killed and wounded, he was sure he had inflicted greater damage on Jackson. Hooker estimated the enemy loss at two to one. Kearny thought it closer to three to one. First thing in the morning Pope would wire General-in-Chief Henry W. Halleck that "the enemy was

*For the next fifteen years Porter attempted to get a new hearing. This finally occurred in 1878. A more objective board convened at West Point, heard new evidence, listened to ex-Confederates, including General James Longstreet, and decided in Porter's favor. He was restored to the army rolls (for purposes of pension and honor) twenty years after his alleged transgression.

driven from the field, which we now occupy." Pope's frustration stemmed from Fitz John Porter's failure to deliver the death blow to the enemy.

"I'll arrest him!" snapped Pope when he learned of Porter's inaction at Dawkin's Branch. His belief Porter would at some point deliberately let him down seemed substantiated. But McDowell interceded. Porter was an overrated general who made a mistake through incompetency, not deliberate motive, he said. Why take such severe action when they were winning a great battle? Pope listened, and yielded. Nonetheless, he wrote Major General Porter a menacing dispatch: "Immediately upon the receipt of this order, the precise hour of receiving you will acknowledge, you will march your command to the field of battle of today and report to me in person for orders."

Porter's corps turned out of its blankets at 3:00 a.m. and began a sleepy trudge to the battlefield.

Pope made no plans or changes in position during the night. He had decided to wait for August 30. He was deeply troubled about the condition of his army. The troops were exhausted, famished, lacking commissary supplies. At dawn, a courier arrived from the Manassas telegraph station with a message from Major General William Buel Franklin, written at McClellan's direction. Pope read the words, crumpled the paper in his fist, and without a word to anyone, walked away from his officers for a short distance before turning around to return.

"What is it, General?" asked one of the staff. Pope handed him the note. Washington was well aware of his acute supply problem. Several times Pope had requested rations and forage. McClellan's reply, through Franklin, was that his requested supplies would be loaded when Pope sent cavalry to Alexandria as an escort to the railroad trains. In the middle of battle, it was a petty, impossible condition. One of his friends on the staff later recalled he only knew Pope to feel downtrodden once: "That was when he got that damned dispatch from McClellan at Alexandria telling him that he and his army could go starve."

In the morning hours of Saturday, August 30, Pope called his commanders together at his Buck Hill headquarters. The night before, McDowell gave him Buford's message about the seventeen regiments passing through Gainesville, but Pope placed no credence in it. He was still under the delusion Jackson, and Jackson alone faced him. His impulse was to follow up on Kearny's previous afternoon's success and resume attacking. He felt this would be a safer course than retreat. McDowell and Heintzelman were to assail the Rebel left, aided by Porter, whose corps was due to arrive shortly.

But by noon, the August 30 plan of operations had undergone considerable revision. Pope and several of his chief subordinates had come to the fantastic belief the enemy was retreating. Information came from Hatch's front along the Warrenton pike that John B. Hood's division was gone. (This was true. Hood had withdrawn to the main Confederate line at 2:00 a.m.) Paroled Union prisoners said the Confederates had been retreating all night long. For a man of action, oddly enough, Pope seemed confused. "General Pope seemed wholly at a loss what to do or what to think," a witness observed.

While Pope was plagued with indecision, McDowell and Heintzelman rode up the Sudley Springs Road to inspect their attack zone. Jackson's line was concealed deep in the woods, and the two generals, seeing no evidence of it, or of Confederate wagon trains (wagons had been parked behind Sudley Church the day before), hastily deduced Jackson had gone. Franz Sigel, whom they met on the way back to headquarters, had come to the same conclusion.

Pope cut them off before they could speak: "I know what you are about to say, the enemy is retreating." Pope was himself again. Based entirely on reports from Hatch's front, Pope had come to the same erroneous conclusion they had: Jackson had had enough and was pulling out. McDowell and Heintzelman confirmed this belief. The attack plan was dropped. Pope now thought in terms of pursuit.

By the oddest, ironic contrast, Lee had the feeling Pope might retreat. Except for a desultory exchange of cannon shots, the Federal side of the battlefield was perfectly calm. Occasional grass fires lifted white smoke toward gathering clouds. Lee's thoughts, as he sat down to write a report to Confederate President Jefferson Davis, were not on the probability of a battle, but on more marches to maneuver the Yankees out of Virginia. His moves so far, he said, had "drawn the enemy from the Rappahannock frontier and caused him to concentrate his troops between Manassas and Centreville. My desire has been to avoid a general engagement, being the weaker force, and by maneuvering to relieve the portion of the country referred to."

If the Federals did not attack that day, Lee decided Longstreet should create a diversion in the afternoon while Jackson slipped across the Bull Run at Sudley Springs after dark, and once again thrusted at the enemy's rear. If they did attack, Lee was confident the Yankees would be repulsed in two hours.

Jackson also began to doubt there would be a battle. He rode to the right of his line to watch for Federal movements, but could detect little. "Well," he said to Colonel William Smith Hanger Baylor of his old brigade, "it looks as if there will be no fight today, but keep your men in line and ready for action."

Pope, after a full morning of hesitation, determined to begin his pursuit and strike Jackson's rear guard. Porter's corps reached the Stone House about 9:00 a.m. and relaxed in the fields near the John Dogan place. There hungry men husked and boiled corn until Southern artillery burst shrapnel around them and officers ordered the fires extinguished. Since Porter's corps had done next to nothing on August 29, Pope reasoned these soldiers would be freshest. About 11:30 a.m. he dispatched a verbal order to Porter: "Attack, King [Hatch] will support."

At noon, realizing more coordination would be needed, he dictated a written general order placing McDowell in charge of the pursuit of the supposedly retreating Confederates. Porter's corps, followed by Reynolds' division, and King's old division, now commanded by John Hatch, were to push west along the Warrenton pike. Ricketts' division, which had at last reached the field after a circuitous retreat from Thoroughfare Gap via Bristoe and Manassas, was to cross the Bull Run at Sudley Springs and turn west on the Haymarket Road. (This route roughly paralleled the pike several miles north.) Heintzelman's corps would follow Ricketts. The remainder of the army—Sigel's, Reno's, and Banks' men and the Federal wagon train at Bristoe—would wait in reserve.

No sooner was this order written, than the Union command became aware they had guessed wrong about

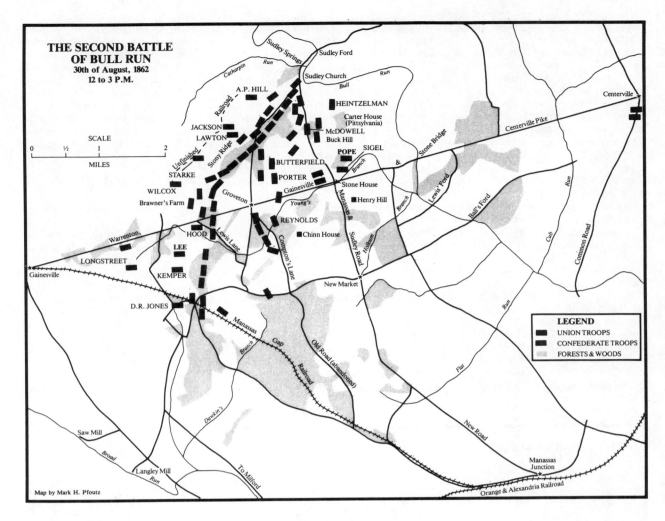

THE SECOND BATTLE
OF BULL RUN
30th of August, 1862
12 to 3 P.M.

SCALE

0   ½   1   2
MILES

LEGEND
UNION TROOPS
CONFEDERATE TROOPS
FORESTS & WOODS

Map by Mark H. Pfoutz

the Rebels.

Ricketts, before he could lead the northern procession, had to put his division back together. When it arrived that morning, McDowell detached two of its brigades to relieve Philip Kearny's men. "Apparently no opportunity for dividing and scattering commands was to be lost," one of Reno's officers disgustedly observed. Rebel artillery commenced beating on one of Ricketts' brigades as it began to assemble. Another brigade was skirmishing with the enemy. Ricketts came to McDowell firmly convinced the Rebels "had no intention of retiring." Heintzelman's corps met Confederate fire too, when it attempted to move.

McDowell ordered Ricketts to abandon pursuit and resume his position: Reynolds' Pennsylvania Reserves, meanwhile, broke camp and fell into marching formation. Some men, too weak to participate, were permitted to go to the rear. The hungry 3d Regiment was told sadly by its colonel there were no rations for issue, only cartridges. Moving out with these

men (the Pennsylvania Bucktails) covering the front, Reynolds kept just south of the pike. He had his troops wade Young's Branch, step over corpses from Hatch's evening fight, and enter the woodlands near Groveton.

They bumped into Longstreet's Confederates again. Sporadic skirmish fire began. The Bucktails requested a supporting regiment, then another. Some Rebel sharpshooters had climbed trees and were sniping from the foliage. Their locations were revealed by smoke puffs. The Pennsylvanians huddled into small squads and blew them from their nests with short bursts of fire.

Reynolds became suspicious, especially when one of his regiments fled across a clearing and flopped down to take cover. Rebel infantry was preparing to attack, their colonel reported; they were masked by a line of cavalry pickets. "Impossible!" snorted Reynolds, riding into the clearing to see for himself. One glance was enough. The enemy seemed to be waiting at right angles to his flank.

The report was correct. Reynolds whirled his horse around just as the opposite woodline erupted with shots. The general escaped, but his orderly was killed.

McDowell, underestimating the magnitude of the uncovered peril, ordered Reynolds to pull back slightly to a defensive position. Porter was notified of the change; if he needed support, Pope would send him Sigel's troops. But Sigel, too, was suspicious of a Confederate presence south of the pike and conveyed the information to Pope. Pope digested the report, then, with a wave of his arm, instructed the aide to return to General Sigel and have him send a brigade and a battery to "the bald hill."

"What bald hill?" asked Sigel. "He said, the bald hill," responded the officer, mimicking Pope's arm jesture. Sigel ordered Brigadier General Nathaniel McLean's Ohio brigade to Chinn Ridge, a treeless plain topped by a whitewashed frame farm house, a mile in Reynolds' rear. There they

203

could be of no immediate help, whatever, to Reynolds.

By early afternoon Pope and most of his senior generals were conscious that the Confederates had not retreated as they had at first supposed; and some of them were also vaguely aware of an enemy menace brewing behind the woods south of Groveton. The only result Pope's noontime pursuit order produced was confusion, especially in Porter's corps. These men still believed they were to sweep over Jackson's rear guard.

Against light skirmish fire, two great divisional columns of Porter's Peninsula veterans closed in on the strip of woods bordering the Groveton-Sudley lane. This day the volunteer division was commanded by Brigadier General Daniel Butterfield. (During the night General Morell with two brigades, because of a misunderstanding, had marched to Centreville instead of the battlefield. Butterfield would miss them.) Butterfield's division lay down in the woods. Brigadier General George Sykes' division of Regulars halted in the fields on their left. From behind the railroad grade across a meadow came brisk musket fire.

"Now, men," cautioned a Federal sharpshooter officer, "if there are any here who think they are going to have an easy time on this skirmish, change your tune now." These were the marksmen of the 1st United States Sharpshooter Regiment, a group of men who each could shoot ten consecutive shots into an 8-inch bull's eye at 200 yards. They rushed over the field, making for the cover of a dry stream bed about half way across. "There was very little chance for a man to escape being hit at this place," one of them said, "even if he lay very low." Minié bullets smacked into the dirt bank or whizzed close overhead. Bullets riddled their knapsacks. Three infantry regiments were rushed out to help their pinned-down comrades.

Porter and Butterfield observed how the Rebel-held railroad grade ran off diagonally to the left of their corps' front. The outlook was bleak. An enfilade fire from the right was checking progress. To the southeast, Confederate batteries posed trouble. Belatedly, Porter called for Hatch's division to come up on his right. It was done "slowly and in a confused manner." Hatch would lead. After Butterfield's division took the railroad grade, it was to wheel left and go for the enemy's artillery. It was three o'clock in the afternoon when the Union attack finally got rolling.

Finished On Familiar Ground

"Here they come" the Confederates warned one another. They shifted their cartridge boxes to the front of their uniforms for quicker access. The Yankees came pouring out of the woods giving "three deafening cheers." For a moment they wavered in the lane as Confederate bullets peppered their ranks. They scaled a rail fence, then formed into regimental fighting lines. Colonel Bradley Tyler Johnson rushed his Virginia regiments out of seclusion to join his skirmish line at the "Deep Cut," where the railroad excavation was

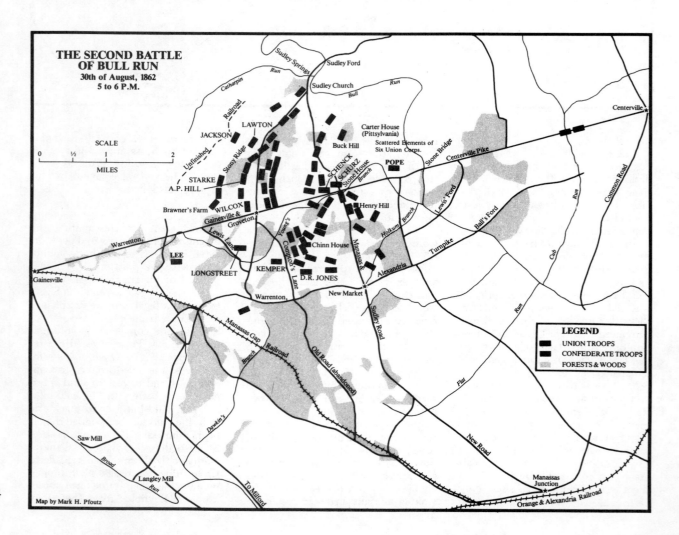

THE SECOND BATTLE OF BULL RUN
30th of August, 1862
5 to 6 P.M.

LEGEND
UNION TROOPS
CONFEDERATE TROOPS
FORESTS & WOODS

Map by Mark H. Pfoutz

204

lowest. The Stonewall Brigade, all that remained of it, hurried forward from thickets on Johnson's left.

W.W. Blackford, the cavalry engineer, rode forward to watch the Federal attack sweeping across the front of Colonel Stephen D. Lee's artillery battalion. Later he wrote: "The advance began in magnificent style, lines straight as an arrow, all fringed with glittering bayonets and fluttering with flags. But the march had scarcely begun when little puffs of smoke appeared dotting the fields in rapid succession just over the heads of the men, and as the lines moved on, where each little puff had been lay a pile of bodies, and half a dozen or more staggering figures standing around leaning on their muskets and then slowly limping back to the rear."

Colonel Leroy Stafford, on Johnson's left, had his Louisiana brigade protected by a high embankment. They poured a deafening volley over it. The noise was followed by the frantic rattling of steel ramrods. "We all knew," said a 24th New York private, "that our only hope lay in getting there before they could reload their guns. Over half our men had now fallen, but the rest swept on in an unbroken wave." The 24th scrambled up to the top of the bank, delivering their own volley, and causing a convulsive shudder in the Louisiana ranks. A mounted Union officer, sword raised high, got clear to the top. From the astonished Southerners came the spontaneous cry, "Don't kill him!" But bullets plunged into both horse and rider and they both went down in a heap.

The 50-yard gap in the embankment to Stafford's left was where peacetime railroad architects had envisioned a trestle. The place was called "the dump." Jackson protected this weak area with a motley collection of stragglers and other petty ne'er-do'-wells; "I suppose as much for punishment as for the real benefit they might be," speculated Captain William C. Oates, an Alabaman. The right of Oates' 15th Alabama obliqued their fire to lend a hand.

The attacking Union forces, hugging the embankment slope, poked their rifles over their heads and pulled the triggers without exposing themselves. The defenders, short of cartridges, hurled cannonball-size rocks down on them. "The flags of the opposing regiments were almost flapping together," said Oates.

"The shouts and yells from both sides were indescribably savage," a 24th New York lieutenant wrote. "It seemed like the popular idea of pandemonium made real, and indeed it is scarcely too much to say that we were really transformed for the time, from a lot of good-natured boys to the most blood-thirsty of demoniacs."

Back on Johnson's front, the Yankees in Butterfield's division lost a great number of men to a crossfire: from Southern artillery on their left, and from small arms fire from in front and on their right. Some regiments changed direction under fire in order to approach the Rebel line more squarely. Up a slope they clambered to a short plateau where, as a Michigan sergeant said, "the slaughter commenced." The 17th New York sprawled on the ground and fired. Most of the other regiments stood erect, exchanging bullets with Confederates sheltered in the Deep Cut. Colonel Johnson reported he "saw a Federal flag hold its position for half an hour within ten yards of one of the regiments in the cut and go down six or eight times."

Though the Yanks melted fast, the Virginians began to run out of ammunition. They took it from the cartridge boxes of their dead and wounded comrades. They picked up stones and threw them, the range was that close. (Lieutenant Lewis Randolph, a grandson of President Thomas Jefferson, was reported to have killed a Federal with a rock.) The Union regiments would stand the punishment for as long as they could, then break, and flee for protection at the base of the slope. While officers reformed them for another attempt, the Confederates ran forward to retrieve their supply of stones.

All the while, S.D. Lee's battalion of eighteen cannon pounded on the exposed Union flank. They burst shells and case shot among Union reserves trying to advance and support the attacking forces. Then they drove them back into the woods. Federal counter-battery fire was ineffective; only two batteries fired and did nothing to neutralize the Confederate cannon. A feeble lunge toward the Rebel guns was blasted with discharges of canister at 200 yards.

There was no hope of Federal assistance from the rear. A wounded lieutenant under the embankment watched the reinforcements advance, "many of them holding their arms before their faces, as though to keep off a storm." They broke under the metallic hail, tried to reform, then fled for their lives.

A Confederate staff man rushed to Jackson's side reporting Colonel Bay-lor was shot. His successor requested reinforcements.

"What brigade sir?" asked Jackson, missing the connection.

"The Stonewall Brigade," he answered.

"Go back," commanded Jackson, "give my compliments to them, and tell the Stonewall Brigade to maintain her reputation." Jackson began wondering whether his soldiers could hold out much longer. He signaled a message to R.E. Lee requesting reinforcements.

General Longstreet, galloping to the front, learned of Jackson's plight. With one look out across the smoky plain at what S.D. Lee's guns were doing to Porter's flank, Longstreet called for a pair of his own batteries and placed them near where the Union's John Gibbon had positioned his on August 28. As the first battery began to boom, Longstreet received a request from Robert E. Lee to send a division to Jackson. "Certainly," he replied cheerfully, "but before the division can reach him, that attack will be broken by artillery fire."

The Union assault forces began retiring, losing as many men retreating across the open meadow as when they advanced. They could not break into the railroad bed, they could not be reinforced, they could not remain in an untenable position any longer. Unaccountably, Porter had made the attack with only half the troops he had available; Sykes' entire division and two brigades of Hatch's were never sent into action.

At this point, General McDowell committed a colossal blunder. Sigel's corps was near the J. Dogan house directly in Porter's rear. Reynolds' division was south of the turnpike protecting the Union left. With ample evidence Longstreet's Confederates were facing Reynolds, McDowell sent a hurried, thoughtless call to run the division across the pike to bolster Porter. Lieutenant Charles Hazlett's battery of U.S. Regulars was all that was left to cover the Union flank.

Hazlett was horrified by what he saw happening. Not even pickets were being left behind. An orderly was sent galloping for help. From Sykes' division came about 1,000 men, his volunteer brigade: the 5th New York and 10th New York Infantry, Colonel G.K. Warren commanding. No sooner had they hustled into the woodlands and deployed on Hazlett's left than Longstreet began the great Confederate counterattack.

Anticipating the order from Gen-

. . . 500 Shots Were Fired At That Yank. . . . He Pulled Up On A Knoll Out Of Range, Turned Around And Waved His Cap. The Confederates, Appreciating His Daring, Responded With A Cheer

Drawing by Dale Gallon

eral Lee, Longstreet seized the initiative at precisely the right time and place. Porter was repulsed; the Federal left was in a state of confusion. Longstreet struck with 28,000 fresh Confederates where Pope and McDowell had only 1,000 New Yorkers to oppose them. Five divisions swept forward along a two-mile crescent. General John B. Hood's Texans led the great charge.

The six companies of the 10th New York on the skirmish line barely had time to shoot before they were overrun. They rallied on their 5th New York comrades, standing erect in a clearing, rifles at the ready. The 5th's men were dressed like French Zouaves: tasseled fezzes, flashy blue jackets, bright red pantaloons, and white gaiters. They were about to set a ghastly record.

Hood's 5th Texas and Carolinian Major General Wade Hampton's "Legion" staggered a moment under a point-blank zouave volley, then surged ahead, firing as they came, swarming around the zouaves' flanks. "It looked like a slaughter pen" around the colors, said a survivor. The New Yorkers' colonel fell from his saddle; he was wounded seven times that day. An officer's stampeded horse dragged its rider across the ground. Hazlett's guns were positioned in such a way that they could not possibly help. The battery was hastily limbered up and withdrawn.

The zouaves were right behind. As they fled for the rear, some men darted in a zig-zag fashion to avert a shot in the back. Those who turned to fire a last time were usually shot themselves. In fifteen terrible minutes, the 5th New York suffered the highest percentage of men killed outright in a single Civil War battle — 124 slain, 223 wounded, out of 490 men present. An irreverent Texan described them as "gaudy corpses."

After dispatching the zouaves, Hood's division next slammed into the rear of Reynolds' men, catching Union Brigadier General C.F. Jackson's brigade, in column, headed for the north side of the pike. Caught surprised, the Pennsylvanians tried to make a stand, but the Texans destroyed the brigade and captured four cannon.

The great Southern V-shaped vise began to close relentlessly. As Longstreet's left swept ahead, his right ponderously wheeled to the northeast. The ground there was uneven, cut by gullies, ravines, and long hollows, with the upper slopes covered with trees and undergrowth. Longstreet's divisions would hit not as one solid mass, but as a series of brigade-sized punches and flanking attacks. Although parts of Stonewall Jackson's Confederate force emerged from their railroad cut stronghold, their depleted condition prevented them from keeping up with Longstreet's pace.

Sykes' U.S. Regulars gave ground grudgingly. Gibbon's now-veteran Black Hats covered Hatch's backward move, always facing to the front. They backed up to a defensive line the erstwhile Germans Sigel and Schenck had drawn up near the J. Dogan place. There they lay down, the Confederates coming from the woods cautiously.

"Gott in Himmel! General, vhy you no zay schoot by my battery!" screeched one of Sigel's artillerists. "I vill be disgraced by New York. By Jesus Christ, vhy you no zay schoot?" Gibbon told him to shut up and obey orders. When the Rebels came within easy range, he barked the fire command. Canister knocked them down like tenpins. "Set 'em up in t'other alley, boys," a Wisconsin Irishman shouted, "they are all down on that."

Pope and McDowell worked frantically to get enough forces in front of Longstreet to stop him. McDowell sent Brigadier General Zealous B. Tower with his own and Brigadier General George Hartsuff's brigades of Ricketts' division to Chinn Ridge. Sigel sent Brigadier General Robert Milroy's brigade, followed soon after by Krzyzanowski's and a Colonel John Koltes' men. As soon as Reynolds reached the north side of the pike, his two remaining brigades were rushed toward an old Battle of Manassas site, the Henry Hill. Sykes' Regulars and the one serviceable brigade of Jesse Reno's division followed them. Pope moved his headquarters there too. For the moment, however, the only Yankees in front of Longstreet were Colonel Nathaniel McLean's four Ohio regiments and a battery of New York artillery.

The 75th Ohio boys were occupying themselves by taking pot shots at some Texans reforming in the thickets off their right flank. Apparently they were not conscious of the whooping sound coming from the woods in front. Out of the trees burst Brigadier General Nathan G. "Shanks" Evans' brigade of South Carolinians, two ranks deep and 75 yards away. Their objective was Pope's "bald hill," the Chinn Ridge. The Ohio regiments fired by file: Two men at a time discharged their rifles from one end of the line to the other. The batterymen switched from shell to canister, then, double-shotted canister. Evans' soldiers recoiled under the furious blasting, but quickly returned for a second try, reinforced now by Brigadier General Micah Jenkins' South Carolina brigade.

Then two Virginia brigades—Colonel Eppa Hunton's and Colonel Montgomery Corse's of Brigadier General James L. Kemper's division—moved up from the south, threatening the Federal flank resting by a corn field fence in front of the Chinn house atop the ridge. Hunton's brigade halted momentarily to dress its ranks. Union Colonel McLean was ordering a section of the New York battery to turn and blast them when someone yelled those were reinforcements. McLean peered hard through the thick gray smoke, but all he could detect was that they wore dark uniforms, like Federal blue. He probably guessed they belonged to Milroy's Union brigade, last seeen moving laterally across the valley of nearby Chinn's Branch behind McLean's rear. He was unfortunate in his belief; Milroy had actually halted and reversed his march. Hunton and Corse charged toward the side of the house and sent a deluge of bullets into the Yankees' flank. The 73d and 25th Ohio fell back over the ridge crest for shelter, but Confederate artillery, in their rear, jarred them with banging shells. General Schenck, who for the longest time did not know Sigel had detached McLean from his division, rode into the action rallying his men and was hit by three bullets in rapid succession. The last one caused him to be carried off the field delirious.

As McLean gave the order to retreat, reinforcements took over. Tower's four regiments fought bravely, but ineffectively, unable to deploy under demoralizing pressure. Among these troops, in Hartsuff's brigade, was the 12th Massachusetts of Colonel Fletcher Webster, son of the great statesman, Daniel Webster. These men got back on top of the ridge, but could not hold it; Webster was killed and they were forced back with the others.

Charging the Union battery, Lieutenant Colonel F.G. Skinner, a giant of a man riding ahead of his 1st Virginia, nearly decapitated a Yankee cannoneer with one powerful slash of his sword. He killed another with a thrust, before an infantryman plunged a bayonet into him, driving him backward out of the saddle. Wounded so seriously that later, parts of three ribs had to be removed, Skinner shrugged off attempts to aid him, exclaiming, "Bah! Witness gentlemen, I took this battery."

Swarming down the slope, the Virginians were attracted by a test of their marksmanship, a moving target. To save his piece from capture, a Federal artillery driver dashed between the dry creek bed of Chinn's Branch and advancing Confederate troops. A stream of bullets was directed his way as he whipped his lead horses, the gun bounding behind. He steered along the brink of the creek bed, Rebels yelling, shooting, and closing the range with every step. "Let the man alone and shoot the horses," hollered a captain. "You are shooting too high," he screamed. "Shoot the horses!" The captain estimated 500 shots were fired at that Yank, and yet somehow he escaped. He pulled up on a knoll out of range, turned around and waved his cap. The Confederates, appreciating his daring, responded with a cheer.

Koltes' and Krzyzanowskis' men then charged into the fight with abandon; coupled with Federal artillery fire from around Dogan's house, they made Longstreet's attack sag momentarily.

The Confederates had plenty of guns of their own, leap-frogging from one ridge to another, delivering a few rounds until the Federals were out of range, then repeating the process. General Robert Lee reigned up next to one of these, the Rockbridge Battery, and was told one of the cannoneers wanted to speak with him—not an unusual request in the Confederate army. "Well, my man, what can I do for you?" he said pulling down his binoculars. "Why General, don't you know me?" Under the grime covering him Lee did not see at first it was his youngest son, Private Robert E. Lee, Jr.

South and east of the main battle area, near New Market Crossroads, in back of a building called the Conrad house, Confederate Brigadier General Beverly H. Robertson, with

Battles and Leaders

Stubborn Union troops make a stand at Henry Hill and prevent a rout.

a brigade of troopers, hoped to swing around Pope's rear and intercept the Yankees' retreat. The 2d Virginia Cavalry galloped in the van. Rebel Colonel Thomas T. Munford spied a lone squadron of Yankee horsemen strung out along the base of a ridge. When he took the bait, ordering a charge, two of Brigadier John Buford's Federal regiments trotted over the crest, and Munford found himself in

a wild saber-swinging melee. "Go for the Colonel," cried a Union sergeant. But as he delivered a saber slash his horse went down and Munford caught only a glancing cut. Stuart, with the 7th and 12th Virginia, thundered to the rescue, overwhelmed Buford's disorganized troopers, and sent them fleeing for Lewis' Ford over Bull Run, leaving 300 prisoners in Confederate hands.

It was getting late in the afternoon. Gathering dark clouds threatened an evening rain. Pope, his generals, and men were beaten. Their only salvation was to keep open the route of retreat across Bull Run and its Stone Bridge. If the Confederates seized control of the bridge approaches, all was lost.

North of the turnpike, to conform with the retirement of the Union left, Sam Heintzelman began pulling his corps east of the Sudley Road to the vicinity of the brown Carter mansion, called Pittsylvania. Sigel, in the Federal center, abandoned the Dogan house plateau area. Along the length of the Warrenton Turnpike for miles, from the Stone House across Bull Run toward Centreville, there was a tangled throng of Union army wagons, broken batteries, ambulances, fragmented infantry units, and confused, defeated men.

All that stood between them and destruction at the hands of James Longstreet was one last Yankee line, drawn up in ranks near a pile of rubble. A year before it had been the dwelling of old Mrs. Judith Carter Henry, a civilian victim of the First Battle of Manassas. The defenders were the two serviceable brigades of the Pennsylvania Reserve Division (it had done a great deal of fruitless marching so far but not much fighting), Robert Milroy's brigade, a brigade of Jesse Reno's corps, and a patchwork of companies, squads, and individuals who refused to quit.

CWTI Collection

A contemporary photograph of the Stone House on the field at Manassas. Built in 1828, it stands today unaltered by time and the tangled fighting of 120 years ago.

Beyond the Sudley roadway they watched Longstreet's exultant Rebels crush or push aside whoever tried to stop them.

Infected with victory, the Rebels began ascending Henry Hill, nearer and nearer, their officers urging them on. Against the setting western sun they "came on like demons emerging from the earth."

General John Reynolds drew his breath and hollered, "Forward, Reserves!"

Two charging lines collided head-on at the Sudley Road, the Pennsylvanians jumping into the eroded depression for shelter. In the evening there was bitter fighting again. It equaled any that had gone before it. Reynolds seized the flag of the 2d Pennsylvania and, as if charmed, galloped the length of the front untouched. The Rebels brought up their reserve division, Richard H. Anderson's, and extended their right east of the road. In the nick of time, Federal George Sykes arrived with his Regulars and took over from Reynolds, skillfully pulling the flank back to keep it out of the enemy's reach. A volunteer regiment fired by mistake into the Regulars' backs, and at the height of the crisis an artillery battery panicked and bolted for safety. But, this time the Yankees could not be moved.

At long last the sun went down and the Rebels fell back to Chinn Ridge and went into bivouac. Lee and his generals gathered around a camp fire. There, Hood exclaimed Confederate battle flags moving forward that afternoon had been a thrilling sight. Lee answered gravely, "God forbid it should ever see our colors moving in the opposite direction."

At eight o'clock Pope ordered a general withdrawal to Centreville. Banks was instructed to destroy everything at Bristoe that could not be transported and march for Centreville, also. An odor of black powder smoke polluted the air, and as the darkness deepened, a steady rain began to fall, soaking the tired soldiers to the skin and turning the road to a thick paste. Reflecting on their adventures and misadventures long afterward, many old Union veterans remembered the retreat to Centreville as the gloomiest, most miserable single night of the whole war.

The rank and file seethed with anger. They knew they had fought as well as the Confederates; they had been out-generaled and mis-generaled. Of all the lies Pope ever told, perhaps his greatest was the dispatch telegraphed to General-in-Chief Henry Halleck from Centreville that evening. After outlining the facts, Pope had the gall to write: "The troops are in good heart, and marched off the field without the least hurry of confusion." True, there was no panic as there had been after the first defeat, but there was a great amount of confusion. And there was ugly talk.

"Scoundrel!" a soldier called to McDowell. "Traitor!" yelled another. One infantryman said loudly he would rather put a bullet through McDowell than Stonewall Jackson. And Pope got his share. A Horace Greeley reader hailed him with "Go west, young man. Go West!"

Preparing For The Future

Next morning, Sunday, August 31, Pope had his army in the old Confederate fortifications along Centreville heights. Major General William Buel Franklin's corps had arrived the night before. Major General Edwin V. Sumner's was coming in from Alexandria too, giving Pope 20,000 fresh troops to make a new fight if he wanted.

First he believed he did: "I shall attack again tomorrow if I can; the next day certainly." Then his mood changed to despair. He inquired if Halleck felt "secure about Washington should this army be destroyed." He hinted darkly about "unsoldierly and dangerous conduct" by some of McClellan's old Army of the Potomac officers.

Pope's talk of this conduct filtered down to the ranks. Franklin's reinforcements treated Pope's disspirited men with contempt and scorn; they lined the route of retreat and "greeted us with mocking laughter, taunts and jeers," said one of McDowell's officers. "They held us back," a Wisconsin soldier told the Black Hats. When General Franklin was questioned why it took three entire days to march from Alexandria to Centreville, he replied he had McClellan's orders in his pocket.

Three miles to the west, Longstreet's Confederates drew the grisly task of undertakers. The casualties were nearly equal: the Union lost about 20 percent of their strength, the Confederates about 17 percent. Pope's 70,000 lost about 1,750 killed, 8,450 wounded, and 4,250 captured or missing. Lee's 55,000 lost 1,550 killed, 7,750 wounded, and about 100 unaccounted for. The battlefield was horrible. Clods of mud were heaped in the shallow trenches and graves, for there was much work and very little time. Hundreds received no burial at all. The Confederate army had to move.

Stonewall Jackson already had his tired men slogging north on another circling maneuver. Lee had beaten the Federal army badly, but he had not destroyed it as he had hoped. He wanted to try again before they retreated to the safety of the defenses of Washington. Jackson crossed Bull Run at Sudley Springs and headed for the Little River Turnpike, where he turned sharply to the right on the route to Fairfax, eight miles in Pope's rear. Roads were muddy, rations again short, troops fatigued, and by day's end Jackson had covered only ten miles. The next day, September 1, the weather was dismal and the going even slower. Late in the day, near a Virginia country estate named Chantilly, the Federals came from the south looking for a fight.

Pope, aware something was afoot north of him, began withdrawing toward Fairfax, at the same time dispatching troops to block the Little River Turnpike. Brigadier General Issac Steven's division marched cross-country and attacked immediately. Jackson faced his three divisions south to meet him. When Steven's line crossed a fenced cornfield advancing toward a Confederate held woodline, the gathering dark clouds rolled with thunder, lightning split the sky, and rain came down in torrents. Stevens pushed his line forward in the downpour until he fell dead, shot through the temple. The attack came to a soggy halt.

The driving rainstorm made it impossible for soldiers to load without soaking their cartridges. But when one of A.P. Hill's colonels requested his outfit be relieved because his rifles were useless, the army's commander, Jackson, sternly replied the enemy's ammunition was just as wet as his.

One-armed Phil Kearny splashed to the front at dusk and tried to get the Union attack going again, but the conditions were so bad, the men so miserable, even he could get no response. Galloping through the storm he rode into a Confederate skirmish line and was shot to death before he could escape. "Poor Kearny," said A.P. Hill, viewing the body. "He deserved a better death than that."

After Kearny fell, the inconclusive fighting sputtered to an end in the darkness. The Federals lost two of their best generals and about 1,000 men, the Confederates about half as many. Jackson's maneuver was thwarted, and the Federals slipped off to Fairfax.

On September 2 Old Pete Longstreet's corps joined the troops and the whole army rested. Stuart reported the Federal army heading for Washington. Fortifications there were much too strong for a successful assault, and the suffering Confederate supply situation compelled Lee to look toward Maryland, beyond the Potomac. He could not remain where he was, idle. Western Marylanders were pro-Southern. They might provide recruits and provisions. With the defeated Federal army recovering in Washington, Lee believed he would have time for his own army to refresh itself in the enemy's territory before they marched out for a fight.

In scarcely three months since taking command, Lee had moved the war from the suburbs of Richmond to the environs of his opponent's capital. Washington lived on rumors while Pope's army was out of communication. Then muffled gunfire shook the breezes coming out of the southwest from Virginia. A bulletin from the Treasury Department first announced a great victory. At Secretary of War Edwin Stanton's call, surgeons and male nurses were urged to journey to the battlefield and minister to the Federal wounded, said to number 10,000. Then came shocking news of a military disaster.

Frightened and bewildered crowds gathered. Some said the Army of the Potomac had refused to fight; some of its officers, supposedly, deliberately caused the defeat. One wild rumor said McDowell had committed a treasonous act and Franz Sigel had shot him. General Schenck's arriving ambulance was surrounded by an agitated crowd. "Why, General, is that you?" "Yes," replied Schenck un-

covering his wound, "and they have shattered me." All across Washington it was repeated; Schenck had said "our army is scattered."

President Abraham Lincoln called his personal secretary John Hay from his bedroom—"Well, John, we are whipped again, I'm afraid."

All the while the great engagement took place in Virginia, a different sort of battle was being waged across the Potomac. While Jackson's Confederates feasted on Federal supplies at Manassas Junction, General George McClellan had arrived at Alexandria, and reported for duty to Halleck. Part of his assignment was to forward reinforcements from his own Army of the Potomac to Pope, his despised rival. Halleck agreed to his suggestion to have Edwin Sumner's corps protect Washington, but he wanted William Franklin's sent to Pope as soon as possible. McClellan ordered Franklin to move, then countermanded the order. There was no cavalry escort, and the corps' artillery had no horses; the corps was not in fighting condition.

While Pope's soldiers were storming the blazing railroad embankment, McClellan reported he heard Lee with 120,000 Rebels was about to descend on the capital. He wanted to know if Halleck was certain Franklin should leave the capital. Halleck sent preemptory orders for Franklin to move at once. Franklin's force "crawled" ten miles to Annandale and halted. Halleck angrily telegraphed, "this is contrary to my orders." McClellan cooly wired back he had obeyed orders; henceforth Halleck should be more specific with his instructions, "for I have simply exercised the discretion you committed to me."

While Pope's beaten troops retreated across Bull Run, Halleck collapsed in bed "utterly tired out."

Lincoln was among those who believed McClellan had wanted Pope to

fail. In proposing alternatives for Washington's safety, McClellan had used the phrase "leave Pope to get out of his scrape."

Secretary of War Stanton, who had been passive since Halleck came east, sent a demand to Halleck's office for a full record regarding McClellan's movement from the Peninsula to northern Virginia, and he asked if any slackness had endangered national security. Halleck's reply was, all things considered, McClellan could have moved faster. Stanton and Treasury Secretary Salmon Chase prepared a protest for other cabinet members' signatures. Addressed to Lincoln, it demanded McClellan's dismissal. Chase's real opinion was that McClellan should be taken out and shot.

Lincoln, however, had his ear to the political ground. McClellan and his vision of the Union cause was espoused by the Democratic party, and McClellan was beginning to be regarded as the leader of the opposition. Lincoln needed support from the Democrats for recruits and war legislation. Furthermore, the army, upon whose strained shoulders the nation depended, was devoted to this general. The army wanted McClellan, and if any part of the current rumors were true, it might not fight for anyone else. Indeed, there was no one else. Pope was finished. Halleck had collapsed under pressure. "There is no man in the Army," concluded Lincoln, "who can man these fortifications and lick these troops of our's into shape half as well as he."

On September 2, after a stormy night, General McClellan was at an early breakfast at his house on H Street when the president and General Halleck came and asked him to take command of Washington and the troops falling back from Manassas. For the time being, the future was his.

Troops of the 2d Michigan Infantry regiment, veterans of Second Manassas, strike solemn poses for the camera. Many were veterans of McClellan's Peninsula Campaign and the earlier horrors at the First Battle of Bull Run.

ANTIETAM

Text by Edward J. Stackpole
Designed by Frederic Ray

212

AS NIGHT fell and the sounds of fighting faded along the crest and eastern slope of South Mountain on Sunday, Sept. 14, 1862, Gen. Robert E. Lee made a reluctant decision. He would withdraw his Army of Northern Virginia from Maryland and give up his first major invasion of the North without fighting a showdown battle with the Union Army of the Potomac.

At 8 p. m. he sent this message to Lafayette McLaws, who commanded two of the six Confederate divisions besieging Harpers Ferry:

> General: The day has gone against us and this army will go by Sharpsburg and cross the river. It is necessary for you to abandon your position [on Maryland Heights] . . . ascertain the best crossing of the Potomac, and if you can find any between you and Shepherdstown, leave the Shepherdstown Ford for this command . . .

Lee's soldierly language did not reveal his disappointment. In crossing the Potomac after his overwhelming victory at Second Manassas on August 30, he had expected to (1) win Maryland to the Southern cause, (2) eliminate the Federal garrison at Harpers Ferry before the Army of the Potomac could reorganize, and (3) with his communications thus secured, move deep into Pennsylvania in hopes of winning a major victory on Union soil, a victory that would bring foreign recognition of the Confederacy.

But Maryland had responded coolly to Confederate appeals. Maj. Gen. George B. McClellan had restored the morale of the Army of the Potomac, reorganized its units, and put its 87,000 men in the field much sooner than expected. Even worse, a Union soldier had found a copy of Lee's detailed march orders at Frederick on the morning of September 13 and had delivered it to McClellan. These orders spelled out how Lee would divide his army to capture Harpers Ferry and carry out other missions before making a bold thrust into Pennsylvania.

AS A RESULT of this Union luck, the Army of the Potomac now was making an attack on the gaps of the South Mountain range which sheltered the scattered Confederate units. Unless Lee withdrew quickly across the Potomac, it seemed the Federals would clear the outnumbered Confederate defenders from the passes and defeat his army in detail.

As he dictated his note to McLaws, Lee had one piece of good fortune to reflect on. A Confederate sympathizer had overheard a Union staff discussion of the lost orders and had tipped him off quickly that McClellan knew about the divided state of the Confederates. Thus Lee had been able to plug the mountain gaps and force McClellan to deploy his army. He had been lucky, too, in that McClellan had not been faster in carrying out his announced plan "to cut Lee in two and beat him in detail." Over-estimating Confederate strength at "120,000 or more men" (Lee really had only about 43,000), McClellan delayed the march of his 18 divisions for 17 hours after reading the lost orders.

But now the ponderous strength of the Federals was being exerted against the South Mountain passes. Stonewall Jackson, with six divisions, was still involved in the siege of Harpers Ferry. Lee seemed to have no choice. He ordered Maj. Gen. James Longstreet to withdraw his three divisions from the passes to Sharpsburg, Md. preparatory to crossing to the southern bank of the Potomac.

WHY THEN was the Battle of Antietam fought on September 17? Why did Lee change his mind about giving battle on the north side of the Potomac? He did so because of a message that came from Stonewall Jackson at Harpers Ferry the night of September 14. Jackson reported that the Federal garrison of 11,000 men probably would surrender the next morning and that most of his men could rejoin Lee soon after. This news restored Lee's fighting spirit. Even before Longstreet had disengaged his three divisions from the Federals on South Mountain, Lee had decided to concentrate his scattered army *north* of the Potomac, near the village of Sharpsburg.

Thanks to McClellan's sluggish pursuit, Longstreet, covered by Stuart's cavalry, was able to reach Sharpsburg during the morning of September 15. There on the high ground west of Antietam Creek, Lee assigned positions to his three divisions for defense and settled down to await the arrival of the six divisions under Jackson, Walker, and McLaws. It was a magnificent bluff. On that day Lee had only 18,000 effectives at Sharpsburg, after deducting casualties suffered at South Mountain. But Lee understood McClellan and had so far recovered his poise as to predict that his opponent would not attack on either September 15 or 16. Although the Federals outnumbered him more than four to one, Lee felt sure that "Little Mac" would have every man and gun placed to his satisfaction before committing his army. The two additional days of grace should find the Confederates fully reassembled, although even then at a strength disadvantage of at least two to one.

The major part of the Army of the Potomac on the afternoon of September 15 was within easy striking distance of Sharpsburg, having followed Longstreet's column by a few hours. A vigorous attack could have driven Lee into the Potomac, but McClellan figured that his troops were tired and should be given a night's rest. The following day was spent in placing his infantry and artillery in position for attack and then personally inspecting the entire line. While McClellan dallied, Jackson's corps (less A. P. Hill's and Walker's divisions) came on the field

THE DUNKER CHURCH—Hundreds of men on both sides died in the see-saw fighting that raged around this small church. This photograph from the Library of Congress, by James Gardner, shows some of the dead left on the field.

BRIDGE ACROSS THE ANTIETAM—This is one of the stone bridges which crossed Antietam Creek in the vicinity of where the battle of Sept. 17, 1862 was fought. This was the "middle bridge" where the Boonsboro Pike crossed.

(by midday September 16), which left only three of Lee's nine divisions (McLaws, Anderson, and A. P. Hill) still absent. The Federal advantage was dissolving hour by hour and still McClellan waited.

THE Confederate position at Sharpsburg was tactically advantageous for defense except for some terrain limitations. The battle area was in a bend of the Potomac and only three miles from Shepherdstown. The left of Lee's curving line rested on the Potomac, the right on Antietam Creek, a stream 60 to 100 feet wide that was fordable at a number of points and crossable at three stone arch bridges, located at varying distances of a mile and upwards from the Confederate line of defense. Space for maneuver was limited, but Lee had the advantage of interior lines. The enemy would find it difficult to outflank him. The position nevertheless was exposed to artillery fire from the ridges east of Antietam Creek and vulnerable in the event of a serious reverse, for with the Potomac at his back Lee would then be in trouble, the ford at Shepherdstown being his only nearby escape route.

ANTIETAM CREEK was a natural dividing line between the opposing armies. The Confederates made no attempt to destroy any of the stone bridges, possibly because Lee wanted to force the Federals to approach in column so as to present concentrated targets for his artillery. The battle area, aside from the town itself, where five important roads converge, was mostly open country, but with patches of woods here and there. The cultivated farm lands and certain of the woods were soon to achieve an historic status, but of the stone bridges only the one southeast of the town was to gain distinction.

UPON his arrival on the scene McClellan had established his headquarters in the garden of the Pry House, situated to the north of the Boonsboro Road about midway between Keedysville and Porterstown. Atop a hill overlooking the Antietam approximately two miles by air from the eastern end of Sharpsburg, the position commanded an excellent view of that portion of the battle area not obscured by woods and the north-south ridge on whose reverse slope nestled the little town of Sharpsburg.

Lee selected a small grove just north of the Boonsboro Road on the western edge of town, in which to pitch his headquarters tents.

About 2 p.m. on September 16, McClellan ordered Maj. Gen. Joseph Hooker to take his I Corps (three divisions) across the Antietam at the upper bridge and nearby fords to a position perpendicular to the Hagerstown Road from which to launch an attack against the left of Lee's line. Hooker was told that he would be supported by Maj. Gen. Joseph K. F. Mansfield's XII Corps (two divisions). Hooker's approach march was executed in broad daylight without any attempt at concealment, with the result that Lee was given advance information of the point toward which McClellan was aiming his punch.

Meade's division, in the lead, ran into Confederate pickets about sunset, resulting in a minor skirmish at about the time that Federal guns opened fire on the Confederate lines from the hills east of Antietam Creek. Thus alerted, Lee directed Longstreet to send Hood's division to counter the Federal infantry and told Jackson to move his troops into line on the left, facing north. A serious clash was prevented by darkness, when Hooker's corps halted. About midnight Mansfield's XII Corps followed Hooker and bivouacked about a mile northeast of the I Corps. Meanwhile, McClellan sent word to Maj.

Gen. William B. Franklin to bring his two-division VI Corps up from Pleasant Valley.

September 17 dawned gray and drizzly as Hooker's I Corps formed ranks and moved south to the attack, Meade's division in the center and guiding on the Hagerstown Road, with Doubleday and Ricketts on the right and left respectively. The sun soon dissipated the mists, and the troops were able clearly to see their objective, a whitewashed brick Dunker Church a mile or so to the front, which stood out in contrast against the dark-green background of the West Wood at the point where the Smoketown Road joined the Hagerstown Turnpike. Between the two roads as they approached a junction stood a field of tall corn, flanked on the east by another wooded area (the East Wood). It was over this terrain that Hooker's extended divisions marched to open the bloodiest single day's battle of the Civil War.

Awaiting the Federal attack on the left of Lee's line were two of Stonewall Jackson's divisions, his own under J. R. Jones and Ewell's under Lawton, covering the Hagerstown Turnpike and area on either side. D. H. Hill occupied the center of the four-mile line farther south, while on Hill's right the responsibility for the defense rested with Longstreet, only three of whose divisions, Hood's, D. R. Jones', and Walker's, were on hand. McLaws and Anderson were coming, but meantime Lee would have to stave off repeated Union attacks with what he had available, approximately 28,000 effectives, supported by 200 guns. The defense of the mile of terrain between Jackson's left and the looping Potomac River was assigned to the cavalry of Jeb Stuart, whose horse artillery under such able artillerymen as Pelham, Chew, and Hart created the illusion that the thin line was solidly held—by the simple but effective device of shifting gun positions between bursts of fire.

THE UNION ARMY'S great strength superiority and the confident feeling among the troops that they now had the vaunted Army of Northern Virginia on the run were together a pretty fair guarantee that aggressive leadership would have promptly paid off in driving Lee off the Sharpsburg ridge and into the Potomac.

The overly cautious McClellan didn't see it that way. He had a plan, which he apparently kept pretty much to himself at the time, but explained in his post-battle report in this fashion: "to make the main attack on the enemy's left—at least to create a diversion in favor of the main attack, with the hope of something more by assailing the enemy's right—and as soon as one or both of the flank movements were fully successful, to attack their center with any reserve that I might then have in hand."

The plan was a conventional one and entirely feasible, except in several rather important respects. No ground reconnaissance or probing operation had been undertaken to ascertain the strength or weakness of Lee's defense line. Nor were his corps commanders taken into McClellan's confidence so they might accomplish their missions in a co-ordinated drive. McClellan's self-sufficiency presumably dictated a policy of keeping battle control in his own hands, despite the fact that his command post at the Pry House was too far removed for that to be effective.

For some inscrutable reason during the first two years of the war, Union army commanders were wont to employ the piecemeal method of attack. No evidence exists that at Sharpsburg McClellan even considered a co-ordinated attack in which each corps would be given a mission to fit in with the overall tactical conception. On the contrary, each corps was committed by successive oral orders from headquarters, without informing the other corps commanders, and without instructions for mutual support. After the same pattern, with one or two

OPENING OF THE BATTLE—The Battle of Antietam began with an attack on the Confederate left by Hooker's division. Here, in a sketch by F. H. Schell, the Federals are shown fording Antietam Creek the day before the attack.

215

WHERE CONFEDERATES CONFERRED—Lee held a conference in Sharpsburg with Longstreet and D. H. Hill in this house, which was the residence of Jacob H. Grove. Lee's headquarters, however, were in a tent pitched in a small grove on the right of the Shepherdstown Road, just outside of the town. (From "Battles & Leaders")

exceptions, the corps commanders in turn duplicated the McClellan method by sending in their own divisions to the attack in the same piecemeal fashion.

Hooker's approach march preceding contact with Jackson's toughened veterans was facilitated by his corps artillery, which from well-sited positions at the southern edge of the North Wood poured a heavy rain of shells over the heads of the advancing bluecoats into the ranks of the Confederates. At the same time, from across Antietam Creek, General Hunt's rifled Parrotts threw their shells into the Confederate line with devastating effect. As the guns roared their initial greeting from two directions, Mansfield's XII Corps moved out after Hooker, guiding on the Smoketown Road, both divisions in a single line with Williams on the right, Greene on the left.

HOOD'S Texas and Mississippi division, after the skirmish of his pickets with the leading elements of Meade's Union division on the evening of September 16, had been pulled back to give the men their first opportunity in several days to cook a hot meal. Hood was consequently not in position to assist Jackson in repelling Hooker's opening attack, which made rapid progress for a time. In the early stages the weight of the Union assault, 9,400 strong, drove back in confusion brigade after brigade of the Confederates. Jackson was in trouble, but when he called on Hood to get back in the fight, the fiery Texans came charging into the flank of Gibbon's detached brigade, which had outrun the rest of the Union I Corps and was just emerging from Miller's corn-

field, now covered with Confederate dead. Gibbon recoiled, but Rickett's division on Meade's left made steady progress and gradually drove the Confederates back into the West Wood. Doubleday on the right, west of the turnpike, got nowhere, and lost heavily on account of shells from Stuart's horse artillery.

By 7 o'clock the fighting had become general in the area of the cornfield, the Dunker Church, and the West Wood. The battle lines surged back and forth with local successes and failures occurring in such rapid succession that it was difficult for either side to tell who was winning. Losses were enormous; shells crashed indiscriminately on Federals and Confederates alike; blue and gray regiments melted into scattered fragments as the early morning hours passed and the casualties steadily mounted.

Although Hooker's attack had crested and then receded, Jackson's situation remained critical. Another Union corps could be seen moving to the attack. Lee began shifting troops from the right of his line to meet it, a risky undertaking which could have been fatal if McClellan had displayed equal field generalship. One of D. H. Hill's brigades from the center and Walker's division from the right were summoned to Jackson's support. Since there were no reserves, all Lee could do in this crisis was to transfer troops from those parts of his line which were not then under Federal pressure.

Hooker's attack had lost momentum in the face of Jackson's stubborn defense and Hood's counterattack, but when Mansfield led his Federal XII Corps of 6,500 men into the fight he was under the mistaken impression that the I Corps was getting the better of it. A former Inspector General of the Army, the 59-year-old Mansfield was an imposing figure with his flowing white locks and towering stature. As he approached the East Wood, Hooker galloped up and shouted that his own divisions were being driven back—Mansfield must hold the East Wood to check the advancing Confederates.

THE PRY HOUSE—McClellan had his headquarters in this house. This position offered a good view of the battle area but it lay two miles from Sharpsburg, north of the Boonsboro Road about midway between Keedysville and Porterstown. (From "Battles & Leaders")

HOOKER'S ATTACK—The facing map shows the start of the battle at daybreak on September 17. Hooker's I Corps, led by Meade's division, is striking straight south, followed by Ricketts and Doubleday.

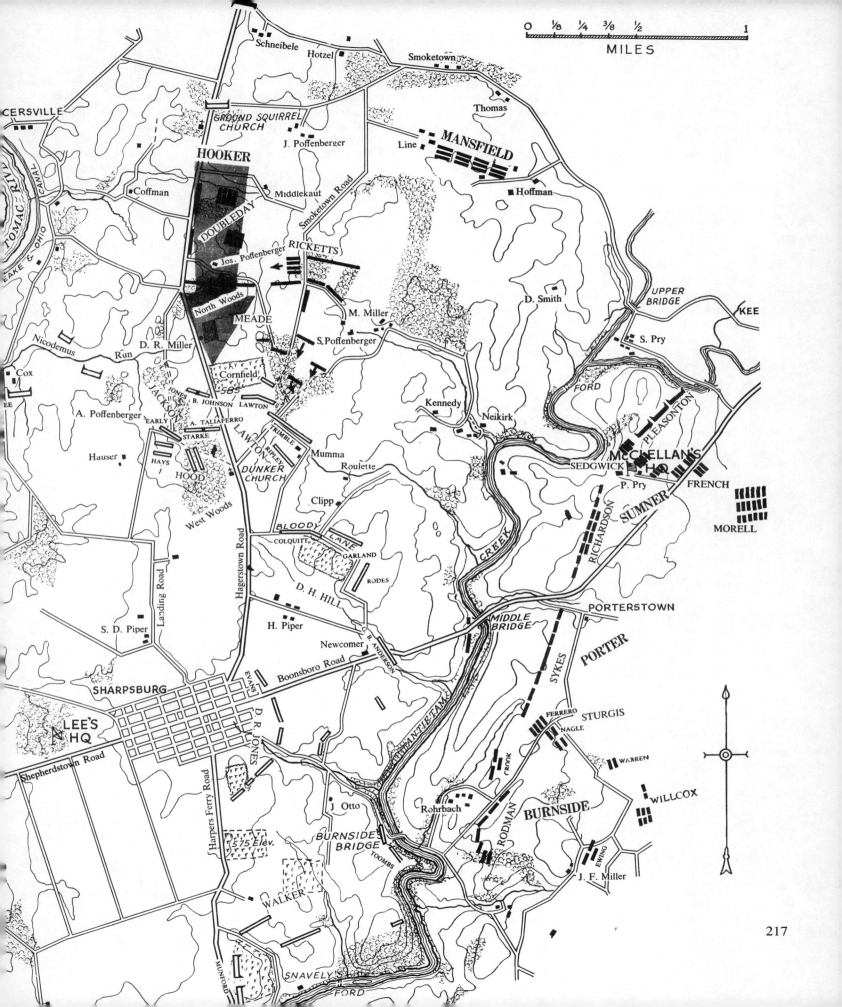

O 1/8 1/4 3/8 1/2   1
MILES

CERSVILLE

POTOMAC RIVER

CHESAPEAKE & OHIO CANAL

Schneibele   Hotzel
GROUND SQUIRREL CHURCH   Smoketown
                                                        Thomas
                    J. Poffenberger   Line   MANSFIELD
HOOKER   Hoffman
    Coffman   Middlekauf
                Smoketown Road
DOUBLEDAY
              RICKETTS   D. Smith
        Jos. Poffenberger   UPPER BRIDGE
    North Woods   KEE
              MEADE   M. Miller   S. Pry
Nicodemus   D. R. Miller   S. Poffenberger   FORD
    Run   Kennedy   McCLELLAN'S HQ
Cox   Cornfield 585   Neikirk PLEASONTON
                JONES B. JOHNSON LAWTON   SEDGWICK
EE A. Poffenberger EARLY A. TALIAFERRO   P. Pry   FRENCH
              STARKE   SUMNER
    Hauser   HAYS JACKSON LAWTON TRIMBLE Mumma   MORELL
              HOOD DUNKER RIPLEY Roulette
                    CHURCH
              West Woods Clipp
                    BLOODY LANE CREEK
                COLQUITT GARLAND
    Landing Road Hagerstown Road RODES
                    D. H. HILL   PORTERSTOWN
    S. D. Piper   H. Piper   MIDDLE BRIDGE
              Newcomer B. ANDERSON   SYKES PORTER
              Boonsboro Road
SHARPSBURG EVANS   FERRERO STURGIS
LEE'S HQ D. R. JONES   NAGLE
                                          CROOK   WARREN
Shepherdstown Road Harpers Ferry Road   WILLCOX
                                          RODMAN BURNSIDE
              J. Otto   Rohrbach
              575 Elev.
              BURNSIDE BRIDGE TOOMBS   EWING
                                          J. F. Miller
    WALKER
              ANTIETAM CREEK
MUNFORD SNAVELY'S FORD

217

Believing that Hooker's men still held the East Wood, Mansfield rode forward to reconnoiter and received a fatal Confederate bullet in the stomach. Brig. Gen. A. S. Williams, senior division commander of the Corps, took over and renewed the attack, while the I Corps withdrew to its initial positions to regroup under Meade (Hooker having been wounded in the foot).

WILLIAMS' own division, under Brig. Gen. S. W. Crawford, advanced toward West Wood while Greene followed the ridge leading to the East Wood, so that the two divisions diverged as they advanced. Crawford took heavy punishment from the Confederates in the West Wood, but Greene, meeting lighter opposition, cleared the East Wood and flanked Hood in turn out of the Miller cornfield. Ultimately (after Sumner's II Corps had joined the fray) Greene gained a precarious foothold in the West Wood near the Dunker Church, where he held a spearhead position until shortly after noon, expecting every minute that reinforcements would move up to enable him to consolidate his gains.

SLAUGHTER in the CORNFIELD—The situation about 7 a. m., when Hooker's attack had reached its height, is indicated here. The fighting is swirling around the West Woods and in D. R. Miller's cornfield. Mansfield's XII Corps is coming in to join Hooker. About this time Mansfield is fatally wounded, being succeeded by Brig. Gen. A. S. Williams. Hooker is also wounded, and is succeeded by Meade.

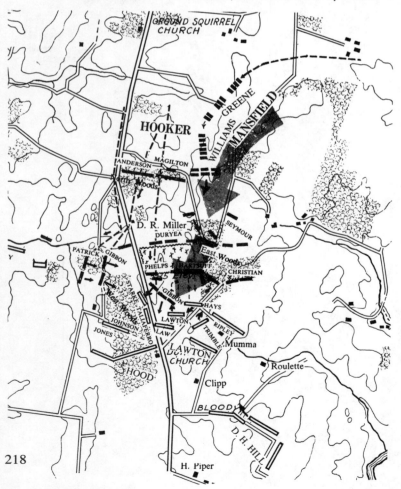

Short one of his brigades, which had earlier been detached, Greene took into the battle fewer than 2,000 men, but they were all well trained and had had previous battle experience. And they showed it, under their aggressive old leader (Greene was 61), whose penetration of Jackson's defense, if followed up by supporting troops, might have changed the course of the battle. The divergent attacks by the two divisions of the corps had created a wide gap. Crawford had fought his division out, Greene could do nothing further without reinforcements, and so this, the second of successive corps attacks, ground to a halt.*

NOW CAME the third of McClellan's piecemeal attacks. Maj. Gen. Edwin V. Sumner's II Corps attempted what the I and XII had failed to accomplish. Sumner, who received McClellan's order at 7:20 a.m. to cross the Antietam in support of the two corps already engaged, commanded the largest corps in the army, three divisions with a paper strength of over 18,000, more than 15,000 of them fighting men. But only Sedgwick's and French's divisions moved out together, shortly after 7:30. Because of indifferent staff work at corps or army level it was 9:30 before Richardson got the word. Advancing in column of divisions, each in line of brigade columns, the 10,000 men of the two divisions moved across country in so orderly a fashion, colors flying as though on parade, that the waiting Confederates made no effort to conceal their admiration.

When the center of the corps reached a point opposite the Dunker Church, the columns at a given signal changed direction by the left flank and were at once in battle formation to advance to the attack with divisions abreast, Sedgwick on the right, French on the left. Greene's division of the XII Corps had not yet made its penetration of Jackson's line, but the gap between Williams (Crawford) and Greene had already occurred and it was through that gap that Sedgwick advanced, while French moved up on Greene's left.

Sumner came on the field without being told just where to go or what his specific mission might be, other than to support the attack. The I Corps had been put out of circulation and the XII had had about all it could take without help. The two division commanders of the II Corps led their troops in the general direction of the Confederate line, Sedgwick heading for the West Wood, while French guided more in a southwesterly direction, where Confederate Gen. D. H. Hill, a rugged fighter, held the center of Lee's line.

---

*The author is indebted to Dwight E. Stinson, Jr., former National Park Service Historian, Antietam National Battlefield Site, for permission to use herein the results of his detailed "Analytical Study of the Action of Greene's Division," which clarifies much of the confusion that has existed in various accounts of the battle. According to Mr. Stinson, the movements and actions of that undersized division throughout the better part of the morning represented the Union key to the battle, serving as the central but unrecognized connecting link between the right and left of the Federal attacks, without regard to corps zones.

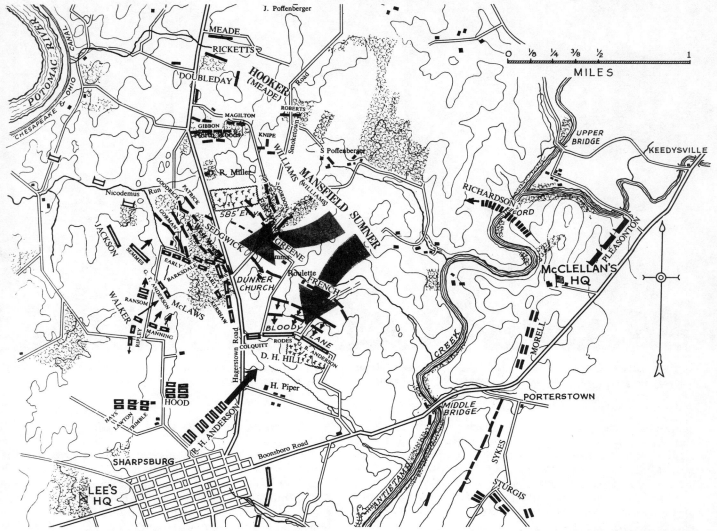

FEDERAL ARMY IS COMMITTED PIECEMEAL—The situation is shown from about 9 to 9:45 a. m. Sumner's corps has been thrown in, and with Mansfield's (Williams') is pressing the attack toward West Woods and also the sunken road (Bloody Lane). Lee's divisions are in a critical condition, with heavy losses, and being assailed by successive heavy blows. But McLaws is deploying, having just arrived from Harpers Ferry, and Anderson has nearly reached the battle line. This is the moment when Burnside should have attacked on the south.

DURING the successive attacks by the I and XII Corps, the Federals had succeeded in clearing the East Wood and Miller cornfield of Confederates, whose line then changed from one facing north to one facing generally east, extending through the West Wood. Unaware that Greene's division of the XII Corps held a front line position on the Mumma farm, and that as Sedgwick and French advanced they would overrun Greene's line unless they fanned out to right and left of him, Sumner directed the advance of his corps as though Greene didn't exist. This oversight was shortly to prove fatal to Sedgwick's division through failure to provide the flank protection that Greene's division could have afforded.

The forward movements of Sumner's two divisions were observed by the watchful Jackson, who realized the threat from this powerful new force on his front and did everything possible to meet it. Sedgwick was peppered by artillery as he approached the Hagerstown Road from open country to the east, as Jubal Early, commanding what was left of Ewell's division after Lawton had been wounded, was hustled over from the extreme left with but 600 men to strengthen the line in the West Wood and around the Dunker Church.

It was at this critical moment, about 10:30 a.m., that Walker's division arrived from below Sharpsburg, together with McLaws' division, just up from Harpers Ferry after a hard march. Stonewall Jackson, never willing to admit defeat, had drafted orders for a counterattack in anticipation of just such an opportunity as now offered. Sedgwick by this time had penetrated the West Wood and there was nothing in front to stop him. Suddenly the shrill Rebel yell rang out as McLaws' brigades, just arriving, dashed forward at the double, stopped, and poured heavy volleys of musketry into the flanks of Sedgwick's division. Not a planned ambush, this nevertheless took the Federals completely by surprise, with no chance to change direction.

The effect on Sedgwick was disastrous, 2,200 of his men being killed and wounded in not much more time than it takes to tell it. Sedgwick himself received his third wound of the day, whereupon his leaderless troops faded rapidly to the protection of the solid phalanx of Federal artillery batteries posted in the North Wood. The Union guns in front of Jackson's sector all during the morning battle served as the rock against which Confederate counterattacks dashed themselves in vain and

219

CONFEDERATE ARTILLERY—In this painting by Capt. James Hope, Confederate guns commanded by Col. Stephen D. Lee prepare to meet the advance of Sedgwick's division. The Dunker Church may be seen at upper left.

behind which a succession of retreating Union brigades and divisions were halted and reorganized. It was this artillery that stopped McLaws in his pursuit of Sedgwick, caused him to lose 40 per cent of his men, and forced his retirement to the cover of the West Wood.

That ended the battle on Jackson's front. In five hours of desperate, deadly in-fighting, two Union corps and part of a third, six divisions in all, representing one-third of McClellan's army, had been unable to break Jackson's line. Yet they had inflicted terrible punishment on the Confederates, whose casualties in that period ran to 6,000 killed and wounded against 7,000 for the attackers.

NOW the second phase of the Battle of Antietam commenced in earnest, as the center of gravity of the contending armies shifted southward, where along a sunken lane D. H. Hill was fighting gamely to hold in check the growing strength of Federal units who were pouring into that zone more by force of circumstance than plan. French's division of Sumner's II Corps made progress against Hill until R. H. Anderson's Confederate division came to his defense.

On the Union side, Sumner's third division under Richardson, arriving late, added 5,000 reinforcements to French's attack. The fighting raged in the "Bloody Lane" (Sunken Road) and contiguous fields from 10 until 1 o'clock, swirling back and forth over the Roulette farm and Piper's cornfield even more viciously than around the Dunker Church. This was Longstreet's fight, and when there was defensive battle to be waged "Old Pete" had no peer. But accurate counterbattery fire from Hunt's efficient Union guns across Antietam Creek had done their work so well that all but 12 of Lee's guns had been put out of action on this part of the front. French and Richardson between them finally overcame the tenacious Confederate resistance; the field was cleared of defenders, Bloody Lane and the ridge beyond the cornfield were firmly secured by the Federals, and the second phase of the battle terminated.

The two Federal divisions paid a high price for their victory, with division commander Richardson receiving a mortal wound and Union losses amounting to almost 3,000; but the Confederates, although their casualties exceeded those of Sumner's divisions, were still able to hold grimly their somewhat retracted original line. They were "badly whipped," in Longstreet's words, but they wouldn't admit the fact, and since McClellan didn't seem to know when or where he was ahead of the game, it became evident that Lee was as yet far from licked.

WHILE THE BATTLE on Jackson's front was still in progress about mid-morning, McClellan had sent Franklin's VI Corps across the creek with Slocum's and Smith's divisions, 10,000 men in all. Coming up to General Sumner, who seemed to have lost some of his martial enthusiasm, Franklin suggested accurately that it appeared as though the Confederates on Lee's left were played out, and that a strong counterattack by his fresh divisions could carry that part of the field. Influenced no doubt by his own lack of success and Sedgwick's disaster, Sumner dissented and was supported in his opinion by McClellan himself, who appeared on the field at that moment. Consequently Franklin's offer to attack was rejected, with the result that Slocum's division took no part in the battle, while Smith's played only a minor, supplementary role by plugging a gap in the Union line, without material influence on the overall outcome.

A. P. HILL TO THE RESCUE—Burnside has finally forced a crossing at the stone bridge which now bears his name, and his divisions are slowly advancing toward Sharpsburg. At this juncture, so critical for Lee, A. P. Hill's division arrives from Harpers Ferry, and shortly is launched in a counterattack against Burnside's flank. This stops Burnside, and soon McClellan gives up any further effort to attack.

DURING THE EVENING Lee's generals rode in from their several posts to the Commanding General's headquarters tent, to confer on plans for the following day. All knew how close to disaster the army had come, and none had any illusions as to the fate that might still befall it. Battle losses and march stragglers had reduced Lee's strength to 30,000 men or less, while McClellan's army, after losses, still exceeded 62,000 able-bodied soldiers, almost one-third of whom had not been engaged in the battle.

It was apparent from their reports that all the generals, including Jackson, were convinced that a retreat to Virginia was both logical and inevitable, but Lee calmly informed them that the army would remain in its present position for another day; if McClellan chose to attack they would meet it. Psychological warfare? Perhaps, but it was more than a mere bluff, which Lee did not believe McClellan would have the courage to call. Clearly he hated the thought of retreat, an admission that his invasion had failed, and he may still have hoped for another opportunity to try the outflanking maneuver around the Federal right that he had wanted Jackson and Stuart to undertake on the afternoon of September 17. It was not enough that he had deprived McClellan of a victory, for militarily the Battle of Antietam was a stalemate.

But a stalemate was a new experience for the Army of Northern Virginia, one that its Commanding General did not relish.

DURING the early morning of September 18 two additional Union divisions under Generals Couch and Humphreys reached the field, but according to McClellan they were tired and "needed rest and refreshment" before he would ask them to fight! The contrast with A. P. Hill's Light Division needs no comment. Said McClellan: "After a night of anxious deliberation and a full and careful survey of the situation and condition of our army [this from his after-battle report], the strength and position of the enemy, I concluded that the success of an attack on the eighteenth was not certain."

Having demonstrated to both armies his moral ascendancy, Lee commenced his retrograde movement after midnight September 18-19. No attempt was made by McClellan to interfere with the movement across the Potomac ford below Shepherdstown. It was not until Lee was safely across the river with his entire army, including trains and the wounded, that the Union commander lifted a finger even to harass the withdrawal.

THROUGH THE CORNFIELD—Union soldiers charging through D. R. Miller's cornfield at Antietam are shown in this drawing from "Battles & Leaders." Fighting raged in this vicinity during the early hours of the battle.

FREDERICKSBURG

Text by Edward J. Stackpole
Designed by Frederic Ray

FREDERICKSBURG, Virginia was shrouded by a dense fog that reduced visibility almost to zero in the wintry, pre-dawn darkness of Thursday, December 11, 1862. Pickets of Brigadier General William Barksdale's Mississippi brigade, Confederate Army of Northern Virginia, shivered in the raw morning air as they stood guard along the banks of the Rappahannock River at the eastern edge of town. General Robert E. Lee's watchdogs had for some time been waiting for Major General Ambrose E. Burnside, newly appointed commander of the Union Army of the Potomac, to commence the long-awaited crossing of his vast body of troops.

Early that morning the nocturnal quiet was suddenly broken by the sharp bark of two Confederate cannon posted on the range of hills immediately west of Fredericksburg. With this signal from Read's battery, Major General Lafayette McLaws, responsible for the immediate security of the town, alerted the sleeping Confederates of Longstreet's corps to the fact that the Union army was at long last on the move.

THE PROSPECT of action that would end the suspense of waiting day after day must have quickened the pulses of the men in ranks. The opposing armies had been fully assembled in the Fredericksburg area, facing one another across the Rappahannock, for ten days, during which the Federal commander deliberated in a welter of uncertainty as to when, where, and how to initiate his offensive.

This period of watchful waiting was lightened by an occasional snowball fight on the Confederate side of the river, with at least one evening of conviviality when several bored Union bands, near their end of the partly demolished railroad bridge, decided to break the monotony. Tuning up their instruments, the combined bands broke into "Hail Columbia" and "The Star Spangled Banner" without eliciting any reaction from the Confederates. Finally they struck up "Dixie." That broke the ice, figuratively speaking, and caused much cheering and laughter on both sides of the river. But the friendly concert proved a costly bit of fun for the Federals because it aroused the suspicions of McLaws, who promptly put his men to work digging additional rifle pits from which his sharpshooters would later be able to pour a lethal fire against Burnside's bridge-building engineers.

Burnside's Initial Actions

AFTER the Battle of Antietam, fought on September 17, 1862, the two armies faced each other warily across the Potomac. Why were they now, nearly three months later, still confronting each other on opposite sides of a river, but seventy-five miles farther south?

Though Major General George B. McClellan had dallied in place almost two months after the advantage he had gained at Antietam, he finally moved ponderously southward; early in November his army of 120,000 men occupied the positions shown on Map 1. This placed "Little Mac" between the widely separated wings of Lee's 90,000-man army, so that by striking each successively he might have defeated Lee in detail. But he couldn't do it. He was too slow.

Four regiments were sent over in boats to secure a lodgement in Fredericksburg and drive Barksdale's men far enough away from the river to permit the pontoon bridges to be completed. ("Harpers")

224

Lee, knowing this, was unworried. Lincoln had the same opinion of the snail-like McClellan. His patience exhausted, the President relieved McClellan and placed Burnside in command of the Army of the Potomac.

Burnside, after assuming command on November 7, proposed an entirely different strategy for the coming campaign. It was to feint toward Culpeper Court House, then move the entire army rapidly to Falmouth, where he would cross the Rappahannock on pontoon bridges that Secretary of War Stanton would ship from Washington, following which his army would advance on Richmond. It was the same old "on to Richmond" obsession that had blinded previous Union generals to the basic fact that, as Lincoln repeatedly pointed out, the principal objective of the army was to engage and defeat the enemy in battle rather than strive to capture the Confederate Capital.

ONE OF BURNSIDE'S first acts upon taking command was to reduce the number of generals reporting directly to him. He did this by grouping the several infantry corps into wings that he called "grand divisions," each having two corps of three divisions plus artillery and a cavalry brigade. Major General Edwin V. Sumner commanded the Right Grand Division, Major General Joseph Hooker the Center Grand Division, and Major General William B. Franklin the Left Grand Division.

Overruling General-in-Chief Henry Halleck's preference for McClellan's plan of campaign, the President approved Burnside's proposal on November 14, even though his own judgment coincided with Halleck's. No doubt Lincoln concluded that Burnside showed promise of positive action, in contrast to McClellan's inactivity. Halleck's telegram to Burnside, quoting the perceptive Lincoln, stated: "The President thinks the plan will succeed if you move rapidly; otherwise not."

Initially Burnside displayed the celerity Lincoln desired. Within hours after receiving the President's message he started Sumner's grand division towards Falmouth, followed the next day by the rest of the army. Sumner covered the forty miles in less than three days, arriving at Falmouth on the 17th. On the 20th the entire army was assembled in the new area. The pontoons had not arrived, but Sumner on the 17th could have waded the river at one or more of the upstream fords had Burnside so ordered. Burnside won the race with Lee for Fredericksburg only to throw away this prime advantage by his obstinacy

---

Map 1. THE CONCENTRATION AT FREDERICKSBURG.
The routes of the several corps of both armies are shown from the beginning of Burnside's march on November 14 until both armies were facing each other across the Rappahannock at Fredericksburg. This map shows clearly that with an abler commander than McClellan or Burnside the Federals were in position prior to this march to strike either Longstreet at Culpeper or Jackson at Winchester before the other could intervene.

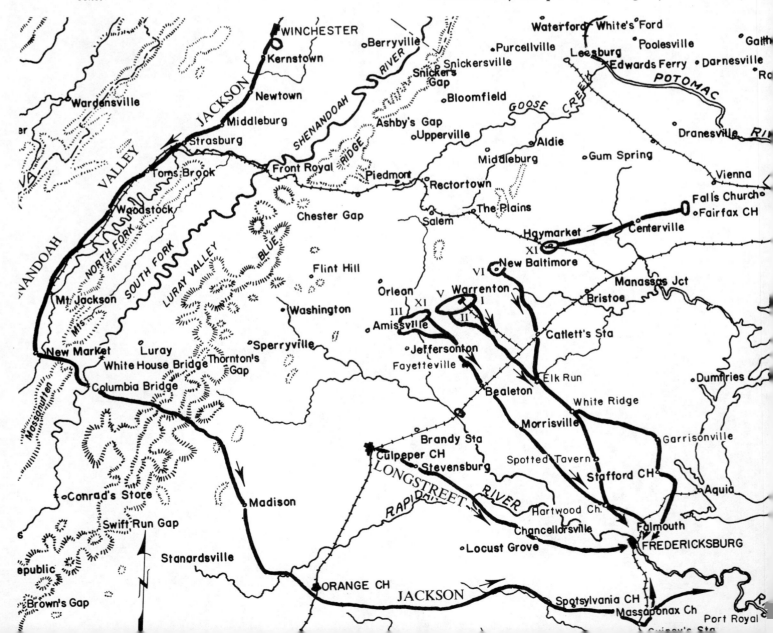

McClellan turning over command of the Army of the Potomac to Burnside. From an A. R. Waud drawing in "Harpers."

in waiting for the bridging material. Two days later, with Longstreet in possession of Fredericksburg, the rains descended, the river rose rapidly, and by then it was too late.

Lee's Reaction

WORD of the Federal change of command reached General Lee while he was considering how he would react to the several possibilities open to McClellan's invading army. Burnside's march on Fredericksburg rather than southwest toward Culpeper Court House came as a surprise, so that Sumner's wing was already at Falmouth before Lee could be certain that Fredericksburg was indeed the major Union objective. Only then had Longstreet been ordered to move in haste, from Culpeper, and at the same time Jackson's corps was directed to leave the Shenandoah Valley for Orange Court House, where he would halt, still thirty-five miles from Fredericksburg, until Lee could re-evaluate his own strategy in the light of Burnside's next move. On November 26, almost a week after the Union army had reached Falmouth, Lee wrote Jackson to bring his divisions to Fredericksburg. They arrived December 1, having marched approximately 150 miles in twelve days.

Rather than make a stand at Fredericksburg, Lee would have preferred to fight thirty miles farther south, along the line of the North Anna River, which he believed offered a more favorable opportunity to turn the defensive into a counteroffensive. But Jefferson Davis, concerned as ever about the safety of the Capital, thought differently, and Lee did not press the point.

Uncertainty as to where Burnside would cross, if he should finally make that decision, prompted Lee to dispose his forces to meet any contingency. It seemed probable, because of the topography and the presence of Federal gunboats at Port Royal, that the main effort would be an attempt to turn Lee's right flank in the area below Fredericksburg. In order to provide against the most likely Federal actions, Lee disposed Longstreet's corps along the high ground west of the town, from the Rappahannock to Hamilton's Crossing, to serve as the Confederate fixed defense. To the south, Jackson's divisions were spread over a wide area, in positions of maneuverable readiness; at Guiney's Station on the Richmond, Fredericksburg & Potomac Railroad; at Yerby's, three miles to the right rear of Longstreet's right flank; at Skinker's Neck; and opposite Port Royal. Stuart's cavalry brigades were posted in observation on either flank of the 20-mile-long Confederate line.

227

Snow ball fight between Confederate units prior to the Battle of Fredericksburg. These were organized affairs, involving large units and conducted with all the seriousness and attention to tactical detail of a real battle. This drawing, from "Battles & Leaders," is by A. C. Redwood, a Confederate veteran.

Burnside's Preliminary Orders

ON December 9 Burnside issued a warning order to his three Grand Divisions to prepare to cross the river on Thursday morning, December 11, in accordance with the following plan: The troops would cross at three points simultaneously as soon as the engineers finished laying the pontoon bridges, two of which were to be at the northern and one at the southern extremities of Fredericksburg; two more just below the mouth of Deep Run, about one mile below the town. Three of the five bridges would have approaches prepared for artillery, designated batteries of which were to follow the infantry into the combat zones. (Later a bridge was added at Deep Run.)

The attack was to be two-pronged, with Sumner's Right Grand Division slated to take Fredericksburg and then attack the Confederates on their ridge position beyond the town. Meanwhile Franklin's Left Grand Division would occupy the plain south of Fredericksburg, then maneuver the Confederates off their high ground near Hamilton's Crossing. Hooker's Center Grand Division would be held in reserve,

prepared to intervene wherever the attack needed bolstering.

BURNSIDE summoned his generals and their staffs to a conference on December 10, at which he discussed additional details as to their actions once they had crossed the river. Instead of issuing clear, concise, and definite written orders, Burnside is reported to have given the commanders long, rambling, and vague instructions of a general nature. If he had a well-rounded plan in mind, it was not revealed to these officers, and there is considerable doubt as to whether he was clear in his own mind as to how the attack would be pressed after the crossing had been accomplished. Burnside certainly deserves criticism for this; and his subordinates were at fault, too, in not asking enough questions to resolve their doubts and problems.

During this conference Burnside did learn, however, that his officers lacked confidence in his plan. The most outspoken critic was Brevet Brigadier General Rush C. Hawkins, a brigade commander in Getty's division of the IX Corps, Burnside's former command. In reply to a casual inquiry as to what Hawkins thought of the plan he had just outlined, Hawkins replied, "If you make the attack as contemplated, it will be the greatest slaughter of the war;

there isn't infantry enough in our whole army to carry those heights if they are well defended." Colonel J. H. Taylor of Sumner's staff added, "The carrying out of your plan will be murder, not warfare." Even that seasoned campaigner, Major General Darius N. Couch, while more restrained in his judgment, nevertheless reported that "there were not two opinions among the subordinate officers as to the rashness of the undertaking."

Though Burnside showed no inclination to change his plan, these outspoken comments must have jarred him and further weakened what little self-confidence he still possessed.

The Crossing

THE actual throwing of the bridges by the Federal engineers was scheduled to start at daylight December 11, but the noise made in moving the bulky equipment into position reached the ears of Confederate pickets in Fredericksburg while it was still dark. General McLaws, convinced that the long-awaited crossing was about to commence, at about 5 a.m. had ordered two guns to fire a prearranged warning signal.

Through the early morning haze Confederate sharpshooters watched for the pontoniers to appear. Then the crackle of Rebel musketry rang out, toppling the leading Federal engineers into the water and spurring the rest back into the protection of the fog. Again and again the undaunted bridge builders attempted to advance their equipment, but each time they were driven back. Covering fire from Federal infantry along the bank was ineffective against the Confederates, protected as they were in pits and behind walls and buildings.

THE TENSE DRAMA continued halfway through the morning, both sides withholding artillery fire for fear of striking their own men. The muzzles of Brigadier General Henry J. Hunt's guns on Stafford Heights could not be depressed sufficiently to blast out Barks-

Pontoon train en route from Aquia to Falmouth. ("Harpers")

Engineers attempting to lay a pontoon bridge under the cover of a heavy artillery bombardment. ("Harpers")

dale's riflemen, while Lee's artillerymen could not see the river line, their view being blocked by the houses and further obscured by the fog. Finally, however, the Federal guns bombarded Fredericksburg for two and a half hours, firing sixty shells a minute for a total of 9,000 rounds. Fires sprang up all over town, but as soon as the firing ceased the undamaged Confederates popped up from their cellars and rifle pits and resumed their deadly work.

The Federals finally realized that they could not lay the bridges during daylight under such accurate fire. General Hunt proposed that volunteers ferry over a strong enough force to drive away the sharpshooters, establish a small bridgehead, and form a screen to protect the engineers. Four regiments—from Michigan, Massachusetts, and New York—accepted the call. The leading elements jumped into pontoons and paddled rapidly across. In a short time they had established their bridgehead, losing only one man killed and several wounded.

ALTHOUGH bitter street fighting continued through the remaining hours of daylight, Federal infantry poured across the completed bridges in a steady stream, fanned out to widen the bridgehead, and finally forced Barksdale to withdraw his 1,600 men from the town.

While all this was taking place at the upper bridges

opposite Fredericksburg, two others at Deep Run, for the use of Franklin's Grand Division, were completed by 11 a.m., with but little opposition from the Confederates. Had Burnside been more alert and allowed discretion to his subordinates, Franklin could have passed a couple of divisions over quickly, then swung north and driven out by the flank the sharpshooters who for long hours had blocked the laying of bridges in Sumner's sector. But Franklin delayed crossing until 4 p.m., five hours after the completion of the lower bridges. Even then, after several brigades were across, countermanding orders were received, with the explanation that the construction of the three upper bridges had been delayed. So back across the river marched Franklin's advance elements, leaving a single brigade on the southwest shore to cover the crossing of the main body of that Grand Division the next day. That night another bridge was laid at Franklin's crossing.

Burnside's Battle Orders

AS the Union divisions moved into position behind their artillery on Stafford Heights and opposite Deep Run, and the engineers struggled vainly to complete the bridges, Burnside issued his first written battle orders. These had been belatedly completed early that morning of December 11, about the same time the engineers were pushing the first pontoons into the water. That Burnside was merely feeling his way toward battle is evident in his fragmentary messages, which were surprisingly imprecise and incomplete. The essence of the order to Sumner was:

> Your first corps, after crossing, should be protected by the town and the banks of the river as much as possible until the second corps is well closed up and in the act of crossing; after which you will move the first corps directly to the front, with a view to taking the heights that command the Plank road and the Telegraph road, supporting it by your other corps as soon as you can get it over the river. General Hooker will immediately follow in your support, and will see that your right flank is not troubled.
>
> General Franklin crosses below, as you are aware, thus protecting your left. The extent of your movement to the front beyond the heights will be indicated during the engagement.

Franklin received this gem:

> General Sumner will, after crossing the river, move immediately to the front, with a view to taking the heights which command the Plank and Telegraph roads. I have ordered General Hooker to hold himself in readiness, as soon as he has crossed the river, to support either General Sumner's column or your own. After your command has crossed, you will move down the old Richmond road, in the direction of the railroad, being governed by circumstances as to the extent of your movements. An aide will be sent to you during your movements.

TO HOOKER, commanding the army reserve, Burnside passed along the instructions already addressed to the two other wing commanders, while directing him to hold himself in readiness to support either column; then added: "Should we be so fortunate as to dislodge the enemy, you will hold your command in readiness to pursue by the two roads." The order incidentally neglected to specify what roads were meant; and the phrase "should we be so fortunate" is not indicative of confidence.

These were no more than movement orders, indi-

Barksdale's Mississippians opposing the laying of the pontoon bridges at Fredericksburg. (BL)

Advance skirmishers of Sumner's Right Grand Division driving Barksdale's men from Fredericksburg. Looting seems to have commenced. Alfred R. Waud in "Harpers."

231

cating that Burnside intended to put his army in close contact with the Confederates on their side of the river without immediately committing them to battle. The orders were silent on how either Sumner's or Franklin's divisions were to react if the enemy should become active while Burnside prepared and issued further instructions. Those to Franklin in particular, considering the fluidity of his assignment, afforded the more striking example of how *not* to start an offensive. It was Burnside's intention that this largest of his grand divisions, with a strength of more than 46,000 men comprising six divisions, would make the main effort that he counted on to dislodge

Maj. Gen. Ambrose E. Burnside (LC)

Map 2. THE VALLEY OF THE RAPPAHANNOCK, SHOWING LEE'S DISPOSITIONS ON DECEMBER 10.
Jackson's corps is on the right, the divisions being indicated by numerals, as follows: 1. D. H. Hill; 2. Early; 3. Taliaferro; 4. A. P. Hill. Longstreet's corps was occupying the ridge west and southwest of Fredericksburg, from the river on the left to Hamilton's Crossing on the right. His divisions are indicated as: 5. Hood; 6. Pickett; 7. McLaws; 8. Ransom; 9. R. H. Anderson. Stuart's cavalry is located as shown, the brigades being: 10. W. H. F. Lee; 11. Fitzhugh Lee; 12. Hampton; 13. Rosser. The Federal army was in camps north and southeast of Falmouth, generally back about a mile and a half from the river.

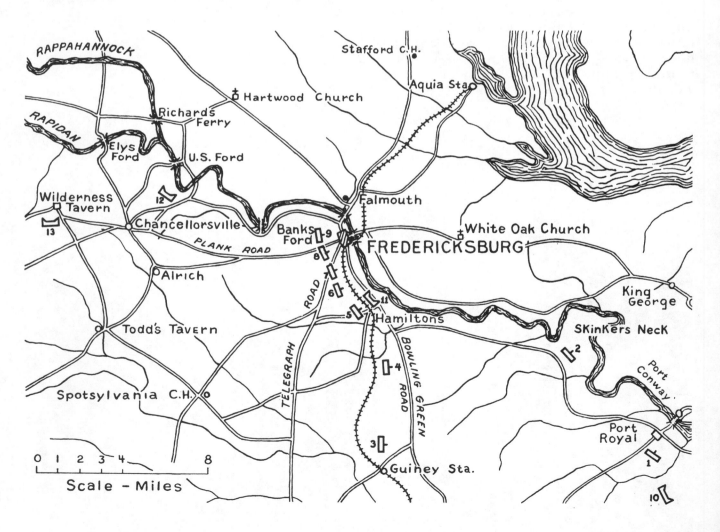

232

Lee's army from its position. Therefore he was derelict in not giving Franklin a more specific directive for the attack. At the very least he should have indicated his objective in clear, unmistakable language, then left it to the wing commander to execute the mission in his own way.

The halting efforts of the Federal army, with its commanding general attempting to direct its every action by remote control and with virtually no co-ordination between wings, accomplished just about what might have been expected. Instead of briskly effecting the passage of the river in the early hours of December 11, and advancing at once to the attack in accordance with clearly defined orders that would allow reasonable discretion to the wing and corps commanders, forty-eight hours went by before either Sumner or Franklin received word to put into effect the confusing, fragmented messages that came down from army headquarters.

Contrast in Leadership

THE striking contrast between the generalship of Lee and Burnside can be noted in virtually every facet of the army commander's sphere of activity— strategy, overall tactical direction, logistical planning, the ability to make decisions, the issuance of clear operational directives, the fixing of objectives, and in the maintenance of troop morale. In the important task of making troop dispositions for battle, about the only positive measure that Burnside ordered was the siting of artillery along the dominant position on Stafford Heights, actually the work of General Henry Hunt, easily the best artillerist in either army. On that high ground across the river, the army's Chief of Artillery placed 147 of his 312 guns, covering the five crossing points.

The real problem would arise later when the Federal forces would undertake to storm the strongly defended Confederate line on the high ground west of Fredericksburg. To reach those heights after passing through the town, Hunt's guns would have to displace forward, a dubious undertaking. Some of the longer-range artillery on Stafford Heights, such as the rifled 3-inch guns and Parrotts, especially the 20-pounders, had effective ranges of from 2,000 to 3,000 yards and could deliver counterbattery fire against Longstreet's artillery on the ridge opposite Fredericksburg, but much of the Confederate line below the town was beyond effective range. Only around Hamilton's Crossing, on the right of Jackson's position, could Hunt expect to do any real damage to the enemy artillery, and then only at extreme range and against uncertain targets concealed in the ridge's heavy woods. The solution would have to be to cross the divisional artillery with the infantry and, hopefully, to employ the field pieces to the best advan-

tage, as accompanying guns with their respective infantry units or for use in counterbattery fire on targets of opportunity.

IN employing his numerous cavalry, Burnside followed the precedent established by earlier Union army commanders who never learned how properly to use the mounted brigades. As a result they, and Burnside, dissipated the cavalry strength instead of assembling a strong mounted force on the critical left flank to seize the key terrain along the river east of Hamilton's Crossing, from which Franklin could have more effectively launched his enveloping attack. Except for several half-hearted attempts at battle reconnaissance, which accomplished nothing, Pleasonton's cavalry would sit out the Battle of Fredericksburg.

Lee's plans and dispositions, after Burnside's rapid surprise march to Falmouth, which suggested that the new Federal commander might be a more aggressive opponent than McClellan, were based on the presumption that his opponent would probably undertake a turning movement on the south flank from the direction of Port Royal, where he would have room to maneuver. Consequently Lee decided on a flexible defense, so disposing his forces as to encourage Burnside to expend his strength in attacking the Confederate defense heights, after which Lee would launch a counterattack to drive him back across the river.

Lee anticipated that there would be two key defense positions in the forthcoming battle. The best remembered would be the stone wall along the sunken road at the foot of Marye's Heights. The other, Hamilton's Crossing, was a tactically significant cross-road that marked the southern terminal of the seven-mile-long range of hills that formed the backbone of Lee's defense. Both landmarks became the center of attention for Federals and Confederates alike. Most of the fighting and killing would occur in their vicinity.

ON THE RIDGE west of Fredericksburg, Longstreet's guns were zeroed in on the likely river crossing points, and his infantry guarding the heights had familiarized themselves with the fields of fire across the open fields and roads the Federals would be forced to use to reach the Confederate positions. In 1862 the armies in Virginia had not commenced to dig the extensive fieldworks that became the vogue in late 1863 and especially in 1864.

At Hamilton's Crossing the Mine Road from the west joined a new military road, recently built by the Confederates behind the ridge, and another road from the south that crossed the main line of the Richmond-Fredericksburg railroad at that point to join the Richmond Pike, a much-travelled highway paralleling the Rappahannock about midway between the ridge and the river. Massaponax Creek, a wide and marsh-fringed stream that is marked as a river on modern maps, about 800 yards south of Hamilton's, anchored the right flank of the Confederate line, and it was this maneuverable area upon which General Lee concentrated his attention as the more sensitive, vulnerable sector.

IN EQUALLY striking contrast to the sedentary Burnside, Lee spent much preparatory time in the saddle visiting corps and division commanders, examining the siting of his 275 guns and correcting faulty battery positions, making certain that the guns would be able to deliver enfilade fire across their front, and scrutinizing closely the features of the terrain. Having initially established his command post at Hamilton's Crossing, on the arrival of Jackson's corps Lee moved his headquarters to the highest elevation in Longstreet's sector, an ideal observation post that overlooked both the town and the open terrain to the south. This hill, on Telegraph Road, which marked the approximate center of his defense line, thus became the point from which Lee directed the defense, and which thereafter became known as Lee's Hill.

From this point the Confederate commander frequently trained his binoculars on Stafford Heights, where the Federal artillery had emplaced nearly half its guns, and on which was to be seen Ferry Farm, the boyhood home of George Washington. There was also Chatham (the Lacy house), which Lee had frequently visited in his youth, but more importantly where he had courted his future bride, Mary Custis. At the time of the battle, the Lacy house was serving Federal General Sumner as his field headquarters.

FROM his observation post on the hill Lee watched the Federal artillery shell Fredericksburg on the morning of December 11, but the efforts of the enemy engineers to lay their pontoon bridges could not be seen from that point. Seemingly unconcerned by the unfolding events of the day, even after he had received reports that the bridges had been successfully completed and Federal troops were crossing on both upper and lower bridges, Lee made no move to recall Stonewall Jackson's four divisions, two of which would have to march ten to fifteen miles. Lee evidently interpreted the troop crossing at Deep Run as a feint to cover a larger movement from the Skinker's Neck-Port Royal area. In any event, he would wait for Burnside fully to expose his hand before summoning Jackson.

Only after darkness had fallen on December 11 did Lee decide to send for two of the divisions of the Second Corps, which had been at Yerby's and at Guiney's Station. These two units, A. P. Hill's division and Taliaferro's, upon arrival were ordered to extend Longstreet's line to the right, relieving Hood's division of the First Corps, which had been stretched thinly to the south pending the arrival of Jackson's corps.

ON THE MORNING of December 12, with a heavy fog again concealing the terrain, Lee again deferred the calling up of Jackson's more distant divisions. Sporadic firing from the guns on Stafford Heights were the only sounds to disturb the morning calm. When the fog lifted about noon, Lee rode off to the right with Jackson in an effort to discover what "those people over there" might be up to. A member of Stuart's staff, the huge Prussian volunteer Major Heros von Borcke, joined the two generals and reported that the Federals were massing in front of the Confederate right, that he had seen them himself and would be happy to take the generals to a place where they could observe the large enemy concentration. This was vital intelligence, so off the three horsemen rode, toward Deep Run. Dismounting at von Borcke's suggestion, as they approached the place where he had spotted the enemy, the distinguished trio crept along a covered ditch to within rifle range of the Federal troops, where they halted to peer through their field glasses. As far as the eye could see, Lee and Jackson observed regiment after regiment of Blue infantry moving down from the Federal side of the river and crossing two of the bridges, while over the third, in tight column, came artillery and wagon trains.

That was all Lee needed to know. It was now clear that Burnside's pivot would execute a holding attack to keep Longstreet occupied at Fredericksburg, while the major attack, as expected, would be

directed at the more vulnerable Confederate right flank, although not in the wide sweeping movement that Lee had feared. Burnside's now-revealed plan was, in Lee's judgment, vastly more advantageous to the defenders than a turning movement from the vicinity of Port Royal, which might well have forced the Confederate leader to disengage in the face of a superior force and fall back the thirty miles to his originally planned line on the North Anna River.

Urgent orders were immediately dispatched to Jackson's two absent divisions, D. H. Hill's at Port Royal and Jubal Early's at Skinker's Neck, to march at once. When they arrived, during the night of December 12, Jackson assigned them to positions on the ridge, so that by daylight, December 13, the Confederate defense line was fully manned all the way

from the Rappahannock northwest of Fredericksburg to Hamilton's Crossing. Stuart's two cavalry brigades and horse artillery covered the mile-wide open space on the army's right flank between Hamilton's and the river. Lee was covering so wide a front that no units were available as a general reserve, but each corps had local reserves.

WHEN HIS divisions were all posted, Lee's keen tactical sense and appreciation of the military uses of terrain became apparent. Longstreet's corps of approximately 40,000 men occupied a frontage of five miles, while Jackson's 39,000 were positioned in depth within the space of only two miles. Faced with no danger from a Federal turning movement, Longstreet could defend against a frontal assault with less density per man-yard of front, but Jackson's

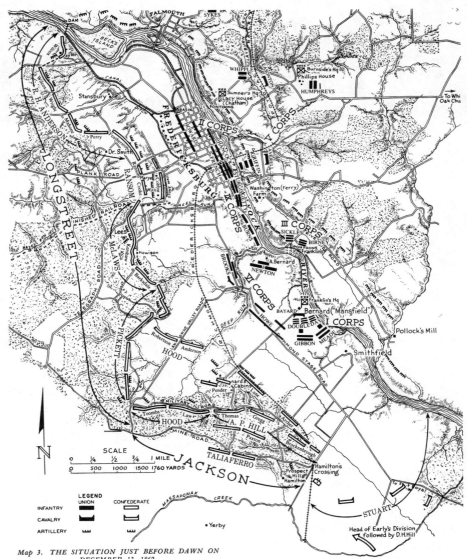

Map 3. THE SITUATION JUST BEFORE DAWN ON DECEMBER 13, 1862.

Federal divisions selected to make the attack have crossed the river and are bivouacked in the positions shown. The Confederates, having watched or heard them cross, are aware that an attack is pending, but are uncertain as to where the main effort, if any, will be made. But by now Lee is satisfied that there will be no wide turning movement to the south, in the Port Royal area, and he is moving Jackson's two flank divisions up to the vicinity of Hamilton's Crossing, where they will arrive about daybreak. The positions of Hunt's reserve artillery east of the river are indicated though the

names of the batteries are not shown. Similarly the Confederate battery positions are shown by symbols which do not necessarily indicate the number of guns in each emplacement. It will be noted that a sixth pontoon bridge is now in place, making three at Franklin's crossing site. This bridge was built late on the 11th. There were few displacements of artillery during the battle, except for the release of some of the organic batteries accompanying the attacking Federal divisions. Therefore, for simplicity, artillery positions will not be generally repeated on succeeding maps.

BELLE PLAIN, one of two Federal bases on Potomac, whence supplies received by water were transshipped by rail or wagon to Falmouth. (LC)

assignment was one that called for flexibility and a readiness to shift troops on short notice to counter possible penetrations or flank action. The new military road that the Confederates had constructed transversely along the rear of their position had been ordered by Lee with that very possibility in mind.

The positions of the major components of the opposing armies at daylight, December 13, was as shown on Map 3, except that Early's and D. H. Hill's divisions (shown approaching on the right) had arrived and moved into their assigned slots; Early in the third line abreast of Taliaferro and in rear of A. P. Hill's two front lines; D. H. Hill south of the Mine Road west of Hamilton's Crossing. The latter division served as corps reserve, in a position of readiness which might become the front line if the Federals should succeed in penetrating or enveloping Jackson's line.

More of Burnside's Incompetence

DURING the late afternoon of December 12, General Franklin, informed that Burnside was coming over for a conference, had summoned his corps commanders, John F. Reynolds and William F. Smith,

to join him at his field headquarters, the Bernard house, formerly a large plantation known as Mansfield. While awaiting Burnside's arrival, the three generals compared notes and decided unanimously that the only sensible attack plan for their wing would be to form up in two assault columns on either side of the Richmond Road and to turn Lee's right flank, no matter what the cost. When Burnside arrived and the plan was submitted to him, all three generals received the distinct impression that he had given his tacit approval, which would be transmitted in the form of written orders as soon as he returned to his headquarters. So they stayed up half the night, working out specific action details for their divisions and waiting for the expected orders. Finally the three tired generals turned in for a few hours' rest, still uncertain as to what battle orders they should transmit to their divisions.

At 7:45 a.m. December 13, the delayed orders arrived, but Franklin and his two chief lieutenants were startled to discover that their own plans were useless. Instead of approving Franklin's attack plan, the new dispatch repeated Burnside's original directive about keeping the Left Grand Division "in position for a rapid movement down the old Richmond road," adding only the instructions "to send out at once a division at least to pass below Smithfield to seize, if possible, the height near Captain Hamilton's, on this side of the Massaponax, taking care to keep it well supported and its line of retreat open."

IT IS DIFFICULT to avoid the conclusion that Burnside had only a vague conception of the size and complexity of his task, but as army commander he could hardly admit to his subordinates that he didn't quite know what he was doing. Obsessed with the idea that his plan of action would force Lee to relinquish his hold on the high ground and commence a retreat to the south, Burnside had also ordered Hooker to send two divisions to await orders at the bridges used by Franklin's wing, prepared to support the latter in the main effort. These divisions, with Bayard's attached cavalry, brought Franklin's strength to about 54,000, which in Burnside's view was ample to do the job.

But there were two major flaws in the plan: in ordering a single division to penetrate Lee's line, Burnside was committing his major striking force piecemeal, the besetting sin of Union commanders. And the very tone of the order was one which could hardly be construed as aggressive, inspiring, or even positive in its implications. Troop commanders should not tell their men to seize a position *if possible,* or to *keep their line of retreat open.* It is little wonder that the Army of the Potomac was becoming disheartened in the face of repeated evidence of incompetence at army headquarters, in a situation in which its chances of being extricated would depend chiefly on sheer guts.

ONCE the die was cast so that no choice remained to Franklin, orders were issued and the Left Grand Division stirred. For the directed attack with a view to piercing Lee's line, Franklin designated the corps

THE pontoon bridges at Franklin's Crossing. The hills occupied by Stonewall Jackson's command are seen in the distance. (LC)

of General John Reynolds, who in turn selected his smallest division, only 4,500 men under the command of Major General George G. Meade, a capable leader whose Pennsylvanians constituted one of the best outfits in the army. John Gibbon's division was assigned to support Meade's attack, while Reynolds' remaining division under Abner Doubleday, as corps reserve, was told to deploy as left flank protection between the Richmond Road and the river, at a refused angle facing south. All the other divisions of Franklin's wing would merely stand to arms in readiness.

The deployment of Franklin's massive force began while the plain between the river and the Confederate position was still covered by the dense morning fog, which again served the Federals well in concealing their movements from the Confederates on the hill. The latter could hear a variety of noises in front of them, even the occasional sharp bark of commands all along the front, but they could see nothing through the curtain of fog.

The Action Near Hamilton's Crossing

ABOUT 10 o'clock the brilliant rays of the sun rapidly dispelled the mists, disclosing an exciting panorama to the grayclad audience on the heights. The bright sun was reflected from thousands of flashing bayonets; officers dashed up and down on galloping horses as adjutants were observed moving to the front of their regiments and reading battle orders; a strange anachronism to the modern day veteran, but a blood-tingling extravaganza that would never be forgotten by the men of Jackson's corps who occupied the front row seats.

At 8:30 a.m., forty-five minutes after receiving Burnside's order, Meade's division moved out in a

237

southeasterly direction, crossing the fields in column of brigades, followed by Gibbon's division on Meade's right rear. After paralleling the river for about 600 yards, Meade turned right, heading directly for the Richmond Road which here as at other points was sunken, with six-foot banks on either side. When the heads of the columns reached the fence-bordered road, they came under direct fire from several of Jackson's guns (Walker's battery) as well as enfilading fire from two guns of Stuart's horse artillery, under the command of young Major John Pelham, stationed at the point where the Mine Road crosses the Richmond Pike. Continuing the advance in spite of this fire, Meade finally was forced to pause while still 600 yards from his first objective, the railroad skirting the base of the high ground on which Jackson's men were posted. Pelham's two guns, served audaciously by that young officer, were manipulated so rapidly and effectively, in the face of the potentially overwhelming Federal force on his immediate front, that Meade's advance was held up for two hours. Only when a large number of divisional artillery batteries that had crossed with Franklin's wing poured such a heavy fire on Pelham that one of his guns was disabled and the destruction of the other became an eventual certainty, would he withdraw, but even then it required a peremptory order from Stuart, to force him to pull his two guns out of action. Meade then resumed his advance, assisted by Federal counterbattery fire that partially neutralized the effect of Walker's guns from Jackson's ridge.

JACKSON'S infantry remained carefully concealed in their woods on the ridge, and his artillery withheld its fire during the morning, even after the fog had lifted, rather than waste shells in attempting to reach for Franklin's assembled masses at the extreme range of the Confederate guns. When Meade resumed the advance, however, shortly before 1 p.m. and after the removal of Pelham's annoying guns, the gunners on Jackson's right opened vigorously, hoping to slow the Federal attack and weaken the Blue lines before they could reach the railroad and cover of the protecting woods. Four batteries with Reynolds' corps immediately trained their guns and returned the fire of the Confederate guns, at the effective range of 1,000 yards. For almost an hour the artillery slugging match continued, until the Federal guns were silenced to avoid dropping their shells among Meade's men as they neared the enemy position.

About a mile below Deep Run could be seen a point of woods that jutted into the open plain, an easily noted reference point that Corps Commander Reynolds had pointed out to Meade as his initial objective. Fortuitously, as it happened, this particular section of woods afforded a more gradual ascent for

On the Picket Line
Federal Advance Against Jackson's Corps

THE MIST still clung to the river and the lowlands as the army began to cross the stream. Our brigade was among the first to cross, and upon reaching the opposite bank, halted for further orders. As the mist rolled away and the sun made its appearance, it was a magnificent sight to watch the troops, many of them in new uniforms, marching from all directions toward and across the bridge and then double-quick up the opposite bank.

In crossing a pontoon bridge men are cautioned not to keep in step. A pontoon bridge is not a very substantial structure, therefore any regularity of step would tend to sway it from its moorings.

We then marched along the bank of the river in an easterly direction about half a mile and halted; whereupon the colonel was asked by General Gibbon if he could deploy his whole regiment as skirmishers at once, and being promptly answered that he could, he was directed to do so. The ground in front of us was a flat, unobstructed plain of considerable extent, where every man of the regiment could be seen as he deployed. On our right was a Vermont regiment and on our left a Pennsylvania regiment, also deployed as skirmishers. These three regiments constituted the skirmish line of the Left Grand Division, and it advanced firing at will and slowly driving back the Rebel skirmishers toward their main body. After dark we arrived at the Bowling Green Road which, being a sunken road, afforded us protection from the enemy's fire. Here we remained all night as a picket guard for the I Corps. The regiment was divided into three reliefs, each of which was sent out in turn some distance beyond the road and within talking distance of the Rebel pickets.

DURING the night the enemy set fire to some buildings near by, illuminating a considerable extent of country, while hundreds of men of both armies swarmed to the fences to watch and enjoy the sight.

All night long we could plainly hear the sound of axes in the enemy's camp, which we subsequently learned were being used in the preparation of obstructions against our advance in the morning.

While we were deployed as skirmishers a captain of one of the companies observed a man, who up to this time, had always failed to be present on any important occasion, endeavoring to escape to the rear. The captain called out in a loud voice, "C———, get into your place, and if you see a Reb, SHOOT HIM!" A few minutes later the man disappeared and was not seen again until the "surgeon's call" was established in camp, some days later.

An incident happened shortly after our skirmish line returned to the Bowling Green Road that afforded us a great deal of amusement. The boys had just started fires for coffee when a young officer, whose new uniform suggested recent appointment, approached and with arbitrary voice ordered fires to be put out, at which the colonel exhibited an asperity of temper that surprised us, who had never seen him except with a perfectly calm demeanor. Our experience on the picket line had taught us how to build fires without attracting attention of the enemy, and we were not pleased that a fledgling should interfere with our plans for hot coffee. The colonel's remarks were quite sufficient for our guidance, so we had our fires and our hot coffee, while the officer went off about his business.

ANOTHER incident occurred to add to the occasion. Our pickets, as already stated, were so near to those of the enemy that conversation was easily carried on. One of the Rebel pickets was invited to come over and make a call, though the invitation might have appeared to him like the spider to the fly. After some hesitation and the promise that he would be allowed to return he dropped his musket and came into our lines and was escorted to one of the fires, probably to his great delight, inasmuch as coffee and hardtack was cordially offered him, being not so abundant in the South as to allow a distribution of it as an army ration. "If thine enemy hunger, feed him; overcome him with good." Fill him with lead, good lead, was what we tried to do most of the time. After that he enjoyed our hospitality as long as he dared and then returned.

On the following day while we were halted at the Bernard house, who should be brought in as a prisoner but this same man, who was greeted with shouts of welcome and friendly shaking of the hand. Some years later, a member of the regiment, while travelling in Ohio, became acquainted with a man tarrying at the same hotel. After supper the two sat down to talk, and very soon the conversation drifted to the war, when it was discovered that each had served in the war, though on opposite sides. The Southerner, learning that his new-found friend was a member of the 13th, remarked that it was rather a singular coincidence, for "I was entertained by that regiment once at Fredericksburg and a right smart lot of fellows they

were." And then he told what had happened. As our comrade was present at that battle, and a member of the company that did the entertaining, he was perfectly familiar with the facts, whereupon mutual expressions of pleasure followed and an adjournment for "cold tea."

—13th Massachusetts History

Map 4. THE ATTACK OF REYNOLDS' CORPS. ACTIONS ON THE SOUTH FLANK UP TO ABOUT 1:30 P.M.

As described in the text, Meade's initial rush penetrated A. P. Hill's center, turned the flanks of and partially broke up Lane's, Archer's, and Gregg's brigades, and gained the new military road. Gibbon advanced only to the railroad. His men, seeing that no one on their right was advancing, and not being told that they were not to be supported by a general advance, were wavering and drifting to the rear. A. P. Hill has requested help from Early, and it is on the way, as the sketch shows.

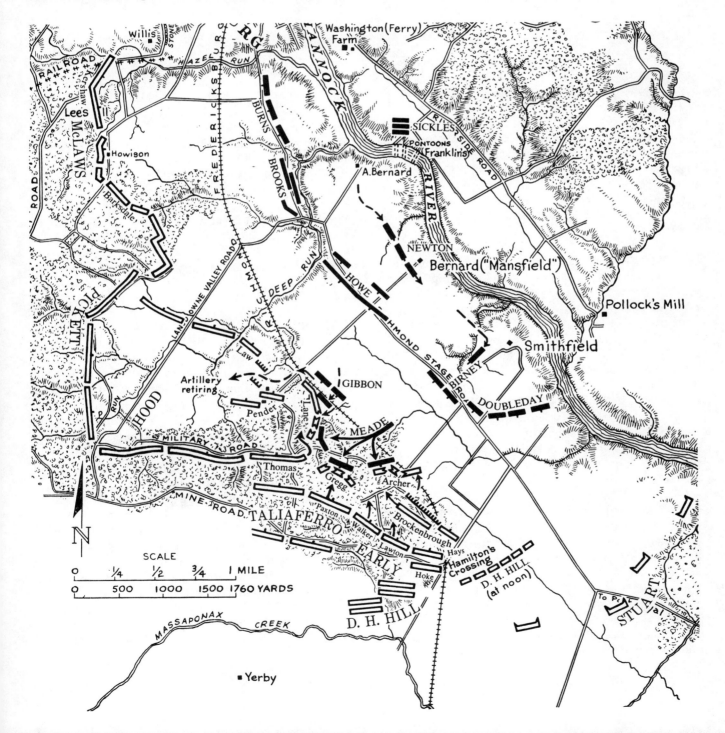

Meade's men charging across the railroad a mile northwest of Hamilton's Crossing. (BL)

the attackers than other parts of Jackson's line. The bulk of the Confederate artillery here appeared to be massed in the vicinity of Hamilton's Crossing, in view of which Reynolds' plan called for Meade's division to turn left, after gaining the crest, in the hope of immobilizing and perhaps destroying these guns.

WITH Gibbon's division advancing on Meade's right rear, the latter's leading assault echelons rushed the hill, broke into the Confederate line, took several hundred prisoners, and then paused for breath as they reached the military road that ran along the rear of the Confederate line. It looked like the breakthrough that Burnside had hoped for, and so it might have been if more adequate preparations had been made and communicated to those charged with the performance. The fault was primarily Burnside's, but Franklin must bear a share, in spite of the restrictive character of the army directive. For, once committed to the fight, it was inexcusable that supporting divisions were not rushed forward to exploit Meade's initial success.

Gibbon's division advanced only as far as the railroad, discovered that no other troops were on their right, and began to waver. By this time the able Confederate general, A. P. Hill, reacting to the break in his line, sent for help to expel the invaders. Early's division and other brigades were dispatched by Jackson to plug the gap. Moving at a run, the Confederate brigades counterattacked just when Meade's formations were somewhat disorganized after their successful dash through the woods and up the slope. By midafternoon Meade's division, suffering heavy casualties and unsupported by Franklin's idle divisions, was driven back in confusion, the men making their way to their own lines, singly and in groups. Reynolds, Meade, and other officers tried unavailingly to halt the retreat, and there is no telling how many of the Pennsylvanians would have got back alive had it not been for a rescue party in the shape of Birney's division of the III Corps, which had crossed the river on Franklin's summons and was thrown into action at the critical moment. As the men of Meade's and Gibbon's divisions streamed to the rear across the plain, Birney struck the right flank of the pursuing Confederates, drove them back in turn, and inflicted a loss of more than 500 killed and wounded.

IN SPITE of Franklin's objections to Burnside's plan for his heavily reinforced left wing, once he became locked with the defending Confederates and had committed Reynolds' corps and later a division of the III Corps, there was little excuse for his failure to engage at least some of his unemployed divisions to support and exploit Meade's penetration of Jackson's line. Even Doubleday's division of Reynolds' corps was allowed to remain in place, east of the Richmond Road, as an immobilized flank guard facing Stuart's Confederate horsemen.

Franklin's lack of initiative was especially noteworthy in the case of Smith's VI Corps of 25,000 men, the largest in the Union army, which was deployed along the Richmond Road with its right on either side of Deep Run, two divisions in the line and one in support. About all this corps did during the entire afternoon was to engage its organic artillery in lively duels with Confederate guns on the ridge, while the main body of its infantry sat out the battle, with one exception. That was a spirited bayonet attack by

240

With the Skirmishers of Gibbon's Division

ABOUT 9 o'clock in the forenoon we were again deployed as skirmishers, and ordered to advance over the fence into the damp clayey soil of the ploughed ground beyond, the enemy firing and slowly retreating.

Our batteries were speedily brought into position and began shelling the woods, while the enemy's guns in turn, opened upon us. We were between two fires, and the greatest caution was necessary to prevent a needless loss of life. Very soon we were ordered to lie down as close as possible to the earth in the soft clay, rolling over on our backs to load our guns. We were now engaged in the very important service of preventing the enemy from picking off the men of Hall's 2d Maine Bat-

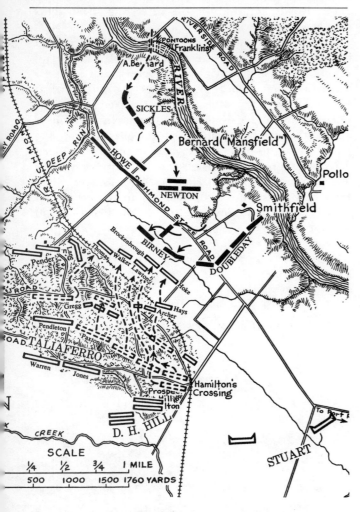

Map 5. THE CONFEDERATE COUNTERATTACK. SITUATION ABOUT 2:30 P.M.

Early's prompt and vigorous counterattack struck Meade at a time when his brigades had become attenuated and had lost cohesion in the woods. The Federals were driven down the hill, out into the open, and back half way to the road. Gibbon's division became involved in the rout. The Confederates were stopped by several batteries of light artillery posted on the rise from which Meade had launched his assault, and by Birney's division, just arrived. Newton has arrived in support and Sickles, also sent for, is approaching. Doubleday is held in check by the threat of Stuart's cavalry. Meade's and Gibbon's broken units are streaming back through Birney's lines, to be re-formed on the ground where they had bivouacked the previous night.

tery, then shelling the enemy from a position slightly elevated from ours in our rear. In order that this battery might do effective work it was ordered to point its guns so as to clear us by one foot. This was a terrible position to be in. An earnest protest was sent back to Captain Hall, asking him to elevate his pieces, or every man of us would be killed. Suddenly a shell or solid shot from his battery struck the cartridge box of one of the boys while he lay on his stomach. Some of our number crawled out to where he lay and dragged him in. He lived about six days, having been injured in the hip. It was bad enough to be killed or wounded by the enemy, but to be killed by our own guns excited a great deal of righteous indignation.

ABOUT ONE O'CLOCK a general advance was ordered. Those on the left moved first and then came our brigade. As skirmishers we advanced in front of our division until the firing became so rapid that we were not only of no advantage, but interfered with the firing of our troops, so we were ordered to lie close to the ground while our troops passed over us. Toward night we were withdrawn to the Bernard house, which had been turned into a hospital, and replenished our empty boxes with ammunition.

Our losses were three men killed, one officer and twelve men wounded, making a total of sixteen.

As we were withdrawn from the skirmish line to the rear our appearance excited a good deal of mirth among the old soldiers, who knew too well what rolling round in the mud meant, for we were literally covered with the clayey soil that stuck to our clothing like glue. We had had a pretty hard time of it, as after each time we fired, we turned over on our backs to reload our guns. Hours of this work told on our appearance as well as our tempers, so when some of the men of a new regiment asked us why we didn't stand up like men and fight, instead of lying down, we felt very much like continuing the fight in our own lines.

TO BE THROWN out as skirmishers in front of a line of battle seems more dangerous than when touching elbows with your comrades in close order, but as a matter of fact it is not generally attended with so great a loss. It is a duty requiring, when well done, nerve and coolness on the part of both officers and men. You are at liberty to protect yourself by any means that may be afforded, such as inequalities of the ground, a bush, a tree, a stump, or anything else that you may run across as you advance. The fire which you receive is usually from the enemy's skirmishers, and is less effective than when directed toward an unbroken line.

You are supposed to load, fire, and advance with as near perfect coolness and order as you can command because on that depends the amount of execution you are able to perform. It is no place for skulkers, as every man is in plain sight, where his every movement is watched with the closest scrutiny. As soon as the skirmish line of the enemy is driven back, the main line advances, and very soon the battle begins in earnest; whereupon the skirmishers form in close order and advance with the rest of the line, except in cases like the one just related, when it was necessary to replenish the boxes of ammunition.

We had acquired a good deal of proficiency by constant drilling for many months in this particular branch of tactics, long before we were called upon to put our knowledge into practice. We growled a good deal at the colonel in the early days of our service for his persistence but we had already realized how valuable a lesson he had taught us. There were occasions that will be later seen, when this kind of service was very dangerous, but as a whole, our losses on the skirmish line were lighter than some other regiments, and we think it is not unfair to attribute the fact to the thorough instruction we had had. It was the old story—the oftener a man does a thing, the better he can do it.

History of 13th Massachusetts

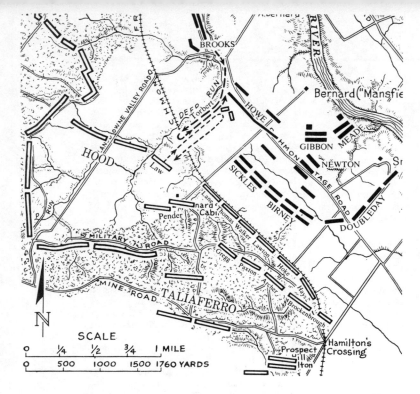

Map 6. *ACTIONS ON THE SOUTH FLANK FROM ABOUT 3 P.M. TO DARK.*

Virtually the only action of Howe's and Brooks's divisions is that shown on this map. Torbert's brigade made a short run up Deep Creek, captured 15 prisoners, then was chased back by Law's brigade of Hood's division and severely punished. This map also shows the general disposition of all units on the south flank at the end of the day's fighting.

Colonel Alfred Torbert's brigade of Brooks's division, which about midafternoon tried to drive the Confederates from a railroad cut on their immediate front at the Lansdowne Valley road, about 600 yards in advance of Brooks's position. Torbert succeeded in driving back a regiment of Pender's brigade (A. P. Hill's division), but was in turn attacked and forced to withdraw by Law's brigade of Hood's division. Other than that single foray, no further effort was made by Smith's corps either to back up Torbert or to test the Confederate defense for weak spots.

The Federal attack had lacked both power and depth, and although Reynolds managed to hold the railroad line for several hours, it soon became apparent that this particular effort had failed. By late afternoon the troops were withdrawn and reformed in the shelter of the Richmond Road, from which the attack had been launched in the morning. Instead of a major, well-supported turning movement against Lee's right flank, the engagement had turned out to be a relatively ineffectual one in which only part of each of the opposing forces was involved. That it was sanguinary, however, is reflected in the casualties: 4,861 on the Federal side, approximately 3,400 on the Confederate.

242

Sumner Attacks Marye's Heights

WHILE Franklin's reinforced grand division was being deployed on the open plain below Fredericksburg and Meade's assault division was marching up the hill and down again, affairs on the north flank were brought to a head. It will be recalled that Burnside's explanation of his plan of action was for Franklin to maneuver Lee's right into an untenable position and then, at an appropriate time, he would give Sumner to the north the go-ahead signal to push two divisions "in the direction of the Plank and Telegraph Roads, for the purpose of seizing the heights in rear of the town."

The Federal army commander evidently reached the conclusion, after several hours had passed and Franklin had made only slow progress, that an early success on that front would not be achieved. For at 11 a.m., three hours after Sumner received his orders, Corps Commander Couch received a dispatch, over a recently installed field telegraph circuit from the Lacy house, to put the troops in motion. Couch designated French's division for the advance via the Telegraph Road, with Hancock's to follow, while Howard's division was formed up in a position of readiness, to move towards the Plank Road if and when released by Couch.

AT NOON French's leading brigades moved out from the center of town, as described by Couch (the corps commander):

". . . by two parallel streets, the one on the right, which was Hanover Street, running into the Telegraph road, and both leading direct to Marye's Hill, the stronghold of the enemy. On the outskirts of the town the troops encountered

a ditch, or canal, so deep as to be almost impassable except at the street bridges, and, one of the latter being partly torn up, the troops had to cross single file on the stringers. Once across the canal, the attacking forces deployed under the bank bordering the plain over which they were to charge. This plain was obstructed here and there by houses and fences, notably at a fork of the Telegraph road, in the narrow angle of which was a cluster of houses and gardens; and also on the parallel road just south of it, where stood a large brick house. This cluster of houses and the brick house were less than 150 yards from the stone wall, which covered also as much more of the plain to the left of the brick house. A little in advance of the brick house a slight rise in the ground afforded protection to men lying down, against the musketry behind the stone wall but not against the converging fire of the artillery on the heights."

Thus the Federals were under fire, either from musketry or artillery or both, from the moment they debouched from the edge of town—and to a certain extent they took casualties from artillery even while in the streets. They lost many men while still in column before they could double-time over the two bridges on the canal to the slight cover on its far side; and their losses increased from musketry fire as they advanced in line beyond this swale.

Longstreet had assigned the divisions of R. H. Anderson, Robert Ransom, and McLaws to the defense of the range of hills extending from the Rappahannock on the north almost to Deep Run on the south, with McLaws on the right and Ransom supporting him in the area between the Plank and Telegraph Roads. It was on McLaws' front, where the stone wall at the foot of Marye's Heights afforded the Confederates their most effective defensive positions, that the major fighting would occur.

Lieutenant Colonel E. P. Alexander, commanding a battalion of Longstreet's artillery, had confidently declared that the fields between the western edge of the town and the high ground where the Confederates awaited attack were so thoroughly targeted by the artillery on the ridge and the muskets of the infantry at its foot that "not even a chicken could live to cross." It was a grim but prophetically accurate appraisal, one that Burnside might have made for himself with a modicum of imagination and appreciation of terrain, in addition to taking the precaution of conducting a few reconnaissances.

The Sunken Road Makes History

GENERAL Cobb's Georgia brigade and the 24th North Carolina Volunteers of Cooke's brigade manned the sunken road with its protective four-foot stone wall, both of which were invisible to the attackers, who had no idea what a formidable obstacle stood in their way. When this road was built, the dirt had been thrown to the far side, thus concealing the existence of the wall from those approaching it from the town. These units, in preparing their reception for the Federals, formed two successive lines in their narrow, protected causeway so that a continuous band of musket fire could be laid down on the attackers, one line loading while the other fired.

The congestion in the streets of Fredericksburg, and the confusion caused by the intermingling of

Troops crossing on Sumner's lower bridge, just downstream from the ruined railroad bridge. ("Harpers")

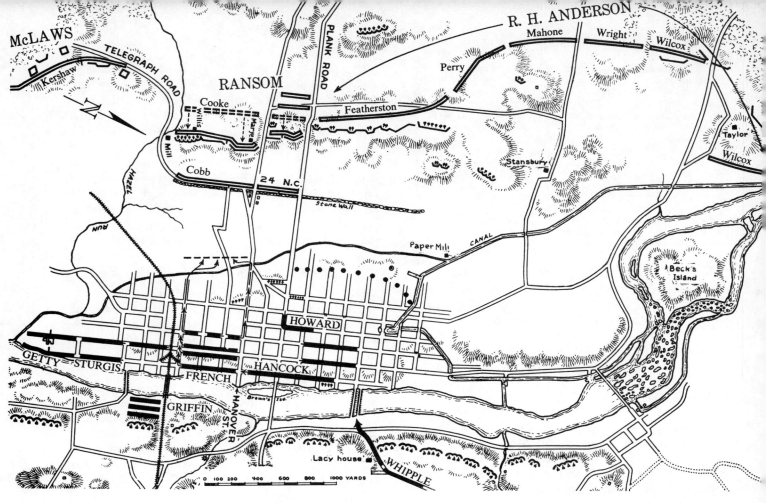

Map 7. ACTIONS ON THE NORTH FLANK, ABOUT 11 A.M. TO NOON.

Federals: French's division formed up about midmorning in the streets where his brigades had spent the night. Three regiments detailed as skirmishers moved at 11 a.m. toward the front, marching in two columns—the right via Hanover Street and the left on a street parallel to the railroad. They trotted from the western exits of the town, across the bridges over the sluice, turned left and right, respectively, faced into line and advanced. They were met by heavy artillery fire from Marye's and Willis' Hills, but continued to dash forward. The skirmishers were followed by the brigades in the order 1st, 3d, and 2d, at intervals of about 150 yards. Then came Hancock's division in the same formation. Meanwhile Howard had formed his brigades on the right of Plank Road, having been told that he would attack on the right of French and Hancock. But these orders were countermanded and his men were held in column in the streets, ready to advance. Sturgis' division also formed up in the streets, preparing to move out in column along the railroad. Whipple's division moved down from its bivouac north of the Lacy house, crossed over the upper bridge, and commenced taking over picket duty in the northwest portion of the city from Howard. Getty's men remained crouched at the lower end of the town near the river.

Confederates: Longstreet's defense was largely entrusted to McLaws, supported by Ransom. Cobb's brigade was behind the stone wall at the foot of the heights, with the 24th North Carolina Volunteers of Ransom's division occupying that portion of the front between Plank Road and the extension of Hanover Street. The remainder of Ransom's division was held back of the artillery on the heights; but when the Federals appeared, Cooke's brigade was rushed forward to the crest, from where they reinforced the small-arms fire of the troops behind the wall. At least initially, the greatest damage to the advancing Federals was caused by the Confederate artillery firing from Marye's and Willis' Hills.

large masses of infantry and artillery, proved a serious handicap to the attackers. Nineteen divisional batteries of artillery had crossed with the foot soldiers, ten of them assigned to Couch's corps, but only seven of the nineteen found the opportunity to fire their pieces, either before or during the actual assaults.

The converging gun fire of the Washington artillery descended on the advancing Federals as soon as they emerged from the shelter of the buildings in the town. It was so destructive that it undoubtedly accelerated the rate of the Federals' advance as they dashed across the narrow bridge of the drainage ditch to the comparative security, however fleeting, of the depression in the ground beyond the ditch. But the effect of the gunfire, though devastating, was less than that of the blinding sheets of musket fire that assailed them as soon as they came within range of the grimly waiting Confederates behind their stone wall.

THE ADVANCE of French's division from the western exits of the town was accompanied by only two guns, manned by heroic cannoneers, who did their best, even though it was of little real help to the charging infantry. The only effective artillery support came mainly from a few of Hunt's long-range guns across the river, but even that was of limited assistance because of the necessity for ceasing fire when the Blue infantry entered the fire-swept zone in front of the wall.

For some strange reason it did not occur to any of the Federal generals that there were other parts of the Confederate defense line that might have been approached with better chance of success, at least after observing how the leading attack waves were being mowed down before reaching the stone wall. Instead, brigade after brigade was rushed headlong into disaster in monotonously bloody succession, all directed at the same limited objective and over ground covered with a rapidly increasing number of dead and wounded. It was as though the stone wall possessed some sort of awful, magnetic attraction that with difficult ground on the flanks, funneled its victims into a valley of death from which there could be no escape.

IN THE FACE of the withering hail of bullets from Cobb's infantry in the sunken road, the guides of the leading brigade of French's division succeeded in planting their guidons within 100 yards of the wall. Encouraged by the sight, the men of the brigade grimly continued to advance, ignoring heavy casualties, until they were only sixty yards from the Confederate muzzles. At that point flesh and blood and courage could take no more, and the lines melted

A. C. Redwood sketch of the Washington Artillery firing on the Union troops charging Marye's Heights. Note the excellent observation and open field of fire enjoyed by these batteries. (BL)

away. The brigades that followed, those that remained of French's division, then Hancock's, rushed successively across the killing ground, each one cresting a bit closer to the wall, until Hancock's final charge, which was stopped only forty yards from the wall. By that time McLaws had rushed additional regiments from Ransom's division into the sunken road so that the Confederates were using four relays of infantry, with a resulting speed-up in the rate of fire, delivered point-blank in the faces of the charging Federals.

Two Union divisions in the space of a single hour had been decimated in the fruitless sacrifice, and the plain over which they advanced was covered with the dead and wounded, adding up to 3,200 casualties alone in the divisions led by French and Hancock.

AS GENERAL COUCH watched the slaughter from the cupola of the Fredericksburg Court House, it finally dawned on him that there might be a better way to execute Burnside's order. Howard's division was the only one that remained under his control, so Couch ordered Howard, who had lost an arm at the Battle of Fair Oaks, to take his division off to the right in order, if possible, to flank the stone wall by piercing the Confederate line beyond its protection. Without taking time to send out a reconnaissance patrol to determine a feasible route of ap-

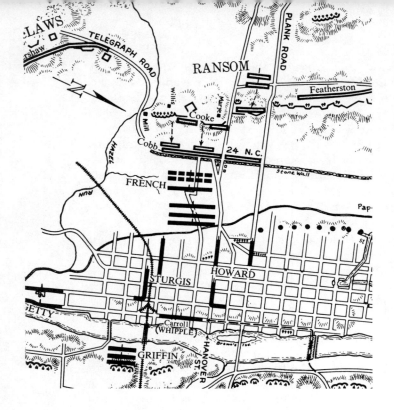

*Map 8. THE SITUATION ON THE NORTH FLANK
FROM ABOUT NOON TO 1 P.M.*

Federals: This sketch shows the charge of French's and Hancock's divisions against Marye's Heights. The picture may be likened to successive waves of a surf dashing against a shore, breaking up, receding, leaving a thin line on the sand to mark their farthest reach. Each Federal brigade suffered heavily from artillery fire as it came in sight at the edge of the town, then encountered long, tearing sheets of musketry volleys as the men neared the stone wall. The leading guides planted their guidons within 100 yards or so of the stone wall, but the lines for the most part melted away. Couch says that the plain seemed to be alive with men, some lying down, others running about, while a steady stream of wounded was returning to the town. Whipple, who crossed the river about noon, has used one brigade to take over picket duty on the right from Howard. His 2d Brigade (Carroll) has moved down to the left behind Sturgis. Howard, having received orders to support Hancock, is moving two brigades to the left toward Hanover Street.

Confederates: Two of Cooke's regiments ran down the slope into the sunken road with Cobb's men. Ransom has brought the remainder of his own brigade to the crest just south of Plank Road. Cooke is wounded. Cobb suffers a cut artery in the leg and bleeds to death quickly despite surgical aid. Mc-Laws orders Kershaw to bring up his entire brigade and to assume overall command in place of Cobb.

---

*Map 9. THE SITUATION ON THE NORTH FLANK
FROM ABOUT 1 P.M. TO 2:30 P.M.*

Federals: The remnants of French's and Hancock's divisions are scattered in front of the stone wall. Survivors who have drifted to the rear are being rallied in the small ravine along the ditch. Sturgis is following Hancock, Ferrero's brigade in the lead. Nagle's brigade starts to deploy on the left, then sidles to the right oblique and follows Ferrero. Howard, deployed on the right with two brigades, is advancing; his third brigade is held in reserve on the right of the Plank Road. Griffin's division, coming in as part of the Fifth Corps reinforcing the Ninth Corps, has crossed the bridge and is moving forward on the left; Carroll's brigade of Whipple's division, ordered to support Sturgis, has joined Griffin instead and is moving forward with him. Sykes has moved down to the upper bridge. Humphreys is still in bivouac.

Confederates: Kershaw has moved two of his regiments to the top of Marye's Heights thence down into the sunken road to reinforce Cobb's regiments. Three additional regiments are following to the top of the hill. Ransom has brought his regiments forward to the crest and one of them is in the sunken road reinforcing the 24th North Carolina.

The attack on Marye's Heights as seen from the Confederate side.

proach, Howard started his regiments across the lone bridge used by his predecessors, with instructions to change direction after crossing. The hapless soldiers of his division, however, in angling off to the right, ran into marshy ground which caused them to veer to the left, so that they soon found themselves headed for the selfsame stone wall and in as deep trouble as those who had gone before. Result: 900 additional casualties.

Unwilling to admit failure, or mentally incapable of modifying his suicidal tactics, Burnside from his remote headquarters across the river kept sending orders to continue the attack. Perhaps he thought the Confederates would run out of ammunition, or lose heart, if he kept hammering at them. He still had two uncommitted corps, Willcox's IX and Butterfield's V. (Whipple's division of Stoneman's III Corps had already been attached to Couch and was standing by awaiting orders.)

IN THE COURSE of the afternoon all seven of these divisions, having been directed to support Couch either by attachment or as collaborators, were poured into the cauldron, wholly or in part, some directly against Marye's Heights, others a short distance to the south of it. All to no avail, as the casualties mounted and the troops began to wonder whether their absent commander was in full possession of his senses.

Burnside Loses His Head

EVERYTHING had gone badly for Burnside, who chose to remain throughout the battle on Stafford Heights across the river, where he could neither see nor get the feel of the fighting. All he could think of, seemingly, was that his original plan would succeed and therefore required no modification in spite of the disheartening reports that flowed in to his headquarters from all parts of the field. His unwillingness to allow the least discretion, or departure from his orders, to his grand division commanders, was equalled by a lack of that flexibility of mind that is so necessary in adjusting to battle conditions as they develop, including a willingness to modify preconceived tactics and unhesitatingly discard plans that prove unworkable. But these changes of pace cannot be made irrationally, or without adequate communication with subordinate commanders. For example, when Franklin's battle was slow in developing, Burnside decided to throw Sumner's divisions into repeated canalized attacks against the unyielding Marye's Heights, without even coordinating the change of plans with Franklin.

As the divisions on the north flank successively bloodied themselves against Longstreet's hard anvil, and the dead and wounded piled up in the narrow zone before the stone wall, Burnside in desperation ordered Franklin to charge the enemy with his whole force in an effort to take the pressure off the right

247

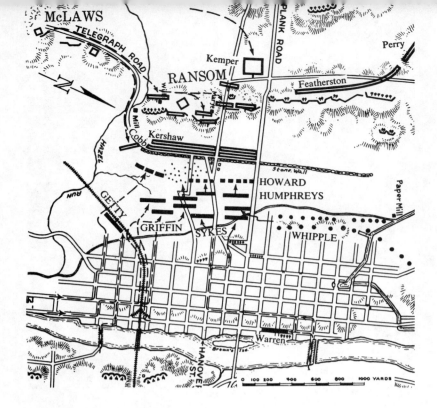

Map 10. SITUATION ON THE NORTH FLANK FROM ABOUT 2:30 P.M. TO DARK.

Federals: Howard's two leading brigades have reached a line near the stone wall. His third brigade has been moved to the left of the Plank Road in the shelter of a ravine. Humphreys crossed the river shortly after 2:30 p.m. and formed a battle line in the ravine, to the right and left of Hanover Street. At dusk he advanced in a bayonet charge, which was repulsed. Meanwhile Griffin, with Carroll's brigade attached, has advanced astride the railroad for a short distance then driven straight for the stone wall. His brigades attacked successively but were repulsed. Sykes moved to the upper bridge at 2 p.m., crossed at 4 p.m., moved out Hanover and George Streets, and formed line with two brigades in the ravine. At 5 p.m. Getty advanced on the left in a column of brigades. His leading brigade almost reached the stone wall before being thrown back. The supporting brigade remained behind the railroad embankment. By dark the foremost elements of the Federals in this sector were pinned to the ground in front of the stone wall. Another irregular line was in the ravine.

wing. Franklin disregarded the order, stating afterward that it came too late; but by then, it may be, he and his generals had made up their minds that *any* order from army headquarters could not be trusted or considered intelligent.

CONCURRENTLY with this order to Franklin, Hooker was directed to renew the attack against the stone wall with the two uncommitted divisions of his reserve wing. While these divisions were crossing the river, Hooker did what Burnside himself should have done, rode to the front to see the situation for himself and to confer with Couch and the division commanders whose men had already attempted what everyone but Burnside had now concluded to be impossible.

Hooker's opinion was that further suicidal sacrifices should be ruled out. He then rode back to the eastern bank to dissuade Burnside, who refused to entertain the recommendation that the order be revoked. By the time Hooker had crossed the river for the second time it was late afternoon, foreshadowing

Confederates: Kershaw's three remaining regiments are placed in position near Marye's house. A battalion is moved forward to the gap in the unfinished railroad embankment on the right of Willis' Hill in order to stop any Federal advance up Hazel Run. At 4:30 p.m. the Washington Artillery Battalion, being out of ammunition, is replaced by Alexander's battalion. Ransom, fearful that his left flank would not be supported by Featherston, asked for reinforcements. Kemper's brigade of Pickett's division was sent to him at 4:30, and two of its regiments were placed in the sunken road to relieve the 24th North Carolina. Other readjustments of units were made after dark. The Confederates had repulsed the Union attack so easily and with so little loss to themselves that Lee could hardly believe there would be no renewal of the attack the next day.

HOT WORK FOR HAZARD'S BATTERY.

an early December twilight that would shortly reduce visibility to the point where Hooker might safely defer ordering a further assault on the premise that it could not be effectively completed before dark.

WHILE Hooker was visiting the army commander, one of his divisions, Humphreys', had already crossed to the town and was in formation, prepared to take up the assault, when Hancock advised Couch that his men had just noticed some Confederates apparently leaving their position. Although this movement was only the relief of one artillery battalion by another, the Federal generals interpreted it as the start of a general withdrawal, and Couch promptly told Humphreys it was a good time for him to attack. Humphreys immediately ordered his men to fix bayonets without taking time to load their muskets, and

Hazard's Battery B, 1st Rhode Island, going into position. About 3:30 p.m. he placed his six guns on a low crest only 500 yards from the Confederates. Hazard fired rapidly on the Confederates on Marye's Heights until Humphreys asked him to stop so that the infantry could advance through. Hazard's losses were heavy. Though most of the horses were down, the men preserved the old artillery tradition by dragging away the guns by hand. Gen. Howard, who watched the action, said, "Captain Hazard's conduct was equal to anything I ever saw on the field of battle." (BL)

A. R. Waud sketch of the attack by Hooker's Center Grand Division. This was an on-the-spot drawing, and therefore represents quite accurately the appearance of the scene. This shows clearly that the tactics of 1862 were concerned more with keeping a parade-ground alignment of troops than in taking advantage of folds of the ground or using dispersed formations to minimize losses. ("Harpers")

led them toward the stone wall. Whether the cold steel gave them courage, or they covered the ground more rapidly because they didn't have to stop to load their pieces, they did manage to approach closer to the Confederate line than any of the previous attackers. But they, too, failed to reach the wall, and their wave likewise crested and receded, leaving 1,000 additional dead, wounded, or missing.

The Federal casualties in front of the stone wall had now mounted to 6,300, following the sixth and last (Humphreys') contribution to the senseless slaughter. This marked the end of the day's fighting, with twilight already covering the battlefield as Hooker ordered his troops to fall back from their advanced position with the sardonic comment in his battle report: "Finding that I had already lost as many men as my orders required me to lose, I suspended the attack."

As soon as the semi-darkness made it safe for a man to stand erect without attracting Confederate fire, Sykes's heretofore unused division moved out to within a stone's throw of the Confederate position, to serve as a shield against enemy interference with the painful Federal task of pulling back from close contact and removing as many wounded as possible during the hours of darkness. Some undirected, sporadic firing from nervous Confederates occurred during the night, but no forward movement was undertaken by either side, which was understandable after more than five hours of active combat in so small a sector, where no more than 6,000 Confederates and twenty guns had withstood the driving attack of seven Federal divisions whose battle strength exceeded 40,000 men.

Kershaw's troops defending the stone wall at the foot of Marye's Heights.
A. C. Redwood

On the left is a modern view of the Marye house, taken by Ralph Happel and reproduced by courtesy of the National Park Service. The building is now a part of Mary Washington College. On the right is a photograph of the Marye house taken during the Civil War.

After the Battle

THE night of December 13, after the battle, was bitterly cold for Sykes's men, forced to snatch what fitful sleep they might on the cold, damp ground less than 100 yards from the stone wall. But it was much worse for those wounded who were not evacuated, many of whom during the night died from their wounds and exposure. Blueclad corpses by the hundreds, stiffened by death and the chill of the night air, were rolled into positions where they served as parapets for the living.

At daylight the usual morning fog allowed the front-line men of both armies to move about, restoring circulation and smoking with impunity, until the sun broke through to expose a macabre sight. Where hundreds of blueclad dead had dotted the field could be seen only naked white bodies. Many thinly clad Confederates, having decided that these Federals had no further use for clothes, thought the living might as well replenish their own wardrobes.

As the fog rolled away, Sykes's men were startled to discover how close to the lethal stone wall they had spent the night, but they were even more surprised to see their enemy casually moving about only a few yards away, cooking breakfast, cleaning muskets, and performing other peaceful camp chores. The Confederates saw them at the same time, grabbed their guns, and opened fire, as Sykes's exposed lines

hit the dirt, almost as one man. Their position was unenviable, to put it mildly; they had not been ordered and were not expected to attack, and they couldn't retreat from what little protection was offered by their shallow swale without inviting certain death from the sharpshooting Confederates. So they stayed where they lay, all through the doubly long hours of December 14, until the welcome relief of the second night of their ordeal ended their misery by enabling them to fall back to the shelter of the buildings in Fredericksburg.

IN THE MINDS of the Union generals the feeling was universal that another attack would be attempted on Sunday, December 14, although Burnside had not yet divulged his intentions. Either that or Lee's army would counterattack to drive them out, since one or the other would naturally be expected to take the initiative. One officer, however, had positive views and the fortitude to express them in opposition. At nine o'clock on the evening of the battle, in a conference with several generals including Butterfield, Meade, and Humphreys, the outspoken Rush Hawkins again inveighed so vehemently against another attack that he persuaded the others and was promptly designated as their spokesman in an attempt to bring Burnside around to the same view.

So they all repaired to the Phillips house, where

251

they found Sumner, Hooker, and Franklin, who in turn listened to Hawkins' estimate of the situation and were convinced. Burnside at the time was not at headquarters, but at 1 a.m. he entered the room with the abrupt announcement, as Hawkins related the incident: "Well, it's all arranged; we attack at early dawn, the IX Corps in the center, which I shall lead in person." Seeing Hawkins, he added, as though on the spur of the moment: "Hawkins, your brigade shall lead, with the 9th New York on the right of the line, and we'll make up for the bad work of today [yesterday]."

The dead silence that met this statement seemed to astonish Burnside, but after questioning the others and finding none to approve, he said, lamely, that since he was alone in his opinion, the attack would not be made. The following day he called another council to consider whether to stage a general retreat or simply withdraw from the plain while retaining possession of Fredericksburg. The consensus was that there should be no retreat and no further attacks for the time being. The army would hold the ground it presently occupied and at once initiate defensive measures.

Then ensued, for the second time in a month, an uneasy period of watchful waiting between the two armies, as each rested on its arms expecting the other to renew the battle. Sooner or later, something was bound to happen, but neither Lee nor Burnside seemed anxious to shift from their defensive postures.

SUNDAY the 14th passed with only an occasional exchange between opposing skirmishers. So did Monday, and still neither army showed any intention to move. Lee was puzzled, believing that Burnside would certainly now attempt the turning movement that he had expected in the first place, to counter which Lee reshuffled the position of his divisions for greater flexibility.

On the afternoon of the 15th Burnside sent a flag of truce with the suggestion that time out be taken to allow his men to bury the dead that cluttered the ground in front of Marye's Heights. Lee consented and the gruesome work was accomplished without the Confederates being able to determine whether Burnside's action foreshadowed a resumption of the battle or a Federal withdrawal.

That night the rains descended and the winds blew. Next morning wondering Confederate scouts who reconnoitered the Federal lines discovered that the entire Union army had quietly recrossed the river under cover of darkness. The storms had drowned the noise of the retreat from the Confederates. It was conducted so efficiently, quietly, and rapidly, and the bridges were taken up with such alacrity, that the Federals were able to regain some measure of

self-respect after their defeat. On the other hand, considerable chagrin was felt by Lee and his generals, in spite of their satisfaction at having so easily and cheaply repulsed Burnside's hosts, that their enemy had been allowed to escape without punishment.

An Appraisal of the Battle

THE Battle of Fredericksburg served to illustrate, to an unusual degree, the controlling influence of competent top generalship on the one hand; and conversely, how little superiority in manpower and weaponry contributes to battle success for the army that is burdened by ineffectual leadership.

The scales were heavily weighted in favor of the Confederates, despite their lesser strength, simply because Ambrose E. Burnside, inexperienced as an army commander and lacking the vital ingredient of self-confidence as well as that of his subordinate commanders, was pitted against the best general in either army, by any criterion, the experienced Robert E. Lee.

Granted that Lee was fortunate in having lieutenants such as Jackson, Longstreet, and Stuart, nevertheless it was he who bore the responsibility, planned the strategy, coordinated the tactics, evaluated the characters and limitations of the opposing generals, and assigned to his corps commanders the missions that they consistently executed so superbly.

During the heavy fighting of December 13, in the restricted area on both flanks, the ease with which Burnside was defeated is revealed in the fact that only four of Lee's nine infantry divisions, a small percentage of his 275 pieces of field artillery, and none of Stuart's three brigades of horse cavalry, had become actively engaged.

LEE MADE proper use of his numerous cavalry after contact, assigning to Stuart the job of protecting Jackson's right flank and at the same time denying maneuver space to Franklin's Grand Division between Hamilton's and the river. Burnside, however, merely attached elements of his cavalry to his three grand divisions and gave them no further thought. Nor did Sumner or Franklin employ them any more effectively. More imaginative wing commanders would have been alert to seek useful missions, such as harassing Longstreet's rear on the north flank, or sending Bayard's strong cavalry force to keep Stuart occupied on the south flank, thus releasing Doubleday's division to strengthen Reynolds' attempted penetration of Jackson's line.

Lee and Longstreet were justified in their belief that the latter's position was virtually impregnable, an opinion shared by most of the Union generals except Burnside. It must therefore have amazed the battle-experienced Confederate leaders to find their opponent desperately beating his head on so narrow a front against their unyielding stone wall, while the largest part of his army stood passively by on the open plain, after failing on the first attempt to split Jackson's line wide open.

At no time during the fighting on December 13 or subsequently, until the Federals had recrossed the river, did it occur to Lee that Burnside would so readily acknowledge defeat, after his initial repulse, particularly after a Federal soldier had been captured with a message disclosing that Burnside had ordered a renewal of the attack for the following day.

THE ONLY principle of war that Burnside succeeded in putting into effect was when he made an unexpectedly fast march from Warrenton, and finally, although in reverse, when he withdrew his entire army from close contact without Lee's knowledge. In between, the entries on the Burnside ledger were all on the liability side, an accounting which Lincoln correctly analyzed by removing him from command a few weeks after the battle.

In reviewing Burnside's strategy, it is difficult to understand his reasons for deciding to march his entire army directly from the Warrenton area to Falmouth, preparatory to crossing the river on pontoons, rather than employing the more expeditious and infinitely simpler method of crossing the Rappahannock and Rapidan at one or more of the upper fords (as Hooker was to do in April 1863), and then moving overland, with a minimum of obstacles, to the occupation of Fredericksburg as the initial objective. In either case, if he had proceeded without pausing, he would have been unlikely to encounter effective

opposition from the Confederates, nor should he have had serious difficulty in establishing his base of supply at Aquia Landing and concurrently occupying Fredericksburg and the high ground to the west before the rains could cause a rapid rise of the Rappahannock River.

ON THE Confederate side, Lee followed his usual strategy, refusing to be hurried until all the cards were on the table and he could appraise Burnside's probable intentions. The Confederate commander's ability to concentrate his forces at a time and place of his own choosing, without apparent concern for what might appear to be his own temporary disadvantage, had been demonstrated repeatedly, most recently at Second Manassas and Antietam. Seemingly unconcerned that some day a thoroughly capable opponent might take advantage of the situation (so far such a Union general had failed to make his appearance), Lee correctly assumed that Burnside would not attack until the additional facilities required at his supply base at Aquia could be built. Consequently he felt no need to hasten the concentration of his army at the critical point. As it turned out, Jackson's corps reached Fredericksburg ten days before Burnside finally made ready to cross the river.

WHERE BURNSIDE would decide to effect his river crossing became the subject of a major guessing game by both sides, because the narrow, winding course of the river offered numerous opportunities above, at, and below Fredericksburg. Lee knew perfectly well that he could only hinder, not prevent, the crossing in the face of Burnside's heavy concentration of artillery on Stafford Heights, but he was equally sure that he could make it hot for Burnside once he got across.

Franklin's divisions recrossing the Rappahannock during the withdrawal. ("Harpers")

In trying to make up his own mind, Burnside's vacillation was painful to behold. The longer he hesitated, the more confused he became and, if his lack of mental clarity can be judged by his subsequent decisions and orders, he never did develop an intelligible plan for the conduct of the battle. A single incident, characteristic of the shallowness of his tactical perception, illustrates how blind Burnside was to realities. While riding along Stafford Heights with the commander of the VI Corps, he told General Smith "in the strictest confidence," as Smith later put it, that "he knew where Lee's forces were and expected to surprise them and occupy the hills before Lee could bring anything to bear against him."

His basic plan for the army attack was equally naive and unrealistic. He imagined that by sending one division to frontally attack Longstreet opposite Fredericksburg, and another in the same manner against Jackson, these two widely separated divisions could succeed without massive support in piercing the Confederate line at two points, with the effect of forcing Lee's army to evacuate the ridge and hasten off to Richmond. At once thereafter, according to the visionary Burnside, Franklin and Hooker would be all ready to promptly pursue, intercept, or whatever.

BURNSIDE'S amazing blindness to the military facts of life was similarly displayed in the area of communication with his subordinate commanders. When the battle commenced, about all they understood was that when Burnside should give the word, the two divisions earmarked for the penetration attack were to head for the enemy lines. Nothing more than that!

At a later Congressional committee meeting, before which both Burnside and Franklin testified, Burnside stated that he had learned about the new military road the Confederates had constructed, that he wanted possession of it as a means of separating Lee's two wings, and that his instructions to Franklin anticipated that the latter would capture the road as a prelude to an aggressive assault by Sumner against Longstreet's position. One searches in vain for anything in either Sumner's or Franklin's orders that conveyed any such meaning.

FRANKLIN in turn testified that he interpreted the order which he received at 7:45 a.m. December 13, as calling for what he described as "an armed observation to ascertain where the enemy was." He also stated: "I put in all the troops that I thought it proper and prudent to put in. I fought the whole strength of my command, as far as I could, and at the same time keep my connection with the river open."

Franklin may have interpreted the order too literally, but was certainly less than accurate in the statement above quoted. Smith's corps of three divisions was not used, and Franklin had been negligent in not promptly calling into service two of the three divisions of the III Corps (Hooker's wing), which were waiting at the river for the express purpose of being employed as needed. When he did belatedly bring Birney into the action the results suggested how much more he could have done had he not been almost as mentally inflexible as Burnside himself. Instead of "fighting the whole strength of his command," as he stated, he had actually put only three divisions, one-third of his available strength, into the attack.

Franklin may have been obtuse, uncooperative, and unaggressive, and Hooker could have shown a more constructive attitude, but the fact remains that the primary responsibility for the fiasco rested on Burnside for poor planning and even worse execution. With more speed, normal coordination, an evidence of aggressiveness from the top and a confident, experienced army commander, a night crossing followed by a well-organized dawn attack in strength to outflank Lee's right, would at the very least have made Fredericksburg a less one-sided battle.

LEE'S CONDUCT of the defense was well up to his usual standards, the victory at Fredericksburg adding one more to his string for the year 1862. Nevertheless Lee made one major miscalculation with respect to Burnside. He overestimated his opponent's ability as an army commander to such an extent that it caught the usually perceptive Lee unprepared to turn the Federal defeat into what might have become a debacle. Understandably Lee gave Burnside credit for a normal degree of military know-how, even though this was his first campaign as army commander, and the natural corollary to that assumption would be that the December 13 attack was only the preliminary to a second-day assault on a broad scale, employing the troops who were not engaged in the first phase. When Burnside made no further attempt for two days, and then quietly recrossed the river without being discovered, Lee forfeited the opportunity to stage a counterattack that could conceivably have seriously hurt the Army of the Potomac and created interesting strategic possibilities that might have made Fredericksburg a really profitable victory for the South.

The campaign as a whole had proved to be a major exercise in mutual frustration, causing casualties of some 18,000, only one-third of whom were Confederates, and solving nothing. Both armies were right back where they had been on December 10. Lee's superiority had again been demonstrated, against inferior opposition it is true, and Burnside was marked for removal. But the incomplete victory gave Lee little satisfaction, considering his not inconsiderable losses, the destruction of homes and buildings in Fredericksburg, and the escape of the Federal army.

CHANCELLORSVILLE

Text by Joseph P. Cullen
Designed by Frederic Ray

ON A RAW, WINDY DAY in early April 1863, President Abraham Lincoln and Major General Joseph ("Fighting Joe") Hooker sat astride their horses as the Army of the Potomac, encamped on Stafford Heights overlooking the city of Fredericksburg and the Rappahannock River, passed in review. The ground was soft with melting snow, and the mud flew from the horses' hoofs. A reporter for the New York *Herald* described the scene: "Out upon a little swell of upland were crowded the President and his staff of generals, and over all the plain stretched the columns of the army. In the distance were the camps, the river, the spires of Fredericksburg, and the frowning batteries beyond; behind, miles of mud-walled villages, long, white-topped baggage wagons, and cannon on the hills. The sun danced on the bayonets and rifles and lingered in the folds of the flags; then the shadows drifted over the plains and melted away with the music."

Lincoln had come to visit the army for a few days, not only "to get away from Washington and the politicians," as he quaintly expressed it, but also to check on rumors about morale being low. Hooker's recent appointment as commander in chief of the army, replacing Burnside after the disaster at Fredericksburg in December, had not been particularly popular, as the President well knew. Consequently, when he appointed Hooker he told him, "I think that during General Burnside's command of the army you have taken counsel of your ambition, and thwarted him as much as you could, in which you did a great wrong to the country. . . . I much fear that the spirit which you have aided to infuse into the army, of criticizing their commander and withholding confidence from him, will now turn upon you. . . . Neither you nor Napoleon, if he were alive again, could get any good out of an army while such a spirit prevails in it."

After reviewing the troops, visiting with the sick, and talking with many of the officers, Lincoln was pleasantly surprised to find that morale was generally high. Hooker had realized his first job was to restore morale and discipline to the demoralized Union army, and in this he showed administrative ability that few suspected he possessed. Abandoning Burnside's unwieldy Grand Divisions, he reorganized the army on a corps level, forming the cavalry into a separate corps. The quality and quantity of the rations was increased, camp sanitation and living conditions improved, deserved furloughs granted. By the spring of 1863 the Army of the Potomac, numbering about 130,000 men, was certainly the largest and best equipped and supplied army the country had ever seen. "The finest army on the planet," Hooker called it.

Lincoln was reassured about the army, but he was still not convinced about its commander. It was not so much Hooker's constant boasting that bothered the President, as "Fighting Joe" had always been regarded as a braggart. "My plans are perfect," he had stated after his appointment to top command. "May God have mercy on General Lee for I will have none." But Hooker also had a reputation as a tough, aggressive corps commander, a good combat soldier, and

Repulse of Jackson's men at Hazel Grove by Federal artillery under (then) Brigadier General Alfred Pleasonton. (From B&L)

256

Lincoln was hoping that he would take this superb army and use it aggressively against the enemy. All he now heard from his general, however, was what he was going to do when "I get to Richmond." This brought forth Lincoln's mournful remark to his secretary, "It is about the worst thing I have seen since I have been down here." And he also stated in his characteristic way that "the hen is the wisest of all of the animal creation because she never cackles until the egg is laid."

Although a civilian with no formal military train-ing, Lincoln was acutely aware, unlike most of his generals, that the army's objective was not Richmond, it was the Confederate army. Now he feared that Hooker did not understand the problem, that his plan probably was to outmaneuver the enemy, à la McClellan and the Seven Days, with Richmond the major objective. Thus, as he departed for Washington, with a premonition of disaster, the President gave Hooker and Major General D. N. Couch, second in command, some sound advice. "In your next fight, gentlemen," he told them, "put in all of your men."

Review by President Lincoln of the cavalry of the Army of the Potomac in April 1863. Original drawing, A. R. Waud. (LC)

LEE'S PROBLEM

Across the river Lee's Army of Northern Virginia had its problems also, although of a different nature, to be sure. The winter had been long and unusually severe, with extreme cold and intermittent snow lasting into early April. Many of the men lacked blankets, while others wore coats and shoes that were in tatters. Horses were gaunt from lack of forage, and finally scurvy began to appear among the men when the ration was reduced "to 18 ounces of flour, 4 ounces of bacon of indifferent quality, with occasionally supplies of rice, sugar, or molasses." Each regiment sent out daily details to gather sassafras buds, wild onions, garlic, and poke sprouts, but the supply obtained in this manner was negligible. From his headquarters camp near Fredericksburg Lee wrote the Secretary of War that he feared the men "will be unable to endure the hardships of the approaching campaign."

This shortage of supplies, due primarily to the lack of efficient transportation and the general ineptitude of the commissary general, Colonel Lucius B. Northrop, also had a direct effect on the numerical strength of the Army of Northern Virginia. Lieutenant General James Longstreet, with Pickett's and Hood's divisions, had been sent south of the James River to contain the Federal forces at Newport News and in North

Carolina, but his primary mission was to gather desperately needed supplies for Lee's army. When Longstreet completed the mission, Lee planned to recall him and mount an offensive against Hooker in order to relieve the pressure on the other Confederate forces in Tennessee and North Carolina and still keep Richmond covered. "I think it all-important," he wrote President Davis on April 16, "that we should assume the aggressive by the 1st of May. . . . If we could be placed in a condition to make a vigorous advance at that time, I think . . . the army opposite us could be thrown north of the Potomac."

In the meantime, however, Longstreet's absence reduced Lee's force to something over 60,000 effectives. If the Union army advanced before Longstreet could join him, Lee faced the prospect of having to fall back to the North Anna River, about halfway between Fredericksburg and Richmond, something he did not want to do because then the vital forage and provisions in the Rappahannock Valley would be lost. But to recall Longstreet now would mean that Lee, lacking provisions, would be unable to undertake an offensive. Therefore he decided to leave Longstreet's force south until its mission was accomplished. If necessary, he would face a Union advance with an inferior force.

In late April the weather turned warm and springlike. Across the river constant activity could be observed in the Union camp. The Federals sent an observation balloon aloft every day, weather permitting; cavalry raids across the upper Rappahannock

258

increased in number and intensity. Then on April 23 the Federals made a crossing and demonstration against Port Royal on the lower Rappahannock on the Confederate extreme right. This did not particularly disturb Lee, however, as he recognized it for what it was, a feint. He told Lieutenant General Thomas J. ("Stonewall") Jackson that he believed the "purpose is to draw our troops in that direction while he attempts a passage elsewhere," and "I think that if a real attempt is made to cross the river it will be above Fredericksburg." Until such time as some definite move on the part of the Federals could be ascertained, Lee had no intention of shifting any of his troops. Jackson's corps held the extreme right from Hamilton's Crossing to Port Royal. McLaws' division of Longstreet's corps, posted on Jackson's left, stretched from Hamilton's Crossing to Banks's Ford above Fredericksburg. Farther up the river Stuart's cavalry watched the various crossings, supported by Anderson's division of Longstreet's corps.

HOOKER'S PLAN

Finally, late in April, Hooker put the Army of the Potomac in motion, in furtherance of a bold plan. He would take at least three corps up the Rappahannock to Kelly's Ford, twenty-five miles northwest of Fredericksburg, then cross both the Rappahannock and the Rapidan Rivers to get on Lee's left flank and rear. Two corps would demonstrate actively in front of Fredericksburg to hold the Confederates in their defensive positions, while the remaining two corps would be held ready to go wherever the best opportunity might present itself. An essential part of the plan was for Stoneman's cavalry corps to precede the infantry by about two weeks, crossing the upper fords of the Rappahannock and, sweeping down upon Lee's lines of communication to Richmond, cut railroads and canals, block roads, and intercept all supplies. As it was known that the Confederates had great difficulty in keeping more than four days' rations on hand, Hooker believed that if Stoneman was successful Lee would run short of provisions, and with three Federal corps on his left and rear would be forced to retreat, thus giving the Federals a moral victory, at least.

Map 1. HOOKER'S PLAN. *Although generally excellent, this plan had two flaws. First, Sedgwick's secondary or "holding" attack was designated only as a "strong demonstration." Lee was never deceived by a feint. Sedgwick, however, did make a full-scale attack that might have achieved its purpose had Hooker himself done his part in the over-all scheme. Second, the timing of the grand cavalry raid was faulty. The Federal cavalry—especially under Stoneman—at this time was incapable of keeping the Confederate supply line interrupted for two weeks or more, even if it succeeded in penetrating the enemy rear areas deeply enough.*

Maps below and elsewhere, prepared by Col. Wilbur S. Nye, originally appeared in *Chancellorsville: Lee's Greatest Battle* by Lt. Gen. Edward J. Stackpole and are reproduced here by courtesy of Stackpole Books, Harrisburg, PA.

It was an excellent plan with more daring and imagination than any Union commander in the East had ever shown before. Hooker, in effect, was splitting his army in the front of a brilliant and feared adversary, but if this were executed efficiently and aggressively it would almost guarantee the destruction of the Army of Northern Virginia. It was a risk well worth taking!

HOOKER'S OPENING MOVES

On the morning of April 13 Stoneman moved out at the head of 10,000 finely equipped and conditioned troopers to swing far out to the right, cross the Rappahannock, and fall on the unsuspecting Confederate rear. Before Stoneman left, Hooker reminded him that "celerity, audacity, and resolution are everything in war. Let your watchword be fight, fight, fight."

But after two days' march the skies opened up and halted the column. "During the night of the 14th a severe rain commenced and continued without cessation for thirty-six hours, which prevented the command from crossing the river," Stoneman reported. "The rain continued, with short intervals of fair

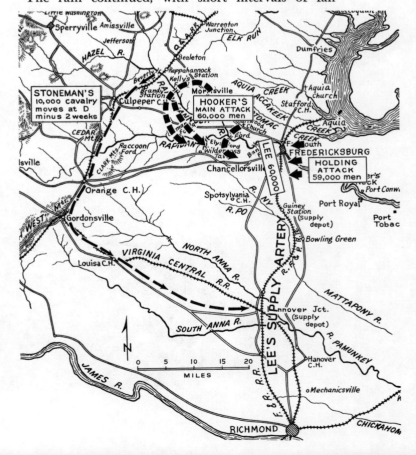

weather, and the river remained impassable for cavalry until the 28th of April, during which time the whole command remained in the vicinity of Warrenton Junction, on the Orange and Alexandria Railroad." Owing to this delay the battle would be over before Stoneman really got active, and his subsequent operations would have little or no effect on the outcome.

With this disruption of his timetable, Hooker became impatient and when the rains finally subsided he put his original plan into operation. Initially he displayed a boldness that augured well for the success of the campaign. On the morning of April 27 Meade's V, Howard's XI, and Slocum's XII Corps started up the Rappahannock, well screened from Confederate observers by the topography. Each man carried sixty rounds of ammunition and eight days' rations (twice the normal amount) of hardtack, salt pork, coffee, sugar, and salt. Each ration weighed three pounds. For the first time in the East, 2,000 pack mules were used instead of the usual supply wagons, to speed up the movement. "For miles nothing could be heard but the steady tramp of the men," wrote one campaigner, "the rattling and jingling of canteens and accouterments, and the occasional 'close-up-men-close-up' of the officers."

At dawn the next day Hancock's and French's divisions of Couch's II Corps marched to Banks's Ford, where a demonstration was made to keep the Confederates confused, while the road to United States Ford, farther up the river, was repaired. The third division of the II Corps, Gibbon's, was left behind because its encampment at Falmouth, directly across the river from Fredericksburg, was in full view of the Confederates and to withdraw it would have alerted them to the fact that some unusual movement was taking place. The other reserve corps, Sickles' III, was ordered to join Reynolds' I and Sedgwick's VI Corps below Fredericksburg where the Federals made

Pontoon bridges erected for Sedgwick's VI Corps to cross the Rappahannock in Hooker's planned diversionary move. (HW)

a strong demonstration in an attempt to hold the Confederates in their defensive positions until Hooker could complete his turning movement.

During the night of the 28th and early morning of the 29th, the three Federal corps crossed the Rappahannock at Kelly's Ford. Slocum and Howard then marched to Germanna Ford on the Rapidan, while Meade crossed lower down the river at Ely's Ford. Moving east, they uncovered United States Ford and were joined by Couch's two divisions. By early evening on the 30th, all were encamped around the rendezvous point, Chancellorsville (not a town, merely a farmhouse), a strategic crossroads at the edge of an area known as The Wilderness. Here Hooker joined them, establishing his headquarters at the Chancellor house. Receiving word from Sedgwick that although he had thrown two bridges across the Rappahannock below Fredericksburg the Confederates showed no disposition to attack, Hooker then ordered Sickles' III Corps to join him at Chancellorsville, which it did early next morning, via U.S. Ford.

THE whole plan had been executed perfectly. According to Couch, "It had been a brilliantly conceived and executed movement." The corps commanders realized that Hooker had successfully outflanked Lee and thus secured a great opportunity to destroy the Confederate army. Even the men in the ranks sensed they had stolen a march on the Confederates for the first time, and their confidence in Hooker increased. Major General Carl Schurz, commanding the 3d Division of Howard's XI Corps, reported that during the move "all orders were executed by officers and men with promptness and alacrity, and the men marched better, were in better spirits, and endured the fatigues and hardships of the march by night and day more cheerfully than ever before. I have never known my command to be in a more excellent condition."

In gaining this advantage, however, Hooker had split his army and it was now vital that he uncover

Banks's Ford, just a few miles above Fredericksburg, in order to place the two wings within easy support of each other, and to insure a safe route of retreat if necessary. Also, most of his men were still in the dark thickets of The Wilderness, a dense forest of second-growth pine and scrub oak, with numerous creeks, gullies, swamps, heavy tanglefoot underbrush, and few farms or open spaces. A few miles east toward Banks's Ford and Fredericksburg, however, would bring them to open areas where they could maneuver efficiently and bring their great preponderance of artillery to bear.

From Chancellorsville there were three roads that could be used. The Orange Turnpike, which passed through Chancellorsville from the west, and was the best and most direct road to Fredericksburg; the Orange Plank Road, which went southeast from Chancellorsville and then swung left to rejoin the Turnpike about five miles away; and the River Road, which ran almost north from Chancellorsville and then turned east, paralleling the Rappahannock to Banks's Ford and on to Fredericksburg. With Banks's Ford in Hooker's possession and his columns operating in favorable terrain, the Army of the Potomac would be in a good position to destroy Lee's army

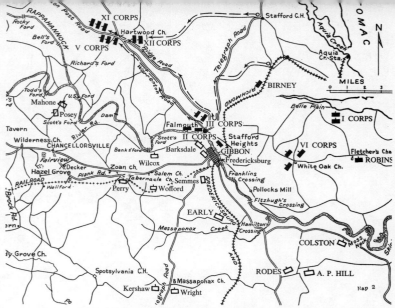

Map 2. Start of Hooker's Turning Movement. On April 27, 1863 Hooker's strong right wing started its march around Lee's left flank. Three corps reached Hartwood Church, undetected by Lee, and two others were ready to depart from the Falmouth area. The I and VI Corps are still in their camps.

Lee's army is spread over a wide front, watching the river crossings. Jackson's corps, on the right, occupies the front from Moss Neck to Telegraph Road. Two of Longstreet's divisions are to the left; the other two, on a detached mission near Suffolk, are unavailable during the campaign.

Map 3. Movements on April 28, 1863. This shows Hooker's march from Hartwood Church to Kelly's Ford where, beginning at 10 p.m., the XI Corps starts crossing the Rappahannock. The remainder of this corps and the V and XII Corps are closing up and waiting for their turn to cross. Two divisions of the II Corps have marched from Falmouth to Banks's Ford, throwing out Carroll's brigade to U.S. Ford to cover their flank. The I and VI Corps have marched down to their assigned crossing sites, and the III Corps has been shifted over between them.

Lee has made no material change in his dispositions. His first intimation of Hooker's threatening moves was a message from Stuart on the evening of the 28th that a Federal force of all arms (indicating a major unit) was moving up the Rappahannock in the direction of Kelly's Ford.

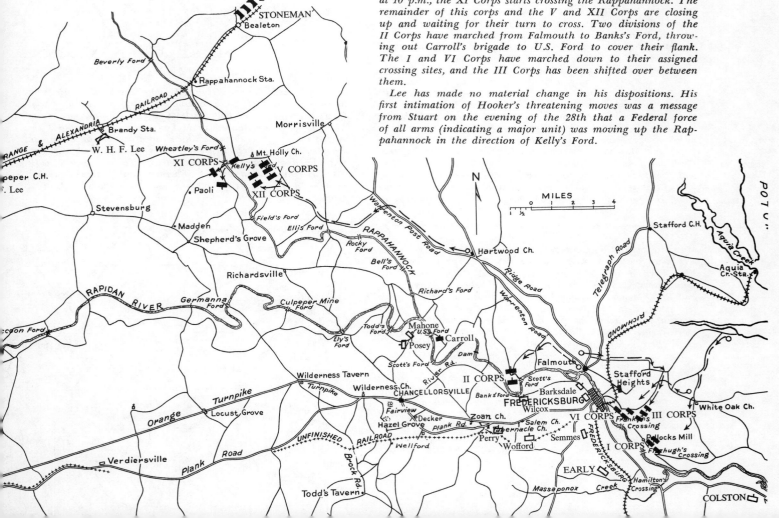

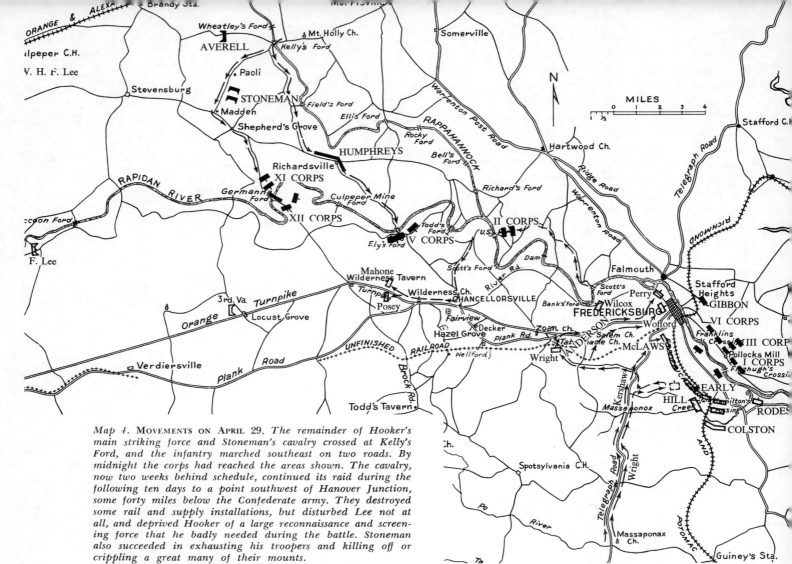

Map 4. MOVEMENTS ON APRIL 29. *The remainder of Hooker's main striking force and Stoneman's cavalry crossed at Kelly's Ford, and the infantry marched southeast on two roads. By midnight the corps had reached the areas shown. The cavalry, now two weeks behind schedule, continued its raid during the following ten days to a point southwest of Hanover Junction, some forty miles below the Confederate army. They destroyed some rail and supply installations, but disturbed Lee not at all, and deprived Hooker of a large reconnaissance and screening force that he badly needed during the battle. Stoneman also succeeded in exhausting his troopers and killing off or crippling a great many of their mounts.*

Lee, on April 29, only partially informed by his cavalry of the Federal movements, was beginning to react. He was still inclined to believe that the Federal main effort might be made near Fredericksburg, although he previously reasoned that it would be near Chancellorsville. During the day he made a number of readjustments. Anderson was ordered to bring Posey and Mahone down from where they were covering U.S. Ford, and take positions west of Chancellorsville. Colston, Hill, and Rodes, of Jackson's corps, were moved over to the Hamilton's Crossing area. Early deployed in the old intrenchments along the railroad and McLaws occupied the high ground at

Lee's Hill and Marye's Heights. Wright was brought up from Massaponax Church to a reserve position in rear of Early, then later to near Tabernacle Church. Kershaw was also brought north and added to McLaws' line, and Wofford was moved from near Tabernacle Church to a position on the Plank Road overlooking Fredericksburg. Perry, of Anderson's division, was placed on the extreme left, at Dr. Taylor's. Stuart, with Fitz Lee's brigade, marched to Raccoon Ford. Three squadrons of the 3d Virginia Cavalry were pushed forward to Locust Grove.

Map 5. FEDERAL CONCENTRATION NEAR CHANCELLORSVILLE—MOVEMENTS UP TO 2 P.M. APRIL 30. *Meade's V Corps started from Ely's Ford at daylight, with Sykes's and Griffin's divisions; Humphreys' division was still en route between Kelly's Ford and Ely's. Meade, encountering a detachment of Rebels to his left front, detached Sykes toward Todd's and U.S. Fords to clear up the threat on that flank, meanwhile continuing the march with Griffin's division toward Chancellorsville. He arrived there at 11 a.m. and called in Sykes.*

Slocum's XII Corps marched from Germanna Ford, followed, at an hour's interval, by Howard's XI Corps. He brushed part of Stuart's cavalry aside at Wilderness Tavern and arrived at 2 p.m. at Chancellorsville. Here he was greeted by Meade, who was jubilant that Hooker had succeeded in getting a large force on Lee's flank and rear. Slocum sourly said that a new order from Fighting Joe directed them to stop and take up a defensive position.

Anderson has blocked the Turnpike at Tabernacle Church, with cavalry out to the front.

262

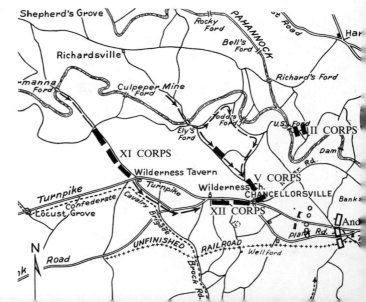

when it retreated from Fredericksburg, as the Federal commander believed it would have to do, with Sedgwick and Reynolds in hot pursuit. And Lee, in retreating would, in effect, be executing a flank movement across Hooker's front, a movement generally regarded as suicidal if performed in front of an aggressive enemy. As Hooker boasted: "I have Lee in one hand and Richmond in the other."

LEE'S COUNTERMOVES

But as darkness settled down that last day of April, Lee had finally decided on a plan of his own, and it did not conform at all to what the Federal commander hoped he would do. Before daybreak the previous day, Lee had been aroused by one of Jackson's staff officers sent to inform him that under cover of a heavy fog the Federals had thrown pontoon bridges across the Rappahannock just below Fredericksburg. Riding through the fog to Jackson's position, Lee found that the Federals had indeed crossed the river and driven back Jackson's pickets but were making no attempt to advance, although a large force could be observed on the other side of the river making preparations as if to cross. Everything seemed to indicate a general offensive, so Lee in a precautionary move withdrew all troops to the heights back of the river.

The Rappahannock at Fredericksburg takes a wide swing to the south to cut between two elevated ridges. If the Confederates tried to oppose the crossing, Federal artillery would have been looking down their throats. As Lee explained in his report: "As in the first battle of Fredericksburg, it was thought best to select positions with a view to resist the advances of the enemy, rather than incur the heavy loss that would attend any attempt to prevent his crossing."

As the morning wore on, however, and the Federals showed no inclination to attack, Lee became more convinced than ever that Hooker's main effort would be made in some other area. This view was confirmed when cavalry chief Major General J. E. B. ("Jeb") Stuart reported later that morning that a large Federal force had crossed at Kelly's Ford. A few hours later he informed Lee that he had captured prisoners from the V, XI, and XII Corps, and that heavy enemy columns were crossing the Rapidan at Germanna and Ely's Fords. Lee now believed that by the next day the entire Army of the Potomac would probably be south of the Rappahannock. In a dispatch to Jefferson Davis he stated: "Their intention, I presume, is to turn our left, and probably to get into our rear."

BUT not entirely sure of the strength of the turning column, Lee was reluctant to make any major shift of troops until he could be more confident of where the major engagement probably would take place. In the meantime, however, he realized he had to do something to protect his left flank. A glance at the map showed him that the roads on which the Federals were advancing converged at Chancellorsville, from where several roads led directly to the rear of his position at Fredericksburg. Consequently, he ordered Anderson, whose brigades were guarding two fords immediately above the city, to advance his division towards Chancellorsville to cover the roads; and Stuart, in danger of being cut off by the Federal column, was ordered to rejoin the main force as soon as possible, delaying the enemy wherever he could. And he ordered McLaws to be ready to move his division at a moment's notice in case Anderson might need help. Now all Lee could do was wait to see what the next day might disclose.

Anderson moved out that night about 9 p.m. in a drenching rain and by early morning of the 30th had selected a strong position on a high rise a few miles east of Chancellorsville at the intersection of the Mine and Orange Plank Roads near Zoan [also called "Zoar" and "Zion"] Church. His left extended across an unfinished railroad and his right crossed the Orange Turnpike. Lee then ordered him to throw up strong fortifications and to extend his line in case additional troops were sent to him.

Accompanied by Jackson, Lee spent the morning carefully studying his intelligence reports and observing the lack of activity on the part of the Federals across the river at Fredericksburg. Finally convinced that the troops in front of the city were merely a diversion, he told his officers, "The main attack will come from above."

The question now was, what should he do about it? As Lee saw it, there were only two courses open to him: Either retreat southward or attack the Federal forces at Chancellorsville with the main part of his army. Retreat was definitely the easiest and safest course of action to take, but Lee undoubtedly reasoned that that was exactly what Hooker expected him to do, consequently he was reluctant to consider it. Also, by retreating now he would lose the desperately needed supplies and forage that the Rappahannock Valley could produce and, as he had stated in March when he argued against the evacuation of the Rappahannock line, "It throws open a broad margin of our frontier, and renders our railroad communications more hazardous and more difficult to secure." This consideration must have weighed on his mind now, but he was also seriously worried about his lack of strength. As he telegraphed Jefferson Davis on April 30, "If I had Longstreet's division [sic], would feel safe." [Lee was referring to the divisions of Pickett and Hood that Longstreet had taken on a detached mission to the Suffolk area.—Editor]

ABOVE: Hooker's army on the march to the battlefield of Chancellorsville. From an original sketch by Edwin Forbes. (S)

Even without these absent divisions, however, Lee decided to take the gamble. If it came to the worst, he believed he could always retreat and join Longstreet at the North Anna River. He hoped, however, that the unexpected nature and suddenness of his attack might surprise the enemy enough to disconcert him and force him to change his plans.

"It was, therefore, determined to leave sufficient troops to hold our lines," Lee wrote, "and with the main body of the army to give battle to the approaching column. Early's division of Jackson's corps, and Barksdale's brigade of McLaws' division, with part of the Reserve Artillery, under General Pendleton, were entrusted with the defense of our position at Fredericksburg, and, at midnight on the 30th, General McLaws marched with the rest of his command toward Chancellorsville. General Jackson followed at dawn next morning with the remaining divisions of his corps."

The renowned Jackson, always conscious of the value of time in battles, had his men moving long before daylight by the light of a brilliant moon that near dawn fortunately was obscured by a dense mist, concealing his movements from the ever-present Federal observation balloon.

BELOW: A Union battery posed for this photo made on the bank of the Rappahannock just prior to the Battle of Chancellorsville. From "Miller's Photographic History of the Civil War."

HOOKER VACILLATES

That morning, May 1, the Federal corps commanders at Chancellorsville were impatiently awaiting orders to advance. They realized that Hooker had outflanked Lee, but a delay now could lose all the advantages gained by the successful maneuver. With the aid of the bright moonlight, the troops should have been moving out before dawn, with no enemy in front of them but Anderson's division. But the sun came up, and the morning got hot, and still they did not move. Hooker, who until that morning had been all vigor, energy, and activity, suddenly became hesitant and cautious. Yet the only opposition he had encountered so far had been in a minor cavalry skirmish the night before between the 6th New York Cavalry and the 5th Virginia Cavalry on the road from Chancellorsville to Spotsylvania Court House.

Finally, about 11 a.m., Hooker gave the order to advance; but at 11 o'clock Anderson and McLaws were also moving out, supported by Jackson who had just arrived. Although Hooker by his vacillation had thrown away a great advantage, the day could still be won if the Federals with their superior numerical strength advanced vigorously and launched a determined and sustained offensive.

265

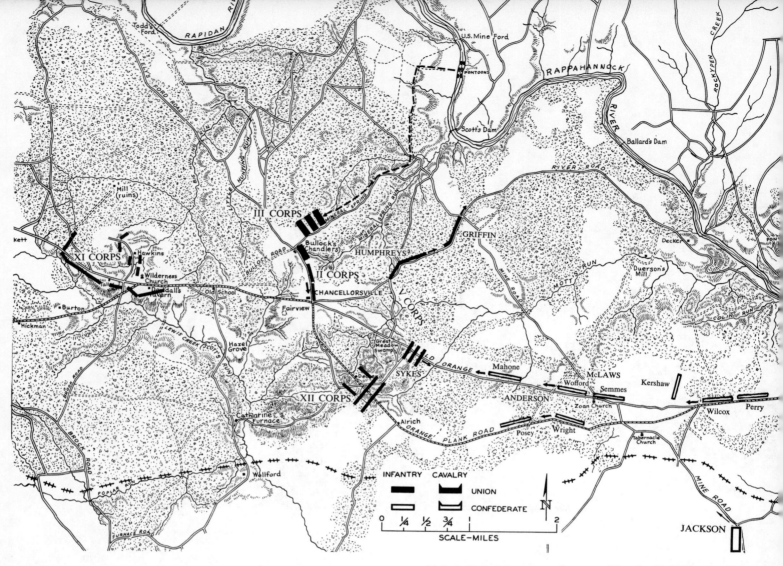

INFANTRY CAVALRY

▬ ⊔ UNION

▭ ⊔ CONFEDERATE

0   ¼ ½ ¾   2
SCALE-MILES

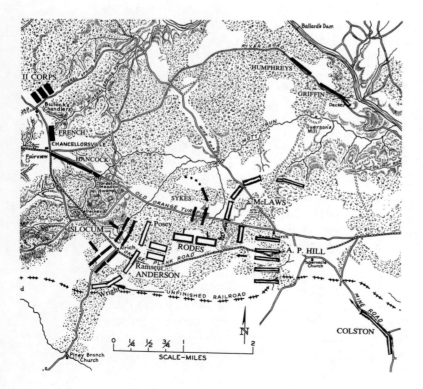

0   ¼ ½ ¾   2
SCALE-MILES

Map 6. The Advance to Contact, May 1. *At 11:30 a.m. two divisions of the V Corps have marched east on the River Road and the other division, Sykes's, is advancing on the Turnpike. Couch, commanding the II Corps, has directed that French's division move from its bivouac north of Chancellorsville to Todd's Tavern, six miles south of Wilderness Church. But this unit's passage was blocked at Chancellorsville by the XII Corps moving on the Orange Plank Road. On the 30th Hooker had taken Sickles' III Corps away from Sedgwick's concentration below Fredericksburg and added it to his own force. It had crossed at U.S. Ford on the morning of the 1st and was now moving toward Chancellorsville. The XI Corps was in the defensive position it had taken up on the evening of the 30th.*

On the Confederate side, Anderson's men had left their trenches along the line: Tabernacle Church-Zoan Church and were advancing west in two parallel columns as shown. Jackson's, shifting west from Hamilton's Crossing, is approaching on Mine Road.

The opening gun of the Battle of Chancellorsville has been fired, and in a few minutes Sykes will be fighting Mahone.

Map 7. The Situation at 1:30 p.m. May 1. *The Confederate advance has isolated Sykes. Hooker, now at Chancellorsville, orders him to withdraw; Hancock is brought forward to cover the movement. Slocum, who had advanced a half mile, is also ordered to retire. Griffin and Humphreys, not informed until after 5 p.m. of these developments, reached Decker's. An order from Meade caused them to retrace their steps at a killing pace.*

Rodes, at the head of Jackson's column, swung off the Plank Road and faced north against Sykes's flank. A. P. Hill came up in support, with Colston in reserve.

Meade sent two divisions (Griffin's and Humphreys') out on the River Road, leading to Banks's Ford, and another division, Sykes's, down the Orange Turnpike, followed by Hancock's division of Couch's corps. Slocum moved out on the Orange Plank Road, to be followed by Howard's corps. Sickles' corps was held back of the Chancellor house in reserve. Two miles out on the Turnpike Sykes ran head-on into McLaws, who had formed line of battle with his division astride the Pike; and Slocum's skirmishers tangled with Anderson on the Plank Road. Soon the area echoed to the roar of cannon, the crack of

musketry, and the angry, confused shouts of men trying desperately to kill each other. Then Anderson, on McLaws' left, sent Wright's brigade up an unfinished railroad south of the Plank Road, outflanking Slocum on his right, but not driving him back.

In the center, however, Sykes found himself partially outflanked on both his right and left when his advance carried him ahead of Slocum on his right and Meade's divisions on his left. He then fell back in an orderly manner behind Hancock, who took his place.

By 1 p.m. Slocum had advanced to the Alrich [often misspelled "Aldrich"] house, and was deployed astride the Plank Road with Geary's division on the right and Williams' on the left. Although outflanked on his right by Wright's brigade, the advance of Howard's corps behind him would in turn take Wright in flank. Meade's two divisions on the River Road had met no opposition and were within sight of Banks's Ford, the immediate objective.

Map 8. Situation up to Midnight, May 1. From dark until midnight the opposing armies held the positions shown, except Wilcox's brigade, which owing to changing orders was kept marching back and forth between Duerson's Mill and the Turnpike. The divisions of Hill, Rodes, and Colston, except for Ramseur's brigade, have been kept "well in hand." Anderson's and McLaws' divisions, however, are somewhat intermingled.

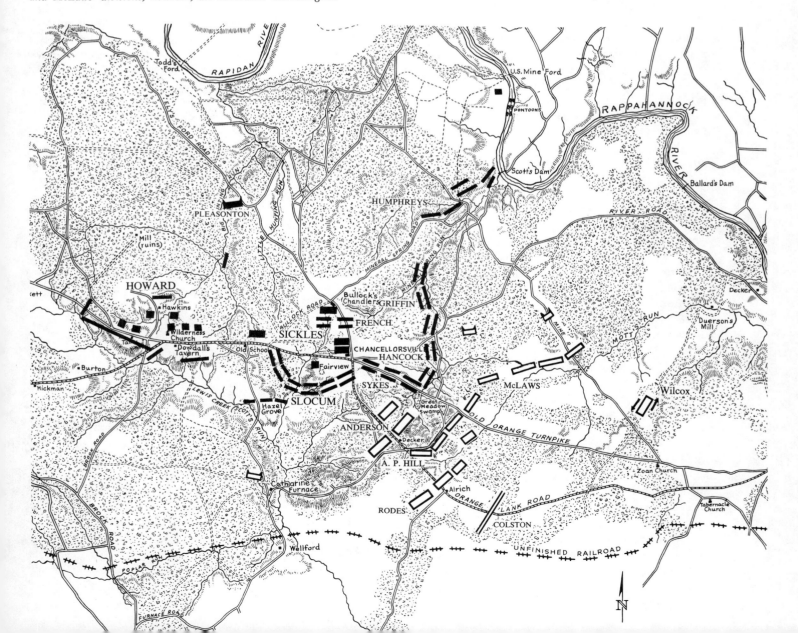

HOOKER ABANDONS THE OFFENSIVE

Then, to the consternation of the corps commanders, came Hooker's order for everyone to retreat to his original position! Fighting Joe was not willing to risk a fight, even with his superior numbers and artillery.

"The position thus abandoned was high ground," Couch reported, "more or less open in front, over which an army might move and artillery be used advantageously." Meade grumbled disgustedly, "If he can't hold the top of the hill, how does he expect to hold the bottom of it?" In a circular order to the corps commanders from army headquarters later came the excuse for the hasty retreat. "The major-general commanding trusts that a suspension in the attack today will embolden the enemy to attack him."

So by dark that evening most of the Army of the Potomac was entrenched in a defensive position around Chancellorsville. The terrain generally lent itself to defensive actions, rather than offensive, even though the superior Federal artillery could not be brought to bear effectively. It was rolling country covered with dense thickets and woods, with few open spaces, and commanded by two knolls south of the Turnpike at Hazel Grove and Fairview. The land between this position and the enemy was cut up by small streams, sharp ravines, and numerous marshes and swamps. Meade's V Corps held the left of the line, with its left resting on the Rappahannock, and facing east. Then came Couch's II, Slocum's XII, and Sickles' III Corps, curving around the Chancellorsville crossroads and stretching out along the Turnpike, facing east and south. The army's right flank was held by Howard's XI Corps, strung out about a mile west of Wilderness Church and generally facing south.

IT WAS now evident to every soldier in the ranks that the Army of the Potomac had suddenly gone on the defensive; and the men began to doubt the ability of their commanding general. "Troops were hurried into position," according to Couch, "but the observer required no wizard to tell him, as they marched past, that the high expectations which had animated them only a few hours ago had given place to disappointment."

When Couch went to headquarters Hooker tried to assure him that everything was just as he wanted it. "It is all right, Couch," he said. "I have got Lee just

268

Hooker's headquarters at Chancellor house on May 1, 1863. (S)

where I want him; he must fight me on my own ground."

Couch, however, was not convinced. "The retrograde movement had prepared me for something of the kind," he stated, "but to hear from his own lips that the advantages gained by the successful marches of his lieutenants were to culminate in fighting a defensive battle in that nest of thickets was too much, and I retired from his presence with the belief that my commanding general was a whipped man."

Major General Abner Doubleday, commanding the 3d Division of Reynolds' I Corps, believed that

BELOW: Action Friday afternoon, May 1, near the Chancellor house. This drawing (LC) by A. R. Waud is described in "Harper's Weekly" as follows: "The enemy made a vigorous effort to storm our position on the crossroads at Chancellor's. The house is on the right; about it the orderlies, servants, and pack mules of the headquarters—General Hooker and his staff, with Captain Starr's lancers. Slocum's battle line is formed in front, supporting the batteries near the burned chimney, which was surrounded by cherry trees in bloom. In the foreground are columns moving up to take part in the struggle."

"Hooker probably thought if Lee assailed a superior force in an entrenched position he would certainly be beaten; and if he did not attack he would soon be forced to fall back on his depots near Richmond for food and ammunition. In either case the prestige would remain with the Union general."

In any event, Hooker had no desire and no plans to attack, and thus by abandoning the offensive and assuming a defensive attitude he voluntarily surrendered the initiative to his opponent. This despite the fact that one clear lesson from all the campaigns of the great military commanders in history was that generally the defensive posture should not be assumed except as a temporary means, with the plan of passing to the offensive as soon as more favorable conditions obtained. The strength of the offensive lies in retaining the initiative, maneuvering at will so as to secure surprise, and to mass superior power at the opponent's weak point.

In retrospect, it is clear that Hooker lost the Battle of Chancellorsville on May 1. Initially he lost it by his hesitancy in moving out when he had Lee outflanked; then by his premature withdrawal before making any serious effort to carry out his plan; and finally by his unwillingness to assume the offensive at any time. Years later, on a visit to that open area

Lee and Jackson in the famous "cracker box" council on the night of Friday, May 1. Drawing by W. L. Sheppard. (B&L)

east of Chancellorsville, Hooker exclaimed grandly, waving one arm in the air, "Here, on this open ground, I intended to fight my battle. But the trouble was to get my army on it." He carefully neglected to mention that his army had been on it, but that at the first sign of a little opposition he hastily withdrew.

LEE DECIDES TO ATTACK

After the Federal forces' sudden and unexpected withdrawal, Lee rode out to his right to inspect the Federal left and see if an attack there might be feasible. He credited Slocum's withdrawal on the right to Wright's flanking movement up the unfinished railroad, but he was puzzled as to why Meade's divisions on the Federal left had retreated with no opposition in their front. Perhaps the enemy's left was weak and should be attacked. Instead, he found that "the enemy had assumed a position of great natural strength, surrounded on all sides by a dense forest filled with a tangled undergrowth, in the midst of which breastworks of logs had been constructed, with trees felled in front, so as to form an almost impenetrable abatis. . . . It was evident that a direct attack upon the enemy could be attended with great difficulty and loss, in view of the strength of his position and his superiority of numbers."

Darkness was approaching by the time Lee finished his reconnaissance and returned to his headquarters,

270

still undecided as to what action he should take. Here he conferred with Jackson, who expressed the belief that the Federal action had been either a feint or a failure, but in either event he insisted that "By tomorrow morning there will not be any of them this side of the river."

Lee, however, was not convinced. Then "Jeb" Stuart joined them with a report from Brigadier General Fitzhugh Lee that the Federal right extended west beyond Wilderness Church, was not resting on any natural obstacle, and seemed ill-prepared to resist a surprise attack. "It was, therefore, resolved," Lee reported, "to endeavor to turn his right flank and gain his rear, leaving a force in front to hold him in check and conceal the movement."

The risk was high, for the attacking force would have to make a flanking march of some twelve miles across the front of the Union army, traditionally one of the most dangerous military maneuvers. It was decided that Jackson would make this wide envelopment with his entire corps, some 28,000 men, thus leaving Lee with only Anderson's and McLaws' divisions to hold Hooker's whole force in check while the march was being made. Stuart's cavalry would screen Jackson's movement.

It was a bold and seemingly desperate gamble, but Lee apparently was willing to take the risk in order to seize and hold the initiative. That he was aware of the dangers involved and the possibility of failure is evident in what he wrote to Jefferson Davis: "It is plain that if the enemy is too strong for me here, I shall have to fall back, and Fredericksburg must be abandoned. If successful here, Fredericksburg will be saved and our communications retained. I may be forced back to the Orange and Alexandria or the Virginia Central road, but in either case I will be in position to contest the enemy's advance upon Richmond. . . . I am now swinging around to my left to come up in his rear."

JACKSON'S MARCH

It was almost dawn when Lee's conference broke up. The fading stars gave promise of a clear, hot day. Shortly after 7:30 a.m. the head of Jackson's column moved out past the crossroad near Decker's, to the southwest. A local guide had been found who knew a seldom-used woodcutter's road through the woods, which in turn led to a better road that ran northward beyond the Federal right flank and would put the column on the Orange Turnpike, well west of the enemy's position.

As the climbing sun burned down, the column, six miles long, wound its way across the Union front. Anderson and McLaws were ordered to press strongly against the Federal left to prevent reinforcements

being sent to their right, but Lee ordered them "not to attack in force unless a favorable opportunity should present itself."

Shortly after sunrise that morning Hooker rode out to inspect his lines. When he reached Howard's XI Corps on the west flank he found the three divisions spread along the Turnpike, generally facing south. Brigadier General Charles Devens' division held the extreme right, with only two regiments facing west at right angles to the Pike. Hooker seemed satisfied with the disposition of the troops and remarked about the unusually strong breastworks built by Devens. "How strong," he said to Howard, "how strong." And yet General Schurz, commanding the 3d Division of Howard's corps, later would report: "Our right wing stood completely in the air, with nothing to lean upon, not even a strong echelon, and with no reliable cavalry to make reconnaissances, and that, too, in a forest thick enough not to permit any view to the front, flank, or rear, but not thick enough to prevent the approach of the enemy's troops."

Map 9. START OF JACKSON'S FAMOUS FLANK MARCH. *As was often the case with him, Jackson did not get an early start. The head of his column did not pass the crossroads at Decker's, on the Plank Road, until 7:30 a.m. (This late start, and its slowness, was to mean that he would not launch his attack against the XI Corps until too late to exploit his initial success before dark.)*

Federals at Hazel Grove spied Jackson's column when, at 8 a.m., it was near Wellford, and Hooker later had Sickles attack the column near Catharine Furnace. During the entire march, however, Hooker failed to appreciate the significance of the movement—he thought the Rebels were trying to get away.

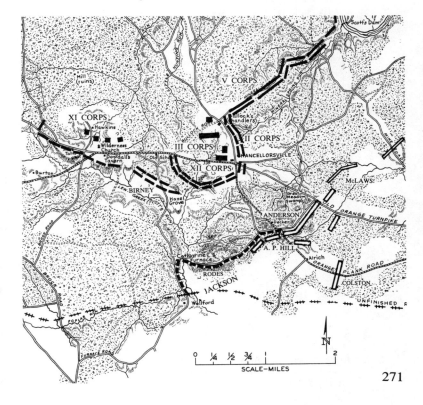

271

Hooker's headquarters at Chancellorsville on Saturday a.m., May 2. Picture faces south. From sketch by Edwin Forbes. (B&L)

ON returning to his headquarters at Chancellorsville Hooker was informed of strong demonstrations being made by the enemy in front of Meade's V Corps on the Federal east flank. Then, shortly after 9 o'clock, Federal observers posted in tall trees reported a heavy Confederate movement westward on the Catharine [usually misspelled "Catherine"] Furnace Road in front of Sickles' III Corps. Sickles immediately requested permission to attack, but Hooker was not yet willing to commit himself. He hoped, and tended to believe, that the movement signified that Lee was retreating to Gordonsville. Either that, or the Confederates might be preparing to attack his right flank. If he really believed the latter, he should have ordered Sickles and Slocum to attack immediately in front in order to break up the movement, and then ordered Meade to swing around and get on the Confederate rear. Instead, at 9:30 the following order was sent to Howard:

I am directed by the Major-General Commanding to say that . . . the disposition you have made of your corps has been with a view to a front attack by the enemy. If he should throw himself upon your flank, he wishes you to examine the ground and determine upon the positions you will take in that event, in order that you may be prepared for him in whatever direction he advances. He suggests that you have heavy reserves well in hand to meet this contingency. The right of your line does not appear to be strong enough. No artificial defences worth naming have been thrown up, and there appears to be a scarcity of troops at that point, and not, in the General's opinion, as favorably posted as might be.

We have good reason to suppose that the enemy is moving to our right. Please advance your pickets for purposes of observation as far as may be safe, in order to obtain timely information of their approach.

Howard later denied receiving this order, but admitted frankly that even if he had he would not have changed position without specific instructions to do so. The order was general in nature, he said, with no sense of urgency; Hooker had inspected the lines just a few hours previously; and Howard was firmly convinced that the heavy woods on his right would prevent any major attack from that direction. Yet he sent a message to Hooker's headquarters that stated, in part, "I am taking measures to resist an attack from the west."

But according to Schurz, "All the precaution that was taken against a flank attack . . . was the construction of a small rifle-pit across the Chancellorsville road in the rear of my division, near the house [Dowdall's Tavern] occupied by General Howard as headquarters."

AT 11 o'clock Devens reported a westward movement of the enemy in strength in his front. Still

Hooker hesitated. The previous night he had ordered Sedgwick to send Reynolds' I Corps to Chancellorsville, and when it arrived he would have approximately 90,000 troops at his immediate command. Even if Lee, instead of retreating, was preparing to attack his right, Hooker apparently felt secure in his defensive position and had no plans to attack. As the day wore on, with no word of a Confederate offensive anywhere along the line, Hooker convinced himself that Lee was fleeing to save his army. So, about 1 p.m., he ordered Sickles to "advance cautiously toward the road followed by the enemy, and harass the movement as much as possible." The word "attack" was not even mentioned, and only Sickles was ordered to move. Strange orders, indeed, for a commanding general who earlier had informed his cavalry commander that the secret of success in battle was to "fight, fight, fight."

At 2 o'clock Couch reported at headquarters, where Hooker greeted him with the exclamation: "Lee is in full retreat toward Gordonsville, and I have sent out Sickles to capture his artillery." Couch, who already believed that Hooker was a whipped man, thought to himself: "If your conception is correct, it is very strange that only the Third Corps should be sent in pursuit."

Map 10. Movements Between 1:30 p.m. and 2 p.m. May 2. This shows the march of Jackson's command around Hooker's army. Birney, of Sickles' III Corps, has moved his division south from Hazel Grove to attack the tail of Jackson's artillery column. Posey's brigade of Anderson's division and Thomas' and Archer's brigades of A. P. Hill's division are hastening to aid the 23d Georgia, which has been assailed by Birney. The remainder of the III Corps is coming to join Birney.

Jackson has just joined Fitzhugh Lee at Burton's farm, and is observing the disposition of Howard's unalarmed troops along the road near Dowdall's Tavern. Jackson sends word to Rodes, who had started to turn northeast at Hickman, to continue north and halt with the head of his column at the Turnpike three-quarters of a mile west of Luckett's. Colston and A. P. Hill are following Rodes. The cavalry is moving between the main infantry column and the enemy; the trains are on the outside route.

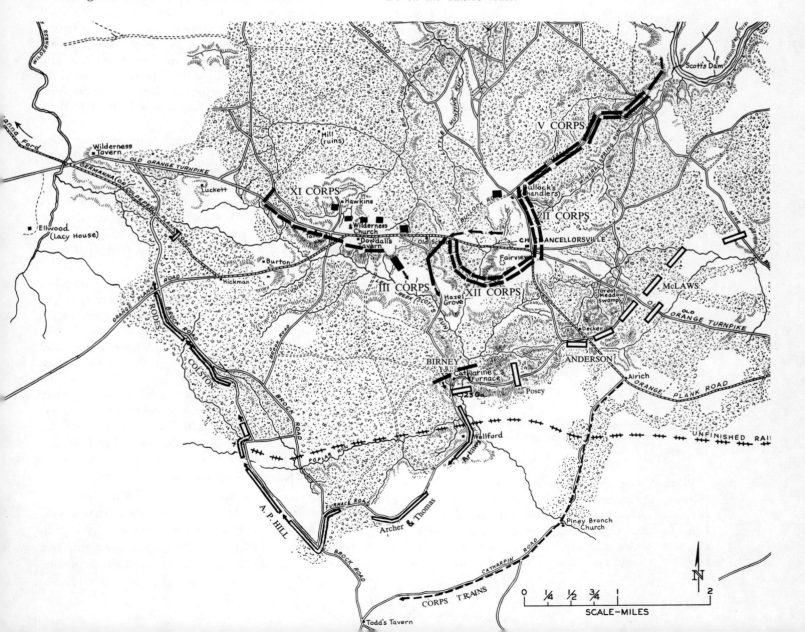

Donalds Tavern - Howards Hd. Qts. [handwritten caption]

It is impossible, of course, to know what Hooker really did believe at this point, and there seems to be only one logical explanation for his actions, or lack of them. He was not willing, apparently, to disrupt what he considered a strong defensive position to risk an attack under any circumstances. He was hoping to win a great moral victory, which is the way Lee's retreat would be regarded in the North, without fighting a battle or risking his army or reputation. This, of course, was waging war in the classical European tradition of maneuvering rather than fighting.

Sickles moved out with two divisions. About 2:30 he hit Jackson's rearguard near Catharine Furnace and killed or captured most of the 23d Georgia Regiment. A veteran of the 8th Pennsylvania Cavalry reported: "Passing to the left of the Chancellorsville House, we crossed our line of battle at the edge of a wood and came up with a reconnoitering party that had captured the 23d Georgia. We had heard that Lee was retreating, and supposed that this unfortunate regiment had been sacrificed to give the main body a chance to escape; but while we were commiserating the poor fellows, one of them defiantly said, 'You may think you have done a big thing just now, but wait till Jackson gets round on your right.' We laughed at his harmless bravado." Not only the generals thought Lee was retreating; even the men in ranks believed it.

WHEN Lee learned of this attack on Jackson's column, he immediately dispatched Posey's brigade of Anderson's division to the support of Wright's brigade near Catharine Furnace. This successfully checked Sickles' advance, and as Sickles stated in his report: "Ascertaining from a careful examination of the position that it was practicable to gain the road and break the enemy's column, I so reported to the general-in-chief, adding that as I must expect to encounter a heavy force and a stubborn resistance, and bearing in mind his admonition to move cautiously, I should not advance farther until the supports from the Eleventh and Twelfth Corps closed up on Birney's right and left."

Hooker then ordered Barlow's brigade, 2,500 men, of the XI Corps over to support Sickles' right, although he knew this was the only force Howard had in reserve, and despite his earlier order to Howard that morning that he should "have heavy reserves well in hand." If Howard needed any convincing, this move certainly must have assured him that in Hooker's mind at least there was no thought of any attack on his right.

About the same time that Sickles was capturing the 23d Georgia, Jackson's leading regiment, the 5th Alabama, was already forming for the attack across the Turnpike west of Hooker's right flank. As the other Confederate regiments gradually came up and formed in the woods, the Union pickets were aware that something big was afoot. Junior officers of the line tried to alert corps headquarters, but Howard, by now imbued with Hooker's belief that Lee was fleeing, and convinced that the woods were too thick on his right for a major assault, refused to take any action.

Colonel Noble, commanding the 17th Connecticut Infantry, later reported: "Horseman after horseman rode into my post and was sent to headquarters with the information that the enemy were heavily marching along our front and proceeding to our right; and last of all an officer reported the rebels massing for

274

Howard's line at the moment of Jackson's attack on the evening of May 2. A. R. Waud's pencil drawing (LC) shows a part of the XI Corps line along the Old Orange Plank Road just before it caved in and was overrun. In the center of the picture is Dowdall's Tavern, Howard's headquarters. Across the pike (indicated by the line of troops) and to the right in the woods, is Wilderness Church, a landmark in the battle.

Map 11. JACKSON'S DEPLOYMENT. Archer and Thomas reached Catharine Furnace at 3:30 p.m. to assist the 23d Georgia. An hour later they resumed the march. Meanwhile Anderson's and McLaws' divisions, under Lee's immediate charge, kept up a lively demonstration to divert the Federals' attention from Jackson's march.

Sickles was having a private war of his own near the furnace. He saw a chance of cutting off part of the Confederate column, but needed help. Barlow's brigade of the XI Corps was sent to him. Slocum wheeled Williams' division around to assist. Sickles intended an advance against the flank and rear of Anderson, but Jackson launched his attack on the XI Corps before this could be executed.

Jackson had reached the Turnpike at 2:30 p.m., turned east at Luckett's, and deployed astride the Pike in the formation shown. The deployment was completed at 5 p.m. whereupon Jackson told Rodes to move out—although the last three brigades of Hill's division were not up.

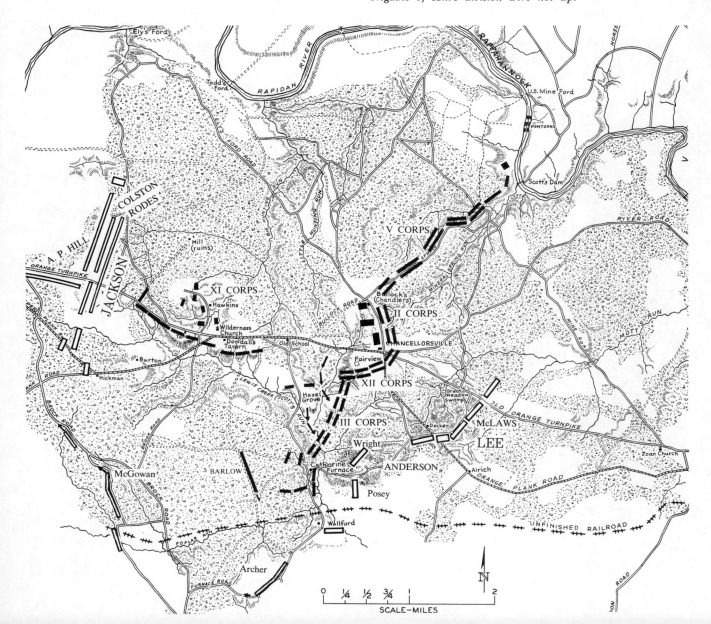

attack. Howard scouted the report and insulted the informants, charging them with telling a story that was the offspring of their imaginations or their fears."

In desperation, one officer in command of some pickets sent a final message to Howard that the enemy was forming in strength in the woods on his flank, and ended with, "For God's sake make disposition to receive him."

About this same time Hooker sent Sedgwick, back at Fredericksburg, a telegram: "We know that the enemy is fleeing, trying to save his trains."

By 5 p.m. all of Jackson's troops were up, and were eager to attack. But to be sure that they all moved forward in good order, Jackson spent almost an hour deploying them for a mile or more on either side of the Turnpike. In front was Rodes's division, with Colston's division 200 yards behind, and A. P. Hill's in the rear to support the other two. When Rodes reported he was ready, Jackson said calmly, "You can go forward, sir."

JACKSON STRIKES HOWARD

Most of the men in Howard's corps, their muskets stacked, were preparing supper, some were playing cards, others sleeping. Then the woods suddenly

Confederates carrying Howard's breastworks in Jackson's surprise attack on XI Corps. Drawing by W. L. Sheppard. (B&L)

echoed with bugle calls and the grayclad regiments, exploding into action to the sound of the fearful Rebel yell, proceeded to roll up Hooker's right flank.

"Its first lively effects," Howard described the assault, "appeared in the startled rabbits, squirrels, quail, and other game flying wildly hither and thither in evident terror, and escaping where possible into adjacent clearings." The first fierce rush struck the two regiments of Colonel Leopold Von Gilsa's brigade and his two guns on the pike, the only Federal force actually fronting in the direction of the attack. Devens' division, taken in flank, was driven back in disorder on Schurz's division, which in turn fell back in confusion and panic on Steinwehr's division.

"The noise and the smoke filled the air with excitement," according to Howard, "and, more quickly than it could be told, with all the fury of the wildest hailstorm, everything, every sort of organization that lay in the path of the mad current of panic-stricken men, had to give way and be broken into fragments."

Schurz in his report stated: "To change the front of the regiments deployed in line on the old Turnpike road was extremely difficult. In the first place, they were hemmed in between a variety of obstacles in front and dense pine brush in their rear. Then the officers had hardly had time to give a command when almost the whole of General McLean's brigade, mixed up with a number of Colonel Von Gilsa's men,

came rushing down the road from General Devens' headquarters in wild confusion, and, worse than that, the battery of the First Division broke in upon my right at a full run. This confused mass of guns, caissons, horses, and men broke lengthwise through the ranks of my regiments deployed in line on the road. . . . The whole line deployed on the old Turnpike, facing south, was rolled up and swept away in a moment."

And a soldier in the 13th Massachusetts Volunteers remembered that "along the road it was pandemonium; on the side of the road it was chaos."

IN THE deep, purple shadows of dusk the initial charge began to lose its momentum as scattered Federal units were brought into line to stem the tide. "Gathering up such troops as were nearest to the scene of action," Couch reported, "with Berry's division from the Third Corps, some from the Twelfth,

Hays' brigade of the Second, and a portion of the Eleventh, an effectual stand was made." Sickles was immediately ordered back from Catharine Furnace, several batteries were placed on Fairview, a knoll 750 yards west of Chancellorsville, and Brigadier General Alfred Pleasonton's brigade of cavalry, which had remained with the army, was ordered to Hazel Grove, a low but commanding hill just south of the Turnpike. Here his artillery, with other batteries from the III Corps and supported by Major General Amiel Whipple's division, enfiladed Jackson's right.

Their alignment broken by the charge through the woods, the darkness, and the growing resistance to the attack, the Confederates halted to reform. A confused clamor could be heard as officers and men sought to find their companies and regiments, now inextricably mixed, by the dim light of a rising moon. But Jackson, sensing his advantage, had no intention of stopping now. He ordered A. P. Hill to relieve Rodes and Colston and to prepare for a night attack. When Hill reported to him, Jackson directed: "Press them; cut them off from the United States Ford, Hill; press them." And then Jackson went forward on the Turnpike in the darkness to study the situation at first hand. Returning to his lines he and his aides rode into the 18th North Carolina Regiment, braced for an expected attack from the Federal cavalry,

Map 12. JACKSON FRACTURES THE XI CORPS. *This shows the situation at 7:15 p.m. May 2, with the XI Corps fleeing the scene of its disaster. By 7:15 Sickles had broken off his movement to the south and had faced his three divisions back toward the Turnpike to stem the Confederate tidal wave. The first unit sent north to help Howard, the 8th Pennsylvania Cavalry, made a heroic but costly charge and was caught up in the general rout.*

Federal artillery at Hazel Grove and Fairview is firing effectively. Sykes has moved northwest along the Ely's Ford Road. The I Corps, snatched early that day from Sedgwick, has reached U.S. Ford and is headed south into the battle.

Barlow's brigade of Howard's corps has not yet received orders to stop its advance southward to attack Jackson's supposed retreat.

Jackson's assault has lost its initial momentum. The front line units have become disoriented and intermingled in the darkening woods. Jackson, soon to be shot down by his own troops mistaking him for a Federal, has ordered Hill to pass through Rodes and renew the attack.

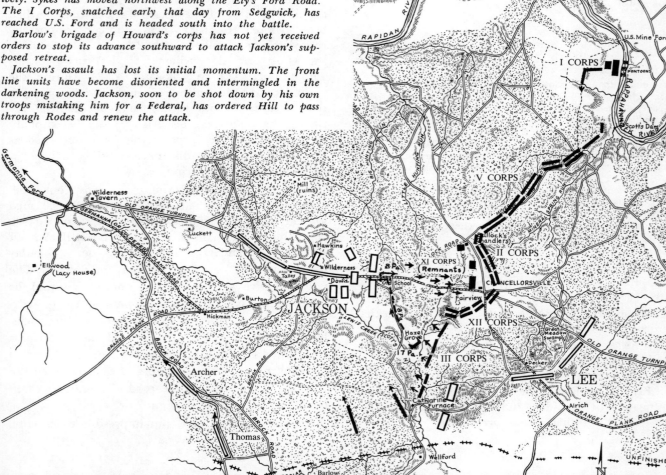

This drawing by A. C. Redwood shows the panic-stricken stampede of the XI Corps from position on the Plank Road. (B&L)

where he was shot and mortally wounded by his own men, thus ending any chance for another major assault before dawn. Command then fell to Hill, and when he was wounded by Federal artillery, Stuart took command of the corps.

Stuart, who arrived on the field at 10 o'clock that night, later reported:

I found, upon reaching it, A. P. Hill's division in front, under Heth, with Lane's, McGowan's, Archer's, and Heth's brigades on the right of the road, within half a mile of Chancellorsville, near the apex of the ridge, and Pender's and Thomas' on the left. I found that the enemy had made an attack on our right flank, but were repulsed. The fact, however, that the attack was made, and at night, made me apprehensive of a repetition of it, and necessitated throwing back the right wing, so as to meet it. I was also informed that there was much confusion on the right, owing to the fact that some troops mistook friends for the enemy and fired upon them. Knowing that an advance under such circumstances would be extremely hazardous, much against my inclination, I felt bound to wait for daylight.

THE FEDERALS REORGANIZE

By 11 p.m. the Federal XI Corps had been reformed north of Chancellorsville, Slocum and Sickles were in position across the Turnpike behind strong breastworks, Meade held the left flank securely based on the Rappahannock, and Reynolds' I Corps, after a 30-mile march, held the Federal right flank along the Ely's Ford Road, the right flank of the corps resting on the Rapidan and facing west generally. One veteran of that corps remembered: "Notwith-

standing fatigue and weariness, we began at once to build earthworks, as every man felt that his own safety as well as that of the army might soon be at stake. Knives, bayonets, plates, and dippers were enlisted, and by continuous activity substantial breastworks were completed when daylight appeared."

Hooker, with the addition of the I Corps, was actually stronger after Jackson's attack than he had been before. Howard's corps, though temporarily routed in panic, suffered only 2,412 casualties during the whole campaign, whereas Sickles' corps, for example, lost 4,119 and Slocum's 2,824. During the night Howard reorganized his men, and by morning they were ready and willing to fight, if given the chance. As Couch expressed it: "It can be emphatically stated that no corps in the army, surprised as the Eleventh was at this time, could have held its ground under similar circumstances."

With the arrival of Reynolds' I Corps from Fredericksburg, Hooker had approximately 90,000 men around Chancellorsville to oppose Lee's divided 48,-000. Thus most of the advantages were still his; but the Union commander had lost his nerve the day before, and he was thinking only of defense. The only offensive action taken, if indeed it could be called that, was a panic-stricken message sent to Sedgwick at 9 p.m. ordering him to capture Fredericksburg immediately, drive the enemy off Marye's Heights back of the city, and proceed at once on the Turnpike to Hooker's relief, to "attack and destroy any force he may fall in with on the road . . . and march to be in our vicinity at daylight."

An easy order to give, but impossible to execute.

As Couch pointed out, "It was 11 p.m. May 2d when he [Sedgwick] got the order, and twelve or fourteen miles had to be marched over by daylight. The night was moonlit, but any officer who has had experience in making night marches with infantry will understand the vexatious delays occurring even when the road is clear; but when, in addition, there is an enemy in front, with a line of fortified heights to assault, the problem which Sedgwick had to solve will be pronounced impossible of solution."

LEE'S ATTACK ON MAY 3

There is no question that Lee's strategy and tactics had been successful. His whole movement had been a model of maneuvering, screening, and massing superior forces at the opponent's weak point. But the fact remains that as of 10 p.m. that night Lee had actually gained no material advantage. His situation was just as critical as while the flanking march was being made. The Army of Northern Virginia was still split into three parts, with Sickles' corps and most of Slocum's between Lee and Stuart. And if Reynolds' comparatively fresh corps had moved out aggressively and attacked Stuart's left flank, while Meade simultaneously threw his V Corps at Lee's right flank, in all probability the Confederate army would have been destroyed. As the caustic Couch observed: "It only required that Hooker should brace himself up to take a reasonable, common-sense view of the state of things, when the success gained by Jackson would have been turned into an overwhelming defeat."

Lee was well aware of his potentially dangerous position. At 3 a.m. on May 3 he ordered Stuart, now commanding Jackson's corps, to resume the attack as soon as possible so as to unite the two wings of the army. Thirty minutes later he sent still another

Major General Oliver O. Howard trying to rally his men during the rout of the XI Corps at Chancellorsville. He lost his right arm at Fair Oaks. Drawing by R. Zogbaum. (B&L)

279

→

message to Stuart, stressing the urgency of the situation. "General: I repeat what I have said half an hour since. It is all-important that you still continue pressing to the right, turning, if possible, all the fortified points, in order that we can unite both wings of the army. Keep the troops well together, and press on, on the general plan, which is to work by the right wing, turning the positions of the enemy, so as to drive him from Chancellorsville, which will again unite us. Everything will be done on this side to accomplish the same object. Try and keep the troops provisioned and together, and proceed vigorously." And later in a note to the wounded Jackson he wrote: "Could I have directed events, I should

Map 13. THE MAY 3 FIGHT FOR CHANCELLORSVILLE. This shows the situation at 7:30 a.m., as A. P. Hill's division (under Heth) advances against Fairview on the south of the Pike and Berry's division to the north of it. Archer's brigade has wheeled against Sickles' withdrawing column but is repulsed. Lane and Pender have crashed against the juncture of Berry's and Williams' divisions. Lee is wheeling Anderson's and McLaws' divisions to come abreast of Heth and make contact with the latter's right.

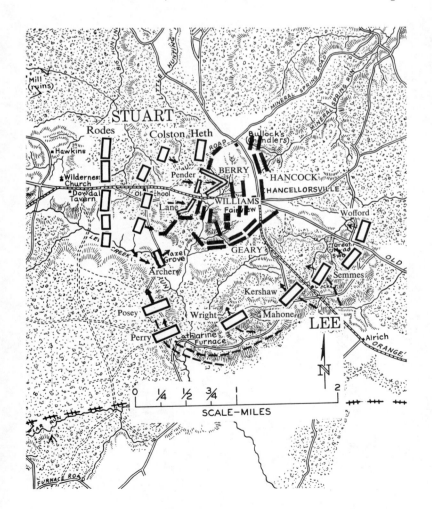

have chosen for the good of the country to be disabled in your stead."

At the first gray streaks of dawn Stuart sent Hill's division forward on the Turnpike, swinging his right flank, Archer's brigade, around to the south against Sickles' right, fighting desperately to hook up with Anderson's left. Colston was in the second line, Rodes in the third. Anderson, with his right resting on the Plank Road, pivoted his division on that point and swung his left flank, Posey's and Wright's brigades, forward from the vicinity of Catharine Furnace, against Sickles' left and Slocum's right. Meanwhile McLaws, between the Orange Plank Road and the Turnpike, moved straight ahead against Slocum's left and Couch's right.

THEN, suddenly, Hooker made it easy for the Confederates. The key to Sickles' position was the high ground at Hazel Grove which, since Pleasonton's cavalry had been withdrawn to Chancellorsville,

Whipple's division now held. But in order to strengthen his new, shorter defense line around Chancellorsville, Hooker ordered Whipple to be withdrawn from Hazel Grove and placed behind Berry's and Birney's divisions, straddling the Turnpike just west of Chancellorsville.

Stuart immediately saw that Hazel Grove was key terrain. Within a few minutes he had placed thirty pieces of artillery on it, and these guns soon began to play with devastating effect upon Sickles' troops and Geary's division of Slocum's corps. Sickles was forced to fall back, and with shouts of joy and excitement Stuart's right and Anderson's left linked up. Lee reported: "As the troops advancing upon the enemy's front and right converged upon his central position, Anderson effected a junction with Jackson's corps, and the whole line pressed irresistibly on."

For several more hours on May 3 the fighting raged furiously. Hill's men twice captured the knoll at Fairview and twice were thrown back; but with the Con-federate artillery at Hazel Grove pouring in a deadly fire, the third time Fairview was captured and held. The Chancellor house was hit and set on fire and a cannon ball, striking a wooden pillar on which Hooker was leaning, hurled him to the ground and temporarily disabled him.

"The woods had caught fire in several places," wrote an observer, "the flames spreading over a span of several acres in extent where the ground was thickly covered with dry leaves; and here the conflagration progressed with the rapidity of a prairie-fire, and a large number of Confederate and Federal wounded thickly scattered in the vicinity, and too badly hurt to crawl out of the way, met a terrible death."

281

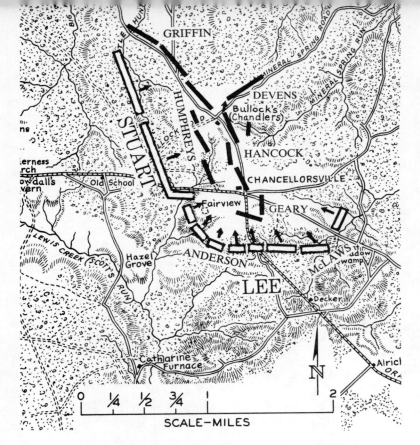

Map 14. THE CONFEDERATES CAPTURE CHANCELLORSVILLE. *The situation at 10 a.m. May 3, as Lee's two wings unite for the final drive to capture Chancellorsville. Hooker, in a semi-stupor, has ceased to function, and his divisions, though still full of fight, reluctantly pull out to the north.*

HOOKER IS DEFEATED

Almost out of ammunition and their requests for reinforcements refused, Sickles and Slocum were slowly driven back and the Federal front gradually melted away and passed to a new defensive line north of Chancellorsville, which Hooker's engineers had laid out the night before. In effect, the new position did nothing more than cover the bridgeheads across the Rappahannock. By 10 a.m. May 3 Lee was in full possession of the field, and by noon the Army of the Potomac was in its last defensive position before retreating across the river.

Hooker was reluctant to inform Washington of the results of the three days of fighting. In fact, for two days he had deliberately kept President Lincoln in the dark. Now, at 1:30 p.m., Major General Daniel Butterfield, his chief of staff, took it upon himself to let the President know something. "From all reports yet collected," he informed Lincoln, "the battle has been most fierce and terrible. Loss heavy on both sides. General Hooker slightly, but not severely wounded. He has preferred thus far that nothing should be reported, and does not know of this, but I cannot refrain from saying this much to

you." This, of course, told the President nothing, except that someone was fighting somewhere.

The anxious Lincoln frantically telegraphed Butterfield: "Where is General Hooker? Where is Sedgwick? Where is Stoneman?"

Finally at 3:30 p.m. Hooker reported: "We have had a desperate fight yesterday and today, which has resulted in no success to us, having lost a position of two lines, which had been selected for our defense. . . . I do not despair of success. . . . If Sedgwick could have gotten up, there could have been but one result. . . ."

It is interesting to note that while Hooker did not "despair of success," he offered no plans or information as to how this success was to be achieved in his present position, nor did he explain why, after ordering Sedgwick with 24,000 troops to come to the aid of the right wing of an army with 90,000 troops, he now withdrew the entire wing to a safe defensive position, leaving Sedgwick and his men to take care of themselves as best they could.

Lee was anxious to capitalize on the victory, but most of the men were scattered in confusion and many of them had been fighting since before dawn. He wisely halted to rest and to reorganize for a new attack. He stated in his report: "The enemy had withdrawn to a strong position nearer the Rappahannock, which he had previously fortified. His superiority of numbers, the unfavorable nature of the ground, which was densely wooded, and the condition of our troops after the arduous and sanguinary conflict in which they had been engaged, rendered great caution necessary. Our preparations were just completed when further operations were arrested by intelligence received from Fredericksburg." This intelligence was that Early had been driven off the heights at Fredericksburg, and a Federal force under Sedgwick was even now marching on Lee's rear.

Dilger's battery of Federal artillery on the Plank Road slowing Jackson's advance, Saturday evening, May 2. (B&L)

Rescuing the wounded from the burning woods. Many men were not so lucky. Based on wartime sketch by Edwin Forbes. (B&L)

SEDGWICK'S BATTLE AT FREDERICKSBURG

When Sedgwick at 11 p.m., May 2 received Hooker's order to cross the river at Fredericksburg and advance on Chancellorsville he immediately put his corps in motion even though he realized it undoubtedly would be impossible to reach Chancellorsville by daybreak, unless the Confederate force in his front had withdrawn. Of that he had no evidence. Also, it seemed apparent that Hooker either forgot or ignored the fact that on May 1 he had ordered Sedgwick to cross the river and make a demonstration down the Bowling Green Road, which Sedgwick had done with his whole command. "The [new] order to cross at Fredericksburg," Sedgwick reported, "found me with my entire command on the south side of the river, ready to pursue by the Bowling Green road," and he was already more than three miles beyond the city. "To recross for the purpose of crossing again at Fredericksburg, where no bridges had been laid, would have occupied until long after daylight. I commenced, therefore, to move by the flank in the direction of Fredericksburg, on the Bowling Green road."

But in the dark and unfamiliar country it took time to brush the Confederate pickets out of the way, and the column was slowed by the usual constant halts and false alarms of a night march in the presence of an enemy. It was close to daylight on May 3 when the advance reached the quiet streets of Fredericksburg. As the bright morning dawned, the dread Marye's Heights, the scene of Burnside's horrible disaster in December, came into view. "Several regiments were speedily moved along the open ground in the rear of the town toward the heights," a staff officer recorded, "and this movement discovered the enemy in force behind the famous stone wall at the base of the hill. They were protected by strong works and supported by well-served artillery. It was at once felt that a desperate encounter was to follow, and the recollections of the previous disaster were by no means inspiriting."

On reaching the town, Sedgwick ordered Gibbon's division of Couch's II Corps, which had been left at Falmouth, to cross and take position on Sedgwick's right and try to outflank Early's left. He sent Howe's division to the south of Hazel Run to turn the Confederate right, and he held Newton's division in the center to await the results of the turning movements. Gibbon, however, was stopped by the canal and heavy artillery fire, and Howe found the terrain such that he could not move to his right. Consequently, Sedgwick concluded, "Nothing remained but to carry the works by direct assault."

Map 15. SITUATION ON SEDGWICK'S FRONT AT 7:30 A.M., MAY 3. *During the early morning hours Sedgwick's VI Corps moved north from its pontoon bridges at Franklin's old crossing site, prepared to assault the Confederate works on the heights west of Fredericksburg. The bridges were then moved upstream, one to the position near the railroad bridge, the other to near the Lacy house. Gibbon's division, which was to cross at the latter bridge, was delayed in getting across, but at 7:30 a.m. was in the position shown. Newton's division led the VI Corps north into Fredericksburg, followed by Burnham's Light Division (a small provisional unit). Opposition was slight. Howe followed as far as Hazel Run, and Brooks as far as Deep Run, when skirmishing in his rear caused him to halt and face southwest.*

The Confederates' fieldworks on the heights were occupied by Early's division. Wilcox came up to the vicinity of Taylor's Hill just in time to stall Gibbon's advance.

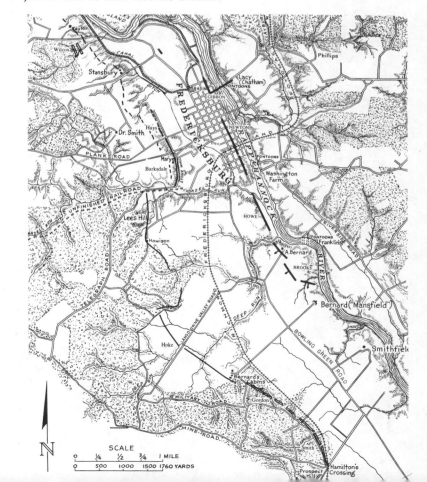

IT was now 10 a.m. and Major General Gouverneur K. Warren, who was at Sedgwick's headquarters as Hooker's representative, urged an immediate attack against Barksdale's brigade on the heights in the center of the Confederate line. Newton then formed three columns of assault in the center, based on the Plank Road, and at 11 o'clock Sedgwick, with much apprehension because the memory of the tragedy of the previous December was still fresh in his mind, gave the order to advance.

An observer noted: Both columns and line, in light marching order, advanced at double-quick without firing a shot. The enemy kept up an incessant artillery fire, and the noise was deafening. Their musketry fire was reserved until our men were within easy range. Then a murderous storm of shot from the stone wall, and grape and cannister from the hill, burst upon the columns and line. For a moment the head of the left column was checked and broken. The column on the right was also broken . . . Then, as if moved by a sudden impulse and nerved for a supreme effort, both columns and the line in the field simultaneously sprang forward. Along the wall a hand-to-hand fight took place, and the bayonet and the butt of the musket were freely used. The stone wall was gained and the men were quickly over it . . . and immediately after the wall was carried the enemy became panic-stricken. In the flight they threw away guns, knapsacks, pistols, swords, and everything that might retard their speed.

Map 16. SEDGWICK'S ATTACK AT FREDERICKSBURG. *This shows the VI Corps capturing Marye's Heights between 10:30 a.m. and 11 a.m. May 3.*

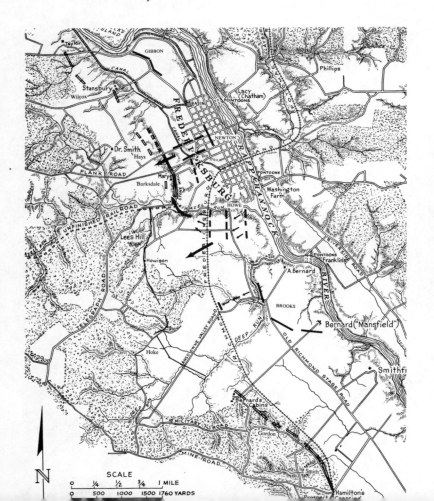

Attack on Sedgwick at Bank's Ford, Monday evening, May 4. From sandbag battery near Falmouth. Drawing, Edwin Forbes.

It was all over in fifteen minutes, as Early's troops retired along the Telegraph Road in confusion toward Richmond. It was a welcome but costly victory, as Sedgwick suffered almost 1,000 casualties.

Although he was still under orders to proceed as quickly as possible to Hooker's relief at Chancellorsville, Sedgwick now halted to reform and to rest Newton's division, exhausted by the night march, the weight of several days' rations and sixty rounds of ammunition, and by the heat, fatigue, and excitement of battle..

Brooks's division, which had been left to guard the bridges three miles lower down the Rappahannock, was now ordered up. Aware of the casualties Newton had suffered in the brilliant charge, Sedgwick was anxious to have Brooks, whose men had seen no action, take the lead in the move to Chancellorsville. Consequently it was 3 p.m. before Brooks moved out, followed by Newton and Howe.

Salem Church, from photograph made after the war. View is from the Plank Road. On the left is what remains of the Confederate trenches. The bricks on the four sides of the church are spotted with bullet marks, especially on the line of the upper windows toward the road, evidence that many Union soldiers aimed high. This church sheltered many Fredericksburg families during Burnside's battle. (B&L)

BATTLE OF SALEM CHURCH

The Plank Road running west from Fredericksburg passed through a gently rolling country with a series of low hills and sharp ravines at right angles to the road. Wilcox's brigade of Anderson's division, which had marched from Banks's Ford to Barksdale's assistance but arrived too late to help, now fell back slowly in front of Brooks, using the advantage of the terrain to impede the Federal advance. About four miles out, however, at Salem Church Wilcox halted and threw up breastworks across the road. The church, a small, unpretentious red-brick building, was situated on a long ridge covered with thick woods and tanglefoot underbrush. This position commanded the open approaches from the east. Here Wilcox was joined by McLaws with his three brigades and Mahone's brigade of Anderson's division, sent by Lee when he learned that Early had been repulsed and a Federal force was marching on his rear. The brigades of Kershaw and Wofford went into line on Wilcox's right, those of Semmes and Mahone on his left.

Coming up on this strong position, Sedgwick immediately deployed Brooks astride the road, and Newton on his right, and ordered an attack without waiting for Howe to come up. "After a sharp and prolonged contest," Sedgwick reported, "we gained the heights, but were met by fresh troops pouring in upon the flank of the advanced portion of the line. For a short time the crest was held by our troops with obstinate resistance, but at length the line was forced slowly back through the woods." Then darkness settled like a gently restraining hand over the field and the fighting stopped. When Howe came up, Sedgwick wisely had him form line of battle in the rear, facing east and south, and with his left flank resting on the Rappahannock protecting the Banks's Ford area. Sedgwick was now convinced that if Hooker did not attack to relieve the pressure on his front, he would have to retire across the river.

SHORTLY after dawn the next morning, May 4, Early, with his division reformed, advanced on the Telegraph Road to Fredericksburg and recaptured Marye's Heights and the adjacent hills without dif-

---

Map 17. BATTLE OF SALEM CHURCH. This map also shows the position to which Hooker withdrew on May 3.

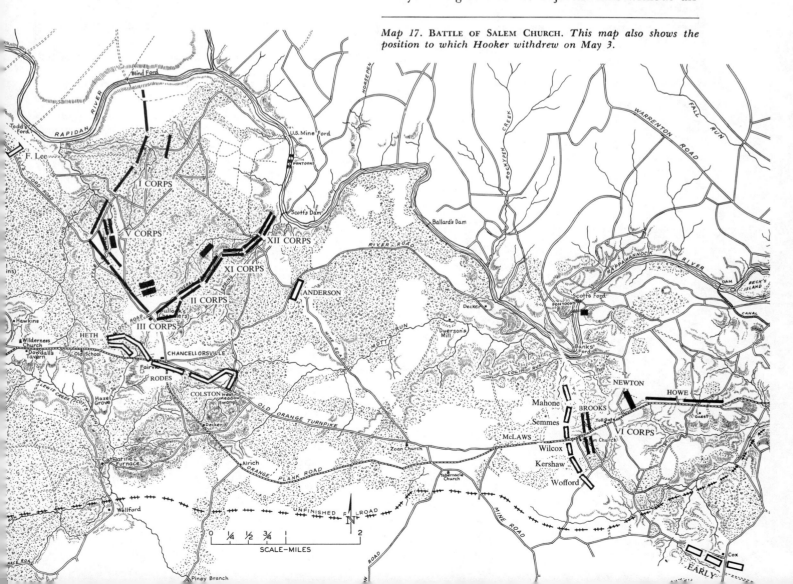

The 29th Pennsylvania (of Kane's brigade, Geary's division, XII Corps) in the trenches under artillery fire, Sunday, May 3. From an original drawing by W. L. Sheppard. (B&L)

Map. 18. THE ATTACK ON SEDGWICK, MAY 4. *Anderson has marched from his position west of Salem Church to participate in Early's attack on Sedgwick's left flank. Gibbon has withdrawn to his bridge.*

ficulty. Gibbon retired back across the river to Falmouth to protect the Federal camp and the supply line to Aquia Creek. Lee then ordered Early to march immediately to Salem Church so as to hit Sedgwick on the left and rear, while McLaws and Wilcox assailed him in front. McLaws, however, reported to Lee that he did not believe he was strong enough to make a frontal assault on the Federal position. Consequently, Lee decided to reinforce him. Showing his complete contempt for Hooker, he sent Anderson with his remaining brigade to Salem Church to swing around McLaws' right and effect a junction with Early marching out from Fredericksburg. This left Lee with only Jackson's three divisions and Stuart's cavalry to hold Hooker's force of approximately 90,000 men.

Anderson reached Salem Church about noon and continued on around McLaws' right flank to join Early. But, according to Lee, "Some delay occurred in getting the troops into position, owing to the broken and irregular nature of the ground and the difficulty of ascertaining the disposition of the enemy's force. The attack did not begin until 6 p.m., when Anderson and Early moved forward and drove General Sedgwick's troops before them across the Plank road in the direction of the Rappahannock."

McLaws failed to move in conjunction with Anderson and Early because, he claimed later, of the rapidly descending darkness and dense fog. Hence the attack fizzled out and Sedgwick's force crossed the river to safety that night under cover of darkness, after suffering approximately 4,500 casualties.

IT had been a trying day for Sedgwick. Believing that the Confederate force in his front had been reinforced by Lee, he was at a loss to explain why Hooker had not advanced to trap the enemy between them, and he was particularly disturbed because he had heard nothing from the commanding general. Early that morning he had sent a dispatch to army headquarters: "I am anxious to hear from General Hooker. There is a strong force in front of me, strongly posted. I cannot attack with any hope of dislodging them until I know something definite as to the position of their main body and ours."

Although Sedgwick was not aware of it, the main Confederate force was actually in his front. Finally he received a message from Hooker's headquarters telling him that he must look well to the safety of his corps and that if necessary he could fall back on Fredericksburg or retire across Banks's Ford. But, as Sedgwick reported, "to fall back on Fredericksburg was out of the question. To adopt the other alternative, except under cover of night, was especially so, for the enemy still maintained his position on Salem Heights, and was threatening my flank and rear from the direction of Fredericksburg."

Thus, facing in three directions, Sedgwick was forced to await attack, "determined to hold the position until dark and then fall back upon Banks's Ford." He frankly informed Hooker at 9 o'clock that morning (May 4) that "It depends upon the condition and position of your force whether I can sustain myself here." At 11 a.m. he sent another message: "The enemy threatens me strongly on two fronts. . . . Can you help me strongly if I am attacked?" The answer he received, signed by Hooker himself, stated: "I expect to advance tomorrow morning, which will be likely to relieve you. You must not count on much assistance without I hear heavy firing."

Hooker Withdraws Across The River

Hooker had no intention of trying to advance the next morning or any other time. In effect, the VI Corps was being abandoned to its fate, while the main force of the Army of the Potomac, within three miles of it, did nothing. As Couch bitterly explained it: "Some of the most anomalous occurrences of the war took place in this campaign. On the night of May 2d the commanding general, with 80,000 men in his wing of the army, directed Sedgwick, with 22,000, to march to his relief. While that officer was doing this on the 3d, and when it would be expected that every

A. R. Waud describes this drawing as showing "an old mill near the front used as a hospital for Slocum's corps and as a rendezvous for skedaddlers." (HW) An examination of Map 17 indicates that the mill was on Mineral Spring Run.

effort would be made by the right wing to do its part, only one half of it was fought (or rather half-fought, for its ammunition was not replenished), and then the whole wing was withdrawn to a place where it could not be hurt, leaving Sedgwick to take care of himself."

And during the night of May 4-5, as Sedgwick was hastily crossing the river, Hooker, safe in a snug retreat north of Chancellorsville, called a meeting of his corps commanders. In a feeble explanation for his actions, Hooker told them that his main responsibility was to protect Washington, and that therefore he had no right to jeopardize the army. He then wanted to know if the corps commanders would vote to stay and fight, or retreat across the river. Although a majority voted to stay and fight, Hooker took upon himself the responsibility of withdrawing the army to the other side of the river. As the conference broke up Reynolds exclaimed angrily, "What was the use of calling us together at this time of night when he intended to retreat anyhow?"

Retreat of the Union army across the Rappahannock at United States Ford. From original drawing by Edwin Forbes. (B&L)

287

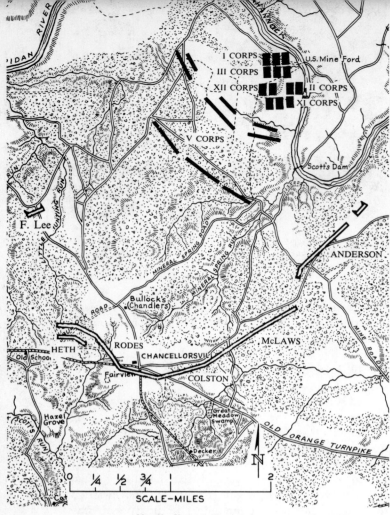

Map 30. HOOKER'S WITHDRAWAL

Map 19. HOOKER'S WITHDRAWAL, EARLY ON MAY 6.

The withdrawal began the next day and continued into the night. By May 6 everything was safely transferred to the north bank of the Rappahannock, and the Battle of Chancellorsville was over. The Federal loss in killed, wounded, and missing was approximately 17,287; Confederate losses are estimated at 12,821.

COMMENTS

Unquestionably this was Lee's best fought battle of the entire war. Yet there was a striking similarity between his plan and Hooker's. They both divided their forces in the enemy's front to execute brilliant flanking movements. The main reason one succeeded and the other failed was not because of any difference in the two armies, but in the two commanders. One had the courage and conviction to execute his plan regardless of the circumstances; the other did not. One was willing and even anxious to fight; the other desired to avoid any decisive action. Hooker's basic plan really had as its major objective forcing the *withdrawal* of Lee's army, rather than the *destruction* of the Confederate force. There was nothing in it that

even anticipated a major attack or battle. Hooker simply did not have the nerve to commit the Army of the Potomac to a decisive test. As Couch succinctly phrased it: "In looking for the causes of the loss of Chancellorsville, the primary ones were that Hooker expected Lee to fall back without risking battle. Finding himself mistaken, he assumed the defensive, and was outgeneraled and became demoralized by the superior tactical boldness of the enemy."

While Richmond rejoiced at the brilliant victory, the deep despair in Washington was summed up by Lincoln's anguished cry, "My God! What will the country say?"

BUT the situation for the North was not as bad as it first seemed. In a sense, the Army of the Potomac had not been defeated, only its general. At no time during the battle had it been committed to action as an army. Over 40,000 troops had done no fighting at all, despite Lincoln's admonition to use all the men. The Federal losses were promptly made good by new recruits, and the Army of the Potomac was soon stronger than ever. Although few people recognized it at the time, while the North was losing battles it was at the same time inexorably winning the war by consistently whittling away at Southern resources.

And while Richmond celebrated, the truth was that the South had gained little if anything from the victory. Perhaps Lee alone realized this. His triumph was not an unmixed blessing. He had suffered a 22 percent loss whereas Hooker had lost only 13 percent of his strength. Since the recuperative power of Hooker's army was greater than his, and since Lee had not gained ground nor driven the invader from Virginia, his victory was a barren one. Lee was greatly depressed. In addition, he mourned the death of Stonewall Jackson, his "great right arm." In announcing it to the army he said: "The daring, skill, and energy of this great and good man are now lost to us."

To adjust the command structure of the Army of Northern Virginia and close the gap created by the loss of Jackson, Lee changed from a two-corps to a three-corps army, and placed A. P. Hill and R. S. Ewell in command of the troops formerly under Jackson. Both were to fail him repeatedly. He was never again able to take full advantage of his own aggressive fighting spirit and that of his troops.

Lee's great victory had two noteworthy effects: It removed any lingering objection on the part of the Richmond administration to his proposed invasion of Pennsylvania, and it confirmed him in his belief that his men were invincible. He said so, after Gettysburg, to explain his failure there. Thus the Battle of Chancellorsville led directly to Gettysburg, the turning point of the war.

Detail from *The Battle of Shiloh* by Thure de Thulstrup
(1848-1930). The painting depicts the fierce fighting at the Hornets' Nest
on April 6, 1862. Published with permission of the Veterans of the
Seventh Regiment, New York.

A Historical Times reenactment photograph by Ohio native Robert L. Klausmeier, Jr. captures a cavalry charge as it might have appeared to men on the battlefield.

A Prang lithograph from the Library of Congress after Thure
Thulstrup's depiction of a Federal charge toward Dunker Church.

The climax of Pickett's Charge against the Union center on Cemetery Ridge on the afternoon of July 3rd is vividly depicted in this portion of the Gettysburg Cyclorama by the French military artist, Paul Philippoteaux. The artist came to Gettysburg in 1881 to study the field and interview veterans of the battle. Working from sketches and photographs of the terrain made at Gettysburg, he and five assistants completed the giant, circular painting in Paris in 1884. It measures 360 feet in circumference and is 27 feet high. First hung in Boston, it came to Gettysburg in 1913, and was purchased by the Federal Government in 1942. For 50 years it was displayed in a damp, unheated building and there deteriorated badly. It was restored and rehung in the new Visitors Center at Gettysburg in 1962. In the center of the cover painting can be seen Confederate Brig. Gen. Lewis A. Armistead falling at the head of his troops, mortally wounded. (Armistead was actually on foot). To the left is the copse of trees, the focal point of Pickett's attacking troops. Lt. Alonzo H. Cushing is seen dying at his gun in the left middleground.

Detail from a poster illustration by H. Charles McBarron showing
the U.S. Infantry attack on Stockade Redan on May 19, 1863.

Detail from *The Battle of Lookout Mountain* by James Walker
(1818-89). Reproduced courtesy of the Department of Defense, Washington, D.C.; photograph by Wayne C. O'Neill, U.S. Army Photographic
Agency.

Detail from "The Surrender of Lee to Grant" by Louis Mathieu Guillaume
(1816–1892), which now hangs in the courthouse at Appomattox Court House
National Historical Park.

GETTYSBURG

Text by Edward J. Stackpole
Designed by Frederic Ray

The Prelude to Gettysburg

By Col. Wilbur S. Nye

EARLY in 1863 the Confederate Army of Northern Virginia and the Union Army of the Potomac were facing each other across the Rappahannock River at Fredericksburg, Va. Gen. Robert E. Lee was hoping to repeat his 1862 invasion of the North. As he was to explain it later: "An invasion of the enemy's country breaks up all his preconceived plans, relieves our country of his presence, and we subsist while there on his resources. The question of food for this army gives me more trouble and uneasiness than everything else combined; the absence of the army from Virginia gives our people an opportunity to collect supplies ahead."

Attractive supplementary advantages would accrue. The constant threat to Richmond would be lifted and Maj. Gen. Joseph Hooker lured from his intrenched position and his army brought to battle on terrain favoring Confederate victory. This would ease the pressure in Tennessee and Mississippi where Grant and Rosecrans were endangering Confederate forces. Lee might even capture Harrisburg, capital of Pennsylvania, and strike from there toward Philadelphia or Baltimore. Such strategy could isolate and strangle Washington, center of the Federal war effort and site of the U.S. Treasury. The Northern peace party, already clamoring for a negotiated settlement of the war, would be encouraged and strengthened. Military victory might change the complexion of the diplomatic situation and, as had been hoped in 1862, bring about European recognition of the Confederacy. Altogether, a thrust into Pennsylvania promised great rewards.

GENERAL Hooker's spring offensive in the Chancellorsville area (April 28-May 5) interrupted Lee's planning and preparations. Although President Davis favored his plan, final approval by the government was not secured until mid-May. In the meantime Lee was getting his army ready. The most difficult task was to obtain the return of troops that were in the coastal regions reinforcing Maj. Gen. D. H. Hill in repelling a Federal incursion. Hill and the Richmond authorities were reluctant to give them up but Lee, by pointing out that his army as constituted was too weak, secured the return of two brigades.

Another serious problem was posed by the mortal wounding at Chancellorsville of Lt. Gen. Thomas J. (Stonewall) Jackson, Lee's "great right arm." Lee felt that Jackson was irreplaceable, but in selecting a successor he took advantage of the opportunity to convert his two oversize corps into three; and thus two corps commanders had to be found. Richard S. Ewell was given command of Jackson's old corps, the Second, and A. P.

Hill that of the new Third Corps. Other changes in key personnel had to be made.

In addition to reorganizing the infantry, Lee reorganized and as far as possible rearmed his artillery, and resupplied it with better ammunition. He rehabilitated and augmented the cavalry, assembling it as a strong division under Maj. Gen. J. E. B. (Jeb) Stuart near Culpeper Court House.

Lee's achievements in administration and organization during the amazingly short space of three weeks have been little noted, being obscured by his greater renown as a tactician and strategist.

As soon as his reorganization was completed and he had collected enough rations to last his troops until they could subsist at the enemy's expense, and when he was reasonably sure that the Federals were not about to advance against Richmond, Lee started his Great March. McLaws' division of Longstreet's corps departed for Culpeper on June 3, followed during the next two days by Ewell's corps. A. P. Hill's corps was left at Fredericksburg to guard the army's rear until it had shaken itself free of hostile contact, and to beguile Hooker into thinking Lee was still in his old camps.

WAR

With all its desolating evils is upon our Good Old Commonwealth! The Rebel Invaders are upon our Soil, and with Fire and Sword desolating the once happy homes of our people.

Come to the Rescue!

A PUBLIC MEETING

Of the Citizens of the TWENTY-FOURTH WARD will be held

THIS EVENING

Wednesday, June 17th, 1863,

On the Lot adjoining the Armory,

38th & Bridge Sts.

PROMINENT SPEAKERS

will be in attendance. Now is the time to come forward and join in the efforts to drive the invaders from our soil.

YOUNG MEN!

Let not the blush of shame, in after years, tingle on your cheeks, when you recount to your children the trials and perils of 1863, and are asked, "Were you ready to defend your country in the hour of danger?" You must not answer No!

POSTERS such as this one from Kean Archives appeared throughout Pennsylvania in June, 1863. Despite repeated appeals, however, only a fraction of the 50,000 militia quota assigned the state actually reported in time to be of any use.

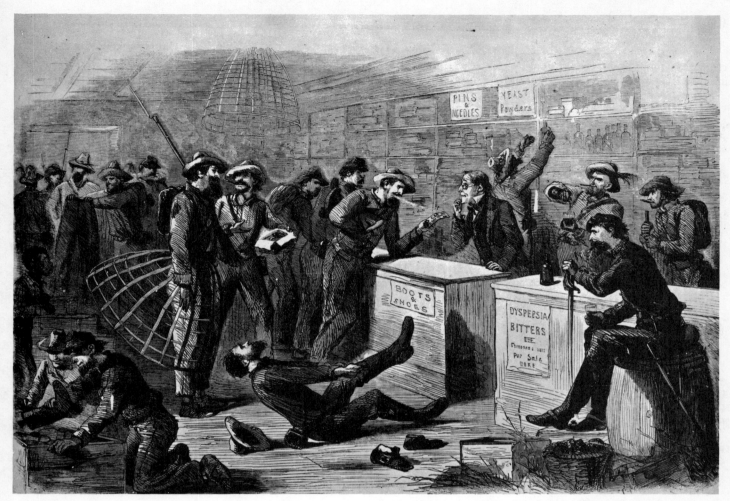

MEANWHILE, north of the Rappahannock, "Fighting Joe" Hooker had fallen into general disfavor following his defeat at Chancellorsville. Although President Lincoln still liked him personally, Secretary of War Stanton and General-in-Chief Halleck were determined to oust him as soon as this could be accomplished without political repercussions or damage to the army's morale. Lincoln finally acquiesced. Immediately after Chancellorsville he had asked Hooker, "What next?" Fighting Joe's plans, if he really had any, did not satisfy Lincoln, who told him to remain on the defensive for the time being.

Initially neither Lee nor Hooker had a clear idea as to what the other was up to. This was unusual for Lee, and was caused by the inability of the Confederate spy apparatus at Baltimore to penetrate Washington at this time, and to a general tightening of security in the Army of the Potomac. In the battle of wits between the two commanders, however, Lee's deductions were almost always more accurate than Hooker's because the latter was handicapped by a steady stream of false dispatches and absurd analyses from his cavalry chief, Maj. Gen. Alfred Pleasonton, whom some perceptive Southern commentators dubbed "The Knight of Romance." Although in the latter part of May and early June there were numerous indications that something ominous was stirring south of the Rappahannock, Pleasonton thought Lee was only preparing to launch his cavalry, perhaps reinforced by infantry, on a raid into Maryland. The eventual target was supposed to be the Pittsburgh industrial complex. Pleasonton infected Halleck and Stanton with this notion,

CHEERFUL INVADERS—Many a southern Pennsylvania storekeeper found himself in the predicament of the one pictured in this contemporary illustration. Forced to open their stores by Southern soldiers, they were paid in Confederate money.

to which all three clung tenaciously even after evidence to the contrary was piling up.

At the time Lee's march was getting under way, Hooker's balloon observers and signal officers on Stafford Heights reported changes in the Confederate camps and a dust cloud moving west in the Chancellorsville area. Two deserters who came into Falmouth on the night of June 3 said their division was under marching orders.

This did not look like a cavalry raid. Furthermore, editorials in the Richmond press had been speculating openly on the imminence of a new offensive by Lee, and the War Department had received several letters from Union people living in the South predicting such a move. In an effort to verify these reports and rumors by obtaining identifications, Hooker on June 5 sent a division across the river south of Fredericksburg. Prisoners taken were all from Archer's brigade, which had been in that locality for months. Nothing significant was learned.

HOOKER now concluded that Lee would cross the Rappahannock at the upper fords and follow his 1862 invasion route through Manassas and Leesburg, crossing the Potomac at Edwards Ferry and heading for Frederick, Md. There was always the possibility that he might turn east toward Washington. Hooker thought that the best riposte was to thrust straight at Richmond or at least to

291

attack the tail of Lee's column at Fredericksburg. He asked Lincoln to let him take this action.

Lincoln disapproved, pointing out that Lee's army was Hooker's true objective and that he ought to cling to it, moving on interior lines if Lee undertook a turning movement, and keeping his army always between Lee and Washington. Though historians have applauded Lincoln's concept and jeered at Hooker's, Lee's own statements show he would have hastened back to cover Richmond had Hooker's proposal been followed.

The Federal demonstration on June 5 delayed Lee for one day. When he saw that it was of minor importance and could be neutralized by A. P. Hill, he ordered Ewell to resume the march. Ewell's divisions closed around Culpeper Court House on the 7th; two of Longstreet's divisions and Stuart's cavalry were there also.

After reviewing Stuart's command the next day, Lee planned that Ewell's march be resumed on the 9th, screened by Stuart. The other elements of the army would follow at appropriate intervals.

This program was interrupted by a cavalry battle at Brandy Station.

GOVERNOR Curtin of Pennsylvania was early convinced that a major invasion was scheduled, with his capital, Harrisburg, as the initial objective. At least partly to placate him, the War Department created two new military departments in Pennsylvania, with Maj. Gen. W. T. H. Brooks in command of the western one and Maj. Gen. Darius N. Couch, the eastern. Curtin and Couch, denied material Federal aid, tried desperately to raise a militia corps but popular response was disappointing until near the end of June.

Even the panic in Cumberland Valley generated by the tidal wave of refugees fleeing ahead of the Confederates failed to bring forth any substantial number of minutemen. New York state came to the rescue of Pennsylvania with 26 regiments of state guard between June 15 and July 3. General Couch sent troops, as they became available, to threatened points on the enemy routes of approach. But as anticipated, these units melted away when the veteran Confederates appeared, or even before.

EWELL had resumed his advance on the day after the fight at Brandy Station. His 23,000 troops with their long wagon trains and artillery passed through Chester Gap for 18 hours on June 12—all undetected by the Federals. This shows that Pleasonton was conducting a shallow, timid reconnaissance and that the myopic Union high command was befogging its own vision with preconceived ideas.

Winchester was held by a reinforced Federal division under Maj. Gen. Robert H. Milroy. Although cautioned repeatedly by his superiors to withdraw to Harpers Ferry, he fatuously insisted that he could hold out indefinitely against any force the Rebels might send against him— meaning the three cavalry brigades in the Shenandoah Valley. He was flabbergasted when Ewell's corps confronted him on Saturday afternoon, June 13. But he still failed to evacuate Winchester.

In a neat double envelopment executed late Sunday and before daylight Monday, Ewell scooped up half of Milroy's division and sent the remaining debris whirling across the Potomac. Simultaneously Rodes' division with Jenkins' cavalry brigade attached chased away Federal detachments at Berryville, Bunker Hill, and Martinsburg. On the 15th Jenkins waded the Potomac at Williamsport and penetrated Pennsylvania as far as Chambersburg. Rodes stayed at Williamsport for a few days to allow the rest of the corps to catch up. Both he and Jenkins were collecting and sending rearward thousands of cattle and horses and tons of other seized supplies.

BY HOLDING Hooker to a strategic defensive Lincoln had handed the initiative to Lee. Fighting Joe could only make countermoves. That these were up to eight days tardy was not due to lethargy on the part of Hooker but because he lacked timely and accurate information of his enemy. Pleasonton told him much that was wrong and little that was correct. Nevertheless several sources placed Hood's division on the lower Rapidan near Verdiersville as early as May 27 and other infantry units of unknown strength near Culpeper Court House by June 8. Hence Hooker was satisfied that the Confederates were moving in strength toward his right flank. He reacted by shifting the mass of his army, during June 11-13, to the Bealeton-Catlett's Station area.

Two days later it was clear that Ewell had reached Winchester and some enemy troops were as far north as Williamsport. Hooker quickly broke what little contact he had with the Confederates at the crossings of the upper Rappahannock and moved his forces along the Orange and Alexandria Railroad to a line roughly from Leesburg on the north to Thoroughfare Gap on the south. There he sat for nearly 10 days, facing west and waiting for Lee to strike through or around him toward Washington.

HOOKER'S abandonment of the Rappahannock line was a signal for Lee to take like action. On the 15th and 16th Hill's and Longstreet's corps, with Stuart's cavalry screening the march, headed northwest toward the Shenandoah Valley. Longstreet's great corps moved stealthily through the foothills east of the Blue Ridge while A. P. Hill followed Ewell's route through Chester Gap to Front Royal and from there to near Berryville. Longstreet blocked Ashby's and Snicker's Gaps until Hill was safely through the mountains, when he passed through the gaps and camped near the other corps. Stuart remained east of the mountains screening the defiles and battling Pleasonton's cavalry.

On June 24 A. P. Hill's corps started crossing the Potomac at Shepherdstown and Longstreet's at Williamsport. The crossing was completed on the 26th and the two corps reunited at Hagerstown then moved toward Chambersburg, with Hill in the lead. Ewell, who had occupied that town on the 24th and 25th, moved on to Shippensburg and entered Carlisle on the 27th. Before reaching Chambersburg he had sent Steuart's brigade, with Gilmor's Maryland cavalry battalion, to McConnellsburg and back through Fort Loudon and Roxbury to rejoin the corps west of Carlisle. This detachment collected many horses and cattle and other supplies, since this was the chief occupation of Ewell's troops. The Confederates were now living high and fulfilling Lee's hopes of a thorough-going replenishment of his larder from enemy stocks.

FEDERAL observers on the mountaintops north of Harpers Ferry had been watching the long gray columns moving north across the Potomac, and had noted, without understanding their significance, the many wagons returning south loaded with supplies. Also frequent reports from along the leading edge of the invasion wave reached Washington via General Couch in Harrisburg. Hooker was forced to shift his army again to keep it between the enemy and Washington. During June 24-27 he funneled his troops across the river at Edwards Ferry and fanned out into Maryland east of South Mountain and around Frederick. He blocked the passes lest Lee come that way.

On the night of the 28th General Hooker was relieved from command of the army by Maj. Gen. George G. Meade. Halleck and Stanton had finally harvested his scalp by goading him into asking to be relieved.

On that date Hill and Longstreet were around Chambersburg, the former poised to go through the mountains and on east and the latter to follow Ewell. Ewell, now at Carlisle, had previously sent Early's division through Gettysburg to York, where he was collecting tribute in cash and goods from the citizens. Gordon's brigade had gone that afternoon to Wrightsville to capture the bridge over the Susquehanna. On his approach the defending militia fled their breastworks west of the town and skipped nimbly across the bridge, burning it behind them. The conflagration lighted up the valley very prettily in the deepening dusk.

From Carlisle, Ewell sent Jenkins to within three miles of Harrisburg to scout out the river crossings and their defenses. Jenkins' cavalry and artillery exchanged harmless shots with W. F. (Baldy) Smith's militia for several hours at Oyster's Point on Sunday and Monday. About noon on the 29th Jenkins went to nearby high ground to peer through his glasses at Baldy Smith's new earthworks on a ridge west of the bridge, then sent an optimistic report to Carlisle. Ewell already had Rodes' division primed to march on Harrisburg that afternoon.

ON SUNDAY night, June 28, General Lee, sitting in his tent in a wood a mile east of Chambersburg, was wondering why he had not heard from Stuart since the 24th. He frowned too over his lack of information about the Federal army, which he thought was still in Virginia. He had just sent orders to the corps commanders for the next day's operations. Ewell was to take Harrisburg, with Longstreet in support.

Hill was to follow Early's route, cross the Susquehanna, and cut the Pennsylvania Railroad between Harrisburg and Philadelphia. The collection of supplies remained an important task for all units.

At 10 p.m. General Lee learned from Longstreet's agent, Harrison, who had just arrived after passing through the Federal army, that that army, with Meade in command, was at Frederick, Md., with one corps near South Mountain.

Lee was incredulous, then concerned. This could mean that the Federals were about to cross the mountains in his rear and cut his line of communications. This must be kept open for ammunition resupply and for evacuation of prisoners and casualties. He was ever aware, too, that, though unlikely, the Federals might suddenly take a notion to turn around and go after Richmond, now weakly defended.

GENERAL Lee quickly changed his program. He sent orders to his corps to assemble east of the mountains near Cashtown and take up a battle position. He would either

ANDREW G. CURTIN—Governor of Pennsylvania in 1863, he foresaw danger of a Confederate invasion and tried to alert the Federal Government to it. (Photograph from Kean Archives.)

HARRISBURG'S DEFENSES—In this drawing from the Library of Congress, which first appeared in the "New York Illustrated News," citizens are erecting breastworks on the west shore of the Susquehanna River for the protection of Harrisburg, the Capital of Pennsylvania and a railroad center. A Confederate cavalry brigade came within three miles of the city.

accept battle there or feint toward Washington. He was confident that the latter course would relieve any Federal threat toward his rear or the Confederate capital. Hill and Longstreet accordingly were to move east through the pass, and Ewell was to return to Chambersburg, thence move to Cashtown. Early would retrace his steps to the latter area.

Before morning the general realized that these movements might cause a jam in the Cashtown pass. At 7:30 a.m., therefore, he sent another courier with a dispatch to Ewell instructing him to march to Cashtown or Gettysburg as circumstances dictated, but going by way of Heidlersburg rather than Chambersburg.

Ewell received the first message about 2:30 p.m., June 29. He canceled Rodes' advance on Harrisburg and started Johnson's division toward Chambersburg. Necessary instructions were sent to Early at York. The second order came before dark and was duly transmitted to Early. It was too late to have Johnson return to Carlisle, so Ewell sent him orders to turn south at Greene (now Green) Village and take the Black Gap road to Greenwood, thence over the Cashtown pike to east of the mountains. No urgency having been expressed by Lee, Rodes' division was permitted to remain in place that night. They started for Heidlersburg at 6 a.m. on the 30th, arriving at sunset; Early's division came to the locality soon afterwards.

Jenkins was left near Sporting Hill, some five miles west of Harrisburg. This could not have been to protect Ewell's rear, for the danger lay far to the southwest. Apparently Ewell, a bit absent-minded in times of stress, forgot Jenkins. The latter came on that night, after a skirmish with the militia at Sporting Hill in which he lost some men, and reached Petersburg (York Springs) at 2:30 a.m. on July 1. He reached Gettysburg after the fighting for the day was over.

EWELL'S final march to the battle began at a leisurely pace. With Rodes' division he took a road toward Mummasburg, but when near Middletown (Biglerville) he received messages from Lee and Hill that turned him south toward Gettysburg. Evidently contact was expected there. They arrived on Oak Hill overlooking the fighting on McPherson's Ridge at about 12:30, and Rodes was fully committed an hour later.

Early had marched down the Harrisburg pike, also at an unhurried gait, because Ewell had wanted him to be echeloned to the left rear. He felt no urgency because the sound of battle did not reach him until he was almost in sight of the town. But when he reached the high ground overlooking the valley of Rock Creek, he saw the Federal XI Corps deploying and at the same time a staff officer from Ewell galloped up and told him to attack. It was about 2:30, and two-thirds each of Hill's and Ewell's corps were soon in the fight.

294   A. P. HILL had camped around Cashtown on the 30th, one of his brigades reaching the outskirts of Gettysburg briefly during the afternoon, then withdrawing to Marsh Creek when they saw Federal cavalry. On the morning of July 1, Hill's corps resumed the march eastward and was soon engaged.

Johnson's division of Ewell's corps reached the battlefield at sunset. McLaws' and Hood's divisions of Longstreet's corps came up between 9 p.m. and midnight and bivouacked in the fields along the pike west of Herr's Ridge. Pickett's division remained at Chambersburg until the next day, arriving at Gettysburg in the early evening.

GENERAL Meade started his army north from Frederick on June 29. His information of the enemy was fragmentary and changing rapidly as reports came in from his cavalry and from Couch via Washington. He knew that Stuart was somewhere to his east, that Ewell was at Carlisle and Early at York. The rest of Lee's army was supposed to be near Chambersburg.

Meade's formation in five columns abreast provided quick deployment to the front or either flank, but indicated no disposition on his part to turn westward in the direction of the enemy. He reconnoitered a defensive position along Pipe Creek from which to cover his base of supplies at Westminster, Md. and be able to block any move of his antagonist toward Washington. His whole posture was one of alert caution.

On July 1 General Couch reported that the Rebels had withdrawn from Carlisle and York and were assembling either at Chambersburg or Cashtown. But by the time Meade had that information, Buford's cavalry, then the I Corps, had been attacked just west of Gettysburg. He began to hasten his other troops on the roads converging at Gettysburg. But he still didn't know whether he would stand there or along Pipe Creek.

The Battle of Gettysburg has been called an accidental collision. It was not quite accidental, since major parts of both armies were proceeding on a collision course. It is true, however, that neither Lee nor Meade sought a general battle at Gettysburg.

The men who fought and died there on July 1 determined that.

MAJ. GEN. JOSEPH HOOKER was relieved of the command of the Army of the Potomac and replaced by Maj. Gen. George G. Meade while the army was moving north to intercept the Confederate Army of Northern Virginia then engaged in an invasion of Pennsylvania. Here is printed General Orders 67 which General Meade issued on June 28, 1863, just three days before the Battle of Gettysburg:

> By direction of the President of the United States, I hereby assume command of the Army of the Potomac . . . As a soldier in obeying this order—an order totally unexpected and unsolicited—I have no promises or pledges to make.
>
> The country looks to this army to relieve it from the devastation and disgrace of a foreign invasion. Whatever fatigues and sacrifices we may be called on to undergo, let us have in view constantly the magnitude of the interests involved and let each man determine to do his duty, leaving to an all-controlling Providence the decision of the contest.
>
> It is with diffidence that I relieve in the command of this army an eminent and accomplished soldier, whose name must ever appear conspicuous in the history of its achievements, but I rely upon the hearty support of my companions in arms to assist me in discharge of the duties of the important trust which has been confided in me.

THE CAVALRY of "Jeb" Stuart conducted in the Gettysburg Campaign what was tantamount to a separate invasion of Maryland and Pennsylvania—an adventure t h a t was spectacular, showy, and almost fruitful at the beginning. But it proved to be a whimsical, unhappy, altogether barren invasion in the end. Perhaps the high point was when the gray-clad horsemen threw momentary terror into Washington, by appearing on the outskirts of the sprawling city, even to where they could discern the dim outline of the majestic United States Capitol.

They baffled and enraged Secretary of War Stanton afresh, agitated General-in-Chief Halleck, gave Lincoln deeper concern, and cut all ties for a time between the Federal Government and the Northern army that was driving up through Maryland to intercept Lee's main army. They won some cavalry brushes and captured provisions aplenty. But they failed in their primary function, which was to supply Lee with intelligence about his enemy's movements, and thereby they compelled the Southern commander to begin the battle of Gettysburg gropingly, hesitatingly, almost as though he were blindfolded.

WHAT would have happened at Gettysburg or in a battle fought elsewhere had Stuart's men been at their familiar places by Lee's side and in his front during the invasion is anybody's guess. The advantages obtained by the Southern army on the first two days of the battle, when Stuart was still absent, and when Lee fought without much understanding of the extent of the Northern concentration, were sufficiently impressive to persuade many students that had Stuart filled his expected and customary role, and had Lee maneuvered and battled knowingly instead of searchingly and illy informed, the Gettysburg story would have had a different ending.

And had Lee won a decisive victory at Gettysburg, it is possible, as all the world knows, that the South would have achieved independence and become, for a period at least, a separate nation. So much as that was the decision resting in Jeb Stuart's saddles as he pressed his men mercilessly through Maryland and southern Pennsylvania on their third ride around the rear of the Federal army, repeating in much less inspiring fashion their performances in the Peninsular and Sharpsburg campaigns.

The preliminaries of Stuart's ride are well known to the seasoned buff and may be explained briefly for the less ardent student. On June 22 Stuart's brigades were continuing to cover Ashby's and Snicker's Gaps after fending off the Federal cavalry that had been trying to break through the screen and uncover Lee's main force, which was then resting on the Shenandoah River near Berryville. Lee was about to close Hill's and Longstreet's corps up on Ewell's, then approaching Chambersburg, Pa. Desiring to place Stuart in proper position to cover the further advance of the army, Lee issued directly and

through Longstreet a number of orders to Stuart, written and verbal, and there was no doubt about Stuart's duty to gain contact with Ewell and protect his right flank as he moved north and east. But the most significant order was the last one, which allowed Stuart to decide whether he could fulfill his mission by passing around the rear of the Federal army and disrupting its communications and supply. The order was delivered at midnight June 23, to Stuart's headquarters at Rector's Crossroads, Va., in a driving rainstorm. Stuart read it by a flickering light under a tree and the words which clearly made the greatest impact on him were those that he would be "able to judge whether you can pass around their army without hindrance." Having argued earlier in favor of a ride around the Federal rear, he considered this ample authority for such a movement. Before he went back for a few hours of sleep, he directed his adjutant to prepare orders for the movement.

ALL of the 24th was required to assemble at Salem, the chosen rendezvous, the three brigades Stuart decided to take on the expedition. In accordance with Lee's instructions he left two brigades, Robertson's and W. E. Jones's, to cover the gaps and guard the rear of the army until it had crossed the Potomac.

When Stuart headed eastward before daylight on June 25 to pass across Hooker's rear and cut in between the Army of the Potomac and Washington, he unexpectedly struck the middle of Hancock's II Federal Corps moving north in column across his line of march. Hooker, now aware that Lee was crossing the Potomac, was moving north toward Frederick, Md. to conform. Stuart sent a

295

messenger to tell Lee what he had seen. This might have tipped off Lee on the 25th to what he failed to learn until the night of the 28th—that his antagonist was shifting to southern Maryland. But, unknown to Stuart, the courier never reached Lee.

Owing to this encounter with a large Federal force, Stuart had to move farther south than expected. Since he was traveling light, without wagons to carry grain, he had to stop for half a day to graze his horses. This delay, and others that would occur during the next few days, were to prevent his rendezvous with Early near York, Pa., as planned by Lee. On the 26th he moved to Wolf Run Shoals on the Occoquan Creek, where he crossed on the 27th and in the evening struck the Potomac at Great Falls, 12 miles above the Federal Capital. He forded the river in the darkness a short distance upstream from the cataract, where the tumbling water was so deep that the cannon and caissons disappeared beneath the surface. The men held the ammunition above their heads to keep it serviceable. Well before dawn on June 28, Stuart's cavalry, consisting of the brigades of Fitz Lee, Chambliss, and Hampton, were in Maryland. They were separated from Lee's army by two mountain ranges and the Army of the Potomac, which was concentrating at Frederick.

STUART was delayed again while his horses grazed on the lush Maryland pastures untouched by the ravages of war. Then about noon he startled the town of Rockville, eight miles from the District of Columbia line, on the highway between Washington and the Federal army headquarters at Frederick, by appearing suddenly as though out of the sky with his dusty gray squadrons. The noontime congregations were leaving church and the streets of the town, where sentiments apparently were divided, were lined with the enthusiastic and curious observers and by bevies of eager young ladies from the Rockville Female Academy, who clapped their hands, requested buttons, and seemed ardent secessionists. When one of the regiments halted, they rushed up and cut the buttons from the cavalry jackets with their own knives or scissors.

While Stuart's men were exchanging glances with the fair of Rockville, an unsuspecting Federal train of 150 wagons loaded mainly with forage for horses but with lesser supplies of whisky, bacon, hams, and sugar came lumbering up from Washington en route to Meade's army in Frederick. Had there been time to establish an ambuscade the entire convoy would have been captured. As Chambliss's troopers attacked the guard at the head,

the rear teamsters turned their wagons about and lashed the mules back toward Washington. A detachment of Chambliss's men pursued them but they had a good lead and an overturned wagon blocked the road. Not until the determined Southern troopers could look out from a hill across the city of Washington did they abandon the pursuit. Thus 25 wagons escaped behind the defenses. The portion of the convoy captured numbered 400 teamsters and guards, 125 wagons, and 900 mules.

This dash marked Stuart's closest approach to Washington. It threw the city into a frenzy of fear and preparation. Whitelaw Reid, one of the best of the Northern correspondents, was in Washington making his way to the Army of the Potomac to cover the Gettysburg campaign, and compared the conditions he saw to what they were after Bull Run:

"All night long, troops were marching; orderlies with clanking sabres clattering along the streets; trains of wagons grinding over the bouldering avenues . . . The quartermaster's department was a bee-hive; everything was motion and hurry."

In Baltimore the alarm bells sounded and Maryland home guards hurried to duty.

ONE OF Stuart's most disconcerting actions at Rockville was cutting the telegraph line. When contact was severed between the Federal Government and the army, rumor supplanted intelligence. For all the city knew, Meade could have encountered all or portions of Lee's army, fought a battle, won a victory or had his force destroyed. True, the blank-out was temporary, but it was sufficiently grievous to cause Secretary of State Seward to aver that the government was in extreme peril, and for Halleck to tell General Couch in Harrisburg via the wire that remained open to the Pennsylvania capital that he had lost all touch with the army.

Escorting his captured wagons, which were a godsend at first because of the grain they supplied for his mounts, the Confederate cavalry leader headed north on what was quickly to become one of the most gruelling, ener-

JEB STUART—Students of the Gettysburg Campaign still argue about whether he was justified in making his fruitless and exhausting ride around the Union army. (Photograph from the Cook Collection, the Valentine Museum, Richmond, Va.)

vating rides in the whole course of the war. Stuart, who was supposed to supply Lee with intelligence, could not gather enough for his own purposes, though he talked with the Marylanders and read every newspaper that came into his hands. He had no contact with General Lee and did not know where the moving elements of the Confederate army were.

STUART, one of the most resourceful and aggressive officers developed in this war, was capable of driving his men relentlessly, and this he now did. None had greater ardor for the Confederate cause than this handsome, blue-eyed, reddish-whiskered horseman, who, above his fondness for ladies and flowers, or banjos and gaiety, worshipped achievement and loved renown.

His virtues were simple, as uncomplicated as the man himself. Because he had promised his mother when he was 11 years old never to drink, he refused liquor that might have eased his pain when, 10 months later, he lay dying. He was inordinately proud of the fine, rich beard that had the warm glint of his best sorrel mount, and he enjoyed elegance of dress with the open exuberance of youth. He had shown himself to be bold in his planning, quick to improvise, and sly as a catamount— a leader his group of hell-for-leather riders followed with pride.

Stuart, according to popular fancy, wore the heavy red beard to conceal a weak chin. A look at his West Point graduating picture will destroy that legend because his face was more attractive and possibly stronger without it. But it did give him age, keep him in harmony with the Army fashion, and save shaving time, which was important to one always on the go.

AFTER brushing aside a small Federal detail at Cooksville, Md., Stuart ripped up the Baltimore and Ohio railroad at Hood's Mill and burned the bridge at Sykesville, thus severing transport about midway between Harpers Ferry and Baltimore and cutting one of the two trunk railroad lines between Washington and the West. He read in a newspaper that Jubal Early, commanding Ewell's advanced division, had reached Wrightsville on the Susquehanna River and therefore headed through Westminster. There, on the Baltimore-Gettysburg Pike, he beat off a spunky attack by two companies of the 1st Delaware Cavalry, which lunged headlong into the Confederate brigades that had the numerical superiority to gobble up the little force.

"The impudent daring of a few rebel horsemen" startled Baltimore, it was related, the reports of their proximity being carried into the city "by swift-running fright."

Stuart reached Westminster June 29, the day Lee's couriers were hurrying to recall Ewell's scattered corps from the Susquehanna and cause the army to assemble near Cashtown. That night he moved on to Union Mills, where he stopped for a few hours of rest. Already the troopers were falling from their saddles from want of sleep and the captured mules were becoming almost unmanageable from lack of food and water.

Still ignorant of the general situation, though warned by his scouts that enemy cavalry were in Littlestown, to his left, Stuart dragged on to Hanover the next morning, hoping soon to meet Early. Instead he ran into Judson Kilpatrick's Federal cavalry division, that was just passing through Hanover. Stuart's leading brigade charged on sight, driving on through the town one of Kilpatrick's rear regiments, and taking possession of the streets briefly. But part of the Federal division countercharged, driving out Chambliss, whom Stuart could not support promptly because the captured train was between Chambliss and the next brigade. There was little more close fighting during the day, the two forces glaring at each other from positions above and below the town. Weighted down with the captured wagons and animals and a horde

First Occupation of the Town

IT IS not generally known that Gettysburg was twice occupied by Confederate soldiers during the Southern invasion of 1863. Five days before the battle there, part of Early's division passed through the town on its way to York, Pa. and Wrightsville where there was a bridge across the Susquehanna which General Lee wanted seized.

Pausing briefly in Gettysburg on June 26, 1863, Early demanded that the town officials furnish 60 barrels of flour, 7,000 pounds of pork, 1,200 pounds of sugar, 600 pounds of coffee, 1,000 pounds of salt, 10 bushels of onions, 1,000 pairs of shoes, and 500 hats or pay $10,000.

Dr. David Kendlehart, president of the borough council, notified Early that "it is utterly impossible to comply." He said all the town fathers could do would be to "request the stores to be opened and the citizens to furnish whatever they can of such provisions . . ."

Being under orders to hasten to York, Early did not press the requisition. In York, however, he collected $28,000 indemnity from the local government. On July 1, Early's division again occupied Gettysburg, this time on the heels of the routed XI Federal Corps.

297

HANOVER, PA.—Stuart's horsemen tangled with Kilpatrick's cavalry division in the streets of this town on June 30, 1863. This sketch was made just after the battle by Benson J. Lossing, author of a three-volume history published in 1866. "Here the battle began and continued down the street seen near the center of the picture," Lossing noted.

of prisoners picked up along the way, Stuart preferred not to become embroiled before he could form juncture with Early. During the night he moved off to the east through Jefferson, and headed toward York.

WHEN Stuart reached the vicinity of York, Early, of course, was gone. He was on his way west to join Ewell at Heidlersburg, and had missed Stuart by only a few miles. Stuart now felt that his only course was to go to Carlisle or Shippensburg, where General Lee had indicated the army would probably concentrate before advancing across the Susquehanna. Stuart knew nothing about the changed plans, and had no knowledge of Lee's whereabouts.

There was no time now for jest or banjos. Finally he reached Carlisle on the night of July 1, after the first day of the battle of Gettysburg had passed into history. He shelled the town when it refused to surrender and fired Carlisle Barracks. At Carlisle he learned that Lee was fighting a battle so he headed south.

Some points are not customarily recalled about Stuart's groping ride. One is the fact that he covered 70 miles on

June 30 and July 1, and fought for several hours at Hanover. This was achieved in 36 hours, on jaded mounts and escorting a lumbering captive wagon train.

ANOTHER point is that Stuart never did find Lee. Lee found Stuart. On the night of July 1 the anxious commanding general had Maj. Harry Gilmor dispatch eight picked horsemen over the Pennsylvania countryside by different roads, with instructions to locate Stuart. James D. Waters, a Marylander, told the story of it. They carried sealed orders, which they were to destroy if they seemed likely to be captured, directing Stuart to ride at once to Gettysburg. Waters was the fortunate courier who located Stuart at Carlisle and gave him Lee's orders. Stuart rode to Gettysburg that day, July 2, while the main actions of the battle were being fought, and reported to Lee at army headquarters near Seminary Ridge about 11 o'clock that night.

Another point is that Col. Charles Marshall, Lee's chief-of-staff, who had prepared the orders issued to Stuart in Virginia, thought they had been so grossly violated by the cavalry chief that he should be court-martialed and shot. That is what he recommended to General Lee.

The nearest Lee ever came to censuring Stuart was the rebuke implied in the greeting when they met that night, "Well, General Stuart, you are here at last."

Stuart's ride around the Federal army was unfortunate for the South and many think it was one of the important elements contributing to Lee's defeat. But there is not a reasonable doubt that he had ample authority to make it. He violated no orders. He merely guessed wrong and in warfare that is sometimes the worst thing a general can do. Furthermore, even if he had not been delayed en route, but had succeeded in placing himself on the front and right of Ewell's corps, as called for in his orders, he would still have been of little value to Lee. For he then would have been as distant from the Federal army as Ewell was—until July 1 completely out of contact. The simplest and most impartial summary that can be made is that the Confederate cavalry was not properly employed during the Gettysburg Campaign. It was diverted from what should have been its most important duty—reconnoitering the enemy.

298 CARLISLE BARRACKS—Arriving at Carlisle, Pa. on July 1, 1863 and finding it re-occupied by Union militia who refused to surrender the town, a part of Stuart's command burned the U.S. Army Barracks there. The Confederates also shelled the town. Ruins of the barracks may be seen in this drawing which appeared in "Frank Leslie's Illustrated Newspaper" on July 18, 1863. (From Kean Archives.)

The Battle of Gettysburg

BY EDWARD J. STACKPOLE

THE GRAY LIGHT of dawn was beginning to outline trees, fences, and scattered farm houses along the Chambersburg pike near Willoughby Run, 1½ miles west of the little crossroad town of Gettysburg, Pa. The time was shortly after 5 a.m. Wednesday, July 1, 1863.

Troopers of Union Brig. Gen. John Buford's 1st Cavalry Division, Army of the Potomac, on night picket duty along a wide arc thrown out north and west of the town the evening of June 30, had been warned to keep a sharp lookout on the roads from both directions. Gen. Robert E. Lee's invading Army of Northern Virginia, whose main body was known to have been in camp near Chambersburg, Pa., 28 miles west, was reported on the move. Some Confederate infantrymen had approached to within half a mile of Gettysburg the preceding afternoon, but had withdrawn when they saw Federal cavalry.

As the darkness faded, a Corporal Hodges, 9th New York Cavalry, on picket duty west of McPherson's Ridge, observed shadowy figures moving down the road toward him, about 500 yards away. As Hodges moved cautiously forward for a closer look, the Confederates opened fire! The Battle of Gettysburg was under way!

The men in gray constituted the advance element of Archer's brigade of Heth's division, Lt. Gen. A. P. Hill's corps, which had reached

Cashtown, eight miles west of Gettysburg, during the night. The Confederates were unaware that a sizable force of veteran Union cavalrymen already occupied Gettysburg, where Heth's men had hoped to "requisition" shoes to replace their own, badly worn by the long march from Virginia. They anticipated no serious opposition from the untrained militia they thought were defending the town.

BUFORD'S cavalry division, screening the advance of the left wing of Maj. Gen. George G. Meade's army, had been carefully schooled and admirably equipped for its historic mission. A practical general, Buford regarded as outmoded the combat methods that had characterized the Southern cavalry under Jeb Stuart—the mounted charge with saber and pistol. Buford felt that the horse afforded mobility for rapid movement, but the troopers fought more effectively when dismounted.

Neither Lee nor Meade had enough information of the other's strength or dispositions on June 30 to decide when or where to engage, let alone how to fight the all-out battle that both knew to be imminent. The actions and orders of both army commanders during the previous 48 hours indicate that the first concern of each was to concentrate his army.

Lee especially had cautioned General Hill, commanding the advance corps, not to bring on a general engagement until the marching divisions of Lt. Gen. James "Old Pete" Longstreet's corps from Chambersburg and those of Lt. Gen. Richard S. "Dick" Ewell's corps from York (28 miles east) and Carlisle (21 miles north) could reassemble at Cashtown. Here, east of South Mountain, the

BUFORD'S MEN—This drawing by H. Charles McBarron, Jr., outstanding military artist, originally appeared in "The Infantry Journal." It shows dismounted troopers of Buford's cavalry division on the morning of July 1, 1863, along McPherson's Ridge west of Gettysburg. They are contesting the advance of Heth's Confederate infantry division.

Confederate army would be in a position to maneuver as a whole and attack with hope of success and some degree of safety for its line of supply down the Cumberland Valley.

ON THE opposite side the newly appointed Meade was playing a cautious hand, mindful of his dual instructions to protect Washington and Baltimore as well as to seek out Lee, whose army had been moving at will across South-Central Pennsylvania. The advance of the Army of the Potomac northward from Frederick, Md. had therefore been conducted on a front of about 15 miles so that on the morning of July 1, although well in hand, it was far from being concentrated. No battle orders were contemplated until the situation could be developed and Lee's movements determined.

Thus the Battle of Gettysburg started as an unplanned meeting engagement between the advance party of a Confederate infantry corps and the pickets of a Union cavalry division. And, since troops coming up from the rear usually march to the sound of gunfire, divisions were deployed and thrown into the fight as fast as they converged on Gettysburg from all points of the compass.

July 1—The First Day

WHEN the opening shots were fired, Generals Lee and Meade, the army commanders who between them controlled more than 170,000 officers and men, were each more than a dozen miles away. Lee on his horse Traveler rode with Longstreet in the midst of the latter's foot soldiers along the Chambersburg pike toward the eastern exit from South Mountain at Cashtown. Meade remained at Taneytown, Md. where he had established his headquarters in the belief that he would probably fight a defensive battle along the high ground above Big Pipe Creek, 12 miles southeast of Gettysburg and just across the Maryland state line.

By the time he reached Herr Ridge, General Heth, commanding Hill's leading division, had deployed Archer's and Davis' brigades in line astride the Cashtown pike, Archer on the right. Opposing them, and in position on McPherson's Ridge, were four dismounted squadrons of Gamble's brigade of Buford's cavalry division. The remainder of Buford's division, Devin's brigade, was farther north, near the Mummasburg road. Initially Heth's attack with two brigades was a reconnaissance-in-force to feel out the enemy strength. Buford continued to feed more strength into his line, trying to win time for infantry reinforcements to come up.

Heth advanced slowly behind his skirmishers until he had reached Herr Ridge. Gamble's dismounted troopers and Calef's six-gun Battery A, 2d U.S. Artillery, fighting determinedly, delayed the Confederate advance until at least 10 a.m., at which time the leading division of Maj. Gen. Abner Doubleday's I Corps came up from Marsh Creek and relieved the Union cavalry. Soon it was corps versus corps, with the lines ever lengthening as Hill's divisions extended their flanks to overlap the Union's defense and Buford shifted Devin's brigade to the east to delay two divisions of General Ewell's corps, approaching Gettysburg from the north and northeast along the Carlisle and Harrisburg roads.

MAJ. GEN. John F. Reynolds, distinguished Pennsylvanian in command of Meade's left wing of three corps, who was the first of four Union generals to give their lives on this battlefield, had taken vigorous charge of the situation as soon as he rode up at the head of his leading division. Recklessly exposing himself at the very forefront of the action, he was instantly killed at the eastern edge of McPherson's Woods but not before he had sent an urgent message back to Maj. Gen. O. O. Howard to speed the three divisions of his XI Corps to the scene. This message reached the leading division, Schurz's, then at Horner's Mills, about 10:30 a.m. The division marched rapidly, reaching Gettysburg shortly after 12:30. By 2 p.m. the long column of the XI Corps had closed up, one division being posted on Cemetery Hill, south of town, the other two deployed in the flat fields north of Gettysburg, where Devin's brigade of Buford's cavalry division had been observing the advance of Rodes' division of Ewell's corps from the north.

By that time Rodes' division had lined up on Oak Ridge, north of the then Federal right flank, and were on the point of linking with A. P. Hill, while Early's division of Ewell's corps was still three miles to the northeast on the Harrisburg road. Exploiting the gap between the Federal I and XI Corps, Rodes moved south out of the wooded portion of the ridge and prepared to assault.

Carter's artillery battalion, from a position near the site of the present Peace Light monument, began to shell the Federal troops along an unfinished railroad cut, causing Doubleday to shift three brigades to meet the threat to his right flank.

ROBERT E. LEE—The commander of the invading Confederate Army of Northern Virginia, he had absolute confidence in the ability of his lean veterans. He had decisively won four of his previous five general engagements with Union armies. Antietam, fought Sept. 17, 1862, was a tactical draw but a strategic defeat for him. (From Kean Archives.)

GEORGE GORDON MEADE—This capable officer assumed command of the Union Army of the Potomac only three days before the Battle of Gettysburg began.

301

ABOVE—Brockenbrough's Confederate brigade here is attacking Stone's brigade, Pennsylvania Bucktails, around McPherson's barn (which still stands west of Gettysburg). This illustration from "Battles & Leaders" was drawn by A. C. Redwood, a former Confederate soldier.

BELOW—This original sketch by Alfred Waud depicts Maj. Gen. John F. Reynolds at the instant he was struck by a Confederate bullet at McPherson's Woods. Commander of a wing of the Union Army of the Potomac, Reynolds was a highly popular and able general. (Library of Congress.)

Death of Reynolds
Gettysburg

Rodes' attack was repulsed along the east edge of Oak Ridge, but that prong which drove toward the railroad cut made progress. Nevertheless Rodes suffered very heavy casualties, two of his brigades being nearly destroyed. Concurrently A. P. Hill was stepping up the tempo of his attacks from the west against Doubleday's corps, finally succeeding in enveloping the Federal I Corps at McPherson's farm and driving them back to the Seminary.

CONFEDERATE strength on the battlefield was growing faster than Union. The Battle of Gettysburg seemed likely to end within a matter of hours, with Lee in control of all the important terrain. Those Federals not already casualties would be driven back on the marching columns of Meade's five uncommitted corps.

At 2:30 p.m. Jubal Early's division, arrived at last on the high ground across Rock Creek from the County Almshouse, made a slashing attack from the northeast against Howard's right flank north of Gettysburg, causing it to crumple. This threw the entire line of the XI Corps into confusion, which soon turned into a disorderly rout back to the town. Early pursued the beaten divisions through the clogged streets of Gettysburg, capturing thousands. He then stopped to reorganize, and sent part of his victorious troops out the York road to protect his flank against a reported threat that never materialized. The attack of A. P. Hill was pressing the Union I Corps back from Seminary Ridge, and the Federals were in danger of being cut off by Rodes' advance south toward their rear. After heavy fighting that left many dead and wounded on the grass in the fields on all sides of the Seminary, the survivors of the I Corps retreated to Cemetery Hill. The day's casualties: Union, 10,000, Confederate, 7,000.

All day long and far into the night of July 1 the numerous divisions in blue and in gray with their supporting artillery had been snaking along the roads that converged at Gettysburg like the spokes of a wheel. The men of both armies were driven at a rapid pace by their officers to get there first, but without knowing just where they were going or what they would meet when they got there, except that the barking of the field pieces and the crackle of musketry sounded like the real thing.

GENERAL MEADE, at distant Taneytown until late that night, exercised no influence on the first day's fighting beyond sending Maj. Gen. Winfield S. Hancock, commanding II Corps, forward as his deputy to size up the situation. Hancock was the fifth Union general officer in top field command on this first day, the vagaries of battle having placed the responsibility successively on Buford, Reynolds, Doubleday, O. O. Howard, Winfield S. Hancock, and finally Slocum (Maj. Gen. Henry W. Slocum, commanding XII Corps), before Meade would appear in person to take up the reins. It had been Hancock's afternoon role to restore order in the shattered Union ranks, stabilize the defense on Cemetery Ridge, and advise Meade that Gettysburg was the place for him to fight his battle, already one third over.

General Lee had reached the field about noon or shortly after. At Cashtown he had found A. P. Hill, who, suffering from a chronic liver ailment, was feeling far from well and unable to give him any information. The troop buildup and the fighting were both so fluid and unpredictable that Lee could initially do little but observe. Far enough forward, however, to watch the disciplined withdrawal of the I Corps following the rout of the Union XI Corps, he noted the confused troop movements of the Federals on Cemetery Ridge and appreciated the importance of pressing his advantage.

Once again the ability of Lee's divisions to effect rapid concentrations at the point of conflict was being demonstrated. The Federals were obviously in such deep trouble, pressed from three directions, that the Confederate commander discarded his earlier fear of bringing on a general engagement until the entire army was assembled.

Lee promptly sent word to Ewell "to attack that hill (Cemetery) *if practicable,*" in the mistaken belief that Ewell would do as "Stonewall" Jackson had been wont to do, make the day's victory complete by driving the enemy from the field. Ewell, however, was accustomed to specific rather than discretionary orders and Lee's message only confused him. He was tired after a hard day and the infected stump of the leg he had lost at Second Manassas was bothering him. Furthermore he felt his corps was not in shape to resume the attack. Rodes had suffered very heavy losses. Early was holding the town and 4,000 prisoners with two brigades, his other two being two miles or more out the York road. Thus at the moment Ewell had no force with which to pursue. So he waited until his third division, under Johnson, arrived, about 8 p.m. He then ordered Johnson to send a party to reconnoiter Culp's Hill, which overlooked Cemetery Hill. But it was occupied, and it was 4 a.m. before Ewell had enough information to make a night attack. Ewell called off the operation.

BY NIGHTFALL that first day, with the fighting practically over, the Confederates had assembled some 35,000 troops, at least 10,000 more than the Federals. Within a few hours, however, three more Union divisions had reported in against only two of Lee's, and from that time on Meade's relative strength progressively improved. By daylight, July 2, he could count 68,000 men to Lee's 60,000, and by 4 p.m. of the second day Sedgwick's 15,000 had completed their long march from Manchester, Md. to give Meade a strength of 97,000. Pickett's division and Stuart's cavalry also arrived, late on July 2, to bring Lee's total to 75,000.

As the hours passed, Meade carefully weighed the reports coming in from Buford, Reynolds (until his death), and Hancock. He became convinced that the entire Confederate army was concentrating at Gettysburg. Without waiting for Hancock's final recommendation, at 4:30 p.m. July 1 he discarded his tentative plan to await Lee's attack on the Pipe Creek line and sent word to all corps commanders to march on Gettysburg without delay.

Riding up from Taneytown through the darkness, Meade reached Cemetery Hill about midnight July 1, to find his army organizing the Cemetery Ridge portion of the fishhook defense line with every means at their command. Having escaped disaster by a hair's breath, but now reassured by newly arrived units, the confidence of the basically sound Army of the Potomac returned as the men contemplated the natural strength of their

"HOLDING THE LINE" is the title of this painting by Gilbert Gaul. While it was not meant to depict the Battle of Gettysburg specifically, it does illustrate the desperate, stand-up fighting that took place there on the first two days.

. . . The Battle of Gettysburg; A Long Pause As Both Sides Bring Up Additional Troops

position. What they saw was a relatively short, convex line, with flanks fastened on wooded and boulder-strewn hills, and with interior lines that provided quick communication and covered facilities for rapid troop shifts.

Lee's position was less advantageous, having evolved by accident in the course of throwing troops into battle as they arrived from several points of the compass. At the close of the first day's fighting the Confederates occupied a line running from part way down Seminary Ridge on the right, thence along the unfinished railroad and eastward through the town of Gettysburg. Johnson later prolonged this line about 9 p.m. to the high ground north of Benner's Hill. Lee's line was concave and posed serious problems of communication and coordination, but at the same time afforded a wide choice for the general in determining how and where to continue his offensive tactics.

July 2—The Second Day

J. E. B. STUART, Lee's cavalry commander, had broken contact with the main Confederate army seven days before to ride behind the Union army, cross central Maryland and advance into Pennsylvania by a separate route. Therefore Lee had been unable to learn Meade's strength on the march. Now the woods and heights of the Union fishhook prevented his observing the Federal units on the field. On July 2 Lee wanted Ewell to attack the Union right, but after separate morning conferences with Longstreet and Ewell, during which the former tried unsuccessfully to impose his own tactical concept on Lee (viz: to undertake an active defense and invite an attack by Meade), Lee decided, in view of Ewell's reluctance to take the initiative, to revise his battle plan. He would threaten both enemy flanks, Ewell from the north, Longstreet from the south. Ewell would make a demonstration against Meade's right, to be converted into a real attack if opportunity offered, while Longstreet, making the main effort, would attack diagonally up the Emmitsburg road, a maneuver which Lee mistakenly believed would result in rolling up Meade's line. A. P. Hill's job was to demonstrate on the center, chiefly with artillery fire, to keep the enemy occupied.

Nothing worked as planned. Lee was conscious of the need for an early resumption of the attack, to keep Meade off balance and to strike him before he could receive further reinforcements. But Longstreet was uncooperative, even obstinate in his effort to change Lee's tactics, and Ewell seemed equally lethargic. The morning hours passed with both armies inactive. In the early afternoon Union Maj. Gen. Dan Sickles further upset the Confederate program, already badly disarranged by Longstreet's delay in moving his troops into their jumpoff position. Sickles' III Corps had been assigned to the Union left on Cemetery Ridge, his own left flank to rest on Little Round Top, the Union anchor on the south. Sickles thought he saw a better position about three quarters of a mile to the front, and, after sending out a strong reconnaissance group, including Berdan's sharpshooters, to probe the Confederate position, became convinced that he was right. Without securing Meade's permission, he moved his entire corps forward about 1 p.m. and took position at the Peach Orchard, his right division extended northward along the Emmitsburg road, his left refused at an obtuse angle, extended southeastwardly to the vicinity of Devil's Den, an area of enormous boulders. The result: Little Round Top unoccupied, both his own flanks and Hancock's left (on Cemetery Ridge) exposed, and Meade's scheme of defense sadly upset.

THE Confederates, however, were slow to take advantage of the Union weakness. Longstreet, already short Pickett's division, was unwilling to attack until Law's brigade of Hood's division arrived. Law, after a 24-mile forced march, reached Herr's Ridge about noon, but his men had to be given 30 minutes rest. Longstreet then consumed 3½ more hours in marching and countermarching west of Seminary Ridge. So it was 4:30 p.m. when he finally started his infantry attack, which was badly conceived and launched in fragmentary fashion without sufficient preliminary ground reconnaissance. He found one of Sickles' divisions directly in his front. Furthermore, Hood was not permitted to work around south of Round Top, as he wished to do. This disposed of Lee's idea that the attack would be a flanking operation. When fully launched, however, the Confederate assault was fiercely pressed, and again the Union defenders came close to disaster. Little Round Top would unquestionably have been captured except for the alertness of Brig. Gen. Gouverneur K. Warren, who, finding the hill undefended, moved troops to its summit. Sickles' corps was so badly chopped up that it would never again be employed as an entity; and the bloody fighting spread over the landscape until it engulfed the Rose buildings, the Wheatfield, Devil's Den, the valley of Plum Run, and the slopes of Little Round Top.

For four long hours the battle raged between the opposing ridges, with a display of raw courage on both sides that has never been exceeded by American troops anywhere. The fighting was confused and without pattern, surging back and forth, unpredictably, over a wide area. It was Longstreet's fight all the way, and Lee's "Old War Horse" was at his best once he put his mind to it. But this became Meade's fight also, and he performed in a masterly fashion, rushing up reserves, plugging gaps, shifting troops, meeting each tactical crisis as it arose.

Losses were heavy on both sides, but when the sun had set and the contestants rested on their arms, the Union position on Cemetery Ridge remained intact, although Longstreet's divisions held all the ground in front, including Devil's Den, the Wheatfield, and the Peach Orchard. Lee had no intention of giving up the attack, nor would he relinquish the initiative that he had held from the very beginning, and would maintain until the rear guard of his army splashed across the Potomac on its return to Virginia 11 days later. Conversely, Meade's attitude was wholly defensive throughout the campaign, and not without justification as he weighed his instructions from Washington and the outcome of earlier battles—battles in which Lee's army had

WARREN ON LITTLE ROUND TOP—The Chief Engineer of the Army of the Potomac, Brig. Gen. G. K. Warren, discovered the danger to Little Round Top just in time to summon Federal troops to defend it. This picture from "Battles & Leaders" was sketched on the scene by Alfred R. Waud, who was present at Gettysburg as a special artist for "Harper's Weekly."

'The Savior of Little Round Top'

WHEN Gen. Daniel E. Sickles advanced his two divisions to the Peach Orchard on July 2, 1863, he left Little Round Top unoccupied except for a signal station. Prompt action by Gen. G. K. Warren, chief engineer of the Union Army of the Potomac, prevented this key hill from being seized by Hood's Confederates.

Here are excerpts from General Warren's account of how he discovered the threat to Little Round Top and what he did about it:

JUST BEFORE the action General Meade sent me to the left to examine the condition of affairs, and I continued to Little Round Top. It was used only as a signal station. I saw that this was the key of the whole position. Our troops in the woods in front of it could not see the ground in front of them; therefore the enemy would come upon them before they would be aware.

The woods west of the Emmitsburg road furnished a concealed place for the enemy to form, so I requested a battery just in front of Little Round Top to fire a shot into those woods. The sound of the shot whistling through the air reached the enemy's troops, causing them to glance up in that direction. This motion revealed to me the glistening gunbarrels and bayonets of the enemy battle line, already formed and far outflanking our troops; his line of advance to Little Round Top was unopposed. This discovery was intensely thrilling and appalling. I immediately sent a dispatch to General Meade to send a division at least to me. He directed the V Corps to take position there. The battle was beginning at the Peach Orchard, and before a single man reached Round Top, the enemy moved on us in splendid array, shouting confidently.

WHILE I was still alone with the signal officer, the musketballs began to fly around us. He was about to withdraw, but, at my request, remained and kept waving his flags. Seeing troops going out on the Peach Orchard road, I rode down the hill, meeting my old brigade. The commander had already passed, so I took the responsibility to detach Colonel O'Rorke's regiment, which moved at once to the hilltop.

Lieut. Charles E. Hazlett, 5th Artillery, now arrived with his battery of rifled cannon. He planted a gun on the summit, explaining that though he could do little execution, he could give confidence to the infantry, and that his battery was of no consequence compared with holding a position. He stayed there till he was killed.

I was wounded slightly with a musketball while talking with Lieut. Hazlett; and seeing the position saved though the whole line to the right and front of us was melting away under the enemy's attack, I left the hill to rejoin General Meade near the center of the field, where a new crisis was at hand.

always proven to be a formidable opponent in spite of inferior numbers and weapons.

BY THE end of the second day it began to be evident to both armies that the pattern of almost unbroken Confederate victories had somehow changed. Fighting for its life on its own soil seemingly had infused a new spirit in the Army of the Potomac. Indifferent performance by the Confederate corps commanders was partly responsible, but whatever the cause, after two days of bitter infighting Meade's veterans were now confident that they were capable of throwing back any further attacks.

There would be one more test of strength before the books closed on the second day's contest. Up on Ewell's front, opposite the extreme right flank of the Union fishhook on Culp's Hill, a strange calm had prevailed during the daylight hours. Here Ewell's divisions covered two miles of frontage, from the western limits of Gettysburg, through the town itself and on to the east in a curving line that terminated on Brinkerhoff Ridge, a northern extension of Wolf Hill. These dispositions placed the Confederate left flank only a mile in rear of Meade's headquarters, located at the center of the Union line just off the Taneytown road.

During the afternoon battle for the Round Tops, Meade had found it necessary to take the calculated risk of denuding Culp's Hill of the better part of Slocum's two divisions to bolster the defense on the opposite end of the line, leaving only Greene's brigade to defend that critical flank. Fortunately for the Union cause, Ewell's planned attack in conjunction with that of Longstreet failed to materialize because Brig. Gen. Henry J. Hunt's effective artillery outgunned the Confederate's in that area and caused Ewell to delay his infantry attack. Not

until Longstreet's fight was sputtering to a halt on the Union left did the bemused successor to Stonewall Jackson decide that the right hour had arrived, and again it was too late. Twilight was gathering on the slopes of Cemetery Hill when two of Jubal Early's brigades finally attacked, Johnson's division being already engaged. In the gathering darkness they gained the crest and broke through the sector manned by Howard's XI Corps, the key to the Union defense on Cemetery Ridge. At this critical moment Hancock again rose to the occasion, sending one of his brigades under Carroll to the rescue. Fighting fiercely in the darkness, lit only by flashes from muskets in the melee, Carroll plugged the gap; then with additional help from various units of the I and XI Corps the aroused Federals counterattacked, driving Early's two unsupported brigades back down the hill.

WHILE the fight for Cemetery Hill was in progress, Johnson's division moved down the slopes of Benner's Hill and east thereof, crossed Rock Creek and assaulted the east slopes of Culp's Hill, which had been almost entirely deserted when Slocum's divisions were shifted to the Union left. To meet this attack, General Greene, 63 years of age and a grouchy, rugged scrapper, stretched his already brittle brigade line even thinner. However his men were in trenches and behind rock walls, and, in the darkness, Confederate control broke down. Greene's volleys were effective, while his own losses were light. One of Johnson's brigades did succeed in placing troops in unoccupied trenches just above Spangler's Spring, and thus were within a few hundred yards of the Baltimore pike, squarely on the Union right rear and nearly athwart Meade's supply lifeline to the southeast. Although John-

IN THE WHEATFIELD—This area south of Gettysburg changed hands several times in the furious fighting of the second day. From the Library of Congress, this painting is by F. D. Briscoe. It is titled "The Whirlpool in the Wheatfield."

ON CULP'S HILL—Here the 29th Pennsylvania is depicted forming in line of battle about 10 a.m., July 3, preparatory to driving the Confederates from their foothold in this area along the Federal right.

Overlooked by many historians, the action in this sector was particularly heavy. This drawing from "Battles & Leaders" is by W. L. Sheppard, a former Confederate soldier.

son was at the moment unaware of this accomplishment, it would become apparent with daylight.

Meade at this stage was thinking clearly. With the stabilization of his still unbroken defense along Cemetery Ridge, he began patching the quiltwork. First he ordered Slocum to return to his original position on the extreme right. Then he called his corps commanders to a council of war in the Leister House to discuss plans for the next day. At this conference it was decided that the army would stay to fight it out on the same line.

The practicability of attacking was ruled out by all the corps commanders except Howard, who advised watchful waiting until 4 p.m. the next day, but favored a counterattack then if the Confederates had not resumed the offensive. At the close of the meeting, Meade remarked to General Gibbon, temporarily in command of Hancock's II Corps, that if Lee should again attack on the morrow, it would be on the front of the II Corps, the center of the Union line.

July 3—The Third Day

ALTHOUGH recognizing that his corps commanders on July 1 and 2 had failed to take advantage of favorable battlefield situations, Lee remained confident and was determined to push the fight to a conclusion. His only other choice was to withdraw, since he could not live off the country indefinitely and realized that his line of supply to Virginia might be cut at any time.

His estimate of the situation on the night of July 2 was erroneous in several respects. He reasoned that the Union army's morale must have suffered from its near-disaster on each of the first two days, but such was not the case. He believed that Meade had been forced to weaken his right and center in repelling Longstreet's

assault, from which it would appear that the Union center was vulnerable. There, thought Lee, Meade's back could be broken and the battle won. Never had the Confederate commander made a less accurate appraisal. Although he expressed an appreciation of Meade's capabilities, he probably expected Meade to do as his predecessors had almost invariably done—find excuses for giving up the fight when the final Confederate pressure was applied. Lee must not have realized that the entire Union army had arrived to give Meade a 20,000-man edge in combat strength despite heavier losses, or that the 25,000 in Sedgwick's and Slocum's corps had not yet been seriously engaged. Of supreme importance, however, was the fact that Union morale *had* recovered and was now at a high peak.

The Confederate commander's plan for July 3 was in effect a continuation of the second day's attack, with important modifications. Lee had attempted without success to turn Meade's right flank, then his left. Believing that the enemy must be weak somewhere, he decided, in what he visualized as the conclusive effort, that Longstreet should make a massive frontal assault on the Union center while Ewell would continue to assail Meade's right flank. Stuart had finally arrived with his cavalry. His part would be to circle east of Gettysburg to cover the army left, prepared to exploit the expected infantry breakthrough at the center.

LEE'S timetable directed that the battle be opened "in the early gray of the morning," but once again, for the third successive day, his plans would miscarry. During the night Ewell had sent three additional brigades to support Johnson's division in the projected attack against Meade's extreme right flank on Culp's Hill. But Meade overnight had redisposed his more numerous artillery with the aid of additional batteries brought up from General Hunt's ample reserve. To cover the front of the Union center, where Meade anticipated Lee's main attack, the Federal guns were sited to provide powerful bands of overhead crossfire; and at the same time the firing positions were strengthened on all the prominent elevations from which fire could be directed against a probable assault upon Culp's Hill

At 4:30 a.m. Union artillery along the Baltimore road opened heavily on Johnson's position, a precarious one because he had been unable to support it with artillery on account of the steep slope and dense woods. To escape the punishing bombardment, Johnson's infantry was forced to advance, only to run into Geary's Union division which, with the rest of Slocum's corps, was eager to recover its own trenches, purloined by the Confederates during the former's absence.

Thus the third day's battle got underway. The Confederates attacked repeatedly, each time being driven back by Slocum's determined brigades. So terrific was the Union artillery and musket fire that the foliage of the luxuriant forest on Culp's Hill was swept away as though by a hurricane, some of the trees being found later imbedded with 200 or more bullets.

For seven hours the battle raged about Culp's Hill and Spangler's Spring, until 11 a.m., when the Confederates, having sustained very heavy casualties and gained no ground in the process, withdrew, leaving a carpet of dead and wounded in front of the Union trenches.

THE FEDERALS had won the first round on July 3. Slocum's XII Corps was again in full possession of Culp's Hill, the Union right flank had again been anchored, the army rear was no longer in jeopardy, and the road to Baltimore remained securely in Union hands.

Longstreet had passed the night of July 2 bedded down with his troops on the field, using his saddle for a pillow. Early the next morning General Lee rode out to consult with his senior lieutenant, possibly to make sure that he would promptly carry out the attack order Lee had sent him the previous evening. There opposite Little Round Top, where his First Corps was in close contact with the Union defenders, Longstreet renewed his earlier arguments in favor of a maneuver around Meade's left flank. This time he went so far as to tell Lee flatly that the frontal attack his superior had ordered was certain to fail in the face of Union strength on Cemetery Ridge and his own men's exposure to enemy gun fire as they crossed the open fields to close with the Union infantry on the heights. Lee, however, was impressed by the fact that Wright's brigade, if supported, could have broken through the center of the Federal position on Cemetery Ridge on the evening of July 2. That portion of the Union line appeared to be lightly held, and to a degree this was true even on the 3d.

Lee made one concession to Longstreet's insistence that he could not safely disengage his own two divisions from their present position. He agreed to substitute two of A. P. Hill's divisions for the assault, but Longstreet would remain in command. As revised, the attack would be made by Pickett's division of Longstreet's corps plus elements from all three of A. P. Hill's divisions, more than 13,000 men in all. The infantry advance from Seminary Ridge would be preceded by a massive artillery bombardment aimed chiefly at the Union guns on Cemetery Hill.

When (hopefully) these should be neutralized, Pickett's men were to move to the attack. Lee personally pointed to a copse of chestnut oaks on Cemetery Ridge, in the area occupied by Hancock's Union II Corps, and directed that the infantry advance toward that prominent terrain feature.

PREPARATIONS for the attack took much longer than Lee expected, as the reluctant Longstreet seemingly made no effort to hasten them. And so it came about that the battle for Culp's Hill had been over for two hours when at 1:07 p.m. two Confederate guns near the Peach Orchard barked the signal to commence the bombardment.

At once some 140 guns opened along the two-mile line of Confederate field pieces. As though by reflex, 80 Federal guns immediately responded, to initiate the most stupendous artillery duel ever witnessed on the American continent. Quickly the battlefield was covered with a pall of smoke and dust, through which little could be seen but the flashes from the gun muzzles and the exploding shells that tore into men and horses on the opposite ridges.

Meade's headquarters, several hundred yards in rear of the "clump of trees," was endangered by many of the Confederate shells that overshot the ridge. Heavy losses occurred among units of the Union reserve artillery, supply and ammunition trains, and the medical services. But the front line troops of Hancock's corps suffered little damage, most of the shells clearing the forward

---

The Death of Jennie Wade

WHEN *the Battle of Gettysburg broke out, 20-year-old Jennie Wade was at the home of her sister, a Mrs. McClellan, who lived on Baltimore Street at the foot of Cemetery Hill. There was a new baby in the McClellan home and Jennie was helping her sister with its care.*

There was no heavy fighting in the immediate area but a Federal picket line did run behind the little brick house. There was intermittent skirmishing between it and Confederate outposts in the town proper.

On the morning of the third day, while Jennie stood in the kitchen kneading dough, a bullet pierced two wooden doors and struck her in the back, killing her instantly. The cries of her sister and mother attracted Federal soldiers who carried Jennie's body to the cellar. Later she was buried in a coffin some Confederate soldiers had fashioned for an officer.

Jennie was engaged to a Cpl. Johnston Skelly who, unknown to her, had been wounded two weeks earlier in the Battle of Winchester. News that he had died in Confederate hands came several days after the Southern army had withdrawn from the Gettysburg area.

JENNIE WADE HOUSE—It was in this house on Baltimore Street that Jennie Wade was killed on July 3, 1863.

slope of the ridge where the men lay on their arms awaiting the certain infantry assault.

For almost two hours the artillery duel continued without pause. Then Union artillery commander Hunt ordered his batteries to cease firing in order to cool the guns, conserve and replenish ammunition, and switch certain damaged batteries, in preparation for the new targets that were momentarily expected.

ON THE Confederate side artillery ammunition was fast being used up. For that reason, and also because he observed 18 Union guns being withdrawn (Hunt was merely effecting a relief), Col. E. P. Alexander, who directed the bombardment, dashed off a hectic message to Pickett: "For God's sake come quick; the eighteen guns are gone; unless you advance quick my ammunition won't let me support you properly."

Pickett rode up to Longstreet, saluted, and inquired: "General, shall I advance?" Unwilling to take the responsibility of ordering what he felt would be certain death for thousands of Pickett's men, with no compensating gain, Longstreet averted his eyes and barely nodded. It was enough for Pickett, who on his coal-black charger then rode to the center of his line and gave the command: "Forward, guide center, march."

As the long gray lines moved out from the protection of the swale behind Spangler farm and Seminary Ridge, instinctively correcting their alignment as though on dress parade, a sudden dramatic hush fell on the battlefield. In three lines the Confederates marched forward at route step, across the open fields and toward the Emmitsburg road, their fluttering battle flags adding a brilliant touch of color to the impressive scene.

The batteries of the II Corps held their fire because they had only canister at their guns and could not fire effectively until the Confederates were much closer. The Union batteries at other points, particularly on Little Round Top and Cemetery Hill, opened at once. Soon the Confederates neared the Emmitsburg road, lined on both sides with sturdy farm fences to be broken down by the skirmishers. It was at that critical moment that all of Hunt's guns were unleashed with devastating effect, unhindered now by the Confederate artillery which was forced to cease firing to avoid killing their own men. Converging crossbands of fire from Union batteries on Cemetery Hill and Little Round Top joined their destruction to that of the II Corps batteries, all the guns targeted on Pickett's hapless foot soldiers.

WATCHING the pageant from Cemetery Ridge and holding their fire until the enemy were within effective range, Hancock's infantrymen paid silent, grim tribute to the magnificent courage of the Confederates as they marched steadily forward, the lines closing doggedly as the shells knocked out huge segments of the attacking force. Longstreet had been right—it was sheer suicide, but there was no faltering as the heroic Confederate veterans continued to advance regardless of losses.

Only a few hundred of the 13,000 who started the charge reached the Union position through the hell of cannon fire and musketry. Over the stone wall went that intrepid handful, but inevitably, were either killed, driven back, or captured. More than 7,000 lay dead or wounded in the no-man's land between the two ridges, as other

THE BATTLE OF GETTYSBURG—LONGSTREET'S ATTACK UPON OUR LEFT CENTRE

ABOVE, PICKETT'S CHARGE—This dramatic woodcut of Pickett's assault against the Union center on the afternoon of July 3, 1863, was made from an original drawing by Alfred Waud. Appearing in "Harper's Weekly" on Aug. 8, 1863, it is the only drawing made by an eyewitness. Waud labeled his original sketch: "Battle of Gettysburg. Longstreet's attack upon the left center. Blue Ridge in distance."

309

thousands limped dejectedly, but still defiant, back to their starting point.

General Lee met the disorganized survivors as they streamed back to Seminary Ridge. "This was all my fault," he said to them, and added: "It is I that have lost this fight, and you must help me out of it the best way you can."

The Aftermath

WITH the containment and turning back of Stuart's cavalry by Gregg's countercharging Union horsemen east of Gettysburg, the Battle of Gettysburg came to an end. The only question that remained was whether Meade would exploit his success in repulsing Lee. Hancock, Pleasonton, and Howard strongly favored a Union counterattack, but others, like Hunt, believed that was just what the Confederates wanted, an opportunity to inflict the same punishment they had just suffered.

Meade's decision not to counterattack is still warmly debated. It is doubtful that the Union commander, having fought his army defensively for three days and barely having escaped defeat several times, thought seriously about passing to the offensive. Nor had his staff been instructed to plan for such a contingency, so far as is known; which of itself may seem odd to today's strategists and tacticians, accustomed to the presence at army headquarters of huge staffs, trained to be always ready with flexible operational plans.

On the evening of July 3 Lee recalled Ewell's divisions from their Gettysburg-Culp's Hill position and Longstreet's divisions from the vicinity of Devil's Den, to shorten his line and concentrate his artillery against the attack that the Confederates hoped would come the following morning. But he had already decided that he must now take his army back to Virginia without further fighting, unless it be on Meade's initiative.

PLANS for the return march were developed with great care. The Confederate army which had roamed the Maryland and Pennsylvania countryside for weeks almost at will, had lost a third of its initial strength of some 75,000 men, leaving but 50,000 effectives, including many slightly wounded who had not fallen as prisoners into Federal hands and could still wield a musket if need be. About noon on Saturday, July 4, it started to rain. By late afternoon the downpour became torrential, converting the dirt roads into mud holes and running streams, and requiring Herculean efforts to put the wagon trains, most of them loaded with the wounded who were unable to walk, on the road to Chambersburg. Many wounded, however, were left behind.

By Saturday night it was clear that Meade's army would not attack. With the trains well on the way, Lee gave the order to move, taking about 4,000 Union prisoners along with the retreating column, which followed the Fairfield road. Two brigades of cavalry protected the trains on the Chambersburg road; two others covered Monterey Pass, beyond Fairfield; and the remaining two, under Stuart, marched by way of Emmitsburg to secure the army left flank and to cooperate with Ewell's rearguard in fighting off Federal harassment.

Sunday, July 5, was half gone before Meade finally became convinced that Lee's army had departed. He then sent a cavalry brigade to follow the Confederates heading for Chambersburg, and started Sedgwick's corps down

BELOW—In this U. S. Army photograph of a diorama on display at the West Point Museum, Robert E. Lee (mounted) is meeting the survivors of Pickett's shattered division as they straggle back from their unsuccessful assault on the Union center. General Pickett is standing, hat in hand, in front of Lee, who assumed full responsibility for ordering the attack in which approximately 7,000 were killed, wounded, or captured.

the Fairfield road to establish contact with the enemy main body, already many miles ahead.

THE UNION army marched slowly south, keeping east of the mountain range, but without starting soon enough or moving fast enough to overtake Lee. Meade himself did not leave Gettysburg until July 7. Unhurriedly, almost casually, the Union army finally turned west at Frederick, and in due course found the Confederates in a defensive position in the neighborhood of Williamsport, Md., waiting for the swollen Potomac to subside. On July 13, ten days after the battle, Lee recrossed the river, virtually unmolested.

Lincoln was anguished over Meade's failure to pursue and attack Lee promptly and vigorously after the battle, when the opportunity appeared at hand to destroy the Confederate army either on the march or when trapped north of the Potomac by the high water. On July 14, the President wrote a reproving letter to Meade which on second thought he decided not to send. This was the gist of the letter:

"I do not believe you appreciate the magnitude of the misfortune involved in Lee's escape. He was within your easy grasp, and to have closed upon him would in connection with our other late successes [meaning the capture of Vicksburg] have ended the war.

An Appraisal of Lee's Failure

GENERAL Lee's kindly words to the officers and men of Pickett's command on July 3, as the survivors straggled slowly back to their own lines, were intended primarily to soothe feelings wounded by defeat. But his readiness to take the blame to himself may also have reflected from deep within him a feeling that victory would have been his had he exercised the more positive leadership of which he was capable.

Admittedly overconfident in the belief that his men were invincible, Lee evidently expected his corps commanders to function smoothly and effectively as heretofore, not fully realizing that A. P. Hill and Ewell, inexperienced in corps command and in poor physical condition, were unlikely to duplicate Stonewall Jackson's

SOUTHERN PRISONERS—These three Confederates captured at Gettysburg were photographed in front of a wooden breastwork on Cemetery Ridge. (From the National Archives.)

fiery exploits without close supervision and detailed attack orders.

The impression is widespread that the absence of the cavalry under Stuart deprived Lee of the "eyes of the army." It was Stuart himself who was missed; more than half of the cavalry was available to Lee and could have been utilized for reconnaissance had Lee not felt so dependent upon his capable lieutenant.

At Gettysburg Lee was below par in his field generalship. His physical strength and probably his mental powers were adversely affected by a severe attack of dysentery. His orders were vague, and left too much to the judgment and discretion of his subordinates, all of whom at one time or another either took direct issue with their commanding general (Ewell and Longstreet) or were dilatory in executing his expressed wishes (all three corps commanders). There was a serious lack of coordination between corps and between divisions and brigades within corps. Part of this was due to terrain and the distance between units, part to inadequate signal communications, part to pre-attack arrangements, and part to inadequate control by commanders at all levels from army to brigade.

THERE was an unusual lack of thorough terrain reconnaissance at all stages of the battle. Such precautions are vital to the attacking force. In this battle the Union army held a strong ridge position based on interior lines and Lee knew neither the size of Meade's army nor his troop dispositions, beyond what he could see from Seminary Ridge. Even worse, he chose to disregard the evidence brought to him through battle reconnaissance by Longstreet's officers (chiefly from Hood's division) on the afternoon of the second day, which, if acted upon, might have changed the course of the battle.

In evaluating the probable reactions of his opponent, Lee gave too little weight to the fact that the Federals were fighting to defend their own soil, under a competent, experienced general officer. Burnside's disaster in front of the stone wall at Fredericksburg could not have been present in Lee's mind at Gettysburg. Otherwise he would have given more weight to the firepower of Meade's veteran infantry, defensively deployed on high ground behind a stone wall, with both flanks securely anchored. He also neglected to take into account Hunt's superiority in artillery, which had been demonstrated in previous battles. Or perhaps he thought the enemy guns could be neutralized by a powerful preliminary bombardment. Had Lee properly assessed these factors, he might never have ordered Pickett's frontal assault, particularly after Longstreet took such an obstinate stand in opposition.

Finally, the manner in which his opponent, General Meade, conducted the defense was a potent influence in thwarting Lee's attacks on the second and third days. Meade's troop dispositions were sound, but his most effective action was in meeting successive crises by promptly and skilfully shifting troops about like chessmen as he countered his opponent's moves. Although it cannot be said that Meade succeeded in checkmating Lee's king, the game ended with the former's castles (Culp's Hill and the Round Tops) still in position and many more chessmen on the board than remained to the Confederates.

Lee never blamed others for his failure at Gettysburg. In taking the full responsibility on his own shoulders he said, in effect, that he was overconfident and that proper coordination had not been attained.

311

Union dead on the Battlefield of July 1st.

More than 50,000 men killed, wounded, and missing ... Ten leading generals dead ... Both armies crippled ... The countryside littered with the bodies of soldiers and horses ... Crops trampled and fences shattered ... Relatives flocking in to seek sons and brothers ... Every building a hospital ...

This was:

The Aftermath of Gettysburg

By Robert D. Hoffsommer

BATTLE STATISTICS by themselves are cold, colorless figures. To say that the Union casualties at Gettysburg were 3,155 killed, 14,529 wounded, and 5,365 missing; and the Confederate losses 3,903 killed, 18,735 wounded, and 5,425 missing (the usually accepted Livermore figures) is simply stating facts. To realize the real horror, imagine the dead and wounded men, including many listed as missing, evenly distributed over the 25 square miles of the entire battle area. Result: more than 1,600 men to every square mile! Or for a simpler exercise of imagination, conceive that of the approximately 160,000 men who fought at Gettysburg, better than one out of every four lay dead or agonizingly wounded at the end of the three days' carnage.

In addition to these losses in fighting men—the privates and their company and regimental officers—each army suffered irreplaceably in higher leadership. Four generals —Reynolds, Zook, Weed, and Farnsworth—died for the Union; the Confederacy lost Pender (severely wounded, died July 18), Barksdale, Semmes, Garnett, and Armistead, and at Falling Waters, in the retreat, Pettigrew.

The list of badly wounded generals is equally appalling. For the North that roster would include Hancock, Sickles, Barlow, Paul, Gibbon, and Graham; for the South: Hood, Trimble, Kemper, Scales, Jenkins, and Anderson. The less severely wounded general officers would make a list of similar length. Generals were battle line officers in those days.

The battle crippled both armies. Never again could Lee mount a major offensive; he had left too many of his finest fighting men in trench graves at Gettysburg. For the North, the unwilling draftees and unreliable bounty men brought in later were hardly equivalent replacements for the men who died on McPherson's farm and the slopes of the shallow valley between the famous ridges. It was the last great battle of the volunteers in the East.

WHAT was the battlefield like, when the three days of slaughter ended and the two armies moved out in retreat and pursuit? Neither side lingered long to tidy up. Lee began his retreat in the tremendous thunderstorms of July 4; Meade started his slow pursuit two days later. They left a macabre scene of nightmare desolation, a vast charnel house of unburied, festering dead whose contorted, bloating bodies lay in fields and woods littered with the infinite debris of battle. There were shattered guns and caissons, broken muskets, cartridge boxes, canteens, torn and bloody fragments of clothing, and gaping knapsacks, battered daguerreotypes, rain-sodden letters, and testaments lying pathetically in the mud beside the slit or turned-out pockets of their owners, discarded where the battlefield ghouls had dropped them in their robbing of the dead. And over the town and the surrounding fields the sickening smell of corruption was already rising like an almost palpable miasma. It was a horror that would linger almost to that November day when Abraham Lincoln would ride up Baltimore Street on a horse too small for his lanky height to dedicate the final resting place of the Union dead.

J. Howard Wert, a young man living at the time on the outskirts of Gettysburg, left a description of the battlefield in the Rose farm area as he saw it in the three days immediately after the battle. In his *Monuments and Indications,* one of the first battlefield guide

SCENES such as this were commonplace around Gettysburg after the battle. Here some of the dead of the 24th Michigan, a part of Meredith's Iron Brigade, await burial. These men were killed in the action around McPherson's woods on the first day of the battle. All told, more than 7,000 men were killed at Gettysburg. Others died later of wounds. (Library of Congress photograph.)

books, he tells vividly of the shattered orchards, the torn-down fences, the trodden battleground litter of equipment, and the horror of the unburied and half-buried dead, lying so thick that in places the bodies dammed the rain-swollen streams into ponds. He describes the hundreds of Confederate burials around the Rose house and writes of trench graves with 75 to 150 bodies laid in like logs of wood.

TRENCH burials were the rule. What we would call decent, individual graves were rarities. There were simply too many dead for the tired survivors to do more, often, than throw a few shovelsful of earth over their comrades or the enemy dead. Where bodies lay fairly close, the burial details usually dug a shallow hole for one body, rolled it in; dug another hole beside it, covering the corpse with the excavated earth; rolled another body into the new hole; dug again, covering the second body with earth from the third hole, and so on until all were buried.

Monstrous trench graves scarred the battlefield wherever the killing had been at its worst: the area south and east of the Rose house; southwest of the Wheatfield, where now are thick woods; along the edges of the Wheatfield; in the Valley of Death before Little Round Top; in terrible profusion in the fields immediately west of the "High Water Mark" of Pickett's Charge; on Oak and McPherson's Ridges, and near the railroad cut; and on the slopes of Culp's Hill. One "reliable farmer" reported to Samuel Weaver, supervisor of the later Union reburials in the National Cemetery, that he witnessed the burial of over two hundred in one trench.

In the days immediately following the battle hundreds of friends and relatives from as far as Ohio and Massachusetts swarmed over the fields seeking missing loved ones, hampering and nullifying the work of the soldier burial squads by reopening graves and leaving exposed the decaying bodies in their frantic search. Dozens of undertakers did a large and lucrative business in sheds and tents, preparing bodies for shipment to the soldiers' home towns. Not all the Union dead lie in the National Cemetery.

Burial of all the thousands of dead artillery and cavalry horses and wagon train mules was out of the question. Some were buried, but most of them were dragged into huge heaps and burned, and the foul smoke of these cremations hung for weeks over the countryside.

THIS MUCH for the dead. The more than 21,000 wounded posed an infinitely more complicated problem, made more difficult because of Hooker's June 19 order cutting down the Medical Department's transportation to about two wagons per brigade in the forced march up from Virginia. Later, Meade's countermanding order permitting only hospital and ammunition trains to accompany the army was fumbled by the Chief Quartermaster; not until late July 2 did any of the corps hospital trains begin to arrive at Gettysburg, with the sole exception of the XII Corps train, which came with the Corps.

In the brief scope of this article we shall consider only the Union hospitals; moreover, the bulk of Lee's wounded, over 12,700, went south in that famous 17-mile wagon train of suffering, and those remaining were cared for largely in Union hospitals.

When the fighting began, regimental aid stations were set up just behind the lines. An example is the 32d Massachusetts station, marked with a plaque in the woods about 40 yards southwest of the Wheatfield. Another (regiment unknown) was located in the Ziegler's Grove-Bryan house area. From these stations wounded were taken back to their divisional hospitals, located out of cannon range along the low ground of Rock Creek east of Cemetery Ridge. There the overworked surgeons hastily sorted out the men who might be saved, setting aside the hopeless cases. Head and abdominal wounds were considered mortal; young Cornelia Hancock, working as a volunteer nurse, describes a little wood carpeted with head-wounded men set aside to die. The bone-shattering effect of the Minié bullet required amputation of arms and legs; after-the-battle descriptions are full of gruesome pictures of heaps of severed limbs.

HOMES, churches, schools, the Lutheran Seminary, Pennsylvania College's "Old Dorm," the county almshouse and courthouse, and practically all farmhouses and barns in the vicinity were commandeered for the wounded. The whole countryside became a huge hospital area. Under the direction of Drs. Jonathan Letterman and Henry Janes, some 1,106 Army medical officers plus a large number of medical cadets and local and area doctors served in the above places and in the seven consolidated corps hospitals. The latter were tent establishments set up after the battle along a line that ran from Powers' Hill south one mile, thence east across Rock Creek to the White Church (St. Marks) on the Baltimore pike. The flooding of Rock Creek in the heavy rains following the battle drowned many helpless wounded and necessitated relocating several hospitals.

As early as July 8 the authorities began shipping out all wounded who could be moved. These were sent into Gettysburg for train transportation, mainly to Baltimore, York, and Harrisburg. In this move human nature revealed itself at its worst. There are numerous accounts

POST-GETTYSBURG ADVERTISEMENT—With more than 7,000 killed outright and hundreds more dying of wounds, Gettysburg offered morticians and coffin-sellers a booming business. This advertisement is from Kean Archives, Philadelphia.

of farmers who charged exorbitantly to convey wounded men to the station; the railroad company allotted filthy freight and cattle cars to the job, showing a callous disregard for everything but collection of the money due it for transport. This situation was soon remedied by the medical officers, but there is an angry report in the *Official Records* on conditions as Medical Inspector Edward P. Vollum found them.

ON THE credit side for humanity must be mentioned the scores of noble women from Gettysburg and surrounding towns who gave themselves unsparingly to feed and care for wounded Federal and Confederate alike. Similarly, the civilian-manned U. S. Sanitary Commission did splendid work in furnishing needed supplies of food, medicine, and equipment, and was particularly valuable in setting up a "lodging hospital" in a field just north of the tracks and station (still there) of the Western Maryland for the wounded soldiers awaiting, often overnight, the trains that took them from Gettysburg.

By the last week of July only 1,995 Union and 2,922 Confederate wounded remained. A general hospital named Camp Letterman was established about a mile east of town in Wolf's Woods along the York Road. Between August 5 and 11 all Confederate wounded were transferred there; on August 12 the Union wounded were evacuated from the corps hospitals, so that by the 18th all hospitals outside of Gettysburg were broken up. Almost exactly three months later Camp Letterman, with the removal of the few remaining patients, ceased to exist.

SO THE WOUNDED were gone, except for those still being cared for in Gettysburg homes and farms; but the

dead remained. During the week following the battle, Pennsylvania's Governor Curtin visited the field and was horrified at the condition of the half-buried and unburied dead. He approved a plan to remedy this, at least in part, presented by local attorney David Wills. This suggestion involved purchase by the state of land for a cemetery for the Union dead, their reinterment, and an invitation to the 17 other Union states whose soldiers died in battle and in the hospitals to join proportionately in the expense of reburial and care of the cemetery.

Curtin promised legislative support and instructed Wills, as his agent, to proceed at once. Wills' first action was to purchase 17 acres on Cemetery Hill, adjacent to the local Evergreen Cemetery, at a cost of $2,475.87. Next he commissioned William Saunders, an outstanding landscape artist, to lay out the cemetery grounds. Saunders' plan utilized the natural lay of the land, sloping as it did to the north and west from a central point, to set the lines of graves in concentric arcs curving around the center point where the present national monument stands. This arc arrangement allowed for radiating segments, to be proportioned in size to the number of each state's dead, with equal prominence.

ON OCT. 15, 1863 Wills advertised for bids on two contracts: removal of the dead from their battlefield graves, and reburial in coffins supplied by the Quartermaster General. A local man—F. W. Biesecker—submitted

the low bid of $1.59 per body for both contracts, and the removal of the dead began on Tuesday, October 27. By the contract terms, no more than 100 bodies could be moved in one day. Thus when Lincoln dedicated the ground on November 19, he spoke from a stand erected on the national monument site to an audience grouped in a cemetery less than a third completed. A hard winter interfered at times with the work so that Samuel Weaver, supervisor of exhumations, was unable to report completion of the task until March 18, 1864. Although the commonly accepted figure is 3,512, 3,564 Union dead were reported reburied—not the full total, since many were interred in Evergreen Cemetery and others were removed to their home towns.

More than a fourth—979—lie in graves marked "unknown." (Neither army had any system equivalent to our modern "dog tag" identification.) Next in order are New York with 867 and Pennsylvania with 534. The other states range from Michigan (171) to Illinois (6).

One of the pathetic features of the reburials was the collection of 287 packages of personal belongings found on the bodies. The contents ran from diaries, combs, daguerreotypes, gun wrenches, knives, and testaments down to—in one case—"the bullet that killed him."

So at last the battlefield was cleaned up, but long before the new grass appeared to hide the raw earth of the graves, the first steps were being taken to make Gettysburg a national shrine to American courage and devotion.

DEAD HORSES—Edwin Forbes, famous Civil War artist who drew this sketch furnished by the Library of Congress, made this notation about the below scene: "Caisson and battery horses—near the grove of trees, 2nd Corps front, scene of Pickett's Charge."

VIEW TOWARD CULP'S HILL—The earthworks on the side of the hill mark the position of Wadsworth's division. In the foreground are lunettes which protected Reynolds' Battery (Battery "D"), 1st New York Light Artillery. (Library of Congress photograph.)

ABOVE, LEE'S HEADQUARTERS—This drawing from "Battles & Leaders" shows the house used as Robert E. Lee's headquarters at Gettysburg. Lee slept in a tent nearby.

AT LEFT, THE TOWN OF GETTYSBURG—This was Gettysburg as it appeared in 1863. This photograph, taken by the Tyson brothers, is looking east from Seminary Ridge. (Kean Archives.)

BELOW, THE CHAMBERSBURG PIKE—A. P. Hill's corps and most of Lee's army approached Gettysburg along this road. Looking west from the first day's battle area, this photograph shows the Lutheran Seminary to the left and the cut of the unfinished railroad to the right. (Kean Archives.)

VICKSBURG

Text by Stephen E. Ambrose
Designed by Frederic Ray

AT A TIME when the Civil War went badly for the Union, President Abraham Lincoln looked at a map and commented to a visitor, "See what a lot of land these fellows hold, of which Vicksburg is the key . . . Let us get Vicksburg and all that country is ours. The war can never be brought to a close until that key is in our pocket."

By October 1862, the Federals had gained control of the Mississippi River from its mouth upstream to Port Hudson, in Louisiana, and from the river's sources down to Vicksburg, Mississippi. As long as the Confederates held the 130-mile stretch between those two towns, they could maintain communications with the western third of their nation and draw reinforcements and supplies. By denying the use of the great waterway to the Union, they prevented the reopening of normal traffic between the Northwest and New Orleans.

Lincoln was right. Vicksburg was the key and until that key was in the Federal pocket the war would continue. But wresting it from the Confederates seemed an impossibility.

WITH a population of nearly 5,000, the town stood on a 200-foot bluff on the eastern bank of the Mississippi, just downstream from where the river made a hairpin curve. Between there and Memphis the line of bluffs ran far inland, and the area adjacent to the river was low and swampy.

Across the river the ground was often inundated, and always nearly impassable for an army. From the north, the Yazoo River blocked the landward approach. To the east and south, staunchly Confederate Mississippians inhabited the countryside.

Soon after a Federal fleet seized New Orleans in April 1862, the Confederates began fortifying Vicksburg, first with batteries below the town to command the river approach from the south. Later, they mounted guns above the town and along the river, making Vicksburg impregnable to an attack from the water and creating a long gantlet past which boats found it dangerous to run. With good reason Vicksburg became known as the Gibraltar of America.

Long before Lincoln made his comment about Vicksburg, Ulysses S. Grant recognized its importance and began pondering how to secure this key that would both lock off the trans-Mississippi territory of the Confederacy and unlock the southern hold on the "Father of Waters."

NO ONE knows for sure just when Grant conceived his strategy for penetrating the heartland of the Confederacy by stabbing south along the great waterways leading into it. A visitor to the small Union headquarters at Ironton, Missouri in the summer of 1861 found the shabby, insignificant-looking new brigadier sitting under a tree in front of a cabin, drawing lines with a red pencil on a map. Grant explained that these were the invasion routes the high command should adopt and pointed out that one ran down the Mississippi past Vicksburg.

Two years were to elapse before Sam Grant was in a position to put his ideas into effect, but he never abandoned them.

The little spring beside which Grant dreamed his dreams now bubbles from a swale in the lawn of a Catholic school, and there is a simple shaft erected by his comrades of the 21st Illinois to mark the nearby site of his headquarters. But the greatest monument to this quiet little man is the fruition of

Vicksburg was vital to the South in the Ci

those early plans which he converted into one of the most decisive campaigns of all time.

IT IS a classic campaign, one that professional soldiers still study. With the single exception of air power, it contained the major elements of warfare later exemplified in World War II. There were mobile forces and even partisans striking far behind the lines of the main forces, and joint (Army-Navy) operations on a scale not seen again until the landings in North Africa in 1942. There were amphibious assaults, forced marches, pitched battles, field engineering of great resourcefulness, logistical triumphs, and intelligence and counterintelligence activity of a sophisticated nature. Finally, there was a siege in which courage and endurance were commonplace, and imaginative approaches to diverse problems were everyday occurrences.

STRATEGY OF THE CAMPAIGN

The scope of the campaign, the size and type of problems encountered and overcome, and its strategic importance are together enough to make it unique. But above all else, Vicksburg stands out because of the way in which one man dominated the entire campaign. Seldom in history has an individual so totally imposed his will upon his own forces,

ar. The Confederates defended it fiercely. (KA)

those of the enemy, and an operation. Ulysses S. Grant and Vicksburg are names that history will link together forever.

The campaign gave Grant an opportunity to show his skill in nearly every aspect of the soldier's trade. For each test he proved he was prepared and capable. His outstanding characteristic was flexibility of mind; he was always able to change his plans when confronted with a change in the situation. His relations with all but one of his chief subordinates were excellent. He was superb in handling troops. If throughout the long winter of 1862-63 he was not able to keep his superiors—a crabby General in Chief and an impatient President—completely satisfied, he

did convince them that a change in commanders would be a mistake. He solved a potentially explosive political problem with tact, delicacy, and understanding. He was keenly aware of the vital importance of logistics and saw to it that his men were never critically short of food or without ammunition. Though not an inspirational leader, he was ever steady and generated confidence and trust. In this campaign he managed his frontal assaults capably and broke them off before they became blood baths. His ability to maneuver large bodies of troops over great distances was truly outstanding.

FITTINGLY, Grant himself began the strategic campaign that culminated in the fall of Vicksburg when, in February of 1862, he captured Forts Henry and Donelson in northwestern Tennessee. Thus began the operations to open the Mississippi River, a task that would be the major objective of the Union forces in the West for the next year and a half.

Grant took command of the Department of the Tennessee on October 25, 1862. General in Chief Henry W. Halleck informed him that substantial reinforcements would soon come to the theater. It was characteristic of Grant that he started his campaign within a few days, and that he never turned back. His plans were flexible and he tried various routes of approach, but he kept his face ever toward his objective.

ON NOVEMBER 4 Grant started from Bolivar, in south-central Tennessee, with the idea of advancing along the axis of the Mississippi Central Railroad to Jackson, the capital of Mississippi. The Confederate forces facing him, commanded by Lieutenant General John C. Pemberton, fell back behind the Tallahatchie River. When this line, which Pemberton fortified, was outflanked by Federal cavalry and an infantry force from Arkansas that crossed the Mississippi at Helena, the Confederates retreated to Grenada and began digging in south of the Yalobusha River. Pemberton's retreat was almost a rout. Grant remarked after the war that had he known this he would not have been so meticulous in maintaining his supply lines and staying so close to the railroad, but would have moved right on to Jackson. But, being unaware of the enemy situation, Grant advanced cautiously, stopping to rebuild bridges, repair the railroad, and bring up supplies to advance depots. Although his cavalry made a dash into Holly Springs on November 13, his infantry did not arrive there until the 29th. By December 5 he still had not reached Grenada.

Perhaps Grant's reluctance to display the kind of boldness that had won him Forts Henry and Donelson was the result of a confused command system, one that made it difficult for him to advance

Ruined Depot of Shreveport and Texas Railroad.   Court-house.   Washington Hotel.   Uncle Sam House

with confidence. He was not sure at this time that he was being supported by the authorities in Washington. Essentially the high command there consisted of three men—President Lincoln, Secretary of War Edwin Stanton, and General in Chief Henry Halleck. Lincoln and Stanton were politicians who, with no prewar military experience, had handled well the administrative details of the largest war in which the United States had ever been engaged. Inevitably they were irritated when their generals were unable to use the large numbers of men they had raised and armed to conquer the South. Thus they were receptive when, in August 1862, John A. McClernand, an Illinois Democrat wearing a major general's uniform, had come to them, cursed the West Pointers for being too cautious, and said he could give them Vicksburg by Christmas. Lincoln and Stanton arranged for McClernand to raise a private "army" in the Northwest, with which he would launch an attack down the Mississippi River against Vicksburg. Even though he would be in Grant's theater, he would operate independently.

Evidently Lincoln and Stanton were embarrassed by what they had done, or else they feared the West Pointers would sabotage the operation, for they hesitated to tell Halleck about it and when they did they ordered him to keep it secret.

EVERYTHING was at cross-purposes. Halleck approved of neither the plan nor McClernand, whom he considered a pompous, foolish person and a poor general. Grant and his most esteemed subordinate, Major General William T. Sherman, distrusted McClernand as a soldier and disliked him as a man. McClernand in turn was outspoken in his contempt of all West Pointers.

Eventually Halleck spoiled McClernand's grandiose plans through a complex series of machinations that had a simple goal: to deprive McClernand of the force he was enlisting. As fast as McClernand raised troops in the Northwest, Halleck sent them to Memphis, where they were in Grant's Department and thus quite properly under the latter's control.

By early December Halleck had managed to tell Grant obliquely most of the "secret" (which had been discussed in the newspapers anyway), and Grant sent Sherman to Memphis to organize the new levies into units. The object was then to get them on their way to Vicksburg before McClernand became aware that he was being euchred. The latter, full of suspicion and indignation, finally hastened to Memphis, but he was too late.

INITIAL THRUSTS SOUTHWARD

Grant's plan had called for a single, overland thrust on Jackson and Vicksburg. He now changed it, possibly (at least in part) to thwart McClernand. The Union forces would make a two-pronged attack, one Grant's original overland drive and the other Sher-

322

man's amphibious effort down the river.

Three divisions of Sherman's force left Memphis on December 20, just a few days before McClernand arrived. All of Halleck's, Grant's, and Sherman's moves had been carried out more or less surreptitiously. For Grant this was risky; he did not yet have the press and public opinion solidly behind him, and the Government attitude was unknown. One aspect of the situation did give him reassurance: it had become obvious that Halleck was going to support him all the way. Halleck and Grant had had their differences early in the year, when Grant served under the other in the West, but now when it was a choice between McClernand and Grant, Halleck made his preference clear.

Grant might also have drawn comfort from the Confederate command structure had he known it. Pemberton, a native of Philadelphia and a graduate of West Point, had in mid-October assumed command of the Confederate forces in Mississippi and East Louisiana. A nervous man, Pemberton was unsure of himself and incapable of furnishing bold, aggressive leadership. When Grant started south Pemberton reported to Richmond that his situation was desperate. His statements caused such keen concern in the higher Southern echelons that President Jefferson Davis himself went west by rail to confer with Pemberton and inspect the defenses of Vicksburg. He was accompanied by General Joseph E. Johnston, whom Davis had appointed to command

all forces between the Appalachians and the Mississippi. Considering the communications system available to Johnston, this was an impossibly large theater to control. An additional complication was that Johnston and Davis, both Military Academy graduates, hated each other.

Johnston vainly tried to avoid the assignment, protesting that no one could effectively control such a theater. He then asked Davis for more troops. Davis told him to transfer them from the other major army in his command, Braxton Bragg's, which was in Tennessee. Johnston argued that it would be easier and wiser to pull reinforcements from Arkansas, where Lieutenant General Theophilus T. Holmes had 20,000 men. Davis agreed; then to Johnston's disgust he wrote a friendly note to Holmes "suggesting" that he send some men. No troops came.

Before Davis returned to Richmond, Johnston had one more conversation with him. A pessimist by nature, Johnston must have sounded like a veritable Cassandra. He said the theater was too large, each of the two armies too small, and they were too far apart to support each other. All was lost. Davis told Johnston to do the best he could, and left.

Map 1. General area of operations during the Vicksburg Campaign. October 1862—July 1863.

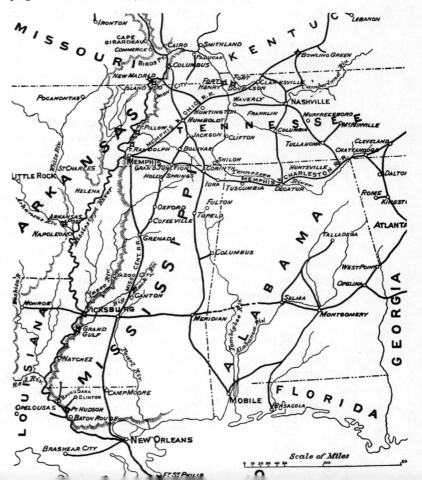

Major General Ulysses S. Grant, USA. (LC)

GRANT and Sherman, meanwhile, had paused to regroup. Major General Earl Van Dorn, commanding Pemberton's cavalry, and at the front facing Grant, decided to avoid a head-on collision. He slipped past Grant's left flank, got into his rear, and wrecked his supply base at Holly Springs. The Confederates destroyed or carried away a million dollars' worth of rations, forage, and ammunition.

Grant decided he had better pull back to Memphis and Grand Junction, where he could get fresh supplies by water from the big Union supply base at Columbus, Kentucky. Then he would rebuild the railroad from Memphis to Grand Junction which, because of its damaged condition, he had not used before, and repair any fresh damages caused by Van Dorn on the line. After a new supply reserve had been accumulated he would resume his overland advance. During the retrograde movement Grant restricted his men to short rations and sent out wagons fifteen miles on both sides of the road to scour the country for food and forage. To his amazement he found that even this narrow zone would support his force for two months.

Grant tried to inform Sherman of this withdrawal, but his wire communications to the rear had been torn down by Rebel raiders commanded by Brigadier General Nathan B. Forrest. Pemberton, unknown to

Sherman, reinforced the garrison at Vicksburg. Still, on December 21, Sherman learned that Van Dorn had captured Holly Springs. He might have guessed that this would cause Grant to turn back; but Sherman was determined to push on. He was so intent on reaching Vicksburg before McClernand that in his hurry to get away he had left behind part of a pontoon train. In the fighting that followed, this error of Sherman's cost the Union dearly.

SHERMAN arrived on the Yazoo eight miles north of Vicksburg on December 26. For three days he debarked his four divisions and worked them through the difficult swamps and bayous to a position from which he could assault across Chickasaw Bayou against the ridge just north of Vicksburg. He made this attack on the 29th. The Confederates, thanks to reinforcements which the suspension of Grant's overland drive had released, easily repulsed the Union troops with severe losses. Sherman fell back to Milliken's Bend.

There, on January 2, McClernand finally caught up with the expedition. In a towering rage he showed Sherman his orders from the President placing him in command. Sherman at once relinquished the command and, in his own words, "subsided into the more agreeable office of corps commander."

McClernand named his force "The Army of the Mississippi." He eagerly agreed to Sherman's suggestion that he move the army back up the Mississippi to the mouth of the Arkansas River, then steam up that stream to take the main Confederate position on it, the Post of Arkansas. McClernand had independently planned a similar campaign before he caught up with Sherman. Both generals felt this move necessary to relieve a growing threat to their right flank and rear, for the Confederates were preparing to descend the Arkansas with gunboats capable of raiding Union shipping. Indeed, one supply boat had already been captured.

McClernand got under way quickly, before Grant could interfere (Halleck had finally obtained from Lincoln orders that placed McClernand under Grant's general direction). On January 11 McClernand captured the Post of Arkansas. He then wrote Grant proposing that he penetrate deeper into Arkansas.

Grant was furious. He told McClernand to get back to the Mississippi immediately. He also wired Halleck that McClernand had gone off on a wild goose chase. Halleck telegraphed Grant: "You are hereby authorized to relieve General McClernand from command of the expedition against Vicksburg, giving it to the next in rank or taking it yourself." McClernand returned to Milliken's Bend. Grant arrived there on January 29. The next day he took personal command of all forces operating against Vicksburg.

WHEN Grant took command, McClernand protested bitterly. He had already told Lincoln, "I believe my success here [at the Post of Arkansas] is gall and wormwood to the clique of West Pointers who have been persecuting me for months. How can you expect success when men controlling the military destinies of the country are more chagrined at the success of your volunteer officers than the very enemy beaten by the latter in battle?" Lincoln, who was learning to rely more upon his professional advisers, especially Halleck, ignored the communication.

Grant's first act was to divide his forces into four army corps. He split McClernand's Army of the Mississippi into the XIII Corps under McClernand and the XV Corps under Sherman. His own forces were distributed into the XVI Corps (Hurlbut) and the XVII Corps (McPherson). Grant assigned to the XIII Corps the duty of garrisoning the Arkansas bank of the Mississippi. McClernand thought this was an attempt to relegate him to a subsidiary role in the campaign. He sent to Lincoln through Grant a formal complaint, citing Lincoln's original intention that he should command the expedition. Meanwhile in his personal contacts with Grant, McClernand was clearly insubordinate—and insufferable.

Grant wisely chose to ignore him and go on with his business, disregarding McClernand's insubordination. Grant realized that McClernand was an im-

Lieutenant General John C. Pemberton, CSA. (LC)

The head of the canal opposite Vicksburg cut by Grant's army. Although the project was a failure, the hard work toughened the Federals. (From a sketch by Henry Lovie in "Frank Leslie's.")

portant politician in Illinois, that Lincoln desperately needed the support of War Democrats, that McClernand was among the first members of Congress from the Democratic Party to pledge himself to a vigorous prosecution of the effort to save the Union, and that he had given up his seat in Congress to take the field. Such men are rare enough in any war, and Grant felt that he should make every effort to overlook McClernand's faults.

CAMPAIGN OF THE BAYOUS

By the time Grant assumed command winter rains had made the land around the river's banks impossible for any but the most limited operations. Still, Grant felt he could not stand idle for three months. Grant had good reasons for conducting a vigorous bayou campaign, although he was sure none of his efforts would be fruitful. The North had become discouraged. It was common talk, even among strong Union men, that the war would prove a failure. The elections of 1862 had gone against the Republicans. Voluntary enlistments had practically ceased. Had the North's second largest army stood idle over the winter or fallen back it would have fed the already rampant defeatism.

As Grant explained later, "It was my judgment at the time that to make a backward movement . . . would be interpreted by many of those yet full of hope . . . as a defeat, and that the draft would be resisted, desertions ensue, and the power to capture and punish deserters lost. There was nothing left to be done but to *go forward to a decisive victory*. This was in my mind from the moment I took command."

Through the winter Grant kept the troops busy, as he made four attempts to reach the high ground east and south of Vicksburg. The engineers tried to dig a canal that would divert the Mississippi and thus leave Vicksburg high and dry. The men labored for weeks in an effort to provide a water route from Lake Providence south to the Ouachita and then to Red River, which would allow the gunboats and transports to get below Vicksburg without having to run the Confederate batteries. Two attempts were also made to get into and along the Yazoo River above Vicksburg.

All these efforts involved an enormous amount of material and tremendous exertion by the troops. If they did no practical good in terms of the campaign itself, they nevertheless were of great benefit. The activity kept the generals from conspiring among themselves while the men, being constantly busy, had little time to grumble. The work gave newspaper reporters something to write about and stimulated the North's interest and morale. Perhaps most important, when spring came and Grant finally set

out, the troops he commanded were in good physical condition. Their muscles were hard, they were used to life in the field instead of the soft life of a permanent camp, and they had learned to get along on short rations.

GRANT BYPASSES VICKSBURG

At last, in late March, the river began to recede, the roads to dry out, and Grant concentrated his troops at Milliken's Bend, Young's Point, and Lake Providence "preparatory to a final move which was to crown the long, tedious, and discouraging labors" with success. By March 29 Grant had evolved his plan. He told Halleck he would move his army south of Vicksburg in barges and small steamers, through the series of bayous west of the Mississippi. Some overland marching would be necessary, but it should not be difficult in the drier weather. At the same time Rear Admiral David D. Porter's gunboats and large transports would run past the Vicksburg batteries. They would meet the troops south of Vicksburg and ferry them across the river. Grant had discussed the plan with Porter, who then approved it. This was fortunate for the army, since Porter's command was independent, and Grant could not give him orders. McClernand also agreed with the plan, but Sherman and McPherson strongly urged Grant to return to the overland approach east of the river.

Two months later, when Grant was besieging Vicksburg, he overheard Sherman telling the visiting governor of Illinois, "Grant is entitled to every bit of the credit for the campaign; I opposed it. I wrote him a letter about it." In his letter Sherman had said that by crossing the river south of Vicksburg, Grant would be putting himself voluntarily in a position that an enemy would be willing to maneuver for a year to get him into. Grant chose to regard the letter as unofficial and did not keep a copy. Years later Sherman himself gave a copy to Grant's biographer, General Adam Badeau, who printed it.

WHEN Halleck received Grant's plan he approved it, with the proviso that Grant should help Major General Nathaniel P. Banks before moving on Vicksburg. Banks, operating out of New Orleans, was attacking Port Hudson. Grant replied that once across the river he would send a corps to aid Banks, and Halleck was satisfied. As a diversion, Grant sent a small cavalry force, under Colonel Benjamin Grierson, on a raid through central Mississippi. Grierson's justly famous raid, which began on April 17 and ended on May 2, was a huge success. He broke railroad lines at a number of crucial places, frightened the citizenry, and caused Pemberton to send the Confederate cavalry and a division of infantry after him in a hopeless chase.

Another, almost as important a diversion, was the dispatch, early in April, of Major General Frederick Steele's division to Greenville. Going ashore, the Federals drove inland to Deer Creek and then turned south, inflicting much damage in an area from which Pemberton's commissary drew much of its hogs and hominy. To counter this thrust, Pemberton's subordinate at Vicksburg, Major General Carter L. Stevenson, ordered out a strong column. Steele then retired and reported back to Grant at Milliken's Bend. Because of this expedition, Stevenson gave scant notice to intelligence reports telling of a Union advance southward from Milliken's Bend.

As a secondary diversion Grant left Sherman at Young's Point; late in April Sherman made a feint on the Yazoo that held some of Pemberton's force in place.

Throughout April, Grant's main force, led by McClernand's XIII Corps, worked its way down the west bank of the river. The area was flat bottom-land cut by numerous bayous. Road construction was a hard, muddy, disagreeable task that required much corduroying. The troops had to improvise a number of bridges, using whatever material was at hand and their own ingenuity. By April 29 McClernand's and Major General James B. McPherson's corps had joined at Hard Times, where they met Porter's fleet, which in a spectacular movement had passed the batteries at Vicksburg.

Although the Federals had been moving south since the last day of March, Pemberton had done little to meet the threat. He did not even know about Grant's movements until April 17 and not until the 28th did he foresee a Union attack on Grand Gulf. Even then he sent the local commander, Brigadier General John S. Bowen, only some 5,000 reinforcements, raising Bowen's total force to 9,000—far inferior to Grant's more than 24,000 men. Pemberton had been begging Johnston for reinforcements, but disagreements at higher levels—Johnston wanted to take men from Arkansas, while Davis said he should make transfers from Bragg—prevented action.

Pemberton, however, could have done much more with what he had. But he was besieged with reports of the great damage being done by Grierson, had an exaggerated idea of Grierson's strength, and had consequently sent all his cavalry and thousands of infantry after the Yankee raider. He kept a large force north of Vicksburg to meet the threat Sherman posed, and hesitated to weaken the garrison at Port Hudson for fear Banks would pounce on the fort (this last was partly Davis' fault, as he had repeatedly stressed the importance of Port Hudson).

THE result of the poor intelligence work was that just when Pemberton should have been concentrating to meet and oppose Grant's crossing of the river, he had his force dispersed all over the state. Pemberton's subsequent discomfort was primarily due to his own indecision.

On April 29 Porter, at Grant's request, bombarded the Grand Gulf batteries. Grant hoped to cross his troops in the transports and assault craft, but the batteries proved too strong and, after consultation with Porter, Grant decided to land farther downriver. He planned to go to Rodney, but when a Negro informed him that a good solid road led inland from Bruinsburg he decided to cross there. On April 30 Grant got McClernand's corps and part of McPherson's corps across.

It would be impossible to improve on Grant's own description of his feelings at this point: "When this was effected I felt a degree of relief scarcely ever equalled since. Vicksburg was not yet taken, it is true, nor were its defenders demoralized by any of our previous moves. I was now in enemy territory, with a vast river and the stronghold of Vicksburg between me and my base of supplies. But I was on dry ground on the same side of the river with the enemy. All the campaigns, labors, hardships, and exposures from the month of December previous to this time that had been made and endured, were for the accomplishment of this one object."

GRANT MOVES TO ISOLATE VICKSBURG

From this point on, until the siege began, Grant moved with amazing speed. Brushing the Confederates aside with short, hard blows wherever he met them, he moved his force inland to Jackson, then westward to Vicksburg. He hardly ever took the obvious route, always left himself with alternatives, and kept Pemberton thoroughly confused. No other campaign of the Civil War, and few others in all military history, were so successful at such small cost. In view of this operation, it is difficult to explain the prevalence of the widely held view that Grant was slow and deliberate—a bludgeon general rather than the wielder of a rapier.

As soon as Grant was across the river he ordered Sherman to bring the bulk of his force south. Leaving Major General Frank Blair's division to guard his depots and supply line west of the river, Grant then set out inland with McClernand's corps and part of McPherson's.* The troops marched along the

---

*Grant's force numbered around 24,000 men; when Sherman joined him, on May 8, his strength was about 34,000. Pemberton had nearly 40,000 at all times; but while Grant was concentrated, Pemberton's force was badly scattered. Further, Pemberton received no substantial reinforcements, whereas by the end of the campaign Grant had over 75,000 officers and men.

Rodney road south of Bayou Pierre toward Port Gibson, a small village where there was a network of roads leading to Grand Gulf, Vicksburg, and Jackson. McClernand, in the lead, hoped to beat Bowen to the bridge over Bayou Pierre on the route that led to Grand Gulf, but he had wasted valuable time because of poor staff work. His men had not received their three days rations prior to crossing the river and he had to wait while they were issued. By the time he reached Thompson's plantation, five miles west of Port Gibson, it was after midnight.

In any case the Confederates were already there. Brigadier General Martin E. Green and an advanced detachment of Bowen's force had arrived late in the afternoon and taken up positions to contest the Yankee advance. Because the cavalry was off chasing Grierson, Bowen had no firm idea where the Federals were, but he guessed that they would try to cross the bayou and invest Grand Gulf. Therefore he sent one brigade to hold the bridge and cover Port Gibson, while he prepared to move with the other as necessary.

FOR General Green the night of April 30-May 1 passed slowly. All was silence about him. No scouts had reported in; he began to fear that Grant had taken a wholly unexpected route, or perhaps even reembarked his troops for another try at Grand Gulf. At 12:30 a.m. the tension became more than he could bear, and he rode forward to make sure that Lieutenant Tisdale and his outpost were alert.

Coming up to the Shaifer house he found a small area of chaos. Mrs. A. K. Shaifer and the other women of the house had panicked at the news the Yankees were coming. They were frantically trying to load their most valuable household effects into a wagon in which they proposed to flee to Port Gibson. The panic of the ladies allowed the overwrought Green to get control of himself. He calmly told them that the Yankees could not possibly arrive before daylight, and that they therefore had plenty of time to load their wagon.

He had hardly spoken the comforting words when a crash of musketry shattered the stillness. One ball smashed through the west wall of the house and several more buried themselves in the wagon-load of furniture. A brief horrified silence gave way to shrieks of dismay. Abandoning both household goods and dignity, the ladies scrambled into the wagon and whipped the team frantically toward Port Gibson and fancied safety. Green, both chagrined and amused, ordered Tisdale to contest the Yankee advance, then galloped back to make sure that the gunfire had alerted his command. The land campaign for Vicksburg was underway.

During the remainder of the night the troops exchanged sporadic fire with little result. The night was so dark and the country so broken that Brigadier General Eugene A. Carr, senior Union commander on the spot, decided to wait until dawn before deploying his division further.

BATTLE OF PORT GIBSON, MAY 1, 1863

Dawn revealed to General Carr a terrain of incredible complexity. It was an utter maze of ridges, each more or less flat-topped and of equal height, but running in all directions. Each ridge was separated from its neighbor by a steep-sided ravine filled with a jumble of trees, vines, and immense and almost impenetrable cane brakes. The ridge tops were chiefly cultivated fields except where there were groves of trees around plantation buildings. Visibility was excellent from the ridge-tops but the ravines were jungles that closed tightly about men moving through them, so that each man's world was a tiny green-walled room only a few yards across.

McClernand, nervous, eager, and excited, rode up at daybreak. He had just passed a fork in the road and had no idea which of the routes before him led to Port Gibson. The inevitable Negro "contraband" appeared to explain that both did, and that at no point did the two roads, which followed ridges, diverge more than a mile or two. They were separated, however, by a deep vine- and cane-choked ravine, so that one flank could not reinforce the other except by marching back to the junction of the roads. Bowen's men were in position on both roads, hoping to hold off McClernand until reinforcements under Major General William W. Loring could arrive from Big Black Bridge.

The old Mississippi River bed as it now appears from Fort Hill. The Water Battery lies in the center of the picture. (Courtesy Vicksburg National Military Park.)

Magnolia Church on the Port Gibson battlefield. (Margie Bearss collection.)

McClernand immediately decided to attack along both ridges and simply push the Confederates out of the way. He put the divisions of Hovey, Carr, and A. J. Smith on the right flank and that of Osterhaus on the left.   With an entire corps passing through one road junction there was not much room for maneuver, and it took a few hours to get everyone into position. Neither attack got off until after 8 a.m. By then Bowen himself had arrived. Instantly recognizing that he had the whole of Grant's army in front of him, he sent couriers to the rear to bring up all possible reinforcements.

IN RETROSPECT this was the critical moment of the Vicksburg campaign. Grant was still involved in an amphibious operation. His force was inevitably divided, with one of his three corps still on the west bank of the river and over half of another still engaged in disembarking and in unloading the transports. If Pemberton could have struck while Grant was thus off balance, with one foot in the water and the other on land, he certainly would have spoiled Grant's plans and he might have even destroyed his army.

But Pemberton utterly failed to take advantage of the opportunity. Because he had voluntarily given up his cavalry he was operating in the dark. Not until the battle had been joined did he learn that contact had been made. Then he sent elements of two divisions toward Port Gibson and telegraphed Johnston, demanding reinforcements. Johnston at once wired back: "If Grant's army lands on this side of the river, the safety of Mississippi depends on beating it. For that object you should unite your whole force."

As always, Johnston's strategic insight was impeccable. His advice, however, was worthless. Pemberton had five divisions scattered through the triangle formed by Port Gibson, Jackson, and Vicksburg. He had only one division and two brigades of another at the scene of the opening battle. He was simply in no position to prevent Grant from establishing himself on the east bank. Pemberton must have winced the next day when Johnston again wired him: "If Grant's army crosses, unite all your forces to beat it. Success will give you back what was abandoned to win it."

Johnston had been ill, and in any case never had his heart in the campaign. He approached it with the attitude that the result was a foregone conclusion, never showed any enthusiasm for his assignment, made no real effort to control or direct Pemberton, and was so weighted down with pessimism that he evidently felt that sending more troops to Pemberton was simply to waste them. There is no evidence that he ever made a determined attempt to get reinforcements to the hard-pressed Pemberton. In a typical "my hands are tied; there is nothing I can do" message to the Confederate War Department the day after the Battle of Port Gibson, he transmitted Pemberton's call for reinforcements and commented,

329

The Perkins house (now abandoned) still stands on the Port Gibson battlefield. It first served as Grant's headquarters and later was used as a hospital. (Photograph by Ken Parks.)

"They cannot be sent from here without giving up Tennessee."

THE upshot was that Bowen was left by his superiors to fight his battle alone. Grant, meanwhile, reached the field just as the battle was getting into full swing and inspected both flanks in person. McClernand's progress was slow but steady. He could not begin to deploy all his troops on one road, and in any case Confederate fire made a direct advance along the ridge unprofitable. He therefore sent men into the ravines on both sides to attempt to outflank Bowen. Once in the ravine, however, the smoke of battle, coupled with the vines and underbrush, made it virtually impossible to maintain any sense of direction, and regiments found themselves moving at odd angles to the direction their officers supposed. Great gaps opened at some points, while at others regiments jammed up. Still the weight of the advance was enough to force the enemy to give ground.

On the left Brigadier General Peter J. Osterhaus, a Prussian who was the most distinguished of the foreign-born generals who served the Union, was having great difficulty. At 8:15 he had tried to rush the Rebel position. He had gained about 400 yards, then had come to a sudden stop when he hit the main enemy lines. When he found time to check his position, Osterhaus discovered that his attack had carried his men into the middle of a concave system of ridges, and that the diverging movements caused by peculiar arrangement of the ravines had opened huge gaps in

Rain during the night of May 13-14 turned roads into mudholes for Grant's artillery. Drawing by Edwin Forbes. (LC)

his lines. The 42d Ohio faced the middle of the Rebel line with the 49th Indiana on an odd eccentric to the left. Between the Hoosiers and the 118th Illinois on their left there was a gap of more than 200 yards. A well-led Confederate counterattack might roll up his entire line.

But the Rebels had no fresh troops. Grant meanwhile, as soon as McClernand's men had passed the road junction, rushed elements of McPherson's corps forward. Throughout the day McClernand begged Grant for more men. Grant consistently insisted that McClernand, who had sent Brigadier General Alvin P. Hovey to help Carr, on the right, already had more men on his very limited front than he could use effectively. A brigade of Major General John A. Logan's division (which had crossed the river that morning) reached the Shaifer house about noon and Grant ordered it to support McClernand's right. Logan's next brigade to reach the field was sent to assist Osterhaus.

WHILE Union reinforcements reached the field in division strength, Bowen received his only reinforcements—about one and a half brigades coming up from Grand Gulf and Vicksburg. Osterhaus, with a superiority of over three to one, moved some troops into the ravine on his left, and sent a series of skirmish lines forward. There was a great deal of noise, tremendous confusion, and clouds of smoke before the Confederates fell back.

On the right McClernand, never a subtle general but a firm believer in applying the greatest strength

in the smallest space, prepared a direct frontal smash. He concentrated so many men on his narrow front that the regiments were stacked up two, three, and four deep. The two leading regiments got within eighty yards of the Confederate artillery before the men had to seek shelter. Two more regiments followed, the men shouting and forming a single irresistible mass. The Confederates had two batteries double-shotted with canister for a last telling volley, but before the gunners could fire their pieces the Yankee swept over them, capturing two guns of the Botetourt Virginia Artillery. Gleefully the Union men manhandled these guns around and fired them at the backs of the fleeing Rebel troops.

McCLERNAND'S column moved forward along the Rodney road. About a mile beyond Magnolia Church the vanguard encountered a strong force of Confederates posted in a deep hollow. Here Bowen had deployed the brigade (William E. Baldwin's) that had just arrived from Vicksburg, after marching forty-four miles in twenty-seven hours. The half brigade (Francis M. Cockrell's) that had come from Grand Gulf that morning would constitute Bowen's reserve.

In this difficult country it took several hours for McClernand and his three division commanders to form their troops in line of battle. The Federals then advanced into the cane-choked hollow, but within minutes the enemy checked their forward progress. Bowen in the meantime had taken a desperate gamble. He sent Cockrell with his two regiments

far to the left. Taking advantage of the terrain, Cockrell was able to assail McClernand's right, which was not refused, and roll up one Union brigade. To counter this thrust McClernand was compelled to rush artillery and infantry to his right. Superior numbers soon told, and the Confederate success was nullified. But by this time dusk was at hand, and the day's fighting was over.

It had taken all day but the Confederate position was finally gone. Bowen had fought magnificently; no other Confederate leader would do as well in the campaign to follow. A West Point classmate of McPherson and the ablest general in Pemberton's army, Bowen was a severe disciplinarian. His jet black hair, bushy eyebrows, and luxuriant chin beard tended to draw attention away from his sleepy eyes and rather frail constitution. He was unable to withstand the rigors of the siege, contracted severe dysentery, and survived the campaign by only a few days. But he had made his contribution; it could have been decisive. For eighteen hours he had held up Grant's entire army, inflicting over 800 casualties. Had he received any help at all, Bowen might have driven Grant into the river. But Pemberton had let his best chance go by.

GRANT rode up to McClernand's headquarters just after the successful assault at Magnolia Church. Governor Richard Yates of Illinois was there; together the three men rode forward to inspect the captured position. The men cheered lustily as they passed along the line. Grant was impassive as always, but the cheers were heady to McClernand and Yates. The two politicians were so overwhelmed by the sight of all those voters that they simply had to stop and make brief congratulatory addresses to the troops. Yates said a few words, then McClernand shouldered him aside and exulted, "A great day for the Northwest!"

Grant watched quietly, then suggested that perhaps the advance should be resumed. McClernand, beaming, agreed, and got the pursuit started. Bowen had led part of his force over Bayou Pierre to cover Grand Gulf (which he evacuated the next night), while the remainder slipped northeastward over the Little Bayou Pierre, (South Fork of the Bayou Pierre) and then took a more northerly route toward Vicksburg, crossing Big Bayou Pierre (the Bayou's north fork) at Grindstone Ford. He fired the three bridges behind him. When darkness fell Grant let his weary men make camp.

The next morning Grant moved through Port Gibson to Little Bayou Pierre; he at once set his men to work bridge-building. Lieutenant Colonel James H. Wilson, two years out of West Point and soon to achieve fame as a cavalry leader, supervised the construction. Using material obtained from wooden buildings, stables, fences, and the like, and going into the water himself to work as hard as the men, Wilson quickly had the bridge finished. Grant crossed, and by evening of that day (May 2) had reached Bayou Pierre.

A Bold Decision

Grant had planned to solidify his position around Grand Gulf and south of the Big Black, then send McClernand's corps to assist Banks at Port Hudson. Once that operation was completed, Grant would move north with his entire army reinforced by that of Banks. But on May 3 Grant learned that Banks was on a chase up Red River and would not be ready to invest Port Hudson for several weeks.

The news was extremely frightening. Grant had bet everything he had on this campaign only because he was convinced he could move faster than the Confederates. Outwardly taciturn, he was filled with an inner tension, a compulsion to get moving. The trouble was that he had no assured line of supplies. The road from Milliken's Bend down to Hard Times was so bad and so exposed to attack that Grant hesitated to supply his army that way. Material could not be brought up from New Orleans as long as the guns at Port Hudson were still firing. Transports and barges could run the batteries at Vicksburg, but only at what would be an increasing cost as the Confederate gunners improved with practice.

Grant made the boldest decision of the war. He declared that he would move inland without occupying the countryside. He would have the men carry enough hardtack, coffee, and salt to get by on, load his wagons to the bulging point with ammunition, and depend on the countryside for whatever else he needed. He did arrange to have heavily-guarded supply trains come out of Grand Gulf each day.

Grant's next problem was where to attack. McPherson, on May 5 had conducted a reconnaissance north of the Big Black River which revealed that Pemberton had finally concentrated his troops and was having them dig in to oppose an attack from the south. Grant may have known that Johnston was attempting to build up a force at Jackson, that President Davis had dispatched troops from the East, and that any reinforcements to Vicksburg had to come through Jack-

son. He therefore adopted a favorite Napoleonic maneuver and advanced so as to get between the two forces, hopefully to destroy the weaker one first, then turn on the stronger.

BY MAY 7 Grant had McClernand up to Big Sand Creek with McPherson at Rocky Springs. Sherman had reached Hard Times, crossed the river to occupy Grand Gulf, and caught up with the other two corps in a couple of days. On May 11 Grant pushed Sherman's corps out in front of McClernand's, which had halted near Cayuga, while McPherson prepared to advance on Raymond from Utica. Sherman and McClernand marched together to Auburn, where McClernand branched out almost straight north on the Telegraph Road toward Edwards' Station while Sherman moved on eastward to Dillon's plantation. If it proved necessary, Grant had lateral roads available so that any one corps could support another at any time.

Still, Grant was taking a risk. If Pemberton had organized the countryside so that spies and scouts could be reporting, or if he had retained his cavalry for reconnaissance, he might have descended quickly on the nearest Union corps and isolated and destroyed it. But he had neglected to make either of these elementary preparations and as a result was completely in the dark about Grant's movements. He was, in addition, under orders from Davis to hold Vicksburg and from Johnston to concentrate and attack Grant. Under the circumstances he decided to take an indecisive course, which suited his temperament in any case, collect his forces along the Big Black River, and await developments. He did send Bowen forward to occupy Edwards' Station and a brigade, Brigadier General John Gregg's, from Jackson to Raymond.

One of the great myths of the Civil War is that Grant cut loose from his supply line when his army began its march inland from the Hankinson's Ferry-Willow Springs area. It was May 14 before the last train moved out of Grand Gulf. If Grant had been repulsed at Champion Hill, another train escorted by an infantry brigade would have been called up from Grand Gulf.—Edwin C. Bearss

332

When Gregg marched into Raymond on the afternoon of May 11 the populace hailed his men as saviors. The village seethed with rumors of the approach of a Yankee column from Utica. Gregg asked where he could find the headquarters of Colonel Wirt Adams, expecting to find the cavalry commander busy receiving reports on the enemy's movements. Gregg's request was met with blank stares—Adams had exactly five men in the village.

Adams' absence was due to a masterpiece of ambiguity by Pemberton. The latter, after ordering Gregg to Raymond, had sent a messenger to Adams: "General Gregg is ordered to Raymond. Direct your cavalry there to scout thoroughly, and keep him informed." What Pemberton meant was that Adams should take all his cavalry to Raymond and carry out this mission. Adams, however, read the message to say that the cavalry he already had in Raymond (five men) should scout thoroughly and keep Gregg informed. Adams therefore proceeded with his original plans and, while Gregg marched into Raymond, rode into Edwards' Station.

The result was that a Union corps was bearing down on an unsuspecting Rebel brigade, and again the Yankee forces, though outnumbered in the area, had overwhelming superiority at the point of contact. In the engagement that followed, the Southerners again showed that given equal numbers they were more than equal to their enemy. In part this was due to a misreading of the situation by McPherson, who overestimated his opponent's strength, a natural mistake—he just could not believe that a brigade would challenge a corps to pitched battle. He therefore advanced cautiously, enabling Gregg to engage the Union regiments piecemeal.

THE battle itself, on May 12, was even more confused than that at Port Gibson. The Confederates kept attacking, wildly hitting advancing Union regiments and forcing them to retreat. On two occasions John A. Logan personally rallied his men. Once the 20th Ohio, seeing a Texas regiment sweep down upon its flank, began to waver and prepared to run. Logan dashed up and with "the shriek of an eagle turned them back to their place." One Ohioan gave Logan his just due: "Had it not been for Logan's timely intervention, who was continually riding up and down the line, firing his men with his own enthusiasm, our lines would undoubtedly have been broken at some point."

The whole battlefield was a bowl of dust and smoke; no one could see what was really going on. The Confederates would probably not have fought had they known what they were up against. Considering some of the things they did, however, it is possible that a knowledge of the odds would have simply spurred them to greater efforts. For example, late in the day Colonel R. W. MacGavock found himself on a bare spur just as a pause occurred in the battle. As the smoke and dust lifted, he and his men were exposed to McPherson's entire corps artillery. Joyfully switching fire to the only visible target, the Union gunners began to rake MacGavock's ranks with shell fire. Meanwhile a blue line of infantry, sharpshooters thrown out in advance, began to come up the hill. MacGavock realized that if he fell back the entire Southern position would go with him. If he stayed, he would be cut to pieces by the Yankee artillery and the charging infantry.

Panoramic view of the battlefield of Raymond, situated about three miles southwest of Raymond along the Utica Road. The view is from the commanding ridge which was occupied by Federal forces during the battle. (Photo by Margie R. Bearss)

He could think of only one thing to do. A tall, commanding man who habitually wore a long gray cloak with a brilliant scarlet lining, MacGavock dramatically threw his cloak back. There he stood, a compelling crimson figure, at the head of his troops. Every eye on the battlefield turned toward him. He waved his arm forward and shouted for a charge. At that instant a Union sharpshooter cut him down, but his men rushed forward with irresistible force, screaming for vengeance. They broke the Yankee line and sent it running.

SOMEHOW this was not the way a battle between a brigade and a corps was supposed to go; in the end inevitably the weight of the Union attack made itself felt. The Confederates slowly fell back, even though Gregg continued to find the best defense was a good offense. Whenever a Yankee regiment appeared, the Rebels facing it would move forward threateningly, making as much noise as possible. Soon, however, the Confederates found themselves nearly surrounded, with the enemy well around both flanks. Gregg retired.

One Confederate brigade had held up a Union corps for half a day, at a cost of 515 casualties. McPherson suffered almost an equal loss in killed and wounded, but because his missing total was only 37 his casualty list ran to only 442.

The bone-weary, hot, dusty, thirsty 20th Ohio led the Union advance into Raymond. Coming into the shaded village from the brazen sun, they were astonished to find a tremendous picnic spread beneath the stately live oaks along the streets. The ladies of Raymond had prepared the feast for Gregg's soldiers, to be eaten upon their "return from victory." Gregg had moved through the village so fast, however, that the men had not touched the food. The boys from Ohio gratefully took their places and by the time the following regiment reached town the food was gone.

GRANT received McPherson's report of the battle while at Sherman's headquarters. He knew from his scouts that Pemberton was concentrating at Edwards' Station, partly to block the Federal movement to Vicksburg, partly to pose a threat to the Grand Gulf-Raymond road over which Grant was bringing up reinforcements and the heavily guarded trains. During the day, Sherman in the center and McClernand on the left had forced their way across Fourteen Mile Creek, as they turned their columns toward the Vicksburg-to-Jackson railroad. Grant also knew that a couple of Confederate regiments coming all the way from the eastern seaboard had reported to Gregg after he had retreated through Raymond. More would be coming and their route would be via Jackson. If Pemberton were finally going to

concentrate all his units, Grant wanted his pulled together too. He also wanted to cut Pemberton off from any possibility of receiving outside aid, and at the same time destroy the communications and manufacturing center of Mississippi, which was Jackson. Grant therefore "decided at once to turn the whole column toward Jackson and capture that place without delay."

Grant issued his orders on the night of May 12. He directed McPherson to Clinton, almost directly west of Jackson and astride the Vicksburg-to-Jackson railroad; once McPherson had occupied Clinton he would sever Pemberton's direct communications with Johnston, who was building up a force in the capital. Grant told Sherman to start at 4 a.m., marching through Raymond toward Jackson. McClernand would follow and occupy Raymond.

Grant was now deep in hostile territory, with large enemy forces on either side of him. The Union troops were in the position Sherman had said the enemy would be willing to maneuver for a year or more in order to get them into. Meanwhile General Banks, on Red River, was pleading for reinforcements.

GRANT had been in a similar position in February 1862, at Fort Donelson. Then as now he did not panic. (The modern slang expression is an excellent description of Grant in such a situation: "He kept his cool.") Neither did he take foolish chances. He kept his troops in supporting distance of each other, making constant reconnaissances to enable each corps to know at all times where the most practicable routes were in case it became necessary for them to concentrate. More important, he moved so rapidly, as well as audaciously, that he had the Confederates constantly and thoroughly confused.

Crocker's division at the Battle of Jackson on May 14, 1863. From a drawing by battlefield artist Theodore R. Davis. (HW)

McPherson reached Clinton early on May 13. The men immediately cut the telegraph line and began destroying the railroad. Sherman got into Raymond before the last of McPherson's command had left. McClernand had the most difficult mission; his spearhead, which had forced its way across Fourteen Mile Creek, was in contact with the formidable force Pemberton was concentrating at Edwards' Station. To keep the Confederates off balance while he broke contact, McClernand bluffed an attack, and the Confederates began digging in. McClernand, covered by this feint, sent three of his divisions eastward across Bakers Creek, and by the time Pemberton and his generals realized what had happened, McClernand's corps had stolen a day's march on them.

McClernand reached his encampment in good order. The next morning, May 14, McPherson marched at dawn for Jackson; so did Sherman. When the two corps reached the Confederate entrenchments around the city they would be about two miles apart. McClernand sent one division to Clinton, another behind Sherman, and a third to Raymond.

JOHNSTON GIVES UP JACKSON

By the afternoon of the 13th Grant's position was as nearly perfect as the human mind and hard marching could make it. He had two corps threatening Jackson; a division, Hovey's, at Clinton that could either hold off Pemberton or reinforce McPherson; another division behind Sherman for support; a division at Raymond that could take either road and reinforce Hovey or Sherman; and two more divisions (one of which, Blair's, had recently crossed the river) farther back within one and one-half day's march of Jackson. These last divisions, under Mc-

Clernand's command, were threatening Pemberton and, if not needed at Jackson, were one day's march from there on their way to Vicksburg and on two different roads leading to that city.

The Confederate position, by contrast, approached the ludicrous. Johnston, who had arrived in Jackson on the evening of the 13th, had nothing like enough men to hold off two corps. Although the total Confederate strength in the whole area of operation was still greater than Grant's, the third battle of the campaign was about to be fought with the Union forces—who were invading and were in the heart of enemy territory—again in great superiority. Grant stood squarely between the two Rebel armies. Johnston ordered Pemberton to move on Clinton, where the two separated forces could unite. Pemberton, however, had other ideas. He was considering moving southeast to attack and destroy Grant's trains and the two divisions guarding them.

Within Jackson, Johnston had only some 6,000 men to defend the capital. "I am too late," he wired the Secretary of War. At 3 a.m. on May 14 he issued an evacuation order, even though he then was facing two corps, which had not yet begun their final advance on Jackson. In short, Johnston's pessimism was so great that he decided to retreat before any pressure was exerted and before he could possibly be certain that the Union concentration was aimed at Jackson.

AT 5 A.M. McPherson and Sherman started out for Jackson. It had rained most of the night; with daybreak the rain began to fall in torrents, turning

335

the roads into sheets of mud. At places along McPherson's route the road was covered by a foot of water. The wheels of the ambulances, guns, and limbers quickly converted the road into a bottomless quagmire, through which the artillery horses strained in vain to pull the heavy caissons. The sodden infantrymen put their shoulders to the wheels. Curses quickly lost in the sound of falling water rang out whenever an officer or courier dashed past on his horse and splashed sheets of mud and water on the straining infantrymen.

Despite everything the men moved forward. By midmorning they had reached the outer Confederate lines. McPherson's leading division, Brigadier General Marcellus M. Crocker's, deployed. McPherson sent word back to the following division, Logan's, to hurry forward. Just then the rain abated slightly and McPherson organized an immediate assault. As he prepared to give the order to charge, another terrific downpour commenced, with the water coming down in buckets. McPherson, afraid to allow his men to open their cartridge boxes lest the water ruin the ammunition, called off the attack to wait for the rain to subside.

Sherman's vanguard, meanwhile, had worked its way forward and had reached Lynch Creek, which was nearly overflowing. A small Confederate force covered the bridge. As soon as he heard the enemy artillery contesting his advance Sherman rode forward, made a hasty reconnaissance, and ordered an immediate attack. Just then the rain ceased. It was 11 a.m. The men dashed forward, crossed the bridge, and drove the Rebels back. By early afternoon Sherman had forced the enemy into the main Jackson entrenchments (dug earlier by slave labor and citizen volunteers), where his assault came to a halt.

GRANT was with Sherman, and the two officers conferred on the next move. Sherman pointed out that the enemy trenches extended as far to his left as he could see. To the right his vision was obstructed, and he decided to send a scouting party to reconnoiter in that direction. Sherman, Grant, and some staff officers, standing in front of a cottage as they talked, presented an obvious target to the Rebels. Just as the scouting party rode away several shells whistled over the infantry line and exploded nearby. Neither Grant nor Sherman turned a hair.

The scouts, led by Sherman's chief engineer, Captain Julius Pitzman, found that the trenches to the right were unmanned. Pitzman returned to the main force and gathered up the 95th Ohio for a flanking operation. As the regiment was placing its flag as a symbol of victory on the earthworks, an old Negro ran up to the men waving his hat and yelling at the top of his voice, "I'se come to tell you-all that the

Rebels is left the city, clear done gone. You jes' go on and you will take the city."

With considerable difficulty the Ohio soldiers got the old man calmed down enough to ask him, "Why are the Rebs still firing their battery if they have left the place?"

"Ho!" he laughed, "there is only a few cannoneers there to work the guns to keep you back."

The Negro offered to guide them and the men agreed to follow. Sure enough, he led them right into the unsupported and unguarded rear of the Southern artillerymen. Shouting joyfully, the Yankees surged forward, through the backyards and over fences, pounced on the Confederates, and bagged themselves six guns and fifty-two prisoners. Sherman could now walk into Jackson.

THE northern jaw of the Union pincer was prepared to close. When the rains let up, Crocker decided not to waste time on such an inferior force, especially one that was challenging him two miles outside its earthworks. He sent his whole line charging forward on the double with banners unfurled, bayonets fixed, and the men cheering wildly.

The Rebels resisted for a few minutes, then retreated to their main trench system. Shortly after they arrived they pulled out of the city. Johnston had already left; Gregg was in command. Gregg, learning that Sherman had closed up against the Jackson fortifications, and of the repulse of the men facing McPherson, and receiving a message that the army's supply train had left Jackson en route to Canton, decided he had done enough. He ordered his remaining men, except for a number of artillerymen manning the guns, to retreat along the Canton road and protect the rear of the wagon train. It was these artillerymen whom Sherman's troops captured.

At 3 p.m. McPherson learned that the enemy had vanished from his front. He sent Crocker's division on into the city while directing a brigade of Logan's division to march cross-country and attempt to cut

off Gregg's retreat. Either the brigade did not march fast enough (the men had been marching or fighting in deep mud since 5 a.m.) or the order did not reach them soon enough. In any case Gregg escaped.

Raising the Stars and Stripes over Jackson, Mississippi after Johnston's evacuation. Drawing by Theodore R. Davis. (HW)

AT 4 P.M. Grant, McPherson, and Sherman met in the Bowman House to exchange congratulations, count the cost of victory, and plan new blows against the enemy. The Union forces had 299 casualties, the Rebels 845. In addition, the victors had captured seventeen cannon.

If Grant had been thinking of savoring his victory and letting his men rest for a day or two, McPherson gave him news that dispelled this notion. General Johnston had the previous day sent an order to Pemberton, dispatching it via three messengers. One of the couriers was widely known as a fire-eating Rebel civilian whom the Union authorities had expelled from Memphis some months earlier for making public statements threatening and disloyal to the Union. His expulsion and subsequent flight into Confederate-held territory had received considerable publicity. Actually the man was an undercover Federal agent, and the whole affair had been stage-managed. He became a trusted Confederate mes-

senger, and when Johnston sent him with orders to Pemberton, he took them first to McPherson. Thus the latter had the order before Pemberton, and showed it to Grant.

Grant eagerly grabbed the message. It directed Pemberton to proceed to Clinton and strike at Grant's rear. Johnston would try to unite with him there. Grant knew that Johnston's force was retreating to the northeast, but Pemberton did not. Presumably Pemberton would obey orders and should soon be setting out for Clinton.

Grant decided to concentrate at Bolton, the nearest point where Johnston could swing around and effect a junction with Pemberton. He told McPherson to march at earliest dawn and sent a courier to McClernand. After giving the tidings of the fall of Jackson, Grant ordered McClernand to "turn all your forces toward Bolton Station, and make all dispatch

Destruction of Confederate property in Jackson, one of the few towns in Mississippi. Drawing by Theodore R. Davis. (HW)

in getting there. Move troops by the most direct road from wherever they may be on receipt of this order."

One can only stand amazed at Grant's ability. The Confederates did not concentrate at Bolton or Clinton, which would have been their best move, so no battle was fought there. Had they done so, however, Grant would have fought them on at least equal terms—with his fresh troops in the forefront.

Grant told Sherman to occupy the rifle-pits around Jackson, and to destroy the railroad tracks in and about Jackson, and all the property belonging to the enemy. The conference then adjourned, and Grant retired for the night to sleep in the bed Johnston had occupied the night before.

BY 10 A.M. on May 15 all of McPherson's corps had gone and Sherman was ready to begin the destruction. The chief purpose was to eliminate Jackson as a communication center, since Grant did not have enough troops to leave an occupying force. Sherman therefore started with the railroads. He would line a regiment up in single file parallel to the tracks. At a given signal everybody would bend over, grab a tie, and heave, thus turning up on edge a section of track equal in length to the regiment. The men then piled up the ties, placed the rails on top of the pile, and started a fire. When the iron was cherry red in the middle, teams of brawny soldiers would grab the ends and twist the rails around a convenient tree. The results were called "Sherman's neckties."

Sherman burned all the factories in the town, many of the public buildings, and some private ones. His men found a supply of rum; the inevitable result was indiscriminate burning, against which Sherman protested bitterly.

During the morning Grant and Sherman visited a large textile factory. The plant manager and the employees, most of them women, simply ignored the presence of the two generals and went on working. The looms were producing tent cloth with C.S.A. woven into each bolt. Grant meditated on this industrious scene for a few minutes, then turned to Sherman and suggested that the girls had done work enough. Sherman told the girls they could leave, taking with them all the cloth they could carry. He then burned the factory.

BATTLE OF CHAMPION HILL

Sherman spent the night of May 15-16 in Jackson, marching for Bolton on the 16th. The Confederates re-occupied Jackson but the Union mission had been accomplished. Jackson was now worthless as a transportation center, her war industries were crushed, and the Confederate concentration that had

aimed at saving Fortress Vicksburg was scattered to the winds. And Grant, now well concentrated, was marching due west towards Vicksburg.

Pemberton, meanwhile, had finally started to move. He had so far committed the inexcusable blunder of doing nothing. When he received Johnston's order to strike Grant's rear at Clinton, Pemberton held a council of war. There, incredibly, he raised with his commanders the question, "Should we obey the theater commander's order?" A heated discussion followed. A majority voiced a desire to march to the southeast and destroy Grant's trains and the two divisions guarding them. Pemberton himself wished to hold the line of the Big Black, repulse the Federals, and then counterattack. Sensing the mood of his generals and soldiers, Pemberton announced he would ignore Johnston and strike out for Auburn and cut Grant's supply line.

The next morning, May 15, Pemberton set out. The rains, however, had swollen Bakers Creek, and

at the Raymond crossing the stream was unfordable. The Confederates spent most of the afternoon in waiting for the water to subside. Pemberton finally turned northeast and marched his troops into the main Vicksburg-Jackson road, where a bridge crossed the creek. They then marched eastward, turned into a plantation road, and after a seven-mile detour, the head of the column was back on the Raymond road. It was after midnight before the rear brigades had crossed Bakers Creek. When the army camped the troops lay down where they halted. Six miles separated the vanguard from the rear guard.

EARLY the next morning, May 16, Pemberton received a later order from Johnston, one written after the fall of Jackson. Again Johnston wished to attempt to unite the forces at Clinton. This time Pemberton decided he would do as ordered; he sent a message to that effect to Johnston.

Grant, meanwhile, had McPherson and McClern-

and converging on Champion Hill. The two contending armies were unaware on the night of May 15-16 that they were camped within four miles of each other. At 5 a.m. two railroaders reported to Grant that Pemberton was at Edwards' Station preparing to move east. His force was estimated at 25,000 men.

Grant's first thoughts were to get up reinforcements. He had planned to leave Sherman in Jackson for two days, in order to complete the destruction of the city. Now he sent orders to Sherman to move as soon as possible westward, and to put one division with an ammunition train on the road immediately. Sherman was to tell the division commander to march with all possible speed until he reached the rear of McPherson's corps.

The Battle of Champion Hill, the chief engagement in the Vicksburg Campaign. From a sketch drawn by a Union officer. (FL)

IN sharp contrast to the way in which orders were acted upon in the Confederate army, Sherman had a division on the road within an hour, and his other division was soon out of Jackson. A. J. Smith's and Blair's divisions on the 15th had marched from Auburn to Raymond. Passing out of Raymond, they had advanced a short distance up the Edwards road and had camped. Hovey's division of McPherson's corps had marched westward from Clinton. A clean-shaven politician from Indiana who had received a promotion for his good work at Shiloh, Hovey had spent the night at Bolton. McClernand sent Hovey forward, while Grant, who was preparing to ride forward from Clinton, sent a message to McPherson to clear his wagons from the road and follow Hovey as closely as possible. McClernand had two roads available for his four remaining divisions; Grant told him to move on the enemy by both, but cautiously and with skirmishers to the front to feel for the enemy.

A. J. Smith, leading McClernand's advance on the southernmost road, was the first to encounter the enemy's pickets. Shortly thereafter, Osterhaus, spear-heading McClernand's column on the middle road, and later yet, on the Vicksburg-Jackson road, bumped into the Rebels. McPherson, hearing the scattered fire, tried to hurry his men forward, but Hovey's wagons were occupying the road and delayed the advance. McPherson sent word back to Grant at Clinton, describing the situation. Grant immediately mounted his horse and rode forward. In a short time he had got the wagons off the road and cleared the way for McPherson. By then, too, Hovey's skirmishing had increased in intensity, and now amounted almost to a battle.

CHAMPION HILL,* Pemberton's accidental choice of a battlefield, was well suited to the defense. One of the highest points in the region, it commanded all the ground to the north and southwest. The position would be especially formidable against attack by columns advancing via the Raymond and Middle roads. As contact was made early with General McClernand's columns advancing via these roads, Pemberton concentrated his troops along the ridge extending to the southwest and commanding Jackson Creek. To reach the Confederates' main line of resistance, McClernand's troops would have to deploy and advance across fields commanded by Pemberton's artillery.

---

*The owners of the property prefer this usage to the usual form, Champion's Hill. Incidentally, if Pemberton had got across Bakers Creek farther south, he would not have disrupted Grant's movements but would have saved his army. Grant was moving straight west and was inclined to let Pemberton get away if he could capture Vicksburg cheaply.

The following quote is from "A Child at the Siege of Vicksburg," by William W. Lord, as it appeared in "Harper's Magazine," December 1908:

A bombshell burst in the very center of that pretty dining-room, blowing out the roof and one side, crushing the well-spread tea table like an eggshell, and making a great yawning hole in the floor, into which disappeared supper, china, furniture, and the safe containing our entire stock of butter and eggs.

It was not until midmorning that Pemberton and his generals learned of Hovey's approach. To meet this threat to their left, the Confederates rushed several brigades to hold the ridge extending northwestward from the crest of Champion Hill. Fronting this ridge were several ravines which ran north, then westerly, terminating at Bakers Creek. These ravines were overgrown with trees and underbrush. The weakness of this position was its length. So long as Pemberton was compelled by the presence of McClernand's troops on the Raymond and Middle roads to keep one half of his army posted on the ridges west of Jackson Creek, he would be unable to commit sufficient troops to hold the entire ridge overlooking Bakers Creek. Thus Pemberton's left flank rested in the air.

AS THE two armies confronted each other the stage was seemingly set for the climax of the campaign. After months (indeed, almost a year) of maneuvering in the west, the two major forces stood directly opposite each other. Pemberton had his troops on the field well in hand, but before the day was over he undoubtedly would wish that he had with him the two divisions he had left to hold the Vicksburg area, when he marched out to battle Grant. Pemberton's total strength on the field was about 23,000, opposed to Grant's 32,000.

To the winner of the battle that followed would go the final victory in the campaign for the Mississippi River. Champion Hill is thus, at first blush, one of the decisive battles of the Civil War.

Such a view of Champion Hill is superficial.

While Grant, through superior strategy and maneuvering ability, had gained a distinct advantage by splitting Pemberton and Johnston, all could be lost if he were defeated at Champion Hill. At this time Grant was deep in hostile country with a formidable force under Pemberton to his front and Johnston's rapidly growing army in his rear. By the 15th Johnston's scattered brigades outnumbered Sherman's two divisions at Jackson. In addition, there were two fresh Rebel divisions in Vicksburg, which on the morning of the 16th were as close to Champion Hill as Sherman. Grant, like Lee at Gettysburg, had to carry his ammunition with him. A two days' battle would have exhausted his supply of artillery ammunition.

If Grant were checked at Champion Hill, he would have to pause to regroup, and this would have allowed the Confederates to bring up fresh troops. The next battle would have found many of his batteries with nearly empty caissons. If Grant should decide to turn aside following a repulse at Champion Hill, he would either have to head for Grand Gulf or the Yazoo. Such a march would expose his flanks to Confederate attack.

As for the approach of Sherman's corps, it would have had little effect if Grant had been routed. Sherman's troops did not reach the Bolton area until long after dark on the 16th. The officers had pushed the men hard, and thousands had straggled. Some regiments in Tuttle's division melted to company strength. A thorough examination of diaries and journals offers convincing evidence that it would have been late on the 17th before Sherman's two divisions could have effectively interfered at Champion Hill.

WHEN the battle opened, Pemberton's men, who had been marching and constructing earthworks for the past two weeks, were tired but eager to come to grips with the Yankees. McPherson's, on the other hand, had been marching and fighting for more than eight straight days. McClernand's were not quite so hard pressed, but they too had done their share of tramping over the countryside. Sherman's, coming up in reserve, had done more marching than either of the others. In addition, the Union troops had been living on hardtack, fresh meat, and coffee for over a week. When the day ended, however, it was the Confederates who were exhausted, the Yankees who were ready for more. Grant's winter campaign to make the men work, in order to get into peak physical condition, had paid off.

As soon as Grant had cleared the road for McPherson he sent word to McClernand to push forward and attack. "These orders were repeated several times," Grant later recalled, "without apparently expediting McClernand's advance." The main weight of the battle therefore fell on Hovey and Logan.

Grant's criticism of McClernand may have been colored by personal feelings. It was about 2:30 before McClernand received the orders. He then issued instructions for his division commanders "to attack the enemy vigorously and press for victory." It was the division commanders who really failed to push the attack. Grant gives full credit to Hovey, whose division was, after all, a part of McClernand's corps. If McClernand is to be blamed for the failure of his other division commanders, he should in all justice receive part of the praise heaped on Hovey.

By 10:30 Hovey's and Logan's divisions advanced to attack the Confederate left. Hovey on the left at 11:30 charged up out of a hollow and wrested from the Confederates a battery posted on the crest of the salient angle. (Brigadier General Alfred Cumming's Georgia brigade opposed Hovey's advance.) Pushing on, Hovey's men captured a second battery at the crossroads. Logan's division in the meantime was locked in a savage contest with S. D. Lee's Alabamians. On the extreme Union right, a brigade led by John Stevenson turned Pemberton's left, held by Seth Barton's Georgians, and captured two batteries. By 1:30 Pemberton's left had been mauled and hurled back almost a half mile with the loss of sixteen guns and several thousand prisoners.

THE Rebels of Bowen's division counterattacked with great dash and elan. Most of Pemberton's troops had stood helplessly by the past couple of weeks while Grant marched all through Mississippi, or so it seemed; now, unleashed, they fought as only men in a desperate situation can fight. At one point in the battle Colonel Francis Cockrell, commanding a Confederate brigade, led a charge holding his reins and a large magnolia flower in one hand while he brandished his sword with the other. The men followed, shouting gleefully.

The result of these attacks was to drive Hovey back, and he had to relinquish his captured guns. For the rest of the day the battle on Champion Hill raged, increasing in intensity. Hovey sent out innumerable pleas for reinforcements; he lost nearly one-third of his division. Hovey later called Champion Hill "a hill of death," and added that "I never saw fighting like this."

Grant did what he could to help. Crocker's division of McPherson's corps arrived just as it seemed that Bowen's Missourians and Arkansans would destroy Hovey's division and capture Grant's ordnance trains parked near the Champion house. Grant rushed one brigade into the breach torn in the Union line by the onrushing Rebels and bolstered Logan with a second. Hovey meanwhile got three batteries in action where they enfiladed Bowen's advancing lines.

THE advance by John Stevenson's brigade of Logan's division had carried it to a position from which, if he made a direct forward movement over open fields, he could get directly in Pemberton's rear and eliminate all possibility of escape. He did slide forward a little and got near the road leading down to Bakers Creek. Grant, who had been with Hovey, rode up, but neither he nor Logan realized the significance of Stevenson's position. Just at that

341

The Battle of Black River. Drawing by Theodore R. Davis. (HW)

moment a messenger arrived from Hovey with another plea for reinforcements—Pemberton had reinforced Carter Stevenson on Champion Hill after noting McClernand's disinclination to attack. Grant told Logan to rush John Stevenson to Hovey's aid, which uncovered Pemberton's line of retreat. Years later Grant admitted, "Had I known the ground as I did afterwards, I cannot see how Pemberton could have escaped with any organized force."

With Crocker moving into the breach the Confederate position on Champion Hill began to crumble. McClernand, meanwhile, had started to increase the pressure on the Confederate right. At the same time another brigade (Ransom's, of McPherson's corps), which had crossed the river at Grand Gulf a few days before, came up on the Rebel's right.

BY 4 P.M. Pemberton decided to withdraw. He had lost nearly 4,300 men, while inflicting on Grant losses of 2,400. As in all previous engagements the Confederate enlisted men had fought well, and the regimental and brigade commanders, along with one division commander, Bowen, had done good work. At the higher level dissension and incompetence had spoiled the effort. Early in the battle one division commander, Loring, said he would "be willing for Pemberton to lose a battle provided that he would be displaced," and Loring and other generals openly laughed at Pemberton's orders. Another Confederate officer said Pemberton was "to all appearances—so far as my judgment could determine—as helpless and undecided as a child."

Pemberton left Loring to cover the retreat. The withdrawal began smoothly enough, but soon took on the aspects of a rout. Organization was lost, men fled for Vicksburg's fortifications as individuals, officers galloped about frantically trying to find their units, while artillerists looked for their guns. One Confederate officer confessed that what he saw on Champion Hill "made it look like what I have read of Bull Run," and the dispirited soldiers chattered wildly that the Yankee-born Pemberton "has sold Vicksburg."

Carr drove across Bakers Creek, swung to the southwest, and was able to shell the Raymond road, along which Loring's division would have to pass if it were to rejoin Pemberton. Finding the Federals on his flank and rear, Loring drifted off to the southeast, made a forced march to Crystal Springs, during which his men abandoned their cannon and supply wagons, and finally moved north to join Johnston at Jackson.

ACTION AT BIG BLACK

Pemberton rode through the already prepared breastworks guarding the Big Black and sent a fresh brigade in to man the works. He left instructions to move all the wagons to the left bank and to clear the roads for the passage of the defeated army. Then, thoroughly exhausted, he crossed the river with his staff, established his headquarters at Bovina, and settled down for a night's rest.

The men of Carter Stevenson's division were the first to reach the river; after their day with Hovey and Logan they were much too weary to do more fighting and they crossed the river. When they reached Bovina, Stevenson let the men flop down beside the road. They were instantly asleep.

Bowen's division came next. One of Pemberton's aides told him to defend the bridgehead until the whole force, including Loring's division (whose position was unknown to the Confederate main force) was across the river. Bowen's men, bone-tired and almost out of ammunition, were still—like their commander—of sound spirit. They filed into the trenches to extend the line.

AT THE same time, Sherman was on the road from Jackson to Bolton. He reached the Bolton area at 2 a.m. on the 17th; after four hours' rest he had the men on the road again, taking a route north of that followed by Grant's other two corps. Grant's idea was to send Sherman around to the left of the Confederate line, then have him swoop in behind Pemberton and keep him from getting back to Vicksburg. McPherson and McClernand would pursue the Confederates by the direct road to Vicksburg.

Grant's advance division, Eugene Carr's of Mc-Clernand's corps, began the pursuit at 3:30 a.m. (staff work in the Yankee divisions was outstanding, as was discipline; almost every day of the campaign the men were in full march when the sun rose). Shortly after daybreak they bumped into the main Confederate position. The east bank, where the Confederates were drawn up, was low bottom-land, with a bayou running irregularly across its front. The bayou was grown up with timber, which the Rebels had felled into the ditch, and there was a foot or two of water in it. The position was naturally strong; it had been strengthened by using cotton bales and throwing dirt over them to make breastworks. Carr came up almost on the exact center of Bowen's line; his left brigade (Benton's) anchored its left near the railroad, while his right brigade, under Michael Lawler, occupied the woods between Benton's right and the river, which at this point flows from east to west.

IF May 16 and Champion Hill belonged to Hovey and Logan, May 17 and the Battle of the Big Black was Lawler's. A mountainous man, weighing over 250 pounds, he fought in his shirt sleeves and sweated profusely. So huge was Lawler that he could not make a swordbelt go properly about his waist and wore his sword suspended by a strap from one shoulder. Grant once said of him, "When it comes to just plain hard fighting I would rather trust old Mike Lawler than any of them." A native of County Kildare, Ireland, Lawler was a veteran of Winfield Scott's advance from Vera Cruz to Mexico City. Lawler and his regiment had been mustered into service by U. S. Grant, then a captain serving on the staff of the Adjutant General of Illinois. He enforced discipline in his young heroes by knocking down recalcitrants with his fists, feeding emetic to drunks in the guardhouse, and by threats of violence to officers and men alike.

This morning Lawler moved his brigade through the woods to within 400 yards of the enemy line. There, next to the river, was a meander scar, a scar deep enough to hide his brigade. From it he could launch a short, quick assault on the Confederate left center. To get to it, however, he would have to cross an open field exposed to fire from some detached rifle pits. Lawler did not hesitate. Leaving one regiment behind to protect his artillery, he dashed across at the head of the other three. Losing only two men, he was now safe and snug almost within a stone's throw of the Southern works. Lawler, after calling up the regiment left to protect the artillery, massed his four regiments in columns of battalions, with the brigades on a two-regiment front so that his attack would be a narrow battering ram rather than spread out in the usual manner. He told the men not to bother to fire, but to keep moving forward until they reached the enemy parapet. When his preparations were complete, he had the regimental commanders order "Fix bayonets." Pouring sweat, he heaved his great bulk up on his horse, jammed the animal in the flank with his heels, leaned forward to help his horse clear the scar, and bellowed "Forward!"

The regiments roared out of their shelter and ran toward the Confederate line. The dumbfounded Rebels barely had time to get off one volley before the assault column hit them. The charge was one of the shortest of the Civil War—it lasted just three minutes.

Completely outmanned, with bayonets and the stocks of muskets raining down on their heads, the Rebels fled. Lawler had broken the entire Confederate line south as far as the railroad. All along that line Rebels were scampering to the rear, desperate to get across the river before they were cut off.

The Indiana regiments and the Illinois units came over the barricade north of the railroad and captured a gun. Private James S. Adkins of the 33d Illinois, exhilarated by the bloodless victory, leaped astride the gun tube, waved his elbows up and down at his sides, and crowed like a rooster. Then, curious, he tugged at the lanyard. The gun went off, hurling a shell close over the heads of the units coming up in support, and bucking Adkins head over heels into the dirt. Miraculously, no one was hurt.

GRANT was near the middle of the Union line. Shortly before the charge began, a staff officer rode up and gave him a letter of May 11 from Halleck. In it the General in Chief ordered Grant to return to Grand Gulf and to co-operate from there with

343

Banks against Port Hudson, then return with the combined force to besiege Vicksburg. Grant quietly told the officer that the order came too late. Grant had served under Halleck before, and he realized that the General in Chief would not have given him the order if he had known Grant's position. The officer insisted that Grant had to obey, and was increasing the intensity of his argument when the sounds of an attack broke forth. Grant later described what happened: "Looking in that direction, I saw Lawler in his shirt sleeves leading a charge upon the enemy. I immediately mounted my horse and rode in the direction of the charge, and saw no more of the officer who had delivered the dispatch."

The Confederates on the west bank, before all the retreating men got across, fired the turpentine-soaked railroad bridge and the steamer *Dot*. Pemberton had ridden up from Bovina; he took one look and immediately decided against making a further stand along the Big Black. He just had too few men to prevent the Union troops from crossing. Sadly he ordered his division to withdraw the twelve miles to Vicksburg. Riding back to Bovina with a staff officer, he morosely muttered, "Just thirty years ago I began my cadetship at the U. S. Military Academy. Today, the same date, that career is ended in disaster and disgrace."

Grant's men spent the rest of the day (Lawler's charge ended at 11 a.m.) cleaning up the battlefield and building bridges over the Big Black. They had

Ruins of the Civil War railway bridge across the Big Black River under the present-day bridge. (Photo by Margie Bearss.)

captured 1,752 prisoners, 18 cannon, 1,421 stand of small arms, and 5 battle flags, at a cost of 39 killed and 237 wounded. The bridge building, as always in Grant's army, was superb. McPherson himself directed the construction of one of the four. He used bales of cotton to make a pontoon bridge. General Ransom supervised the building of another. He had trees felled on opposite banks of the river, dropped them into the water so that their tops interlaced. Taking lumber from nearby buildings, he then laid a roadway across the trees. Working through the night, the army had four serviceable bridges ready on the morning of May 18.

GRANT'S PINCERS CLOSE ON VICKSBURG

That morning Grant sent his three corps forward, McClernand's on the road paralleling the railroad, and McPherson's and Sherman's along the Bridgeport road. About three miles northeast of Vicksburg, Grant, who had pushed ahead, overtook Sherman's vanguard and turned it into the Graveyard road while a staff officer was left to point out the route McPherson was to take—the Jackson road. As the three corps approached the city, McClernand's would be on the left, McPherson's in the center, and Sherman's on the right.

By late afternoon on the 18th, Sherman's advance was in contact with Confederates posted on the ridge fronting Vicksburg defenses. Before darkness put a stop to the fighting, Sherman had discovered a road branching off from the Graveyard road and leading toward the Yazoo. Steele's division was turned into this road. Under the cover of darkness, Pemberton recalled the troops that had been contesting Sherman's approach, and they took position alongside their comrades on the earthworks extending from Fort Hill to Stockade Redan.

STEELE'S division early on May 19 resumed its advance. Grant and Sherman soon joined Steele. Grant was anxious to secure a base of supplies on the Yazoo above Vicksburg and Steele was headed straight toward Walnut Hills—the Confederate defensive position which Sherman had tried unsuccessfully to carry the previous December. So impatient were Grant and Sherman that they moved past the advance column and were riding well up with the advanced skirmishers. The enemy still occupied some detached works along the crest of the hill, although Pemberton had already decided to shorten his lines, and made no serious attempt to hold Walnut Hills. Shots rang out, and minie balls

A Federal's Recollection Of Vicksburg

Colonel Manning Force of the 20th Ohio Regiment, told of his experiences during the Vicksburg Campaign in an address in 1885 before the Ohio Commandery of the Loyal Legion. Following are excerpts from his address.

ON APRIL 25, Logan's division marched. The 20th Ohio had just drawn new clothing, but had to leave it behind. Stacking spades and picks in the swamp, the troops took their places in the column as it appeared, taking with them only the scanty supplies they had there. Six days of plodding brought them over nearly 70 miles to the shore of the river opposite Bruinsburg. I find in one of my letters: "We marched 6 miles one day, and those 6 miles, by evening, were strewn with wagon wrecks and their loads, and half-buried guns. At a halt of some hours, the men stood in deep mud, for want of any means of sitting. Yet when we halted at night, every man answered to his name and went laughing to bed on the sloppy ground."

Troops were ferried across the river to a narrow strip of bottom land which intervened between the river and the lofty-precipitous bluff. A roadway, walled in with high vertical banks, cut through the bluff, led from the river bottom up to the table land above. A small force could have held this pass against an army; but it was left unguarded, and the army marched up.

A Regiment in the Battle of Raymond

ON THE 12TH OF MAY, the 17th Corps marched on the road toward Raymond, Logan's division leading, Dennis' brigade in advance. The 30th Illinois was deployed with a skirmish line in front, on the left of the road, the 20th Ohio in like manner on the right. About noon we halted; the 20th Ohio in an open field, bounded by a fence to the front, beyond which was forest and rising ground. An unseen battery on some heights beyond the timber began shelling the woods. The 1st Brigade came up and formed on our right.

All at once the woods rang with the shrill Rebel yell and a deafening din of musketry. The 20th rushed forward to a creek and used the farther bank as a breastworks. The timber between the creek and the fence was free from undergrowth. The 20th Illinois, the regiment next in line to the 20th Ohio, knelt down in place and returned the fire. The enemy advanced into the creek in its front. I went to the lieutenant colonel, who was kneeling at the left flank, and asked him why he did not advance into the creek. He said, "We have no orders." In a few minutes the colonel of the regiment was killed. It was too late to advance, it was murder to remain; and the lieutenant colonel withdrew the regiment in order behind the fence. I cannot tell how long the battle lasted. I remember noticing the forest leaves, cut by falling rifle balls, in thick eddies, still as snowflakes. At one time the enemy in our front advanced to the border of the creek, and rifles of opposing lines crossed while firing. Men who were shot were burned by the powder of the rifles that sped the balls.

IN TIME the fire in front slackened. We ceased firing and advanced. The ground rose into a hill beyond the creek; dead and wounded were found there where they had fallen or crawled behind trees and logs. We emerged into open ground upon a hilltop, and were greeted by cheers of the brigade below at the crossing of the creek. The enemy was in retreat. A battery covering its retreat fired upon us. I made the men lie down behind a ridge, and the exploding shells sprinkled them with earth while the 1st sergeants were making out reports of casualties. Notwithstanding the admirable protection of the bank of the creek, 20 percent of the regiment were killed or wounded.

Soon the column advanced. We fell into place when it came up, and were halted on the hither side of Raymond. In a few minutes the earth was sparkling with fires, over which coffee was making in tin cups, and little chunks of salt pork were boiling. The sweet savor told that supper was nearly ready, when orders came to march through the town and go on picket on the farther side. Every man picked up his smoking cup, and the stick which bore his sizzling bit of salt pork, and we incensed the town with the savory odor as we marched through.

The 20th Ohio at Champion Hill

Champion Hill is a considerable eminence about a mile across from east to west. It is steep; its sides are roughened by knobs, gullied by ravines, and covered with forests. Low, flat land encircles the north and west faces. Hovey, following the road, attacked the northeast face; Logan's division, following, debouched upon the low land north of the hill. The 20th Ohio, being in advance, deployed, marched near to the base of the hill, and lay down to wait until successive regiments should arrive and form the line. A part of the enemy's forces, high upon the hill, kept up a dropping fire, and every few minutes a soldier would rise, bleeding, and be ordered back to the hospital to have his wounds dressed. There was in front of the line a very large and tall stump. The adjutant, Bryant Walker, and I, sending our horses away, stood behind this stump and observed that its shelter made a species of shadow of the fire. We found we could pace to and fro 50 yards, keeping in line with the stump; and while the rifle balls rattled against the stump and whistled through the air, we were shielded.

By the time the line was formed, a hostile line advanced from the timber at the base of the hill to confront us. We charged, pushed them into the timber and up the slope, and took position in a ravine parallel with a ravine in which the enemy had halted in our front. The firing was very heavy.

McPherson kept extending his line to his right, till Pemberton's line of retreat was endangered, and his army, abandoning the field, pushed in disorder for Vicksburg.

Rations Were Short

In 18 days Grant had marched 200 miles, won five battles, four of them in six days, inflicted a loss of 5,000 killed, wounded, and missing, captured 88 pieces of artillery, compelled the abandonment of all outworks, and cooped Pemberton's army within the lines of Vicksburg; while he had opened easy and safe communications with the North. During these 18 days the men had been without shelter, and had subsisted on 5 days' rations and scanty supplies picked along the way. The morning we crossed the Big Black I offered five dollars for a small piece of corn bread and could not get it. The soldier said the bread was worth more to him than money.

Life in the Trenches

On May 22 the 20th Ohio moved in support of the 1st Brigade of Logan's division. The brigade reached the base of an earthwork, too high and steep to be scaled, and could neither advance nor retreat. The 20th was placed in a road-cut which was enfiladed by one of the enemy's infantry intrenchments. But by sitting with our backs pressed against the side of the cut toward

Vicksburg, the balls whistled by just outside our knees. At sunset the company cooks came to us with hot coffee. They succeeded in running the gantlet, and the garrison could hear the jingling of tincups and shouts of laughter as the cramped men ate their supper.

After dark we were recalled and placed on the slope of a sharp ridge, with orders to remain in place, ready to move at any moment, and with strict injunction not to allow any man's head to appear above the ridge. There we lay two or three days in line. Coffee was brought to us at meal times. Not a man, those two or three days, left the line without special order. The first night Lieutenant Weatherby, commanding the right company, reported that the slope was so steep where he was that the men, as soon as they fell asleep, began to roll down hill. I had to give him leave to shift his position.

WHEN lying there, it sometimes occurred to me, what a transformation it was for these men, full of individuality and self-reliance, accustomed always to act upon their own will, to so completely subordinate their wills to the will of other men, many of them their neighbors and friends at home. But their practical sense told them that an army differs from a mob only in discipline, and discipline was necessary for their self-preservation. They had also perceived that military obedience is a duty enjoined by law, and in obeying orders, they were obeying the law.

One day when there was a general bombardment, I was told a soldier wished to see me. Under the canopy of exploding shell I found a youth lying on his back on the ground. He was pale and speechless—there was a crimson hole in his chest. As I knelt by his side, he looked wistfully at me. I said: "We must all die some time and the man who meets his death in the discharge of duty is happy." A smile flickered on his lips, and I was kneeling beside a corpse.

Fraternization

At night it was common practice for the pickets on both sides to advance unharmed, and sitting together on the ground between the lines pass the night in chat, banter, and high discussion. A watch was always left in the lines, and when an officer of either side came along on his tour, warning was given, the conference ceased, and the men on both sides slipped back to their places. When day came, work was resumed.

General Leggett was transferred to command the 1st Brigade, and I was assigned to his vacated place. The saps were made wide and deep enough for the passage of artillery, and batteries were constructed near the besieged works. General Ransom had a battery so close that the embrasures were kept covered by mantlets. A gun would be loaded and pointed, and then fired just as the mantlet was removed. The first time a gun was fired from it, a storm of rifle balls poured through the embrasure. A gunner jumped on the gun and shouted back, "Too late!"

When the working parties carried the saps to the base of the works, the besieged used to light the fuzes of 6-pound shells, and toss them over the parapet. They would roll down among the working parties and explode, sometimes doing serious damage. A young soldier of Company C, 20th Ohio, named Friend, on detached service in the division pioneer corps, devised wooden mortars. A very small charge of powder in one of these would just lift a shell over the enemy's parapet and drop it within. After the surrender, there was much inquiry from the garrison how they were contrived.

whistled past the generals' ears. Ignoring them, Grant and Sherman rode to the crest of the ridge.

Sitting there on their horses, they took possession of the most important single piece of real estate in the Confederate States of America. As long as Pemberton held that chain of hills no Union force could approach Vicksburg from the upper Mississippi. For a year and a half the western armies of the United States had concentrated their effort on gaining control of these few square miles. As Sherman and Grant watched the men spread out over the heights, they felt the most intense satisfaction. Grant could now reopen his communications with the north, receive supplies and reinforcements, and conclude the campaign.

Sherman turned to Grant and said, quietly, that up to this moment he had felt no positive assurance of success. Now he realized that this was the end of one of the greatest campaigns in history. Vicksburg was not yet captured, and much might still happen, but whether captured or not, the campaign was a complete success.

Johnston agreed. He telegraphed Pemberton to cut his losses and get out. "If Haynes' Bluff be untenable Vicksburg is of no value and cannot be held," Johnston wrote. "If therefore you are invested in Vicksburg you must ultimately surrender. Under such circumstances, instead of losing both troops and place you must if possible save the troops. If it is not too late, evacuate Vicksburg and its dependencies and march to the northeast."

Pemberton held a council of war, which concluded that it was impossible to withdraw—a strange conclusion, considering that McClernand's force, on Grant's left, extended only a little south of the Southern Railroad of Mississippi. Pemberton decided to ignore not only Johnston's good advice but, once again, a positive order. When informed of Pemberton's decision, Johnston exhibited remarkable self-restraint—he advised Pemberton to hold out while he attempted to gather a relief force. His labors, however, were in vain.

BY June 4 Johnston had gathered a force of 31,000, and between them he and Pemberton outnumbered Grant. At this time he was notified by the authorities in Richmond that no more reinforcements could be diverted to Mississippi. Instead of boldly seizing the initiative, while the Confederates had numerical advantage, Johnston allowed one of his division commanders to go on leave. Not until June 22, when this officer returned from leave, did Johnston organize his army to take the offensive. At this time, thousands of reinforcements rushed from points as far away as Central Kentucky and Rolla, Missouri, had reported to Grant. The Federals now held a decisive

A Union assault on defenses of Vicksburg on May 19, 1863. From a Prang chromolithograph by Swedish artist Thure Thulstrup.

numerical advantage. As time for the Vicksburg defenders ran out, Johnston continued to drag his feet. It was July 1 before he put his troops in motion.

The threat of a move by Johnston against his rear forced Grant to keep forces on the Big Black guarding the crossing. On June 22 when reports, which were later proved untrue, reached Grant that Johnston had forced his way across the Big Black, he rushed additional troops eastward and placed Sherman in charge of a seven-division army. Sherman's task was to smash Johnston should he cross the Big Black.

ASSAULT OF MAY 19

On the morning of May 19 Grant, figuring that the Confederates were so demoralized by the events of the past two weeks that they would crumble at the first sign of pressure, ordered a general assault. On the left and in the center the Union troops managed to gain some important positions for gun emplacements, but did not even come close to driving the Confederates out of their trenches. Obviously the Rebels could still fight. Sherman, on the right, learned this lesson best.

The key position in the enemy works opposite Sherman was the Stockade Redan complex. He gave Frank Blair's division the job of taking it. The ground in front of the redan was exceedingly rugged, consisting of a ravine covered with timber that Confederate working parties had cut six months earlier. Attempting to charge through this area, the men found it impossible to maintain a line of battle. As the Rebels poured small arms and artillery fire upon

them, they instinctively searched out a place of concealment and stopped there, pinned down.

On Blair's right the 1st Battalion, 13th U. S. Infantry, tried a charge. When the commander called out "Forward!" the Regulars sprang across the hill behind which they had formed. Charging on the double, they passed through a deadly beaten-zone that was being swept by canister and shell. Men began to fall, some killed instantly, others with an arm or leg torn off. Crossing the ravine, the Regulars were caught in a crossfire between the enemy in Stockade Redan and those in the 27th Louisiana Lunette on the left of the stockade.

Color Sergeant James E. Brown was shot through the head and killed. Another soldier instantly picked up the colors, and was immediately shot. In all, five different men were killed or wounded as they sought to carry the colors forward. The Regulars closed to within 25 yards of the Stockade Redan, began to falter, and finally scrambled back for cover behind fallen timber and stumps.

AFTER the battle a count revealed that the flag of the 13th U. S. Infantry had 55 bullet holes in it. The battalion had lost 43 percent of its personnel in the attack. Sherman called its performance "unequaled in the Army" and authorized the regiment to insert "First at Vicksburg" on its colors.

There were other acts of heroism that day. Sherman decided he could not withdraw his corps until it was dark; meanwhile the men fired by volley at any Confederate who stuck his head above the parapet. The Rebels replied by cutting short the fuzes of their shells, then rolling them down the hill into the Yankee masses. Occasionally the Union men could catch the shell and throw it back; more often it ripped apart legs and arms.

Late in the afternoon the Yankees discovered they had almost exhausted their ammunition. Volunteers raced through the felled timber to fill boxes and hats with the cartridges rifled from dead and wounded men. Orion P. Howe, a 14-year-old musician in the 55th Illinois, volunteered to go to the rear and order up fresh supplies. While dashing through the timber he caught a minie ball in his leg. Undaunted, he staggered on. At the point of exhaustion he reached General Sherman himself and reported on the critical ammunition shortage. Sherman called for volunteers to lug the heavy boxes of cartridges forward, and every man of the nearby Company C, 12th Iowa, stepped forward. Musician Howe was subsequently awarded the Medal of Honor for his services on that bloody day.

At dark, the Union troops withdrew. Grant's attempt to storm his way into Vicksburg had failed. He had gained some advance artillery emplacements and some good staging areas for use in future attacks, but at a fearful price. He had lost 157 killed, 777 wounded, and 8 missing, as against a total Confederate loss of about 250.

GRANT TRIES AGAIN

Following the failure on the 19th, Grant could either accept the situation and settle down for a siege operation or he could try another assault. He decided upon the latter course. Both he and his army were rather cocky at this point; five times they had met the Confederates in battle and routed them. The repulse of the 19th was an obvious fluke. The lesson of the campaign seemed to be that when Yankees attacked, Rebels ran. There were other more substantial reasons for another try. Johnston, in Grant's rear, was busily raising a relief force, and Grant wanted to destroy Pemberton's army before Johnston could come to his aid. If Grant could take Vicksburg immediately, he would not have to call upon Halleck for reinforcements and could, in fact, send men to the other theaters of war. Finally, in Grant's own words, "the first consideration of all was—the troops

believed they could carry the works in their front, and would not have worked so patiently in the trenches afterwards if they had not been allowed to try."

The attempt was to cost them dearly. Pemberton's men, given a decent chance, could fight as well as any men on earth. And, in their entrenchments, they were powerfully placed. One of McPherson's staff officers described the position: "A long line of high-rugged, irregular bluffs, clearly cut against the sky, crowned with cannon which peered ominously from embrasures to the right and left as far as the eye could see. Lines of heavy rifle-pits, surmounted with head logs, ran along the bluffs, connecting fort with fort, and filled with veteran infantry." On the slopes in front of the works were felled trees, with their tops interlaced, forming an almost impenetrable abatis. "The approaches to this position were frightful—enough to appall the stoutest heart."

Still Grant—and his men—wanted to try, and on the morning of May 22 they did. Grant had his corps

Inside the Federal lines at Vicksburg, May 22, 1863. From an on-the-scene sketch by battlefield artist F. B. Schell. (FL)

348

commanders set their watches by his, then called for a simultaneous assault at 10 a.m. The attack would be preceded by a heavy preliminary artillery bombardment. Sherman would aim at the Stockade Redan, McPherson at the stronghold on either side of the Jackson road, McClernand at the defenses flanking the railroad and Baldwin's Ferry road.

Sherman, who had failed in his direct attack across the ravine in front of Stockade Redan on May 19, decided to attack directly down the Graveyard road. He would spearhead his attack with a "forlorn hope," consisting of 150 volunteers. These men, carrying timbers in their hands, would move at the double down the road and fill in the ditch fronting the stockade.

THE attack moved off promptly at 10 a.m. The "forlorn hope" came through a curve in the road at full speed. The road at that point cut through a hill, then turned directly toward the redan. When the "forlorn hope" emerged from the extremely narrow cut they were 150 yards from the enemy and presented a perfect target. The Rebels cut loose, and most of the men were either killed or wounded. The remainder took cover in the ditch in front of the stockade. The 30th Ohio followed, to suffer the same fate. On their heels came the 37th Ohio. When that regiment started to emerge from the cut most of the men took one look and "bugged out," throwing themselves on the ground and refusing to advance farther. This choked the narrow cut, and Sherman's assault ground to an abrupt stop. Sherman made no further attacks that morning, even though only slightly more than 1,000 of his nearly 15,000 men had been engaged. After his experiences of the previous December and of May 19, he had had about enough of assaulting Fortress Vicksburg.

In the center McPherson never got any organized attack going. He put only 7 of his 30 regiments into action, and they all except those of John Stevenson's brigade stopped at the first sign of opposition.

Things went better on the left. McClernand sent

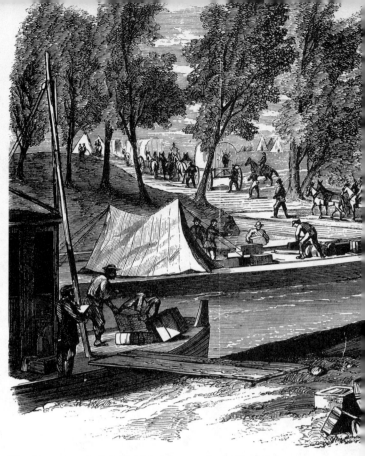

Landing supplies for Grant's army at Chickasaw Bayou on the Yazoo River, north of Vicksburg. Sketch by F. B. Schell. (FL)

Carr, who had the advantage of having Lawler's brigade in his division, storming the 2d Texas Lunette and the Railroad Redoubt. The 99th Illinois carried its flag across the Confederate works at a point 50 yards south of the lunette. Lawler, charging the Railroad Redoubt, drove the 30th Alabama out of its rifle pits and planted several Union colors there. Elsewhere McClernand's men pushed up to, although not through, the Rebel lines.

The enemy was soon able to contain the penetration McClernand's corps had achieved, and the Yankees were unable to do much about it. If Sherman and McPherson were guilty of not making strong enough commitments that morning, McClernand made the mistake of throwing everything he had into the first rush. With no strategic reserve he was unable to exploit his opportunities, and in fact could barely hold what he had gained.

WITH his entire corps engaged, McClernand appealed to Grant to have Sherman and McPherson resume the attack, arguing that he could achieve a breakthrough with more help. Grant thought McClernand was exaggerating his success (or so at least he claimed later), but felt he could not ignore the request and ordered Sherman and McPherson to renew their assaults as a diversion in favor of McClernand. At 3 p.m. Sherman sent Mower's brigade spearheaded by the 11th Missouri charging down the Graveyard road four abreast. As the regiment emerged from the fatal cut in the road it was riddled by Confederate fire. Those Missourians who were not killed dashed forward and took cover in the ditch alongside the survivors of the "forlorn hope" and the 30th Ohio. Sherman suspended the attack.

McPherson launched a half-hearted assault on the 3d Louisiana Redan, which got nowhere.

McClernand, meanwhile, was stuck. He could neither go forward nor disengage. At 5:30 counterattacking Confederates recovered the Railroad Redoubt.

Passing the Buck, *by Col. Manning Force*

ON MAY 3 our brigade found a road leading northeast toward Hankinson's Ferry. When we reached the road I was standing with Generals McPherson, Logan, and Dennis, the corps, division, and brigade commanders, respectively. McPherson said, "General Logan, you will direct General Dennis to send a regiment forward with skirmishers well advanced, rapidly toward the ferry."

General Logan said, "General Dennis, you will send a regiment forward, with skirmishers well advanced, toward the ferry."

General Dennis said, "Colonel Force, you will take your regiment forward with skirmishers well advanced, rapidly toward the ferry."

Finally, at nightfall, McClernand pulled his troops back. He was the only corps commander who really made an effort that day; if Sherman and McPherson had attacked with the same energy, the assault would probably have worked. But they did not, and later they—and Grant—were unduly skeptical about McClernand's penetration, which they claimed was a figment of his imagination. But in fact McClernand did get into the Rebel works and his report to Grant was accurate.

GRANT'S position in this affair is a strange one. If he really intended to try a full-scale assault, he should have been angry with Sherman and McPherson.

In any case Grant, in his report written on May 24, was quite unfair to McClernand. He showed a pettiness most uncharacteristic of the Commanding General. "General McClernand's dispatches misled me as to the real state of the facts," Grant said of the events of May 22, "and caused much of the loss. He is entirely unfit for the position of corps commander, both on the march and on the battlefield. Looking after his corps gives me more labor and infinitely more uneasiness than all the remainder of my department." Assuming that Grant really felt that strongly, that he did not immediately relieve McClernand can only be regarded as amazing. If McClernand was that bad, Grant was extremely derelict in his duty (not to mention his responsibilities to the troops in McClernand's corps) when he kept McClernand in command.

FALL OF McCLERNAND

McClernand smoldered. He was sure that if Mc-Pherson and Sherman—and of course Grant—had properly supported him his corps would be in Vicksburg. He was not, therefore, in a receptive mood when Colonel James Harrison Wilson visited him with an order from Grant directing him to send some troops to watch the crossings of the Big Black.

McClernand read the order, then snapped, "I'll be God-damned if I'll do it. I'm tired of being dictated to—I won't stand it any longer, and you can go back and tell General Grant." He added some more remarks of a similar character, then began to curse West Point generally. Wilson heatedly pointed out that McClernand was not only insulting the commanding general but Wilson himself, as Wilson was an Academy man, and offered to get off his horse and use his fists to get McClernand to apologize. The middle-aged general sized up the colonel in his mid-twenties and muttered, "I was simply expressing my intense vehemence on the subject matter, sir, and I beg your pardon."

Wilson, of course, reported the whole affair at Grant's headquarters, to everyone's great delight. Thereafter whenever anyone was heard using profanity—and it was a hard-cursing headquarters—Grant would laugh and explain, "He's not swearing—he's just expressing his intense vehemence on the subject matter."

McCLERNAND'S end came a couple of weeks later. He wrote an order of congratulations to the XIII Corps which, with some help from his headquarters, got into the papers. This violated a standing War Department regulation to submit such papers to army headquarters before publication; worse, McClernand had implied in the order that the XIII Corps alone had been responsible for the success of the campaign. Sherman bitterly remarked that the order was really addressed "to a constituency in Illinois," and McPherson said it was designed "to impress the public mind with the magnificent strategy, superior tactics, and brilliant deeds" of McClernand.

Grant asked McClernand if the order as published was genuine. McClernand said it was and he was prepared to stand by it. Grant finally decided to act and on June 18 relieved McClernand, putting E. O. C. Ord in his place.

Following the May 19 assault Grant held a conference with Porter and arranged for some good landing places along the Yazoo for transports and supply ships. He wired Halleck to say he was ready to receive reinforcements and supplies, which the General in Chief immediately began to send.

ONE afternoon a day or so later Grant took a ride along the rear of his fighting lines. Men began to glance at him as his horse moved slowly past. The soldiers generally did not love Ulysses Grant, nor were they awed by him—he was much too matter-of-fact a man to inspire such emotions. Besides, nothing about his personal appearance suggested greatness. The soldiers did respect him as a soldier, and as a man. He was the kind of person who invited honesty and was obviously approachable.

When Grant rode by a soldier who had looked up stared at his commanding general for a moment, then said in a conversational tone, "Hardtack." Other soldiers glanced at Grant and took up the call; soon everyone in the vicinity was yelling "Hardtack! Hardtack!" at the top of his lungs. They were not expressing a deep-rooted hatred of Grant, or anything like that, nor were they blaming him for the bland diet they had been on for the past month. They were saying that they were terribly proud of what they had done, especially considering the conditions under which they had marched and fought, but now the time had come to create a more regular existence. In short, it was time that Grant, who had done so well so far, get them something better to eat than a straight hardtack and meat diet.

Grant reined in and told the soldiers he had made all the arrangements and they would soon have fresh bread and coffee. The men laughed and cheered. The bond between Grant and the Army of the Tennessee had been strengthened.

351

Grant was very good at this sort of thing. Men in an Illinois regiment remembered that one evening Grant strolled out, sat down by their campfire, and "talked with the boys with less reserve than many a little puppy of a lieutenant." Grant assured the boys that he had everything under control, said that Pemberton was a "northern man who had got into bad company," and insisted that the Union position could be held even if Johnston raised 50,000 men.

THE SIEGE

The siege went forward. Grant's basic plan was to hold on until starvation forced Pemberton to surrender—the classic strategy of siege warfare—but he also wanted to end it as soon as possible, in order to release his troops for other theaters. In addition, the sooner Pemberton surrendered the sooner Grant could turn Sherman loose on Johnston, who had raised a relief expedition.

June, therefore, was an active month. Most of the work was designed to get the Union lines closer to those of the Confederates, so that the next time there was a general assault the troops would not have to cross a quarter-mile or so of rough terrain before reaching the enemy works. Grant had his engineers plan approach trenches and mines (which could be used to blow gaps in the Confederate position), which the men then dug. The whole thing anticipated the more sophisticated trench warfare of the Western Front in World War I.

The only trained engineers in the Army of the Tennessee were the West Point graduates, and most of them were high-ranking officers with other duties. The few full-time engineers discovered, however, that the Western soldiers were handy jacks-of-all-trades who could do almost any thing. One professional engineer declared that in the enormous task of constructing trenches, saps, batteries, and covered ways he could safely rely on the "native good sense and ingenuity" of the common soldier. "Whether a battery was to be constructed by men who had never built one before," he declared, "a saproller made by those who had never heard the name, or a ship's gun carriage to be built, it was done, and after a few trials well done . . . Officers and men had to learn to be engineers while the siege was going on."

AS SOON as Grant established his base on the Yazoo, the General in Chief began to feed him reinforcements. By June 18 Grant's army was up to 77,000. Pemberton had no more than 30,000, all plagued by illness and malnutrition, and his supply of food and ammunition was strictly limited. Grant's lines ran from the Yazoo to the lowlands along the Mississippi above the city to the banks along the river to the south—twelve miles of camps, trenches, and gun emplacements on the hills and ridges. So tightly did Grant hold the ground that a Confederate defender wrote despairingly, "When the real investments began

a cat could not have crept out of Vicksburg without being discovered." Among other things, this meant nothing—especially no artillery ammunition—got in to Pemberton, so that on top of all their other difficulties his men were forced to endure the constant Yankee artillery bombardment without being allowed to reply in kind. They did, however, have a good supply of powder and minie balls. One Yankee wrote home to say that although the Rebels had not fired a cannon for seven days, at least fifty rifle bullets had whizzed over his head in the last ten minutes.

Taking pot shots at the Union lines was about all the Confederates could do. For the rest of their defense, according to one Yankee officer, was "far from being vigorous." The defenders seemed content to "wait for another assault, losing in the meantime as few men as possible."

THE waiting was hard, both because the Confederates were short of nearly everything and because of the Union bombardment. Food was so short that the citizens of Vicksburg and the soldiers defending it were soon reduced to eating mule meat and pea bread.* Medical supplies were almost non-existent. Water was so scarce that officers posted guards at wells

---

*In my eleven years at Vicksburg it was impossible to find a single primary document telling of eating rats, although statements to that effect appear in some histories. The origin of the rat story is with men of several Louisiana regiments who ate muskrats. Indeed, these men were eating muskrats before the investment.—Edwin C. Bearss

The Bombardment of Vicksburg

That night of the 13th we remained on the boat, which was anchored to trees on the shore. The boom, boom, of the mortar fleet every two minutes, the splash of the water against the sides of the boat, and the shrill saw-file notes of the myriads of insects on the shores kept one's eyes and ears open, so that sleep was almost impossible. The writer, with some others, sat on the bow of the boat till a late hour watching the shells as they fell into Vicksburg. We timed the shells as they left the mortars on their aerial flight, and found that it took about eighteen seconds for them to land in the city. Bombs do not pass so rapidly through the air as do shot or shell from cannon. The shell from the mortar passed at a considerable elevation—sometimes at an angle of forty-five degrees—making a curve like that of a rocket, and could be traced by the fire of the fuse till it exploded or dropped to the ground. When it did not explode in the air, it was easily dodged by an experienced veteran.

Most of the inhabitants of Vicksburg lived under ground during the siege, because the city was situated on bluffs of hard clay; and consequently comfortable rooms could be quite readily excavated. On a visit to the city after its surrender, the writer went into several of these subterranean rooms, and found them fitted up with the best furniture, removed from the houses, where nothing had been safe.

From "History of the Sixth New Hampshire Regiment in the War for the Union," Captain Lyman Jackman, historian, Amos Hadley, Ph.D., Editor. Concord, N. H. Republican Press Association, Railroad Square, 1891.

to make sure none was wasted "for purposes of cleanliness." On top of these privations, the citizens were forced to burrow underground or live in caves to avoid the well-nigh constant shell fire, which came both from Grant's artillery and Porter's fleet.

The ground was well suited to the building of caves, for it consisted of a deep yellow loess of great tenacity. Perpendicular banks cut through the ridges stood as well as if made of stone, and the citizens cut rooms for themselves in the embankments. In some cases two or more rooms were cut out, carpeted, and furnished with tables, chairs, and kitchen equipment.

IN TERMS of some of the sieges of the 20th century, most especially that of Leningrad, conditions inside Vicksburg were not so terrible. They were, however, bad enough—certainly the worst any large group of Americans have ever been asked to undergo. The citizens compiled a proud record. There was some complaining, but no pressure on Pemberton from the city to surrender and end the suffering. The people got by, as people under siege have done since war began, by joking about their condition. They even had a newspaper, which by the end was being printed on the blank side of wallpaper. The citizens of Vicksburg, in short, endured.

←

The Siege of Vicksburg, showing the struggle in the crater of the 3d Louisiana Redan after the explosion of the Federal mine on June 25. The Rebels held the line. By F. B. Schell. (FL)

A July 4th to Remember

MEN in combat frequently are unable to assess the historical significance of the events of which they are a part. At Vicksburg, however, Grant's men knew they were engaged in a momentous undertaking. Because the siege lasted so long they received copies of Northern newspapers on a regular basis and thus knew that they were being talked about all over the world. Most of the men were from the Northwest, and the Mississippi River held a special fascination for them—they spoke and thought of it in almost mystical terms. The opportunity to participate in the campaign to open the Father of Waters was, they knew, a rare one, and few of them doubted that this was the most important thing they would ever do in their lives.

My great-great grandfather, Sergeant Pleasant W. Bishop of the 94th Illinois, expressed this feeling well. On July 4, 1863, early in the morning, he began a letter to his wife and children. "Since yesterday evening," he began, "there has been to some extent a cessation of hostilities between our forces & the rebels." He noted that the pickets had been "together all along the line *shaking hands,* trading pocket knives, exchanging papers, etc., etc." Rumors were flying, but Bishop found it difficult to evaluate them. He found it especially hard to believe that the Rebels were really existing on mule meat. Looking about him, Bishop reported that "the rebs have their white flags floating in many places," and a report had it that one was flying on the court house, "but I have lost all confidence in *'reports.'*"

AT THAT moment Bishop received orders to prepare to march. He broke off his letter, to resume it again on July 6. "Glorious news," he began. "I thank my God that I was permitted to *celebrate* the 4th of July by marching (at the head of Co. I) inside of the fortifications of Vicksburg." He examined the fortifications with a soldier's practiced eye and pronounced them formidable, reported that the mule meat stories were true, and thanked God for His blessings. "I would say that while I rejoice that Vicksburg is ours, it gives me no pleasure to see the destitution and the sufferings of fellow mortals in the rebble army, yet such must be their conditions unless they lay down their arms, and cease to fight against their God by fighting against their country. But I have been looking them over now for two days (feds and confeds being all mixed up together inside of the fortifications) and I find them to be just like people in other parts of the world, some of them are *men of sense* and some are not."

Bishop said the Yankees had been sharing their rations with the Rebels for the past two days, and were glad to do it. In a comment that speaks volumes for the efficiency of the Union high command, he added, "We have always had plenty to spare, for which I feel truly thankful."

THE possibility of an attack by Johnston must have been an active topic of conversation with the troops, for Bishop bragged that "our division inside these fortifications could whip all the Southern Confederacy . . . You can just tell our friends that the rebs' old Whistling Dick (a large gun they call by that name) is ours now, and I think he will whistle a tune they won't like to hear in taking the place."

No attack came, and the North held securely to the city and the river. For Pleasant Bishop, and for thousands like him, that hot afternoon was the greatest 4th of July they would ever celebrate, and the grandest in the nation's history.—**Stephen E. Ambrose.**

The troops on both sides did the same. On the picket line Johnny Reb and Billy Yank discussed politics, the siege, and philosophy, traded coffee and hardtack for tobacco, and got to know each other. Occasionally they sent personal messages back and forth. Each army contained regiments from Missouri; one day the picket at Stockade Redan agreed to informal short truces. This area, when soldiers in blue and in gray might visit briefly a relative or friend on the other side came to be called "Trysting place."

While the pickets got to know each other, under their very feet Grant's army dug tunnels. The Confederates counter-mined, but without success. Grant exploded the first mine, near the Jackson road, on June 25. The explosion of the mine was a signal for a heavy bombardment all along the line, accompanied by small arms fire. The mine blew off the top of a hill and created a crater into which an assaulting column charged, only to be checked by Confederates posted behind a parapet previously constructed to the rear of the work. A desperate battle ensued for possession of the crater. After twenty hours, Grant had McPherson recall his men, and another mine was commenced. On July 1 this mine was exploded. When this occurred, one of the Negroes who was countermining was thrown all the way into the Union lines. When asked how high he had gone, he replied, "Dunno, massa, but t'ink about t'ree miles." General Logan confiscated the Negro, who thereafter worked in his headquarters.

GRANT exploded another mine on July 1, again without significant results. His engineers, meanwhile, had pushed forward everywhere, so much so that at some points only ten yards separated the two forces. Within a week or so Grant would be able to simply overwhelm the defenders, sending his men over the top and into the Confederate lines so fast that the Rebels probably would not even get off a volley. Grant set July 6 as the date for the final rush.

Johnston had plans of his own. On July 1 he finally put his 32,000 men and 78 cannon in motion toward Big Black. He had no illusions about any great victories; he did hope to so distract the Army of the Tennessee that Pemberton could break out.

Pemberton circularized his generals to see if that was possible, asking specifically if their men could stand a battle and a long hard march. Most of the generals thought not. Their men could hold the lines a while longer, but a campaign in the field was impossible. Brigadier General Louis Hébert summed it all up: "Forty-eight days and nights passed in trenches, exposed to the burning sun during the day, the chilly air at night; subject to a murderous storm of balls, shells, and war missiles of all kinds; cramped

The arrival of General Grant at the Rock House just inside the Confederate line on July 4. Here he had a brief conversation with Pemberton, before riding on down the Jackson road to the Warren County Courthouse. The Rock House still stands. Sketch by Theodore R. Davis (BL). Note: Pemberton's headquarters were not at the Rock House, they were at the Willis-Cowan House. It also still stands.

up in pits and holes not large enough to allow them to extend their limbs; laboring day and night; fed on reduced rations of the poorest kinds of food, yet always cheerful . . ." All but one of Pemberton's generals told him it was time to surrender.

SURRENDER

At 10:30 a.m. on July 3, under a flag of truce, two horsemen approached the Union lines. One was a colonel on Pemberton's staff, the other General Bowen, who had fought so ably at Port Gibson and Champion Hill. Bowen was an old friend of Grant's, which may have influenced Pemberton's decision to send him on this mission. The Confederates carried a letter from Pemberton to Grant proposing an armistice and the appointment of commissioners to write a surrender formula. Pemberton knew that Grant wanted to get the whole business over in a hurry, and this knowledge gave him, he felt, bargaining power.

Bowen gave the note to A. J. Smith, who took it to Grant. The Union commander hoped to repeat his triumph at Fort Donelson and at the same time simplify matters, so his reply was short and to the point: "The useless effusion of blood you propose stopping . . . can be ended at any time you may choose, by the unconditional surrender of the city and garrison."

Bowen took the message to Pemberton at 3 p.m. Pemberton, Bowen, and a staff officer rode out. Grant, Ord, McPherson, Logan, and A. J. Smith, accompanied by several of Grant's staff, went forward to meet them. Grant and Pemberton walked away from the main group and had a conference near a stunted oak tree. Pemberton, excited and impatient, asked what terms Grant offered; Grant replied that he had said everything he had to say in his letter. Pemberton replied "rather snappishly" that in that case the conference might as well end immediately. Grant thought so too, and they walked back to mount up. Grant suggested that if he and Pemberton withdrew, per-

haps four of their subordinates (Bowen and Montgomery for the Confederates, McPherson and A. J. Smith for the Union) might be able to work out a satisfactory arrangement. Bowen patched things up, and before parting the two commanders agreed that at ten that night Grant would send another letter through the lines, one containing his final terms.

AT DUSK Grant called a meeting of all the corps and division commanders in the area—the nearest thing he ever had to a council of war. There was much to discuss. Vicksburg was unquestionably doomed—that was not at issue. The attack scheduled for July 6 would certainly be successful. But why pay the price? All Pemberton really wanted was to make sure his men were paroled instead of being sent north to a prison camp. Grant's officers urged him to make a deal, especially since shipping thirty thousand prisoners up the Mississippi would be an intolerable strain on Porter's fleet (something Pemberton already knew, as his intelligence service had intercepted and decoded messages wigwagged back and forth between Porter and Grant). Grant reluctantly agreed to abandon his unconditional surrender formula, and wrote to Pemberton proposing that the Southerners stack their weapons, give their paroles, and then go off to such camps for exchange prisoners as the Confederate authorities might suggest. Pemberton, who hoped that Grant would give generous terms in order to consummate the surrender on the nation's birthday, asked for some other minor concessions. Grant refused, and the deal was finally made.

Grant was later much criticized for allowing the Rebels to make their paroles. The critics contended that all, or most of Pemberton's 30,000 men would soon be fighting again. Grant's reply was that "I knew many of them were tired of war and would get

Interview between Grant and Pemberton to settle upon final terms for the surrender of Vicksburg and the Confederate garrison. (HW)

355

home just as soon as they could." Grant was mistaken, because many of the Confederates were back in ranks by November. A number of Carter L. Stevenson's soldiers were captured at Missionary Ridge, for instance.

ON THE morning of July 4 white flags began to flutter over the Confederate works. Logan's division and Sanborn's brigade were the first units to march into the city. Logan and Sanborn posted guards to keep unauthorized persons from entering or leaving and took charge of the captured people and property.

Sherman immediately moved his corps to the east in order to drive Johnston off. He took time to scribble a note to Grant before departing. "I can hardly contain myself," he exclaimed. "This is a day of Jubilee, a day of rejoicing to the faithful, and I would like to hear the shout of my old and patient troops." But duty called. "Already my orders are out to give one big huzza and sling the knapsack for new fields."

Grant, typically, was more subdued. Greatness can take many forms, assuming one shape with a Douglas MacArthur, another with an Andrew Jackson. It is most appealing, perhaps, when couched in directness and simplicity. At the conclusion of the most momentous and successful campaign on the North American continent, the architect of victory sent the following report to the War Department: "The enemy surrendered this morning. The only terms allowed is their parole as prisoners of war. This I regard as a great advantage to us at this moment. It saves, probably, several days in the capture, and leaves troops and transports ready for immediate service. Sherman, with a large force, moves immediately on Johnston, to drive him from the state."

IN HIS operations during May 1863, Grant used the classic ingredients of military success—surprise, speed, and power: *Surprise* of Pemberton, who could not believe that Grant would move independently of a protected supply line; dazzling *speed* in which his divisions marched upward of 200 miles in two weeks, fighting five battles; and the application of superior *power* at each successive, critical point. As historian Francis V. Greene wrote: "We must go back to the campaigns of Napoleon to find equally brilliant results accomplished in the same space of time with such small loss."

It is true that Pemberton was outclassed. Yet his soldiers, when given the benefit of good leaders such as Bowen and Gregg, fought with their customary skill and elan. As Grant said of them, when negoti-ating surrender terms with Pemberton, "Men who have shown so much endurance and courage will always challenge the respect of an adversary." Again, he offered a line of thought that does not often occur to our people: Americans do not fight wars to make permanent enemies, but ever strive to convert their ex-foes into allies. Grant suggests this in his statement: "The men had behaved so well that I did not want to humiliate them. I believed that consideration for their feelings would make them less dangerous foes during the continuance of hostilities, and better citizens after the war was over . . . [Therefore] when they passed out of their works they had so long and so gallantly defended, between the lines of their late antagonists, not a cheer went up, not a remark was made that would give pain."

INSTEAD, individual Yanks shared the food in their haversacks with Johnnies, and Grant ordered his commissary to issue ample rations to Pemberton's troops and to the citizens, both in the city and throughout the countryside recently passed over by the armies.

Tactically and strategically the results of the campaign were among the most decisive of the war. Abraham Lincoln, his cabinet, and the people in the North were enheartened after the previous long months of defeat and discouragement. The Confederacy, after Gettysburg and Vicksburg, never regained the military initiative. From hindsight, perhaps, the final outcome of the war was now inevitable. The commander at Port Hudson, on learning of the fall of Vicksburg, surrendered to General Banks. President Lincoln could now say, "The father of waters rolls unvexed to the sea."

As a Defender Saw the Siege

The following excerpts are from the regimental history of the Third Regiment, Louisiana Infantry, by W. H. Tunnard, published in 1866.

Vicksburg, May 17, 1863. The day dawned clear and warm. The troops left Snyder's Bluff for aye late at night, and proceeded toward Vicksburg, an intermingled line of wagons, artillery, and infantry. The night was very dark, yet the men pushed forward as rapidly as possible along the valley, wading streams and sloughs on the route. They were in most excellent spirits, and very enthusiastic. They considered Vicksburg an impregnable stronghold, and experienced a peculiar pride in the prospect of defending it.

May 18. This morning the regiment reached the Hill City, and was immediately placed in the intrenchments. These intrenchments were constructed on the crests of a line of hills, extending in a semicircle completely around the city, and about a mile in its rear. The whole country was a succession of abrupt hills, intersected by deep, narrow defiles. The regiment was placed near the centre of the line, on the left of the Jackson road, as it emerges from a deep cut through a hill.

Procuring spades and pickaxes, the men went to work with a desperate energy, which rapidly constructed works on the gap in the line. Rumors and particulars of the disasters which had befallen our troops, poured in on our men as they took their respective positions. Numbers had fallen into the enemy's hands, and many pieces of artillery had been lost. Yet our brigades, fresh from camp, felt no despondency, and the shadow of defeat darkened not their brave spirits as they quietly waited for the foe. On the afternoon of the 18th the skirmishing began some distance outside of the line of works. Our forces were steadily driven back, until they reached the protection of our guns. The enemy hesitated as they reached the line of woods skirting the cleared ground in front of the breastworks. It was only momentary, however, and the spattering reports of the small arms approached nearer and nearer. The next day was clear and warm. The enemy succeeded in establishing their position, and the siege commenced in earnest. About 1 p.m. the cannonading became terrific, the musketry deadly and heavy. The enemy charged the intrenchments on a portion of the lines, and were driven back with fearful slaughter, our own loss being very light.

May 20. At 1 a.m., the silence of the starlit night was broken by the roar of heavy guns. A huge ironclad approached from below, and commenced a furious bombardment of the city, which was rapidly responded to by our heavy batteries. Below lay the fleet of the enemy, and above, the river was dotted with a huge fleet of transport and war vessels. On the peninsula the white tents of the enemy's encampment were plainly visible. Such was the panoramic view in front of Vicksburg on the third morning of the siege. At early dawn the mortar fleet of Commodore Porter opened fire on the beleaguered city, adding to the tremendous din their hoarse bellowing, accompanied with the fearful screams and tremendous concussions of their huge, exploding missiles.

An incident during the siege of Vicksburg, showing the cave home of noncombatants. From a drawing by artist Howard Pyle originally published in "Harper's Monthly Magazine" 1908.

Huge caves were excavated out of the precipitous hillsides, where families of women and children sheltered themselves. Fair ladies hurried with light tread along the torn-up pavements, fearless of the storm of iron and lead, penetrating every portion of the city, as they attended to the necessities of their brave, wounded, and dying protectors. The annals of history can furnish no more brilliant record than did the heroic women of Vicksburg during this fearful siege.

May 21. The firing continued rapid and heavy all day, the mortar shells tearing the houses into fragments and injuring several citizens, including one lady. The enemy in front of the Third Regiment were slowly but surely contracting their lines, and the fire of their sharpshooters was particularly accurate and deadly. Their batteries concentrated their fire on every one of our guns that opened on their lines, and speedily dismounted them.

In conversation with the enemy (then a common occurrence, from the proximity of the lines), a member of Company E named Masterton, a Missourian of huge dimension familiarly known in the regiment as "Shanghai," found some acquaintances and was invited into the enemy's lines with the assurance that he would be allowed to return. The invitation was immediately accepted, and he trusted himself to the honor of the foe. He was cordially welcomed, and all the delicacies and substantials, which the Federals possessed in such profusion, were furnished him. After a feast, accompanied with a sociable chat and several drinks, he was permitted to return, very favorably impressed with the generosity of the Yankees. The evening chats, after the day's deadly sharpshooting, revealed the fact that there were members

357

of both armies who were personally acquainted and, in one instance, two members of the Third Regiment found a brother in the regiment opposed to them.

May 22. The bombardment continued unabated from all sides of the beleaguered city, and was more rapid and furious than heretofore. Nearly all the artillery along the lines was dismounted.

May 24. The enemy succeeded in establishing themselves directly beneath one of our parapets, above which stood the undaunted and heroic men of the Third Regiment. They immediately commenced undermining this portion of the line, with the intention of blowing it up. As the sound of their voices could be distinctly heard, our brave boys began to annoy them by hurling upon them every species of deadly missile which human ingenuity could invent. Twelve-pounder shells were dropped over the breastworks among them, and kegs filled with powder, shells, nails, and scraps of iron. A more deadly, vindictive, and determined species of warfare was never waged.

May 25. Another clear and hot day, and a continuation of the usual music along the lines. In the afternoon a flag of truce was sent into the lines, requesting a cessation of hostilities for the purpose of burying the dead. The effluvia from the putrefying bodies had become almost unbearable to friend and foe, and the request was granted, to continue for three hours.

Now commenced a strange spectacle. Flags were displayed along both lines, and the troops thronged the breastworks, gaily chatting with each other, discussing the issues of the war, disputing over differences of opinion, losses in the fight, etc. Numbers of the Confederates accepted invitations to visit the enemy's lines, where they were hospitably entertained and warmly welcomed. They were abundantly supplied with provisions, supplies of various kinds, and liquors. Of course, there were numerous laughable and interesting incidents resulting from these visits. The foe were exultant, confident of success, and in high spirits; the Confederates defiant, undaunted in soul, and equally convinced of a successful defense.

May 27. Clear and very warm. The firing was very brisk. About 11 a.m., the gunboats approached our batteries, both from above and below, while all around the lines a tremendous, rapid cannonading began. The roar of artillery was terrific in its volume of sound. The *Cincinnati*, one of the finest ironclads in the enemy's fleet, boldly approached our upper batteries, but was repeatedly struck and compelled to return. As she turned in the stream a ball penetrated her hull, and she was only able to reach a sand bar in the bend, when she went down. This combat was witnessed by hundreds of ladies who had ascended to the summits of the most prominent hills in Vicksburg. There were loud cheers, the waving of handkerchiefs, amid general exultation, as the vessel went down.

May 28. Still clear and warm. A courier succeeded in reaching the city with 18,000 caps which were much needed. Heretofore, the Third Louisiana were armed with the Confederate Mississippi rifles furnished them at Snyder's Mills. These arms were almost worthless, often exploding, and so inefficient that the enemy boldly exposed themselves and taunted the men for their unskillful shooting. On this day, however, the regiment was supplied with Enfield rifles of English manufacture, and Ely's cartridges, containing a peculiarly shaped elongated ball and the finest English rifle powder. These guns had evaded the blockade at Charleston and had never been unboxed. Beside the rifles, every man was furnished with a musket loaded with buckshot, to be used in case of an assault in close quarters. The men were so elated at the change in their weapons that they began a brisk fire in their eagerness to test their quality. The foe soon discovered the change, and there was a hasty retreat to the shelter of their rifle-pits, and the protection of their earthworks.

June 4. Heavy firing, as customary. Day clear, and very warm. The ration furnished each man was: peas, one-third of a pound; meal, two-thirds or five-sixths of a pound; beef, one-half of a pound, including in the weight bones and shanks; sugar, lard, soup, and salt in like proportions. On this day all surplus provisions in the city were seized, and rations issued to citizens and soldiers alike. To the perils of the siege began now to be added the prospect of famine. The gaunt skeleton of starvation commenced to appear among the ranks of the brave defenders.

June 11. Morning dawned cloudy. The day cleared off cool and pleasant. Below the city two gunboats floated lazily at anchor, while above not a vessel was in sight. In front of the Third Louisiana the enemy planted two ten-inch columbiads, scarcely a hundred yards distant from the lines. Their terrible missiles, with their heavy scream and tremendous explosion, somewhat startled the boys, being a new and unexpected feature in the siege.

June 14. W. McGuinness, mentioned among the wounded today, was shot through the right eye as he was looking through one of the pipes planted in the earthworks to observe the effects of his shooting. He was seen by one of the enemy, who fired at him with deadly aim. McGuinness recovered, but lost his eyesight and a piece of the bone from the side of his face.

The ironclad gunboat "Cincinnati," sunk at Vicksburg. (HW)

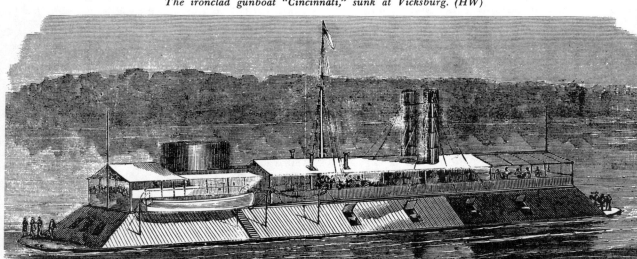

June 15. Day cloudy and threatened rain. The firing was very rapid, and shot and shell flew into and over the place in every direction. The enemy seemed to feel in a particularly lively humor. They made a charge on the breastworks held by the Twenty-seventh Louisiana Infantry, on the left of the position occupied by the Third Louisianans, in a mass four columns deep. They were repulsed and terribly slaughtered. A small rifle-gun, planted on the side hill, immediately in the rear of the Third Regiment, enfiladed their advancing columns, making great gaps in the ranks—as the balls literally ploughed a passage through their dense array of men. This episode in the usual monotony of the siege infused new life and spirit into the Confederates.

June 25. Just after noon the enemy sprang the mine beneath the Third Regiment, which they had been so long preparing. Six Mississippians working in the countermine were buried alive in the earth. This countermine counteracted the force of the explosion. The enemy immediately charged in heavy columns into the gap made in the works, when a fierce hand-to-hand struggle ensued. Hand grenades were freely used in this fierce struggle.

June 27. Cloudy and very warm, and the place full of rumors. At this period, the fortieth day of the siege, Vicksburg presented a fearful spectacle, having the appearance of being visited with a terrible scourge. Signs wrenched from their fastenings; houses dilapidated and in ruins, rent and torn by shot and shell; the streets barricaded with earthworks and defended by artillery over which lonely sentinels kept guard. The avenues were almost deserted, save by hunger-pinched and wounded soldiers, or guards lying on the banquettes, indifferent to the screaming and exploding shells. The few stores that were open looked like the ghosts of more prosperous times, with their empty shelves and scant stock of goods, held at ruinous prices. "Ginger beer," "Sweet cider," "Beer for sale," glared out in huge letters upon placards or the ends of barrels, seemingly the only relief to the general starvation. Palatial residences were crumbling into ruins, the walks torn up by mortar shells, the flower-beds trodden down, the shrubbery neglected. Fences were torn down and houses pulled to pieces for firewood. Even the enclosures around the remains of the revered dead were destroyed, while wagons were parked around the graveyard, horses tramping down the graves, and men using the tombstones as convenient tables for their scanty meals, or a couch for an uncertain slumber. Dogs howled through the streets at night; cats screamed forth their hideous cries; an army of rats, seeking food, would scamper around your very feet, and across the streets and over the pavements. Lice and filth covered the bodies of the soldiers. Delicate women and little children, with pale, care-worn, and hunger-pinched features, peered at the passerby with wistful eyes from the caves.

June 28. Another Sabbath morn. The Catholics of the city held services in their cathedral, notwithstanding the danger. As the congregation was emerging from the building, the enemy across the river discovered the unusual number of people in the streets, and instantly opened on them with a Parrott gun. As the shells came screaming wickedly through the streets, exploding or entering the building, men, women, and children hastily sought shelter to escape the danger. Several persons were struck by fragments of shells, but fortunately no one was killed.

Meat at this period became exhausted, and orders were issued to select the finest and fattest mules within the lines, and slaughter them for the purpose of issuing their flesh as food to the troops; a half pound per man was the ration of this new species of flesh. Several Spaniards belonging to the Texas regiments were jerking this meat for future consumption.

Mule flesh, if the animal is in good condition, is coarse-grained and darker than beef, but really delicious, sweet, and juicy.

July 1. At 2 p.m. the enemy exploded the mine beneath the works occupied by the Third Louisiana Infantry. A huge mass of earth suddenly flew upward with tremendous force and a terrible explosion, then descended upon the gallant defenders, burying numbers beneath its falling fragments, bruising and mangling them horribly. It seemed as if all hell had suddenly yawned upon the devoted band, and vomited forth its sulphurous fire and smoke upon them. The regiment at this time was supported by the First, Fifth, and Sixth Missouri Infantry, upwards of a hundred of whom were killed and wounded. Others were shocked and bruised, but not sufficiently to more than paralyze them for a few moments. At first there was a general rush to escape the huge mass of descending earth. Then the survivors, without halting to inquire who had fallen, hastened to the immense gap in the works to repel the anticipated assault. The enemy, taught by a dearly-bought experience, made no attempt to enter the opening, not daring to assault. An immense number of 12-pounder shells thrown from wooden mortars descended among the troops, doing fearful execution. The fire was tremendous, rapid, and concentrated, yet there was no flinching among those brave Southerners.

July 3. The morning was clear. The cannonading was terrific, and a storm of iron hail was poured upon the city. The hospitals seemed a special mark for the enemy's shot and shell. In the afternoon a heavy storm cloud gathered in the north and northeast, hanging like a funeral pall over the city. A flag of truce went out to the enemy's lines, and rumors began to prevail that the place was about to be surrendered. The brave garrison indignantly denied such a contingency, yet scarcely knew what to believe. Affairs looked very gloomy.

July 4. A day memorable in the annals of American history was destined once again to be made memorable as a day both of rejoicing and humiliation to those who had besieged and defended Vicksburg. Early in the day it became known that negotiations were pending for the surrender of the Southern stronghold. A perfect storm of indignation burst forth among the troops. What? Surrender? And that, too, on the 4th of July, above all other days? Impossible! Alas, it became too true.

The receipt of this order was the signal for a fearful outburst of anger and indignation. The members of the Third Louisiana Infantry expressed their feelings in curses loud and deep. Many broke their rifles against the trees, and scattered the ammunition over the ground where they had so long stood battling bravely and unflinchingly against overwhelming odds. In many instances the battle-worn flags were torn into shreds, and distributed among the men as a precious and sacred memento that they were no party to the surrender.

When the appointed hour, 10 a.m., arrived, the surrender was effected in conformity with the published order. The troops were marched outside the trenches, along whose line fluttered white pennants, arms were stacked. In sullen silence they returned within the lines and sought convenient camps in the rear of the intrenchments, where they might give free expression to their pent-up feelings. Soon along the entire lines Federal soldiers paced where so recently arose the sulphurous smoke and deafening din of fierce battle.

The siege of Vicksburg was at last ended.

. . . When the Federals first appeared . . . no word of exultation was uttered to irritate the feelings of the prisoners. On the contrary, every sentinel who came upon post brought haversacks filled with provisions, which he would give to some famished Southerner, with the remark, "Here, Reb, I know you are starved nearly to death."

359

Above—One of the parks of artillery captured at the surrender of Vicksburg. The Methodist church is shown in the front and the Catholic church (with the high steeple) in the rear. (KA)

Below—Fort Hill on the north side of Vicksburg overlooking the Mississippi. Here were located the powerful Confederate batteries which commanded the river. (KA)

CHICKAMAUGA

Text by Glenn Tucker
Designed by Frederic Ray

IF, AFTER GETTYSBURG, the Southern Confederacy ever had a clear invitation to win the war and gain independence, it was lost, not in defeat, but spurned in an hour of glorious victory in the deep woods at Chickamauga.

There the rewards of two days of some of the most desperate fighting of American history were shamefully sacrificed by the hesitation of leadership. There a triumph so signal as to be almost unparalleled in this grim war between the two sections was cast aside not through any reluctance of the gray-clad soldiers to continue the fight and reap the full harvest of their success, but by the incapacity of the commanding general of the Southern army, who was so out of touch with reality he was not even sure that a victory had been won!

Chickamauga, a word taken from the ancient Cherokee meaning "River of Death," is an appropriate name for this sanguinary, unplanned, almost uncontrolled clash of two great, groping armies, struggling with fervent zeal and ghastly sacrifice for the prize of Chattanooga, the rail center and heart city of the Middle South.

How desperately fought this battle truly was may be seen from the bare statistics. The combined casualties during the two days of fighting — on the 19th

and 20th of September, 1863 — were 37,129. They compare with total combined casualties of 23,582 at Sharpsburg (Antietam), known as the "bloodiest day of American history," where the fighting was confined largely to a single day. They compare with the reported casualties of 43,454 (perhaps more than 50,000) for the three days and the larger armies that fought at Gettysburg.

SOME HIGH POINTS

In truth, mere ground that few had ever heard of, much of it near worthless ground that lay uncultivated, vine-strewn, thicket-matted — stretches that had never known a saw nor heard the ring of the axe of man — was more recklessly fought for than almost any other of the world's acres. No ground was more coveted than those Georgian wastes, broken by a few cleared fields, running for five miles along the LaFayette Road between Lee and Gordon's Mill on the south and the McDonald house and Reed's Bridge road to the north.

It was a battle of peculiarly individualistic generals, Rosecrans and Bragg. Both are arresting studies in human behavior and the reactions of taut men under stress; neither is yet fully understood, despite the voluminous writing about them.

Major General William S. Rosecrans made a fatal mistake. (U.S. Signal Corps photo No. 111-B-3646 in the National Archives)

General Braxton Bragg could not believe that he had won. (KA)

Battle of rugged Pap Thomas, clinging doggedly to a convenient hill which ever after has been famous, named after the log cabin home of old man George Washington Snodgrass, near which Thomas slept with his portents and forebodings on the night of the 19th, using the knot of a tree root for a pillow, and where he held his line obstinately and heroically on the 20th until the grace of darkness relieved him of Longstreet's incessant hammering.

Battle of blunt and stormy Longstreet, newly arrived with five veteran brigades from the Army of Northern Virginia, who massed his attack and launched it in depth, and, like a tornado slashing a pathway in the woodlands, cut through the Federal right center, aided fortuitously by a momentary gap created by a misunderstanding and an ambiguous order. Longstreet broke Rosecrans' army into parts and drove substantially half of it — the better part of four divisions — with four division commanders, two corps commanders and the Union army commander himself from the field, back through McFarland's Gap into Rossville and the Chattanooga defenses.

Battle of Bushrod Johnson, the Ohioan in gray who pierced the Union center; of clear-visioned Nathan Bedford Forrest, whose pleas after the Confederate triumph that "every hour is worth ten thousand men," awakened in Bragg no quick response; of the gallant Cincinnati brigadier general and poet, William H. Lytle, whose lyric strains and battlefield fate were like those of Joyce Kilmer and Alan Seeger of a later war, who preferred to hold his brigade and die rather than follow his division commander Sheridan from the field.

Battle of the Hoosier ironmaster John T. Wilder, a sensational factor because his mounted infantrymen had armed themselves at their own expense with the new Spencer repeating rifles. Seemingly ubiquitous on the field was his efficient artilleryman, the young Greencastle and Lafayette, Indiana, druggist, Eli Lilly, whose triple charges of canister and grape caused Wilder to exclaim "it actually seemed a pity to kill men so."

Battle of the lovable, dashing Ben Helm, Lincoln's favorite brother-in-law, commander of the "Orphan Brigade," an intrepid Blue Grass aggregation also known as the "Blood of Boone," perhaps the most romantic unit of the Confederate Kentuckians. Helm fell from a Kentucky Unionist's bullet on the gory morning of the second day. His death, though he was an enemy of the Union, cast the Executive Mansion in Washington into the deepest gloom, and gave Lincoln probably as much anguish as any other event of the war.

THE PRESIDENT had offered Helm, who was a graduate of both West Point and the Harvard Law

Major General George H. Thomas, "Rock of Chickamauga." His stubborn stand saved the Union army from complete rout. (LC)

Lieutenant General James Longstreet. His men made the crucial breakthrough of the Union line. (Cook Coll., Valentine Museum)

School, and was a distinguished young representative of Blue Grass wealth and culture, son of a governor and descendant of earlier noted statesmen and famed pioneers, a Federal commission. But Helm had talked on that same day with reserved but inspiring Robert E. Lee, and had sided with the South.

"I feel like David of old when he was told of the death of Absalom," the grief-stricken Lincoln lamented to his caller and close friend, Judge David Davis, when he had word that Helm had died on this sanguinary field.

Battle of the "Bloody Pond," stained when the wounded soldiers crawled down and drank, and of driving thirst at night in the fields and dark woods where the masses of Unionists, cut off from Chickamauga Creek, were crowded into an area that had only a few weak wells and shallow springs, altogether inadequate for such numbers. "How we suffered that night no one knows," wrote a Federal officer. "Water could not be found. Few of us had blankets and the night was very cold." Some relief was provided by the 19th Mounted Indiana Infantry, which collected 1,000 canteens, filled them at Crawfish Springs three miles south, and brought them to sufferers at midnight.

"We had vermin in our clothing," wrote a soldier who lost his coat and went through the battle in his undershirt. "We did not take our socks off until they were rotten, and only removed our shoes once a week."

Battle that revealed the stanchness of the American character, where men of both sides submerged their individual identities and heedlessly threw their lives and fortunes into their causes, as a duty unsought, and often little understood, but nonetheless an overpowering duty. Battle of the vacant chair and the mother's anguish, about which nearly every Southern schoolboy once knew in the lines of the old song:

> One lies down at Appomattox
> Many miles away
> Another sleeps at Chickamauga
> And they both wore suits of gray. . . .

IN ONE respect Chickamauga was more similar to First Manassas than to any other battle. In no others were major Union armies put to such complete rout. Brice's Cross Roads was comparable but on a smaller scale.

Perhaps the two most obvious opportunities for the South to win a standoff war followed First Manassas, where the approaches to Washington were open and the city occupied by little more than a rabble; and Chickamauga, where able and aggressive Southern generalship might have taken the Army of Tennessee past Rosecrans, huddled in Chattanooga, and Burnside in Knoxville, and carried it to the Ohio, bringing the scattered Union forces behind it for the test in Kentucky of a second Perryville.

365

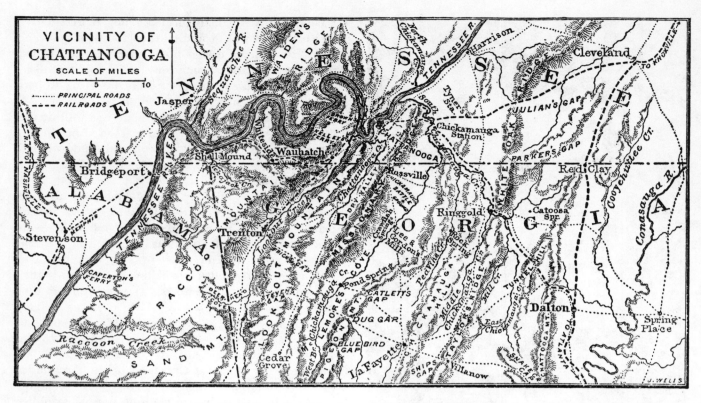

Theater of operations during the Chickamauga Campaign.
(From "Battles & Leaders, III, 640)

These things are clearer in aftersight, and it may be contended that the vast industrial and manpower superiority of the North made Southern independence impossible at this stage of the war; still, as is often demonstrated, bustling industries, teeming immigration, and monetary wealth are no substitutes for victory on the battlefield and a hot pursuit of the vanquished. Jackson, Forrest, Hancock, and others understood this well, and history abounds with examples of the triumph of weakness over strength. So it might have been after Chickamauga, this battle of the last opportunity, the last clear chance.

ROSECRANS' BLUNT DEMANDS

The campaign that culminated in the Battle of Chickamauga began at Tullahoma, Tennessee, into which Bragg had retired when Rosecrans advanced from Murfreesboro on June 23, 1863.

William Starke Rosecrans, commanding the Army of the Cumberland, had settled down in Murfreesboro on January 5, after the battle of Stone's River. At Murfreesboro he engaged in what was derisively termed "masterly inactivity." But the fault was more that of the War Department than the commanding general. He called loudly for the mules, horses, and equipment urgently needed for an advance, but the department was so indifferent that this became known as the "stepchild army."

Chief of Staff Halleck kept the wires hot with messages urging more aggressive action and Rosecrans burned them as blisteringly with appeals and impertinences demanding the transportation facilities that would make feasible an advance into the heart of the Southland. Secretary of War Stanton heartily disliked Rosecrans and it is fair to say that this was a factor in the bad blood and low-key cooperation between the department and one of the largest Federal armies.

Rosecrans consulted with his officers. Thomas,

A panoramic view showing the Chattanooga region as it appears from Point Lookout, high point on Lookout Mountain. (B&L)

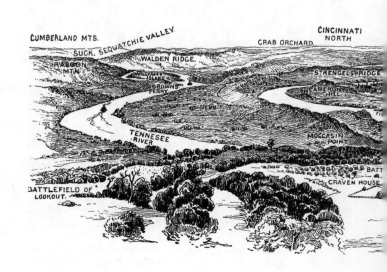

366

whose judgment few would question, agreed with the commanding general that the army could not move without adequate transportation. So did the other corps commanders. Only Chief of Staff James A. Garfield, who commanded no troops, voted for a prompt forward movement, about which Major General David S. Stanley, who had commanded the Union cavalry at Stone's River, said Garfield sought "cheap glory." Garfield wrote confidentially to his friend in Washington, Secretary Chase, about it, complaining of the delay, which was scarcely his role as chief of staff and the officer presumably closest to Rosecrans.

WHEN at length on June 23 Rosecrans felt ready, he conducted a series of brilliant strategical movements, perhaps unequalled and certainly unsurpassed for boldness and effectiveness in the Northern armies during the four years of war. By them he ousted Bragg from Tullahoma, and then from Chattanooga, a mountain-rimmed citadel with a wide river in its front, a stronghold which many regarded impregnable. He did this without losing a man in taking the town, and with the death of only six in the campaign, four of these by accident. The swift, sure procession of adroit flanking movements, which took the Army of the Cumberland over three mountain ranges in three weeks, startled the entire South, distressed Richmond, and caused rejoicings in the North like those that followed Gettysburg and Vicksburg.

Bragg Thoroughly Baffled

Rosecrans' capture of Chattanooga on September 9, 1863, disclosed at its best his customarily dexterous handling of his army. Bragg was deprived of any reasonable opportunity to fight for the possession of the city, even had he been disposed to risk a battle or a siege.

He was simply outmaneuvered. Coming down through the Cumberland Mountains, the Union commander gave indication of a wide sweep to the left and a passage of the Tennessee River above Chattanooga. That would have appeared good judgment, for Major General Ambrose E. Burnside had arrived in East Tennessee with what was presumed to be a supporting army, and was on the left, where Rosecrans might be expected to make a juncture. Elements of Burnside's army captured Cumberland Gap and a neat bag of prisoners on September 9, 1863, and Burnside meantime had occupied Knoxville, 114 miles from Chattanooga, on September 6, three days before Rosecrans took Chattanooga.

Rosecrans' apparent swing to the left was merely a feint, well executed by elements of Crittenden's corps, aided by Colonel Robert H. G. Minty's cavalry brigade and the mounted infantry brigade of Colonel John T. Wilder of Thomas' corps. The Federals showed themselves frequently upstream, simulated the building of pontoons, pounded on empty barrels as though constructing boats, mounted batteries, shelled the city, and ingeniously baffled Bragg into maintaining a sharp watch and massing his troops upstream on his right, when all the while the menace was downstream on his left.

THERE, in late August and early September, Rosecrans' army crossed on pontoons, by pirogues, and at length by a hastily constructed trestle bridge. It passed over the river at or near Bridgeport and Shellmound, only twenty-five miles by air from Chattanooga, but hidden and remote either over the intervening mountains or by way of the winding river. For seven days the two great corps of Thomas and McCook, consist-

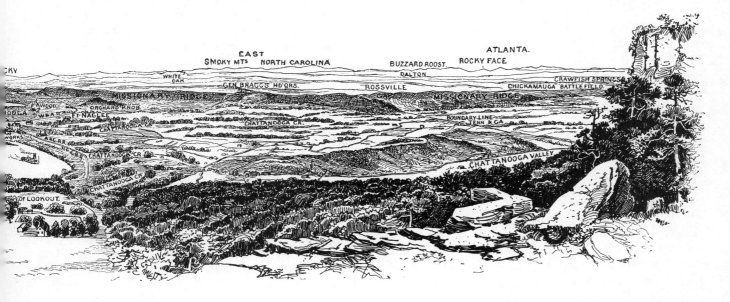

Col. Edward M. McCook commanded Union cavalry division. (LC)

But Bragg, though never popular, was not altogether stupid. When he saw he was flanked by the long swing of the Federal army to his left, and its crossing downstream and march into north Georgia, where it threatened his supply lines, he, too, resorted to stratagems. These were to emphasize to the now confident Rosecrans that the Confederates were in full and headlong retreat toward Rome and Atlanta. Bragg sent out scouts to be captured and give this false information. He imparted to country people and mountain dwellers the tale of woe that he was in full flight, and they in turn told Rosecrans. Rosecrans tended to believe the stories, and why not? Had not Chattanooga, the great prize sought in the campaign, fallen like a dead duck at an eager huntsman's feet? Were there not visible evidences that Bragg was baffled?

Success, so often dangerous to an impetuous, emotional man, now had its way with Rosecrans. If Chattanooga had tumbled to his ingenious flanking movements, Rome and Atlanta might be carried. When they were in his hands the communication lines of the South would be effectively severed. The Confederacy would be cut through the middle. A wave of optimism passed through the Federal army and sent its ripples into the Northern cities. "Old Rosey" might soon capture Atlanta. The war might be over by Christmas!

ALL of this went to make up one of the strangest dramas of the war, the covert reinforcement of Bragg to the utter surprise of Rosecrans. Bragg's retreat from Tullahoma deeply agitated President Davis and stirred repercussions through the Army of Northern Virginia, which was nursing its wounds and refitting behind the Rapidan after the tragedy of Gettysburg. Longstreet, prior to Gettysburg, had proposed to both Lee and the Richmond authorities that instead of heading north with Lee, his corps should be detached to reinforce Bragg, and that Joseph E. Johnston's Mississippi army be united with them. Combined, they would sweep Rosecrans aside, march to the Ohio River, and perhaps draw Grant back from Vicksburg to save Louisville and Cincinnati and prevent an invasion of Indiana and Ohio. Longstreet now felt that if Rosecrans overran Georgia the story of the Confederacy would end soon. He renewed his suggestion to Secretary of War Seddon that he go to Bragg. This time Lee and Davis assented. Both Longstreet and Davis preferred that Lee head the relief expedition in person but Lee declined, feeling that his more pressing duty was in Virginia.

ing of seven divisions, operating 300 miles from their "zone of the interior" base at Louisville (and 150 miles from Nashville, the main base in the theater of operations), but carrying with them rations for forty-five days and enough ammunition to fight two large battles, crossed the river behind the security of the Raccoon and Sand Mountain Range, and then Lookout Mountain, without Bragg being fully apprised of what was happening.

Friendly country folk who had watched from the ridges began to bring him more impressive reports than the earlier inklings he had been receiving by hearsay and rumor. He had thought the downstream movement the feint, the upstream the genuine danger, and in this was altogether mistaken. When he learned that Rosecrans was plunging south behind the cover of the Raccoon-Sand Mountain Range, and might debouch at any moment in his rear and interpose the Federal army between his own and Atlanta, he had no course open but to retire.

The 92d Illinois mounted infantry of Wilder's brigade passed around the head of Lookout Mountain, following the curve of the river, on the early morning of September 9, 1863, and rode into Chattanooga without firing a shot. Dust clouds to the south showed Bragg's retreat route.

Had the Confederate War Department acted with alacrity, Longstreet might have arrived in time to save Chattanooga, for the direct railroad line ran through Bristol, Virginia, and Knoxville, to Chattanooga. Before the orders were issued and the rolling stock collected, Burnside had occupied Knoxville and cut the railroad. The transfer had to be made by a circuitous route mainly through Wilmington, North Carolina and Augusta and Atlanta, Georgia.

Longstreet's corps, heavy with Georgians, was elated. The men would get a chance to see their home state, possibly their home towns once more. Many did so on the transfer, even the celebrated and ancient Guards company from as far south as Columbus.

Lafayette McLaws wrote to his wife that the army had been "increasing daily in strength and efficiency" after the defeat at Gettysburg, and had regained its old self-confidence. The assumption was, as G. Moxley Sorrel explained, that when Longstreet left Virginia the Federal army would detach troops from Lee's front, but that Longstreet, having the short route, would arrive first. Meade was counted on to move cautiously and deplete his own army with great deliberation if he had to strengthen Rosecrans'. "His well known prudence and lack of imagination," wrote Sorrel, "might be trusted to keep him quiet during our great strategic coup."

AT FIRST it was judged Longstreet could reach Bragg with two divisions in two days. How inaccurate was this estimate! It depended on utilization of the railroad through Bristol and Knoxville. The more circuitous journey required upwards of ten days. Most of the rolling stock of the Southeastern states was pressed into service for this first transfer of a large army by railroad. (Joseph E. Johnston had transferred a much smaller force over a short distance in the First Manassas Campaign.) Longstreet's men, wrapped in carpets and blankets, filled passenger and freight cars and huddled together on the tops of flatcars and boxcars. They were fed bountifully by women who brought delicacies as they passed through the Carolinas and north Georgia.

The strangest aspect of this transfer was that Rosecrans, the man who would be the most concerned, was the last to hear of it. Richmond and Baltimore buzzed with gossip of an impending troop movement of major proportions, but the wires to Rosecrans were silent. Meade reported to the War Department the sudden disappearance of Longstreet's corps from his front. Stanton, Halleck, or some alert official in the department might have apprehended the danger to Rosecrans and told him about it, then sent him aid. But not until the last moment, when it was too late, were orders issued to units scattered through the southwest to march to the support of Rosecrans.

Burnside in Knoxville turned in the opposite direction and reported to Washington that he was going to Jonesboro (in northeast Tennessee), which brought from Lincoln at the telegraph office the ejaculation, "Damn Jonesboro."

ROSECRANS himself did not accept at full value the report when he finally got it, that Longstreet was reinforcing Bragg. Not until he captured a captain of Robertson's brigade, Hood's division, on the battlefield was he willing to face actualities. Before that Colonel Atkins of the 92d Illinois had brought in a youth who had said he was from Longstreet's corps. Rosecrans "flew into a passion," Atkins said, "and upbraided the lad as a liar, frightening him into speechlessness."

Bragg was further strengthened by the return of elements that had been sent when Joseph E. Johnston's army was assembled at Jackson, Mississippi to succor Pemberton in Vicksburg. These included Breckinridge's veteran division of Hardee's corps; Bushrod Johnson's division, that would play a key role in the battle; and Walker's Reserve Corps which, with additions, aggregated two full divisions. Hardee, after the surrender of Vicksburg, had been sent to command in southern Alabama and the testy D. H. Hill, formerly of Lee's army, had been given a lieutenant general's rank and assigned to command Hardee's old corps, consisting of the divisions of Breckinridge and Cleburne. Bragg, who had left Tullahoma with a force of about 35,000, now had a formidable army of 71,550 officers and men. Rosecrans was outnumbered, having a force of about 57,000.

Bragg might have waited for the arrival of Longstreet's full complement, but chose not to do so. Pickett's division had been left in Virginia, but Longstreet brought with him the divisions of Hood and McLaws, consisting of nine brigades. Only five arrived in time for the battle. The rest were scattered over north Georgia, making their way toward Bragg's army. McLaws was still in Atlanta forwarding his troops and did not reach the field until the day after the engagement ended; his division during the battle was commanded by E. M. Law. Some have thought that Bragg wanted to win a victory with his own army, now that the troops sent to Johnston had been returned, without having to share a triumph with Longstreet and his men. Bragg did try for an engagement two or three times prior to Longstreet's arrival, and began the main battle with Longstreet still absent. Another view is that Bragg went ahead without waiting for Longstreet

Gen. John B. Hood received crippling wound at Chickamauga. (LC)

370   *Major General John C. Breckinridge led a veteran division in Bragg's army. (Cook Collection, Valentine Museum, Richmond)*

because he hoped to catch and destroy Rosecrans' force while it was divided and in rough country.

NEAR TRAP IN McLEMORE'S COVE

His first effort was in McLemore's Cove. His opportunity there developed because Rosecrans in an impetuous movement farther south, such as had won him Chattanooga, caused his army to become gravely extended, whereas Bragg was concentrating in LaFayette, Georgia on Rosecrans' exposed flank. Rosecrans' army soon was strung out from Chattanooga to Alpine, Georgia, along a circuitous route and through mountain passes that left the wings three to four days' marches apart. Crittenden's corps occupied Chattanooga, with divisions thrown south toward Ringgold, and through Rossville toward LaFayette as far as Lee and Gordon's Mills.

Thomas' corps, in the center, crossed the Raccoon-Sand Mountain range and entered Lookout Valley; then the leading division trudged through Stevens' Gap into McLemore's Cove and began a movement toward LaFayette, not knowing of Bragg's concentration there. Crittenden was fifteen and more miles removed from him, out of prompt supporting distance.

Thomas had not wanted to proceed so hastily. He had recommended that the army occupy Chattanooga, refit itself, and consolidate its communications and defenses, then conduct a more orderly advance against Bragg in north Georgia. But Rosecrans, confident, overruled him and directed him into McLemore's Cove, while McCook's corps was laboring far to the south through Winston Gap toward Alpine and Summerville, and Crittenden was extended south of Chattanooga. The army was about like the Army of Northern Virginia at the beginning of the Gettysburg Campaign, when Lincoln observed that Lee reached from the Rappahannock to beyond the Potomac, and commented that "the animal must be pretty slim somewhere in the middle."

BRAGG detected Rosecrans' thinness from his point of observation in LaFayette and determined to trap Thomas' advance units in the cove. Thomas' leading division, Negley's, passed through Stevens' Gap into the cove on September 9. McCook's corps was now forty-two miles to the south and Crittenden's fifteen miles and more to the northeast. When through the pass, Negley marched to Davis' Crossroads near the headwaters of Chickamauga Creek, moving without much caution, because he judged the cove, six to nine miles wide, unoccupied by hostile troops. Ahead of him was Dug Gap over Pigeon Mountain, through which he intended to march for the capture of LaFayette, believing that Bragg, shielded by the Pigeon range, was either unaware of his approach or was in flight.

But Bragg at that very moment was converging on Negley with vastly superior forces, consisting of Hindman's division to the north, supported by the balance of Buckner's corps, and D. H. Hill's corps in his front and to his right, with Cleburne's division in the lead. Bragg issued his attack orders and paced nervously along the crest of Pigeon Mountain awaiting the sound of his guns.

Two events happened that frustrated his carefully laid plans. First, Negley grew suspicious, having learned that Confederates were having lunch at a house a mile to the north. He withdrew to a wood, changed position to face north, and called on Thomas for reinforcements. Thomas, alert to the danger, sent Baird's division hastening over Lookout Mountain to Negley's aid.

THE other event was the reluctance or inability of Bragg's generals to obey his orders. Hill contended that Cleburne was ill, a matter which Cleburne himself did not seem to notice, and that Dug Gap was so barricaded that the obstructions could not be removed. Hindman claimed he was not supposed to attack until Hill had formed a juncture with him in the cove. For the better part of two days the opportunity to destroy Negley, and, in turn, Baird, continued to be neglected, however urgently Bragg called for action. Bragg later preferred charges against Hindman, but they were never pressed after Hindman's brilliant performance at Chickamauga. Nor did Bragg have much to do with Hill thereafter, but placed him under the command of Polk and dealt with him mainly through that general.

Cleburne finally got into the cove, waded through Chickamauga Creek, and tried to cut off the retreat of the two Federal divisions, but reached the entrance to Stevens' Gap only to hear their artillery and wagons lumbering across the mountain. Thomas had extricated them instead of trying to support them. He understood Bragg's opportunity and was appalled by it. Negley's retirement was called "masterly," but Rosecrans seemed unperturbed that 10,000 of his men had been recklessly exposed to 30,000 of the enemy, and judged that Bragg was merely demonstrating to check the pursuit. His scouts still brought false reports that the Confederate army was hastening from LaFayette en route to Rome.

Bragg was no more successful in operating against Crittenden's corps than he had been against Thomas. He issued and reiterated orders for Polk to attack Crittenden, who had now concentrated around Lee and Gordon's Mill, where he was isolated when Thomas retired from in front of Hindman and Hill. Polk merely requested more troops and the opportunity passed, and soon the great battle was impending.

These threats against his center and left caused Rosecrans to recognize reluctantly on the night of September 12 that Bragg was not in flight toward Rome and Atlanta, but was concentrated and distinctly menacing, while he, in turn, was dispersed and vulnerable anywhere along the line. His recourse was to effect the speediest concentration possible. For four days the Federal commander was bringing his scattered army together, while Bragg, baffled when his two fine chances were sacrificed by his unresponsive subordinates, stood by idly at LaFayette. Rosecrans brought McCook back by forced marches on Thomas, who issued again through Stevens' Gap into McLemore's Cove and moved down the cove and Chickamauga Creek to join with Crittenden at Crawfish Springs and Lee and Gordon's.

BRAGG'S BATTLE PLAN

Bragg, having given Rosecrans the grace of four days in which to concentrate, did not wait two or three more until he had all of Longstreet's two fine divisions in hand, and could assume an orderly offensive for the recapture of Chattanooga. He still hoped to catch Rosecrans in a disadvantageous position. But when Rosecrans was about concentrated around Lee

Brig. Gen. James A. Garfield, Rosecrans' chief of staff. (LC)

371

and Gordon's, Bragg determined to cut around his left, and, by moving up the right bank of Chickamauga Creek (which flows north) interpose between him and Chattanooga. If cut off from Chattanooga, Rosecrans would be deprived of any satisfactory line of communications with the North. To extricate himself he would have to go by the laborious routes through the mountain passes, by which two of his corps had come, and reach the Tennessee River at Bridgeport, being exposed to attack by Bragg and harassment by Forrest.

Bragg intended to deliver battle on September 18 but could not get his units into position in time. The delay allowed the advance units of Longstreet's command to reach him, and to fall in under Hood on his left. His plan was for Bushrod Johnson's division, accompanied by Forrest's cavalry and supported by Walker's corps, to move down the Chickamauga, cross at Reed's and Alexander's bridges, which were presumed to be beyond the Federal left flank, find and assail the flank, and roll Rosecrans' army back into McLemore's Cove. Meantime, as the battle advanced, Buckner's corps was to cross at Thedford's Ford, farther upstream, while Polk would cross and attack the Federals at Lee and Gordon's, and Hill's corps would serve as a support still farther upstream.

The plan appeared to be feasible. Bushrod Johnson and Forrest brushed aside Minty's cavalry on Rosecrans' left and took Reed's Bridge by an impetuous charge that prevented the Federals from destroying it. Johnson's division was on the west side of the creek at 4:30 p.m. September 18. Walker's corps was delayed at Alexander's Bridge by Wilder's mounted infantry with their repeating rifles and by Eli Lilly's battery, but Forrest was there and crossings were made above and below the bridge, which eventually was carried at about the time Johnson was crossing downstream at Reed's.

First gun at Chickamauga, September 18, 1863. Confederates open fire upon Federal cavalry who have begun the destruction of Reed's Bridge. From original drawing by A. R. Waud. (LC)

Reed's Bridge (taken about 1890). It here retains its 1863 appearance. Reed's Bridge was a major creek crossing for the Confederates. Johnson's division crossed here after driving off Minty's cavalry.

FORREST, in the fight at Alexander's Bridge, was at his customary place in front of his men, where his beautiful steed was shot from under him — the mount that had been presented to him by the citizens of Rome, Georgia, after he had captured the Federal cavalryman and raider, Colonel Abel D. Streight.

Walker's corps consisted of the divisions of Brigadier Generals States Rights Gist and St. John R. Liddell, which, with Bushrod Johnson's division, gave Bragg three divisions on the west, or Federal side of Chickamauga Creek. Bragg all the while was pressing his army north in order to reach around the Federal flank, while Rosecrans, now understanding his adversary's intention, was moving his army north along the LaFayette-Chattanooga road, roughly parallel with Chickamauga Creek. Wilder, at Alexander's Bridge, finally finding his flanks were threatened by the Confederates who had forded the creek, retired beyond the LaFayette Road.

That night both armies prepared for the full-scale battle each saw was imminent. Rosecrans sent Thomas' corps to the left, to the region of the Kelly log cabin and a clearing called Kelly Field. Crittenden, whose rear Thomas had crossed in a hurried night march, was in the center and McCook's corps, as it arrived by forced marches, took position on the right. Be-

cause of the staggered arrival of the divisions marching from different positions to the concentration, the three Federal corps did not remain intact on the field. Reinforcements of divisions and brigades were continually sent to Thomas, who had the initial point of danger on the left, the flank Bragg was trying to turn.

Intelligence passed slowly in the wooded, thicket-grown area that chance was selecting for one of the most grueling battles of the war. As Thomas marched north to Kelly Field he learned from Wilder of the Confederate crossing at Reed's and Alexander's, but he later was informed by Colonel Dan McCook, who had been sent out from Gordon Granger's Reserve Corps at Rossville to help Minty, that a lone Confederate brigade was isolated west of the creek near Reed's Bridge. The brigade was McNair's, one of Bushrod Johnson's, which later would have a stellar role in the battle. It was not truly isolated, but was in the rear of Johnson's division, marching south.

BRANNAN OPENS THE FRAY

Thomas, at 7:30 a.m. on the 19th, sent his left division, Brannan's, to pick up this stray brigade, and thereby opened the Battle of Chickamauga.

Brannan found that Bushrod Johnson had marched his entire division upstream. He encountered, not a stray brigade, but Forrest's cavalry and Gist's division of Walker's Corps, which now held Bragg's right flank. This first clash at Jay's Mill, at a road convergence upstream from Reed's Bridge, was of a nature that presaged the desperate fighting of the next two days. Croxton's brigade of Brannan's division, which began the assault, sent back a facetious message asking which, of the many brigades in its front, was the one it was supposed to capture!

The battle of the first day was formless and inconclusive. Rosecrans established headquarters on his right, in the Glenn house, where he could dispatch into the action his divisions and brigades coming up on the roads from the south. He could have little influence over the battle there, though he tried to follow it by ear. The New York *Herald* correspondent, W. F. Shanks, poked fun at Rosecrans, who brought out some crude maps of the area and paced back and forth nervously, while his engineer officer tried to locate on the map with a compass the scene of the firing. "Never was anything more ridiculous," Shanks wrote. "When a gun sounded Rosecrans would ask the young widow, Eliza Glenn, where it was, and the country woman would say 'nigh out about Reed's Bridge somewhar,' or, 'about a mile fornenst John Kelly's house.'" (Fornenst was a good, colloquial word meaning beyond, but it seems to have no place in modern dictionaries.)

Divisions arrived on both sides throughout the day, marching north but going into action at the south end of each line. Thus the first day's battle was mainly a series of brigade clashes in the woods, and as the brigades became exhausted and the battle lulled toward the north, it was continued with renewed fury to the south. The armies were moving north but the battle was rolling south. During the afternoon Longstreet's first arrivals under Hood went into action.

The house of Mr. J. M. Lee, Crawfish Spring, Rosecrans' headquarters before the start of the battle and site of the field hospital for the right wing of the Federal army. (From B&L)

STEWART'S SPECTACULAR ADVANCE

Most promising for Bragg was the attack by the division of Major General Alexander P. Stewart, known as "Old Straight," more for his proficiency in mathematics than from his trim West Point bearing. Part of the time he had been Longstreet's roommate at the Academy, and after leaving the service he had been a fellow faculty member with Bushrod Johnson at Nashville University.

His excellent division of three well-led brigades, of Brigadier Generals William B. Bate, Henry D. Clay-

CONFEDERATE LINE OF BATTLE IN THE
CHICKAMAUGA WOODS.

ton, and John C. Brown, was a veteran part of the Army of Tennessee. It struck the Federal center at 3:15 p.m. in column of brigades. The assault caused the recorder of the affair to question: "Did you ever see the destruction of hail storms to a growing cornfield? Did you ever witness driftwood in a squall?" That was what Clayton's Alabama brigade looked like as it closed with Van Cleve's Federal division, with no breastworks for either and rifles being fired almost muzzle to muzzle.

STEWART'S DIVISION was proudly termed the "Little Giants" and here it proved itself worthy of the name. The three brigades pressed back Van Cleve, fought through the burning woods, crossed the La-Fayette Road, and reached the tanyard of the Dyer farm, in the heart of the Federal position. The situation was critical for Rosecrans because the LaFayette Road was the link with Thomas battling under heavy pressure with Walker, now aided by Cheatham on the left. Stewart's division now held a segment of this vital roadway. But the Federal center was saved by the commander of one of Thomas' divisions, Major General Joseph J. Reynolds, who had been Grant's roommate at West Point, and was now one of Rosecrans' stanchest fighters. He posted his fourteen guns to bear on Stewart's men and ordered every infantry unit in the neighborhood to pour in their fire.

Wilder's mounted infantrymen again came to the center of the fray and their repeaters compelled the Confederates to give ground. Negley's division put in its appearance. Before Negley could reach the fighting, Stewart's intrepid division was pushed back to the east side of the LaFayette Road. The jumbled Federal center, now a confusion of units from all three of Rosecrans' corps, was given time to reorganize.

Cleburne Is Beaten Back

The battle rolled farther south for desperate fighting at Viniard's farm, in front of Rosecrans' headquarters at the Widow Glenn's. Then it broke with renewed vigor at the far opposite end of the line, where Cleburne, who had been marching down Chickamauga Creek while the battle roared to his left and had crossed at Thedford's Ford in the late afternoon, made a desperate sunset attack on Thomas' strongly held line.

Thomas had conferred with two of his left-wing division commanders, Baird and Richard W. Johnson, the latter detached from Crittenden's corps, and had personally supervised the placing of the guns in anticipation of a renewed assault. Apprehensive when Stewart crossed the LaFayette Road and dented the Federal center, he had detached Brannan's division from the far left and sent it to the relief of Van Cleve.

There it remained, and came to have a distinct bearing on the fortunes of the second day.

Cleburne was at length repulsed. Darkness settled early in the woods. Orders against campfires that would reveal positions were enforced as rigidly as possible. The moans of the wounded, who could be given little relief, could be heard from the Reed's Bridge Road to Viniard's farm. The weather was unusually cold for late September and both armies suffered from lack of fires and shortage of overcoats and blankets. Perhaps on no other field of the war was the suffering so acute as on the night of September 19.

THE ARMIES lay along roughly parallel lines, the LaFayette Road dividing them except on the Federal left, where Thomas crossed the road to the east and defended a fortified position through the woods, which he continued to strengthen by felling trees and hewing abatis all night. The Federal divisions as aligned roughly from left (north) to right were those of Baird, Richard Johnson, Palmer, Reynolds, Brannan, (recently shifted from the far left), Wood, Van Cleve (recessed), Negley (recessed), Davis, and Sheridan. Facing them, the Confederate alignment from right (north) to left was Forrest, Cleburne, Gist, Liddell, Cheatham (recessed), Steward, Bushrod Johnson, Hood, Hindman, and Preston.

Breckinridge's division, rated among the best, and consisting of the brigades of Daniel W. Adams, Marcellus A. Stovall, and the "Orphan Brigade" under Ben Helm, was reaching, with difficulty in the darkness, the position assigned to it on the far right, where Bragg intended to renew his attack at dawn on the 20th, adamantly adhering to his plan to cut between Rosecrans and Chattanooga and drive the Federals back into McLemore's Cove.

Hood commanded a demi-corps, consisting of the five brigades of the Army of Northern Virginia that had arrived in time for a part in the battle. These were two brigades of McLaws' division, those of Joseph B. Kershaw, who assumed the division as well as brigade command, and Benjamin C. Humphreys. The latter had been Barksdale's, who had fallen at Gettysburg. The other division was commanded by E. McIver Law and consisted of Law's old brigade commanded by James L. Sheffield, Hood's old Texas brigade commanded by Jerome B. Robertson, and the brigade of Henry L. Benning. Bushrod Johnson's division was thrown into Hood's corps while the divisions of Stewart, Preston, and Hindman were formed into Buckner's corps. As it developed, the battle of the second day was fought more by brigades and regiments than by divisions and corps. A St. Louis newspaperman termed it a "soldiers' battle" and that term has persisted because much of the time in the bush and heavy timber the higher officers had little control.

The most significant event of the night was the arrival of Longstreet. Bragg had made no arrangements to meet him when he reached the railhead at Catoosa Station, accompanied by his always reliable chief of staff, Colonel G. Moxley Sorrel, and his chief of ordnance, Colonel P. T. Manning. They waited for their horses that arrived on a second train, then made their way gropingly toward the sound of the firing, without a guide, and narrowly escaping capture by a Federal patrol that accosted them in the bright moonlight. Longstreet parleyed with the Federals, claiming to be a friend, rode quietly away, then with a dash avoided the delayed bullets.

Bragg was asleep in an ambulance but Longstreet aroused him and they talked for an hour. Longstreet, always combative and dominating, must have looked on Bragg with some contempt, though that did not become apparent until the next afternoon, when he had further opportunity to observe the army commander's generalship. Bragg's headquarters reflected a dismal air, which Hood had noticed when he arrived earlier. Longstreet's rank entitled him to high command on the field. Bragg consequently divided his army into wings, assigning Longstreet to command the left and Bishop Polk, also a lieutenant general, to command the right. It was noticeable that he did not divide the army into three elements and assign the remaining lieutenant general, D. H. Hill, to the center. Polk recommended that. Hill served under Polk and commanded a corps consisting of the divisions of Breckinridge and Cleburne. Bragg had not forgiven him for the failure to attack in McLemore's Cove.

THE DOWNGRADING of Hill unmistakably was an element in Bragg's ghastly failure to get the attack under way on time early on the 20th. His plan, as he outlined it to Longstreet, was for Polk to attack on the right at sunrise with Hill's two divisions. The battle would then move down the line through Cheatham's division and Walker's corps until it reached Longstreet, who would attack with Hood's and Buckner's corps in succession. Hood, who had participated with part of his command on the 19th, was elated over Longstreet's arrival. Longstreet was the first general he had met, he said, who was talking in terms of victory.

One detail Bragg had not attended to was to advise Hill that his corps had been placed under Polk. These two generals, Polk and Hill, had on the morning of the 20th one of the greatest opportunities of the war, and proceeded to bungle it. Polk had asked Hill to stop at his headquarters in an ambulance at Alexander's Bridge and had stationed sentries to keep

watch for him. Hill did not find Polk but two members of his staff did come and Polk entrusted the attack order to them. Hill had gone to Bragg's headquarters at the Thedford house after midnight but Bragg was not there, then had passed Alexander's Bridge, a mile away, at 3 a.m., but the sentries had been withdrawn at 2 a.m. He claimed he never saw the attack order until nineteen years after the battle. Perhaps the blame should fall equally on Hill and Polk; at any rate Bragg awoke early on the 20th, confident that the battle was about to begin, when all the while his orders were lost in the mechanics of transmission.

That night Rosecrans held a council of war, through which Thomas dozed. When his opinion was asked he would rouse himself and invariably deliver the same reply, "I would reinforce the left." He understood that Bragg would persist in his aim to get between Rosecrans and Chattanooga. The council settled little. When the business was completed, McCook entertained his fellow officers with a rendition of a mournful melody entitled "The Hebrew Maiden's Lament," a German song about a Jewish girl who sorrowfully rejected the suitor she loved to adhere to the faith of her fathers.

BISHOP POLK DALLIES

The critical moment of the battle of the second day came at 11 o'clock. Until then, the two armies

Longstreet's troops debarking from the trains below Ringgold, Georgia on September 18, 1863. They hastened from here into the Battle of Chickamauga which was already raging. (Reproduced from the booklet "Battlefields in Dixie Land" pub. 1928)

Thomas' bivouac after the first day's battle. The next was to be his great day. From a drawing by Gilbert Gaul in B&L.

were still fighting desperately and inconclusively in the deep woods. Bishop Polk failed to attack Thomas at dawn, as Bragg ordered. He got into action five hours late, at 10 o'clock, just as the church bells were ringing for morning services in Chattanooga ten miles away. Bragg said later that if his orders to Polk had been carried out, "our independence might have been gained."

When Bragg did not hear the guns on the right he sent messengers to Polk to learn the cause of the delay. One of them, Major Pollock B. Lee, told Bragg that he found Polk three miles behind his lines, about an hour after sunup, sitting on the porch of a farmhouse, reading a newspaper and waiting for his breakfast. When Major Lee told him that General Bragg was greatly disturbed, Polk was quoted as replying from his rocking chair. "Do tell General Bragg that my heart is overflowing with anxiety for the attack — overflowing with anxiety, sir."

Polk well before the war was one of the distinguished men of the country, Episcopal Bishop of the South, with his seat in New Orleans; handsome, with erect military carriage and large, intelligent face; close friend of the Confederate President, whom he had preceded by one class at West Point; a natural leader, inspiring by his presence as well as by his devoutness.

HE gave his life to the cause a little later near Kennesaw Mountain; but despite Polk's many high

377

qualities, President Davis' judgment is subject to question for entrusting him with a veteran corps and making him second in command of Bragg's army. One who had been at the top in authority, and the communicant with God for one of the leading faiths of the South, responded with lack of ardor to the severe and straightlaced soldier under whom he had been placed. He did not foment the cabal among the officers against Bragg in protest to that general's retreat after Stone's River, but he lent dignity and prestige to it by writing Davis personally over Bragg's head, a letter in which he told of the disquiet in the army and recommended that a new commander be appointed.

He had remained in the army only five months after graduating from the Military Academy, then turned to his religious studies and career. After thirty-four years as a churchman he was suddenly appointed a major general by his friend Davis. The Confederate cause never profited. He never fully cast aside the robe for the resplendent uniform he customarily wore.

Thomas repulsed the desperate but belated assault of Hill's corps, made by the splendid veteran divisions of Breckinridge and Cleburne, with Cheatham in support. Certainly no blame could attach to the division commanders. Thomas threw in a succession of brigades and called repeatedly on Rosecrans for reinforcements from the Federal right, which was then not engaged. Rosecrans said that to prevent Bragg from getting between him and Chattanooga he would reinforce Thomas with the entire army, if necessary.

Polk and Hill attacked by brigades in succession, and never with Polk's entire wing *en masse*. Instead of making a wider encirclement of Thomas' left, they wasted much power in costly assaults against Thomas' log breastworks.

So it was around 11 a.m. Sometime between 10:30 and 11, probably near 11, Rosecrans had moved his headquarters, or at least some elements of it, to a ridge to the north that turned out to be in the path of Longstreet's breakthrough. Thus in modern military parlance the forward echelon of his headquarters was on this ridge while the rear echelon, consisting, perhaps, of his adjutant general and other staff members (and his "housekeeping arrangements") was still at Glenn's. But at 11 Rosecrans himself was on the ridge, following the battle mainly by ear. He had ridden along the lines in the early Sunday morning of the 20th. He was in many respects a magnetic personality, not unlike McClellan in his ability to inspire and win the affection of his troops. Most of them adored him, invariably cheered him.

"Old Rosey" — a handsome officer, neatly dressed, even nattily dressed, wore black breeches and a fresh blue coat, given a dash of elegance and swagger by his snow-white vest. His intelligent eyes, of dark blue, sparkled and danced with the excitement of battle. Well-read, a brilliant conversationalist, an inventor, an able engineer, he was in almost every respect up to that moment a successful general. He was regarded by his enemies as something of a genius, more to be feared than McClellan, Meade, Grant, or any other leader in the Northern armies. He had been triumphant in nearly all of his past engagements — in West Virginia, where the major credit had redounded to McClellan, at Iuka and at Stone's River, and in maneuvering Bragg out of Tennessee. His battles, unlike those of McClellan, Grant, Hooker, and some others, had been fought usually against superior or fairly equal numbers. Here at Chicka-

A SHELL AT HEADQUARTERS.

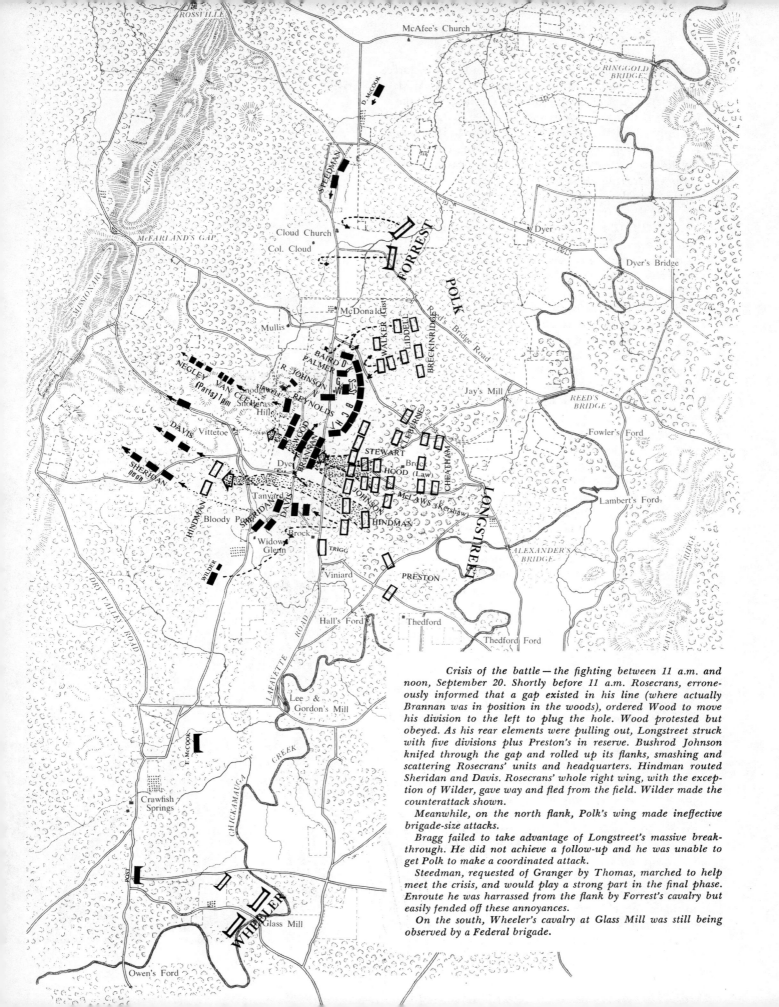

Crisis of the battle — the fighting between 11 a.m. and noon, September 20. Shortly before 11 a.m. Rosecrans, erroneously informed that a gap existed in his line (where actually Brannan was in position in the woods), ordered Wood to move his division to the left to plug the hole. Wood protested but obeyed. As his rear elements were pulling out, Longstreet struck with five divisions plus Preston's in reserve. Bushrod Johnson knifed through the gap and rolled up its flanks, smashing and scattering Rosecrans' units and headquarters. Hindman routed Sheridan and Davis. Rosecrans' whole right wing, with the exception of Wilder, gave way and fled from the field. Wilder made the counterattack shown.

Meanwhile, on the north flank, Polk's wing made ineffective brigade-size attacks.

Bragg failed to take advantage of Longstreet's massive breakthrough. He did not achieve a follow-up and he was unable to get Polk to make a coordinated attack.

Steedman, requested of Granger by Thomas, marched to help meet the crisis, and would play a strong part in the final phase. Enroute he was harrassed from the flank by Forrest's cavalry but easily fended off these annoyances.

On the south, Wheeler's cavalry at Glass Mill was still being observed by a Federal brigade.

mauga he again faced a superior Confederate force.

At the Federal army headquarters (at Widow Glenn's), Chief of Staff James A. Garfield was marking the shifting positions of the Federal division on his improvised headquarters map. Even Garfield must have been confused, for no human being could possibly follow the devious course of the deadly brigade clashes occurring all along the line in the dense, vine-matted woods and jungle-like thickets.

SOMETIME around 10:30 o'clock one of Thomas' aides, Captain Sanford Cobb Kellogg, of Troy, New York, the young nephew of General Thomas' wife, arrived at Rosecrans' headquarters at the Widow Glenn's.

He was the thirteenth courier Thomas had sent that morning to report on conditions on the Federal left and to request more troops. Rosecrans all morning had been weakening his right and center to reinforce his left just as Meade had done on the second day at Gettysburg, and the center of the Federal army at Chickamauga was held by a line of divisions with no adequate reserve.

Captain Kellogg had ridden along the Glenn-Kelly road, then a woodland trail linking the Glenn farm with the Kelly farm. He did not see Brannan's division in line in the deep woods on his left as he passed. He reported to Rosecrans that there was a gap in the line between the divisions of Reynolds and Wood. This would mean that a dangerous hole existed in the center of the Federal army.

Although Kellogg is most frequently credited with it, there is no agreement on who first reported the existence of this supposed gap. Thomas' staff officer, Henry M. Cist, said the report of a gap came initially from Lieutenant Colonel Alexander Von Schraeder, an Ohioan on Thomas' staff, who reported to Thomas that there were no troops on the right of Reynolds, and that a long gap existed between Reynolds and Wood. Von Schraeder did not know that Brannan's division was in position there, slightly recessed from Reynold's front. According to Cist, Thomas at once sent this information to Rosecrans. Cist did not name the messenger but he obviously was Captain Kellogg.

VON SCHRAEDER, incidentally, was an interesting figure. He had eminent military connections. His father had been a lieutenant general in the Prussian army. The son, like many others who came to America in the late 1840's, had implicated himself in revolutionary activities of 1848, and when they collapsed was forced to flee. He reached Cincinnati, where he became a street car conductor. The war brought his military abilities into play and he became Thomas' assistant inspector general and eventually a brevet brigadier general.

Brig. Gen. James A. Garfield, Rosecrans' chief of staff. (LC)

Diorama in Chickamauga Battlefield Visitor Center showing action as Thomas held on Snodgrass Hill, September 20, 1863.

Whether the fault was initially that of the Troy, N.Y. volunteer, Kellogg, or the Ohio Lieutenant Colonel Von Schraeder, the message violently upset the Federal commander, Rosecrans.

One of Garfield's contemporaries and biographers, John Clark Ridpath, gives a picture of the conditions at Rosecrans' headquarters: "The information received at Widow Glenn's up to ten o'clock on the 20th showed that the troops, though wearied, were holding their own. Up to this time General Garfield, appreciating each emergency as it occurred, had directed every movement, and written every order during the battle. Not a blunder had occurred. His clear, unmistakable English had not a doubtful phrase or a misplaced comma. Every officer had understood and executed just what was expected of him. The fury of the storm had so far spent itself in vain."

Thus it was when the aide Kellogg galloped up and informed Rosecrans that there was a hole in his center.

ROSECRANS DICTATES CONFUSING ORDER

Here was the crisis of the battle. All of the resolute fighting being done on the left of the line by Thomas,

who was holding off the piecemeal attacks of Bishop Polk, was as nothing compared with the events of this fleeting instant inside the little log cabin where Rosecrans had paced nervously back and forth, issuing orders, trying to follow by ear the battle he could not see because of the forests. When he heard Kellogg's reports, Rosecrans turned to his staff. Garfield was not on hand at the moment. According to his admiring biographer, if Garfield had been there and if Rosecrans had spoken to him, the order which was about to be issued would never have been written down, because Garfield had been keeping a careful check on the location of each division, and he knew that Brannan was still between Reynolds and Wood, and that there was no gap in the line.

Brannan, it will be recalled, had been on the far left of the line when the battle opened. Later, after helping to repulse Stewart in the center, he had fitted his division into the heavy woods, along the line of a little trail called the Poe Road. At Rosecrans' council of war held on the night of the 19th, an agreement had been reached whereby Brannan would be returned to Thomas if required again on the left. This was the reason why Rosecrans was uncertain as to just where Brannan was at the moment.

Instead of dealing with Garfield, Rosecrans called to his aide, Major Frank S. Bond, and told him to write an order directing Wood to close the gap instantly by moving to the left. This apparently innocent, yet history-making dispatch, said: "Headquarters Department of Cumberland. September 20 — 10:45 a.m. Brigadier General Wood, Commanding Division: The general commanding directs you to close up on Reynolds as fast as possible, and support him. Respectfully, etc. Frank S. Bond, Major and Aide-de-camp."

That was all. But it was the determining factor in a great battle — one of the most desperately fought battles of American history.

AS this was the key situation in one of the most ghastly battles of the war, the order requires further examination. There is the customary difference in details, but there appears fairly general agreement that the order issued, as a result of the false intelligence brought by Captain Kellogg, was worded by Rosecrans himself and taken down by Major Bond as dictated. When he had the order in writing, Rosecrans rode to where Crittenden was mounted with his staff behind the army's right, and gave the order to Assistant Adjutant General Lyne Starling, chief of staff of Crittenden's XXI Army Corps. This account, which was testified to by Starling, partially absolves Rosecrans of the charge that he issued the order to General Wood directly, and not through corps channels, though Crittenden in person did not seem to know the details of it.

ABOVE: Bloody Pond, nameless cattle pond on a backwoods farm until the battle. ("Pennsylvania at Chickamauga and Chattanooga")

BELOW: The Snodgrass house (taken about 1890). This is how it looked in 1863 when Thomas made it famous with his stubborn defense.

Starling said he hesitated when he had the order, not understanding the need for Wood to support Reynolds. There was no firing and the fighting had abated. But Garfield, who called out to him, according to his version, said the object was that Wood should occupy the vacancy made by the removal of Brannan's division, which had been ordered to the left of Thomas.

Starling rode to Wood, gave him the order, and told him the object of it. Wood stated at once that Brannan was in position and that there was no vacancy between him and Reynolds. Starling said he then told Wood "there was no order because there was no object for it." He turned, rode at once to Rosecrans, told the commanding general what Wood had said about there being no gap, and added the information that Wood "had a nice little breastwork in his front and ought not to be moved." He explained further to Rosecrans that the enemy was at the very moment in the act of attacking Wood's line and even while he was there, had driven in Wood's pickets.

IF the account of Starling is correct (it was given at the Crittenden court of inquiry and may have been unconsciously protective of his corps commander, Crittenden, though the chief of staff is not open to any charge of deliberate distortion), the responsibility and blame rests on the army commander Rosecrans. He neither countermanded the order nor rode to Wood's or Brannan's positions to ascertain personally the true conditions. The time was brief but he was only a few minutes away, probably not three minutes at a gallop. Still, Wood obeyed the order with alacrity, little knowing that his scrupulous execution of a written order would bring a storm of wrath down on his head.

Garfield's customary practice was to write an order as he thought it should be issued, then submit it to Rosecrans for approval or alteration. When, in this instance, Rosecrans took over the composition of the order himself, he left the wording vague. The meaning was subject to interpretation. But there was no escape clause, allowing the division commander to exercise his own judgment if circumstances differed. On the face of the order, the only course open to Wood was immediate compliance. That was emphatically the case in view of the fact that he had been severely, even rudely, censored, in the presence of his subordinates earlier in the morning, when Rosecrans felt he had not moved his division with wonted alacrity. Wood was supposed to replace Negley's division, which was to reinforce Thomas. When Negley was slow, Wood was also slow. Rosecrans placed the chief blame on Wood, denounced his "damnable negligence," loosened a torrent of ex-

pletives, as he could do so well when excited. Wood merely saluted and marched immediately. He could scarcely be expected to hesitate over execution of an order an hour or so later.

Particularly was that the case when the order carried the words, "as fast as possible."

WOOD'S SOLDIERLY OBEDIENCE

Wood's division consisted of but two brigades on the battlefield, both stanch and tested and commanded by officers of high merit. They were Colonel Charles G. Harker of the West Point class of 1858, who would be heard of later in the battle and would die in the attack on Kennesaw Mountain the next year; and Colonel George P. Buell, who would have later distinctions including a brevet for gallant service on Missionary Ridge. Wood's other brigade, that of Brigadier General George D. Wagner, had been left behind to garrison Chattanooga. This was one of the divisions which two months later would spearhead the attack and be one of the first, some say the first, to reach the summit of Missionary Ridge, and might therefore be accounted the division which more than any other, made Grant a lieutenant general and, in turn, President.

When Wood issued his orders he gained the customarily prompt response from his brigade commanders and in ten minutes after the departure of Starling the brigades were on the march to the left rear. Harker, who was on the left, moved first, instantly responsive, though, as he said, "we well knew the enemy was in our front ready to take advantage of any false step that we might make." He understood that McCook's corps, which was on Wood's immediate right, was ready to fill the gap caused by the departure of Wood. He marched to the left rear in search of Reynolds, but found Van Cleve's division gone and Brannan being broken, and looked about for the place where he could be of the greatest service. This was happily on what has since been known as "Harker's Hill," because of the notable use he made of it.

Buell followed Harker to the left and rear but was scarcely in motion — he had marched the distance of a brigade front — "when the shock came like an avalanche on my right flank." He was not allowed time to clear his brigade and keep pace with Harker. All about him was near chaos. As he watched, the entire right wing of the army and a part of the center gave way. "My own little brigade," he reported, "seemed as if it were swept from the field. The greater portion of my brigade was cut off from me and driven to the rear."

Down through the decades Wood had been condemned by one school and defended by another because he obeyed the order. He has been accused of vindictiveness, a desire to avenge himself because of Rosecrans' censure of him earlier. He has been charged with stupidity, and with near criminality. But if there was an error, it was in the *order* and not in Wood's *response*. He did what any general ought to do on the battlefield. He obeyed.

Now, instead of the supposed gap reported by Captain Kellogg, an actual gap was created between the divisions of Brannan and Jefferson C. Davis. Wood's departure left a hole in the line a quarter of a mile wide.

LONGSTREET'S BREAKTHROUGH

Gaps have occurred in the lines on other battlefields and not been consequential, but in this instance there was a striking coincidence. At this very instant, at 11 a.m., Longstreet was beginning his massed attack against the Federal right center. Into the hole left by the departure of Wood he poured the divisions of Bushrod Johnson, Joseph B. Kershaw and McIver Law, supported on the right by Alexander P. Stewart and on the left by Thomas C. Hindman. As a general reserve he had the splendid division of William P. Preston, one of whose brigades was commanded by the brilliant young New Yorker, Archibald Gracie. Gracie, like Bushrod Johnson and a good many other officers of Northern birth, was fighting on the Southern side, as Thomas, the Virginian, was in major command of the Union fighting line.

Bushrod Johnson's attack was one of the most spectacular of the Civil War. He cut through Rosecrans' army with the ease of a razor severing a jugular vein. He cut off the Federal army commander from his main body north on the LaFayette Road. He advanced a mile through the center of the Federal position, scattering the fragments of Rosecrans' broken wing to the left and right. The divisions of Sheridan and Jefferson C. Davis collapsed and dashed headlong from the field. They were followed by the larger part of the divisions of Van Cleve and Negley. The right wing disintegrated and the efforts of officers to check the departure of the better part of four divisions was altogether futile. "We'll see you on the other side of the Ohio," some of the fleeing soldiers shouted.

D. H. Hill described the breakthrough and advance of Bushrod Johnson's three brigades: "On they rushed, shouting, yelling, running over batteries, capturing trains, taking prisoners, seizing the headquarters of the Federal commander, at the Widow Glenn's [this may have been the location of his staff; Rosecrans

384

had left the Glenn house], until they found themselves facing the new Federal line on Snodgrass Hill."

WILLIAM M. OWEN of the Washington Artillery of New Orleans, who left such a splendid account of that extraordinary command's activities on many fields, and who was here attached to Preston's division, gave his version of the breakthrough: "Longstreet discovers, with his soldier's eye, a gap in their already confused lines and . . . short and bloody is

the work. We move steadily forward, no halting. The men rush over the hastily constructed breastworks of logs and rails of the foe, with the old-time familiar rebel yell, and, wheeling to the right, the column sweeps the enemy before it, and pushes along the Chattanooga road toward Missionary Ridge in pursuit. It is glorious!"

All the while Bragg did not seem to understand what was happening. Longstreet's attack in depth was a tactical masterpiece, comparable to Winfield Scott Hancock's massed attack with the Federal II Corps at Spotsylvania. But Bragg made no effort to assist Longstreet by ordering a fresh attack with his right. At 2:45 Longstreet said, "They have fought their last man and *he* is running." That might seem to be the situation in his front, but Longstreet did not take into consideration the character of either Bragg or George H. Thomas.

THOMAS RALLIES THE FRAGMENTS

The most stubborn phase of the battle was still to be fought. Thomas collected the remnants of the army's right wing on Snodgrass Hill where he was assisted by the timely arrival of Granger and Steedman with the Reserve Corps, small but resolute, and he held against the triumphant Confederates until he could withdraw under cover of darkness.

Longstreet hammered at Snodgrass Hill through the remainder of the afternoon. While he made occasional inroads to the crest, he was unable to break the stalwart defense, which earned for Thomas the title of the "Rock of Chickamauga." Buell's men, like Harker's, who composed Wood's division, were among the numerous heroic groups of the right wing who tarried to assist Thomas. Famous among the units of Wood's division was Colonel Emerson Opdycke's 125th Ohio, termed the "Tiger Regiment" after the fight on Snodgrass Hill. Opdycke gained later fame in larger commands fighting at Franklin and Nashville under Thomas, but is perhaps best remembered as the commander of "Opdycke's Tigers" at Chickamauga.

Rosecrans, Crittenden, McCook, and Garfield were swept from the field along with their retreating men, as were division commanders Sheridan, Jefferson C. Davis, Negley, and Van Cleve. Garfield returned later in the day with unnecessary orders for Thomas to hold and retire at nightfall. Thomas' retreat was hazardous, but the Confederate army was near exhaustion and he conducted it carefully. Polk's wing remained largely idle.

FOR the Confederates, a second crisis came after the battle had been won. The reluctant Bragg had found any number of reasons why he should not pursue Rosecrans, at a time when pursuit might have saved the Confederacy in the late afternoon of its power. Nearly everyone in the army except Bragg favored quick pursuit. Finally, by the next morning, Bragg also had been won to the obviously correct plan of crossing the Tennessee River above Chattanooga and interposing his triumphant army between Rosecrans in Chattanooga and Burnside in Knoxville. It is clear that both Rosecrans and Burnside would have been compelled to withdraw, unless Burnside, by chance, might have been captured.

Forrest, on Lookout Mountain where he had a good view of the Chattanooga area, pleaded with Bragg through Polk that "every hour is worth ten thousand men." But Bragg had been concerned over his appalling loss of horses in this in-the-woods fighting. From his vantage point Forrest wrote a message

General George Thomas at Chickamauga. Scene is set against a background of Tennessee hills, where battle smoke can be seen. General Gordon Granger, commanding a reserve corps of the Army of the Cumberland, occupied a position several miles from the battlefield awaiting orders. Finally, growing impatient, he said to a staff officer: "I am going to Thomas, orders or no orders," and advanced his troops toward the sound of firing. He is here pictured in the painting by Henry A. Ogden, at the moment of his arrival, shaking Thomas' hand.

to General Polk, saying the Federal trains were moving around the end of Lookout Mountain. Federal prisoners reported that two pontoons had been thrown across the river for the purpose of retreating.

This was the message which, in the opinion of Longstreet, sealed the fate of the Confederacy. Forrest cannot be blamed — he reported what he saw. But Bragg thought Chattanooga was being vacated. Instead of marching around the city, crossing upstream and threatening Rosecrans' communications and line of retreat, he advanced against Chattanooga, found Rosecrans entrenched, and began a protracted siege. The result was his ultimate defeat on Lookout Mountain and Missionary Ridge, by the host of Federal soldiers rushed against him from all directions. His delay gave the Federal armies time to concentrate and never again were they, as at Chickamauga, caught off guard.

CAUSES OF THE DEFEAT

Why did the North lose this battle, which may have prolonged the life of the Confederacy more than a year? The first blame must be lodged against Burnside, who failed to move down from Knoxville, as ordered, to join Rosecrans and shield his left flank, the flank Bragg was trying to turn to reach Chattanooga.

A second cause was the failure of the Federal War Department to send help from Grant's army, units of which were either idle at this period after the capture of Vicksburg, or were being dispersed. The surrender of Vicksburg released Joseph E. Johnston's army, which had been watching ineffectually at Jackson, Mississippi. Some of the best Confederate units in the West, including Breckinridge's division, were returned to Bragg, without Rosecrans receiving any compensating units from Grant. Sherman was idle with his corps in Mississippi and could well have been employed in Tennessee and North Georgia.

Burnside ranked Rosecrans. He has been excused on the ground that he did not want to join the Army of the Cumberland and supersede its commander. But Burnside could have waived the command, by direction of the War Department. A similar situation occurred when Meade sent Hancock to take command at Gettysburg after the death of Reynolds on the first day, though Howard ranked him. Meade issued orders which allowed Hancock the top command, and so the War Department might have done in this instance.

Thus, while Bragg was heavily reinforced, Rosecrans had to fight with substantially the same army he had commanded at Stone's River.

THE third major cause of the defeat was Rosecrans' poor tactical performance. This resulted in part because the battle was fought in the woods and, lacking communications, he lost control. His center and right were in a continual state of flux with units going to help Thomas. Against his weakened right center Longstreet massed his brigades for an attack in depth. Longstreet struck a weak spot and cut through the wide gap with ease, but had the gap not existed, is there not reason to believe that Longstreet could have overpowered McCook's weaker corps?

Rosecrans' failure resulted mainly from lack of an adequate reserve. Granger's corps, which finally gave Thomas some relief on Snodgrass Hill, was inadequate, and had another mission — guarding the Rossville gap — besides that of acting as a maneuverable unit on the battlefield. Rosecrans showed capabilities, often brilliance, in his other battles. In the broader field of strategy he had few equals. His supreme error was in leaving the field while Thomas, with whom he could have gained contact and joined by a circuitous ride, remained. He can be termed "the general of the one mistake." But it was a mistake sufficient to allow his superiors, with whom one of his candid and fiery temperament had not been popular, to relegate him to a quiet sector.

THE BATTLE had a further bearing on the fate of the Confederacy because of the wounding of General Hood, whose leg was amputated on the night of the 20th by surgeons behind the lines. The stump was very short and the instance was one of the few in the war where a man lived with a lower member severed so near to the trunk.

Hood already had been grievously wounded at Gettysburg in an arm that was left near palsied and useless. Many wounded Civil War soldiers knew that when an arm or leg was amputated it continued to hurt. This writer has heard a veteran's account of an instance where a soldier insisted on having his leg dug up and packed with cotton between the toes before being reinterred. Some latter day doctors have diagnosed this pain as the result of fraying of the nerve ends, causing them to send false messages.

Hood suffered severe pain from his two wounds and for it, according to information that has been handed down, constantly took a laudanum derivative, believed by some who have studied his case to have been in sufficient quantity to establish a sort of euphoria, or unrealistic sense of well-being. That is a possible explanation for his belief that he could, in the closing stages of the war, take an army of 30,000 to 35,000 men, march with it to the Ohio, and draw Sherman back from Georgia. The shattering of his army by Thomas at Nashville was perhaps the supreme Confederate defeat of the war, and in different respects it was an outgrowth of Chickamauga.

Finally, in examining the causes of the Federal defeat, attention must be given to coincidence — the play of chance. Longstreet might have crushed Rosecrans' right wing in any event, but the realities are that he did it by taking advantage of the erroneous movement of Wood's division, a movement resulting from a messenger conveying misinformation to the commanding general, and that general's impulsive acceptance of it without making a personal reconnaissance, though he was close at hand.

Nor can any analysis neglect the over-all culpability of the Federal War Department for its failure to give Rosecrans a sufficient warning that Longstreet's corps was leaving Lee's army.

The Men Still Loved "Old Rosey"

Neither Thomas, nor Longstreet, nor Rosecrans, nor Bushrod Johnson have monuments on the battlefield. Perhaps Longstreet and Thomas do not need them, for anyone analyzing the battle will know of their achievements more readily from the written word than from stone. Bushrod Johnson rests in an obscure grave in a village cemetery in southern Illinois, where he went to do farming and grace an enemy countryside with his scholarship, mainly by giving lessons and lending books to farm lads he taught without pay. His is a delightful story that will some day be written more fully, for it has intrigued numerous Civil War buffs.

Rosecrans, the only commander of a major Federal army who has never been given a monument anywhere, lived in the hearts of his soldiers. He went to Congress from California, served as chairman of the House Military Affairs Committee, acquired wealth through his metallurgical enterprises, and had his moment of glory when he returned to the Chickamauga battlefield for the great reunion of blue and gray September 19 and 20, 1889. The barbecue feast was spread over ten acres, on thirty tables each 250 feet long, which on the two sides made 15,000 feet, close to three miles of seating room.

John B. Gordon, governor of Georgia, represented the veterans in gray. He and Rosecrans led the military procession, mounted on high-spirited steeds, with the 4th U.S. Infantry band playing "Dixie." Then they were lifted to a table top, where they spoke. Ten thousand men crowded around "Old Rosey" to take his hand. "Old veterans cried like infants," reported a scribe.

Then, at the final moment, the Rosecrans burial services in 1898, the most prominent personage on the stand was the broken old Georgian, Longstreet, shattered by his wound taken in The Wilderness and by the decades of abuse heaped on him by a coterie of enemies as the man who had lost the Battle of Gettysburg. More than any other, he was responsible for Rosecrans' defeat and relegation to military obscurity, yet was the chief mourner at the final parting.

CHATTANOOGA

Text by Glenn Tucker
Designed by Frederic Ray

Wellington said nothing is so melancholy as a battle won except a battle lost.

So it was after Chickamauga when the Confederate Army of Tennessee, triumphant and bloody, seethed with discord over the lethargy and ineptitude of General Braxton Bragg, its commander.

Gloom, fear, and near despair gripped its adversary, the Army of the Cumberland, as it retreated forlornly into Rossville and on through the mountain gap to Chattanooga, after the disorderly flight of one of its wings, along with its commanding general and two corps commanders, from a field long stubbornly contested, then lost in a twinkling by a chance mistake.

An army without food is better for a time than an army without heart, but Major General William Starke Rosecrans' beleaguered force of upwards of 40,000 exhausted survivors had neither. Morale was shattered; the supply lines were cut.

Only the tardiness of Bragg's pursuit spared the Union army. Spurred on by "Old War Horse" Longstreet, whose left wing had delivered the *coup de main* to the two Federal corps of Major Generals Alexander Mc-

Cook and Thomas L. Crittenden, and implored by the call of the discerning cavalryman, Nathan Bedford Forrest, that "every hour is worth ten thousand men," and importuned even by the Bishop-Lieutenant General Leonidas Polk, whose procrastination on the field had blunted Bragg's attack and possibly dulled his victory, the Confederate commander had buried his dead, counted his surviving artillery horses, taken counsel with his overabundant conservatism, weighed his restraints, and had finally drawn up in front of Chattanooga, having covered the twelve miles from the battlefield in what would have seemed an eon to Lee or Jackson—two and a half days!

On the day after the battle Major General George H. Thomas, who had saved the Federal army by his stubborn stand on Snodgrass Hill, laid out a fairly formidable defensive line across Rossville Gap and the Chattanooga Creek valley. Already the men were changing his nickname from the affectionate "Old Pap" to the more exalted "Old Hero."

Forrest and others believed Thomas' line could be broken or turned by the victory-stimulated Confederates,

but the test was not made. Rosecrans, instead of risking another battle on the outskirts, preferred to sustain a siege in the intrenched inner town. Though he toyed for a time with the notion of evacuating Chattanooga and retiring to Nashville (which might have involved another retreat through Kentucky and race for Louisville like Buell's the year before), he elected to hold fast and await succor. A retirement to Nashville or dash for Louisville would have left Major General Ambrose E. Burnside behind in Knoxville, ripened on the vine for Confederate plucking.

Last into Chattanooga was Cruft's brigade of Palmer's division, Thomas' corps, which during September 21, 1863, the day after the retreat from Chickamauga, had garrisoned the south end of Missionary Ridge. Its right rested on the road at Rossville and its left reached to the point part way up the ridge where Bragg later had his headquarters. When Bragg failed to pursue rapidly, most of the brigade was withdrawn into Chattanooga. Three companies of the 31st Indiana remained as rearguard. Finally only Company A was

left behind. The others, as they left in the darkness, shouted jocular requests to the Company A boys to "send home some souvenirs from [Belle Isle] and Libby Prisons." One sergeant said, as the tread of the last marching columns died away, "the loneliness seemed almost suffocating."

Polk's Confederates were at last coming up and all night the soft, drawling words sounded clearly from their bivouac at the foot of the ridge, while the Southern artillery rattled over the stones, and the heavy tramp of oncoming regiments could be heard from the roads leading from the battlefield. The dull gray of the new autumn day shone at length and with it came a courier with orders for the little company, the last fifty men of Rosecrans' battered army, to retire behind the Federal cavalry videttes three miles south of Chattanooga.

The company, after keeping guard all night, snatched an hour of sleep, then marched, and soon had rejoined thousands of bluecoats digging with spades a half circle of works reaching from the riverbank south to high ground north of the town.

Later that day (evening of September 23), a puff of smoke and a bursting shell gave notice that Polk's corps had reached the vacated crest of Missionary Ridge, while a similar announcement fell short from the top of Lookout Mountain. The siege of Chattanooga, the only investment suffered by a large Northern army during the war (Nashville a year later hardly rates as a siege), and in many respects one of the most peculiar affairs of American history, had begun.

Whether held by a Northern or Southern army, Chattanooga had been regarded as a citadel. It is a natural passageway between North and South. The Tennessee River flows down from Knoxville apparently intent on a course through Georgia, but the tossup of mountains around Chattanooga deflects it abruptly. Making almost an about-face—a sweep spectacular when seen from the peaks—it moves abreast its earlier channel, now churning and tossing northward.

Inside its graceful bend is a mile-wide projection, or virtual isthmus, called Moccasin Point. Here, where the river is so rudely deflected from the Georgia border, it manifests its discomfort by casting aside its former serene and placid surface and vexes itself with a series of what the pioneers called "boiling pots," or "sucks." They render navigation difficult until the mighty stream, comparable in beauty with the Hudson cleaving through the New York highlands, is well into Alabama, and until it is contemplating there the last long turn that directs it gently northwestward to the Ohio.

Chattanooga lay on the left or south bank, just above the coil of Moccasin Bend. The town was not an old

This wartime view of Chattanooga is from the Brady Collection in the National Archives. Lookout Mountain in the background.

The John Ross house, Rossville. Missionary Ridge on right. (NA)

Southern community like Nashville or Augusta, but had technically come into the possession of the United States only twenty-three years before the Civil War, after the ejection of the Cherokee Indians over the "Trail of Tears" in 1838.

Chattanooga is one of the Cherokee's half-anglicized words, derived from *chatta* (crow) and *nooga* (nest), but often given the loftier meaning of "eagle's" or "hawk's" nest. In days before the Revolutionary War, Spanish Roman Catholic priests from St. Augustine, Florida established a mission and school for Indians which long flourished on the ridge overlooking the "crow's nest." The religious outpost caused the height to be called Mission Ridge, later corrupted into Missionary Ridge.

The Indian towns along the nearby creeks were raided and burned by "Nolichucky Jack" Sevier, governor of the ephemeral state of Franklin, in 1793. Returning survivors of the devastation gradually assembled on the river and founded Chattanooga. John Ross, chief of the Cherokee, though only one-sixteenth Indian, built about 1800 a large log house, imposing by frontier standards, near the bold spring of clear mountain water in the pass between Lookout Mountain and the southern break of Missionary Ridge, five miles south of Chattanooga, and the second village of wigwams and huts that grew there took the name Rossville. Chattanooga, at first called Ross's Landing, had attained some importance as a trading post by 1830.

The Cherokee were removed after gold was discovered around Dahlonega, Georgia, and President Jackson had sided with the whites who had encroached on the tribe's southern Appalachian holdings. President Van Buren

sent General Winfield Scott and an army detachment to Missionary Ridge to transport the Cherokee (all except those who hid in the western North Carolina mountains) to reservations beyond the Mississippi. One of Scott's young subordinates who cast his eyes reflectively over the terrain and mused about the unsavory business at hand, who was already dedicating his career to the harassment of his superiors and to inflexible obedience to regulations down to the last punctuation mark, was a lieutenant from North Carolina fresh from the West Point class of 1837, Braxton Bragg.

By Civil War days Chattanooga had grown to be a town of 2,545 citizens with mixed sentiments about secession. The most import structure was the Crutch-field House, rambling hostelry of three stores at Ninth and Broad Streets, conducted by Tom and William Crutchfield, both strong Unionists. (William, during the war, served as a Union scout with an unofficial major's ranking and after the war was a Congress-man from the district.) Possession of the Crutchfield House, the town's tallest building, signified possession of Chattanooga. The commanding general usually used the hotel as his headquarters, and the flag that flew above it would be seen from the surrounding heights.

When war came, the Stars and Bars floated atop Crutchfield's hotel, the town became a Confederate military depot, and the *Daily Rebel* told the news of Lee and Jackson in Virginia. At length, on September 9, 1863, Rosecrans arrived with his Federal army and his maneuvering skill that forced Bragg to evacuate the stronghold without a battle, until the bloody encounter occurred when the two armies stumbled into each other in the woods twelve miles south along Chickamauga Creek. Then the badly worsted Rosecrans came back to the town as a possible sanctuary.

One of the first acts of the beleaguered Union army was to tear down nearly all of the wooden houses. The town lay in valleys and on low hills, one being Cameron Hill, known also as Bell Mountain, in the western portion. There some large residences offered a degree of elegance. But lumber was scarce and the army engineers required it urgently for the bastions and lunettes being erected by Brigadier General St. Clair Morton, chief of engineers.

Within two weeks he had so mercilessly transformed a community of smiling homes and gardens into a forbidding gray fortress that another officer said of him: "If Morton needed earth for a fort, the fact that it was a gold mine would make no difference. He would only say, 'Gold dust will resist artillery—it will do.'" Homes were transformed into blockhouses. As one of the correspondents described it: "Black bastions sprung up in former vineyards; rifle pits were run through graveyards; and soon a long line of works stretched from the river above to the river below the city, bending crescent-like around it, as if it were a huge bow of iron, and rendering it impregnable. For a fortnight the whole army worked on the fortifications, and it became literally a walled city."

Inside the citadel, the men tore down barns, sheds, and fences, along with the houses, and with the boards erected huts along orderly company streets. They used their shelter halves for roofs, which led to the observation that the town was not unlike the village of oldtime Indian days, the tented roofs being similar to wigwams. Day by day the ring of the ax rose to the Confederates on the nearby heights, as the Federal army cut, hewed, drove, and pounded, trying to make itself secure from the long-range enemy fire from Lookout Mountain and comfortable for the oncoming winter.

While he was entrenching in Chattanooga Rosecrans at the beginning made the inexcusable mistake of abandoning Lookout Mountain, which commanded the supply route from the river and railroad at Bridgeport and Stevenson to Chattanooga. As Bragg came up he seized eagerly the looming eminence, assigned Longstreet's corps to garrison it and guard Lookout Valley beyond it, and finally added the division of Major Gen-

"View of Chattanooga and Moccasin Point from the side of Lookout Mountain." This engraving from a photograph appears in B&L.

eral Carter L. Stevenson that had been part of Pemberton's army in Vicksburg, and two brigades of Cheatham's division. These last two brigades were the only ones left behind when the spirited fighting for the possession of Lookout developed.

The Confederate encirclement was not complete but was effective. The great Union army that a week earlier had threatened to take Atlanta and split the Deep South asunder, now needed food and the only means left open to supply it was by a wagon route to the north, over the worst of roads, across Walden's Ridge, a rugged spur of the Cumberland Mountains, thence via the Sequatchie Valley to the army base at Bridgeport and Stevenson, where the rails from Nashville met the river. By yielding Lookout Mountain Rosecrans had allowed Bragg to block the road and water route around Moccasin; all provisions had to be hauled over the miserable land route of sixty miles. The distance was such that the forage mules could haul only about what they required for strength to make the journey.

The army went immediately on short rations. Food conditions could not have been much worse, if as bad, at this stage of the war, in Florence, Salisbury, or Libby

Prisons. As the days passed, famine became a more pressing enemy than Bragg's army, and Bragg seemed content to employ it as his front line ally. The wagon trains lumbered heavily over the Cumberlands back and forth to Stevenson, along a road where the carcasses of dead mules gave grisly evidence that famine was surely winning. Groups of mules might be seen hovering about a small pond where, after drinking, they would die. Ten thousand horses and mules perished of starvation. The army was immobilized. Artillery horses, least needed, were fed less and died first. The batteries were sunk in the mud, stationary except for hauling by manpower.

Horses gnawed their hitching posts, their wagon spokes; some, the tails of other horses. A correspondent found that his mount's only feed was a pine board fence. Too exhausted to stray from it, though unhaltered, the animal finally stretched out and died. Guards had to be posted to keep the soldiers from stealing the thin fare rationed to the most urgently needed draft horses—those engaged in hauling food. The landscape, rolling and resplendent before the armies came, turned bleak and forbidding. Every shrub and blade of grass was devoured.

The men fared slightly better than the mules and horses. By the third week they were restricted to one-quarter rations. The only meat was bacon middling, with little or no lean, the size of three fingers. It was eaten with a four-inch square of hard bread called a "Lincoln Platform," and washed down with thin coffee. Wrote a correspondent: "I have often seen hundreds of soldiers following behind the wagon trains which had just arrived, picking out of the mud the crumbs of bread, coffee, rice, which were wasted from the boxes and sacks by the rattling of the wagons over the stones."

Citizens who remained in the town were even greater sufferers, huddled together in crowded huts under conditions described as worse than any tenement section of New York City. Finally the army fare was reduced to quarter rations for breakfast only. Roasted acorns became a delicacy. Men waited around the feed troughs to catch grains of corn that fell. Wood was scarce. The army shivered in the biting blasts of an early winter.

Bragg sent Wheeler with two cavalry divisions, Wharton's and Martin's, to break the sixty-mile "cracker-box line" by dashing up the Sequatchie Valley to a Federal depot at Anderson's Cross Roads. The raid at the outset was highly effective. He captured or killed horses and mules, destroyed 300 wagons, and burned a large quantity of supplies destined for the starving Federal garrison. Bragg really needed Forrest, who had a better touch in battle, but Forrest had sworn never to serve under Wheeler after they had lost heavily in a joint attack on Fort Henry, against which Forrest had advised; nor would he serve under Bragg either, after Chickamauga.

After his initial success Wheeler sustained a series of sharp defeats by three Federal cavalry detachments under McCook, Mitchell, and Crook, and was fortunate to get back across the Tennessee River with a portion of his command, after he lost 800 mules he had captured. But his destruction of the wagons, followed by a season of heavy rains, was little short of a disaster to the Federal army.

Though famine was Bragg's strongest ally, time was his weakest; and time was running out. Events that were to control the destiny of the half-starved Federal army began to unfold back at the Soldiers' Home in Washington, when Secretary of War Stanton's messenger abruptly awakened President Lincoln with the disheartening news that Rosecrans, from whom so much was hoped, had been defeated and driven back into Chattanooga. Much as he had done when Stonewall Jackson was threatening in the Shenandoah Valley in the spring of 1862, Lincoln began personally the designation and dispatch of succoring forces that could most readily converge on the beleaguered town.

The first decision was to reinforce Rosecrans with two corps from the Army of the Potomac. Major Generals Oliver O. Howard's and Henry W. Slocum's, the XI and XII, were chosen and placed under the command

The Chattanooga Campaign. Dragging artillery over the mountains in mud and rain. ("Harper's Hist. of Great Rebellion")

of Major General Joseph Hooker. Hooker's appointment to head the relief party caused immediate difficulty, because Slocum, one of the most effective of the Federal corps commanders, had been an outspoken critic of Hooker's conduct at Chancellorsville five months before. He promptly resigned, saying it would be "degrading in me to accept any position under him."

Lincoln, adept at adjusting personal relationships, declined to accept the resignation and arranged that Slocum with one division could hold the railroads open behind the lines and not act directly under Hooker's orders. Thus only one of Slocum's divisions participated in the Chattanooga fighting. Hooker's reinforcement, which reached Nashville in the remarkably short time of seven days, consisted of two of Howard's divisions under Adolph Steinwehr and Carl Schurz, and the single XII Corps division under John W. Geary, who had stubbornly defended Culp's Hill at Gettysburg.

As in the case of Jackson in the Shenandoah Valley, Lincoln wanted sufficient troops to counter the unexpectedly triumphant Bragg. He had Halleck telegraph to Grant to send all available troops to Memphis, thence east via the Memphis & Charleston Railroad to cooperate with Rosecrans. Grant, in turn, ordered Sherman in Mississippi to load the troops on transports—all except part of the XVII Corps under McPherson—and steam up the Mississippi River. Sherman, in fact, already was moving in response to an earlier call sent before the Battle of Chickamauga was fought. Grant then was ordered to meet "an officer of the War Department" in Louisville, but as his train was pulling out of the station at Indianapolis it was stopped by a messenger saying Secretary of War Stanton was at hand, and Grant tarried to meet him.

Stanton had a habit, amounting almost to a tic, of constantly wiping his eyeglasses with his handkerchief; but in the opinion of some of his subordinates, such as McClellan and Rosecrans, though he might clean his glasses he never could quite clear away the mist that obscured his thinking. Grant would find him easier to work with than did some of the others.

These transactions were requiring time while the Army of the Cumberland starved behind its trenches. Grant rode to Louisville with Stanton, heard a lengthy review of the military situation on all fronts, including the disappointments over some of the campaigns. Then Stanton divulged the results of the Cabinet meeting that had pondered the problem of extricating the Army of the Cumberland from impending disaster.

Left to Right: Major General George H. Thomas (LC), Major General Oliver O. Howard (LC), Major General George Crook (KA) Major General Gordon Granger (LC).

Lincoln's decision, after the Cabinet members had talked, was to combine the three western armies of the Cumberland, the Tennessee, and the Ohio, under a single commander, Grant, still on crutches thanks to a fall from his horse.

The Cabinet thought that Rosecrans, brilliant but erratic, would have to go. Stanton detested him almost from the beginning, mainly because he treated the Secretary of War as an overly officious clerk, and a harassing one at that. The campaign that had been waged against Rosecrans by the highly articulate Assistant Secretary of War Charles A. Dana, who remained with the army and sent Stanton all the gossip, had been effective. Dana's reports were read aloud at the Cabinet meeting.

The soul of the Army of the Cumberland was in the ponderous form of the clear thinking and decisive but ordinarily self-effacing George H. Thomas. His men, whether he had led a division, a corps, or a separate army, had never yet acknowledged and never would know defeat. From Mill Springs at the beginning to Nashville at the end he was modest and triumphant. Now the "Old Hero," wearing about the only laurels that came to the high Union command from Chickamauga, was suddenly but inevitably and reluctantly about to be catapulted into the leadership of the military wreck that was once the glorious Army of the Cumberland.

Although the Cabinet favored the ouster of Rosecrans, Lincoln was reluctant to see him go. There were numerous

Left to Right: Brigadier General John W. Geary (LC), Major General William B. Hazen (NA), Brigadier General Montgomery C. Meigs (LC), Major General William F. ("Baldy") Smith (NA).

points in his favor that balanced off his ignominious departure from the field at Chickamauga. Finally Lincoln compromised. He left the decision to Grant. He had the War Department issue two orders, one relieving Rosecrans, the other continuing him in command, and gave Grant, the newly appointed commander of the Western armies, the privilege of tearing up one and issuing the other. Grant was not fond of either general but preferred Thomas. He tore up the Rosecrans order and on October 19 forwarded the other to Thomas. Rosecrans left Chattanooga quietly and becomingly, without giving notice to the men, most of whom idolized him even after he had lost at Chickamauga.

Grant upon assuming command received what he regarded as a suggestion from Dana that Rosecrans was considering evacuating Chattanooga. From Louisville he telegraphed Thomas to hold the town at all hazards. Thomas, who rarely made promises, gave assurance by ending his reply with the resolute words: "I will hold the town till we starve."

Back in Virginia General Lee was disproving the frequent expression of latter day recorders that he was concerned only with his own state and did not envision the war on a national scale. When informed of Bragg's triumph at Chickamauga he saw at once that time was of the essence. To Longstreet he dispatched his warmest compliments. To President Davis he expressed hope that the victory would be followed up; that Bragg would operate against the enemy's rear, push the advantage gained, open East Tennessee, and bring Major General Sam Jones, who commanded in southwest Virginia, into the Tennessee operations.

"No time ought now to be lost or wasted," Lee wrote. "Everything should be done that can be done at once." To Longstreet: "Finish the work before you, my dear general, and return to me. I want you badly and you cannot get back too soon."

Meade had heard in early September of Longstreet's departure from Virginia to reinforce Bragg in north Georgia. Sensing an opportunity, he began to menace Lee's left. The VI Corps troops who had been sent to quell the New York draft rioters were returning to the Army of the Potomac. Lee heard trainload after trainload of these regiments arriving to strengthen Meade, then learned after Chickamauga that Meade had detached the bulk of two veteran corps, the XI and XII, to hasten as succor to the penned-up Union army in Chattanooga.

Lee issued orders to Jones to occupy Knoxville, which Burnside had vacated after Chickamauga in order to move belatedly toward Rosecrans and give him some relief. Jones marched but did not reach Knoxville in time. Then Lee struck out on an offensive that took him past Bristoe Station and on to the old lines at Centreville. This was mainly a demonstration in favor of Bragg. His aggressive movement, the first since his return from

General Ulysses S. Grant led the besieged Union forces to victory at Chattanooga. ("Photographic History of the Civil War")

Then-Major General William Tecumseh Sherman was stopped at Tunnel Hill by the stout defense of Cleburne's men. (From LC)

397

"Longstreet reporting at Bragg's headquarters," by A. R. Waud.

Gettysburg, was designed to block any further reinforcements for Rosecrans and Burnside, and to develop any weaknesses resulting from Meade's dispatch of the two corps. One of these, Slocum's XII, had a splendid record in the Union army, culminating in its resolute defense of Culp's Hill at Gettysburg, which was as responsible as any other factor for Meade's repulse of the Southern invasion.

In front of Chattanooga, the Army of Tennessee still muttered rebelliously against Bragg, even more flagrantly than it had when that commander failed to press his prospects after the drawn battle of Stone's River.

While several generals criticised Bragg and signed a petition to have him replaced, the exasperating friction remaining after his removal of Polk was between the commanding general and Lee's "Old War Horse." Reports of their controversy spread through the ranks. It was evident to all from the incident described by one of the officers present at the first stormy session after Chickamauga. One of his men called him over to within hearing range. A group of high generals was assembled, among whom were Longstreet and Major General John C. Breckinridge towering on their mounts above the others. Bragg was afoot. Longstreet and Bragg were talking spiritedly and Longstreet's words were clearly audible.

Bragg held his poise, spoke slowly, in low tones, though Longstreet assailed him angrily. "General," said Longstreet, "the army should have been in motion at dawn today." Bragg's reply was muffled and Longstreet continued: "Yes, sir, but all great captains follow up a victory." The conversation apparently grew more heated for Longstreet concluded: "Yes, sir, you rank me, but you cannot cashier me."

Longstreet worked off his anger in a letter to Secretary

of War Seddon, saying Bragg had done only one thing right—ordering the attack on September 20—but everything else had been wrong. "I am convinced," he wrote, "that nothing but the hand of God can save us . . . as long as we have our present commander." Then he put his finger on the crux of the whole situation: "Can't you send us General Lee? The Army in Virginia can operate defensively, while our operations here should be offensive—until we recover Tennessee at all events. We need some great mind as General Lee's (nothing more) to accomplish this."

Little consideration was given to Longstreet's suggestion—a reiteration of one he had made when he left Virginia—to transfer General Lee temporarily to Tennessee as the person who could now best gather the fruits of the Chickamauga victory. Lee rejected the proposal but his letter to Longstreet on October 26, answering three letters from Longstreet, saying that President Davis, now being on the ground, could take a broad view of the whole situation, did carry the sentence: "I will cheerfully do all in my power." Possibly Lee was not importuned strongly enough to take him, in a desperate hour, to Chattanooga and to the employment of the Army of Tennessee in an aggressive campaign of motion, instead of a siege doomed to failure if protracted.

Apart from their mutual distrust, Bragg and Longstreet were in sharp disagreement over methods. Bragg favored the investment, which he felt might lead to the capture of the entire enemy army; Longstreet still urged by-passing the Federals, operating against their rear, throwing them into retreat, then capturing or dispersing Burnside's army in Knoxville. In the discussion that nearly wrecked the army, Longstreet had the support of virtually all of Bragg's subordinate officers, as well as those from his own corps from the Army of Northern Virginia.

The balance of Longstreet's corps that had been unable to reach Chickamauga in time for the battle arrived immediately thereafter: Lafayette McLaws with the brigades of Brigadier Generals W. T. Wofford and Goode Bryan, and the two missing brigades of Hood's old division, those of G. T. Anderson and Micah Jenkins. When the army began its advance, two days after the battle, Bragg was thinking more of marching triumphantly through Chattanooga with banners aflutter than of heading again toward Kentucky and pulling the invaders after him. As the unsympathetic Longstreet stated it: "The praise of the inhabitants of a city so recently abandoned to the enemy, and a parade through its streets with bands of music and flaunting banners, were more alluring to a spirit eager for applause than was the tedious march for fruitation of our heavy labors."

While Longstreet did not foment the discord that was at the boiling point in Bragg's own Army of Tennessee, a recurrence of the near-mutiny that had agitated the

Left to Right: Lieutenant General Leonidas Polk (NA), Lieutanant General Daniel H. Hill (B&L), Major General Benjamin F. Cheatham. (LC).

officers after the criticised retreat from Stone's River, his concurrence in it and his standing in the Confederacy, gave it such elevation that Bragg was almost a pariah among his own subordinates. Meantime, Bragg's principal quarrel in the Army of Tennessee had been with his second in command, Lieutenant General Leonidas Polk, to whom he wrote two days after the battle, demanding an explanation of why he had failed to attack the Union left, as ordered, at dawn on September 20.

Polk, engaged in troop movements, failed to answer. Bragg gave him three days, prodded him, and this time got a reply he characterized as altogether unsatisfactory. Thereupon he removed Polk from his command and

sent him back to Atlanta. Similarly, he suspended Major General Thomas C. Hindman, who had contributed measurably to the triumph at Chickamauga, and sent him back to Atlanta, giving his division to the capable Brigadier General Patton Anderson.

D. H. Hill, stormy and combative, who nearly always saw the merits of his own way instead of his commander's, was relieved from corps command, replaced by Breckinridge, and the lieutenant general's commission Davis had granted him before Chickamauga was not even sent to the Senate for confirmation. Though one of the South's toughest fighters, he passed from an active combat role. William Bate of Tennessee, who won plaudits at

Left to Right: Lieutenant General James Longstreet (LC), General Braxton Bragg (LC), Lieutenant General William J. Hardee (LC).

399

Chickamauga, strengthened the army by taking command of a division. Forrest's abuse of Bragg to his face was in language which for intemperance probably was never duplicated by a subordinate to a chief. He impulsively walked out to independent command and later triumphs.

Discord was sapping Bragg's effectiveness but not his self-respect or self-confidence. His had been a lifetime of quarreling. He still enjoyed the President's support and shook off his detractors. In the case of Polk, he was undertaking to disgrace the President's old favorite of Military Academy years. The treatment of Polk, the President said, was no less than a "public calamity." He held that Bragg might arrest Polk and prefer charges but did not have the authority to proceed further and pack him off to Atlanta without a trial. Then he gave Bragg, who shared his close friendship from Buena Vista days, much gratuitous advice about his conduct. Bragg, in turn, protested that Polk's disobedience had been flagrant. "I suffer self-reproach from not having acted earlier," he told Davis, but the President pigeonholed the charges.

The army was cast into greater turmoil and shrouded in deeper gloom at this stage when the rumor went around that Polk was to be replaced by John C. Pemberton, a Pennsylvanian in Southern gray, who appeared at Chattanooga. Pemberton's recent surrender of Vicksburg had made him, whether or not justifiably, the most disliked and discredited military figure in the South. Such an appointment would have been a clear provocation for mutiny in an army already rebellious in everything except an overt act. In the end, Lieutenant General ("Old Reliable") William J. Hardee, Davis' West Point classmate, and probably with Stonewall Jackson and Longstreet a part of the triumvirate of the best corps commanders in the Confederacy's experiment in arms, was a compromise who suited everyone. He returned from his independent command in Mississippi to the army that had long known him favorably, to take command of Bragg's largest corps which was strung out for five miles along Missionary Ridge.

Colonel James Chesnut, the President's military secretary, did not overestimate the crisis in command when he telegraphed to President Davis on October 5 that his presence with the army was urgently demanded. Never had a large element of an American army mutinied since the revolt of the Pennsylvania Line under St. Clair's command in the Revolutionary War, but the closest approach undoubtedly was with the victors of sanguinary Chickamauga only two weeks after the enemy had been driven from the field. The clash of personalities sometimes resounds above the din of arms, and campaigns are lost as often by discord as by defeat.

This print is titled "The Army of the Cumberland in front of Chattanooga." The abrupt rise of Lookout Mountain dominates the skyline in this scene early in the siege. (Courtesy of Anne S. K. Brown Military Collection, Brown Univ. Library)

400

President Davis was at Bragg's headquarters by October 9, a rapid railroad journey by the circuitous route imposed by the loss of Knoxville. He had been in Chattanooga before, once to advocate secession to the Tennesseans, and it proved a day of notoriety for innkeeper William Crutchfield. After Davis spoke, Crutchfield the Unionist disputed his words and heckled him with vigor. Pistols were drawn all around and a shootout was threatened. It could have cost the South its emergent political leader had not Tom Crutchfield hurried his brother away and silenced him.

This time Davis quickly entered into one of the most peculiar councils of war ever conducted, in which he gathered the top officers of the Army of Tennessee, together with Longstreet, who stood next to Bragg in seniority, and with Bragg seated before them, demanded that they voice their opinions about their commander's generalship and qualifications to lead a great army. Longstreet was nonplussed, since as senior he would have to speak first, but he was never a man, even with General Lee, to be anything but blunt.

If Davis had a faint notion that he could still any covert denunciation of Bragg by bringing it into the open, he should not have begun with Longstreet, who, though he knew that what he said would alienate him thereafter from the Confederate President, did not hesitate when pressed. He later indicated he regarded the whole procedure improper and gave therefore at first an evasive answer, but when Davis was dissatisfied, he stated that Bragg could be of greater service elsewhere than as commander of the Army of Tennessee. Buckner, Cheatham, Cleburne, and D. H. Hill, who had not yet been dismissed, expressed the same conclusion, Hill speaking "with emphasis." One of his testy temperament would not pass over such a likely opportunity for complaint. Many thought that he had authored the round-robin letter to Davis requesting Bragg's dismissal.

Davis was not appeased. Clearly he had wanted an expression of confidence in Bragg such as he had obtained from Joseph E. Johnston after the Stone's River haggling. He had not expected the unanimous condemnation of one of his choice army commanders. On the next morning he took Longstreet for a walk, and according to Longstreet's version (the only one extant), the Old War Horse offered his resignation for the sake of harmony. Of course, it was declined. Longstreet then must have thrown cold water into the President's face by suggesting that Joseph E. Johnston, the ranking general in the West, be substituted for the nauseous Bragg. Longstreet said the thought increased the President's displeasure. The conference accomplished little more than to confirm some intra-corps transactions, the most important of which was to give Micah Jenkins command of the wounded Hood's division. When they parted Longstreet thought he detected behind the President's gracious smile, "a bitter look lurking about its margin," and felt that clouds were gathering over the headquarters of the First Corps.

Still ruffled, Davis called a second conference at Bragg's headquarters but this time talked more about operations. He asked for ideas. Some good plans were presented as substitutes for a prolonged siege. Already it was known that Grant's troops were being hastened across Mississippi and Tennessee and others were near at hand from the Army of the Potomac, all for the relief

of beleaguered Chattanooga. There was no future in delay. Longstreet favored changing the army's base to Rome, Georgia, marching out to capture Bridgeport, where the Union supply route would be cut, then crossing the Tennessee River and forcing the Union army into either a battle or full retreat. Even Bragg talked some of crossing the river and gaining the enemy's rear. Maps were laid out and scrutinized. But nothing eventuated and, according to Longstreet, Davis left the army more despondent than he found it. He took Pemberton back with him and Hardee arrived to supplant Cheatham, who had held temporary command of Polk's old corps.

Davis' visit, in truth, accomplished nothing. He supported Bragg on all counts and confirmed him in command of the army, which was probably the worst possible course. The only lasting effect of the President's visit probably came from the address he made to a part of the army on Lookout Mountain shortly before his departure. An unusual formation of one of the outcroppings ideally suited for a rostrum had long borne the name of "Pulpit Rock." This the President ascended and with his customarily happy phrases inspired the soldiers. After the Federals captured Lookout and learned of the incident, they changed the designation of "Pulpit Rock" to "Devil's Pulpit," a name that has been more enduring.

Jefferson Davis addressed Stevenson's division from Pulpit Rock on Lookout Mountain. Tripod signal in this 1864 photo erected by officers of U.S. Coast Survey. (Brady Coll., LC)

402

Davis spoke, apparently on the advice of some of the officers, to quiet the apprehension being felt in Stevenson's division, which had surrendered to Grant as a part of Pemberton's army, at Vicksburg on July 4. The division was now back in active service, irregularly, the Federals maintained, because the men had not been exchanged. Davis thought otherwise. If they had not been properly exchanged and were captured with guns in their hands, they were, under the rules of war, liable to the death penalty. What he said was described by a Northern scribe as "a flight of fancy as to what Bragg was going to do, when the proper time arrived, in the way of scattering the vile invaders who ravaged the beautiful valley below." Later developments showed that some trepidation remained with the men of Stevenson's division even after the President's reassurances.

What a strange walk Davis' undoubtedly was with Longstreet. Here was the scholarly President, gifted in the law, gifted in administration, gifted in legislative affairs, gifted presumably in military leadership, who could examine the delicate tendrils of a legal point down almost to abstraction and, given sustained life, prolong an argument into infinity, walking along the mountain ridge with tough, dominating Longstreet, who usually cut through the outer skin and muscle of a problem to see the naked heart, then became impatient of those who sought further assurance by feeling the pulse, lifting the eyelids, and examining the color of the tongue. Personalities could not have offered stronger contrast: the debater and the doer, the pedant who claimed alliance with reason alongside the unflinching disciple of force.

ABOVE: "Sutlers' Row" in Chattanooga, probably 1864. (LC)

BELOW: Thomas' headquarters at Chattanooga. (NA)

As might be expected, there was no meeting ground. The walk helped seal the fate of the Confederacy. On it Davis came to recognize that Bragg and Longstreet could never work under the same yoke. Here, largely to rid Bragg of Longstreet, he committed the major error of the Chattanooga Campaign, determining that they should be parted. Bragg then, with his consent, committed a trifle later that cardinal blunder of dividing his army in the face of a vigilant and increasing foe. He sent Longstreet to Knoxville to capture an enemy force of comparable size, Burnside's Army of the Ohio, while he, Bragg, pursued the investment with little more than the bloody remnants of the army that had fought so desperately at Chickamauga. Longstreet said he acceded to the plan reluctantly, though it freed him from Bragg's irksome presence. He did not know at the time that the author of it was President Davis.

For the moment, however, Longstreet was on hand and to him went the first combat assignment at Chattanooga. He commanded Bragg's left, as Hardee did the right, and Breckinridge, who had borne the heavy load of much of the Chickamauga fighting, the center.

Grant reached Chattanooga on October 23 and at once put into effect the plan that had been developed by Rosecrans and his chief of engineers, Major General William F. ("Baldy") Smith. Much has been made over the authorship of this plan but as one looks at the map, it becomes so simple an expedient that any private in the ranks might well have devised it;

Rapids on the Tennessee River. Steamboat "Chattanooga" being warped up the "suck" at head of rapids. (Brady photo from NA)

it cut off the great Moccasin Point loop of the Tennessee River so as to utilize only the portion of the river not commanded by Confederate guns. The cutoff here was from Brown's Ferry, thence by wagon road to the pontoon crossing at Chattanooga. This meant free passage from the town to the bank well below the area within range of the Southern battery atop Lookout Mountain.

The plan, as carried out, was for two brigades, Hazen's and Turchin's, plus three batteries under Major John Mendenhall, to move on Brown's Ferry, Hazen by boat and Turchin by marching across Moccasin Point. The ferry was just below one of the "sucks," where the

The move that opened the Chattanooga supply lines. Hazen's men landing from pontoon-boats at Brown's Ferry. (From a wartime sketch by T. R. Davis in "Battles & Leaders of the Civil War")

river rushed between gorges and the current at high water was so swift that the sidewheeler river boats of the day could not make headway against it. They had to be warped upstream. More frequently their cargo was unloaded at Brown's Ferry and transported by wagon road across the neck of Moccasin Point, then into the town.

Grant's operation was designed to capture and employ this oldtime high-water route across the neck. It would have to be done by surprise or else Longstreet, who held Bragg's left across Lookout Mountain and into Lookout Valley, between Lookout and Raccoon Mountain, could readily concentrate sufficient men to hold the left bank of the river all the way to the spurs of Raccoon Mountain and the road over it. Secrecy was imperative and was emphasized in the orders. Fairly close timing was required, because the plan called for cooperation between Hooker coming across Raccoon Mountain from Bridgeport, and the two of Thomas' brigades coming separately down from Chattanooga, the one by boat and the other marching across the neck of land.

Hooker, under orders from Thomas, concentrated at Bridgeport and marched into Lookout Valley. Though Corps Commander Palmer accompanied Turchin's brigade, the operation was put under the direction of the chief engineer officer, "Baldy" Smith. He selected fifty details from Hazen's brigade, each being a boatload of twenty-four men—the boats were pontoons—and with Colonel Timothy R. Stanley of the 18th Ohio in charge and Captain Perrin V. Fox, commanding a detachment of the 1st Michigan Engineers, supervising, they pushed off at 3 a.m. and floated silently down the river, hugging the tree-fringed right bank opposite the enemy.

Turchin, marching on the hidden road across the neck, was at the river at Brown's Ferry ahead of them. The little flotilla was observed by Confederate pickets at the ferry, but the troops landed at 5 a.m. in good order, scattered or captured the enemy pickets, en-

Major General Hooker and staff—Lookout Valley, winter 1863-64. (1) Capt. Hall, (2) Gen. Geary, (3) Gen. Butterfield, (4) Gen. Hooker, (5) Gen. LeDuc, (6) Capt. Kibler. (Photo courtesy of Chickamauga-Chattanooga National Military Park)

trenched on a knoll, and immediately, as they labored, resisted a spirited attack by 1,000 of the enemy with three pieces of artillery, before they had established a secure bridgehead on the Confederate side. Turchin crossed by 10 a.m. and the pontoons were laid under Confederate artillery fire. On the next day, October 28, Hooker arrived by the road through Raccoon Mountain and the Union army held the Tennessee River crossing in force.

By capturing Brown's Ferry and commanding the lower Lookout Valley, Grant's army effectively broke the siege, as far as victuals were concerned, though the haul and transfer were still more difficult than any army enjoys. But the "cracker line" was shortened to where it would carry much more than "Lincoln Platforms," and Sherman was coming on. That assurance, plus an abundance of better food, and the appearance of draft animals that began to come down from Nashville following Hooker, lifted the morale of the Federals and eased the restiveness of Lincoln and Stanton in Washington.

Steamers soon began bringing a good supply of vegetables, which the army craved, and other provisions, clothing, and forage for the animals. Hooker now had on hand the complete requirements of an army for land transportation, nor had his teams been starved or overworked. Grant pointed out—it must have been with high satisfaction—that within five days after his arrival in Chattanooga the way to Bridgeport was open, and that within a week the men were receiving full rations. Whatever else might be said about Grant, he was a general of restless action. He saw how the troops were lifted: ". . . an abundance of ammunition was brought up, and a cheerfulness prevailed not before enjoyed in many weeks. Neither officers nor men looked upon themselves any longer as doomed. The weak and languid appearance of the troops, so visible before, disappeared at once."

When Hooker entered Lookout Valley he moved by the railroad station at Wauhatchie, where he left Geary's XII Corps division as a rearguard, then marched down the valley three miles with the XI Corps under Howard to cooperate with Palmer's brigades at Brown's Ferry.

Bragg had discredited reconnaissance reports that numerous Federals (Hooker's two corps) had arrived at Bridgeport, close at hand. Bragg was a chronic doubter. Only when Longstreet led him to the vantage point of Signal Rock, whence he could survey the western country

405

and see the long blue column marching into Lookout Valley below him, did he concede that his own signal corps gleanings had been more accurate than what he had termed them, "sensational."

As darkness came on that night, the Confederate officers could look down on Hooker's campfires disclosing exactly how the Federals had divided their forces between the river and the railroad depot at Wauhatchie three miles up the valley. About 1,500 Federals remained at Wauhatchie while Hooker and Howard went on with 5,000.

Bragg ordered an attack on the weaker party at Wauhatchie. He left the details to Longstreet but took charge of giving orders to the two divisions that were to participate—those of Jenkins and McLaws. According to Longstreet, he changed his mind about sending McLaws but did not inform Longstreet about it.

Jenkins formed his division and designated Law's brigade to hold Howard's main body at the Lookout Creek crossings to keep it from assisting Geary at Wauhatchie. So necessary was this that Longstreet intended that McLaws should reinforce Law with his entire division. As Longstreet described his actions, he waited at the mountain observation point until midnight, then rode to the stepoff point of the attack, and learned there that McLaws had not even been ordered by Bragg to participate. Thus virtually half of the force that was to bag Geary had not been ordered up by Bragg at all.

Longstreet here made the improper assumption, as he acknowledged later, that because McLaws would not appear, Jenkins would not attack. Instead, as he put it, "the gallant Jenkins decided that the plan should not be abandoned." He determined to carry it out with his single division. As this was his only chance to command in a battle in his short and brilliant life he deserves attention.

Micah Jenkins was one of the several young Southerners in Longstreet's corps—Evander Law, Joseph B. Kershaw, Moxley Sorrell, William C. Oates, and others among them—who showed an aptitude for command. He was from Edisto Island off the South Carolina coast—a lad who stood first in his class of 1854 at South Carolina Military Academy, now The Citadel. Then with a classmate, Asbury Coward, he founded and conducted the King's Mountain Military School at Yorkville, South Carolina. He rose in the Southern army from colonel of the 5th South Carolina at First Manassas to command one of Lee's stellar brigades and, by the time of Chattanooga, to lead Hood's division after Hood had his leg shot off at Chickamauga. (Jenkins was killed in the later fighting in the Virginia Wilderness by the unhappy Confederate blast that also grievously wounded Longstreet.)

At this juncture, when Bragg had neglected or refrained from ordering up the reinforcements and Longstreet had departed without countermanding the original attack plan, but when nobody else seemed to believe the attack would

be launched at such a late hour, Jenkins decided to charge Geary with his single division. The battle that ensued was bitterly fought and brutal, and lasted until the streaks of dawn lighted the east, with Jenkins the decided loser. As he wrote about it the next day, he called the odds against him immense and the fight "terrible." That was true of the broad action, but not of his initial encounter, for at first he appeared successful.

Geary was surprised both by the suddenness and the vigor of Jenkins' attack. His three New York regiments, the 78th, 137th, and 149th, and two Pennsylvania, the 27th and 111th, served him well, stood firmly, and finally rolled the Confederates back. Thirty men from the 27th Pennsylvania rushed to Knap's Federal battery when all the horses had been killed or disabled, and dragged a gun to a point where it could arrest Jenkins' flanking column. All officers of the battery were either killed or wounded. The Confederates charged repeatedly for an hour and a half.

In his letter to his wife next day Jenkins told that the creek he had to cross (Lookout) had two bridges, both of which had had their planks removed. The men crossed on the stringers to get between Howard's main body (of 12,000, as he numbered it) and Geary's. Jenkins' entire command numbered about 4,000. His old brigade, all South Carolinians, was under its senior colonel, John Bratton. Jenkins contended that instead of encountering 1,000 Federals as expected, he ran into the XII Corps

Brigadier General Micah Jenkins. (Coll. of Library of Congress)

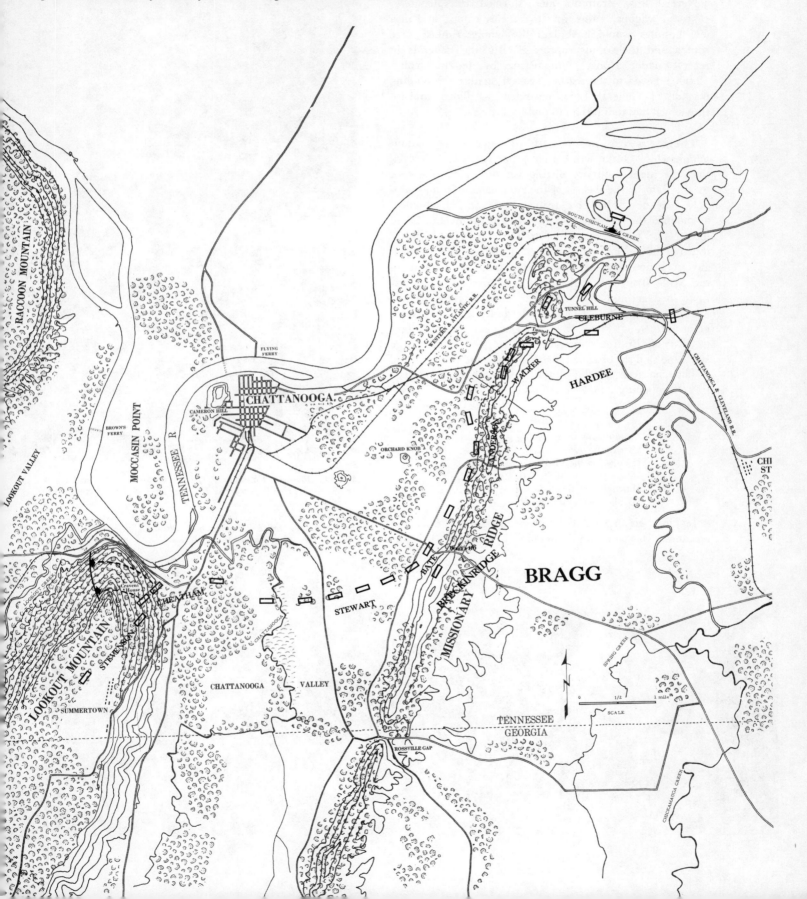

The Battle of Lookout Mountain, November 24, 1863. The three divisions under Hooker have attacked Stevenson and Cheatham and driven them from all but the eastern slopes by evening. They will be withdrawn after midnight. Meanwhile, Sherman has crossed the Tennessee on the right with some resistance from one of Cheatham's brigades, while Cleburne has been moved to meet him.

numbering about 5,000, which had come up in the night prior to the attack.

Nevertheless, Bratton's men stormed in splendidly, captured wagons, trains, and the enemy camp "and in a few minutes would have had the whole Yankee force routed and their guns captured." But the Federals in reserve under Hooker, numbering by Jenkins' count 12,000, moved to the rescue, pressed against the holding brigade of General Law, encircled his flank, and so threatened him that he had to pull back.

There were points of disagreement about Wauhatchie. Grant wrote that "the night was so dark that the men could not distinguish one another except by the light of the flashes of their muskets." In the palpable blackness Hooker's teamsters became frightened, abandoned their teams, and allowed the animals to break loose. The mules, according to Grant, dashed directly toward the enemy and stampeded them. The incident gave occasion for the oft-repeated famous "Charge of the Mule Brigade," a parody on Tennyson's more distinguished account of the British horse at Balaclava. It must have related to Benning's brigade, the only Georgians present. Major J. L. Coker, assistant adjutant general of Bratton's brigade, denied the mule-charge story and said the brigade retired in good order.

The character of the simple burlesque may be seen from the opening stanza:

> Half a mile, half a mile,
> Half a mile onward,
> Right through the Georgia troops,
> Broke the two hundred.
> "Forward the Mule brigade.
> Charge for the Rebs!" they neighed;
> Straight for the Georgia troops
> Broke the two hundred.

Jenkins reinforced Law with Robertson's Texas and Arkansas brigade and Benning's Georgia brigade.

ABOVE: View of Chattanooga from north bank of the Tennessee River. (From "Harper's History of the Great Rebellion")

BELOW: Knap's Pennsylvania battery suffered heavy casualties in what Geary called "Wauhatchie's bloody glen," where his son Edward, an officer in the battery, was killed. (Photo from NA)

When Howard marched to Geary's relief with his main body, Law was brushed aside. With the help of Benning, Jenkins skillfully extricated Bratton and the famed battle of Wauhatchie, a bit overrated because it was the first of the Chattanooga engagements and because of the literature about the charge of the mule brigade, ended. Said Longstreet of the withdrawal: "The conduct of Bratton's forces was one of the cleverest pieces of work of the war. . . ." Jenkins said he had to recall his men "in the midst of success."

Major Coker of Bratton's staff, who disputed the story of the mule brigade charge, as did others, accounted the battle of Wauhatchie of minor importance, as lasting an hour and a half and being a single brigade action, with none but Bratton's men firing a shot, but it did confirm possession of Lookout Valley for Hooker's Eastern army and brought him up facing Lookout Mountain, one of the two keys, the other being Missionary ridge, if Bragg was to keep the Federal army under siege. The Federal loss in killed and wounded was 416. Bratton's brigade loss was 351; the Confederate total, 408. The battle secured the supply line via Brown's Ferry.

For Geary, later governor of Pennsylvania, it was a signal triumph in which he could not have taken much personal satisfaction. His son, a lieutenant in Knap's Pennsylvania battery, was shot through the brain while aiming a piece after most of the other officers and gunners had fallen in their exposed position during the initial Confederate attack.

A striking discrepancy occurs in the accounts with respect to the nature of the night. By one well-established story, Longstreet could be seen clearly atop Lookout Mountain directing the attack. This is of some interest because the Union cryptographers had broken the Confederate signal code and were able to decypher every one of Longstreet's messages.

The circumstance was given high significance to the outcome of the battle and campaign by one of the correspondents present because, as he related it, Geary was heavily outnumbered and would have been driven had he not been able to anticipate each Confederate move.

The promontory on which Longstreet stood, looking westward from Lookout Mountain, was known thereafter as "Signal Rock." Alongside himself Longstreet stationed his signal corps men with their flares, and with them repeatedly signaled down to Jenkins. No doubt it was true that his large form could be seen in front of the flares. "During the whole battle," ran the correspondent's account, "the flaming torch of Longstreet flashed orders that showed his increased desperation, and finally, much to Geary's gratification, he saw it signal the recall. All the while the figure of Longstreet on 'Signal Rock' standing out boldly against the dark back-ground, was plainly visible in the glare of the signal torches to the combatants below."

John S. C. Abbott, who wrote as the war progressed and published his two-volume history in 1866, made a point that "the night, illuminated by nearly a full moon, was almost as bright as day. . . ." It seems more credible that Longstreet at such a distance could be seen by moonlight instead of by the beams of his signal torches. Records of the U.S. Naval Observatory show that on the night of October 28, 1863, the night on which Wauhatchie was fought, the moon had receded only two days from full, having been at full October 26. Thus the John S. C. Abbott account appears more accurate in this respect than Grant's.

Longstreet left Chattanooga on November 5 to force Burnside back into Knoxville, then to besiege him there. He took the divisions of McLaws and Jenkins and was joined later by that of Bushrod Johnson, the division that had been the entering wedge that split Rosecran's army at Chickamauga. Longstreet confronted Burnside with fairly equal numbers at the beginning but as he built his force with the acquisition of Johnson, Jones from western Virginia, and others, Bragg was deprived of 20,000 good soldiers at the very time Grant was strengthening step by step and making formidable the Federal army in the valley below him.

The Confederate commander had no such preponderance of numbers as to warrant his detachment of Longstreet however cordially President Davis may have assented to it. Bragg appears at this point in the campaign to have been naively sanguine. At the time he was losing Longstreet he was losing also his strongest ally, famine, yet he did not undertake to invest Chattanooga by regular approaches, by storming, or by any measure whatever that might lure the Northerners from their position so that he might meet them again in open battle. He merely waited, as he had done at Murfreesboro, then at Tullahoma, for the capricious element of time to assert itself in his favor.

Longstreet, when he heard the rumor that he was to be sent toward Knoxville, could not give it credence. "At the moment," he wrote, "it seemed impossible that our commander, after rejecting a proposition for a similar move made just after the battle, when flushed with victory and the enemy discomfited, could now think of sending an important detachment so far, when he knew that, in addition to the reinforcements that had joined

the Union army, another strong column was marching from Memphis under General Sherman, and must reach Chattanooga in fifteen or twenty days." Longstreet's second thought was that Bragg's move "might, after all, be in keeping with his peculiarities," and took up the plan with the belief he might be given a strong enough force to crush Burnside and be back in front of Chattanooga before Sherman's arrival. But he did tell Bragg the detachment of his force would indeed be hazardous.

Longstreet took the trains to Sweetwater, Tennessee, en route to Knoxville. As soon as Grant learned that he had left Bragg's lines, the Federal commander was eager for action, even though Sherman's corps was as yet at some distance.

Two days after Longstreet left, Grant completed a reconnaissance and was satisfied that he could dislodge Bragg from Missionary Ridge by attacking his right flank, then moving south down the crest of the ridge. Success might bring Longstreet back, since he had not yet reached Knoxville nor gained contact with Burnside en route. Longstreet's departure exercised Washington and Grant was being urged to protect Burnside, who had become almost a liability to the Union side.

Grant ordered Thomas to make the attack on Bragg's right with the Army of the Cumberland. The operation Grant contemplated was precisely the same that Sherman with his fresh army and much other help was to fail in signally later in the month. Thomas, with his 40,000, knew his force was insufficient to hold the Chattanooga lines at the time he was hurling a heavy bolt against Bragg's entrenched lines facing the Union left on Missionary Ridge. Grant on the other hand, thought it possible even to cut Bragg's communications between Dalton, Georgia, and Cleveland, Tennessee, which would sever Bragg from Longstreet. But he was dealing in Thomas with a methodical general who never took the long chance.

Thomas told Grant frankly that the attack would invite disaster. In this opinion he had the support of his chief engineer officer, "Baldy" Smith. Grant yielded, but the incident did not impress him with Thomas' zeal or flexibility. The weight of opinion, however, has remained with Thomas. Colonel Fred Knefler of Beatty's brigade, Wood's division, commented, like others: "There is no doubt if General Thomas had undertaken to execute that order, and at the same time attempted to hold Chattanooga with the limited numbers at his command, he would have disastrously failed."

Grant's disappointment was evident when on November 14 Sherman finally arrived. Grant told his leading lieutenant, as Sherman later stated it, that the defeat at Chickamauga had left the Army of the Cumberland so demoralized "he feared they could not get out of their trenches to assume the offensive." He thought they would fight well after the Vicksburg men supplied the initial impetus.

They remained, as they had been termed for a year, the "stepchild army."

Sherman, leaving Memphis on October 11, moved his corps partly afoot and partly by railroad to Corinth, Mississippi, his progress impeded by Confederate cavalry. A more aggravating cause for his slowness was an order from Halleck to repair the railroad as he went. As he moved from Memphis, he had visions of cutting a swath across north Alabama and southwestern Tennessee that would be a sort of barren bastion protecting Kentucky and the North. The call for haste saved the countryside.

Grant had grown anxious well before Longstreet pulled away from Chattanooga. He wanted Sherman and he wanted him at once. Impatient of the railroad mending, he ordered Sherman on October 27 to stop it, drop everything else and hasten to Stevenson. Sherman had been slowed also by a superabundance of wagons, his belief at the outset being that he would have to haul provisions to the starving army in Chattanooga. Each division marched with its train immediately behind it, which slowed the whole.

Stevenson, Alabama, early Union supply base in the Chattanooga Campaign. ("Harper's History of the Great Rebellion")

The army struggled through rain and mud. Finally the infantry was free of its impedimenta, leaving the wagons to follow. At Eastport, where the Memphis & Charleston Railroad reached the Tennessee River, he obtained abundant supplies which Grant had caused to be collected at St. Louis and sent by boat up the Tennessee. So anxious had Grant become that he sent the orders for Sherman to hasten by a messenger who paddled his craft down the Tennessee past the "sucks" and "boiling pots," over Muscle Shoals, and on to Iuka, Mississippi, where they were handed to Sherman on October 27.

Grant feared the Confederates might be intending to march on Nashville, as Longstreet had suggested, and Sherman's was the only force near enough to be interposed. All was haste now with Sherman. On November 1 he was in Florence, Alabama; on the 14th he rode into Chattanooga ahead of his troops.

Grant, concerned that the single-track railroad from Nashville would be inadequate to supply the several Federal armies that were converging on Chattanooga, plus Burnside's force in Knoxville, ordered Sherman to detach one division, that G. M. Dodge an old-time railroad constructor, to rebuild the railroad linking Decatur, Alabama, with Nashville, so that everything would not depend on a single track between Nashville and Stevenson. That deprived Sherman of a division, but it was an assurance the army would not starve.

On the Union side, the main role in the great drama that was now unfolding was to be played by the "Old Hero's" cast-aside Army of the Cumberland, stripped down to four divisions after Jefferson C. Davis' had been sent to help Sherman, and much of Palmer's XIV Corps, Thomas' old command, had gone to co-operate with Hooker after he had parted with Howard, who came into Chattanooga. To use the theatrical phrase, Thomas, the bit-part player, was about to emerge the star.

First came Orchard Knob, Monday, November 23. The corps of Major Generals Crittenden and McCook that had been worsted and driven from the field at Chickamauga had been consolidated into the IV Corps under Major General Gordon Granger, who had marched to the relief of Thomas on Snodgrass Hill. Two divisions of this corps, Thomas J. Wood's and Philip H. Sheridan's, were paraded in the early morning much as though for a grand review, and such the Confederate onlookers from Missionary Ridge believed to be in progress.

Bragg's forward elements reached to rising ground about a mile in advance of the Federal Chattanooga defenses. They held Orchard Knob, a foothill, that looked out toward Missionary Ridge and was almost a nettle beneath the Union army's underwear, an irritant that would have to be removed before Grant or Thomas could exercise themselves freely and come to grips with Bragg's center.

The demonstration of the two divisions was begun as a reconnaissance in force. It was exploratory, to see how strongly Orchard Knob was held. The divisions left their artillery behind. Absalom Baird's division was stationed *en echelon* in support of Sheridan and Richard W. Johnson's division of the XIV Corps in support of Wood.

Quickly Bragg's spectators were disillusioned of the idea that they were watching a mere pageant, or witnessing a Union chest thumping, or display of power, now that Sherman's reinforcements were at hand. A cannon signaled from Fort Wood and, while most of two great armies observed, the divisions of Wood and Sheridan, with Willich's brigade of Wood's division in advance, rushed the Confederate lines on Orchard Knob. Almost before anyone was aware of what was happening, they overran and captured this strong point of Bragg's front line. Grant was at Fort Wood, with Thomas and others, and could not repress his admiration of the maneuver, or of the élan of the two Cumberland divisions. Thereafter the commanding general had no misgivings about the stanch fighting qualities of Thomas' men.

"Old Hero" Thomas was elated. When he saw the battle standards of Wood's division atop the Confederate ramparts he signaled Wood to hold fast. Though this was merely a feeling movement, the advantage could not be relinquished. His signal corps flag wavers spelled out the words: "You have gained too much to withdraw. Hold your position and I will support you."

The support he sent consisted of Blair's division on the right of Sheridan, who had moved through timber and had not kept abreast Wood, and Howard's corps on Wood's left. The story was told that the unemotional Thomas, when he saw some of his men falling on Orchard Knob, surveyed the terrain through his glasses and remarked with some feeling, "What a beautiful place for a cemetery." He kept it in mind and later caused to be established the one the visitor may see there today.

With Orchard Knob in Grant's possession, the entire army moved forward and intrenched along a new line, which caused rejoicing for several causes. One was that the new works enclosed a much larger area, parts of it heavily wooded. No longer was there crowding. The famine of firewood was ended and loggers at once began felling trees. That very night Orchard Knob sent up red flames from the great fires around which men and officers clustered, warming muscles and sending heat to bones that had been chilled for two months.

Before morning Bridge's Sixth Illinois Battery of Wood's division rolled up behind the infantry. Under cover of darkness, lunettes were added to the field works. The men bivouacked beneath open skies, without shelter, but the fires were a welcome exchange for the dingy, crowded huts and dugouts in the town. By this time the town, according to one description, was a "completely gutted, useless wreck." From Missionary Ridge the Con-

federates tossed shells onto Orchard Knob but the fire was ineffectual and sporadic.

There, along the Orchard Knob line, the Army of the Cumberland, possessing a higher status but still the cast-offs alongside Sherman's men from Vicksburg, passed in idleness the stirring day of November 24, 1863, while Grant was getting his forces into final position for the attack he would launch on the morrow. The plan was simple, with Sherman holding the lead. Bragg's army would be assailed on both flanks. Sherman would attack the Confederate right at the north end of Missionary Ridge. Hooker, who on the 24th was fighting for Lookout Mountain, would cross Chattanooga Creek and valley, take Rossville, and strike Bragg's left at the south end of the Ridge.

Thomas, with the Army of the Cumberland, who was already in position, would be the reserve, would threaten Bragg's center, and assist either Sherman or Hooker. Thomas was not to participate in the initial attack. Grant himself made it clear that "Thomas was not to move until Hooker had reached Missionary Ridge." Grant took his position with Thomas on Orchard Knob and gave orders to him directly. When Sherman became impatient a bit later that Thomas did not coordinate his movements with those of the Army of the Tennessee, he was exhibiting a lack of understanding of Thomas' role in the battle.

Although the Army of the Cumberland had an excellent view of Lookout Mountain and Missionary Ridge, neither end of the ridge was visible from its position in the center. The men could follow the action only by ear except where it might reach a momentarily clear

summit. On the 24th the rain fell, sharply at times, but mostly in intermittent drizzles, and Lookout Mountain was obscured by the mist. The wind blew down in gusts from the north, bitter and searching, chilling especially Thomas' men, who had no huts, no shelter halves, no blazing fires in the heavy wind and rain, and no assigned activity to exercise them and cause them to forget the cold.

All day the heavy mist hung over the peak of Lookout and during most of the day Missionary Ridge was blotted out by the fog. Down where Sherman was getting into position there were bursts of firing and toward Lookout, in Thomas' right rear, the rattle of Hooker's musketry could be heard, rising to a crescendo in the afternoon.

Most eyes were turned in that direction. Sometimes when there were breaks in the mists along the mountain sides, or when the fog lifted sufficiently from the shelvings, they could see blue-clad soldiers working their way up the mountain. The Cumberlanders thought they could distinguish some of their own men, members of Brigadier General Charles Cruft's First Division of Granger's IV Corps, who had been detached to help Hooker. The Federal batteries on Moccasin Point joined in the cannonade of Lookout. Using some of Sherman's horses—the Army of the Cumberland no longer had any—Brigadier General John M. Brannan, commander of the Cumberland army's artillery, hauled forty pieces down to the Point to give Hooker artillery coverage as he stormed up the Lookout slopes. Through the day the cannon roared with their deep voices, but little more destructively than the Confederates' fire through the fog from the mountain shelves and summit.

The "grapevine telegraph," the 1863 name for "scuttlebutt" or "latrine rumor," carried wild stories of victory and defeat along the lines. Finally the dank November day grew duller and darkness came down from the surrounding heights, without anyone being sure of what had happened on Lookout. But the Cumberlanders did get one cheering bit of intelligence: that Sherman had crossed the Tennessee and was in position to launch his assault, which was to be the *coup de grace* of the battle, at daybreak. Grant was so pleased with this development that he sent a telegram to Washington saying the fight had progressed favorably, that Sherman had taken the end of Missionary Ridge, and that Hooker was high up the eastern slope of Lookout. Still, the men knew little, Grant was unduly optimistic about Sherman, and the earnest fighting had not yet begun on Missionary Ridge.

In contrast with the 24th, November 25 dawned bright in the valleys, though a light fog still hung on the summits. The mist was soon burned away. Nearly every eye of the Cumberland Army was turned intently toward the craggy top of Lookout Mountain. The sun's rays appeared suddenly to dissipate the fogginess. Then, simultaneously

413

Hooker's men bridging Lookout Creek. It was here that Hooker's attack bogged down. From a wartime sketch by H. E. Brown. (B&L)

from the entire army, rose a mighty shout. As a Federal colonel described it: "At the point from which rebel batteries had thundered upon Chattanooga for weeks, the Stars and Stripes, gloriously radiant in their gorgeous beauty, were proudly floating in the morning breeze."

The flag was the battle standard of the 8th Kentucky Volunteers, Colonel Sidney M. Barnes commanding, of Whitaker's brigade, Cruft's division, Granger's corps of the the Army of the Cumberland. The division of the castoffs that had been lent to Hooker were the first to reach the mountain top. Cheers rolled back and forth along the lines, especially among the Cumberlanders. Lookout Mountain, believed by Bragg and many others to be impregnable, had been won.

What had happened on Lookout? The Confederates had strengthened their defenses both before and after the departure of Longstreet. Brigadier General John K. Jackson took command on November 14 and drew a formidable line around the Craven house situated on a shoulder of Lookout. Jackson had 1,489 of Edward C. Walthall's brigade and 1,205 of John C. Moore's, both of Cheatham's division. Walthall was above on the shelf and Moore, whose men were poorly armed, was below on Walthall's right.

At foggy daybreak on November 24 Geary, still at Wauhatchie, received Hooker's order to cross Lookout Creek and assail the enemy on the mountain. Geary had three brigades, recently experienced in fighting over rough terrain on Culp's Hill at Gettysburg. They were the brigades of Colonels Charles Candy, George A. Cobham, Jr., and David Ireland. As they stepped off they were reinforced by Brigadier General Walter C. Whitaker's brigade of Cruft's division, Granger's corps, and later by the balance of Cruft's division. Then, still later in the day, came Peter J. Osterhaus' division of Sherman's Army of the Tennessee.

The units are of interest because they represented the three army groups that had been hastily assembled to avert a Union disaster in Chattanooga—portions of the Army of the Potomac, of the Army of the Tennessee, and substantially all of the Army of the Cumberland. Upon

Hooker's advance, Geary held the right, Cruft the center, and Osterhaus the left. Howard's corps had been moved from Lookout Valley to cooperate with Thomas and Sherman.

Hooker's battle for Lookout was effective but not spectacular. Due to the weather it was not as thrilling as Thomas' capture of Orchard Knob. Brigadier General Montgomery C. Meigs, the efficient Georgia-born Quartermaster General of the Union army, who observed such of the fighting as was visible while he was in Grant's party on Orchard Knob, called it the "Battle Above the Clouds," a name that appealed so much to the soldiers and press that it became a fixture, but usually it is awarded no more historical accuracy than the Barbara Fritchie legend or the negotiations under a "famous apple tree" at Appomattox. Still, since a fog is merely a low-lying cloud, and since the fog shrouded the mountainside, the title, one of the most renowned of the war, was not altogether a fantasy of the down-to-earth engineer, Meigs, noted for his practicality.

A coincidental phase of the fighting was that as the battle developed, Grant sent Brigadier General William P. Carlin's brigade of Richard W. Johnson's division, Palmer's corps, to further reinforce Hooker. Carlin's main function was to carry extra ammunition to replenish Hooker's dwindling supplies. Carlin, as night was falling, captured the most readily seen house on the mountain side.

The man who lived here was a well-known ironmaster of that locality, Robert Cravens, and he had painted his house white and it is referred to in the accounts as "the white house." Carlin's capture of it signaled Federal triumph. That night the Confederates withdrew to Missionary Ridge.

The significance of the capture of Lookout Mountain was that it gave Grant a straight line of battle with Lookout on the right, extending to the outer works at Chattanooga, through Orchard Knob, and on to where Sherman had come into position facing the north end of Missionary Ridge.

Grant's plan gave preference to Sherman. Quite naturally he turned to a corps and a general whose methods and responses were familiar to him all the way from Shiloh through Vicksburg. Naturally, as well, he wanted the major glory to go to his own men. He woefully misjudged Thomas, but that was not to become evident until the battle was joined and nearly over. As will be recalled, Sherman was to attack on the northern end of Missionary Ridge and sweep down the crest. Hooker would carry Chattanooga Valley, cross Chattanooga Creek, take Rossville, and sweep up Missionary Ridge from the South. Thomas with four divisions of the Army of the Cumberland would hold the center in front of Orchard Knob and create any necessary diversion required to accelerate the advances of Sherman and Hooker, and assist either. His was to be the more passive role.

Battle of Lookout Mountain, Nov. 25, 1863. Scene from Lookout Valley.
Drawn by T. R. Davis. (HW, Nov. 30, 1867)

The dramatic storming of Missionary Ridge without orders by Thomas' "stepchild" Army of the Cumberland. Confederates a bit late withdrawing guns. ("Harper's Hist. of Great Rebellion")

The plan had some defects, the first being lack of proper reconnaissance. Missionary Ridge at the northern end was presumed to be a continuous range when in truth it was broken into smaller hills with one highly difficult valley before the ascent to the main ridge. An important eminence was Tunnel Hill where the Western & Atlantic Railroad that connected with Knoxville and, when unobstructed, with Richmond, Virginia, passed through the Missionary Mountain range. To the south the ridge was continuous all the way to Rossville Pass.

Another development of the plan, which proved its greatest obstacle, was that just before Sherman assailed the northern extremity, Bragg garrisoned it with Cleburne's division, which became his army's right division under Hardee's right wing command. What ensued here gave warrant to Hardee's later statement: "When Cleburne's division defended, no odds broke its lines; where it attacked, no numbers resisted its onslaught, save only

once, and there is the grave of Cleburne."

Cleburne reached north Missionary Ridge under fortuitous circumstances, with a thin margin of time. When Longstreet moved on Knoxville with 12,000 infantry and a few horses and found that he was supposed to be besieging an army of superior numbers, under Burnside, of 12,000 infantry and 8,000 horses (or so he thought), he called on Bragg for reinforcements. That general, compounding an original error, sent him Buckner with Bushrod Johnson's division, then ordered the division of the Irish-born Arkansan, Pat Cleburne, which was without peer in the Western armies, to go. What Bragg truly had in mind in so wantonly weakening his army at a time when Grant was drastically strengthening his, is anybody's guess, but the distrustful Longstreet gained the impression that the commanding general was out to destroy him when the truth was Bragg was destroying himself. The generals became at heart almost as much at war with each other as with the diligent and gathering foe. One by one Bragg had stripped his own command of nearly every top-ranking general who had recommended his dismissal to President Davis: Longstreet, Polk, Hill, Buckner, and now Cleburne. Bragg paid no attention to

anything that Longstreet recommended, though he was indebted to Old Pete for a glorious victory and might have wanted to share with him counsels about the succeeding steps.

No moment could have been less appropriate for Cleburne to depart from Bragg to join Longstreet. He boarded the cars on November 23, the day Grant was preparing the last details for the grand assault he proposed to begin on November 24. When Bragg saw the Federals in motion and realized his mistake, he telegraphed Cleburne in frenzied haste, caught him at Chickamauga Station, halted him, then ordered him to move in desperate speed to the army's headquarters. By that time the preliminaries of a large-scale battle were already in progress.

Bragg had been proceeding on the theory that because of the formidable nature of Missionary Ridge a weak line could hold it. In even greater indifference, he had weakened his defenses on the right despite evidences of Sherman's concentration there, until the ridge was all but stripped at the north end, and now that was about to become the main object of the enemy offensive.

Cleburne on the morning of November 24, a great day of Chattanooga, was rushed hurriedly to the right. He stationed Lucius E. Polk's Tennessee and Arkansas brigade to hold the Chickamauga Creek crossing just below the confluence of the creek with the Tennessee River, and to the east side of Missionary Ridge. With his other three brigades, those of Lowry, Liddell, and the Texans first under James A. Smith, who was wounded, then under Colonel (later General) Hiram B. Granbury, he fortified himself on a strong line on the ridge. (Granbury and Cleburne were to die within a few paces of each other next year at the Battle of Franklin.) This brigade had been under Brigadier General James Deshler, who fell with 418 of his men killed or wounded at Chickamauga. When General Lee, who had commanded Deshler in western Virginia early in the war, learned he had been killed, he wrote "There was no braver soldier in the Confederacy than Deshler." Now his old brigade, one of Bragg's best, was due for another blood bath.

Cleburne, with a good eye for terrain, had his brigades in strong position after preliminary skirmishing on the night of November 24. He was far up the ridge to the north and had no understanding of Bragg's intentions until he had sent his aide, Captain Irving A. Buck, several miles south to Bragg's headquarters. There Hardee, who was just leaving the council, gave notice: "Tell Cleburne we are to fight; that his division will undoubtedly be heavily attacked, and they must do their very best." Buck reassured Hardee that the division had never yet failed and would not do so on the morrow. The words of both general and captain were prophetic.

That night the moon was in eclipse, a not infrequent attendant of battles. When sufficient light was restored, Cleburne further strengthened his lines. Hardee arrived between 2 and 3 a.m., solicitous about the flank, which all believed Grant would try to turn in the morning. They rode the lines, directed Lucius Polk to occupy an additional hillock, then Cleburne himself determined to cover another spur of Missionary Ridge rising above Chickamauga Creek. The dispositions were important to his defense, which was one of the spectacular features of the oncoming battle.

Smith's and Granbury's brigade of Texans, working busily to complete some new trenches, met the first fire of Sherman's batteries which, with much preliminary skirmishing, told that an attack of major proportions was at hand. At 11 a.m. Sherman assailed Cleburne's lines with his customary impetuousness. He carried the assault forward to within a few yards—fifty paces at best—of Swett's battery that guarded Tunnel Hill. Sherman sent Hugh Ewing's division in first but that was not enough.

Sherman here proved what many Civil War students including his most noted biographer, Lloyd Lewis, have discerned, that he was not a great battle leader. Having at his disposal two corps of the Army of the Tennessee, plus Howard's corps of the Army of the Potomac, and the two divisions of Jefferson C. Davis and Absalom Baird of the Army of the Cumberland, he still could not drive Cleburne who, according to his assistant adjutant, Captain Irving A. Buck, "seemed omnipresent, watching and guarding every point, and providing for any contingencies." All morning Sherman sent in his ample divisions that were, as Buck stated it, repulsed at all points. Grant thought that Bragg was shifting heavy reinforcements to his right, a deduction also of many others, but the fact is that Cleburne fought with no more than his own division, under the general supervision of the right wing commander, "Old Reliable" Lieutenant General Hardee.

Satisfied that the Confederate right was secure, Hardee moved off to the left, to where he quickly summoned Cleburne and Brigadier General States Rights Gist, commanding Walker's old division. An appalling situation had developed in the army's left center.

The roar of battle sounded over the rolling hills of the little town and reverberated from the circle of mountains. In the center there was no assurance that Sherman was doing well on the Union left. Sherman was reported to be holding his own—only that. The rattle of his musketry died down; even the field artillery fire (most of the army's guns were concentrated there) was sporadic and gave the impression the attacks were localized and piecemeal and not one overpowering assault down the crest of the ridge.

There was likewise cause for concern from the army's right under Hooker. He had swept around the foot and

Major General Patrick R. Cleburne (LC)

forward down the mountain summit majestically, but had come up against the simple little matter of crossing Chattanooga Creek, where Cheatham's men had destroyed the bridge after retiring from Lookout, and there was no earthly manner for an army to cross until Hooker could build pontoons. That was a process of hours.

To those in the center, the outlook seemed dismal. The center was being stripped continually of supports. Howard's corps marched from Wood's left to help Sherman; then Baird followed. He had to pass from Sheridan's right and move across the rear of two Cumberland divisions. Grant was determined to crush Bragg's right around Tunnel Hill and was employing the better part of his infantry and artillery in the effort. A man not easily rebuffed, he intended no half measures.

Sherman called repeatedly for Thomas to take up the assault. Grant, nearby, had not yet given the signal. Thomas had three divisions left, Wood and Sheridan from left to right, Johnson in support *en echelon* behind Sheridan. When Howard moved off to Sherman, Wood's left was up in the air, but none worried as they watched the grand spectacle of the large bodies of troops—Howard's corps and Baird's division—marching north with banners waving. Still, there were no cries of victory, no huzzahs along the lines, only depressing uncertainty, perhaps another defeat. The shadows of the late November day lengthened. The sun hung perilously close to the summits of the western ridges.

It was 3 p.m. Two other generals, along with Thomas, were about to take the battle of Missionary Ridge into their hands. They deserve a brief introduction. Philip H. Sheridan's role in the war to this time had been passably good, not distinguished. He weighed 115 pounds, stood 5' 5" and was known in the army as "Little Phil." Bow-legged, by nature a thorough cavalryman, though he now commanded an infantry division, he was devoted to horses. When he was dying on Rhode Island Avenue in Washington and could look out on Scott Circle, he expressed an ardent wish that if he were ever monumented (as other generals were being honored at that time) the sculptor would give him a better horse than Scott's docile animal. He can rest unvexed; the spirited mount he sits astride on Sheridan Circle, supposed to depict him at the moment he reached Cedar Creek from Winchester (the theme of Thomas Buchanan Read's famous "Sheridan Twenty Miles Away") to turn the tide of fleeing Federals and defeat Jubal Early (which many regarded no great task), is often rated the most handsome mount in the capital city.

Sheridan was self-confident to the point of being pertly conceited, though he had been, like the Confederate Lieutenant General A. P. Hill, a five-year man at West Point. Health was something of a factor in both cases. At this stage of the war the quality of his generalship was in as much question as was in later years his birthplace. President Rutherford B. Hayes claimed him for Perry County,

Ground of Cleburne's defense at Tunnel Hill, north end of Missionary Ridge. ("Pennsylvania at Chickamauga and Chattanooga")

Ohio. General Charles Devans, Jr., who delivered his eulogy before the Loyal Legion, said he was born in Somerset, Ohio, where he did spend his youth, and is now handsomely monumented. Some obituaries say he was born in Ireland, as was his father. He wrote in his memoirs that he was born in Albany, New York, the year after his parents reached the United States. The standard biographies accept this, though a man is not always the best authority on his birthplace. New Jersey is given at times.

He was tough and worked his way up through adversities, mainly, perhaps, because of his self-confidence, his willingness to take responsibilities, an understanding that war is a brutal trade. He was roughly handled at Stone's River, and driven from the field at Chickamauga. He saved his reputation partly by turning at Rossville and starting back toward the field, but the battle ended before he got there.

The past was now of little moment, because he was having, like Hooker, a fresh opportunity, and this time under the eyes of the man of destiny, Grant, who could not have been enamored with him yet, because he had preferred at Corinth to leave that uncertain general, then apparently shelved, and join Buell's army in the pursuit of Bragg into Kentucky and the Battle of Perryville. The future appeared more promising with Buell. Thus he worked into division command under Rosecrans, Buell's successor, when he might have been with Grant at Vicksburg.

At 3 p.m. November 25, he had his division in sharp alignment to the right of Wood's, whose reputation likewise was shaky. Wood had appeared (and would do so later) in some of the stirring situations of the war, yet he never seemed to gain the lasting attention to his performance that went to some of the others. Now, at the age of 40, there was a spot on his record, transparent when examined closely, because he obeyed Rosecrans' order, pulled his division out of line at Chickamauga, and opened the gap through which Longstreet drove his massed attack, to scatter the Union right wing and send it helter-skelter back into Rossville and Chattanooga.

Wood had a reputation for extreme diligence. He hastened from West Point, ignoring his leave, to get to General Zachary Taylor and haul up the guns at Palo Alto, then conducted an enterprising reconnaissance and won distinction at Buena Vista. As lieutenant colonel of dragoons he went with Albert Sidney Johnston on the Utah campaign. He was on leave in Egypt and rushed home by the first boat when the Civil War erupted. He held the center and held it firmly in the fast moving battle of Stone's River.

Thomas had confidence in him and that was about as good a recommendation as one could have in this war. He responded to it the next year at Nashville, commanding Thomas' largest corps and the center of the Union army in what not a few have accounted the most complete Union battle victory in the conflict. He was a Kentuckian from Munfordville. Now his division, disciplined and given restored confidence by two months of drill under three highly capable, battle-tested brigade commanders —Willich, Hazen, and Samuel Beatty—stood at attention and dressed with that of Sheridan, each division having a front of two brigades and each brigade a front of two regiments, except Willich's, with a four-regiment front. From the base of Orchard Knob, they looked up the 600 feet to the crest of Missionary Ridge.

A cloud of skirmishers was out in front and each division had one brigade in reserve, the same formation

419

Major General Philip H. Sheridan (KA)

George Pickett had employed in his assault four and a half months before on Cemetery Ridge at Gettysburg. One of the participating colonels confirmed that as the divisions aligned themselves no one seemed to have the impression that they were to storm the forbidding ridge. This was to be only a demonstration in force "to relieve the pressure against Sherman" when the truth was that Sherman was not under pressure, but was himself applying the pressure against Cleburne—unsuccessfully.

All morning and through the early afternoon Grant had been waiting and listening, inwardly disappointed, no doubt, but outwardly composed and mostly silent. When he did turn to Thomas, he disclosed no concern, merely said calmly, "Don't you think it is about time to advance against the rifle pits?" It was half a question, half an order. Thomas took it as an order and as such issued it to the corps commander, Granger, who worded it clearly, so that when it got to Wood verbally it was: "You and Sheridan are to advance your divisions, carry the intrenchments at the base of the Ridge, if you can, and if you succeed, to halt there." Thus Wood wrote it from memory later. Then Granger continued: "The movement is to be made at once, so give your orders to your brigade commanders immediately, and the signal to advance will be the rapid, successive discharge of the six guns of this battery." (Bridges' six 10-pounder Parrott rifle guns.)

Sheridan in turn got the same order. The men had long been waiting for it and they responded with alacrity.

What a transformation! Arms that had been stacked all day were seized; groups that had been idly watching fell into line; and as far to the right and left as the eye could reach, the Army of the Cumberland, or three splendid divisions of it, was beautifully aligned for the massed infantry assault, one of the old-time masterpieces of warfare, (but dying surely with the coming of improved artillery and the repeating rifle). Theirs was the tactic of Lee at Malvern Hill, of Pickett at Gettysburg. Now it was to be employed by Thomas at Missionary Ridge.

Again, let one of the colonels describe it: "There was no trepidation in the ranks of these formidable soldiers as the lines dressed up, as if preparing for a . . . ceremony. There was oppressive silence in the ranks, impatiently intent upon the signal for the advance."

Just then, almost at the moment of the stepoff, Baird's division came up, returning from Sherman. It fell in on Wood's left but was not fully in position when the six signal guns spoke, the sounds everyone had been awaiting. Then the four divisions of the Army of the Cumberland, Wood and Sheridan in front in the center, Richard Johnson and Baird *en echelon* on the right and left, respectively, stepped off. The late afternoon sun glistened off burnished bayonets; muskets were at the carry on right shoulders, the men in solid formation, shoulder to shoulder. All about them the battle had nearly ceased. Hooker was making his bridge across the Chattanooga Creek and was no longer engaged; Sherman was licking his wounds off to the north, biding his time for a fresh assault. Now in the center of the great stage of battle, the scene changed as the fresh cast entered: Thomas, Wood, and Sheridan, in major roles, and in the lesser, Baird and Richard Johnson.

Bragg's army had three defensive positions on Missionary. The first was at the base, consisting of a strong line of rifle pits; another was halfway up, much weaker than the first and intended to give security to those who might be forced from the base. The third was at the physical summit, where in most places the ridge is razorback thin, which meant that the Confederate army had to hold steady or run down the reverse slope, there being no other place to go, no plateau on which to form again and hold. The position was one of the strongest, in that it could be reached only by an arduous climb, yet one of the weakest, in that there were no adequate positions on the crest of the ridge to afford a satisfactory field of fire commanding the western approaches.

Orchard Knob was a salient close to Bragg's pits at the bottom of the mountain. As the two Federal divisions marched, the Confederates in the rifle pits at once opened fire. Behind, Federal guns roared from Orchard Knob at targets on the summit, where groups of Confederates were observed viewing the spectacle through their glasses. The slanting sunrays struck the forbidding cannon which the gray artillerymen were now beginning to serve; lines of Confederate infantry could be observed forming for

battle along the thin crest. The incredible feature of it all was that an extraordinary attack was beginning without anyone, from Grant down to the lowest private, knowing just where it was going. Said one of Beatty's colonels: "There was not the slightest intimation of an intention that the ridge was to be attacked and taken by storm. . . . nothing of the kind was in contemplation." Such was clear from Granger's orders. Such was clear from almost every participant's account noted.

Nearing the rifle pits, the Federal lines halted and fired a volley that thundered along Missionary Ridge and echoed from more distant Lookout. Then the two divisions charged together, keeping their lines fairly well dressed, but rushing impetuously, "like a raging torrent," someone said, "shouting eagerly, boisterously." Some called out, "Remember Chickamauga! Remember Chickamauga!" The great mass of men captured the pits and inundated Bragg's forward position.

The line of Confederates, too thin to withstand such an attack in depth, fell back, those who could, and began laboring up the mountain. Many were captured. Although, as it developed, Bragg's lines were not well engineered, his artillery had not been idle during their two months on Missionary Ridge and had the ranges accurately calculated and tested. Even as the gray-coated infantry struggled upward, the well-served artillery blazed from the ridge, pounding the rifle pits with "frightful precision." The pits gave protection from the front, none from the rear.

It is often true that a battle is won or lost in a twinkling. Here was the crisis of Chattanooga. Here, in fact, was the crisis in the career of Ulysses S. Grant, of George H. Thomas, Braxton Bragg, and other high officers of both armies. And not one of them had the slightest influence in shaping the ensuing course of events. Chance? Coincidence? Providence? Here, many have contended, was the hour of destiny for the American Republic.

The fate of two nations, the old Union and the new Confederacy, was suddenly taken from the grasp of the generals and thrust into the hearts and hands of the farm boys and office clerks, the college students and blacksmiths, the youthful lawyers and factory hands of Ohio, Indiana, Illinois, and a number of other states, who stood during a few fleeting seconds in the Confederate trenches in the midst of the hail of canister and shells sweeping down on them. Nobody had been able to reconnoiter the Confederate trenches. Nor did they calculate how grievously the captors of them would be exposed if this "demonstration" in Sherman's favor, this feeling-out of Bragg's center, ended at the bottom of the ridge.

No army could remain there, Alexander's, Caesar's, Napoleon's—nor that of Thomas. Thus exposed, any army would wither and rapidly disappear. The men had three choices: they could stand and be slaughtered, they could retire, which was foreign to their nature and would bring taunts of the Eastern and Vicksburg soldiers, or they could follow the retreating Confederates up the mountain.

As if by one impulse the entire line swept up the steep slope after the retreating enemy.

Nobody issued an order. None was needed. As Colonel Knefler, commanding the 79th Indiana, Beatty's brigade, Wood's division, explained: " . . . nothing could live in or about the captured line of field works; a few minutes of such terrific, telling fire would quickly convert them into untenable hideous slaughter pens. . . . There was no time or opportunity for deliberation. . . . Something must be done, and it must be done quickly."

421

The common soldier did what Bragg after Chickamauga failed to do. He followed the retreating enemy. Sheridan took out his silver whiskey flask, waved it at the Confederate gunners, shouted pleasantly, "Here's to you," and took a swig, only to be acknowledged by a close shell that scattered the dirt over his uniform. "That's damned ungenerous," he again shouted, and added that he would retaliate by capturing those guns. They were christened after the wives of Confederate generals—Lady Breckinridge, Lady Buckner, and the like. His men, like Wood's, plunged forward instinctively.

The mountain side became half gray with the uniforms of the retreaters, then half blue with the pursuers. Now and then the Confederates halted and turned to loose a blast of musketry. Necessarily the artillery fire from the summit subsided when friend became intermingled with foe. The slope is steep; it has every appearance of being impregnable, but just as the Confederates had pulled themselves up the almost sheer side of Round Top and the formidable incline of Little Round Top at Gettysburg, here the two armies struggled upward, now climbing, now battling with clubbed muskets and rocks, now halting and sending volleys into each other. No exaggeration could be involved in the statement that this mountain combat was as difficult as any fought during the war, perhaps more difficult than Malvern Hill in Virginia, Culp's Hill, Little Round Top, or Cemetery Ridge at Gettysburg, or along the Bloody Lane at Antietam, or Snodgrass Hill at Chickamauga, or anything except possibly the ghastly slaughter in front of Lee's trenches at Cold Harbor during the bloody affair where roughly ten thousand men fell in ten minutes.

One officer could be followed easily by friend and foe because he wore a bright red sash, a beautiful target for a sharpshooter, and waved his glittering sword, giving notice to the world that he commanded. The Confederates quickly got the message and a marksman's bullet crashed into his middle.

Perhaps the improbability of it all was what helped to panic the Confederate division on the summit, which looked down half helpless on the tide of friend and foe that struggled and panted step by step, and bush by bush, toward the crest. The crude and unfinished second line of rifle pits halfway up the steep slope was of little worth. It was overrun after a brief defense. By this time the smoke, the infantry soldier's godsend before the era of smokeless powder, was beneficently wrapping the mountain side. Even through the smoke, there was not much doubt at the top of the ridge, though considerably more back on Orchard Knob, where the high Union command tried to follow every detail, of how the fray was going.

Grant, standing with Rawlins and others, was close to Thomas, who had ordered the Army of the Cumberland forward to the bottom pits, and Granger, the corps commander who executed the movement. All were appalled. Then Grant was highly angered. Visions of Chickasaw Bluff must have passed through his mind. Troops could not storm so forbidding a mountain held by a formidable and up to this time victorious enemy army, well officered, well disciplined, battling to repel an invader from their homeland. Turning to Thomas, Grant inquired sharply, menacingly:

"Thomas, who ordered those men up that ridge?"

The "Old Hero" answered slowly, without excitement, "I don't know, I did not." Granger likewise disavowed it. Thomas, seeing Grant's displeasure, sent his Chief of Staff Joseph S. Fullerton to Wood and another staff officer to Sheridan to learn if they had ordered the men up the ridge. But Thomas told them—and here Thomas'

capacity for command disclosed itself—"if they can take it, push ahead!"

As Grant turned from Thomas, he muttered, as several heard him, that if the assault failed, someone would pay dearly for it!

The exchange brings to mind the declaration of General Douglas MacArthur after a later war that "there is no substitute for victory." Grant's statement showed there would be an accounting for violation of orders, or for exceeding orders, only in case of failure. The test was success. One may have heard the old story of the baseball rookie, who in the last of the ninth, with the score tied, none out, and a man on first, was told by the manager to bunt. Instead, he lashed out a long double and won the game. Returning to the bench to get the manager's warm applause, he received instead a blow on the chin, and a remark, "When I say bunt, I mean bunt."

Not so in warfare. Victory excuses anything—every-thing. When one is ordered to take a trench and wins a battle, all is usually forgiven and a new star appears on the culprit's shoulder. Had he not seen at the front, an opportunity the commander in the rear could not apprehend? In this instance, about 18,000 stars would be merited. Not only Grant, but "Old Hero" Thomas, plus Meigs, Dana, and others, all doubters, but all thrilled with the magnificent sight of the blue coats scaling the heights, were frightened that the effort was too audacious. All seemed convinced the men would be hurled back at the crest. Only Granger, who, like Thomas, disavowed giving the order, appeared sanguine. "When these men get going," he told Grant, "All hell can't stop them!"

Still, Grant reflected doubt. Because of his attitude, a wave of staff officers dashed forward from Orchard Knob to check the advance of the reckless men. But the hail of bullets was too steady for their mounts to penetrate it. 423

Most of them fell or, battle trained as they were, rebelled when the incline became sharp. How fortunate this was for the cause, some of the attackers recalled later. But the order did reach Sheridan's command, caused a trifling delay like a sand hill built by children in front of an advancing wave, and then the blue tide swept past the cautioning aides. No countermanding order reached Wood's division.

For the attackers, the going was a trifle easier as they neared the crest. Occasionally there were areas of dead space not commanded from the summit. Bragg, though he had had plenty of time, had not engineered his main defensive line to the best advantage. The works were generally on the thin topographical crest, and not on the military crest, usually some distance below, free from any shoulders or rises protecting the oncomers. That and the heavy smoke, the wave of retreating Confederates immediately in their front, and the inability of the gunners to depress the artillery—most of which eventualities the Federal high command could have anticipated—were the principal factors that made the assault feasible.

Working toward the summit, color bearers falling right and left, bending forward like men walking into a fierce rainstorm, sinking momentarily into pits and depressions, the "foxholes" of later wars, the stormers at length found themselves immediately in front of the Confederate works, where most of them dropped for a moment, exhausted, protected by the blessings that the artillery could not reach them and that the enemy's infantry fire was abating. Soon they were puzzled by the stillness in the Confederate trenches.

By this time, seeing his men so close to the top, Thomas had confirmed their audacity and ordered the entire line forward, which sent the divisions of Baird and Richard Johnson laboring on the flanks of Wood and Sheridan, giving protection from any enemy movements against the advancing and exposed flanks, such as were disastrous to Pickett when his flanks were enfiladed at Gettysburg.

There was fighting at the summit, to be sure, but it quickly became isolated and sporadic. The advance from the rifle pits at the base to the trenches at the summit was indeed an accomplishment with few parallels. As a participant described it, "Never in the history of our country, in battles on sea or land, was the American flag greeted by such a furious tempest of fire."

But why the sudden calm? Why no counterattack? Why no effort at a flanking movement? The Confederate division on the line where the Federal assault had its full impact suddenly left its works and rushed down the reverse slope of the mountain. Just then a heavy explosion sounded in the Confederate rear. It seemed to shake the mountain like an earthquake. The concussion beat heavily on the eardrums of the blue and gray soldiers. Two ammunition chests of the Washington Artillery of New Orleans had exploded. It seemed to serve as a signal for the half-rested Federal brigades. They rose and dashed with bayonets and clubbed muskets into the Confederate trenches, capturing guns, shouting in exultation, turning the cannon about to fire at the fleeing enemy. The summit in the center of Bragg's army was won.

Colonel Fred Knefler, of the 79th Indiana, mentioned before in this account, was born in Hungary in 1834. He went to military school there, and as a youth carried a musket in Kossuth's army for the liberation of the Magyars from the Hapsburgs. He learned drill, discipline, and the duties of a soldier. When Kossuth's cause failed he came to America, reached Indianapolis, worked as a carpenter, learned to speak beautiful English without the help of a teacher, studied Shakespeare, and eventually won the friendship of General Lew Wallace, later the author of *Ben Hur*, who at the outbreak of war made him his adjutant general. Later Colonel Knefler fought at Chickamauga; later he marched with Sherman to the sea. Now, in Beatty's brigade, Wood's division, as the attack moved against the ridge, he commanded two regiments, the 86th Indiana and his own. At their head, he stormed over the parapet and was credited with leading the first Federal units into the Confederate works.

There was no race track camera nor yet a finish-line tape on the crest of Missionary Ridge that evening and the claimants for first into the works were numerous. Henry M. Cist, the careful chronicler of the Army of the Cumberland, awarded first place to Sheridan's division, but conceded that "almost simultaneously" the crest was won in six places. Sheridan did have favorable ground toward the finish but was slowed a bit by the unhappy injunction brought by the aide to obey orders. Wood in elation when his men were at the top, declared feelingly: "Soldiers, you ought to be court-martialed, every man of you. I ordered you to take the rifle pits and you scaled the mountain!"

In later years when the question was raised of who first entered the main Confederate line, Wood assembled such a impressive sheaf of eye-witness testimony, some from other than his own command, that it has been difficult to assign the credit elsewhere, despite Cist's view and despite the fact that for this performance Grant came to dote on Sheridan instead of his old-time West Point roommate, Wood. Still, what seemed to impress Grant mainly was Sheridan's quick pursuit of the worsted and retreating enemy. Little Phil awaited no orders, as Ewell and Jubal Early did while the precious minutes sped by when they looked up at Culp's Hill and East Cemetery Ridge on July 1 at Gettysburg.

Colonel John A. Martin of the 8th Kansas, Willich's brigade, Wood's division, claimed the honors for his regiment as first to break the Confederate line, as did some of the Ohio men for their units, indicating that there was indeed what was later known as a photo-finish. The fact was that the Confederate line was soft at the point of impact, due in a measure to Bragg's faulty distribution of his troops.

One of Sheridan's conspicuous youths was first lieutenant and adjutant of the 24th Wisconsin, a Milwaukee regiment of Colonel Francis T. Sherman's brigade. Eighteen years old, he won a forecast in the regimental report that he would have "an honorable career." That, he surely did.

He was laboring up the mountain at the head of his regiment when the color bearer fell. Grasping the flagstaff as the line wavered, he rushed forward with great courage and planted the regimental standard on the Confederate works, an act of such signal heroism that he was one of the seven Union soldiers in this battle awarded the Congressional Medal of Honor.

He became a lieutenant colonel at 19 and fulfilled his commander's forecast by rising to be a lieutenant general in the American Army, and its commander in the Philippines. His name was Arthur MacArthur, Jr. His son, likewise a wearer of the Congressional Medal of Honor won in World War I, was General of the Armies Douglas MacArthur, destined to one of the distinguished careers of American military history.

Grant said the Confederate army was thrown into such disorder that the officers lost all control. That clearly was the case except for Cleburne's, Bate's, Gist's, and Stewart's divisions, or with other units that maintained their formation and made a passably orderly withdrawal. Still, Bragg had little to say in praise of his men.

He and Hardee made gallant efforts to rescue his army from disintegration. They tried to form a new line of Gist's, Bate's, and Cleburne's divisions and hold on the right, but the wound in the left center was irremediable. Someone recorded an adjutant's remark at the time of the Federal breakthrough: "I shall never forget the look of anguish on General Hardee's face."

View of Lookout Mountain from the hill to the north. Military road winding over north slope of Lookout was built after Hooker captured the mountain. From a wartime photograph. (B&L)

Hardee, the wing commander, assigned to Cleburne the task of safeguarding the army's retreat across Chickamauga Creek and through Ringgold Gap. No officer could have more ably conducted a rearguard that had to keep its formation and battle frequently and sometimes win, to save a confused, fleeing host.

Cleburne sent off his artillery across Chickamauga Creek. Colonel Hiram A. Granbury, commanding Cleburne's Texas Brigade, was the last to leave the ridge. Night had fallen but by 9 p.m. the last of the division was over the creek save for the pickets, who then crossed without the loss of a man.

The late November night turned bitter cold. Cleburne's heroic division of scarcely more than 4,000 waded Chickamauga Creek through water waist deep and in the early morning of November 26 spread across Ringgold Gap. Here the Chattanooga Campaign ended. Sheridan had followed to the Chickamauga Creek crossing but was halted by darkness, though he captured prisoners, small arms, and artillery and won Grant's hearty commendation. Hooker finally forded Chickamauga Creek without his artillery, captured Rossville, and took some prisoners, but the Confederates retreated before he got into the main action.

Bragg, writing his report a few days later, said: "A panic which I had never before witnessed seemed to have seized upon officers and men, and each seemed to be struggling for his personal safety, regardless of his duty or his character. . . . No satisfactory excuse can possibly be given for the shameful conduct of our troops on the left in allowing their line to be penetrated. The position was one which ought to have been held by a line of skirmishers against any assaulting column. . . ."

More vivid still is the account of Captain Buck:

"The scene of disorder at Chickamauga Station beggars description; it can only be appreciated by one who has seen a freshly beaten army. Regiments were separated from the brigades, the latter from divisions, and com-

manders from commands, and in great part army organization seemed lost. . . . It is difficult for those acquainted with the unflinching bravery of these same soldiers—tried and never found irresponsive to the call of duty upon every field of battle from Shiloh to Chickamauga—to realize, much less to understand, the unaccountable, shameful panic which seized them, and for which no apology can be found."

Unstinted was the praise of Cleburne. Bragg: " . . . Cleburne, whose command defeated the enemy in every assault . . . and who eventually charged and defeated him . . . who afterwards brought up our rear with great success, again charging and routing the pursuing column at Ringgold . . . is commended to the special notice of the Government."

And Hardee: "In the gloom of nightfall Cleburne's division, the last to retire, sadly withdrew from the ground it had held so gallantly. . . ."

Bragg in a letter to President Davis conceding his "shameful discomfiture" claimed the fault was not entirely his, charged that Breckinridge was drunk and "totally unfit for duty" for five days during the crisis of the battle, said it was a repetition of his conduct at Murfreesboro, and implied that Cheatham "is equally dangerous." But he feared "we both erred in the conclusion for me to retain command here after the clamor raised against me." That last, at least, was true.

The Battle of Chattanooga had momentous results.

It confirmed indisputable possession by the Federal army of Chattanooga, the rail center and heart city of the South, a community which more than any other tied the sprawling Confederacy into a nation of accessible parts. It led to the promotion of Grant to lieutenant general and commander in chief of the United States armies. It revealed again the sterling qualities and tactical abilities of Thomas. It launched Sheridan on the notable role he would play in the later stages of the struggle in Virginia. More indirectly,

it led to the promotion of Sherman as the over-all commander of the Western Federal armies.

For the South it was a shattering blow from which the Army of Tennessee never fully recovered. If it did open any beam of sunshine through the clouds looming over the cause of Southern independence, it was in ending Braxton Bragg as an army commander and sending him off to Richmond to become the personal military advisor of his friend, the President. The command passed in a few weeks through Hardee and Polk to the strategically able General Joseph E. Johnston, who succeeded in delaying the collapse of the Confederacy in the West by another year.

Grant in his later writings thought he moulded the battle a little more decisively than was actually the case, and became persuaded in his recollections that he had ordered the movement he so roundly condemned when it was being executed. But it was more a soldier's than a general's victory. Or did it, like so many battles, turn on the whims of the Goddess of Chance? Still, Grant with his simple directness, never made matters more difficult than they were, and did his part with a determined, unruffled calmness, an attitude that was a reassurance to those about him and, in turn, to the army.

Bragg, on the other hand, ratified again Longstreet's comment made after Chickamauga, that almost everything he did was wrong—that almost everywhere he should have done exactly the opposite. Bragg, the subordinate who had come out of the Mexican War with the highest reputation, ended his Civil War career as an army commander with the lowest. A man of such high principles and unfailing integrity deserves pity, more than the violent upbraiding history has accorded him. Few made more enemies needlessly, none struggled more tirelessly than he did to succeed.

Grant regarded his victory as well-nigh epochal: "If the same license had been allowed the people and the press in the South that had been allowed in the North, Chattanooga would probably have been the last battle fought for the preservation of the Union."

Battle of Ringgold, Ga., Nov. 27, 1863. Cleburne stationed his troops on the ridge; their fire was destructive; huge rocks were rolled down the mountain slope; confusion and heavy losses were inflicted on the attacking Federals who withdrew to await reenforcements. Cleburne's command retired unmolested.

426

THE WILDERNESS

CAMPAIGN

Text by Joseph P. Cullen
Designed by Frederic Ray

SHORTLY after midnight the morning of May 4, 1864 the Army of the Potomac, over 100,000 strong, was put in motion from its winter camp around Culpeper, Virginia, heading once again for the Rapidan River. On old maps of Virginia the river appeared as "Rapid Ann" but no one knew for sure whether it was because the unknown woman had a fast gait or simply a reputation for being somewhat skittish. To the veterans in the ranks it didn't really matter, but that river had played an important part in the history of the army. Now many of them wondered how long it would be before they saw it again. Although none of them could know it, they would now cross it for the last time as an army.

The Army of the Potomac had a new leader again, Lieutenant General Ulysses S. Grant. In March President Lincoln had appointed him commander in chief of all the armies of the United States, over one half million men. His headquarters, however, would be in the field with General George Meade's Army of the Potomac, which in effect put Grant in immediate command.

Fresh from his recent dramatic victories in the West, Grant had an excellent working relationship with Lincoln, which was something none of the previous commanders enjoyed. "He doesn't ask me to do impossibilities for him," Lincoln is reported to have said, "and he's the first general I've had that didn't." And before the campaign started he wrote Grant: "The particulars of your plans I neither know nor seek to know. You are vigilant and self-reliant; and, pleased with this, I wish not to obtrude any constraints or restraints upon you. . . . And now with a brave army, and a just cause, may God sustain you." To which Grant replied in part: "And since the promotion which placed me in command of all the armies,

and in view of the great responsibility and the importance of success, I have been astonished at the readiness with which everything asked for has been yielded, without even an explanation being asked. Should my success be less than I desire and expect, the least I can say is, the fault is not with you."

ALTHOUGH new to the East, Grant was fully aware of what had happened in that theater of war. As he stated: "Before this time these various armies had acted separately and independently of each other, giving the enemy an opportunity, often, of depleting one command, not pressed, to reinforce another more actively engaged. I determined to stop this. . . . My general plan now was to concentrate all the force possible against the Confederate armies in the field."

His immediate objective in the East, however, was General Robert E. Lee's Army of Northern Virginia which had spent the winter encamped in the Mine Run area of the Rapidan, just across the river from Culpeper. "To get possession of Lee's army was the first great object," Grant wrote. "With the capture of his army Richmond would necessarily follow." But he had no intention of attacking Lee behind the strong Confederate entrenchments at Mine Run. Instead, he planned to flank the Confederate position by crossing the Rapidan lower down at Germanna and Ely's Fords, thus forcing Lee to come out in the open and fight. Or, failing that, he hoped to get the Army of the Potomac between Lee and Richmond. To do this, however, he would have to risk battle in an area known as the Wilderness, a dense forest of second-growth pine and scrub oak, with numerous creeks, gullies, swamps, heavy tanglefoot underbrush, few farms or open

Federal corps commanders at The Wilderness and Spotsylvania. Left to Right: Generals Winfield S. Hancock, G. K. Warren, John Sedgwick, and Ambrose E. Burnside. (National Archives)

spaces, and most of the roads mere winding trails. Here his preponderance of forces, particularly the cavalry and artillery, could not be used to best advantage. Grant was willing to take that risk. However, as General A. A. Humphreys, Meade's chief of staff, explained, it was hoped "that by setting the whole army in motion at midnight, with its reserve artillery and great trains of over four thousand wagons, it might move so far beyond the Rapidan the first day that it would be able to pass out of the Wilderness and turn, or partially turn, the right flank of Lee before a general engagement took place."

AND so as dawn broke that morning long lines of blue-clad soldiers could be seen once again crossing the Rapidan in the start of a campaign that would not end until the war was over, almost a year later. Before dawn the cavalry had driven the Confederate pickets away from the crossings and by 6 a.m. the pontoons were ready for the infantry and artillery to cross. Gouverneur Warren's V Corps, preceded by James H. Wilson's cavalry division, crossed at Germanna Ford, about eight miles below Lee's position at Mine Run. John Sedgwick's VI Corps followed Warren, while Winfield S. Hancock's II Corps crossed at Ely's Ford, about six miles below Germanna, preceded by David M. Gregg's cavalry division and followed by the artillery, commanded by General Henry J. Hunt. A. T. A. Torbert's cavalry division remained north of the river to prevent the Confederates from crossing and possibly getting in the rear of the Federal army among the wagon trains. The commander of the cavalry was General "Phil" Sheridan. Grant had still another corps at his disposal, Ambrose Burnside's IX, which was left back in the Warrenton area to protect the Orange & Alexandria Railroad from Manassas Junction to Rappahannock Station in case the crossing of the Rapidan should be delayed. He was alerted, however, to be ready to march at a moment's notice once the crossing had been accomplished.

By nine o'clock that morning Lee had been informed of the Federal crossing by the Confederate signal station atop Clarke's Mountain. Although he had anticipated Grant's crossing at the fords, he decided not to contest the crossing for several reasons. One was the powerful Federal artillery, and another was the position of the Army of Northern Virginia. R. S. Ewell's corps was on the Rapidan above Mine Run, with A.P. Hill on his left even farther up the river, while James Longstreet's corps was encamped around Gordonsville, about ten miles south of Hill. Lee apparently believed that he would not have time to bring up a sufficient force to contest the crossing. And he was also concerned about the physical condition of his army. The arms and other equipment were generally satisfactory, but food and clothing had been in scant supply all winter. As General Evander Law wrote later, "A new pair of shoes or an overcoat was a luxury, and full rations would have astonished the stomachs of Lee's ragged Confederates." Not knowing which way Grant might proceed once he was south of the river, Lee nevertheless now ordered Ewell to march east on the Orange Turnpike, while Hill moved parallel with him on the Orange Plank Road. Longstreet was ordered to march for the general area of Todd's Tavern in order to come up on Hill's right. When all arrived Lee would have something over 60,000 troops.

SHORTLY after noon Grant crossed the river at Germanna Ford. Almost immediately he was handed a message from a signal station, which had intercepted a Confederate dispatch, that Ewell was moving forward. Grant immediately ordered Burnside to join the Army of the Potomac, marching by way of Germanna Ford. "Make forced marches until you reach this place. Start your troops now in the rear the moment they can be got off, and require them to make a night march." By mid-

Confederate corps commanders present at The Wilderness and Spotsylvania. Left to Right: Generals James Longstreet, A. P. Hill, and Richard S. Ewell. (All National Archives photographs)

From in front of Dowdall's Tavern: Plank Road in foreground, Wilderness Church on left, Hawkins farm on right. (From NA)

afternoon the II Corps was encamped around strategic Chancellorsville, while the V and VI Corps were on a line running generally north and south just west of the Wilderness Tavern area. To be sure, the Army of the Potomac was not out of the Wilderness, although the II Corps was actually on the eastern edge of it, but it did have control of all the strategic roads in the area. At Chancellorsville the Ely's Ford Road met the Orange Turnpike which ran east and west from Fredericksburg to Orange. A few miles west of Chancellorsville at Wilderness Church the Orange Plank Road took off to the south from the Turnpike and then ran generally parallel to the Orange Turnpike until it rejoined it again just west of Mine Run. At the Wilderness Tavern the Germanna Ford Road leading south crossed the Turnpike. South of the Turnpike, but before it met the Orange Plank Road, the continuation of the Germanna Road crossed Brock Road which led south and then southeast to Spotsylvania Court House.

In effect, then, the whole Army of the Potomac had ground to a halt early in the afternoon and while still in the Wilderness. Nevertheless Grant was not dissatisfied with the progress made. The halt had been made in order that the army not become separated from its long wagon trains, which if spread out in single file would stretch from the Rapidan to Richmond. If Lee's infantry captured or destroyed a large part of the trains by getting between them and the Federal army, Grant would be forced to retreat back across the Rapidan to be resupplied, and that above all he did not want to do. Also, most of the army had been on the march since midnight and many of the men, particularly the recruits, were more than ready to call it a day.

SOME of the veterans remembered later that a sad silence seemed to settle over the army that night in

430

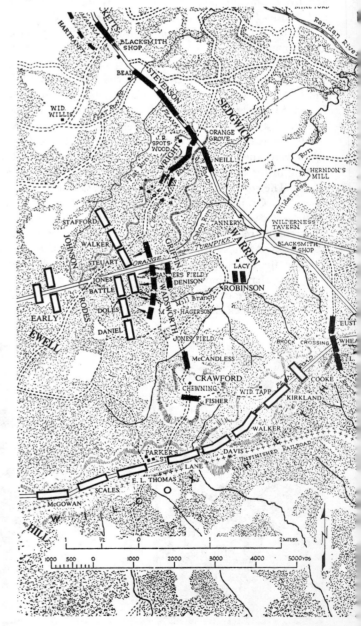

The maps used in this article are reproduced from Edward Steere's *The Wilder*

bivouac. The haunting cry of the whippoorwill echoed through the deep shadows. Occasionally someone stumbled over the bones of the unburied dead from the Chancellorsville battle just over a year before, sapping the morale of the new men in the blue ranks. Around the campfires in the stillness of the woods even the veterans were unusually quiet, haunted by memories or premonitions. One recalled that they all seemed to have "a sense of ominous dread which many of us found almost impossible to shake off." Later in the night the pickets near the Wilderness Tavern heard a rumbling off to the west and guessed that the Confederates were moving somewhere in the night to meet them.

They guessed right, of course. Ewell and Hill were on the move. At 8 o'clock that night Colonel Walter S. Taylor of Lee's staff sent the following message to Ewell: "If the enemy moves down the river, he wishes you to push on after him. If he comes this way, we will take our old line. The general's desire is to bring him to battle as soon as

WARREN'S V CORPS ATTACKS EWELL'S RIGHT AND CENTER

Showing the situation at about 1 p.m., May 5. Johnson and Rodes have deployed to meet Griffin's and Wadsworth's attack, while Heth has ordered a deployment on the line established by Cooke's brigade. Birney and Gibbon are moving north to reinforce the line established by Getty, while Wright is marching to extend Griffin's right.

possible." At that point Lee apparently believed that Grant would either go down river to Fredericksburg or up river to attack him directly. If he moved down river, the movement would of necessity be slow and a large rearguard would be required to protect the wagon trains. Ewell could attack that rearguard until Hill and Longstreet came up, in which case Lee might be able to swing them around to hit Grant in flank, as he had done to Hooker at Chancellorsville. If, on the other hand, Grant came up river then Ewell could fight a delaying action until Lee got behind his entrenchments at Mine Run. It was not until about midnight, when he received reports from his cavalry commander "Jeb" Stuart, that Lee realized Grant was not going to do either. It appeared now that he was going to march south through the heart of the Wilderness. Lee apparently was pleased at this opportunity to strike Grant in flank on the march in an area where Northern numerical superiority would be of small advantage, despite the fact that it would be at least another twenty-four hours before Longstreet could get up, leaving Lee with only two corps for the contemplated attack.

AT the first gray streaks of dawn the next morning, May 5, the vast Federal camp was astir. Hancock marched south from Chancellorsville and then angled slightly west in expectation of uniting his right with Warren, who then moved south from Wilderness Tavern, to be followed by Sedgwick. Warren wisely took the precaution of leaving Charles Griffin's division on the Turnpike facing west to protect his right flank while he started his other divisions south. By now the head of Burnside's corps was approaching Germanna Ford after an all-night march.

Shortly after daylight Griffin reported a strong Confederate force in his front, apparently getting ready to attack. Meade informed Grant at 7:30 a.m.: "The enemy have appeared in force on the Orange Pike, and are now reported forming line of battle in front of Griffin's division, Fifth Corps. I have directed General Warren to attack them at once with his whole force. Until this movement of the enemy is developed, the march of the corps must be suspended. I have, therefore, sent word to Hancock not to advance beyond Todd's Tavern for the present." Grant replied: "If any opportunity presents itself for pitching into a part of Lee's army, do so without giving time for disposition."

Warren's other divisions were now ordered into line south of the Turnpike on Griffin's left and Sedgwick's corps north of the road on Warren's right. But in the dense tangled thickets and heavy undergrowth it took a long time for even couriers to carry messages, and hours to maneuver divisions into positions, so it would be afternoon before Warren would be ready to attack.

By late morning Grant was convinced that it was more than a Confederate reconnoitering force on his flank, so Hancock was now ordered back to protect the strategic Orange Plank and Brock crossroad, where only a thin line of cavalry patrolled it. It would be late afternoon,

431

Harrisburg, 1960) through courtesy of the publisher, The Stackpole Company.

however, before Hancock's troops could possibly get there, which Grant realized, so George Getty's division of Sedgwick's corps was sent to hold the crossroad at any cost until Hancock could come up.

EWELL, meanwhile, came into line of battle across the Turnpike with Edward Johnson's division in the center, Robert Rodes's south of the road, and Jubal Early's to the north facing Sedgwick. When Ewell informed Lee, who was on the Orange Plank Road with Hill, of his position, he was told to base his movements on the head of Hill's column, whose position he could judge by the firing in its front, and not to bring on a general engagement until Longstreet was up, which would not be until the next morning. Ewell, however, was in no position to control events and there was no way for him to prevent the Federals from bringing on a general engagement.

About 1 p.m. as Griffin's men moved west along the Turnpike the air became still and sultry, the dry underbrush crackling beneath their feet. From beyond the trees in their front came the dull popping of the skirmishers' guns. Yellow slits of light began to blink along the regimental lines and little balls of smoke, gray and compact, floated slowly upward in the stifling air. The initial attack hit Johnson's division in Ewell's center and drove it back, but Johnson quickly counterattacked and stabilized his line. As the troops on both sides spread north and south

432

Grim fighting in The Wilderness. This sketch shows more open woodland than was usually the case, where visibility was frequently as low as a few yards, and the difficulty was often compounded by battle haze and the smoke of burning woods.

Federal soldiers rest behind breastworks while their comrades clear a field of fire during a lull in The Wilderness battle.

of the road, they disappeared into the twilight gloom of the dense foliage among the gnarled and twisted tree trunks. Soon the woods echoed to the roar of cannon, the crack of musketry, the angry, confused shouts of men trying desperately to kill each other.

Over on the Confederate right Hill advanced along the Plank Road, quickly driving off the Federal cavalry patrolling the vital Brock crossroad, as Getty's division raced south along the Brock Road in a desperate effort to save it. Getty with his staff was already at the crossroad waiting impatiently for his troops to arrive. One of these officers described what happened next:

> Soon a few gray forms were discerned far up the narrow Plank Road moving cautiously forward, then a bullet went whistling overhead, and another and another, and then the leaden hail came faster and faster over and about the little group until its destruction seemed imminent and inevitable. But Getty would not budge. "We must hold this point at any risk," he exclaimed, "our men will soon be up." In a few minutes, which seemed like an age to the little squad, the leading regiment of Wheaton's brigade, the 1st, came running like greyhounds along the Brock Road until the first regiment passed the Plank Road, and then, at the command "Halt!" "Front!" "Fire!", poured a volley into the woods and threw out skirmishers in almost less time than it takes to tell it. Dead and wounded rebel skirmishers were found within thirty yards of the crossroad, so nearly had they gained it, and from these wounded persons it was learned that Hill's corps, Heth's division in advance, supported by Wilcox's division, was the opposing force.

The Federals had saved the vital crossroad, just barely, but Getty's men were in for a few rough hours as Hill with two divisions (Richard H. Anderson's division was not yet up) attacked furiously. But by late afternoon Hancock's troops began to arrive, David Birney's and Gersham Mott's divisions in the lead, and Grant now ordered Getty and Hancock to attack before Anderson arrived. For the remainder of daylight the fighting continued at a furious pace, fighting such as these two

Major General George Gordon Meade took command of the Army of the Potomac three days before the Battle of Gettysburg.

armies had never seen before and would never see again. Troops could not maneuver in the wild country, battle lines broke into small fragments, nobody could see anything at all. Line officers guessed at the progress of the battle by the sound of the firing. Regiments, brigades, and even divisions inextricably mixed. As Confederate General Law wrote: "It was a desperate struggle between the infantry of the two armies, on a field whose physical aspects were as grim and forbidding as the struggle itself. It was a battle of brigades and regiments rather than of corps and divisions." A Federal soldier remembered that, "As for the fighting, it was simply bushwhacking on a grand scale in brush where all formation beyond that of regiments or companies was soon lost, and where such a thing as a consistent line of battle on either side was impossible." A veteran of the 5th Texas Regiment when captured and asked what he thought of the battle replied: "Battle be —! It ain't no battle! It's a worse riot than Chickamauga was. You Yanks don't call this a battle, do you? At Chickamauga there was at least a rear, but here there ain't neither front nor rear. It's all a — mess! And our two armies ain't nothing but howlin' mobs!"

433

SEDGWICK CARRIES THE ATTACK TO EWELL'S LEFT

This shows Wright's advance to the attack at about 3 p.m., May 5. Warren's division has been pulled back, and Ricketts is marching down the Germanna Plank Road, off the map to the north.

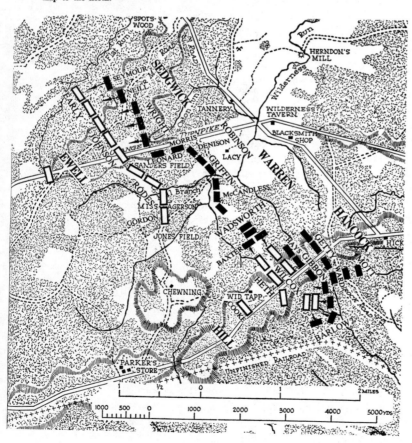

HANCOCK'S DOUBLE ENVELOPMENT CLOSES ON HILL'S CORPS

Showing the situation at about 7:30 p.m., May 5. The two flank attacks close on Heth as Wilcox goes to the latter's relief. On the north the fighting continues. Seymour's attempted envelopment of Ewell's left flank is frustrated by the arrival of Hays and Pegram. Thus Lee wins the race of local reserves. The fighting between Sedgwick and Ewell continues until dark.

The trains of the Army of the Potomac have closed up at Dowdalls Tavern. Johnston's brigade of Rodes' division is still enroute from Hanover Junction; it arrives on the battlefield the morning of May 6.

DESPITE the impossible conditions, Hancock's advantage in numbers began to tell as Hill's men were slowly driven back down the Plank Road in complete confusion. In the hot, still air the musketry smoke clung to the ground before lifting, and through it the guns flashed and crackled as men fired blindly. The noise roared to a crescendo that left them dazed. Regimental and company commanders lost communication and control in the dense forest, amid the underbrush, swamps, creeks, smoke and noise. In some places even companies had to retreat in single file, not knowing who or what was on their left or right. Fortunately for Lee, darkness ended the fighting just as Hill was about to suffer an outright defeat.

Tragic as the fierce fighting had been all day, now a new horror developed as the tinder-dry forest caught fire in several places. "Flames sprang up in the woods in our front," wrote a soldier in the 2d Massachusetts Artillery, "where the fight of the morning had taken place. With crackling roar, like an army of fire, it came down upon the Union line. The wind drove the blinding smoke and suffocating heat into our faces. This, added to the oppressive heat of the weather, was almost unendurable. It soon became terrible. The line of fire, with resistless march, swept the thickets before its advance, then reaching out its tongue of flame, ignited the breastworks composed of resinous logs, which soon roared and crackled along their entire length. . . . The fire was the most terrible enemy our men met that day, and few survivors will forget this attack of flames. . . ." Many of the wounded burned to death that night in the flaming Wilderness.

Despite the heavy fighting all day, the lines were still approximately the same when darkness finally put an end to it. Grant, realizing how close Hancock had come to breaking through that day, ordered him to attack again at 5 a.m. in an attempt to drive Hill back and roll up Lee's right flank before Longstreet's corps could arrive. Sedgwick and Warren were to keep pressure on Ewell to prevent Lee from shifting forces from left to right in order to help Hill. Burnside with two divisions was to fill the gap between Warren's left and Hancock's right and if he succeeded "in breaking the enemy's center, to swing around to the left and envelop the right of Lee's army." His other division was sent to support Hancock directly.

LEE was well aware of how close he had come to disaster that day on his right flank. Consequently, Longstreet was now ordered to make an all-night march in order to reach the field by daylight to relieve Hill's weary troops. Ewell was ordered to open a heavy fire at daylight in the hope that this might relieve the pressure on Hill, at least until Longstreet could get into position. Stuart with his cavalry was ordered to try to get on Hancock's left and rear to disrupt his supply line.

Promptly at 5 a.m. Hancock moved out on the attack and proceeded to drive Hill back. Hancock's men were rela-

*Rescuing the wounded from the burning woods of The Wilderness.
(A.R. Waud drawing in Collections of the Library of Congress)*

tively fresh compared to Harry Heth's and Cadmus Wilcox's, who were "thoroughly worn out," according to General Law. "Their lines were ragged and irregular, with wide intervals, and in some places fronting in different directions. In the expectation that they would be relieved during the night, no effort was made to rearrange and strengthen them to meet the storm that was brewing." Soon the whole line gave way and the Federals rushed forward, driving the Confederates west along the Orange Plank Road. About two miles west of the crossroad was a meager little clearing in the woods around the Widow Tapp farm. Here stood Lee himself among the guns of William Poague's artillery desperately trying to rally the men until Longstreet, expected momentarily, could arrive. Another mile west and the Federals would be around his right flank and among his supply trains, and the whole Army of Northern Virginia would be in grave danger.

But as Hancock's men emerged from the woods into the Tapp clearing, the massed Confederate cannon blasted them back. In the confusion they paused to regroup and reorganize their lines for another attack. Hancock was jubilant. To an officer on Meade's staff he cried, "We are driving them, sir! Tell General Meade we are driving them most beautifully." In reality, however, things were not going as well as Hancock at first believed. Burnside,

Brigadier General James S. Wadsworth, one of the heroes of Gettysburg, was mortally wounded in The Wilderness. (From B&L)

435

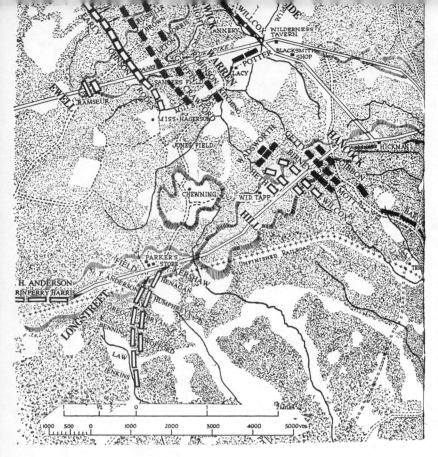

EWELL BEATS MEADE TO THE PUNCH

Hancock, Warren, and Sedgwick attack simultaneously at 5 a.m., May 6. However, Ewell anticipates this by attacking on his extreme left a half hour earlier. Burnside's corps is moving toward the gap between Hill and Ewell. Gibbon has been assigned to the command of a provisional corps of five brigades, posted to cover the Federal left flank.

Longstreet's corps and R. H. Anderson's division are arriving on the field. Johnston's brigade of Rodes' division has just arrived after its long march from Hanover Junction.

The Federal cavalry is on the line: Brock-Furnace Road intersection—Todds Tavern—Piney Branch Church.

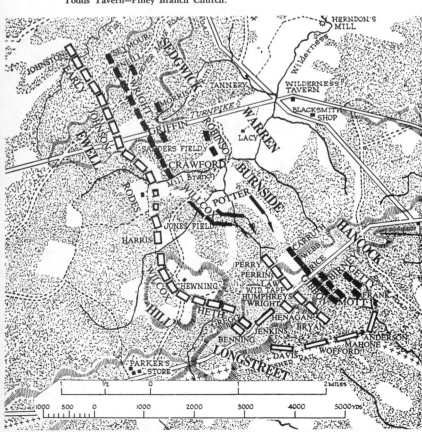

Distributing ammunition under fire to Warren's V Corps

dilatory as usual, was not up and would not be in position to have any effect until the afternoon, and his division sent to support Hancock was just now arriving and would not be in line for several hours yet. "I knew it!" Hancock yelled in anger. "Just what I expected! If he could attack *now*, we would smash A.P. Hill all to pieces!"

HANCOCK was probably right, but at that dramatic moment Longstreet's troops appeared on the field. Seeing the welcome reinforcements, Hill's troops rallied and moved to the left to close the gap between them and Ewell's right and thus were in position to block Burnside across the Chewning plateau. Longstreet advanced along the Orange Plank Road with Charles Field's division on the north and Joseph B. Kershaw's on the south, driving the Federals back, the blow falling primarily on Birney's and Mott's divisions. Finding Hancock's left flank somewhat in the air, Longstreet now swung his brigades south of the road along an unfinished railroad and hit the Federals hard in flank driving them back to their entrenchments around the crossroad. It now seemed as if Lee had an opportunity to roll up Grant's left flank, but Longstreet's

LONGSTREET STARTS AROUND THE FEDERAL SOUTH FLANK

The stalemate on the north flank continues. Burnside, ordered to move by the left flank and attack Longstreet, has begun this movement. Longstreet, after assembling and enveloping force, is moving the brigades in column against Hancock's left and rear.

The remnants of Wadsworth's force, including the heavy artillery brigade under Kitching, have been withdrawn in reserve near the Lacy house, but have been omitted from this map.

troops attacking to the north became mixed up with Hill's facing east and had to halt to straighten out the lines and regroup. During this process Longstreet was wounded and had to leave the field, the command then falling to Anderson.

A temporary lull now settled over the field as both sides tried to organize for another attack. In mid afternoon Grant ordered Hancock and Burnside to attack, but Lee beat him to the punch. Personally taking command of Longstreet's corps, Lee hit Hancock again. But according to General Law, "When at 4 o'clock an attack was made upon the Federal line along the Brock Road, it was found strongly fortified and stubbornly defended. The log breastworks had taken fire during the battle, and at one point separated the combatants by a wall of fire and smoke which neither could pass. Part of Field's division captured the works in their front, but were forced to relinquish them for want of support. Meanwhile Burnside's corps, which had reinforced Hancock during the day, made a vigorous attack on the north of the Orange Plank Road. James Lane's (Alabama) and Edward Perry's (Florida) brigades were being forced back when, Heth's division coming to their assistance, they assumed the offensive, driving Burnside's troops beyond the extensive line of breastworks constructed previous to their advance."

THUS it continued for the remainder of the day, neither side able to gain any permanent advantage. Over on Hancock's far left and rear, the cavalry of both sides had fought a more or less separate battle during the day. When

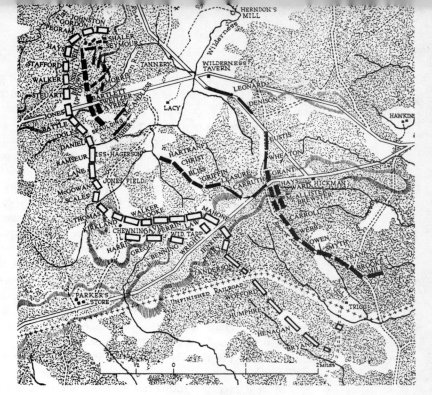

GORDON'S ATTACK

The situation at about 7:30 p.m., May 6. Gordon, supported by Pegram and Johnston, smashes Seymour and Shaler. VI Corps local reserves stop this attack. Crawford's division moves north to reinforce the Federal flank.

Lee now abandons his assault and commences to entrench along his front. On the Federal side, Burnside is also entrenching and connecting with Hancock's Brock Road line. The broken units of Wadsworth's division near the Lacy house have been omitted from this map.

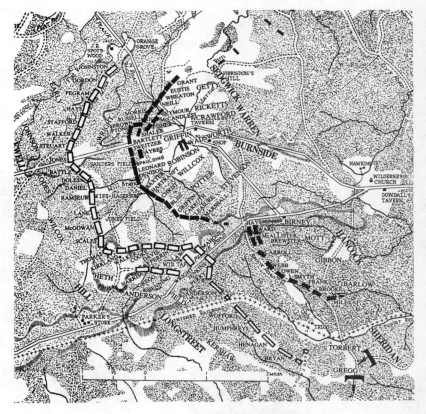

THE MORNING OF MAY 7

By morning of May 7 most brigades have rejoined their divisions, and the corps are again sorted out. Meade has refused his north flank, and both sides are continuing to entrench. Sheridan's cavalry has been relieved of its mission of guarding the trains, being replaced by Ferrero's division. Sheridan withdrew his cavalry, somewhat, after Hancock's reverse on the 6th, but later reoccupied his line covering the Federal south flank. Sheridan is now moving Torbert and Gregg to Todds Tavern, and Wilson (off the map) is at Piney Branch Church. Only light skirmishing occurs on this day. The battle is over.

Grant learned that Stuart's cavalry was attempting to get in rear of Hancock he had sent Sheridan and the Federal cavalry over to stop him. Brisk skirmishes were fought at the intersection of the Furnace and Brock Roads and at Todd's Tavern, with neither side gaining a clear-cut victory. But Stuart was stopped and Hancock's rear protected. And just as darkness fell that night, Ewell ordered an attack on Sedgwick's right flank which was hanging in the air unprotected. A force under General John B. Gordon hit it hard in a surprise attack. Part of James Rickett's division gave way and two generals and a large part of a brigade were captured. But in the darkness and the woods the Confederates became disorganized and the attack fizzled. Gordon later claimed that if he had been supported he could have rolled up Grant's whole right flank, but Early maintained that if the Federals had realized how badly the Confederates were disorganized they could have inflicted serious damage on Ewell's corps. In any event, night closed the fighting, and with it the Battle of The Wilderness.

"More desperate fighting has not been witnessed on this continent than that of the 5th and 6th of May," wrote Grant. The Federals had lost over 15,000 in killed, wounded, and missing; the Confederates, probably about 11,400.

IT was now evident to both Lee and Grant that the two armies were entrenched so strongly that attack by either side would probably be suicidal. As Grant stated,". . . the moment arms were stacked the men intrenched them-selves. For this purpose they would build up piles of logs or rails if they could be found in their front, and dig a ditch throwing the dirt forward on the timbers. Thus the digging they did counted in making a depression to stand in, and increased the elevation in front of them. It was wonderful how quickly they could in this way construct defenses of considerable strength." The same situation, of course, applied to the Confederates also. Consequently, early in the morning of May 7 Grant ordered Meade to "Make all preparations during the day for a night march to take position at Spotsylvania C. H. with one army corps, at Todd's Tavern with one, and another near the intersection of the Piney Branch and Spotsylvania road with the road from Alsop's to Old Court House."

In other words, instead of retreating to lick his wounds as other commanders of the Army of the Potomac had done, Grant again decided to move around Lee's right flank by sliding leftward and southward. And he reported to Washington: "At present we can claim no victory over the enemy, neither have they gained a single advantage." A very accurate and honest description of the situation.

Confederate line waiting orders in a cleared section in The Wilderness. From W.L. Sheppard sketch. ("Battles & Leaders")

SPOTSYLVANIA

Text by Joseph P. Cullen
Designed by Frederic Ray

Battle of Spotsylvania from the Prang chromolithograph by Thure de Thulstrup depicting the fight at Bloody Angle.

S OUTH and slightly east of the Wilderness area was another strategic crossroad at the village of Spotsylvania Court House. The place itself was just a sleepy hamlet, a handful of houses scattered carelessly about a country crossroad, but Federal possession would seriously endanger the Confederate line of communication to Richmond. "My object in moving to Spotsylvania," Grant wrote, "was two-fold: first, I did not want Lee to get back to Richmond in time to attempt to crush Butler before I could get there; second, I wanted to get between his army and Richmond if possible; and, if not, to draw him into the open field."

Shortly after dark on May 7 Warren was ordered to pull out of line and proceed toward Spotsylvania Court House by way of Brock Road, passing behind Burnside's and Hancock's corps. Sedgwick would follow Warren by way of Chancellorsville and the Piney Branch Church Road to where it met the Brock Road. Burnside would march farther east and take the Fredericksburg-Spotsylvania Court House Road. When the rest of the army had moved out, Hancock would follow Warren on the Brock Road. Sheridan and the cavalry had been ordered to clear the way.

During the day the Confederates had been alert for any movement that Grant might make. Lee's scouts informed him that the bridges across the Rapidan had been removed and the area around Germanna Ford abandoned. Obviously, then, Grant was not going to retreat as Hooker had done just a year ago. But when the Federal wagon trains started to move they raised a huge cloud of dust, as the roads were powder dry. So Grant was moving somewhere. If he was just changing base, he could be going to Fredericksburg, but, if he was moving south, his next immediate objective would undoubtedly be Spotsylvania. In either

441

McCool's farm house, within the "Bloody Angle," Spotsylvania. Sketch made from a wartime photograph. ("Battles & Leaders")

event, Lee decided he had better move his army to Spotsylvania, so he ordered a clearing cut through the forest from the Orange Plank Road to the road running from Orange to Spotsylvania in the area of Shady Grove Church. That night Longstreet's corps, now commanded by Anderson, was ordered to take the route to Spotsylvania. Hill and Ewell would follow Anderson as soon as they could.

FOR an army to make an all-night march after two days of brutal combat and one day of nervous alert was no easy task, and much confusion existed that night. Warren reached Todd's Tavern on the Brock Road about 3 a.m., but here he was halted as the road was blocked by Sheridan's cavalry, and a little farther on was Stuart's cavalry. It took several hours to drive the Confederate cavalry off and to clear the road, and as Warren approached Spotsylvania Court House it was becoming daylight. But he never did reach it. The delay had enabled Anderson to take up an entrenched position on a slight rise, about a mile and a half northwest of the vital crossroad. In his *Memoirs* Grant stated:

> But Lee, by accident, beat us to Spotsylvania. Our wagon trains had been ordered easterly of the roads the troops were to march upon before the movement commenced. Lee interpreted this as a semi-retreat of the Army of the Potomac to Fredericksburg, and so informed his government. Accordingly he ordered Longstreet's corps—now commanded by Anderson—to move in the morning (the 8th) to Spotsylvania. But the woods being still on fire, Anderson could not go into bivouac, and marched directly on to his destination that night. By this accident Lee got possession of Spotsylvania. It is impossible to say now what would have been the result

if Lee's orders had been obeyed as given; but it is certain that we would have been in Spotsylvania and between him and his capital. My belief is that there would have been a race between the two armies to see which could reach Richmond first, and the Army of the Potomac would have had the shorter line. Thus, twice since crossing the Rapidan we came near closing the campaign, so far as battles were concerned, from the Rapidan to the James River or Richmond. The first failure was caused by our not following up the success gained over Hill's corps on the morning of the 6th: the second, when fires caused by that battle drove Anderson to make a march during the night of the 7th-8th which he was ordered to commence on the morning of the 8th. But accident often decides the fate of battle.

Warren assumed the enemy in his front was just the Confederate cavalry that Sheridan had driven off earlier, so at 8 a.m. he sent John C. Robinson's division forward to the attack. Robinson, however, received a rude shock when he ran up against Anderson's entrenched troops and was driven back with heavy losses. Warren organized for another attack, but it took time as most of the men were by now near exhaustion after their all-night march. Just before noon he attacked again with his whole corps, but the attack was made piecemeal with one division at a time and consequently failed to dislodge Anderson. Grant, who was anxious to crush Anderson before Lee could get the rest of his army up, now ordered Sedgwick, who was at Piney Branch Church, to Warren's support for another attempt. But Sedgwick for some reason was slow in getting up to form on Warren's left, and it was five o'clock before they could attack. But again the assault was made piecemeal and was not pushed on a wide front, probably because of the physical condition of the troops. During the fight Ewell appeared on the field and came into line on Anderson's right. Hill's corps, now under Early because of Hill's illness, would form on Ewell's right when it reached the field early the next morning.

That night Grant ordered Sheridan and his cavalry to make a raid around Lee's army to disrupt his communications with Richmond, and then to proceed south to re-

442

provision his force from Butler's army south of the James River. Grant hoped that this would force Lee to send Stuart's cavalry after Sheridan, which in effect would protect the Federal supply trains from Confederate cavalry raids. Lee did send Stuart after Sheridan, and in a later engagement of the two cavalry forces at Yellow Tavern, on the outskirts of Richmond, Stuart was mortally wounded.

THE next day, May 9, was spent mostly in getting the remainder of the army into position and entrenching, although sharpshooting and skirmishing was heavy at times, and one of the casualties was the most liked general officer in the Army of the Potmac. In an effort to convince his men in the VI Corps that the sharpshooters "couldn't hit an elephant at this distance," Sedgwick rode forward to an elevated position in his front and fell dead with a bullet in his head. General Horatio Wright then assumed command of the VI Corps.

Later in the day, misled by reports that Lee was withdrawing from the Federal right, Grant ordered Hancock across the Po River to take Lee in flank and rear. Before Hancock could make contact, however, the mistake was realized and he was recalled. In recrossing the river he was attacked by Early whom Lee had sent over from the Confederate right to block Hancock's advance. Hancock extricated himself from this dangerous position and then came into line on Wright's left. Burnside, meanwhile, had come down the Fredericksburg road and now held the extreme Federal left, next to Hancock.

Grant believed that Lee had weakened other parts of his line in order to drive Hancock back, so on the afternoon of May 10 he sent Warren and Wright to attack the left center of the Confederate position. Lee now had Anderson on his left opposite Warren and Wright, Ewell was in front of Hancock, and Early on the right faced Burnside. All were strongly entrenched behind powerful breastworks. There was one weak spot in the line, however. Ewell's entrenchments jutted out in a U-shaped

Brevet Major General Emory Upton. His great hour of combat came when he led the Union assault on "Bloody Angle." (B&L)

salient beyond the rest of the lines. Being elevated, it was a good spot for artillery, which was why Ewell wanted it in the first place, and he placed twenty-two guns there to hold it. It was nearly a mile deep and about half a mile wide. But the Mule Shoe, as the Confederates called it, made an inviting target. Colonel Emory Upton, of Wright's corps, was selected to lead the attack against the west side of the Mule Shoe with twelve picked regiments, to be supported by Mott's divisin of Hancock's corps. Upton ordered the assault to be made with four lines of three regiments each. When the first line breached the salient, he ordered them to fan out to the left and right to take Ewell's troops in flank, while the other regiments coming up behind could go straight ahead through the opening to stop any reinforcements that might be sent up. Also,

Center of Union position at Spotsylvania, May 10. (From B&L)

Spotsylvania Court House, focal point of bloody fighting in The Wilderness Campaign. (Sketch from "Battles & Leaders")

they were to make the initial charge across an open field without stopping to fire and reload.

ABOUT 6 p.m. Upton's men charged out of the woods that concealed them, with a cheer, raced across the open ground and charged into the salient, the fading sun glistening on the steel bayonets. After some brief, but desperate, hand-to-hand fighting, the surprise attack succeeded, the plan working just as Upton had predicted it would. The impregnable line of earthworks had been breached with a narrow but deep penetration, and about 1,000 of Ewell's men had been captured along with several pieces of artillery. Now if Mott's division charged through the opening promptly, the Army of Northern Virginia would be in a critical position. But, as Grant later wrote, Mott "failed utterly." Coming to Upton's support and with only about half a mile to go, Mott's troops came under heavy artillery fire, broke, and then retreated in confusion. There was nothing left for Upton to do now but withdraw. He took his prisoners with him but was forced to abandon the guns he had captured. Grant promoted him to general on the spot, later confirmed by the President.

That night Wright told Meade, "General, I don't want Mott's men on my left; they are not a support; I would rather have no troops there." A few days later the division was broken up and Mott's brigades transferred to Birney's divison.

Elsewhere the attack had not gone any better. Warren was beaten back and Wright could not make any permanent advances. The next day Grant wrote to Washington: "We have now ended the sixth day of very heavy fighting. The result to this time is much in our favor. But our losses have been heavy, as well as those of the enemy. . . . I am now sending back to Belle Plain all my wagons for a fresh supply of provisions and ammunition, and propose to fight it out on this line if it takes all summer."

GRANT had been much impressed with Upton's success, and before starting another flanking movement around Lee's right decided to attack him in his entrenched position once more, using Upton's tactics on a much larger scale against the same position. That afternoon he wrote

an order to Burnside: "Major-General Hancock has been ordered to move his entire corps under cover of night to join you in a vigorous attack against the enemy at 4 a.m. of to-morrow, the 12th instant. You will move against the enemy with your entire force promptly and with all possible vigor at precisely 4 o'clock to-morrow morning. Let your preparations for this attack be conducted with the utmost secrecy, and veiled entirely from the enemy. . . . Generals Warren and Wright will hold their corps as close to the enemy as possible, to take advantage of any diversion caused by your and Hancock's attack, and will push in their whole force if any opportunity presents itself."

In the predawn darkness of May 12 rain set in, wrapping the area in a sullen mist. The drops ticked off the leaves monotonously as Hancock's and Burnside's men formed for the attack, stumbling through the dark and the rain and the mud. Their noisy approach alerted the Confederate pickets that this would be no small attack, and now Ewell's division and brigade commanders were really concerned.

Ewell was well aware that the apex of the salient was his weakest point and consequently had placed the twenty-two artillery pieces there. But Lee, misled by a report that Grant was moving around his right flank again had ordered the guns to the rear to be ready to move quickly if necessary. Alerted by the reports of the pickets, they were now frantically galloping up to the front again in the

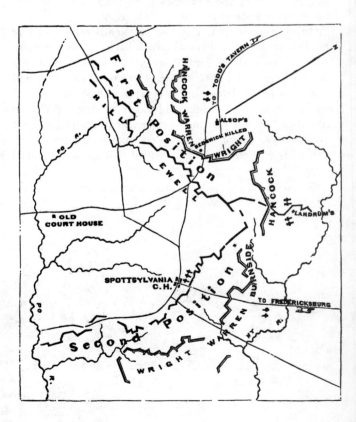

Map of the Battle of Spotsylvania Court House, May 10-12, 1864. ("Lossing's Civil War in America")

444

*Struggle for the salient, near Spotsylvania, May 12, 1864.
(A.R. Waud drawing in Collections of the Library of Congress)*

rainy darkness, and would arrive just in time for twenty of them to be captured without having fired a shot.

IN the early morning rain the massed Federal column hit the apex, Hancock's corps at the center and Burnside's on the east side. Francis Barlow, commanding Hancock's leading division, broke through, closely followed by Birney's division. The blue-clad troops poured through the gap and advanced. Without the necessary artillery support, Ewell's troops were forced back, losing the twenty guns in the process, in addition to General Johnson and about 3,000 of his men, practically the whole division.

But then things began to go wrong for the Federals. Instead of fanning out to the left and right, as Upton's regiments had done, to widen the breach and enable Burnside to come through, they went straight ahead and jammed up. The supporting troops coming in behind them crowded up so closely that organization and control was just about impossible, and the 3,000 prisoners only added to the confusion. The delay enabled Lane's brigade

of Hill's corps (temporarily under Early during Hill's absence), which was immediately on the right of the captured works, to fall back to an unfinished line in the rear and pour a telling flanking fire on Hancock's left, which stopped the advance. Then Gordon's division of Ewell's corps, which was being held in reserve, was thrown in front of the Federal column, slowly forcing Hancock's men back to the Confederate entrenchments in their rear. About 6 a.m. Grant ordered Warren and Wright to Hancock's support, but another breakthrough was not achieved. In the initial assault Potter's division of Burnside's corps momentarily broke through the east side of the salient but was quickly driven out again by Early's troops who came over to their left to support Ewell.

Again, as in The Wilderness, Lee now appeared on the field to rally his men in this critical moment. If the assault succeeded, the Army of Northern Virginia might be cut in two and destroyed piecemeal. All day long and into the night the battle raged along the whole line with increasing fury. One Confederate officer remembered that "there was one continuous roll of musketry from dawn until midnight." Lee made five separate assaults in a vain attempt to recover his position. Although he failed in this,

445

the Confederates did hold so that he could have new works constructed at the base of the Mule Shoe to straighten out his line.

A FEW hundred yards west of the salient the Confederate trenches made a slight bend to the south, known as the "angle," and later as the "Bloody Angle." Here the men of Wright's corps came face to face with Ewell's veterans in a vicious hand-to-hand fight. Clubbed muskets and bayonets were used freely, as the rain poured down in sheets and the trenches ran red with blood. In some places the wounded and dying of both sides were trampled into the mud to drown or suffocate in the frenzied fighting. "The flags of both armies waved at the same moment over the same breast-works," one soldier noted, "while beneath them Federal and Confederate endeavored to drive home the bayonet through the interstices of the logs." Colonel Porter, of Grant's staff, later described the scene as he remembered it. "The battle near the 'angle' was probably the most desperate engagement in the history of modern warfare, and presented features which were absolutely appalling. It was chiefly a savage hand-to-hand fight across the breastworks. Rank after rank was riddled by shot and shell and bayonet-thrusts, and finally sank, a mass of torn and mutilated corpses; then fresh troops rushed madly forward to replace

The struggle for the works at the "Bloody Angle." (From B&L)

446

A COMPARATIVE lull settled over the area for the next several days, as each army tried to catch its breath and the rain continued to pour down. "Since the 3rd we had been marching, fighting, and building earthworks so continuously," wrote a soldier in the 13th Massachusetts Volunteers, "that no opportunity had been afforded to change any of our clothing." On the 16th Grant reported to Washington: "We have had five days' almost constant rain without any prospect yet of its clearing up. The roads have now become so impassable that ambulances with wounded can no longer run between here and Fredericksburg. All offensive operations necessarily cease until we can have twenty-four hours of dry weather." He had suffered over 17,000 casualties at Spotsylvania Court House and he now requested replacements be sent to him. But he did not want anyone in Washington to get the idea that he intended to stop fighting or retreat. "You can assure the President and Secretary of War," he wrote, "that the elements alone have suspended hostilities and that it is in no manner due to weakness or exhaustion on our part."

Grant was gradually getting to know the Army of the Potomac and, more important, the caliber of its generals. He was becoming dissatisfied with Burnside and Warren for their dilatory tactics and lack of drive and initiative. There seems little doubt that had they attacked at Spotsylvania with the force and coordination that Hancock and Wright used, that the Army of Northern Virginia might very well have been destroyed. Of Warren he later wrote: "Warren's difficulty was two fold: when he received an order to do anything, it would at once occur to his mind how all the balance of the army should be engaged so as properly to cooperate with him. His ideas were generally good, but he would forget that the person giving him orders had thought of others at the time he had of him. In like manner, when he did get ready to execute an order, after giving most intelligent instructions to division commanders, he would go in with one division, holding the others in reserve until he could superintend their movements in person also, forgetting that division commanders could execute an order without his presence."

ALTHOUGH he did not seem to realize it, a similar criticism, in a sense, could be levelled against Grant. As General Humphreys wrote later: "There were two officers commanding the same army. Such a mixed command was not calculated to produce the best results that either singly was capable of bringing about. It naturally caused some vagueness and uncertainty as to the exact sphere of each, and sometimes took away from the positiveness, fullness and earnestness of the consideration of an intended operation or tactical movement that, had there been but one commander, would have had the most earnest attention and corresponding action."

the dead, and so the murderous work went on. Guns were run up close to the parapet, and double charges of canister played their part in the bloody work. The fence-rails and logs in the breastworks were shattered into splinters, and trees over a foot and a half in diameter were cut completely in two by the incessant musketry fire. A section of the trunk of a stout oak-tree thus severed was afterward sent to Washington, where it is still on exhibition at the National Museum."

Despite the intensity of the battle, neither side could advance, and later that night Lee's men withdrew to their new line at the base of the salient. Then a tragic silence settled over the bloody field. In the dark woods surgeons were busy amputating by the eerie glow of lanterns. The next day Porter again visited the area of the heaviest fighting. "Our own killed were scattered over a large space near the 'angle,' while in front of the captured breastworks the enemy's dead, vastly more numerous than our own, were piled upon each other in some places four layers deep, exhibiting every ghastly phase of mutilation. Below the mass of fast-decaying corpses, the convulsive twitching of limbs and the writhing of bodies showed that there were wounded men still alive and struggling to extricate themselves from their horrid entombment. Every relief possible was afforded, but in too many cases it came too late. The place was well named the 'Bloody Angle!' "

And Lee by now was getting to know Grant. He had no illusions anymore about Grant retreating, even after his heavy losses in the Wilderness and at Spotsylvania. He was acutely aware that Grant was probably just waiting for replacements before again moving south. On the 18th he sent a long dispatch to Jefferson Davis describing the situation as he saw it: "[Grant's] position is strongly entrenched, and we cannot attack it with any prospect of success without great loss of men which I wish to avoid if possible. The enemy's artillery is superior in weight of metal and range to our own, and my object has been to engage him when in motion and under circumstances that will not cause us to suffer from this disadvantage. . . . Neither the strength of our army nor the condition of our animals will admit of any extensive movement with a view of drawing the enemy from his position." Then he told Davis, "The importance of this campaign to the administration of Mr. Lincoln and to General Grant leaves no doubt that every effort and every sacrifice will be made to secure its success." In effect, he was warning the Confederate Government in Richmond that Grant would get all the replacements and supplies he needed in order to continue to carry the war to the South, regardless of the casualties Lee might be able to inflict along the way. He was also implying that with an election coming up in November, Lincoln could not afford to let the Army of the Potomac retreat again, regardless of its losses. And, although his casualties at Spotsylvania were unknown, Lee informed Davis that if Grant was to be kept away from Richmond the Army of Northern Virginia had to have reinforcements. "The question," he warned, "is whether we shall fight the battle here or around Richmond. If the troops are obliged to be retained at Richmond I may be forced back."

AS early as the day after the hard fighting at the salient, Grant had decided that he would again move around Lee's right flank rather than attempt to attack him in his entrenched position. He wrote to Meade: "I do not desire a battle brought on with the enemy in their position of yesterday, but want to press as close to them as possible to determine their position and strength. We must get by the right flank of the enemy for the next fight." That night, the 13th, Warren and Wright pulled back and marched behind the rest of the army to a new position east of Spotsylvania Court House. The heavy rains then held up further movement. Lee, of course, then extended his right to meet this shift. On the theory that Lee had probably weakened his left and center by this move, Grant agreed to another assault against the salient. On May 18 Hancock, supported by Wright, made a last attempt to break Ewell's line, but this time the attack was blasted by thirty massed cannon and beaten back before it even reached the Confederate position. The next day Ewell tried to find a weak spot on the Federal right flank but was quickly repulsed, although the attack did delay the departure of the Federals for another twenty-four hours. During the night of the 20th the Army of the Potomac once again was put in motion, sliding leftward and southward, always edging closer to Richmond, on the long road to the North Anna, Cold Harbor, Petersburg, Richmond, Appomattox, and the end, the end of the long dying.

Sketch from "Battles & Leaders" titled "Up-Hill Work" shows Union artillery laboring on a typically muddy Virginia road.

448

PETERSBURG

Text by Joseph P. Cullen
Designed by Frederic Ray

Lieutenant General Ulysses S. Grant. This photograph was taken at City Point, Virginia in August 1864. (Library of Congress)

IN MARCH 1864 President Lincoln appointed Lieutenant General Ulysses S. Grant commander in chief of all the armies of the United States. Fresh from his recent dramatic victories at Vicksburg and Chattanooga, Grant now wore three stars—more than any officer had ever worn, except George Washington and old Winfield Scott. He now commanded twenty-one army corps and eighteen military departments, for a total of more than half a million men. In a little more than a month he would turn 42. His appointment would change the whole course and direction of the war.

Of medium height (5′ 8″), Grant was not impressive physically. Round-shouldered with a slovenly posture, his favorite dress was a private soldier's uniform with officer's insignia stitched on the shoulders. A native Midwesterner from Ohio, he was generally looked down on by the more polished Eastern officers in the Army of the Potomac. But the enlisted men quickly noticed one of his strongest characteristics—dogged determination. As one of them noted when Grant galloped past, "He looks as if he meant it." And over in Robert E. Lee's Army of Northern Virginia, General James Longstreet warned, "That man will fight us every day and every hour till the end of the war."

Although he had spent the war so far in the West, Grant was well aware of what had been happening in the Eastern theater. As he stated: "In the east the opposing forces stood in substantially the same relations toward each other as three years before, or when the war began; they were both between the Federal and Confederate Capitals. Battles had been fought of as great severity as had ever been known in war. . . from the James River to Gettysburg, with indecisive results." He planned to change that by putting pressure on all Confederate armies at the same time, something that had never been done before.

LEE'S strategy had always been to "risk some points in order to have a sufficient force concentrated, with the hope of dealing a successful blow when opportunity favors." He believed "as the enemy cannot attack all points at one time. . .the troops could be concentrated. . . where an assault should be made." With its interior, or shorter, lines of communication the South could so concentrate its forces, shifting troops from east to west, or the reverse, as the need arose.

This is exactly what Grant realized and wished to prevent. The way to stop the Confederates from so concentrating, as he saw it, was to put and keep pressure on all points at all times, so that the South would be unable to continue its thus-far-successful strategy. Consequently, he organized a unified plan of operations. General Benjamin F. Butler, with the Army of the James, was to march up the south side of the James river and attack Petersburg or Richmond or both; General Franz Sigel would push down the Shenandoah Valley driving General John C. Breckinridge before him, thereby protecting Washington;

General Nathaniel Banks in New Orleans to march on Mobile; General William T. Sherman to cut across Georgia, driving General Joseph E. Johnston before him, take Atlanta, and if still necessary swing north to Richmond; while General George Meade's Army of the Potomac, with Grant actually in command, pushed to stop Lee's Army of Northern Virginia and capture Richmond. As Grant stated "To get possession of Lee's Army was the first great object. With the capture of his army Richmond would necessarily follow."

LEE was well aware of Grant's determination and ability, and he also realized that this was an election year in the North. He wrote to President Jefferson Davis: "The importance of this campaign to the administration of Mr. Lincoln and to General Grant leaves no doubt that every effort and every sacrifice will be made to secure its success." Consequently, he believed he had to destroy Grant's army before it reached the James River. "If he gets there it will become a siege, and then it will be a mere question of time." To accomplish this, Lee's strategy would be to try to inflict such heavy losses on Grant that either he would abandon the campaign or the North would become tired of so costly a struggle and not re-elect Lincoln, in which event the South hoped for a negotiated peace.

The campaign began in May when the Army of the Potomac crossed the Rapidan River and the Army of Northern Virginia blocked its path in The Wilderness. After a particularly vicious and costly battle Grant, instead of retreating to re-group and re-plan as other Federal commanders had done, executed a left flank movement, still heading south and trying to get between Lee and Richmond. A few days later the two armies clashed again at Spotsylvania Court House in a series of grim battles, but still indecisive so far as major objectives were concerned. Although Grant suffered staggering losses, he was slowly but methodically destroying Lee's ability to wage offensive war.

Again Grant executed a left flank movement to get around Lee, and then, by a series of flanking marches which the Confederate soldiers called the "sidling movement," and the Federal soldiers the "jug-handle movement," Grant worked his way down to the outskirts of Richmond. At the Battle of Cold Harbor in early June he attacked Lee's veterans in their well-entrenched positions but suffered defeat with heavy losses. This battle finally convinced Federal officers that well-selected, well-manned entrenchments, adequately supported by artillery, were practically impregnable to frontal assaults. Consequently, the results of this battle changed the course of the war in the East from a war of maneuver to a war of siege.

GRANT now had to decide what action he would take next. It was obvious that Lee with his numerically inferior force had no intention of coming out from behind his

General Robert E. Lee, commanding Army of Northern Virginia.

451

Pontoon bridge on the Appomattox River below Petersburg, at Point of Rocks, Butler's headquarters. Drawing by Alfred R. Waud. (LC)

entrenchments to fight; it was equally obvious that to attempt to storm those entrenchments again would be nothing less than mass murder. And another left flanking movement was out of the question because Grant had run out of room in which to maneuver. That left only two courses of action open; withdraw to Washington and start all over again, or head south. Grant never even considered withdrawal. On June 5 he wrote to Army Chief of Staff Henry W. Halleck in Washington: "My idea from the start has been to beat Lee's army, if possible, north of Richmond; then after destroying his lines of communication north of the James River, to transfer the army to the south side and besiege Lee in Richmond, or follow him south if he should retreat."

To isolate Richmond Grant needed to cut the railroads which supplied it. Twenty-three miles south of the Confederate Capital stood the city of Petersburg, with a population of about 18,000. Nestling on the south bank of

452   *Grant's crossing of the James River, June 14-16, 1864, one of the most brilliant actions in military annals.*

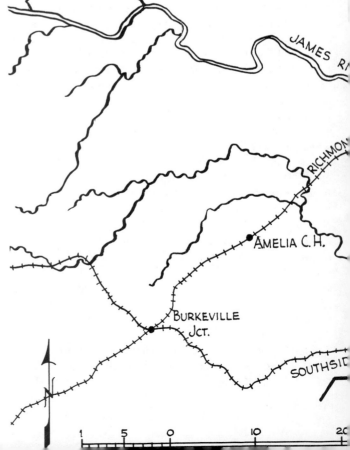

the Appomattox River, Petersburg by 1864 had become the main source of supply for both Richmond and the Army of Northern Virginia. Five railroads converged there, and through it passed a constant stream of war materials and necessities of life from farther south to sustain the war effort. Tracks radiated in all directions. The Richmond & Petersburg Railroad left the city to the north; the Southside Railroad ran west to Lynchburg; the Weldon Railroad connected with North Carolina and points south, and also connected with the Richmond & Danville Railroad (which did not go through Petersburg) at Burkeville, about forty miles west; the Norfolk Railroad; and the City Point Railroad which ran to the hamlet of City Point at the junction of the James and Appomattox Rivers, about eight miles away.

AS early as 1862 the need for fortifications to protect Petersburg was recognized. Work began that summer under the direction of Captain Charles H. Dimmock, and a year later a chain of massive breastworks and artillery emplacements ten miles long stood completed. A huge semi-circle began east of the city on the Appomattox River and ended on the river west of the city, thus protecting all but the northern approaches. The fifty-five artillery batteries were numbered consecutively from east to west. Generally referred to as the "Dimmock Line," its very length and size required a formidable number of troops to man it properly.

Grant's original plan, of course, called for Butler's Army of the James to march up the south side of the James and attack Petersburg. But largely through the ineptness of his Regular Army subordinates Butler, a politically appointed general, was bottled up in a curve of the river at Bermuda Hundred by a much smaller Confederate force and never did reach Petersburg and, although frequent raids on the railroads were made, the damage was usually quickly patched up. It was obvious that if these railroads were to be permanently shut off the Federal forces would have to take physical possession of them. Consequently, Grant decided to by-pass Richmond, move the army quickly across the James River and attack Petersburg before Lee got in position to defend it. With the capture of that railroad center Lee would be besieged in Richmond with most of his supply lines cut and the end of the war would then be a mere question of time, as Lee himself recognized.

On June 6 Grant withdrew General Gouverneur K. Warren's corps from the lines at Cold Harbor and, supported by General James H. Wilson's cavalry division, used it to secure the passages across the Chickahominy River and down to the James. The rest of the army would move behind this screen. On June 7 he sent "Little Phil" Sheridan with the remaining two divisions of cavalry west to raid Charlottesville and disrupt Confederate communications. To counter this, Lee was forced to send Wade Hampton's cavalry after Sheridan, leaving himself without adequate cavalry for reconnaissance. Then during the night of June 12 Grant secretly moved all the troops out of the trenches, without Lee's being aware of the move until the following morning.

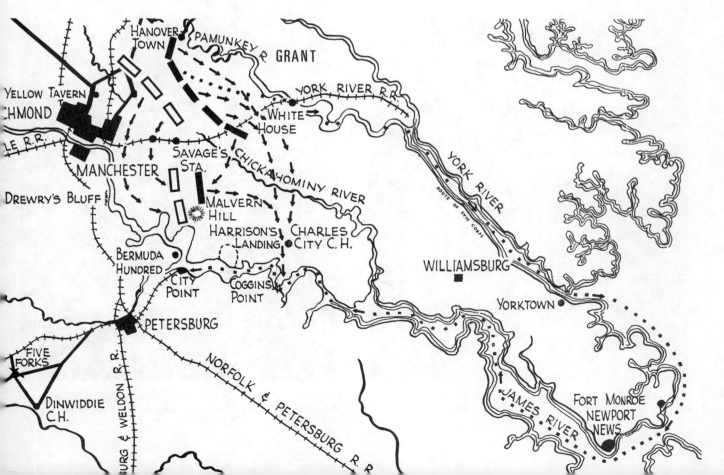

GENERAL William F. Smith's XVIII Corps, which Grant had borrowed from Butler's Army of the James for the fight at Cold Harbor, moved first. Immediately after dark it withdrew from the line quietly and proceeded on a short march behind General Ambrose Burnside's IX Corps to White House Landing on the Pamunkey River, where the troops boarded transports for the return voyage to Bermuda Hundred on the James. General Winfield S. Hancock's II Corps also pulled back at dark and went in the opposite direction towards the Chickahominy behind the screen of the V Corps.

While this move was taking place, Grant went to Bermuda Hundred to confer with Butler regarding the forthcoming attack on Petersburg. It was agreed that Smith's corps, which would be the first to arrive, would, if considered feasible, attack Petersburg, supported later by the II Corps when it arrived. Grant's verbal orders to Butler and Smith may have been definite and dynamic, but his written instructions certainly were not. "I do not want Petersburg visited," he wrote, "unless it is held, nor an attempt to take it unless you feel a reasonable degree of confidence of success." To timid generals like Butler

and Smith, this type of instruction gave them a wide degree of latitude in their interpretation of orders.

Early on the morning of June 15 Smith's troops crossed the Appomattox on a pontoon bridge at Broadway Landing, about a mile above City Point. His corps was below its usual strength as one division was left at Bermuda Hundred and he had suffered heavy losses at Cold Harbor. To bring him up to near normal strength, a small division of colored troops commanded by General Edward W. Hinks had been assigned to the XVIII Corps. All in all, Smith probably had about 15,000 men.

PUSHING westward on the City Point Road, Smith ran into a handful of Confederate cavalry under General James Dearing behind breastworks. This held up the ever-cautious Smith for several hours, so it was almost noon when the head of his column reached the outer defenses of Petersburg on the east side. And these defenses looked formidable indeed, particularly to anyone who had just experienced the awful slaughter inflicted by the Confederates from their entrenchments at Cold Harbor. A long, uneven ridge ran south for several miles, and crest-

Major General George G. Meade, commanding the Army of the Potomac in the long siege of Petersburg. (Library of Congress)

Major General Ambrose Everett Burnside was given the responsibility for the attack at The Crater. (Library of Congress)

454

ing the ridge at intervals were strong redoubts connected by raised breastworks. In front of these breastworks yawned ditches six to eight feet deep and fifteen feet wide, and a few yards out in front of the ditches were felled trees with the branches interlaced. For a half mile or so the ground beyond the slashings was open so it could be swept by fire from the fortifications. Smith decided that a very careful survey was necessary before any attack could take place. "As no engineer officer was ordered to report to me," he stated, "I was obliged to make the reconnaissance in person, and some time was unnecessarily wasted on that account." As a matter of fact, he wasted several hours.

As a result of his survey, Smith concluded that the Confederate works were as strong as they looked, with but one glaring weakness—they were seriously undermanned. The theatrical and controversial General P. G. T. Beauregard commanded everything south of the James with about 9,000 troops, but most of them were at Bermuda Hundred to hold the cork in Butler's bottle. In front of Petersburg he had only about 2,200 men. "These troops," he wrote later, "occupied the Petersburg line on the left from Battery No. 1 to what was called Butterworth's Bridge, toward the right, and had to be so stationed as to allow but one man for every 4 1/2 yards. From that bridge to the Appomattox—a distance of fully 4 1/2 miles—the line was defenseless." He had requested reenforcements that morning and was informed that General Robert Hoke's division was on the way back to him from Drewry's Bluff but would not reach him until later that night. Until then he was on his own. He also warned the Confederate War Department in Richmond that "We must now elect between lines of Bermuda Neck and Petersburg. We cannot hold both."

BY the time Smith had finished his personal reconnaissance it was almost 4 p.m. He believed the Confederate works to be lightly held, so decided to attack by using a succession of skirmish lines rather than a massed assault which could be torn apart by the artillery. If the trenches were lightly held, then the skirmish lines would be sufficient; if they were not, then no method of attack could succeed anyway in Smith's estimation. So he ordered an assault for 4 o'clock. But no one had informed the chief of artillery that an attack was imminent, and he had sent the artillery horses back to be watered. As artillery was considered necessary for the success of the whole operation, the attack had to wait until the horses returned to get the artillery into position. By the time this was accomplished it was 7 p.m. and darkness approached.

Shortly after 7 o'clock Smith attacked and overwhelmed the small force in his front. Entering a ravine between Batteries 7 and 8 the Union soldiers approached Battery 5, one of the strongest Confederate fortifications, from the rear, the direction from which an attack was least expected. Within a few hours Beauregard lost not only Battery 5 but all the line for more than a mile south. The Confederates withdrew to a new line a short distance to the

Incident at Petersburg: the capture of a Confederate cannon by Hinks's Federal Negro troops in the first day's fighting.

rear of the captured works and threw up a hasty entrenchment along Harrison's Creek.

Hinks's colored troops, who had captured six guns and many prisoners, were jubilant, as was Hinks himself. He suggested to Smith that if they continued the attack they could probably walk right into Petersburg. To be sure, it was dark, but the moon was out and its dim light showed the ridges and fields and roads leading into the city. Beauregard also believed this. As he wrote later, "Petersburg at that hour was clearly at the mercy of the Federal commander, who had all but captured it, and only failed of final success because he could not realize the fact of the unparalleled disparity between the two contending forces." Smith, however, had no intention of advancing, being interested only in defending what he had already captured, despite the fact that by now two of Hancock's divisions had arrived on the field.

HANCOCK'S II Corps experienced a most exasperating and frustrating day. By early that morning all his troops had crossed over the James from Wilcox's Landing. The evening before he had received the following dispatch from Meade: "General Butler has been ordered to send to you . . . 60,000 rations; so soon as they are received and issued you will move your command by the most direct route to Petersburg, taking up a position where the City Point railroad crosses Harrison's Creek, where we now have a work." There was no indication that Hancock was to be at any designated area at any specified time; there was no mention of his supporting Smith; there was no word of any impending attack on Petersburg. And, although Hancock could not know it then, Harrison's Creek was behind the Confederate lines.

At 4 a.m. and again at 6:30 Hancock notified headquarters that no rations had arrived. When they still hadn't come by 9 o'clock, he gave the order to move

455

without them. General David Birney's division finally got in motion about 10:30, and then the real trouble started. As Hancock reported: "It is proper to say in this connection that it afterward appeared my orders were based on incorrect information, and the position I was ordered to take did not exist as it was described on my instructions; Harrison's Creek proved to be inside the enemy's lines and not within miles of where it was laid down on the map with which I was furnished to guide me. The map was found to be utterly worthless, the only roads laid down on it being widely out of the way." None of the white natives would or could give him any information concerning the creek, but finally he obtained some Negro guides and the column started toward Petersburg. The day turned excessively hot. "The road was covered with clouds of dust, and but little water was found on the route, causing severe suffering among the men."

THEN between, 5 and 6 p.m., Hancock received messages from both Grant and Smith telling him to hurry to Smith's aid in the attack on Petersburg. Smith, of course, had not attacked yet and would not do so for another hour, but these messages were the first intimation Hancock had received that Petersburg was to be attacked that day. "Up to that hour," he reported, "I had not been notified

from any source that I was expected to assist General Smith in assaulting that city." Regardless of the delay over the rations, he insisted that had he known what was expected of his corps he could have joined Smith by 4 p.m. at the latest, in which case the whole course of the war probably would have been changed. With Petersburg in Union hands Lee's situation in Richmond would have been untenable. As it was, the II Corps did not reach Smith until the attack was over after dark.

And when Hancock's men finally did get there, Smith did nothing with them except to relieve Hinks's men in the captured trenches. When the battle-wise veterans of the II Corps saw what Hinks's colored troops had captured, they concluded that if those inexperienced troops could do that then it meant that Lee's veterans of the Army of

Northern Virginia had not yet reached Petersburg. Consequently, they wanted to attack at once before Lee's men got there, and were furious when all they did was bivouac. As one soldier wrote later: "The rage of the enlisted men was devilish. The most bloodcurdling blasphemy I ever listened to I heard that night, uttered by men who knew they were to be sacrificed on the morrow."

BUT it wasn't just Smith who was hesitant. Grant himself did not seem to understand the situation, nor did Meade, despite the fact that Smith telegraphed Butler that "unless I misapprehend the topography, I hold the key to Petersburg." But the key should have been turned that night because by the next morning the Confederates had changed the lock. Later that night Hancock received

a message from Grant stating that "the enemy were then throwing reenforcements into Petersburg, and instructed me that should Petersburg not fall on the night of the 15th it would be advisable for General Smith and myself to take up a defensive position and maintain it until all of our forces came up." Burnside's IX Corps was expected momentarily, to be followed by Warren's V Corps. But the fighting for the 15th was over.

As darkness settled down that night, Hoke's division began arriving to bolster Beauregard's meager forces in the trenches. Earlier he had informed the Richmond authorities that he could not hold both Petersburg and the Bermuda Hundred lines with the forces presently available to him, and he was hopeful that they would tell him which he should hold. But when no word was forth-

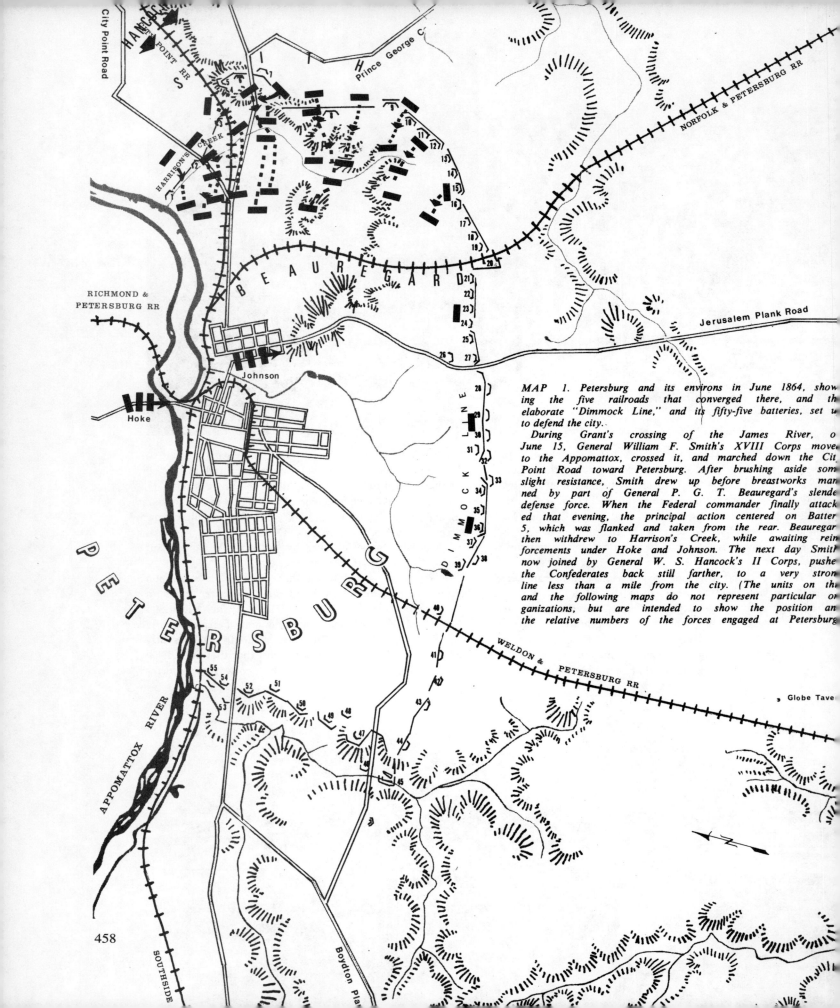

City Point Road

HANCO

POINT RR

Prince George C.

Harrison's Creek

NORFOLK & PETERSBURG RR

BEAUREGARD

RICHMOND &
PETERSBURG RR

Jerusalem Plank Road

Johnson

Hoke

D I M M O C K   L I N E

MAP 1. Petersburg and its environs in June 1864, showing the five railroads that converged there, and the
elaborate "Dimmock Line," and its fifty-five batteries, set up
to defend the city.

During Grant's crossing of the James River, on
June 15, General William F. Smith's XVIII Corps moved
to the Appomattox, crossed it, and marched down the City
Point Road toward Petersburg. After brushing aside some
slight resistance, Smith drew up before breastworks manned by part of General P. G. T. Beauregard's slender
defense force. When the Federal commander finally attacked that evening, the principal action centered on Battery
5, which was flanked and taken from the rear. Beauregard
then withdrew to Harrison's Creek, while awaiting reinforcements under Hoke and Johnson. The next day Smith,
now joined by General W. S. Hancock's II Corps, pushed
the Confederates back still farther, to a very strong
line less than a mile from the city. (The units on this
and the following maps do not represent particular organizations, but are intended to show the position and
the relative numbers of the forces engaged at Petersburg.)

P E T E R S B U R G

WELDON &   PETERSBURG RR

Globe Taver

APPOMATTOX RIVER

SOUTHSIDE

Boydton Pla

coming from higher authorities that night, Beauregard made the decision himself. He ordered Bushrod Johnson's division down from Bermuda to Petersburg, thus uncorking Butler's bottle, and so informed Richmond. "I have abandoned my lines on Bermuda Neck to concentrate all my forces here." This brought his strength up to about 10,000 effectives, as opposed to over 40,000 Federals, and over 60,000 when the IX Corps arrived. The odds were still mighty high against the Confederate commander, but they were better than they had been the day before.

ANOTHER of Beauregard's troubles was that Lee was not yet convinced that Grant had moved his whole army south of the James. As he regarded the safety of Richmond as his first responsibility, he was reluctant to strip the north side of the James of troops in case Grant should mount an attack along that line. Although Beauregard reported fighting the XVIII Corps, Lee regarded that corps as part of Butler's Army of the James and not the Army of the Potomac, and many of Beauregard's reports to Richmond never did reach Lee, as Beauregard at that time exercised a command independent of Lee. The fact is that since the morning of June 13 Lee did not know the whereabouts of the Army of the Potomac or its commander's intentions. He did take some precautions, however, as General Braxton Bragg's dispatch of June 14 to Beauregard attests: "General Lee reports Grant has abandoned his depot on the York and moved to James River, he supposes about McClellan's old base at Harrison's Landing. Lee is on a line from Malvern Hill to White Oak Swamp. He has sent Hoke's division to Drewry's Bluff, with a view to reenforce you in case Petersburg is threatened." In Lee's view that was all he could do until he knew something more definite.

Early the next morning, June 16, Hancock conducted a reconnaissance in force while Burnside's IX Corps came into position on his left. Grant and Meade were both on the south side of the river that morning, and after an inspection of the front Grant told Meade that "Smith has taken a line of works stronger than anything we have seen this campaign. If it is a possible thing I want an assault made at six o'clock this evening." Grant apparently was not the least disturbed that Petersburg did not fall to Smith and Hancock, although he stated years later in his *Memoirs* that he believed it should have been captured on the 15th. And as all his troops were massed on the east side of the city, he seemed totally unaware that there were practically no Confederate troops in the lines west of the Jerusalem Plank Road. As Beauregard admitted later, if Grant or Meade had sent a large force up that road to swing west and then north, "I would have been compelled to evacuate Petersburg without much resistance." But for the time being at least, Grant seems to have been basking in the glow of having deceived Lee completely and successfully outflanked him. Not usually given to boasting, Grant could not help telling Wash-

General Pierre Gustave Toutant Beauregard commanded the first thin defense line at Petersburg. (Photo from National Archives)

ington: "Our forces drew out from within fifty yards of the enemy's intrenchments at Cold Harbor, made a flank movement of an average of about fifty miles' march, crossing the Chickahominy and James rivers, the latter 2,000 feet wide and 84 feet deep at point of crossing, and surprised the enemy's rear at Petersburg. This was done without the loss of a wagon or piece of artillery and with the loss of only about 150 stragglers, picked up by the enemy." All of which was true. By late that night or early the next morning the Army of the Potomac with its more than 100,000 men, 5,000 wagons and ambulances, 56,000 horses and mules, and 2,800 head of cattle, would be safely across the James River. And that night Lee would telegraph in desperation: "I do not know the position of Grant's army."

IT IS a paradox of the war that Grant seldom if ever receives credit for this successful change of base in the face of an aggressive enemy. And yet such an astute military historian as Colonel Mathew Steele has written: "When one considers how unexpected the movement was to General Lee, and how long he was left in doubt and uncertainty; how skillfully all the difficulties of logistics were surmounted, and how quickly the movement was made, one must reckon it, in conception and execution, among the very finest achievements of strategy to be found in our military history."

Unfortunately, however, the staff work and tactics following this great strategic movement were something

Meade reported to Grant: "Our men are tired and the attacks have not been made with the vigor and force which characterized our fighting in The Wilderness; if they had been I think we should have been more successful. I will continue to press."

That night Warren's V Corps came up and held the extreme left of the Federal line, and Grant wired Meade to get it over on the Jerusalem Plank Road. One division of General Horatio Wright's VI Corps also came up. Meade issued his orders that night: "A vigorous assault on the enemy's works will be made tomorrow morning at 4 o'clock by the whole force of the Fifth, Ninth, and Second Corps." Smith's corps and the one division of the VI Corps would be held in reserve ready to support any significant breakthrough.

WARREN moved out early the morning of the 17th toward the Jerusalem Road, ran into heavy skirmishing, stopped to reconnoiter, and never did get going again. On his right there was heavy fighting all day by Hancock and Burnside, with two significant hills captured, the Shand house hill and the Hare house hill; on the latter the Federals would later erect Fort Stedman. But the attack was generally uncoordinated, the tactics and leadership faulty, and again nothing decisive was accomplished, except that Beauregard had held again even though he lost another section of the line.

Time was fast running out now for the Federals. Lee, convinced at last that Grant actually was on the south side of the river, put his army in motion for Petersburg. They began arriving that night and early next morning, with Lee himself on the field by 11:30 a.m. With the arrival of the Army of Northern Virginia the Confederates would have something over 50,000 troops to man the trenches, as opposed to about 90,000 Federals. And during the night Beauregard selected a new line only about a mile in front of Petersburg and withdrew his forces to it under cover of darkness. All night they worked feverishly to fortify and strengthen it. An aide to Beauregard later recalled that "without a moment's rest the digging of the trenches was begun, with such utensils as had been hastily collected at Petersburg, many of the men using bayonets, their knives, and even their tin cans, to assist in the rapid execution of the work."

ANOTHER general assault was ordered by Meade for the morning of the 18th, but it turned out to be more of a fiasco than the previous one. All the divisions were late getting started; first one attacked and then the other; and some never did get going at all until late in the afternoon. Finding the Confederates in their new line seems to have had a confusing effect on the Federal line officers, most of whom believed it should be felt out cautiously before any assault was made. The veterans quickly realized that the Army of Northern Virginia now stood behind those entrenchments, and they had no intention of assaulting them. They knew it would be nothing but Cold Har-

less than brilliant, with both Grant and Meade equally responsible. Hancock and Burnside attacked again that evening as ordered and fought bitterly for over three hours, with little effect. Some more ground was gained, particularly by Birney's division of Hancock's corps, but darkness put an end to it and the Confederates simply threw up a new line during the night. Hancock and Meade both noticed that the men seemed to be wearied and did not attack with their usual persistence.

Federal sharpshooters at work in front of Petersburg. (FL)

bor all over again, and they had had enough of that kind of fighting. One regiment volunteering to make a charge, the 1st Maine Heavy Artillery, suffered the highest losses of any regiment in a single engagement in the entire war. About 4 p.m. this unit, about 850 strong, charged from concealment along the Prince George Court House road. Met by a heavy crossfire, it withdrew in less than thirty minutes with 632 casualties.

In the rear Meade was fast losing his temper in a futile effort to bring about a coordinated attack. Shortly after 2 p.m. he telegraphed Warren and Burnside: "What additional orders to attack you require I cannot imagine. My orders have been explicit and are now repeated, that you each immediately assault the enemy with all your force, and if there is any further delay the responsibility and the consequences will rest with you." But it was far too late by then; the Federals' last chance for success by assault had gone. To another general Meade stated that "It is of the utmost importance to settle today whether the enemy can be dislodged." Now he had his answer—they could not. That night he reported to Grant that "our losses, particularly today, have been severe. . . . It is a source of great regret that I am not able to report more success." In the past four days' fighting the Federals suffered approximately 10,000 casualties in killed, wounded, and missing. And Grant telegraphed back: "Now we will rest the men and use the spade for their protection until a new vein can be struck."

AND SO the decision was made—the war in the East would now be primarily a siege operation. So the campaign that began early in May in The Wilderness ended some six weeks later in the trenches around Petersburg. And in those six weeks Grant had suffered between 60,000 and 70,000 casualties, and Lee's army still stood undefeated, and to some, particularly President Lincoln's political enemies, it all seemed like wasted effort. What they could not understand was that the war would never be the same again. Now it was only a question of time, provided the North did not become impatient and fail to re-elect Lincoln who would support Grant to the end. The failure to capture Petersburg quickly was tragic, to be sure, as it would have shortened the war immeasurably and, thereby, saved many lives, but the fact was that Lee now lay pinned down on the Petersburg-Richmond defense line and could not get out. Never again would he assume the offensive, threatening to win the war by bold, aggressive moves with the famed and feared Army of Northern Virginia. As one Confederate general wrote later, "However bold we might be, however desperately we might fight, we were sure in the end to be worn out. It was only a question of a few months, more or less."

Things remained fairly quiet for several days while the men dug fortifications and trenches and the weather grew hotter. Then Meade ordered the II and VI Corps to extend to the left and march on the Weldon Railroad which Grant was anxious to cut off from Petersburg. Lee himself went over to the right of the line on June 22 to observe the action. General William Mahone reported to him that he believed he saw an opportunity for a flank attack, and Lee agreed. What Mahone observed was a gap carelessly left between the two Federal corps, and here he struck swiftly, rolling up two divisions and capturing over 1,500 prisoners. The Federals then withdrew and the railroad was saved for awhile longer, but Grant's left now extended west of the Jerusalem Plank Road, so that important artery was lost to the Confederates and Lee had to extend his defense line. Now investing Petersburg Grant had the IX Corps on his right, then the V, the II, and the VI held the left of the line on the south. Butler's Army of the James held its position at Bermuda Hundred and was also responsible for the ground the Federals held north of the James River.

THUS the siege of Petersburg, which would last almost ten months, began. Almost every hill and rise of

461

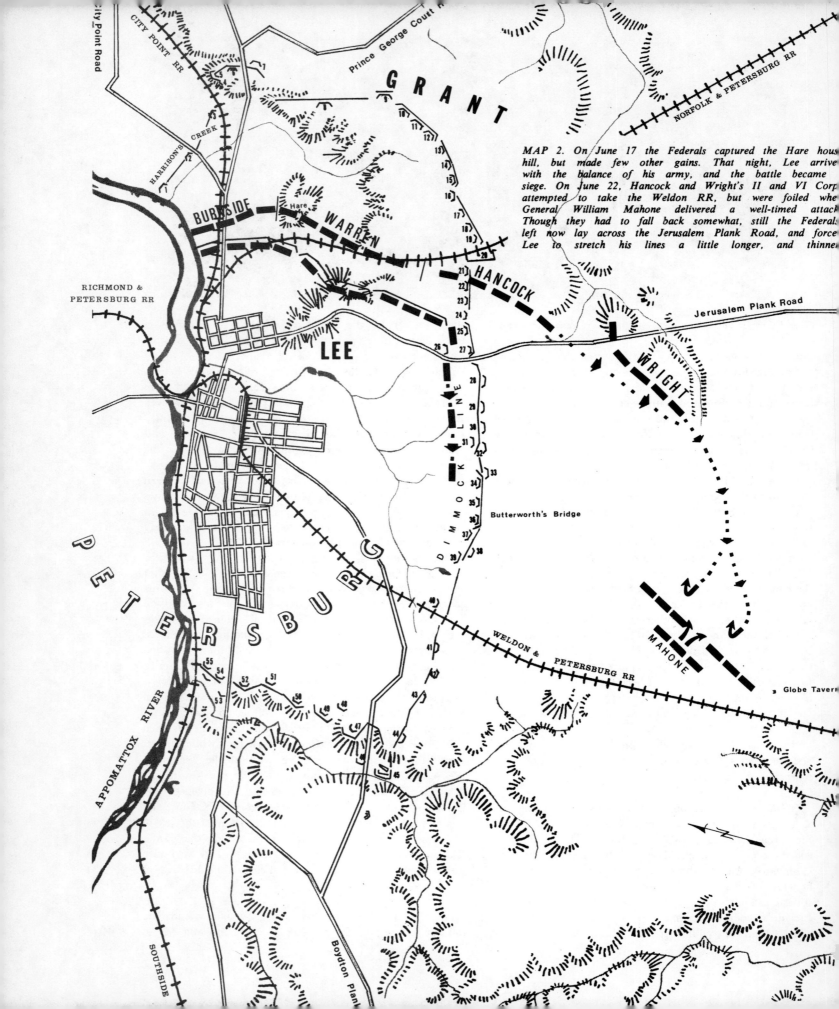

GRANT

City Point Road

CITY POINT RR

Prince George Court H—

NORFOLK & PETERSBURG RR

HARRISON'S CREEK

BURNSIDE

Hare

WARREN

RICHMOND &
PETERSBURG RR

HANCOCK

Jerusalem Plank Road

LEE

WRIGHT

DIMMOCK LINE

Butterworth's Bridge

PETERSBURG

WELDON & PETERSBURG RR

MAHONE

Globe Tavern

APPOMATTOX RIVER

Boydton Plank

SOUTHSIDE

MAP 2. On June 17 the Federals captured the Hare house
hill, but made few other gains. That night, Lee arrive
with the balance of his army, and the battle became
siege. On June 22, Hancock and Wright's II and VI Corp
attempted to take the Weldon RR, but were foiled whe
General William Mahone delivered a well-timed attack
Though they had to fall back somewhat, still the Federals
left now lay across the Jerusalem Plank Road, and force
Lee to stretch his lines a little longer, and thinner

Lieutenant Colonel Henry Pleasants engineered the mine.

ground was capped with a fort and artillery batteries, along both the Union and Confederate lines, and in some places the lines lay less than 400 feet apart. There was little if any chance that any part of either line could be taken by direct assault so long as the defenders remained alert. One Federal soldier wrote later: "In building our works we utilized the dead bodies of the rebels by burying them in the earth which we threw up from the trenches, serving the double purpose of burial and increasing the size of the breastworks." In this vast maze of trenches, forts, redoubts and tunnels the soldiers of both sides lived, suffered, and died. Constant skirmishing and sharpshooting took its deadly toll. Constant shelling back and forth was just another of the nerve-wracking hardships the men had to endure, along with scorching heat and choking dust, then mud and constant wetness, followed by freezing cold and utter loneliness. But in the mud and general filth of the trenches, disease was the greatest killer of all, and one of the most depressing things that had to be endured was complete boredom.

IT was this boredom, more or less, that led to the next significant action. As the days wore on and the awful monotony of siege tactics became apparent to the soldiers, some members of the 48th Pennsylvania Volunteers in General Robert B. Potter's division of the IX Corps, many of whom had been coal miners from

the upper Schuylkill coal region, came up with an idea. In front of their position stood a Confederate work known as Elliott's Salient, a particularly strong point in the line near a ridge called Cemetery Hill. Behind earthen embankments lay a battery of four guns, with two veteran South Carolina infantry regiments stationed on either side. Behind these were other strong defensive works. At this point the two lines lay less than 400 feet apart. One day Lieutenant Colonel Henry Pleasants, the commanding officer of the regiment and a mining engineer by profession, heard one of the enlisted men mutter, "We could blow that damned fort out of existence if we could run a mine shaft under it."

From this and other remarks grew the idea of a Union mine under the Confederate fortification. When Pleasants told his regimental officers, "That God-damned fort is the only thing between us and Petersburg, and I have an idea we can blow it up," they were receptive. The division commander then passed the idea along to Burnside who was agreeable and passed it up to Meade. Meade was lukewarm to the whole idea and his engineer officers thought it all "clap-trap and nonsense" because, they said, the shaft or tunnel leading to the mine could not possibly be ventilated without being observed by the Confederates. But Grant said to go ahead with it.

Work started on June 25, but Pleasants soon discovered that, although higher ups promised all the help he would need, none was forthcoming. "My regiment was only about four hundred strong. At first I employed but a few men at a time, but the number was increased as the work progressed, until at last I had to use the whole regiment—non-commissioned officers and all. The great difficulty I had was to dispose of the material got out of the mine. I found it impossible to get any assistance from anybody; I had to do all the work myself. I had to remove all the earth in old cracker-boxes; I got pieces of hickory and nailed on the boxes in which we received our crackers, and then iron-

"The Forty-eighth Pennsylvania, Colonel Pleasants, mining the Confederate works in front of Petersburg, July 15-20, 1864."

Carrying powder to the mine. From drawing by A. R. Waud. (HW)

clad them with hoops of iron taken from old pork and beef barrels—Whenever I made application I could not get anything . . . . I could get no boards or lumber supplied to me for my operations. I had to get a pass and send two companies of my own regiment, with wagons, outside of our lines to rebel saw-mills, and get lumber in that way, after having previously got what lumber I could by tearing down an old bridge. I had no mining picks furnished me, but had to take common army picks and have them straightened for my mine picks. . . .''

DESPITE the lack of cooperation, the work went ahead day after day. Every night the men cut bushes to cover the fresh dirt at the mouth of the tunnel; otherwise the Confederates would have known what was going on. However, the biggest problem with the 510-foot shaft was ventilation. Generally it had been considered impossible to dig a tunnel for any considerable distance without spacing shafts at regular intervals to replace the polluted air with a fresh supply. In this instance, of course, that was out of the question because of the proximity of the enemy. But Pleasants and his men came up with an ingenious solution, based on the application of the simple physical principle that warm air tends to rise. Behind the Federal picket line and to the right of the tunnel, although connected with it, the miners dug a ventilating chimney. Between the chimney and the tunnel entrance they put up an airtight canvas door. Through the door and along the floor of the tunnel they laid a square wooden pipe. A fire was then built at the bottom of the ventilating chimney, and as the fire warmed the air it went up the chimney, and the draft thus created drew the foul air from the end of the tunnel where the men were working. As the foul air rushed out, of course, fresh air was drawn in through the wooden pipe to replace it.

By July 17 the diggers were directly beneath the battery in Elliott's Salient, twenty feet from the floor of the tunnel to the enemy works above. The average height

464

of the tunnel was five feet, with a base four and a half feet in width, tapering to two feet at the top. By now the Confederates had become suspicious, as the faint sounds of digging could be heard issuing from the earth. Consequently, they sank countermines of their own in an effort to locate the Union shaft. When they failed to locate anything suspicious, their fears diminished, helped along, no doubt, by the belief that it was impossible to ventilate a tunnel of any length over 400 feet without air shafts above it.

THE next step in Pleasant's plan was to burrow out into lateral tunnels at the end of the long shaft. Accordingly, on July 18 work began on two branches extending to the right and left, paralleling the Confederate fortifications above. When completed on July 23, these additional tunnels added another seventy-five feet to the total length of the excavation, for a grand total of a little over 585 feet. Then 320 kegs of black powder, weighing on the average twenty-five pounds each, were placed in the two lateral tunnels in eight magazines. The total charge was thus about four tons or 8,000 pounds. The men sandbagged the powder to direct the force of the explosion upward, and spliced two fuses together to form a 98-foot line.

BY JULY 27 all stood ready with the explosion set for 3:30 a.m. July 30. Burnside submitted his plan of attack, which was to have the division of colored troops now under General Edward Ferrero go in first and fan out to the left and right along the line, then the other

Entrance to Confederate countermine in Fort Mahone. (From LC)

divisions would go forward and take the crest of Cemetery Hill. Grant and Meade, however, objected to this plan on two counts. Meade was afraid they would be blamed for putting the colored troops in first, and Grant agreed, primarily for political reasons. As Grant later stated: "General Meade said that if we put the colored troops in front (we had only one division) and it should prove a failure, it would then be said, and very properly, that we were shoving these people ahead to get killed because we did not care anything about them. But that could not be said if we put white troops in front." Unfortunately this decision was not relayed to Burnside until the night of July 29, which, of course, necessitated last minute changes in his battle orders.

The other objection was to the first division through the gap fanning out to the right and left. Meade, with Grant's approval, changed the orders so that the leading division would charge straight ahead for the crest of Cemetery Hill, the next two divisions advance to the left and right of the crest to protect the flanks, and then the colored division followed by the V Corps, and if necessary the XVIII, would come through for the general advance all along the line. A total of 110 guns and 54 mortars would be alerted to begin a bombardment as soon as the explosion occurred.

Burnside had the commanding generals of the three white divisions draw straws to see who would lead the charge. General James Ledlie of the First Division won the draw. He had been with the division just six weeks.

In the meantime, Grant sent the II Corps over to the north side of the James at Deep Bottom as a diversionary tactic, and Lee reacted to it by withdrawing troops from Petersburg, so that on July 30 the Confederates had only about 18,000 troops in the lines around the city. Then Meade ordered Hancock to make a night march and be in rear of the XVIII Corps by daylight to support the attack if needed. And Meade reminded all corps commanders that "promptitude, rapidity of execution, and cordial cooperation, are essential to success."

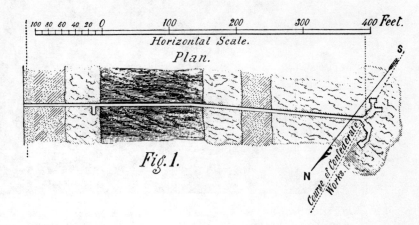

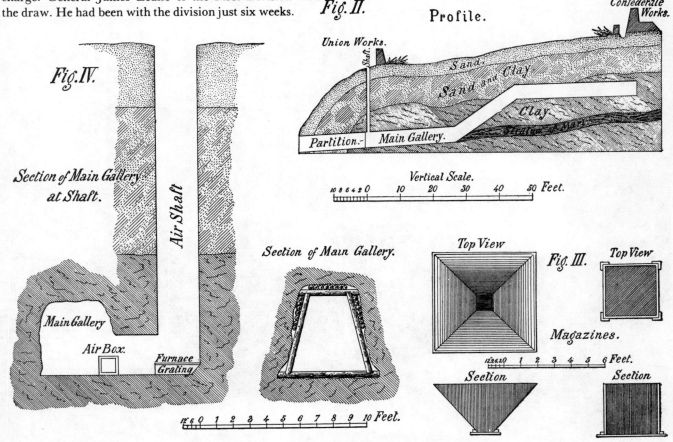

Details of the mine. (B&L)

465

BELOW: "Before Petersburg, July 30, 1864. Explosion of the mine, and charge on the Confederate works." (Both drawings reproduced from "The Soldier in Our Civil War." Vol. II)

ABOVE: "The Fifth Army Corps awaiting the order to advance, after the explosion of the mine, Petersburg, July 30, 1864."

466

Petersburg Railroad   Confederate Fort.   Confederate Mortar Battery.   City of Petersburg.   Ninth Corps B

BY 3 A.M. on July 30 the IX Corps lay assembled in the ravine behind the mine entrance, the First Division at the head of the column. Three-thirty came and went and nothing happened. Then the first grey fingers of dawn began to appear. "Four o'clock arrived, officers and men began to get nervous, having been on their feet four hours; still the mine had not been exploded." Pleasants had lit the fuse at 3:15. By 4:15 he knew something was wrong. Sergeant Henry Rees and Lieutenant Jacob Douty volunteered to crawl in and find out what had happened, and discovered that the fuse had died out at the first splicing. Quickly they relighted it and scrambled to safety. At 4:45 the earth erupted with a terrifying roar. "It was a magnificent spectacle," an officer present remembered, "and as the mass of earth went into the air, carrying with it men, guns, carriages, and limbers, and spread out like an immense cloud as it reached its altitude, so close were the Union lines that the mass appeared as if it would descend immediately upon the troops waiting to make the charge. This caused them to break and scatter to the rear, and about ten minutes were consumed in re-forming for the attack."

But that was just the beginning of their troubles. Incredible as it now seems, no one made provision for ladders for Burnside's troops to get out of their own entrenchments. As Major Houghton of the 14th New York Heavy Artillery reported: "Our own works, which

Brigadier General James H. Ledlie (seated left) and staff at Petersburg. Ledlie was in command of the First Division, IX Corps, at the Battle of The Crater. (Library of Congress)

Explosion of the Mine.

Brigadier General Edward Ferrero. He commanded the Fourth (Colored) Division at the Battle of The Crater. (From NA) 467

The Battle of The Crater. This original drawing by Alfred R. Waud depicts the Fourth (Colored) Division going into action. Regimental colors are being planted on the rim of The Crater in the background. The artist was apparently intending to indicate the detail of the sole of the soldier's shoe for the "Harper's" engraver by drawing the oversized foot. (LC)

were very high at this point, had not been prepared for scaling . . . ladders were improvised by the men placing their bayonets between the logs in the works and holding the other end . . . thus forming steps over which men climbed." Then, after this second delay, the men were not prepared for what they would see at the "crater," the hole caused by the explosion, and it struck them dumb with astonishment. The hole, about 30 feet deep, 60 to 80 feet wide, and 170 feet long, was "filled with dust, great blocks of clay, guns, broken carriages, projecting timbers, and men buried in various ways—some up to their necks,

View of the Confederate works after the explosion of the mine and the battle of July 30, 1864. Sketch by Mullen. (SCW)

others to their waists, and some with only their feet and legs protruding from the earth." The explosion wounded, buried or killed about 278 Confederates and completely destroyed two guns of the battery. Soon one brigade after another of gaping soldiers milled in and around the crater, but no one was moving forward; brigades and regiments soon became inextricably mixed in the confusion. When finally some did try to get out of the crater, they discovered to their chagrin that they again had no ladders and "owing to the precipitous walls the men could find no footing except by facing inward, digging their heels into the earth, and throwing their backs against the side of the crater." Neither Burnside, Ledlie, nor Ferrero were with their troops to lead them on and help bring order out of chaos.

THESE delays proved fatal. In a short time the Confederates recovered from their shock and soon shells poured in on the IX Corps from both the right and left

Brigadier General William Mahone led the successful Confederate defense in the bloody Battle of The Crater. (Photo from LC)

Shortly after 1 p.m. a final charge by Mahone's men succeeded in gaining the outside slopes of the crater. Then some of the Confederates put their hats on ramrods and lifted them over the rim. They were promptly torn to shreds by a volley, but before the Federals could reload Mahone's men jumped into the crater where a desperate hand-to-hand struggle with bayonets, rifle butts, and fists ensued. The scene in the crater was now appalling. As Major Houghton described it, "The sun was pouring its fiercest heat down upon us and our suffering wounded. No air was stirring within the crater. It was a sickening sight; men were dead and dying all around us; blood was streaming down the sides of the crater to the bottom, where it gathered in pools for a time before being absorbed by the hard red clay."

ALTOGETHER Grant suffered some 4,400 casualties in killed, wounded, and missing, as opposed to about 1,500 for Lee. And neither Grant nor Meade was very happy about the way the whole operation had been conducted. Meade's official report to Grant was unusually accurate and detailed:

On the 30th, owing to a defect in the fuse, the explosion of the mine was delayed from 3:30 to 4:45 a.m., an unfortunate delay, because it was designed to assault the crest of the ridge occupied by the enemy just before daylight, when the movement would, in a measure, be obscured. As soon as the mine was sprung the First Division, Ninth Corps, Brigadier-General Ledlie commanding, moved forward and occupied the crater without opposition. No advance, however, was made from the crater to the ridge, some 400 yards beyond, Brigadier-General Ledlie giving as a reason for not pushing forward that the enemy could occupy the crater in his rear, he seeming to forget that the rest of his corps and all the Eighteenth Corps were waiting to occupy the crater and follow him. Brigadier-Generals Potter and Wilcox, commanding the Second and Third Divisions, Ninth Corps, advanced simultaneously with Ledlie and endeavored to occupy parts of the enemy's line on Ledlie's right and left, so as to cover those flanks, respectively, but on reaching the enemy's line Ledlie's men were found occupying the vacated parts, both to the right and left of the crater, in consequence of which the men of the several divisions got mixed up, and a scene of disorder and confusion commenced, which seems to have continued to the end of the operation. In the meantime the enemy, rallying from the confusion incident to the explosion, began forming his infantry in a ravine to the right and planting artillery, both on the right and left of the crater. Seeing this, Potter was enabled to get his men out of the crater and enemy's line, and had formed them for an attack on the right, when he received an order to attack the crest of the ridge. Notwithstanding he had to change front in the presence of the enemy, he succeeded not only in doing so, but, as he reports, advancing to within a few yards of the crest, which he would have taken if he had been supported. This was after 7 a.m., more than two hours after Ledlie had occupied the crater, and yet he had made no advance. He, however, states he was forming to advance when the Fourth Division (colored troops), General Ferrero commanding, came rushing into the crater and threw his men into confusion. The Fourth Division passed beyond the crater and made an assault, when they encountered a heavy fire of artillery and infantry, which threw them into inextricable confusion, and they retired in disorder through the troops in the crater and back into our lines. In the mean time, in ignorance of what was occurring, I sent orders to Major-General Ord, commanding Eighteenth Corps, who was expected to follow the Ninth, to advance at once on the right of the Ninth independently of the latter. To this General Ord replied the only debouches were choked up with the Ninth Corps, which had not all advanced at this time. He,

flanks. The only outfit that actually went forward and got close to the crest of Cemetery Hill was Potter's Second Division, but Lee quickly rushed Mahone's division from farther south into the breach and forced the Federals back. Many, however, got caught in the crater and soon Confederate mortar shells started to drop on them with deadly effect. Meade, observing the scene with Grant, ordered a withdrawal about 9 o'clock, but it was past noon before Burnside transmitted it as he kept insisting that a victory could still be won. Many soldiers by then had chosen to run the gantlet of fire back to their own lines, but others remained clinging to the protective sides of the crater.

Union Fort Morton, opposite The Crater. (LC)

however, pushed a brigade of Turner's division over the Ninth Corps' parapets, and directed it to charge the enemy's line on the right, where it was still occupied. While it was about executing this order the disorganized Fourth Division (colored) of the Ninth Corps came rushing back and carrying everything with them, including Turner's brigade. By this time, between 8 and 9 a.m., the enemy, seeing the hesitation and confusion on our part, having planted batteries on both flanks in ravines where our artillery could not reach them, opened a heavy fire not only on the ground in front of the crater but between it and our lines, their mortars at the same time throwing shells into the dense mass of our men in the crater and adjacent works. In addition to this artillery fire, the enemy massed his infantry and assaulted the position. Although the assault was repulsed and some heroic fighting was done, particularly on the part of Potter's division and some regiments of the Eighteenth Corps, yet the exhaustion incident to the crowding of the men and the intense heat of the weather, added to the destructive artillery fire of the enemy, produced its effect, and report was brought to me that our men were retiring into our old lines. Being satisfied that the moment for success had passed, and that any further attempts would only result in useless sacrifice of life, with the concurrence of the lieutenant-general commanding, who was present, I directed the suspension of further offensive movements, and the withdrawal of the troops in the crater when it could be done with security, retaining the position till night, if necessary. It appears that when this order reached the crater (12:20) the greater portion of those that had been in were out; the balance remained for an hour and a half, repulsing an attack of the enemy, but on the enemy's threatening a second attack, retreated in disorder, losing many prisoners. This terminated this most unfortunate and not very creditable operation. I forbear to comment in the manner I might otherwise deem myself justified in doing, because the whole subject, at my request, has been submitted for investigation by the President of the United States to a court of inquiry, with directions to report upon whom, if any one, censure is to be laid.

GRANT agreed with Meade's request for a Court of Inquiry. "So fair an opportunity will probably never occur again for carrying fortifications," he wrote to Meade the next day. "Preparations were good, orders ample, and everything so far as I could see, subsequent to the explosion of the mine, shows that almost without loss the crest beyond the mine could have been carried. This would have given us Petersburg with all its artillery and a large part of the garrison beyond doubt."

The Court of Inquiry concluded that if Meade's orders had been carried out the attack would have been successful. Burnside was censured for not obeying the orders of the commanding general, specifically regarding a prompt advance after the explosion, and for not "preparing his parapets and abatis for the passage of the columns of assault." As for Ledlie, the Court concluded that instead of leading his troops he "was most of the time in a bomb-proof ten rods in rear of the main line of the Ninth Corps works," and that Ferrero was also in a bomb-proof "habitually, where he could not see the operation of his troops." Burnside and Ledlie later resigned, and Ferrero was transferred elsewhere.

IT WAS certainly evident by now, if not before, that storming the Confederate fortifications by any means was out of the question. But the usual siege tactics, that is, a series of regular approaches by which heavy artillery could get close enough to flatten the enemy's fortifications, would not be effective either against earthen works. And at that rate, both armies could sit there facing each other forever. The only option open, it seemed, was for Grant to continually keep Lee off balance and under pressure with surprise attacks north of the James on the Richmond front, while at the same time extending his left to the west and north, forcing Lee to stretch his thinly held line, until Petersburg was completely encircled and all railroads and roads blocked. If nothing else, this would starve Lee into surrender or force him to abandon Richmond and flee south.

The first move in this new strategy was another attack on the Weldon Railroad. On August 18 Warren's V Corps marched three miles westward and seized the railroad in the vicinity of Globe Tavern, then marched northward towards Petersburg. The next day Lee sent A. P. Hill to attack Warren and recover the railroad. Hill inflicted serious losses and captured 2,700 prisoners, forcing Warren back to the area of Globe Tavern, but here the V Corps held despite repeated desperate attacks by the Confederates. Now Lee's lines were stretched almost to the breaking point, and he had lost another vital line of supply. As an indication of things

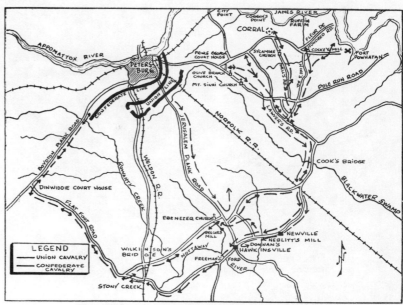
Map of Hampton's "Beefsteak" raid.

General Warren's headquarters at the Globe Tavern. From a contemporary sketch which appears in "Battles and Leaders, etc."

to come, he wired Richmond: "Our supply of corn is exhausted today, and I am informed that the small reserve in Richmond is consumed." Starvation was now a strong possibility. Only the Southside Railroad connected Petersburg with the rest of the South, and the Richmond & Danville Railroad was the only direct connection with Richmond, while Grant with his huge supply base at City Point could haul supplies on the City Point Railroad and now the Weldon Railroad in all kinds of weather.

The Confederate line as reconstructed at The Crater. From a drawing made by Lieut. Henderson after the battle. (From B&L)

IN A desperate move to alleviate the hunger of the Army of Northern Virginia its cavalry commander, Wade Hampton, in mid-September led a daring raid of 4,000 mounted troopers around the entire rear of the Army of the Potomac and succeeded in returning to Petersburg September 17 with over 2,000 head of cattle and more than 300 surprised prisoners, while losing only about 60 of his own men. Although this raised the morale of the Confederates temporarily, it had no lasting effect on the campaign. Grant just continued to tighten the noose and keep the pressure on.

His next move took place just twelve days later. In the pre-dawn darkness of September 29 he quietly slipped Birney, now commanding the X Corps, and Ord's XVIII Corps back across the James in a surprise move against the outer defenses of Richmond. The primary purpose was to prevent Lee from reenforcing General Jubal Early in the Shenandoah Valley. If, however, any weakness was discovered it could be exploited fully, and it might force Lee to weaken some part of the Petersburg line. Ord successfully stormed heavily armed but badly undermanned Fort Harrison on the Varina Road, but Birney was repulsed a mile and a half farther north in a similar attack on Fort Gilmer on the New Market Road. Lee, however, regarded the loss of Fort Harrison as serious enough to demand his personal attention. The next day, with reenforcements rushed from Petersburg, including Generals Archibald Gracie's and Hoke's divisions and four of General George Pickett's regiments, he directed several vigorous assaults against the fort. However, the Federal forces had closed in the rear of the work and also strengthened it and, armed with new repeating rifles, successfully beat back the attacks and inflicted heavy losses on the Confederates.

MEADE took advantage of this diversion to send a reconnaissance in force to the west again, but Hampton's cavalry and Johnson's division of infantry stopped them at the area known as Peebles' Farm. However, Meade had extended his left flank another three miles west of the Weldon Railroad, again forcing Lee to stretch his line of defense. Lee was now holding a 35-mile line from north of Richmond to the west of Petersburg with fewer than 50,000 troops, and with no relief in sight. "The enemy's position enables him to move his troops to the right or left without our knowledge," he informed Richmond, "until he has reached the point at which he aims, and we are then compelled to hurry our men to meet him, incurring the risk of being too late to check his progress and the additional risk of the advantage he may derive from their absence." For the first time during the whole war, Lee now began to sound pessimistic. "Without some increase of strength, I cannot see how we can escape the natural military consequences of the enemy's numerical superiority," he declared. "If things thus continue, the most serious consequences must result."

Grant gave the weary, half-starved Confederates no rest. On October 27 he sent Hancock's II Corps and two divisions of Warren's V, with a cavalry screen, west to the Boydton Plank Road. But when the two Federal commanders carelessly let a gap develop between the two forces, Hampton's cavalry and Generals Henry Heth's and Mahone's divisions quickly struck hard at Hancock at Burgess' Mill, where the road crossed a creek called Hatcher's Run. The Federals were forced to withdraw to their old positions and the Boydton Plank Road remained in Confederate control.

THIS was the last major action of the year, as the two armies settled into the awful monotony of living in the trenches through the cold winter. And as the long winter months of the siege dragged on, the Confederate soldiers began to know real despair for the first time. In the Shenandoah Valley Sheridan had crushed Early's forces at Cedar Creek October 19 and now that indispensable source of supply was lost to the Confederates. Far to the south Sherman had captured Atlanta in September, insuring Lincoln's re-election, and Savannah surrendered December 21. Sherman prepared to march north to join Grant in the spring.

So even the coming of spring could bring no hope to Lee's men, starving and freezing in the filthy trenches. Death, disease, and desertion were slowly destroying the once proud Army of Northern Virginia. In one five-week period that winter 2,934, nearly 8 percent of the effective strength, slipped off in the darkness to go home and not return. Recruiting and drafting could not keep up with the losses. "The men coming in do not supply the vacancies caused by sickness, desertions, and other casualties," Lee admitted sadly. And the caliber of the new men was not what the Army of Northern Virginia was used to, thus tending to destroy the morale of the remaining veterans. But Lee's biggest problem that winter was subsistence. He candidly told the authorities in Richmond, "Unless the men and animals can be subsisted, the army cannot be kept together, and our present lines must be abandoned." He even made a special trip to Richmond to appeal in person to the Confederate Congress, but on his return told his son Custis, "I have been up to see the Congress and they do not seem to be able to do anything except to eat peanuts and chew tobacco, while my army is starving." As one Maryland soldier wrote in January 1865: "There are a good many of us who believe this shooting match has been carried on long enough. A government that has run out of rations can't expect to do much more fighting, and to keep on is reckless and wanton expenditure of human life. Our rations are all the way from a pint to a quart of cornmeal a day, and occasionally a piece of bacon large enough to grease your plate."

EVEN in the dead of winter, Grant wanted to keep Lee off balance. On February 5 he again sent the II and V Corps to take the Boydton Plank Road at Hatcher's Run. This time they had little trouble. Now Lee's line was stretched to over thirty-seven miles, and he had only about 35,000 men fit for duty. Then on March 2 Sheridan destroyed the last remnants of Early's forces at Waynesboro and headed south to join Grant. This development really shook Lee. Now he knew he had to evacuate Petersburg and Richmond and attempt to flee south

to join General J. E. Johnston in the Carolinas. But how to do it was the question.

Lee's answer, characteristically, was to attack. He requested General John B. Gordon to select the target. Gordon picked Fort Stedman, the fortification the Federals erected on Hare's Hill where their lines crossed the Prince George Court House Road. Also it lay near the City Point Railroad, Grant's major supply line. In addition, it was only 150 yards to the east of a strong Confederate position called Colquitt's Salient, with the picket lines only fifty yards apart. And the terrain around the fort was generally level and clear, good for maneuvering and even feasible for cavalry actions. This section of the Federal line was held by General Orlando B. Willcox' division of the IX Corps, with the 14th New York Heavy Artillery holding the fort itself. Lee hoped that with the disruption of the Federal supply line and the capture of a section of his works, Grant would be forced to shorten his line and thus Lee would be able to start part of his army on the road south to join Johnston. It was a daring gamble born of sheer desperation.

LEE left details of the surprise attack to Gordon to work out. In addition to his own three divisions, Lee also gave him troops from Generals Richard Anderson's and Hill's corps, and a division of cavalry under W. H. F. Lee. Almost half of Lee's entire force would be used in

The Confederate attack on Fort Stedman, March 25, 1865 (HW)

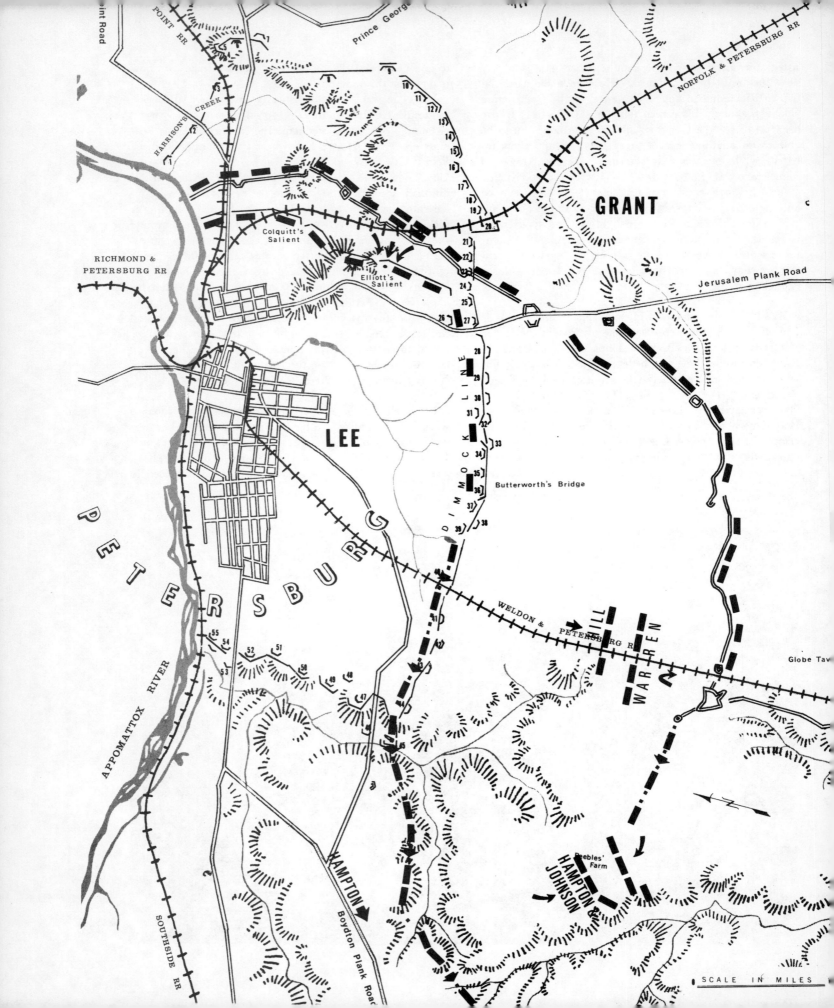

POINT ROAD

POINT RR

HARRISON'S CREEK

Prince George

GRANT

Colquitt's Salient

RICHMOND & PETERSBURG RR

Elliott's Salient

Jerusalem Plank Road

LEE

DIMMOCK LINE

Butterworth's Bridge

PETERSBURG

WELDON & PETERSBURG RR

HILL

WARREN

Globe Tav

APPOMATTOX RIVER

Peebles' Farm

HAMPTON

HAMPTON & JOHNSON

SOUTHSIDE RR

Boydton Plank Road

SCALE IN MILES

NORFOLK & PETERSBURG RR

the gamble. Gordon's plan called for the obstructions in front of the Confederate position to be removed quietly during the night preceding the attack, and the Federal pickets to be overcome without firing a shot. Then fifty picked men were to remove the abatis and *chevaux-de-frise* protecting Fort Stedman, after which three companies of 100 men each, wearing strips of white cloth to distinguish them in the darkness, would rush the fort and then pretend they were Federals so they could hurry to the rear to capture three other forts Gordon believed to be there. The main body of infantry was then to attack to the left and right, up and down the line, while the cavalry charged through and disrupted communications.

At 4 a.m. on March 25 Gordon gave the order to advance. At first the attack went as planned. The Federal pickets were silenced quietly, the obstructions cleared effectively without raising an alarm, and the 300 men swept into the fort to capture the surprised occupants without a fight. They then continued on in rear of the fort while other units started fanning out to the left and right.

But then things began to go wrong. The three other forts the 300 selected men were supposed to capture did not exist, and the futile search for them and the ensuing return to Stedman caused confusion in the Confederate ranks and gave the Federals time to recover from the initial surprise and rally effectively. Soon a hail of shells and musket fire poured into the massed Confederates. They found it impossible to advance farther and certain death to stay where they were. At 7:30 Lee gave the order to withdraw, but rather than face a vicious crossfire on the line of retreat, many preferred to surrender. All told, Lee lost over 4,000 in killed, captured, and wounded, to the Federals' 1,500.

GRANT'S main worry now was that Lee would slip away from him. The day before the Stedman attack he had ordered the II and IX Corps over to the extreme left, preparatory to another attempt to cut the Southside Railroad and encircle Petersburg completely. A few days

Interior of Fort Stedman. A drawing from a photograph. (B&L)

later Sheridan joined the army in front of Petersburg and Grant immediately ordered him over to the left to take command. Sheridan advanced to Dinwiddie Court House where a heavy rainstorm halted him temporarily. In the meantime, Lee had sent Pickett and Fitzhugh Lee over to his right to halt this new threat. On March 31 a portion of Sheridan's force pushed northwest toward Five Forks, eighteen miles southwest of Petersburg. But here Pickett and Fitz Lee the next day stopped them and the Federals withdrew to Dinwiddie. Lee then sent Pickett an order bordering on panic. "Hold Five Forks at all hazards." The Confederates hastily threw up fortifications and prepared to resist to the last. As the beautiful spring day wore on with no indication of another Federal advance, Pickett and Fitz Lee went off to enjoy a shadbake provided by General Thomas Rosser. Late that afternoon Sheridan attacked with his cavalry and infantry and routed the leaderless Confederates, and by dusk held Five Forks and over 3,000 prisoners. The Southside Railroad was less than three miles away. The western end of Lee's defenses had collapsed at last.

THE end came quickly. The next day, April 2, Grant ordered a general assault all along the line, and Lee telegraphed Jefferson Davis: "I advise that all preparations be made for leaving Richmond tonight." Wright's VI Corps broke through on the Confederate right and reached the Southside Railroad first. Other elements swept away the remnants of the Confederate lines along Hatcher's Run, and here A.P. Hill was killed. By midday the entire outer line to the west had been captured with the exception of two forts, Gregg and Whitworth, just in front of the city. Now the city was completely surrounded except to the north across the river. That was Lee's only open escape route and he took it. A desperate last minute resistance

MAP 3. In the months following Grant's first attack, the opposing lines of breastworks and forts grew and gradually extended west. In an attempt to break through the Confederate defenses, on July 30 Grant exploded a mine under the work called Elliott's Salient, but the attack by Burnside that followed was a miserable failure. A few weeks later, Grant extended his lines to Globe Tavern, along the Weldon and Petersburg RR, and sent Warren's V Corps toward the city. Warren was stopped and forced back, but still held the railroad. In an attempt to feed the slowly starving Confederates, Wade Hampton led his cavalry off on the Boydton Plank Road to circle the Federal army and capture over 2,000 cattle in a brilliant raid. Soon after his return, Hampton and Johnson repulsed another attack by Warren at Peebles' Farm, while Lee was forced to stretch his line still more.

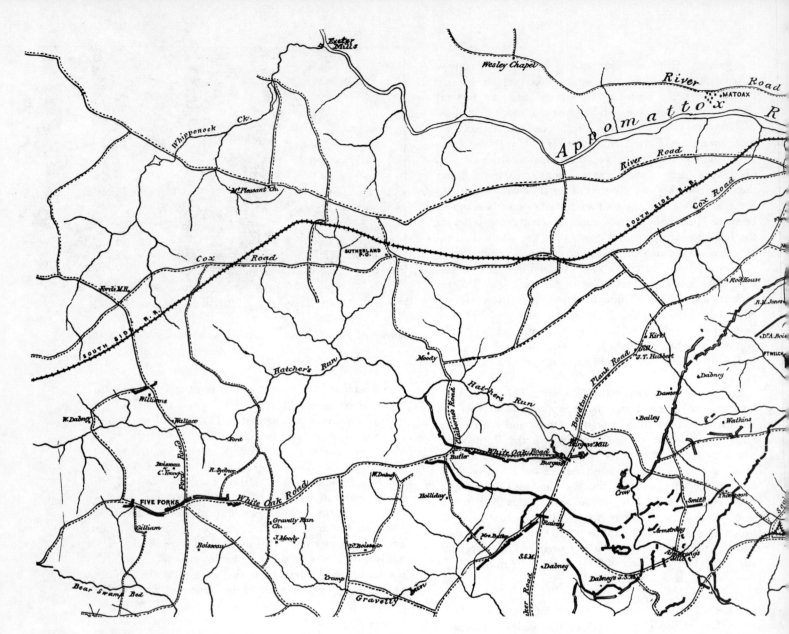

General map of the whole theater of operations during the Petersburg Campaign, June 1864-April 1865. (From A. A. Humphreys, "The Virginia Campaign of 1864 and 1865")

held Forts Gregg and Whitworth and a line between them until darkness, and thus kept the Federals out of the city until Lee had evacuated and headed west in a vain attempt to join Johnston.

MONTHS before, Lee had foreseen the possibilities of such a disaster on his right, and had constructed a chain of inner defenses, designed to protect the main body of his troops in the event of such a crisis. This chain ran from Battery 45 on the main line of defenses to the Appomattox River. To protect this inner line Lee undertook the construction of two forts, named Whitworth and Gregg. Fort Gregg guarded the only approach from the Boydton Plank Road, and no major assaults could be

delivered on the inner defenses so long as the Confederates held it. Laid out in an "L" shape, the fort was protected in the rear by a short palisade and an impassable ditch. The main approach to the fort was guarded by numerous obstructions and a high parapet which ran west and south. Unfortunately, one trench connecting Forts Gregg and Whitworth lay only partially completed, and only a short parapet protected the entire north side of the fort. This narrow access to the fort was ultimately to be its downfall.

At 8:00 a. m. April 2, Forts Gregg and Whitworth were all that stood between the Federal army and Lee's paper-thin inner line. Longstreet was on his way, but the decrepit Weldon & Petersburg Railroad could not get his troops to Lee's support for hours. Fortunately the victorious Federals were at the moment engaged in driving to the Appomattox; their energies had not yet been directed east, but it was only a matter of time. Once

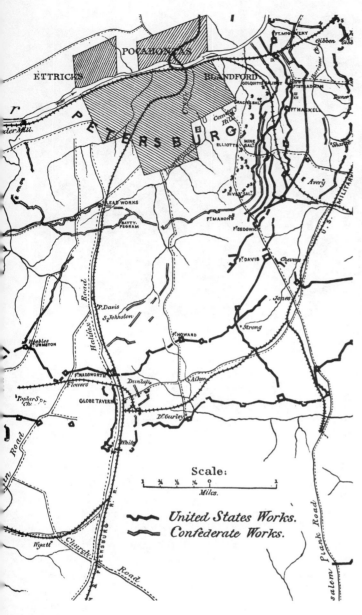

Scale:

United States Works.
Confederate Works.

Forts Gregg and Whitworth. Gibbon prepared two of these divisions, Robert Foster's and John Turner's, for an all-out assault, and finally ordered the advance at 1:00 p.m. when the VI Corps lined up beside him in support. At this time Lee, who fully realized the vital importance of Fort Gregg, sent word to the garrison that "Longstreet is coming. Hold for two hours and all will be well." In fact, as the first attack was being delivered at 1 p. m., the van of Confederate General Charles W. Field's division was entering the trenches, where limited Federal concentrations were being effected. It would be two hours, though, before the main body of Longstreet's men could come up. For these two hours Lee must trade the lives of the Fort Gregg garrison.

Estimates of the number of troops in Forts Gregg and Whitworth vary from 300 to 500. Wilcox, in his official report, put the number at "between 400 and 600." General E.P. Alexander, who in his *Memoirs* said 214 men, including 62 artillery drivers in Fort Gregg, is

they overran the vital inner defenses, retreat would be cut off and they would most likely end the war in the streets of Petersburg. Lee needed time; General Cadmus Wilcox realized this and rallied the remnants of his two shattered brigades, under Brigadier Generals James H. Lane and Edward L. Thomas, at Fort Gregg. Whatever happened, this integral fort must be held until Longstreet could come up and man the defenses upon which the life of the Army of Northern Virginia depended.

AFTER driving successfully through Heth's division to the Appomattox, the Union soldiers paused to re-form and bring up support. Grant, picking himself a tree on a nearby hill, watched the morning's proceedings while pensively whittling and barking out a steady stream of orders. He now ordered three of General E.O.C. Ord's divisions under the command of General John Gibbon to assume the offensive, instructing them to overrun

Lieutenant General Ambrose P. Hill who was killed on April 2, 1865 during the final defense of Petersburg. (NA)

The Federal attack on Fort Gregg, April 2, 1865, from the original sketch by Alfred R. Waud. (Library of Congress)

Major General John Gibbon, commander of newly organized XXIV Corps, led the attack on Forts Gregg and Whitworth. (From LC)

generally considered the most accurate reporter. The only two guns in the fort were commanded by Captain Walter E. Chew of the 4th Maryland Battery and Lieutenant Frank McElroy of the Washington Artillery, the remnants of whose units comprised most of the garrison's artillery force. The infantry consisted of portions of the 12th and 16th Mississippi under Lieutenant Colonel James H. Duncan and various elements from Lane's brigade under Captain George H. Snow. It is doubtful that more than 250 men in all held Fort Gregg; facing them stood over 7000 men of Foster's division. Over in Fort Whitworth, the remainder of the Washington Artillery held three guns; while parts of the 19th and 48th Mississippi, of Lane's brigade also, comprised the bulk of the infantry. Against Whitworth were Turner's 7,000. With both forts open on one side, no more than 300 yards apart, neither could survive without the other.

The Confederate evacuation of Petersburg. ("Harper's Weekly")

478

New York Nov. 2d 1865

Dear Brother David,

I remember well of promising to write from the Rebel stronghold when once it got into our possession, but, we were hurried through it so swiftly after Lees flying columns that I had no time to make my words good. We had a tough march after him for upwards of fifty miles, but brought the stag to bay—The whole road was completely strewn with the debris of Lees flying army. Guns, and caissons were abandoned and left on the road side, whilst every farm house along the route was filled with wounded men. At length Sheridan cut off Longstreets [Ewell's] corps from the main army capturing over eight thousand men. After Lee's surrender which was on the 9th of April, we lay in the vicinity till once the news of Johnsons [Johnston] surrender reached us. When we marched back through Petersburgh to City Point on the James River from thence to Manchester opposite Richmond. Where the whole army of the "Potomac" massed, and on the following morning we marched with the whole army through Richmond on to Washington. It was a glorious day for the Boys, marching through the Rebel Capitol. Four years they had been knocking for admittance and as a newspaper correspondent says "it was peculiarly fit that the army of the "Potomac" so brave and steady and persistent, so long baffled by various fortune, should at last justify their own patient heroism and the national confidence by striking the final blow."

The fighting where we lay in front of Petersburgh was of the most desperate kind, and I cannot be too thankful that I am here uninjured after what I have come through. We lost a good many brave Boys out of the Battery, but the Infantry suffered terribly storming the Rebel works. If you were reading the papers you would see where the Rebels attacked us on the 25th of last March in Fort Steadman, and assaulting us in Fort "Haskell" where we lay. Our fort was just three hundred yards to the left of Steadman which they carried in the first rush. They then tried to carry our fort but were repulsed. It was a wild morning and I never wish to see such sights again.

James Mitchell

GIBBON directed the first attack by Foster's division against Fort Gregg at 1:00 p.m. The Federal troops were in high spirits from their victories in the morning, and expected little resistance from the supposedly disheartened Confederates. At the least, they expected to have no problem overwhelming the tiny garrison with sheer weight of numbers. However, the first assault eliminated whatever doubts the Northerners may have held. Charging across the open field, Foster's Federals came under a killing fire from Fort Gregg, and they had to fall back to re-form. Again they charged, and again they were repulsed. The rebels in Fort Gregg beat off attack after attack, until no one could say for sure just how many separate assaults took place. Gradually the battle became one continuous attack, as the Union troops tried desperately to surround the fort.

Inside Fort Gregg the Confederates fought "like demons." The two field pieces were served magnificently, and Chew and McElroy aided tremendously in beating back the first Federal rushes. As Douglas S. Freeman puts it, the "First Corps artillerymen were proud to claim the gunners in the forts as their own"; the defense of Fort Gregg was one of the high points for Lee's brilliant artillery corps. Wounded men were not exempt from the fighting—they painfully loaded rifles and handed them to comrades with bloody hands. There were no lulls, and for an hour and a half the tiny garrison held off the determined Northerners. In fact, they might have checked the Federals all day had not the enemy, reenforced by two more brigades, managed to surround the entire fort and effect an entry through the narrow gorge opening to the north. After they gained access to the fort, bitter hand-to-hand fighting followed for twenty-five minutes, with the demonic Confederates, wounded included, using the bayonet and knife. At one point six Federal battle flags could be counted on the parapet. Later survivors claimed that those twenty-five minutes were the most infernal and desperate they ever experienced. "We lost all sense of reason," one veteran remembered, "and were driven by a blinding urge to kill. I have never seen men struggling more frantically to clamber up the high parapet. . . and only after 25 or 30 minutes of awful slaughter was that heroic garrison conquered."

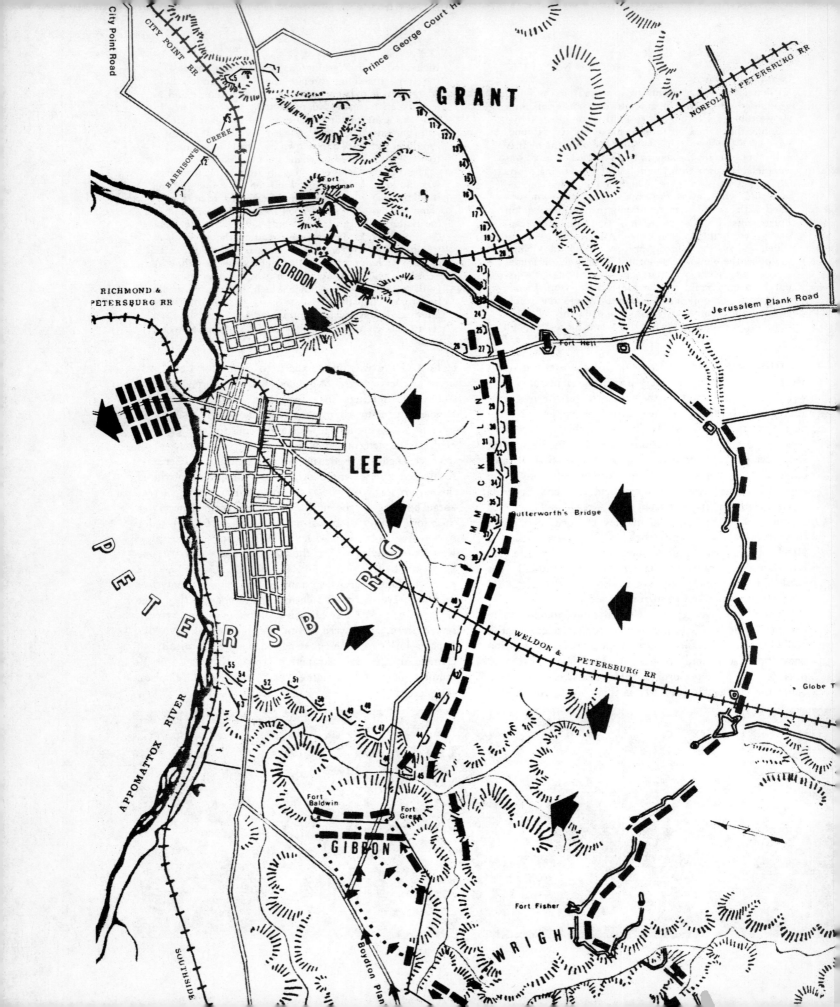

"Charge of the Ninth Army Corps on Fort Mahone, April 3, 1865" is title of this drawing by Alfred R. Waud for "Harper's Weekly."

BY 3:00 P.M. it was all over. About the time of the final successful Union assault on Fort Gregg, Turner's remaining brigade advanced on Fort Whitworth for the first time in the afternoon. It was obvious that Whitworth was untenable with Gregg in Union hands, though, and Wilcox ordered an immediate withdrawal. Federals in

MAP 4. In the spring of 1865 Lee was extended to the breaking point. Hoping that he might force Grant to relieve the pressure on his left, Lee permitted General John B. Gordon to attack. Gordon directed his assault on Fort Stedman. The attack failed and, followed by the disaster at Five Forks on April 1, forced Lee to evacuate Petersburg. On the next day Grant ordered a general assault all along the lines. Wright drove through near the Boydton Plank Road, while General John Gibbon, breaking Lee's line farther south near Hatcher's Run, moved up that road, across Wright's front, to attack the western defenses of the city. There he met a gallant holding action by a handful of Confederates at Forts Gregg and Whitworth. This gave Lee the time necessary to cross the Appomattox and head his shattered, hungry army toward the little courthouse town that bore the river's name.

Fort Gregg, however, quickly turned the two captured guns on Whitworth, causing the Confederate commander, Colonel Joseph M. Jayne, and sixty of his men to surrender.

Confederates and Federals alike paid dearly for the defense and capture of Fort Gregg. Of the brigades Gibbon put into battle, 14,000 troops in all, 122 men lay dead and 592 wounded. The Northern casualties of 714 men more than tripled the size of the entire rebel garrison. The Confederates suffered no less in their Homeric defense; when the smoke cleared 55 were found dead and 129 wounded. Only 30 men remained uninjured in a force of 214; 86% of the Southern garrison were casualties, a figure few units ever approached in a war marked by stupendous mortality rates.

However, if the Union forces gained their objective, so too did the Confederates of Fort Gregg. They gave Lee his precious two hours. Longstreet had come up, Field occupied the defenses of the inner line, the right lay secure, and that evening the Confederates managed to conduct an organized retreat westward. Grant, no doubt influenced by the heroic defense of Fort Gregg, and wishing to prepare for the pursuit of Lee, did not attack the inner defenses after all. Perhaps he saw in the defense of Fort Gregg proof that even with the end only

481

Union occupation of Petersburg after ten months' siege. (HW)

days away, the men of the Army of Northern Virginia would fight with the ferocity that had been theirs for the past three years.

The next morning the Federal troops entered Richmond and Grant was in Petersburg. After a short visit with President Lincoln, who had been in the vicinity of City Point for several days, he sent the Army of the Potomac in pursuit of Lee. The end of the war was now only a matter of days. But the siege of Petersburg had been costly for both sides. Although the exact figures will never be known, it is generally estimated that during the 10-month period the Federals suffered approximately 42,000 casualties in killed, wounded, and missing, and the Confederates about 28,000, not counting desertions.

April 2, 1865 marked the *de facto* death of Lee's attenuated army and the country it sustained. The long siege of Petersburg delayed for ten months, and Fort Gregg for another seven days, the certain fate that awaited, but both demonstrated to the world that although physically the Army of Northern Virginia was dying, its fighting spirit still and forever endured, even on the road to Appomattox.

ATLANTA

By Wilbur G. Kurtz, Sr.

THIS PAINTING by James E. Taylor shows General Dodge, later builder of the Union Pacific RR, ordering Mersey's brigade of his XVI Corps to charge a Confederate column at the Battle of Atlanta. At the extreme right may be seen Fuller's division engaging Walker's Confederate division. (Courtesy of the Atlanta Historical Society.)

O N JULY 5, 1864, the Federal armies of the Cumberland, the Ohio, and the Tennessee, under Maj. Gen. William T. Sherman, approached the Chattahoochee River northwest of Atlanta, hoping to find that their opponent, Gen. Joseph E. Johnston, had already crossed it with his Confederate Army of Tennessee. But they found their paths blocked by strong fortifications on high ground near the river. A bloody repulse at Kennesaw Mountain, eight days earlier, had made Sherman wary of attacking Confederate forts. To bypass Johnston's "river line" he sent his seven army corps upstream, to cross at points beyond Johnston's right.

Atlanta was protected by almost 12 miles of fortifications into which the Confederates could retire, but Johnston had other plans. Midway between those forts and Peachtree Creek he was building an outer line overlooking the valley of Peachtree Creek. When Sherman's right wing, under Thomas, was busy crossing the creek, Johnston intended to send Hardee's and Stewart's (formerly Polk's) corps forward from this outer line to attack the Cumberlanders before they could get ready to fight. The left wing, under McPherson, was too far away to help and Schofield was beyond recall.

Northeast of Atlanta the outer line turned south along the present Highland Avenue. Hood's corps was to stop McPherson as he approached there. Wheeler's cavalry would extend the line on Hood's right. Wheeler was to hold a high, bald hill (later called Leggett's Hill) from which Federal guns could shell downtown Atlanta.

But Johnston did not remain to execute his plans. On July 17 he was relieved from command and Gen. John B. Hood replaced him. The change was not popular with the army.

Hardee had crossed the river at Bolton and gone into bivouac to picket the river. On the 18th he marched his corps into Atlanta on the Marietta road, past Johnston's headquarters. The men had learned that he was leaving, and a feeling of despondency settled down on them. In moody silence they reached today's Five Points and turned north up Peachtree Street (Road). When they reached the outer line, where Peachtree and Spring Streets join, they deployed along it and entrenched. Hardee had three of his four divisions in line: Walker was in the center; Maney was on his left, with his left at Tanyard Branch; Bate's line, on Walker's right, ran to Clear Creek; his fourth division, Cleburne's, was in reserve behind Walker.

Stewart moved from the river into the outer line with his three divisions, Loring on the right, next to Maney, Walthall in the center, and French on the left, west of Howell Mill Road.

Following Johnston's plan, Hood on July 20 made a sortie against the advancing Federals. About 4 p.m., four hours later than Hood had planned, Hardee and Stewart moved to the attack. Along Hardee's front, Walker was astride the Peachtree (Buckhead) Road, Bate was in the Clear Creek valley, and Maney connected with Stewart's right in the valley of Tanyard Branch. Uncleared forests and dense thickets made it difficult to keep in line.

As Loring's division approached the high ground on which the Collier Road led from Peachtree to Collier's Mill, on Tanyard Branch, and then to the Howell Mill Road at the Embry plantation, it had to cross low, cleared ground. Walthall, on Loring's left, advanced over wooded hills. The right of Scott's brigade, next to Walthall's right, moved from the woods to the low ground where Tanyard Branch flowed placidly to the mill. On Walthall's left, French extended toward the mouth of Peachtree Creek, facing Palmer's XIV Corps across the creek.

Hood's delay gave Thomas time to get across the creek and advance to the high ground at Collier Road. Hooker's XX Corps—Williams', Geary's, and Ward's divisions—crossed at Peachtree Road and at the present Northside Drive. Earlier, Newton's division of Howard's IV Corps had crossed at Peachtree Road and moved forward to a high ridge just north of Collier Road. Here Newton deployed his men, with Kimball's brigade west of the road and Blake's (Wagner's) east of it. Goodspeed's battery took position on the road. Bradley's brigade was in reserve, a few hundred yards in the rear.

Geary's division moved up to high ground along Collier Road, just west of the mill, with Williams in his right rear; but Ward's division, between Geary and Newton, was slower in getting across the creek and into position. The resulting gap left Newton dangerously exposed, but he had time to erect barricades and do some digging.

Walker's attack met with deadly fire from Newton's barricaded men. Brig. Gen. C. H. Stevens was killed, and his men strove to avenge him. Although hard pressed, Newton held his ground until Walker was forced to retire to reform his shattered line.

Bate managed to work around the left of Newton's line, over low, swampy ground and through tangles of small growth, and attacked his left rear. But Bradley's brigade quickly formed line of battle along the road, which overlooked Clear Creek. While Bradley's muskets took toll along Bate's front, a storm of canister and case decimated his ranks from guns posted across Peachtree Creek, on his right. He was forced to retire.

On Newton's refused right, Loring's men charged into the gap created by Ward's delay and threatened to engulf Kimball. But Kimball's regiments held firm until Ward could come up and drive Loring back. One of these embattled regiments, the 24th Wisconsin, was commanded by a boy major, Arthur MacArthur, whose son, Douglas, would later win renown.

On Loring's left, a terrible struggle was taking place at Collier's Mill. Scott's brigade, after routing Geary's skirmishers and capturing the 33d New Jersey's state flag, charged into the gap where Tanyard Branch cuts through the ridge by the mill. Col. Benjamin Harrison's brigade, of Ward's division, occupied the higher ground on each side. A battery was sited to sweep the approach. Scott's men were raked with canister and swept by storms of

musket fire from the right and left. Finally they drew back, leaving the ground around the mill thickly carpeted with dead and wounded.

Walthall's men charged across the Embry plantation and into a long, deep ravine to assault Williams' line, posted on the high ground beyond. Although Reynolds' brigade, near the Howell Mill Road, met with some success, enfilading fire from its left forced it back. O'Neal's (Cantey's) brigade, on Reynolds' right, plunged into a section of the ravine between Geary's right and Williams' left, where it suffered heavily from a withering crossfire and was forced to withdraw.

At dark Hardee and Stewart pulled back their beaten men to the outer line. They had lost 4,796 in killed, wounded, and missing. Thomas had lost 1,779. Hood's first sortie had failed. He was not present.

While the Battle of Peachtree Creek raged north of Atlanta, there was also fighting to the east. McPherson's Army of the Tennessee was approaching Atlanta from Decatur. Logan's corps was astride the Georgia Railroad, with Dodge following in reserve. On Logan's left, south of the railroad, Blair moved southwest toward the Bald Hill which Wheeler was defending, and the Flat Shoals Road. Farther to the north, Cheatham's corps (Hood's) was holding back the advance of Schofield's XXIII Corps and Stanley's and Wood's divisions of Howard's IV Corps. Although Cheatham had no difficulty, the pressure on Wheeler grew too great for his dismounted cavalry force. In the late afternoon, Cleburne's division, Hardee's only reserve, was ordered to march to his relief. After a long, hot march, Cleburne relieved Wheeler at midnight.

On the 21st, fighting was suspended along all but Blair's line fronting the Bald Hill. But Cleburne was attacked by Leggett's division of Blair's corps, supported by Gresham's division under Giles A. Smith, with a fury which Cleburne later described as "the bitterest fighting" of his life. Finally, Cleburne's men were driven from the hill by Leggett, whose name the hill now bears. The intrenchments were at once reversed and Atlanta lay within range of Leggett's guns.

HOOD COUNTERED with a move that could have spelled disaster to McPherson's forces, whose left flank had no cavalry screen. He decided to send Hardee's corps on a 15-mile night march to McPherson's rear; a well-placed attack there promised better results than the head-on assault at Peachtree Creek. The ensuing conflict, known as the Battle of Atlanta, is dramatically portrayed on the 400-foot canvas of the Atlanta Cyclorama now housed in a special building in the city's Grant Park.

Hood instructed Hardee to move his corps south through Atlanta that night, swing around to the southeast, and then turn north toward Decatur to strike the rear of McPherson's line. Although the route followed strange roads, Hood expected Hardee to be in position by daylight of the 22d to deliver a surprise attack upon the unsuspecting Federals.

Hardee's march began at dark. Cleburne's division, which had been pulled back into Atlanta after fighting all day, joined the column as it passed through the city. The night was hot and the roads ankle deep in dust. The men slogged along wearily, many of them with empty canteens.

At daybreak Hardee was still far from his destination. Since the country was strange to his officers and he had no maps, he secured two guides. Close to East Atlanta the road forked. Hardee sent Walker's and Bate's divisions up the Fayetteville Road toward Decatur, as Hood had planned. But he sent Cleburne's and Maney's divisions straight ahead toward the Federal left flank.

A short distance farther north the road crossed Sugar Creek. Here Walker halted and decided to turn left, up the creek. In vain his guide, Case Turner, argued that he would be blocked by the large pond at Terry's Mill, but Walker was adamant. He turned and, with Bate following, was soon confronted by the pond. The ensuing confusion attracted unwelcome attention. It was now almost noon, and neither wing of Hardee's corps was where Hood wanted it—behind the Federal line.

During the forenoon, McPherson had ridden to Sherman's field headquarters at the Augustus Hurt (Howard) house, east of Atlanta. He asked that Sweeney's division of Dodge's corps, in reserve behind Logan, be sent across Sugar Creek to fill a gap between the refused left of Blair's XVII Corps and Fuller's division of Dodge's corps, on the extreme left, both of which faced south. In the absence of Garrard's cavalry, which had gone eastward to destroy the rails and bridges near Covington, Sweeney's division would be a welcome addition to that exposed flank. Sherman assented. It was a fortunate decision, for Sweeney's move toward the gap placed his division in position to block Walker and Bate.

Sherman then explained a plan to shift McPherson from the left of the army to the right. On a map, he indicated the line of march. The route would take McPherson behind Schofield's Army of the Ohio and Thomas' Army of the Cumberland, and put him in position to reach for the two railroads which entered Atlanta

through East Point, the Macon & Western, and the Atlanta & West Point. With the Georgia Railroad and the Western & Atlantic in Sherman's hands, Hood depended upon these two roads to supply his army, particularly the Macon & Western.

When Sherman had finished, McPherson rode back to inspect his lines—and to meet his death early in the afternoon.

About noon, Sweeney was moving toward the gap when he halted briefly. He was near Fuller, who had pickets out to his front and left and artillery posted on a hill near where Sweeney had halted. These pickets had been alerted by the confusion at the millpond, and as Walker got clear of the pond and started to ride farther north he was killed. Brig. Gen. Hugh W. Mercer took command of his division. Immediately Bate and Mercer hurried into position but only Bate, on Mercer's right, actually reached a point behind McPherson's line. As they moved forward, they found Sweeney's men formed to meet them. The Battle of Atlanta had begun.

Near Blair's refused left flank, Cleburne had deployed astride the Flat Shoals Road with his right brigade reaching beyond the gap to Fuller's right. Maney deployed on his left. As Cleburne moved forward to attack Blair and Fuller, Maney swung around and attacked Blair's front. Giles Smith's division was swept back upon Leggett's Hill.

When the firing commenced, McPherson galloped to a hill from which he could see the field. He watched Sweeney—on advantageous ground—repulse Walker and Mercer, then hurried to the sound of Giles Smith's disaster.

As Cleburne's right struck Fuller's left, skirmishers pressing forward through the gap saw a Federal general galloping toward them, accompanied only by an orderly. At their cry to halt, he wheeled his horse and attempted to escape. But a shot toppled McPherson from his saddle.

GENERAL JAMES B. McPHERSON, who commanded the Federal Army of the Tennessee, was killed by a skirmisher in the Battle of Atlanta. Only 34, McPherson was highly regarded by Sherman and his fellow Federal generals. (From "Mountain Campaigns in Georgia." Kean Archives, Philadelphia.)

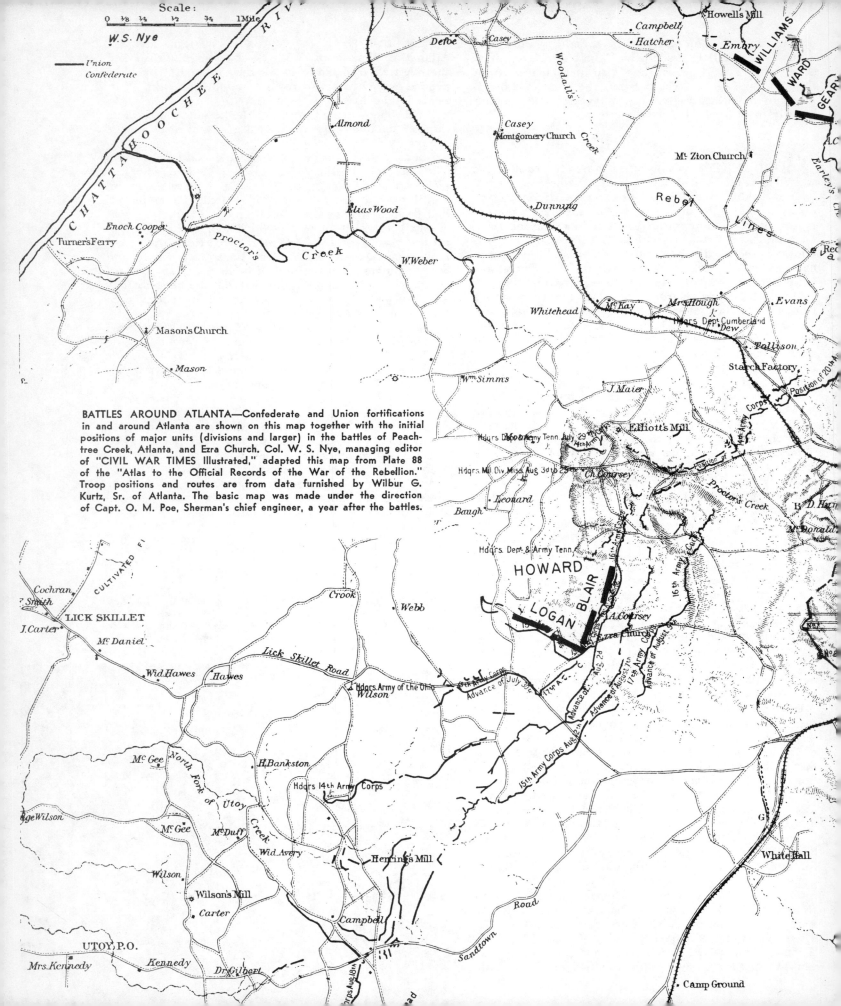

Scale:
W. S. Nye

— Union
— Confederate

CHATTAHOOCHEE RIVER

Howell's Mill
WILLIAMS
WARD
Campbell · Hatcher
Emory
GEARY

Defoe · Casey
Woodall's Creek
Casey
Montgomery Church
Mt. Zion Church

Almond

Rebel

Elias Wood
Dunning
Lines

Turner's Ferry
Enoch Cooper
Proctor's Creek
W. Weber
Whitehead · McKay · Mrs. Hough · Evans
Hdqrs. Dept. Cumberland
Dew · Tallison
Starch Factory
Position of 20th A

Mason's Church
Wm. Simms
J. Maier

Mason

BATTLES AROUND ATLANTA—Confederate and Union fortifications
in and around Atlanta are shown on this map together with the initial
positions of major units (divisions and larger) in the battles of Peachtree Creek, Atlanta, and Ezra Church. Col. W. S. Nye, managing editor
of "CIVIL WAR TIMES Illustrated," adapted this map from Plate 88
of the "Atlas to the Official Records of the War of the Rebellion."
Troop positions and routes are from data furnished by Wilbur G.
Kurtz, Sr. of Atlanta. The basic map was made under the direction
of Capt. O. M. Poe, Sherman's chief engineer, a year after the battles.

Elliott's Mill
Hdqrs. Dept & Army Tenn. July 29
Hdqrs. Mil. Div. Miss. Aug. 3d to 25
Ch. Coursey
Proctor's Creek
Leonard
B. D. Han
Baugh
Mc Donald
Hdqrs. Dept. & Army Tenn.
HOWARD
BLAIR
16th Army Corps
LOGAN
J. A. Coursey
Ezra Church

Cochran
Smith
CULTIVATED FI
Crook
Webb
J. Carter
LICK SKILLET
McDaniel
Lick Skillet Road
Wid. Hawes · Hawes
Hdqrs. Army of the Ohio
Wilson
Advance of July 3d
Advance of Aug. 2d
Advance of August 7th
Advance of August 2
15th Army Corps Aug. 2
White Hall

McGee
North Fork of Utoy
H. Bankston
Hdqrs. 14th Army Corps
ge Wilson
McGee
McDuff
Creek
Wid. Avery
Herring's Mill
Wilson
Sandtown
Wilson's Mill
Carter
Road
Campbell
UTOY P.O.
Mrs. Kennedy · Kennedy · Dr. Gilbert
Corps Aug. 18th
Camp Ground

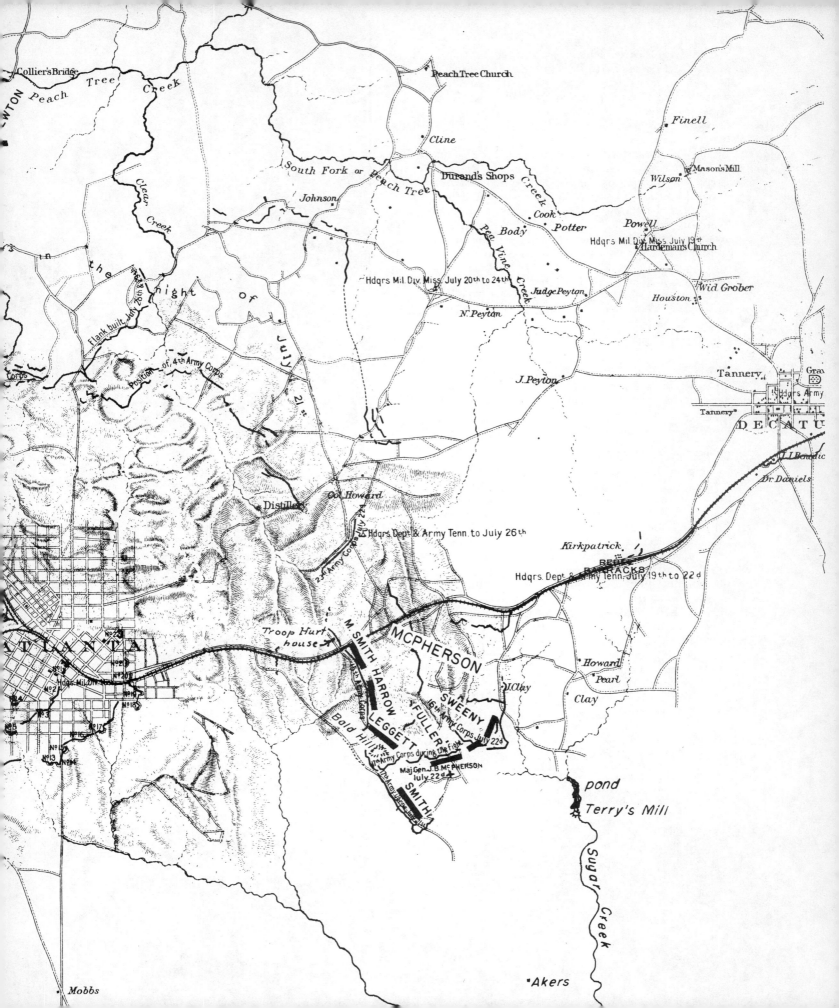

Cheatham's corps had been shifted to the right to attack McPherson's front. Had Hood launched it as Hardee struck the Federal left and rear, his second sortie might have succeeded in wrecking McPherson's army. But again, Hood was not on the battlefield, so Cheatham's attack was delayed. Blair's men reformed on Leggett's left, facing south, and that flank was secured.

Late in the afternoon Cheatham's attack finally got away. It struck M. L. Smith's division of the XV Corps, astride the railroad on the former Confederate outer line, broke Lightburn's brigade at the Troup Hurt house, and captured DeGress' battery of 20-pounder Parrott guns.

Logan, who had succeeded McPherson temporarily, promptly ordered forward Mersey's brigade of Sweeney's division. Mersey's men double-quicked to the scene and, with Smith's reformed brigades, drove back Cheatham's embattled men and restored the Federal line.

When night finally closed the battle, Hood had lost more than 8,000 men. Sherman had lost 3,722. Again Hood had failed.

ON JULY 26, Maj. Gen. O. O. Howard was assigned to the command of the Army of the Tennessee. Maj. Gen. D. S. Stanley assumed command of the IV Corps. Already Howard's new command was en route to the right of the army, as Sherman had planned. By the 28th Dodge was in position on Thomas' right, facing Atlanta, and Logan and Blair had moved beyond him to the vicinity of Ezra Church, in the present Mozley Park, southwest of Atlanta toward East Point.

Stung by his failures, Hood watched Howard's movement, which threatened his remaining railroads. Determined to halt it, he sent Stewart's and S. D. Lee's (Cheatham's) corps against the encircling enemy. The resulting Battle of Ezra Church was a third disaster.

Feeling carefully toward East Point, Howard halted on good defensive ground near the church. Increased cavalry resistance in his front warned him that Hood was aware of his movement. It was a fortunate decision.

Howard's skirmishers found enemy forces approaching on the Lickskillet (Gordon) Road. He deployed quickly, with Logan on the right and Blair on the left. Blair's line was sharply refused to face southeast, making a sharp angle where the two corps joined in front of Ezra Church. Hasty barricades were erected and Logan and Blair awaited the coming storm.

When S. D. Lee's corps arrived, it was deployed facing the XV Corps line. Brown's (Hindman's) division was placed on the left, opposite the right of Logan's line. Clayton's (Stewart's) division moved to his right. Brown had reached the field ahead of his troops and met Brig.

Gen. William H. Jackson, whose cavalry division had been pressed back by Howard's advance. Jackson offered the opinion, however, that the Federal infantry did not appear to be in great force.

Lee's plan was to strike the Federal right flank and roll it back on its left, at Ezra Church. Moving out to the left, to insure a direct blow on Logan's right flank, Brown advanced with three brigades abreast and one in reserve. About 12:30 p.m., his skirmishers pushed forward through dense undergrowth and engaged Federal skirmishers on the Lickskillet Road. Brown's line moved forward, but fences and thickets disrupted his alignment and slowed his advance. He was forced to halt, under fire from the enemy skirmishers. When he advanced again, he drove the skirmishers back into Logan's line. But as he neared it, a withering fire proved Jackson's opinion wrong. After a desperate struggle, Brown was forced to retire.

Ten minutes after Brown moved forward, Clayton advanced. A misunderstanding caused Gibson's brigade to move unsupported against Logan's left. When the defenders saw but one brigade approaching, they swarmed out of their works and shattered Gibson's regi-

THE HEAT of the Battle of Ezra Church is depicted in this drawing from "The Soldier in the Civil War." In this battle, Hood failed in an attempt to smash the Union right and pulled his battered army back into the defenses of Atlanta.

"for severity is unsurpassed by any of the campaign." Lt. Col. Samuel R. Mott, 57th Ohio Infantry, wrote that "the carnage was fearful and the dead and wounded on the field told a tale that must clothe many hearth stones in mourning and sorrow."

But the words of a tired Confederate soldier were the most eloquent of all. In the early dark, one of the skirmishers whom Logan had sent forward again called out—"Well, Johnny, how many of you are left?" The voice that answered might have been speaking for the dying cause:

"Oh, about enough for another killing."

When the losses at Ezra Church were tallied, Hood had lost approximately 5,000 of his remaining men. Sherman had lost 600. And again, Hood had not appeared on the battlefield. Hood had supplanted Johnston because he was a "fighter." He had fought, but the results were to shock even the authorities in Richmond, who had been impatient with Johnston's sensible—but less colorful—policy of preserving his men for the task of holding Atlanta so long as it needed to be held. Now, to the humiliation of three failures was added an admonition from President Davis to avoid attacking the enemy in his entrenchments. With his decimated and dispirited army, Hood faced the dull prospect of conducting a defense. But he soon learned that Sherman was not content with besieging the city. Hood found himself forced to fight for the possession of his railroads.

SHERMAN had found that the fortifications of Atlanta were too strong to assault and too extensive to encircle. Instead of attempting either, he occupied a line facing the city, with his left near the Georgia Railroad and his right probing toward East Point and Hood's vital railroads. His probing forced Hood to extend his own lines to cover East Point.

Meanwhile, Sherman subjected the city to continual shelling. Until August 9, the shelling had been moderate. As his impatience mounted, he had siege guns sent forward. These, together with 50 batteries of field pieces, all emplaced on commanding ground, fired by day and by night. But 30 days of persistent hammering produced no visible results. Hood continued to receive supplies, and spies reported no shortages of food or munitions. The citizens went about their affairs with seeming indifference to the bursting shells. Although most of the families had "refugeed," those remaining lived in cellars, and in caves and "bomb proofs" constructed in their yards and gardens. It appeared that Atlanta would, as Johnston had confidently intended, be held "forever."

As August wore on, the opposing lines crept slowly toward East Point, Hood's finally encircling the town. Continual skirmishing, sometimes amounting to sharp engagements, marked each passing day. On the Sandtown (Cascade) Road, near the south fork of Utoy Creek, a repulse by Bate's division of an attempt by Schofield to break his line resulted in the Battle of Utoy Creek. But on the morning of the 26th the defenders found the trenches opposite them empty. Sherman was gone.

ments. Clayton's attempt to reinforce him was useless. His division, too, was driven back.

It was now 2 o'clock and Lee's attack thus far had failed. But the battle was not over; Stewart's troops were arriving. Walthall's division came first, and deployed in the interval between Brown's and Clayton's shattered remnants. Ordered to retrieve Brown's failure to drive Logan's right from its secure position and back upon his left, Walthall advanced over the same ground that Brown had traversed, his men stumbling over gruesome evidence of the fate of Brown's assault. The dead lay in ominous numbers, and the wounded cried piteously for water. But Walthall, too, failed, and his dead and wounded lay intermingled with Brown's.

Loring was wounded while deploying his division for an assault. Before Stewart could give the order for Walthall to retire, he was struck in the forehead by a spent bullet. Although Stewart had ordered Loring into the fight, Walthall took command when Stewart was wounded and ordered no further assaults. The losses already were appalling—and the men's lives had been spent in vain.

From four o'clock until dark the action was limited to skirmishing. At 10 o'clock, the shattered ranks of Lee's and Stewart's corps moved back to the shelter of the fortifications.

The burden of the battle now had fallen upon Lee's corps and Walthall's division of Stewart's. Despite their crushing defeat, all had fought with the fury of desperation.

The enemy testified to their valor. Col. James S. Martin, 111th Illinois Infantry, stated that the battle

HOOD'S NASHVILLE

CAMPAIGN

By Stanley F. Horn

ONE distinguishing feature of the Battle of Nashville was that it was thoughtfully planned by both sides, and was fought in accordance with those plans. It was not an accidental collision of opposing armies, as at Gettysburg, nor was it the climax of complicated pre-battle military maneuvers as at Chancellorsville or Chickamauga. Neither was there the element of surprise, as at Shiloh. Thomas had decided to leave his fortifications and attack the Confederates in theirs at the first opportunity, and had worked out and explained to his subordinates his detailed plans and tactics for the action when it was launched.

Whatever the other reasons for Hood's failure to win the battle, surprise was not among them. When he advanced his army from Franklin to the environs of Nashville he had no idea of attacking Thomas in his fortified position. His declared plan, fatuous though it proved to be, was to place his army in defensive entrenchments to await attack by Thomas in the hope that such an attack could be repulsed and Nashville captured by a counter-charge. The only question in his mind was as to just when and where Thomas' attack would be made. That he was not at all surprised when Thomas did move is shown by the fact that at 2 a.m. on the morning of December 15 he sent a message to General J. R. Chalmers, commanding the cavalry on his left, warning him that the Federal attack would fall on him in a few hours—a warning which also indicated that Hood had some remarkably accurate information.

THOMAS, always careful in his planning, several days before the battle had issued to his corps commanders detailed orders for an attack at daylight on December 10. With the abrupt change in the weather, with snow, sleet, and freezing temperatures making this movement impossible on that date, he notified the corps leaders on the 9th that "it is found neces-

THIS SKETCH, made by George H. Ellsbury for the Jan. 14, 1865 issue of "Harper's Weekly," purports to show "Charge of Third Brigade, First Division, Sixteenth Corps, at the Battle of Nashville, Tennessee, December 15, 1864." The Battle of Nashville got little attention in the illustrated papers of the day. (Kean Archives, Philadelphia.)

sary to postpone the operations designed for tomorrow morning until the breaking of the storm." Thomas, however, specifically instructed that everything be prepared to carry out the attack as planned as soon as the weather would permit.

On the morning of the 14th, when a welcome rise in the temperature and a warm sun rapidly melted the ice and frozen ground, Thomas completed his plans to attack the next morning. At 3 p.m. he called his corps commanders into a council of war at his headquarters to discuss these plans. They were the same as those for the previously postponed attack. But to make sure that there could be no misunderstanding, Thomas handed to each commander his Special Field Orders No. 342, outlining precisely what each of the units was expected to do.

Overlooking nothing, Thomas had also been closely in touch with Commander Fitch, in charge of the naval forces guarding the river approaches to the city. Thomas wanted to make sure that the Confederates would not cross the Cumberland, bypassing Nashville (which they had no intention of doing), but it was characteristic that he proceeded with such caution.

HOOD, too, had not been idle during the two weeks preceding the battle. Acutely aware of the disparity in numbers between his 23,000 men and the 55,000 combat troops of the Federal commander, he tried desperately but fruitlessly to increase his strength. Hood was actually destined to fight the Battle of Nashville with fewer men than he had at the close of the action at Franklin. In a move that has been characterized by military critics as one of Hood's greatest blunders, he had detached two brigades of infantry and two divisions of cavalry (nearly a quarter of his total force) under General Forrest to operate against the Nashville & Chattanooga Railroad and the Federal garrison at Murfreesboro. From Hood's standpoint, containing the Murfreesboro garrison doubtless was a military necessity, but it now appears that this might have been done with fewer men. Certainly Hood could have better guarded his flanks if he had retained his full cavalry force at Nashville, especially if that cavalry had been under the magnetic leadership of Forrest.

In addition to his vigorous though unsuccessful efforts to increase his strength, Hood was alert in taking all possible steps to have his command at the peak of its efficiency and preparedness. Regular and frequent rollcalls were employed to discourage straggling, and commanding officers were instructed to have their entire lines examined late each evening and early each morning to observe the enemy and ascertain if any changes in their own positions should be made.

ON DECEMBER 10 Hood issued a circular order stating that it was "highly probable that we will fight a battle before the close of the present year," and urging that the troops be "kept well in hand at all times." When the battle began, the order said, the corps commanders were to park all their wagons, except the artillery, ordnance, and ambulances, in the vicinity of Brentwood. In addition to these precautions, corps commanders were to fortify their flanks

496

AT NASHVILLE—Thomas was secure behind fortifications such as those shown in this photograph from the National Archives. This position, Fort Negley, was strongly fortified. The view is to the northeast.

"with strong, self-supporting detached works" to facilitate defense.

Hood, in taking his position before Nashville, placed Stephen D. Lee's corps in the center, A. P. Stewart's on the left, and Cheatham's on the right. The Confederate entrenched line, hastily constructed under adverse weather conditions, was about four miles long, much shorter than the Federal defensive fortifications. The Confederate right wing rested on a deep cut on the Nashville & Chattanooga railroad between the Nolensville and Murfreesboro Turnpikes. Slightly in advance of the main line at this point was a small lunette occupied by the 300 survivors of the brigade of General Granbury, who had been killed

at Franklin. The main Confederate line extended westward across the Nolensville Pike to the principal stronghold of the right flank on Rains's Hill. Extending on to the west, Hood's line ran across high ground, crossing the Franklin Pike where the present battlefield monument stands. Thence the line continued back of Brown's Creek, crossing the Granny White Pike at a sharp angle with the road, then on to Hood's main salient, known as Redoubt No. 1, which crowned the high hill just east of the Hillsboro Pike and north of the present Woodmont Avenue. Here Hood's line turned sharply back southward at almost a right angle to Redoubt No. 2, east of the pike, and on to Redoubt No. 3 across the pike to the west. Further support for Hood's left was supplied by two more detached works west of the pike—Redoubts No. 4 and No. 5—work on which had been delayed by the bad weather and which were incomplete on December 15 when the battle started. Hood's engineers had originally placed his main line in a somewhat more advanced location, but it was considered too close to the Federal works on the left; therefore the engineers established the stronger line to the rear, with its redoubts. This line was occupied as the main line on December 10, the abandoned entrenchment in front of the main salient on the left being lightly occupied as a skirmish line.

AT 4 A.M. ON December 15 the brassy blare of reveille bugles was heard all along the Federal lines, and the movements preliminary to the day's action began. A heavy blanket of fog hung over the city and its environs, and there was a spectral quality to the pre-dawn activities as the troops started to move.

As scheduled, the first movements were on the left, where General J. B. Steedman commanded. Shortly

DEFENDING NASHVILLE—This Library of Congress photograph is looking west from Fort Casino. Note the long breastworks thrown up in front of the tents; also, the long line of stacked muskets.

after 4 o'clock Wood's IV Corps and Schofield's XXIII Corps marched out of the works into their battle positions. As soon as they were out of the line, General Charles Cruft's provisional division of recruits and others was placed in the works commanding the approaches to the city by the Granny White, Franklin, and Nolensville Turnpikes. General John F. Miller's garrison troops occupied the works to the Lebanon Pike on the left; and a little later Colonel James L. Donaldson's armed quartermaster's force, and others under his command, were placed in the works from the right of Cruft to the river on the right, covering approaches to the city by the Hillsboro and Harding Pikes. This rearrangement of Thomas' force provided a continuing defensive line all around the city, manned by troops not taking part in the actual fighting, thus relieving for combat the approximately 55,000 men who were moving out to the attack.

General Steedman, after looking to the establishment of the reserve defensive line in his rear, marched out at 6:30 a.m. with his three brigades under Colonels T. J. Morgan, C. R. Thompson, and C. H. Grosvenor, to make his scheduled attack on the Confederate right. Delayed by the fog, it was 8 o'clock before his 7,600 men made contact with the enemy. Cheatham's advanced skirmish line fell back, but the main Confederate line and the lunette occupied by the 300 men of Granbury's brigade held firm. The assault by Morgan's 3,200 men failed.

Later in the day some of Morgan's men took over a brick house at a safe distance and cut loopholes in the house and brick outhouses from which their sharpshooters kept up a desultory fire on the Confederate line. Colonel Thompson's report shows that after his brigade's preliminary skirmish his men "retired to our position in line," where they were content to remain the rest of the day.

The Federal officers who took part in this action against the Confederate right asserted that they had led Hood to think this the principal point of attack, and even alleged that by their attack they had pinned down Cheatham's corps in its breastworks until the day's fighting was ended. Actually, Hood recognized Steedman's attack as a feint, and during the afternoon withdrew most of Cheatham's force from that flank to strengthen his strongly assailed left—and apparently Steedman was unaware that the troops he attacked in the morning had left his front.

DURING THIS more-or-less sham battle on the Federal left, the main purposeful movement of Thomas' force was developing on the right. There was some confusion in the initial movements of the infantry and cavalry, and it was nearly 10 a.m. before the infantry corps of Smith (about 15,000 men) and the cavalry corps of Wilson (something over 12,000, of whom 9,000 were mounted) were able to start their big sweep against the Confederate left. But when this movement did get under way it was irresistible.

Wilson, whose cavalry on the right was to provide the deciding force in the battle, handled his part of the assignment with efficiency and a thorough attention to detail. A young West Pointer who had graduated into the Engineers, he was quick to learn from experience and was rapidly developing into a first-rate cavalry commander. When he returned from the final conference with Thomas on the afternoon of the 14th, he assembled his division and brigade commanders and explained that the plan of battle called for them to advance on the right of the infantry, turn and envelop the Confederates' left flank and, if possible, strike their rear. To avoid misunderstanding, Wilson personally showed each officer on a map, exactly the ground over which he was to advance, orally reiterated his instructions, and then supplied each with a written copy of the orders.

As a final touch, Wilson conferred with General A. J. Smith (with whose corps he was to cooperate) to correlate their activities so as to avoid any confusion in the initial movements. There was confusion nevertheless. Wilson, in his subsequently published recollections, elaborates on the delay caused by what he considered Smith's (or McArthur's) bungling, as McArthur's division, contrary to what Wilson thought was the arrangement, crossed Wilson's front instead of his rear in getting into position to move out the Charlotte Pike. In spite of this delay, the movement, once started, proceeded like well-oiled clockwork.

THE CONFEDERATES, to meet this attack, had only a token force between their solid left wing on the Hillsboro Pike and the river—a distance of about three miles. Chalmers, in command of the single division of Forrest's cavalry left with Hood, had one brigade

BATTLE OF NASHVILLE—This map by Col. W. S. Nye is a simplification of the official Federal map shown as Plate LXXIII (1) of the Atlas to the Official Records. While it contains some minor inaccuracies, it was chosen because it shows the roads as they existed in 1864. The troop locations have been made by Stanley Horn, as well as the directions of attack of the several Federal corps. These are not the exact routes followed, but give the general axes or directions of movement. The engagements on December 15 and December 16 are shown. The place shown as Traveler's Rest was the Overton house.

498

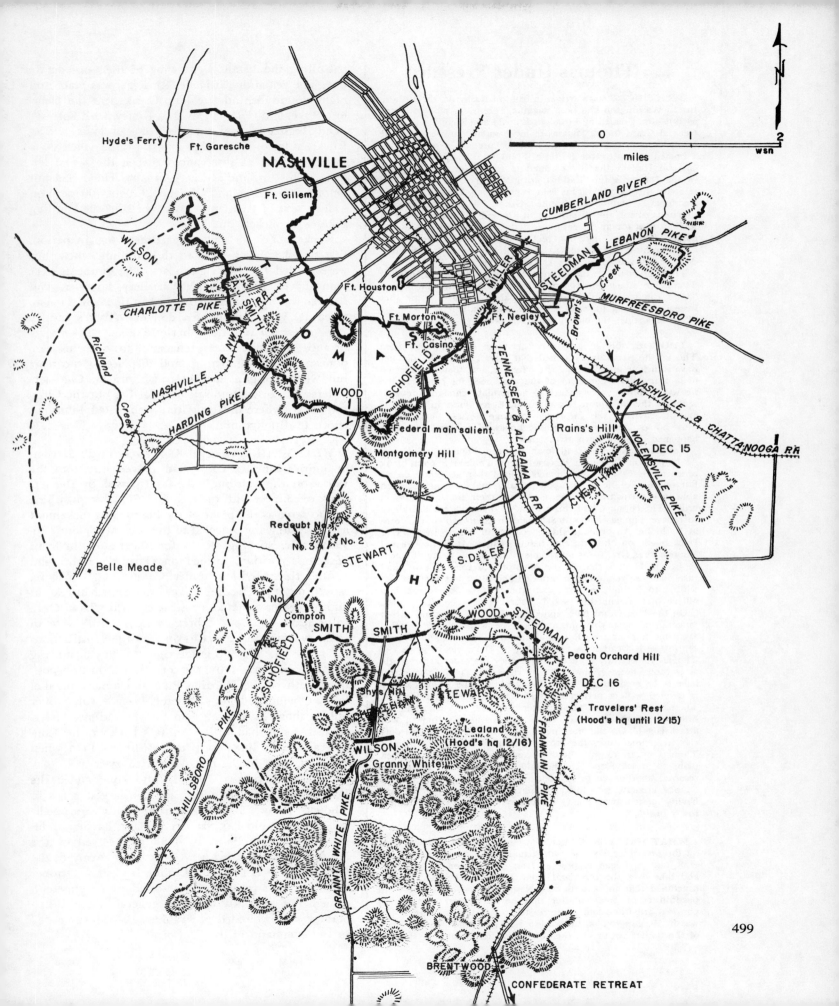

Hyde's Ferry

Ft. Garesche

NASHVILLE

Ft. Gillem

CUMBERLAND RIVER

WILSON

CHARLOTTE PIKE

A.J. SMITH

T H O M A S

Ft. Houston

Ft. Morton

Ft. Negley

STEEDMAN

LEBANON PIKE

NW RR

Ft. Casino

MILLER

STEEDMAN

Brown's Creek

MURFREESBORO PIKE

NASHVILLE

HARDING PIKE

NASHVILLE & NW RR

WOOD

SCHOFIELD

TENNESSEE & ALABAMA RR

Rains's Hill

NASHVILLE & CHATTANOOGA RR

Richland Creek

Federal main salient

Montgomery Hill

NOLENSVILLE PIKE

DEC 15

Redoubt No.

No. 3   No. 2

STEWART

S. D. LEE

CHEATHAM RR

H O O D

Belle Meade

No.

Compton

SMITH   SMITH

WOOD   STEEDMAN

Peach Orchard Hill

SCHOFIELD PIKE

Shy's Hill

STEWART

DEC 16

Travelers' Rest
(Hood's hq until 12/15)

FRANKLIN PIKE

Lealand
(Hood's hq 12/16)

WILSON

Granny White

HILLSBORO PIKE

GRANNY WHITE PIKE

BRENTWOOD

CONFEDERATE RETREAT

499

... Thomas Under Pressure

EVER SINCE Hood's arrival in front of Nashville, the authorities in Washington had been nagging Thomas to move out and assault him. Goaded by President Lincoln and Secretary Stanton, General Grant urged Thomas to move immediately against the Confederates, regardless of his state of preparedness.

Immediately after the Battle of Franklin, Thomas reported to General Halleck that he planned to remain on the defensive in the Nashville fortifications until Wilson could recruit and remount his cavalry. This was reported to Lincoln, and on December 2 Stanton telegraphed Grant: "The President feels solicitous about the disposition of General Thomas to lay in fortifications for an indefinite period 'until Wilson gets equipments.' This looks like the McClellan and Rosecrans strategy of do nothing and let the Rebels raid the country. The President wishes you to consider the matter."

Thus nudged by the armchair strategists, Grant directed Thomas to attack Hood "before he fortifies," commenting that "After the repulse of Hood at Franklin, it looks to me that instead of falling back to Nashville, we should have taken the offensive against the enemy where he was."

THOUGH this long-distance needling must have nettled Thomas, he patiently explained that after Franklin he did not have sufficient force to take the offensive, but that he expected to in a few days. Conscious of the vital need for more cavalry, he was bending every energy to accumulate enough horses to remount the unmounted cavalrymen. Every horse in Nashville and its environs was impressed—carriage horses, work horses, plow horses, even the performing horses of a stray circus that happened to be in town at the time.

Telegrams flew back and forth between Thomas and Grant. At length, on December 6, Grant sent Thomas a point-blank order to attack at once. Thomas replied that he would do so; but on the 8th he wired apologetically that he had not been able to concentrate his troops and get their transportation in order. Thereupon Grant, his patience exhausted, asked Halleck to relieve Thomas and put Schofield in command of the force at Nashville. An order to this effect was drawn up in the War Department on the 9th, but before sending it Halleck wired Thomas that Grant was much dissatisfied at his delay. Thomas replied to Halleck that "a terrible storm of freezing rain" had just come on, rendering an attack impossible; but that he was willing to "submit without a murmur" if it were decided to relieve him. Grant then asked Halleck to suspend the order.

On the 11th Grant telegraphed Thomas: "If you delay attack longer, the mortifying spectacle will be witnessed of a Rebel army moving for the Ohio, and you will be forced to act, accepting such weather as you find. . . . Delay no longer . . ." Thomas respectfully replied: "I will obey the order as promptly as possible, however much I may regret it, as the attack will have to be made under every disadvantage. The whole country is covered with a perfect sheet of ice and sleet." To Halleck, Thomas telegraphed: "The weather continues very cold and the hills are covered with ice. As soon as we have a thaw, I will attack Hood." On the morning of the 14th there was a welcome rise in temperature, the frozen ground began to melt, and Thomas began to put the final touches on his long-deferred plans to attack Hood. In the midst of these preparations he received another querulous telegram from Halleck, telling of Grant's anxiety, to which Thomas replied simply: "The ice having melted away today, the enemy will be attacked tomorrow morning."

WHAT HALLECK did not mention in his telegram was that on the preceding day, the 13th, Grant had ordered Major General John A. Logan to proceed from Washington to Nashville and take over the command from Thomas. Then Grant had concluded that the situation at Nashville was so fraught with possibilities of great disaster that he had better give it his personal attention; and so he started for Nashville himself. He was in Washington on his way to Nashville when he got news of the battle. Logan was then at Louisville.—**Stanley F. Horn**

patrolling the distant right wing of the Confederate line. The remaining brigade, Rucker's, was placed on high ground behind Richland Creek near the Charlotte Pike, and Colonel David C. Kelley, with Forrest's "Old Regiment" and a battery of four guns, was to Rucker's left on the high banks of the river. As a sort of outpost of observance between the actual left wing of his line and Rucker's cavalry, Hood had put Ector's depleted infantry brigade (about 700 men) on a ridge west of Richland Creek, north of the Harding Pike, with pickets out front.

Rucker's brigade, where Chalmers was in person, first tasted fighting early in the morning when they were shelled by Fitch's gunboats. The gunboats were soon driven off by Kelley's artillery, however, and Rucker was not molested further until about 11 a.m. when R. W. Johnson's division of Wilson's cavalry came sweeping out the Charlotte Pike. Rucker's resistance was sufficiently tenacious to give his cannoneers time to limber up and displace to the rear; but when the guns had been withdrawn, Chalmers ordered the brigade to fall back farther out the Charlotte Pike, where until nightfall he resisted Johnson's efforts to dislodge him.

MEANWHILE, General Kenner Garrard's division of Smith's infantry corps had moved out from the works on the Harding Pike, and passed by the left flank to connect with the right of Wood's corps, which was to serve as the pivot of the big turning movement as the right wing wheeled to the left. McArthur's division, after shaking off the few skirmishers in front of Ector's position, formed on Garrard's right; and Smith's third division, under Colonel J. B. Moore, moved out the Harding Pike and formed in rear of Smith's center to act as a reserve to either flank. Once in position outside the breastworks, Smith's veteran infantry swung forward, carrying out their instructions to "touch the left and guide right." Thus advancing and wheeling gradually, the corps was soon in a position south of the Harding Pike and almost parallel to it. Obviously, Ector's skeleton brigade could offer only a show of resistance to this powerhouse drive. In fact, Ector had orders to fall back to the Confederate main line along the Hillsboro Pike when attacked, and this he had done with alacrity.

General Thomas J. Wood, who commanded the Federal center at Nashville, had the largest corps in Thomas' army—13,256 "present for duty equipped." Wood was an old Regular Army officer, having graduated from West Point in 1845 and served in the Mexican War. He had served with the Army of the Ohio and the Army of the Cumberland since October 1861, and was regarded as a sound and competent, though not especially brilliant, general officer. When Stanley was wounded at Franklin, Wood succeeded to the command of the IV Corps.

SPECTATORS—This photograph was made from the northwest corner of the Capitol grounds while the battle was in progress on the first day. The men squatting near the center of the picture seem more interested in the photographer than in the battle. Thousands of civilians watched the battle on the first day. (National Archives.)

With characteristic efficiency and care for details, Wood on the evening of the 14th had briefed his division commanders, explaining to them the next day's intended movements, and had handed to each of them a copy of the orders for the 15th: Reveille was to sound at 4 a.m.; the troops were to breakfast, break camp, pack up everything, and be ready to move at 6 a.m. The orders are interesting as an indication of just how an army corps prepared to move into battle. The exact movement and position of each division were detailed; and, leaving nothing to chance or guesswork, the orders specified:

The pickets on post will advance as a line of skirmishers to cover the movement. The formation of the troops will be in two lines—the front line deployed, the second line in close column by division, massed opposite the interval in the front line. Each division commander will, so far as possible, hold one brigade in reserve. Five wagon-loads of ammunition, ten ambulances, and the wagons loaded with the intrenching tools will, as nearly as possible, follow immediately after each division; the remaining ammunition wagons, ambulances, and all other wagons will remain inside of our present lines until further orders. One rifle battery will accompany the Second Division, and one battery of light 12-pounders will accompany each of the other divisions; the rest of the artillery of the corps will maintain its present positions in the lines.

With only minor fog-induced delay, Wood's men had gone into their designated positions when they moved out of the works early in the morning. From then until shortly after noon the main body of the corps remained inactive, waiting for the adjustment and advance of Smith's and Wilson's forces on their right. Wood's skirmishers, however, had been pushed forward and soon became sharply engaged with the Confederate skirmish line, keeping up a brisk but inconclusive action. Since early morning the guns in Fort Negley and the other forts, as well as the batteries in position along the whole Federal line, had been thundering their salvos, arousing a replying artillery fire from the Confederate positions. This booming of the big guns, Wood commented in a conservative understatement in his official report, "added interest to the scene."

THE BATTLE of Nashville was fought before an exceptionally large "gallery" of civilian as well as military spectators. A participant recalled that "citizens of Nashville, nearly all of whom were in sympathy with the Confederacy, came out of the city in droves. All the hills in our rear were black with human beings watching the battle, but silent. No army on the continent ever played on any field to so large and so sullen an audience."

Shortly after noon, when Smith's wheeling line of infantry had been brought around to a point where it served as a continuation of the right of Wood's line, Wood ordered his men forward. The great sweep of some 40,000 men got under way, and Stewart's men holding Hood's left flank knew that their hour of trial had arrived, as they heard what one of them described as "the sharp rattle of fifty-calibre rifles, sounding like a cane-brake on fire." In somewhat more poetic language, Wood said in his report:

"When the grand array of the troops began to move forward in unison, the pageant was magnificently grand and imposing. Far as the eye could reach, the lines and masses of blue, over which the nation's emblem flaunted proudly, moved forward in such perfect order that the heart of the patriot might easily draw from it the happy presage of the coming glorious victory."

Wood's third division (Beatty), as it swung forward on the shortest arc of the big wheel, was confronted with the works on Montgomery Hill, salient of the advanced skirmish line which had been Hood's main line before that line was moved back on the 10th. From the viewpoint of the attacking Federals, the position looked formidable, but it was actually manned by only a few skirmishers placed there before the battle.

501

Wood, of course, had no idea how strongly Montgomery Hill was defended. He did know, however, that it barred the further advance of his men in this sector and would have to be reduced. So, after ordering a thorough pounding of the position by artillery, Colonel Sidney Post of Beatty's division was ordered to lead his brigade in an assault on this position. They swept up the wooded slope, over the enemy's intrenchments, and the hill was won.

MEANWHILE, Schofield's corps had remained idle just outside the works where it had moved at daylight. General Darius N. Couch's division had formed in the rear of General Smith's left near the Harding Pike, and while Smith was maneuvering into an advanced position during the morning, Couch moved forward behind his left, within supporting distance. The division commanded by General Jacob D. Cox had remained practically stationary to the left of Couch.

Couch was an 1846 West Point graduate, and had served as a corps commander and second in command to General Hooker at Chancellorsville in May 1863. After that battle Couch, refusing to serve further under Hooker, had been given a noncombat assignment. Then in December 1864, he volunteered to serve as a division commander under Thomas, and was assigned to Schofield's corps. Cox was an Ohio lawyer and politician, without prewar military training or experience, but was regarded as able. In active command of the battle line at Franklin, he conducted that operation efficiently. Couch was 42 and Cox, 36.

As Smith's corps advanced, with Hatch's and Croxton's divisions of Wilson's cavalry on his right, his advance drove the Confederate skirmishers before them like a covey of quail. Smith's forward movement bore more to the left than Thomas had expected, so about 1 p.m., Schofield was ordered to swing his corps far around the rear of the advancing line and form on Smith's right, thus allowing the cavalry to operate still more widely and effectively against the extreme Confederate left with its isolated and lightly manned redoubts.

Early in the afternoon, the advancing Federal infantry, cavalry, and dismounted cavalry confronted and overlapped the Confederate line along the Hillsboro Pike. The zero hour had come.

AS THE BLUE JUGGERNAUT rolled across the fields between the Harding and Hillsboro Pikes, General Hood had not been idle. When he saw that he was confronted with the overtures to a full-scale assault on his lines, he moved up his headquarters from Travelers' Rest on the Franklin Pike to Lealand, the home of Judge John M. Lea, just east of the Granny White Pike. Here he began to do everything he could—which was not much—to meet the formidable assault he could see rolling up on Stewart in his weakly defended left wing.

General Alexander Peter Stewart was a native Tennessean, born in 1821, who had graduated from West Point in 1845, but served only three years in the Army. He was given a brigadier general's commission in the Confederate Army in 1861, and had served in the Army of Tennessee since then. He was promoted to major general in 1863, and when General Leonidas Polk was killed in June 1864, was given command of Polk's corps, with the temporary rank of lieutenant general. His men called him "Old Straight."

Stewart, that misty morning of December 15, soon perceived that his position was the immediate objective of the Federal attack, and he began promptly to make the best possible disposition of his inadequate manpower. When he had moved back on December 10 from the Montgomery Hill line to the solid works he now held, based on his main salient at Redoubt No. 1, General Walthall's division was not placed in the line but was put in bivouac, protecting the extreme left of the Confederate infantry line. Walthall was Hood's youngest division commander, only 33 years old, but he was a dogged fighter of great ability. His division had suffered severely at Franklin, one of

his brigades having 432 casualties out of the 1,100 who went into battle. When General Samuel G. French, in failing health, left Hood's army before Nashville, his two brigades (Ector's and Sears's) were assigned to Walthall. Ector had been sent to the relief of Chalmers on the far left, and Sears was placed in the main line, to the left of Loring, holding the salient embracing Redoubts No. 1 and No. 2 to the east of the Hillsboro Pike.

AS SOON as Stewart learned that the Federals were advancing in full strength west of the Hillsboro Pike, he ordered Walthall to prepare for action. Walthall placed a company of infantry and a battery of artillery in each of the redoubts in his immediate front (No. 4 and No. 5), although they were still incomplete. The remainder of his command was put in position behind a stone wall along the eastern side of the pike, extending for the distance between Redoubts No. 3 and No. 4. Ector's retreating brigade reached the Confederate main line in the early afternoon, and Walthall placed it on his left. Even with this extension, however, Stewart's line on his extreme left flank was still not long enough to cover Redoubt No. 5, and he was expressing it mildly when he said in his report, "My line was stretched to its utmost tension."

Stewart appealed to Hood for reinforcements. In response, Hood about noon ordered General Edward Johnson, commanding the left division of Lee's corps, to send Manigault's and Deas's brigades to Stewart's immediate assistance, later sending also the other two brigades of the division, Sharp's and Brantley's—a shift that could be safely made, as Lee's corps was experiencing hardly more than a token attack. Hood also ordered two of Cheatham's divisions on the extreme right to support Stewart, and they started promptly on the march of nearly three miles across country.

THE first collision of the enveloping Federals and the defending Confederates came when Colonel Datus E. Coon, with his hard-riding brigade of Hatch's cavalry division, swinging around the right of McArthur's infantry division, found himself on the exposed flank of Redoubt No. 5, the detached and unsupported outermost outpost of the Confederate left. Coon's men quickly dismounted and with their deadly Spencer repeating rifles moved to the attack. They were supported by the first brigade of McArthur's division and a battery of artillery which immediately opened on the Confederate position. The Confederate guns replied, and there was an artillery duel for about an hour, during which Coon's dismounted troopers and McArthur's infantrymen edged closer to the Confederate works. When they eventually got close enough to charge the redoubt they were met with a burst of canister from the four Napoleon guns on the hill, accompanied by as heavy a musketry fire as a hundred defenders with their single-shot muskets could develop. The result, however, was never in doubt. The fast-shooting Federals swarmed up the hill, over the breastworks and through the embrasures, and literally overpowered the defending force, capturing the guns and practically all the men in the redoubt. As was not unusual during the war, there was some dispute among the victors as to who got there first. Smith said in his report that Coon's men scaled the fortifications "simultaneously with our skirmishers"; but the cavalrymen denied this, saying that the infantry did not get there until after they had the situation well in hand.

Whoever got there first, the Federals had hardly reached the inside of the captured works when they received a salvo from the guns in Redoubt No. 4, and they then turned their attention to this Confederate strong point, which was being invested by the rest of Hatch's and McArthur's divisions.

REDOUBT NO. 4 proved to be not quite so easy a nut to crack as No. 5, although held by no larger a force. It also had a battery of four smoothbore Napoleon guns, manned by 48 men under Captain Charles L. Lumsden, supported by 100 infantry in shallow breastworks stretching a short distance on both sides of the redoubt. Lumsden, a graduate of Virginia Military Institute and, when the war started, commandant of cadets at the University of Alabama, had been ordered to hold the position "at all hazards," and he took his orders literally. Hammered by three batteries of rifled guns from a ridge 600 yards to the west, and almost encompassed by 12 regiments of infantry and two brigades of dismounted cavalry, the Confederate defenders by some miracle of valor clung to their beleaguered position for three hours, banging away with their smoothbores as fast as they could be served. Not until the swarming Federals were actually within the works did Captain Lumsden give the "Take care of yourselves, boys" order, as he and the surviving defenders made off for Walthall's rock wall along the pike.

Meanwhile Schofield had swung his corps around as ordered and was forming on Smith's right, thus making it possible for Wilson to remount his men and move out on a wider arc across the Hillsboro Pike to the left and rear of Walthall's infantry line, commanding both the Hillsboro and Granny White Pikes. Chalmers was still miles away on the Charlotte Pike, pinned down by Johnson's cavalry division, so Wilson was unopposed as he placed his force in position to take a decisive part in the action the next day, although he took no further active part in the fighting on December 15.

WITH the two defending redoubts in his front lost, Walthall's line was now subjected to a blistering bombardment of heavy shellfire from Smith's big guns. Lacking artillery, Walthall was unable to reply; but there was no immediate effort to charge Walthall's thin line as Smith regrouped his divisions on the western side of the pike. During this breathing spell, Walthall tried to strengthen his precarious position by moving Ector's brigade "down near Compton's house" to hold the pike for the protection of the left flank. But after Redoubt No. 5 had fallen and the victorious Federals came streaming down across the pike, Ector's men were driven back to the east and a spearhead of advancing Federals drove in between them and Cantey's brigade, thus isolating Ector's brigade from the ensuing action of Walthall's division.

The Federals driving across the pike into the woods near the Compton house placed a battery on the high hill southwest of the house. Walthall attempted to meet this threat by detaching Reynolds and his brigade from the right of his line to his left, and Reynolds had some temporary success in stemming the Blue tide. But soon the Federals had occupied also the hill west of the Compton house and, shelling Reynolds with the guns on both hills, and threatening both flanks of his brigade with their advancing infantry, drove him back through the woods toward the Granny White Pike.

The reinforcing brigades of Deas and Maningault had meanwhile arrived on the left flank, and were placed in support of Walthall. They were of little or no help. Walthall, to save his men from capture, went into precipitate retreat and the flanking Federals swept northward east of the pike.

Stewart, witnessing the impending debacle on his left, hastily withdrew a battery from his not yet hard-pressed salient at Redoubt No. 1 and placed it on a hill east of the pike where it could sweep the flanking Federals. He ordered the brigades of Deas and Manigault to rally to its support; but says in his report, "they again fled, however, abandoning the battery, which was captured. . . . The other brigades of Johnson's division had come up, but were unable to check the progress of the enemy, who had passed the Hillsboro Pike a full half-mile, completely turning our flank and gaining the rear of both Walthall and Loring, whose situation was becoming perilous in the extreme." Seeing that his position was untenable, Stewart immediately ordered both Walthall and Loring to withdraw, an order which Walthall's men had already anticipated. Loring promptly evacuated his men from the line, leaving Redoubts No. 1 and No. 2 unoccupied and undefended.

MEANWHILE, the third brigade of McArthur's division had been coming up in front of that portion of Stewart's line defended by Redoubt No. 3, west of the pike. As the brigade approached the Confederate position, it came under direct and vigorous artillery fire, which inflicted considerable damage but did not slow the advance. When the men got within striking distance of Redoubt No. 3 they were ordered to storm it, and

thus they reduced the last pocket of resistance on the Confederate line of defense.

McArthur's men, having captured Redoubt No. 3, turned their attention to No. 2 and No. 1, the guns of which had been playing on them as they advanced on No. 3. They were unaware that during the afternoon General Wood had been cautiously approaching Redoubt No. 1. Wood recognized it as the key to the Confederate position, but realized that it would be difficult to carry by frontal attack. He therefore attempted to prepare for a successful infantry attack by a prolonged bombardment of the position by two batteries of his artillery, which almost demolished the Confederate works. He still experienced difficulty in getting his infantry to charge the position; but about 4:30 p.m., Kimball's division did move to the attack and, as Wood says in his report, "rushed forward up the steep ascent and over the intrenchments." Kimball's and McArthur's men each claimed they reached the top first. Neither Wood nor Smith mentions that whichever attacking force had that distinction, it was somewhat of an empty honor, as Loring's defending force was already in retreat, having been ordered by Stewart to withdraw and form along the Granny White Pike.

WHEN the early December nightfall ended the day's action, the elements of the two contending armies were scattered in bewildering confusion. Thomas' units had to a great extent lost their cohesion. On his left Steedman's men were still holding on to the position they had taken early in the day, apparently unaware that Cheatham's forces had been withdrawing from their front all afternoon. Wood, after sweeping over Stewart's salient, had been ordered by Thomas to move east toward the Franklin Pike, reach it if possible before dark, and form his troops across it facing south. Darkness, however, caused Wood to halt his corps shortly after crossing the Granny White Pike to wait until morning. Smith, after driving the Confederate left wing out of its position, had halted for the night in a line between the Hillsboro and Granny White Pikes, and roughly parallel with them. Schofield, on the right, was east of the Hillsboro Pike, with Couch's division entrenched across the hill he had occupied late in the afternoon; and Cox's division, on Couch's right, was roughly perpendicular to him, facing east. Wilson's cavalry divisions were bivouacked on the extreme right, from the Hillsboro to the Granny White Pikes, where they had taken a strong position on the ridge where the road passes through a gap just beyond the old site of Granny White's tavern.

THE CONFEDERATE FORCES were also disorganized and scattered. Cheatham's divisions at nightfall, in the process of being moved to the left, were widely scattered. Bate was already in position on the left, though he arrived too late to take part in the action. Cleburne's division, now under J. A. Smith, was on its way to the left, but bivouacked on the Granny White Pike near Lealand when stopped by darkness. Lowrey's brigade was just starting from its original position on the right. Lee, with the two remaining divisions of his corps, was still firmly holding in the Confederate center, though stretched out in a pitifully thin line. Stewart's battered corps had retired to a position roughly parallel to the Granny White Pike, east of that road, with his left near the Bradford house on the pike. Ector's brigade clung to its precarious resting place on the hill (later called Shy's Hill) where General Hood himself had personally placed it when he encountered its members falling back late in the afternoon.

AT THE CLOSE of the fighting Thomas returned to his headquarters in the city and telegraphed Halleck to tell him of the day's success. "I shall attack the enemy again tomorrow, if he stands to fight," said Thomas in closing his message, "and if he retreats during the night will pursue him." Halleck sent him a gracious acknowledgment; Grant, as soon as he heard the news, sent a telegram saying that "I was just on my way to Nashville, but I shall go no farther"; and then went on to urge Thomas to give the enemy no rest "until he is entirely destroyed." President Lincoln the next morning telegraphed "the nation's thanks"; and, taking his cue from Grant, added: "You made a magnificent beginning. A grand consummation is within your easy reach. Do not let it slip."

Possibly the destruction of Hood's army might have seemed "easy" to President Lincoln and to General Grant; but Thomas, on the ground, knew Hood for the determined, tenacious fighter he was, and knew that there was still work to do "if he stands to fight."

OOD, true to his reputation, did stand to fight; but it taxed his military skill and resourcefulness to improvise an adequate defensive line in the face of a victorious enemy. Working throughout the night and the morning of the 16th, however, he and his engineers did patch together a continuous line in which to meet the expected Federal pursuit. Lee's corps, which had engaged in the least actual combat the preceding day, was moved back on the Franklin Pike to high ground about two miles to the rear. Here Hood established the new right wing of the Confederate army, with hastily scratched-out breastworks and gun emplacements on Peach Orchard Hill just east of the Franklin Pike, and his line extending westward across the pike. Stewart was moved back to a position with his left crossing the Granny White Pike, the main part of his force behind a rock wall, behind which a shallow trench was dug, and his right joining with Lee's left. Cheatham's men were to the left of Stewart, constituting the Confederate left. Shy's Hill, inexpertly fortified during the night, was the salient on this flank, with the rifle pits turning sharply southward to a refused position on the next high hills. The distance from Shy's Hill to Peach Orchard Hill is about two and a half miles as the crow flies, but the meandering Confederate line was about a mile longer. The new line was established about midnight, and the men worked the rest of the night feverishly digging out the best defenses possible.

IN HIS OFFICIAL REPORT, General Thomas, after summarizing the events of December 15, states simply: "The whole command bivouacked in line of battle during the night on the ground occupied at dark, whilst preparations were made to renew the battle at an early hour on the morrow." Thomas does not say, however, just what those preparations were. The net result, however, was that when the Federal forces got into alignment on the morning of the 16th, they had established a continuous line overlapping both Confederate flanks. Schofield was on the right in the position he had taken late in the previous afternoon; to his left was Smith, whose right was opposite the slope of Shy's Hill with his left between the Granny White and Franklin Pikes where it joined the right of Wood, who faced south across the Franklin Pike confronting Lee's position on the Confederate right. Steedman, on the morning of the 16th, after leaving a brigade in his rear to guard the Murfreesboro and Nolensville Pikes, pushed on out the Nolensville Road, eventually taking a position between the pike and the left of Wood's corps. Here he stood until early in the afternoon, when he was instructed by General Thomas to form a junction with the troops of Wood's command and prepare to assault the Confederate right flank.

THE MORNING of the 16th was featured by an exceptionally heavy and continuous bombardment of the whole Confederate line by the superior Federal artillery, particularly severe at Shy's Hill on their left and Peach Orchard Hill on their right. Shy's Hill was subjected to a continuous all-day crossfire from three directions. To reply to this bombardment Bate had only three batteries of smoothbore guns. Lee on the right wing also suffered throughout the day from the guns of Wood's and Steedman's corps, which kept up fire of such intensity that it was considered worthy of special mention in both Federal and Confederate reports.

During the morning and early afternoon the Federals made several feeler attacks on Lee's stronghold on Peach Orchard Hill, but none was successful. Clayton, describing one of these assaults

HOOD'S HEADQUARTERS before Nashville were in the John Overton house shown in this drawing from "Century" magazine.

on his division by Steedman's colored troops, says that the attackers "suffered great slaughter. . . . It was with difficulty that the enthusiasm of the troops could be repressed so as to keep them from going over the works in pursuit of the enemy. Five color bearers with their colors were shot down within a few steps of the works." Holtzclaw reports a "desperate charge" on his line at 10 a.m. and a "determined charge" at noon, both of which were repulsed. Of the losses suffered by the attacking Federals in their second charge, Holtzclaw says:

I have seen most of the battlefields of the west, but never saw dead men thicker than in front of my two right regiments, the great masses and disorder of the enemy enabling the left to rake them in flank, while the right, with a coolness unexampled, scarcely threw away a shot at their front. The enemy at last broke and fled in wild disorder.

Shortly before noon General Thomas in person joined Wood on the Franklin Pike, approved the disposition of his troops, and told him that he wished Wood and Steedman to cooperate in an effort to carry the Confederate works on Peach Orchard Hill. After conferring with Steedman and looking over the ground, Wood concluded that this could be done, in spite of the strength of the position. After careful preparation the assault, led by Post's brigade, was launched at about 3 p.m. The ardor of the attacking force was not dampened by a cold rain that had begun to fall about noon, and they moved forward with "a cloud of skirmishers" in front to draw the fire of the defending line and annoy its artillerists. Nevertheless the attack was repulsed and heavy casualties inflicted. Post was badly wounded and his brigade hurled back.

WHILE THIS ATTACK on the Confederate right was being repulsed, however, things were not going so well on Hood's left. Wilson's hard-driving cavalry brigades had gained the rear of the Confederate left and, fighting dismounted, were putting strong pressure on the defensive line which had been bent back into a fishhook extension of the left wing. Even without this pressure from the rear, the Confederate left was none too strong. Shy's Hill was a formidable looking elevation, but when General Thomas Benton Smith's brigade of Bate's division stretched out to fill the place vacated by Ector's brigade when that unit was withdrawn to be placed in reserve, it was discovered that the works established by Ector's men during the night were improperly located. By some engineering blunder, in the darkness and confusion of the preceding evening, the works were placed so far back from the actual brow of the hill as to give the defending force a limited view and range on the front. This fatal weakness was accentuated by the curvature of the hill and the falling away of the entrenched lines from the angle, making it impossible for the defenders to protect the front of the angle by flanking fire. Also, to make a bad matter worse, there was no abatis or other obstruction to impede the approach of an assaulting party. To add to his discomfiture, Bate was told by Cheatham that it would be necessary for him to stretch his thin line still farther to the left to occupy the position vacated by troops that had been withdrawn to protect the extreme left then in process of being turned by Wilson.

WILSON, who had quickly recognized the value of the position he occupied in rear of Hood's raveled-out left wing, set about capitalizing his advantage. Extending eastward from Schofield's right, Wilson's dismounted skirmishers presented a battle-line a mile and a half long, advancing diagonally across the Granny White Pike, inclining towards Nashville and completely in rear of Hood's left. By noon Wilson's 4,000 troopers (almost as many as Cheatham had left in his whole corps) had pressed their way slowly up the wooded hills in a curving line until they were facing Nashville, parallel with (and in rear of) Hood's main line. Here they were looking down on the backs of Bate's and Walthall's men—a lethal weapon aimed directly at Hood's point of greatest weakness.

Punished by the continuing artillery fire, faced in front and flank by two corps of infantry, and seeing the flanking cavalry-men pouring over the hills in their rear, Cheatham's men were in a desperate plight. The jaws of the Federal vise were closing relentlessly on them. In the words of one of the luckless privates caught in this trap: "The Yankee bullets and shells were coming from all directions, passing one another in the air."

Hood's left wing was doomed. After the battle there were rival Federal claims as to just which unit sparked the advance that closed the jaws of the nutcracker on Shy's Hill. Apparently, however, the movement of Smith's men from the south and Schofield's from the flank occurred simultaneously. Bate's report sums up the climactic action:

About 4 p.m. the enemy with heavy force assaulted the line near the angle, and carried it at that point where Ector's brigade had built the light works; not, however, until the gallant and obstinate Colonel Shy and nearly half of his brave men had fallen, together with the largest part of the three right companies of the 37th Georgia, which regiment constituted my extreme left. When the breach was made, this command—the consolidated fragments of the 2d, 10th, 15th, 20th, 30th and 37th Tennessee Regiments—still contested the ground under Major Lucas; and finally, when overwhelming numbers pressed them back, only 65 of the command escaped. . . . The command was nearly annihilated.

Some of Bate's men did flee to safety, but most of the others who were not killed or wounded stayed resolutely in the line and continued firing until surrounded and captured. Among those taken on the hill were General Thomas Benton Smith and Major Jacob A. Lash, commander of Finley's brigade. General H. R. Jackson, commanding Bate's other brigade, was made a prisoner as he attempted to make his way back from the front line to where his horse had been left.

AS THE ROUTED FORCES of Cheatham's corps fled in disorder through the fields and over the hills in their rear toward the Franklin Pike, the contagion of defeat spread rapidly down the Confederate line—and the equally contagious exhilaration of victory flashed eastward along the Federal works. The triumphant Federals sweeping eastward from their conquest of Shy's Hill swooped down on Stewart's exposed left flank so swiftly and unexpectedly that he had no time to improvise a defense. In the words of one of the officers in French's division:

Realizing their almost hopeless situation, they abandoned their line and organizations and retreated in the wildest disorder and confusion. Many remained in the line and surrendered. In a few minutes the organizations of the corps on the left and center of the army had wholly disappeared, and the routed army rushed over the range of hills to the Franklin Pike.

The men in Lee's corps, on the Confederate right, were taken completely by surprise by the collapse and rout of their left and center. They were flushed with the sense of victory, having just successfully repulsed Wood's vigorous assault on their position and, says Lee, were "in fine spirits and confident of success." Lee's corps, of course, was now forced to retreat also; but its

withdrawal was in more orderly fashion, making it possible to establish a rearguard along the pike. One of the men in the ranks has left an account of how Lee himself, by personal example, contributed to the prevention of panic in his command:

At the time of the break General Lee was sitting, mounted, in the rear of Clayton's division. Over on the left we could see confusion, and a Federal line advancing from the rear and attacking Johnson's division on the left wing of Lee's corps. Everything else had apparently been swept before it. Clayton's division was divided by the Franklin Pike. General Lee rode across the pike, taking both stone fences, followed by one of his staff and two of his escort. He rode until he reached the rear of Stevenson's division of his corps, and rode right into the midst of fugitives and in the face of the enemy who by this time had reached the rear of Pettus' brigade. General Lee seized a stand of colors from a color bearer and carried it on horseback, appealing to the men to rally. . . . The effect was electrical. Men gathered in little knots of four or five, and he soon had around him three or four other stands of colors. The Federals, meeting this resistance, hesitated and halted. (It was late in the evening and misty.) The rally enabled Clayton's division to form a nucleus and establish a line of battle on one of the Overton Hills to the rear, crossing the Franklin Pike in the woods near Colonel Overton's house. Here he was joined by a few pieces of artillery and a little drummer boy who beat the long roll in perfect time, as Gibson's brigade came up and formed a rear guard.

Lee's corps, in event of disaster, had been entrusted with the responsibility of holding the Franklin Pike until the retreating Confederates could use it as an avenue of escape, and this function was performed most capably. As soon as it became obvious that the day was irretrievably lost and that the Confederates' only hope was to save what they could out of the wreckage of defeat, Lee moved with alacrity and efficiency. Informed by Hood that the Federals were already near Brentwood on the Franklin Pike, Lee quickly abandoned the line he had formed across the pike near the Overton house and hastened everything to the rear. At 10 p.m. a new rearguard line was established at Hollow Tree Gap, beyond Brentwood and seven miles north of Franklin. Wood's pursuit was not particularly energetic, and he bivouacked several miles short of the gap when night fell.

THE LAST COMBAT ACTION of the battle was a spirited cavalry engagement on the Granny White Pike about dark. Chalmers, late in the afternoon, rallied his scattered troopers and moved across from the Hillsboro to the Granny White Pike. He formed a line in front of Brentwood to protect the wagons and ambulances collected there. About 4:30 p.m. he received Hood's frantic message to "Hold the Granny White Pike at all hazards," and the brigade was accordingly placed in position across that road, just north of the lane leading to Brentwood. A stout barricade of logs, brush, and fence rails was built.

In the unusual tactical situation now existing, Chalmers was in rear of Wilson, who was in rear of Cheatham's position. Following the collapse of the Confederate left, however, Wilson's victorious and elated troopers had remounted and now came plunging out the pike in pursuit of the fleeing Confederate infantry, through the gathering darkness and the downpour of freezing rain. Only temporarily disconcerted by the unexpected obstacle in their path, the blue-coated riders formed front into line and charged the barricade, thousands against hundreds. Although overwhelmingly outnumbered, the Confederates fought desperately, and what General Wilson later described as "one of the fiercest conflicts that ever took place in the Civil War" ensued.

The battle at the barricade and in the adjoining fields to which it overflowed finally degenerated into a veritable dogfight of individual, hand-to-hand combat, during which Colonel Rucker was wounded, disarmed, and captured. Wilson writes:

> It was a scene of pandemonium, in which flashing carbines, whistling bullets, bursting shells, and the imprecations of struggling men filled the air. . . . Every officer and man did his full duty in the headlong rush which finally drove Chalmers and his gallant horsemen from the field, in hopeless rout and confusion. They had stood their ground bravely, but were overborne at every turn and at every stand by the weight and fury of the Union onset.

Chalmers' last stand had been a desperate and costly one, but it had accomplished its purpose. What was left of his outfit withdrew unpursued to the Franklin Pike, and when the last of the retreating infantry and artillery had passed, the weary troopers camped on the pike with the rearguard for the night. Wilson, his men badly scattered and tired from a full day's fighting, gave orders just before midnight for each command to bivouac where orders overtook it, and to take up the pursuit the following morning.

THE NEXT 10 DAYS were a nightmare of nerve-wracking hardship and struggle for both armies. Alternately marching and fighting, worn down by battle fatigue and sheer physical exhaustion, they somehow managed to carry on an almost continuous running battle from Nashville to the Tennessee River. The weather was abominable—rain, sleet, and snow, with below-freezing temperatures. The wagons and guns quickly churned the roads into seemingly bottomless quagmires which froze into sharp-edged ruts during the cold nights. The heavy rains not only drenched the suffering soldiers but soon flooded the streams and made their passage a serious problem.

Hood's defeat-shocked army was on short rations—mostly parched corn, with an occasional feast of corn pone and fat bacon or perhaps a pilfered pig or pullet. A fortunate few had blankets or overcoats picked up on the battlefield, but most of them had only their threadbare uniforms to protect them from the icy rain that seemed to pierce to the very marrow of their bones. Many had no hats, but it was the scarcity of shoes that presented an especially acute problem. The number of men who were wholly or partially barefooted is almost unbelievable, and Hood's weary veterans left bloody footprints as they stumbled over the frozen ruts.

Thomas' men were well-shod, well-fed and well-clothed, but they had their share of difficulties. And a steady downpour of freezing rain, with muddy roads and swollen streams, will slow down the progress of the most excellently equipped army.

GENERAL FORREST and his men, marching overland from Murfreesboro and driving several hundred head of hogs and cattle, were a welcome addition to Hood's army in Columbia, across Duck River, on the 19th. Here the command of the rearguard was formally assigned to Forrest, and his performance in this capacity was a masterpiece of doing much with little, holding the pursuing Federals at arm's length day after day. On a cold Christmas morning the advance of Hood's weary infantry reached the Tennessee River at Bainbridge, Alabama, near Florence, where the army crossed the river on a pontoon bridge and began the long march to Tupelo, Mississippi, their designated destination. Forrest and the rearguard made a stand at Pulaski on Christmas Day, and on the 26th maneuvered their pursuers into an ambush which, Forrest reported, resulted in their "complete rout" and the capture of one Federal gun. His report concludes: "The enemy was pursued for two miles, but showing no disposition to give battle my troops were ordered back."

That was the last real effort by the Federals to impede the Confederate retreat. Forrest and the last of the rearguard crossed the Tennessee on December 27, and on the 29th Thomas issued general orders declaring the pursuit at an end.

Casualties in the Battle

BATTLE LOSSES AT NASHVILLE—Casualties at Nashville appear to be somewhat light in view of the size and duration of the collision. However, the Federal troops lost many dead and wounded, particularly among colored recruits used in assaulting strong Confederate positions on Rains's Hill on December 15 and on Overton's Peach Orchard Hill on December 16 in diversionary attacks. Confederate reports of killed and wounded are missing, but they are generally believed to be light since they were protected by entrenched positions. The heaviest Confederate loss was in prisoners taken in the swift Federal advance and penetration which surrounded men who were attempting to hold positions to the last in the vicinity of Shy's Hill.

ESTIMATED LOSSES:

	Confederate	Federal
Total Force	23,000	70,000
Engaged	15,000	43,000
Casualties (K & W)	Unknown	3,000
Captured	4,000	100

HOOD'S OFFICIAL REPORT of the battle of Nashville, to General Beauregard, written at Tupelo on January 9, is a masterpiece of half-truths, imparting the news of a disaster in carefully sugarcoated terms. But, sugarcoat it as much as he chose, Hood in his heart knew the bitter truth. His invasion of Tennessee, the last flare-up of aggressive military action by the Southern Confederacy, had ended in disastrous failure. His vision of a victorious Confederate army advancing to the Ohio River was to remain a dream. The Confederate battle-flags would not be seen waving in Cincinnati or Chicago—a possibility Grant had pictured. The Battle of Nashville had decided that, and thereby decided the fate of the Confederate States of America.

It was at Nashville that Hood, wisely or not, had risked all on one cast of the military dice, and lost. For it was by the Battle of Nashville, as one of Thomas' biographers has so well said, that "One of the two great armies of the Confederacy was eliminated from the final problem, and with the total overthrow of that army, the very cause which it had so long and so gallantly sustained was lost."

As a Bugler Saw Nashville

Henry Campbell, a young bugler in the 18th Indiana Battery, wrote the following account of the second day of the Battle of Nashville in his diary:

DEC. 16—I got permission from the colonel to go out and see the battlefield Friday afternoon during the fight. About three miles out I reached the lines, both sides firing vigorously. The artillery made one continual roar. Just as I reached there the charge was made on the keypoint of the Rebel lines, a high, conical-pointed hill. Three or four of our batteries shelled it for awhile. At the signal, the lines advanced in one grand charge in the midst of a terrible storm of bullets and grape. Our brave men knew no faltering. On the brow of the hill as our men came over, the Rebels poured one awful rain of death, but with a wild long shout, our men sprang over the works and fought with their bayonets and butts of their guns.

All of the enemy along this front were captured. They were too close to run. As soon as the success of the charge was seen, our line toward the left began charging, one regiment at a time, in one great tidal wave of victory across the cornfields as far as I could see. The Rebels seemed to know everything was lost, as they threw away guns, blankets, and everything that would hinder their flight.

'Would to God I had never witnessed such a scene' as . . .

. . . Bloody FRANKLIN

Hood wasted 6,000 casualties, including five generals killed, in a series of headlong assaults on Schofield's lines in this tragic prelude to Nashville.

By Hugh F. Walker

THE Battle of Franklin is a "compact" among Civil War battles. In number of men and the time and space covered, it was fought upon a small scale. Yet Franklin ranks as one of the great spectaculars of the war in the West.

Years afterward survivors of Franklin recalled the battle with a sort of painful revulsion, as though the very memory evoked agony. "My flesh trembles and creeps and crawls when I think of it today," wrote Sam Watkins of Columbia, Tennessee. "My heart almost ceases to beat at the horrid recollection. Would to God that I had never witnessed such a scene!"

General Jacob D. Cox, commander of the Federal battle line, put his finger on the thing that made men, especially Confederates, want to forget the battle.

"Hood had more men killed at Franklin, than died on one side in some of the great conflicts of the war," he noted. "His killed were more than Grant's at Shiloh, McClellan's in the Seven-Days Battle, Burnside's at Fredericksburg, Rosecrans' at Stone's River or at Chickamauga, Hooker's at Chancellorsville, and almost as many as Grant's at Cold Harbor."

Captain Robert Banks of the 37th Mississippi, marching across the field on the morning after the battle, wrote of "that sickening, blood-curdling, fear-kindling sight . . . The hell of war was depicted cruelly in the ghastly upturned faces of the dead."

The long, narrow, iron-fenced Confederate cemetery at Franklin is a reminder of that tragic November 30, 1864. Here the fallen sleep under chaste lines of silent stones and sighing cedar trees—424 dead from Mississippi alone.

THE STAGE for battle was set at dawn of that autumn day when Major General John M. Schofield, with two Federal corps, the IV and XXIII, arrived in Franklin, with the advance of Hood's Confederate Army of Tennessee hard on his heels.

Concerned for his seven-mile-long wagon train, Schofield two days before had requested pontoons and bridging equipment from General George H. Thomas at Nashville. But the equipment had not arrived; moreover, of the two bridges across the Harpeth River one was destroyed and the other damaged.

The tired Federal commander considered his situation. The river could not be crossed by the wagon train without many hours of preparation. His men had marched all night, having started on the afternoon of the 29th from Columbia, and were exhausted. Schofield made a quick decision. He would throw up a line of fieldworks south of Franklin and fight, if he must, with his back to the Harpeth River. At the same time he would find means to pass his wagon train across the stream to the Federal fortifications at Nashville, 20 miles to the north.

The town of Franklin, then merely a village, lies in a curve of the Harpeth with the opening to the south. From the river the land rises gently southward for a mile, where it reaches an elevation 40 feet above the square at a point marked then and now by the Carter house, chief landmark of the battle. Through what were then open fields and meadows, so slightly rolling as to appear almost flat, the plain continues another mile and a half to the Winstead Hills. This open field upon which the battle was fought has been likened to the left hand, held palm up and pointed south. The palm represents the village, the little finger and thumb the Harpeth River. The three fingers, from the left, represent the Lewisburg, Columbia, and Carter's Creek Pikes entering the town from the south. The Tennessee & Alabama Railroad also came up from the south, east of the Columbia Pike, and crossed the Harpeth just east of the town and the turnpike bridge.

SCHOFIELD'S works at Franklin were constructed so as to protect his river crossing and line of retreat to Brentwood and Nashville. He directed Cox to throw up a line of fieldworks extending from the river and railroad cut on the left, across the three pikes and bending northward toward the river on the right, the whole about two miles long. Cox's own division was the first to take position in this line, with Brigadier General James W. Reilly temporarily in command. Its three brigades extended from a knoll at the railroad cut westward to the Carter cotton gin and the Columbia Pike. Cox set up his headquarters in the Carter house dooryard.

The Federal line was extended westward to the Carter's Creek Pike by two brigades of Brigadier General Thomas H. Ruger's division under Colonels S. A. Strickland and O. H. Moore, and northwest toward the river by a broken line of light works held by Brigadier General Nathan Kimball's three-brigade division from the IV Corps. As they took position along this line the Federals threw up an earthwork with a ditch in front, topped by headlogs with a three-inch space for rifles. On the left a light abatis of bois d'arc or osage orange was cut from a hedge in front and added to the defenses.

West of the Columbia Pike Ruger's line was strengthened by light logs cut from a locust thicket growing in his front. Except for this grove and the bois d'arc hedge, the ground in front was open and almost level.

UPSTREAM and to the left of Schofield's line the Harpeth was fordable at several places, and the Federal commander expected Hood to launch a flanking attack from that direction. He therefore placed two brigades of Brigadier General George D. Wagner's division, IV Corps, three-quarters of a mile south of the main line to observe Hood's advance. In event of a frontal assault it was to fall back within the main

FRANKLIN BATTLEFIELD—This is how the battlefield looks today from where Hood's headquarters stood. On Nov. 30, 1864, eighteen Confederate brigades advanced on both sides of the road to attack Schofield's army which was drawn up in front of Franklin. (Photograph by Bill Witsell.)

works, but if a flank movement developed, it would swing eastward and check Hood until a new line of battle could be formed.

To guard further against the expected flank movement, Schofield moved a battery of 3-inch rifled guns into Fort Granger, on Figuers' Hill, north of the river near the railroad crossing. This old earthwork, built by Federals earlier in the war, commanded the railroad cut and the ground in front of Cox's division. To its immediate protection was assigned Brigadier General Thomas J. Wood's division of the IV Corps.

Having arranged protection of front and flank, Schofield began work on the bridges, and by midmorning his train began moving slowly across the Harpeth. With this concern eased, the general went to the village home of a Union sympathizer and slept briefly. The exhausted troops, having thrown up the works and eaten their breakfast, dozed on the line in the autumn sun. And it was upon this quiet scene that the head of Hood's army came into view, shortly after noon.

BITTER after his failure at Spring Hill and spoiling for a fight, Hood came over and through the Winstead Hills with two corps, Lieutenant General Alexander P. Stewart's and Major General Benjamin F. Cheatham's, to which was soon added Major General Edward Johnson's division of Lieutenant General Stephen D. Lee's corps. His artillery, except for a battery for each corps, was still in the rear. His cavalry, under the redoubtable Major General Nathan B. Forrest, consisted of three divisions under Brigadier Generals James R. Chalmers, Abraham Buford, and

William H. Jackson, numbering perhaps 6,000 men, and Horn states that Hood had about 20,000 infantry up for the battle—roughly the same number as the Federals had waiting to receive the attack.

Hood's enemies had said the year before in Richmond that he had "the heart of a lion and a head of wood," and his biographer, Dyer, remarked that the general "never was able to think of battle except in terms of long lines of men charging to glory across an open field." These caustic comments, though perhaps exaggerated, nevertheless seem to fit Hood at Franklin. He was to spend the rest of his life explaining away his mistakes on that battlefield.

HIS first error was the decision to form his two corps in line of battle immediately, and charge the Federal works. Cheatham "did not like the looks of the fight," and Forrest strongly advised a flanking movement to the right across the Harpeth. Given a supporting infantry column, the cavalryman asserted,

he could "flank the Federals out in 15 minutes." And despite Hood's denial, there is evidence that Major General Patrick R. Cleburne, his ablest division commander, did not favor the head-on assault.

But Hood was adamant. "No, no," he said. "Charge them out!"

Hood's attitude in this situation is usually ascribed to his crippled physical condition and his bitter disappointment at Spring Hill, where Schofield had escaped him the day before. But the reasons for it go deeper than this, and deserve study. They emerge from the pages of his *Advance and Retreat,* written after the war.

IN the first place, on the morning of the 30th there was bitter feeling between Hood and his officers. Furthermore, the commanding general entertained a poor opinion of his soldiers—the kind words he later lavished on them came after the battle. He felt, and said so, that this army was a cut below Lee's Army of Northern Virginia, where Hood had first won fame as a brigade commander. He conceded that the western troops had the potential to fight as well as Lee's men. But they had been ruined by the leadership of Joe Johnston from Dalton to Atlanta, fighting behind breastworks and falling back. And at Spring Hill he had been irked to see that after a forward march of 180 miles his men were still "seemingly unwilling to accept battle unless under the protection of breastworks."

Hood could see the Federal works at Franklin. He knew they were strong, that the ground was open before them, and that his losses would be heavy. But he did not hesitate to order the charge. He thought, among other things, that it would improve the morale of his army. No other conclusion can be reached from reading his account.

———————————————————➤

THIS IS a section of Howard Pyle's famous "The Battle of Nashville" which hangs in the Minnesota State Capitol in St. Paul. It shows part of a Minnesota regiment attacking Shy's Hill on December 16, 1864.

THE CARTER HOUSE—The Union line at Franklin ran through the yard of the Carter House which has been restored and is operated as a museum. The rear and south side of the brick building are pitted with scores of minie balls. (Tennessee State Library and Archives.)

Some of the men in Reilly's and Strickland's brigades, caught up in Wagner's disaster and misunderstanding their orders, joined in the pell-mell rush to the rear, and Cleburne's and Brown's men poured through the gap on the pike near the Carter house. They took the guns just to the left of the road, but providentially for the Federals they could find no primers, and the guns remained silent.

Suddenly the crucial point of the battle was at hand, with Confederates 50 yards inside the Federal works. For a few minutes Hood was on the verge of victory.

But the break did not spread. Instead it was plugged up by the third brigade of Wagner's division, commanded by Colonel Emerson Opdycke, which had been held in reserve 200 yards behind the main line north of the Carter house. Opdycke's men, needing no orders, charged into the break and fought hand-to-hand with the exhausted, outnumbered Confederates. In a few minutes Confederates inside the works were dead or prisoners and the lines had been restored, though in some places to the rear of the original line of works.

THE DESPERATE CHARACTER of the fighting from the cotton gin to the Carter house has been well described by participants who survived the battle. Writers on both sides noted that men charging into the holocaust of fire walked bent forward, like men breasting a strong wind, heads bent down and caps shielding their eyes from the leaden hail of death.

Of the many brief descriptions of the fighting the following, taken by Crownover from Thatcher's *Hundred Battles*, are the best.

Colonel Wolf, a Federal officer:

I saw a Confederate soldier, close to me, thrust one of our men through with the bayonet, and before he could draw his weapon from the ghastly wound his brains were scattered on all of us that stood near, by the butt of a musket swung with terrible force by some big fellow whom I could not recognize in the grim dirt and smoke that enveloped us.

A member of the 100th Ohio Infantry:

I saw three Confederates standing within our lines, as if they had dropped down unseen from the sky. They stood there for an instant, guns in hand, neither offering to shoot nor surrender—dazed as in a dream. I raised my gun, but instinctively I felt as if about to commit murder—they were hopeless, and I turned my face to the foe trying to clamber over our abatis. When I looked again the three were down—apparently dead; whether shot by their own men or ours, who could tell?

Again and again, as daylight faded into twilight and darkness, the divisions of Cheatham and Stewart renewed their charges. But the high tide of battle, for them, had been reached. They met a solid sheet of flame and lead where the Federal lines, massed four deep behind their works, stood to their guns. As one writer put it, irresistible Confederates came up against immovable Federals.

In some places Hood's men collected in the ditches in front of the works, where they were unable to advance or retreat in the face of certain death. Men held inverted muskets over the parapet and fired blindly into the ditch, exposing only the hand that held the gun.

THE BATTLE was by no means confined to the Federal center. On the left and right things had gone even less well for the Confederates. Forrest's two divisions on Stewart's right pushed back the Federal cavalry early in the fight and crossed the Harpeth. Here, upstream from Figuers' Hill, the dismounted cavalry of both armies fought a pitched battle. The Federals had the advantage of Wood's infantry in support, but this IV Corps division was not engaged. Details of the fight are lacking, but the upshot of it was that Brigadier General James H. Wilson's cavalry could not be dislodged from Schofield's flank, and Forrest's two divisions, having expended most of their ammunition, pulled back across the Harpeth.

A Return to the Carter House

MANY YEARS AGO an aged veteran of Schofield's corps visited the Carter House at Franklin—the first time he had been there since November 30, 1864. Standing on the back porch of the house, and pointing to the door of the family room on the south side, he said: "I was standing in that doorway, making myself as small as I could, while the battle was going on. Rebels at the breastworks started shooting at me. Those minie balls you see in the woodwork there were aimed at me. I returned their fire as fast as I could shoot and reload my rifle, but I didn't have much room, all scrouched up in that doorway, and every time I pulled my ramrod out of the gun barrel it knocked against the wood in the top of the door-frame."

The little dents made in the wood by the sharply withdrawn ramrod were (and still are) plainly to be seen.

"After a little while," he went on, "it got so hot I decided I'd better get inside the house and out of the Rebels' sight. I knocked on the door, but no one opened it. I then tried the doorknob, but it was locked from the inside. But I just had to get into the house, so I broke out the bottom panel of the door with the butt end of my rifle, and crawled through into the room. I tell you I stayed right there till the battle was over and it was safe to come out again." Immediately after the battle, Colonel Carter replaced the broken-out door panel with a piece of sheet-iron, and the patched door, along with the ramrod dents and the imbedded minie balls in the woodwork, may still be seen by today's visitors to the battle-scarred Carter House.

—Stanley F. Horn.

511

Forrest's failure to break up Wilson's units has generally been blamed on his being outnumbered in not having the services of Chalmers' division and Biffle's brigade. But actually he had as many men as on the day of his great victory at Brice's Cross Roads, and Wilson had 2,500 fewer men than Federal Brigadier General Samuel D. Sturgis had on that occasion. One may conclude that the great Confederate cavalryman fought better when campaigning under his own independent command—and so did his soldiers.

ON THE RIGHT of the Confederate infantry Stewart's divisions were crowded to the left by the in-curving river and the high ground near the railroad, with the additional disadvantage of running into the hedge of osage orange, which broke their formations. From a knoll near the railroad track a Federal battery opened on them at almost point-blank range, and from across the river the guns in Fort Granger poured enfilading shells into their lines. From Colonel John S. Casement's brigade Stewart's men received the fire of two companies of the 65th Indiana armed with repeating rifles (probably Spencers) along with a storm of musketry fire. The men in the divisions of Major Generals William W. Loring, Edward C. Walthall, and Samuel G. French were either driven back or pinned in the ditches before the works, where the dead were piled three and four deep.

West of the Columbia Pike Bate's division charged somewhat later than Brown and Cleburne, his right striking Ruger's right and Kimball's left. The left of his line never reached the Federal works. Chalmers' attacks on Kimball's light works were not long sustained, and are described as a "reconnaissance-in-force." To the rear of the Carter buildings Bate's men did effect lodgment in the "outer works" of the Federal line, and remained there until nightfall.

At 7 o'clock, long after dark, Hood sent Johnson's division of Lee's corps stumbling through the locust grove west of the pike in a last-gasp assault upon the works west of the Carter house. But the battle was already lost, and this last charge was another waste of men.

Until 9 o'clock the fighting continued, attackers and defenders firing at the flashes of guns. And then, at last, the weary Confederates drew back, and the front was quiet.

AT 11 O'CLOCK, while most of Hood's army slept on its arms, Schofield began his withdrawal. A house caught fire as Federal soldiers filed out of the works, and for a moment the lines of marching men were darkly outlined against the reddened sky. The fire was soon put out, and the silent retreat continued.

At the crack of dawn Hood's artillery was blazing away at the works as Confederate officers prepared for a new assault. And then the army commander got the news—his stubborn foe had abandoned the field, and the road was open to Nashville.

Wagner's delayed retreat, which shielded the charging Confederates and caused the break in the Federal line, is generally regarded as the blunder which almost gave Hood the victory. It is interesting, however, to note another point of view. James Barr had been a member of Co. E, 65th Illinois Volunteers, stationed across the pike and just south and east of the Carter house. For a few minutes he had been held prisoner by charging Confederates who reached the works, and was released by a Federal countercharge. Barr had an excellent view of the flight of Wagner's men and the Confederate charge into the gap at the Carter house. He wrote:

General Cox censures General Wagner for holding to his advanced position too long, calls his action a gross blunder, etc., but as one of Cox's men I looked upon the matter in a different light.

I think if Cleburne had not struck Wagner's two brigades as he did that his brave lads would have broken our line successfully; but, as it was, his brave men were badly winded with his work with Wagner, which gave Opdyke's and White's men a better chance to check him at the cotton gin.

The way I saw it was this: I was acting as orderly and standing a few paces east of the cotton gin. The first Confederate troops that came in view were Stewart's corps on our left, with Cheatham's corps to the left of Stewart. The Confederate line moved easily and steadily on, until Cleburne was checked for the time by Wagner. The short time lost by Cleburne threw Stewart's line too far in advance. Stewart was the first to receive the fire from our main line, and was unable to carry our works, his men who were not killed or wounded being compelled to retire. Now Cleburne, who had been delayed by Wagner, came up just in time to receive a heavy right oblique fire from the men who had repulsed Stewart's corps. I never saw men put in such a terrible position as Cleburne's division was in for a few minutes. The wonder is that any of them escaped death or capture.

Other writers have spoken of the fury of this oblique fire from the Federal left. Under it Confederate lines are said to have "withered away." In this connection it should be recalled that in addition to the

RESTING PLACE—The bodies of five Confederate generals were brought to "Carnton," southeast of Franklin, and laid out on the rear porch shown in this old photograph furnished courtesy of the Tennessee State Library and Archives. Carnton shows on the map on Page 21 as the McGavock House.

A Confederate's Recollection Of the Battle of Franklin

The memoirs of Captain William C. Thompson, 6th Mississippi, part of which appeared in our November 1964 issue, contain the following account of what he saw during the Battle of Franklin:

ON THE MORNING of November 30 we marched to Franklin, some 20 miles. We fought our way, pressing the Federals to where we could overtake their baggage wagons. They would shoot their fine army mules, cut the spokes out of their wagon wheels, and thus render this transportation useless to us. All this just to keep us from getting their equipment. The Federals also were burning many fine dwellings on the way. It was a sad sight to see helpless women and children looking on, crying to see their homes and all their possessions reduced to ashes.

We reached Franklin at 4 p.m., where the Federals made a stand. General Hood prepared for the fight. Loring's division, composed of Scott's, Featherstone's, and Adams' brigades, was the main element of Hood's force. My regiment still belonged to Adams' brigade.

We went into the fight by brigades in column. General Scott was in front, Featherstone following close, then Adams. The brigades being thus arranged, I could see the movements to the front of us. Scott's brigade charged the Federal fortifications but failed to take the works. Featherstone came to his support and their combined forces made a second assault and again failed. Then Adams' brigade joined forces with the other two and made a third advance.

During our division attack the Federals had a battery planted on the right of Duck [Harpeth?] River that we could not reach. This battery damaged us severely, using canister. The Confederate troops were being mowed down, losing thousands. At the same time the whole division was suffering from galling musketry fire delivered by the enemy entrenched in our immediate front.

Just after the three brigades combined, and in the midst of the enemy artillery fire, I was shot through the right leg. The ground about me was covered with the fallen. I managed with the assistance of the litter men to get to a point where the bullets were not flying so thick. I remained there for the remainder of the night. Suffering great pain, I was also hungry and cold, having had nothing to eat since early morning. That meal was only a piece of corn bread cooked in the ashes of our camp fire. I had but one thin blanket; I lay on part of it and drew the other part over me. The ground beneath was frozen.

MORNING FOUND ME so bad off that I cared little whether I lived or died. I was carried to an operating table where I suffered the torture of having my wound probed for the bullet. The pain was intense but I asked Dr. Aills not to give me chloroform. I said I preferred the pain to the ill effects of this drug. So I gritted my teeth and held on while the doctor dug out the metal. I was then transported to the hospital in Franklin.

On arrival I was put in the officers' ward. Being told that I was the second Thompson to be admitted, I found that my brother, Captain Arthur J. Thompson, had also been in the Battle of Franklin as commander of his company in the 7th Mississippi Infantry Battalion. He had lost his leg just below the knee, besides suffering other wounds. I practically forgot my own pain in my efforts to comfort him.

That afternoon a Mrs. Baugh visited our ward. She stopped by my bed and during our conversation insisted on taking my brother and me to her house. Because of the overcrowding at the hospital she easily obtained permission. She drove us to her house, five miles west of Franklin, where we received the kindest of care.

This memoir was made available by Bill Thompson, a grand-nephew of William Candace Thompson and a former reporter for the Nashville "Banner."

repeaters in Casement's brigade, Cox mentions that two companies in the 12th Kentucky of Reilly's brigade were armed with "revolving rifles," and other troops are mentioned as having breechloading rifles —weapons that could be fired much faster than the standard muzzleloaders.

ACCORDING to one source (H. M. Field), much the same thing happened on the Confederate left. Field, writing in 1890, toured the field with S. A. Cunningham, Major Joe Vaulx of Nashville, Moscow B. Carter and Sam Ewing of Franklin, all of whom had seen the battle. These men said Bate's division was the first to strike the Federal line, where it had to take the whole defensive fire, and had to withdraw. When it is considered that Brown, on Bate's left, had been slowed by Wagner, as had Cleburne, and that Bate could not see Stewart's brigades from his position, all this seems possible. It is also hard to see how such men as Vaulx and Cunningham could have been mistaken as to Bate's premature attack. Carter repeats it, and Field sets it down as a matter of fact. But nowhere else do we find it reported. If it occurred, it explains how Ruger's men, between Bate's first and second attacks, also had time to direct an oblique fire eastward across the field.

THE CONFEDERATE LOSS in general officers is a notable feature of the battle. Adams, Granbury, Gist, Strahl, and Cleburne were killed outright, and Carter mortally wounded. Gordon was captured, and Brown, Manigault, Quarles, Cockrell, and Scott were wounded. Included in the casualties were 53 regimental commanders.

By way of comparison it is notable that Pickett's total loss at Gettysburg was 2,882, while at Franklin the Army of Tennessee lost over 6,000 in dead and wounded. Pickett's men had the advantage of artillery preparation, Hood's did not; Pickett's charge was totally repulsed, while the charge of Brown and Cleburne penetrated deep into the breastworks; Pickett, once repelled, retired from the field, while the Army of Tennessee renewed its charge time after time.

Though it failed to crush Schofield, the Army of Tennessee convinced its commander, that November 30th, that it would fight without protection of breastworks. "Never," Hood reported, "did troops fight more gallantly." They had shown that the men, as well as their commander, belonged to "the school of Lee and Jackson"—an aristocracy of valor in the best tradition of the American fighting men.

BRIGADIER GENERAL O. F. Strahl, soon to die, summed up the Battle of Franklin when he said, just before the charge:

"Boys, this will be short, but desperate." And so it was.

APPOMATTOX

Text by William C. Davis
Designed by Frederic Ray

In the early evening of April 1, 1865, Colonel Horace Porter mounted his horse and rode toward the headquarters of the Army of the Potomac at Dabney's Mills, seven miles southwest of Petersburg, Virginia. As he and his orderly passed groups of men, the aide called out to them the news of a great victory over the Confederates at Five Forks, five miles to the west. But some of the soldiers were unimpressed by the news. "No you don't," one called back while thumbing his nose, "April fool!"

All Fools' Day it was, and as Porter came wildly riding into Dabney's Mills, yelling his good news from the moment he sighted headquarters, not a few onlookers took him to be either overwrought with the spirit of the day, or else just drunk. Porter was neither. He approached the tent of General in Chief U.S. Grant to find him and his staff sitting around a blazing fire. Finally Porter's hearers began taking his shouted reports of a triumph seriously. "In a moment," he later wrote, "all but the imperturbable general-in-chief were on their feet giving vent to boisterous demonstrations of joy. . . . Dignity was thrown to the winds."

Porter rushed to Grant and started vigorously slapping him on the back in congratulation before he remembered himself. Grant, cigar in mouth, exasperatingly calm, only asked how many prisoners had been taken. Then, after hearing from Porter a full account of the victory, and writing a few dispatches in his tent, Grant came out again. He had written to the President and to his subordinates. He had sent out orders that he had waited almost a year to give, directives that meant the final, speedy demise of the Confederate army before him, and of the enemy Capital at Richmond. Calmly, almost as if talking about the weather, he told his staff that "I have ordered a general assault along the lines." Grant was on his way to Appomattox.

For over nine months the Federal Army of the Potomac led by Major General George G. Meade and the Army of the James recently placed under Major General E. O. C. Ord had faced General Robert E. Lee's Army of Northern Virginia and other Confederate commands along an ever-lengthening line of entrenchments and fortifications extending from Richmond twenty miles south, past Bermuda Hundred on the James River, to Petersburg on the south side of the Appomattox River. Encircling the city, the lines of defense had gradually crept to the southwest over the months, stretching Lee's thin ranks of men even thinner as Grant, exercising over-all command of both Federal armies, sought continually to get around the Confederate right flank and cut off Lee's routes of escape. Aside from several severe battles such as The Crater, Globe Tavern, Poplar Springs Church, and Hatcher's Run, there was little to break the seemingly endless tension and monotony of siege life.

Colonel Horace Porter

Lieutenant General Ulysses S. Grant and his staff at City Point, Virginia, only weeks before the opening of the Appomattox Campaign.

516

The Grant of Appomattox—
strong, firm, but unfailingly
compassionate.

As the spring of 1865 approached, both Lee and Grant made plans. Grant's intentions were no secret to an intuitive Lee. The Federal would continue his attempts to cut the Confederates off from their lines of communications to the south, isolating them at Petersburg until surrender was inevitable. Lee, on the other hand, planned to attempt not only a break out of the siege lines, but grand strategy as well for the first and only time since his appointment as Confederate general in chief in January 1865. It was a plan born of desperation and deluded hopes.

With fewer than 50,000 men to face Grant's 112,000, Lee could hardly hope to survive where he was. But if he could join the bulk of his army with the Army of Tennessee led by General Joseph E. Johnston, now facing a much superior army under Major General William T. Sherman in North Carolina, then the two of them combined might perhaps defeat Sherman and be ready to meet Grant soon thereafter. At the same time, however, Lee must be able to leave a force in Virginia strong enough to keep Grant at arm's length while all this was taking place. It is indeed remarkable that a man of Lee's genius would even consider so patently hopeless a plan. But then, there was little else he could do.

As a prelude to his movement, Lee would have Major General John B. Gordon lead an attack on Fort Stedman in the Federal line east of Petersburg. A devastating surprise victory here would draw men away from Grant's left flank off to the west, thereby opening the way for Lee to move south to join Johnston. But Gordon's attack failed, costing Lee 5,000 casualties in the process.

What was worse, it alerted an equally intuitive Grant to Lee's next move. It had been assumed for some time that the Confederates would attempt a linkup with Johnston. Grant had closed off all rail routes out of the city but one, the South Side Railroad which led west to Burkeville. There Lee could hope to take the Richmond & Danville into North Carolina. Obviously, now that Gordon's attack had failed, Lee's only remaining move was to escape via the South Side before Grant captured it, too.

Lee sent his nephew, Major General Fitzhugh Lee, commanding the army's cavalry, off to Five Forks with his entire command. Three brigades of the infantry division of Major General George E. Pickett went with him, along with two other brigades, their mission being to hold Five Forks, a major intersection through which Grant would have to pass in taking the South Side. By advancing from there toward Dinwiddie Court House, Lee hoped to push Grant's left back and away from the railroad.

This same day, March 29, Grant sent the newly arrived cavalry corps of Major General Philip H. Sheridan to Dinwiddie with instructions to take Five Forks, assisted by Meade's V Corps under Major General Gouverneur K. Warren, and pass on to destroy part of the South Side Railroad. The night before, Grant had told Sheridan that he "intended to close the war right here, with this movement."

Brigadier General Wesley Merritt, who helped crush Pickett at Five Forks.

518   **Sheridan and his generals at Dinwiddie Court House, reconnoitering before the attack at Five Forks.**

The Battle of Five Forks as sketched on the spot by *Harper's Weekly* artist Alfred R. Waud.

Pickett, exercising over-all command of the forces at Five Forks, moved south and advanced on Dinwiddie Court House on March 31, a hopeless attack of 10,000 Confederates against at least 12,000 cavalry and Warren's approaching 16,000 infantry. He made surprising progress before night fell, and then came the news that Warren was moving toward Pickett's rear, heading to get between him and the railroad. At 5 a.m. the next morning, April 1, Pickett pulled his command back toward Five Forks, deploying it rather carelessly in the expectation that a diversion from the main Confederate line would prevent Sheridan's advancing against him that day. Then too, though there were better positions available a mile north, he had just received a dispatch from Lee. "Hold Five Forks at all hazards," it said.

Sheridan, meanwhile, despite muddy roads, followed Pickett, "sure that he would not give up the Five Forks crossroads without a fight." As he approached the intersection, Sheridan formulated his plan of attack, intending to assault the whole Confederate front with two of his cavalry divisions led by Brigadier General Wesley Merritt, fake an attempt to turn Pickett's right flank, and send Warren's V Corps around the Confederate left to cut him off from Lee.

The attack was a crushing success, in part because both Pickett and Fitzhugh Lee were absent from the field at a fish fry. Fighting on foot, Sheridan's cavalry held the Confederates at their entrenchments. Then at about 4 p.m., after some apparent delay, Warren moved, at first missed finding Pickett's unprotected flank, but with Sheridan's aid finally found it. Sheridan, ruthless, ambitious, easily moved to resentment, did not like Warren, who lacked the jugular instinct that characterized "Little Phil." Now at the height of the battle, even as Pickett's command was being crushed, Sheridan relieved Warren of his command. Though later exonerated of the charges Sheridan placed against him, Warren was scarred for life.

Major General Gouverneur K. Warren lost his command and reputation to a vindictive Sheridan.

519

So was Pickett. At first skeptical when word of the Federal advance interrupted his fish fry, he finally believed it only when he saw his couriers actually being captured before his eyes by Sheridan's cavalry pickets. Running a terrible gantlet of enemy fire, he rode back to his shattered command, only to join it as all but a few regiments were in full retreat. Fitzhugh Lee was entirely unable to rejoin his command. Instead, the rout went on, Sheridan capturing in all nearly 4,000 Confederates, Five Forks, and a sure path to the South Side Railroad. Pickett never fully lived down the disgrace of his defeat—though R. E. Lee's specific orders to hold Five Forks prevented him from taking better ground elsewhere—-and Lee never forgave him. Curiously enough, however, Lee seems to have uttered no reproach of his nephew, though Fitzhugh Lee was just as culpable as Pickett.

Before the fighting was entirely done, couriers in blue and gray were riding east, one of them, Colonel Porter, jubilantly proclaiming the success to all hearers. The news that went to Lee was just the opposite. Already he had advised President Jefferson Davis that to save his army, and perhaps the cause, he would have to leave his present lines soon. Word of Pickett's disaster, received late in the afternoon, confirmed his advice. Quickly he sent three brigades of Lieutenant General Richard H. Anderson's small command to the right of his line. They would help Fitzhugh Lee's remaining cavalry in an attempt to hold the railroad. By doing so, however, Lee virtually had to abandon three miles of his line near Hatcher's Run—tacit admission to all in the army that evacuation was imminent. At the same time, Lee ordered Lieutenant General James Longstreet, commanding the First Corps in the fortifications around Richmond, to bring Major General Charles Field's division down to reinforce his sparsely manned line. Sending his men by foot, then train, Longstreet and staff rode through the night on horseback. "Our noble beasts peered through the loaded air," wrote Longstreet of the night ride, "and sniffed the coming battle." "The cause," he said, "was lost."

Major General George E. Pickett never regained Lee's confidence after Five Forks.

520

Major General Bushrod R. Johnson and his division were cut off from Lee when Sheridan took Five Forks.

Before dawn the next morning Lee knew this was his last day in Petersburg. "I see no prospect of doing more than holding our position here till night," he wired Secretary of War John C. Breckinridge. "I am not certain that I can do that." He hoped to withdraw his army across the Appomattox and then move west to the Richmond & Danville Railroad near Amelia Court House, thirty-six miles west of Petersburg. There Lee's Petersburg command, Major General William Mahone's division of Longstreet's corps, still facing part of the Federal Army of the James at Bermuda Hundred, and Lieutenant General Richard S. Ewell's troops east of Richmond could all rendezvous for the movement to join Johnston. Orders went out accordingly. "It will be a difficult operation," Lee confided to Breckinridge.

Just how difficult was largely up to Grant, and as April 2 dawned, his "general assault along the lines" bid fair to prevent Lee from making the move at all. The Federal lines advanced before dawn all across the Petersburg front. They emerged from the thick morning fog to crush almost everything before them. By noon all of the western portion of Lee's line had crumbled, except for an outstanding resistance at Fort Gregg. This alone kept Meade's II, VI, and XXIV Corps from rolling up Lee's right into the city of Petersburg itself. Gordon held the city proper against the Union IX Corps. Meanwhile, Lieutenant General A. P. Hill, commanding Lee's Third Corps, had been killed in a chance encounter with two Federal soldiers, and the newly arrived Longstreet assumed temporary command of what remained of Hill's troops.

Cut off from Lee by the Federal breakthrough were the remnants of Pickett's division of Longstreet's corps; the division of Major General Bushrod Johnson, comprising the whole of Lieutenant General Anderson's corps; Major General Henry Heth's division and part of the Light Division of Hill's corps; and Lee's cavalry corps. They would have to cross the Appomattox at Bevill's Bridge several miles to the west in order to reach Amelia Court House, if at all. To an officer near him, as the orders for the evacuation were being executed, a weary Robert E. Lee confessed that "this is a sad business."

By 8 p.m. the movement was under way, though Anderson and the other isolated commands with him had started west some hours before, pursued by Federal cavalry. Lee's artillery went first, heavy, slow wagons and gun carriages, always in bad condition, and now struggling through the mud and darkness. Yet all but ten guns of the mobile artillery were gotten out, and those that remained were spiked or otherwise disabled. Field's division of Longstreet's corps followed, along with Major General Cadmus Wilcox's division of Hill's command, now under Longstreet. Under "Old Pete" Longstreet these divisions crossed the Appomattox and turned west. After them came the rear guard, Gordon's Second Corps, which took a road north of Longstreet's route, and parallel to it.

Major General Phillip H. Sheridan combined talent and utter ruthlessness to perform brilliantly in the last week of the war against Lee.

As Petersburg falls, elements of the Army of the Potomac move into the Confederate stronghold.

Even later that night, and on into the early hours of April 3, Ewell's two divisions left Richmond after Davis and the government escaped on a train that would take them to Danville, 125 miles to the southwest, on the Virginia-North Carolina border. Meanwhile, Mahone's division of Hill's corps, the only remaining troops facing the Army of the James at Bermuda Hundred, pulled out of the fortifications there and marched west. Behind them Richmond was in flames, her people in a panic, and the Federals preparing to occupy the prize they had sought for nearly four years.

No march in the history of the Army of Northern Virginia had been as sad as this one. Defeat, utter and final defeat, weighed heavily on almost every mind. The enemy was behind them and surely pushing west on the south side of the Appomattox, hoping to cut off their retreat to North Carolina. Their gallant Capital, symbol of Confederate resistance and strength against a host of enemy campaigns, had fallen. Ahead lay only the night, gloom, and uncertainty.

Longstreet marched his tired command sixteen miles through the mud before he halted for rest. He, Lee, and a number of other generals took dinner at a plantation house, where their hosts bravely asserted that ultimate victory would still be theirs. Lee was not so sure, and Longstreet ignored the comment entirely as he hacked at his meat with his one good arm. "Whatever happens," said Lee, "know this, that no men ever fought better than those who have stood by me."

For Gordon this night march was even sadder. Behind him in Petersburg he had had to leave his wife. "As the last broken file of that matchless army stepped from the bridge and my pioneer corps lighted the flames that consumed it, there came to me a vivid and depressing realization of the meaning of the appalling tragedy of the last two days," Gordon wrote. "The breaking of Lee's power had shattered the last hope of Southern independence."

The men with Ewell, members of one of Longstreet's veteran divisions commanded by Major General Joseph B. Kershaw, and a largely untested division led by an equally untried major general, George Washington Custis Lee, son of R. E. Lee, marched through the night with the explosions and blazing glow of the

Lee's son, Major General William Henry Fitzhugh "Rooney" Lee was second in command to his own cousin, Fitzhugh Lee, in the army's dwindling cavalry.

522

Major General John B. Gordon fought to the very last. His attack at Fort Stedman was Lee's last major assault of the war.

Capital behind them. In their path were thousands of refugees from Richmond fleeing to escape Grant. They so clogged the road that young Lee's small command was fragmented into a score of small groups, its organization entirely gone.

Daylight on April 3 brought no cessation of the marching. These men, especially those from the lines at Petersburg, were tired, worn from a hunger that had not been fully satisfied in months. The miles came hard to many stiff, blistered, often unshod feet, torturing the muscles of legs for which nine months of normally sedentary siege life had made fast marching a dim memory. Where they could they stopped to rest, to cook what pitiful rations they had brought with them, or to forage the already stripped land for what food could be found. Many of the men and officers alike were sustained by the knowledge—just how it came to them is hard to say—that ahead of them at Amelia Court House supplies would be waiting. Before the evacuation Lee had asked that rations be sent there from Richmond. His men would need them desperately if they were to continue on.

By evening on April 3 Lee had made surprising progress considering the state of his men. Anderson and his fleeing remnant were nearly to Bevill's Bridge and had been joined at last by Pickett himself with a few followers. His whereabouts had been unknown to the rest of the army for two days. Heth and his men, traveling a different route, had finally crossed the river and rejoined the main army. "We moved on in disorder," wrote one of Heth's men, "keeping no regular column, no regular pace." Few spoke, and those who did said little. "An indescribable sadness weighed upon us."

Longstreet, reaching Goode's Bridge on the Appomattox by nightfall, crossed Field and Wilcox. They had intended originally to cross at Bevill's Bridge, to meet the waiting Anderson, but high water made the crossing impossible. In all, Longstreet's men had marched over twenty-five miles since leaving the lines at Petersburg. Singly and in groups they collapsed into troubled sleep, burdened with the weariness of years of their lives now seemingly spent for nothing.

Yet already Lee and his army had achieved something remarkable in the retreat. With these tired, hungry men he had brought off successfully a withdrawal which was one of the most difficult coordinated movements in the war. Longstreet—joined

Grant's supply vessels line the bank of the Appomattox near Petersburg.

523

Lieutenant General James Longstreet and his corps led the advance of Lee's retreating army.

by Heth—and Anderson had met west of Goode's Bridge, holding that crossing while Gordon followed. When Gordon reached the bridge he, in turn, would hold it until Mahone arrived, and Mahone would hold it for Ewell. Each detachment, in turn, helped ensure the crossing of the next, making it possible for what had been five different commands spread over nearly forty miles on April 2 to come together at Amelia Court House two days later, to move as an army once more.

Of course, it helped that Grant was little in evidence on April 3. Instead of directly pursuing Lee, he sent Sheridan west toward Jetersville, ten miles southwest of Amelia Court House, on the Richmond & Danville Railroad. If the Federal horse could reach it before Lee arrived at Amelia, then the Confederates' best avenue of escape to Johnston would be cut off. Lee would have no choice but to keep marching west toward Lynchburg and then try to turn south and reach Johnston on foot. (No trains were running on the Danville line, but Lee did not know it.) The longer and farther Lee marched, the weaker he would become, and the less fight there would be left in him. There was more than just strategy in Grant's plans. There was humanity. When he took Petersburg immediately upon Lee's evacuation, Grant was in the city while hundreds of Confederates were still crossing the bridge over the Appomattox. He could have opened on them with his cannon, disrupting their retreat severely. But he did not. "I had not the heart to turn the artillery upon such a mass of defeated and fleeing men," he said, especially since "I hoped to capture them soon." If at all possible now, he would bag Lee by maneuver, not by pitched battle.

After securing his position in Petersburg on April 3, Grant met with President Lincoln, who had come up from City Point on the James River. Meanwhile, Richmond was being occupied, and jubilation coursed through the Army of the Potomac which had so long sought, and so long been denied, these prizes. But time for elation was short, for Grant sent Meade's II, V, and VI Corps off to the west to follow Sheridan and directed three divisions of Ord's Army of the James, with Meade's IX Corps, to parallel Sheridan several miles to the south, heading toward Burkeville. Should Lee somehow get past Sheridan, Ord would still have the Danville line cut.

524 A Federal pontoon bridge spans the Appomattox River west of Petersburg.

The Federal army entering the Confederate capital, Richmond.

When April 4 dawned, despite losses at Fort Stedman and Five Forks, and isolated commands unable to join him, Lee faced the prospect of soon having almost 30,000 men concentrated at Amelia Court House, 30,000 hungry men. Yet they set out with a will, anxious to reach their destination, and their expected rations. Their pace quickened somewhat at the sound of firing off to the south. It meant that Sheridan was there. Longstreet skirmished with him throughout the day, but no real fighting took place and Lee was not much worried by the Federal cavalry's presence. He felt that he could overcome it in a fight if he must. It was Grant's infantry that he hoped to avoid. As for Sheridan, his only object at this point was to slightly harass and delay Lee while the infantry corps were marching ever west toward Jetersville.

Spirits were high enough among the Confederates that Lee could mildly scold a young officer who appeared with his uniform carelessly put on that morning. The young man took the reprimand in silence and was about to leave, when the general called him back to explain. "I meant only to caution you as to the duty of officers, especially those who are near high commanders," said Lee. "You must avoid anything that might look like demoralization while we are retreating."

Riding with Longstreet's advance, Lee reached Amelia Court House at about 8:30 a.m. What he found was heartbreaking. Despite an abundance of ammunition and ordnance stores, not a single ration was there awaiting his famished troops. He had ordered 350,000 rations sent out from a reserve accumulated in Richmond. The Danville line was still open between the Capital and Amelia on April 2-3— Davis and his cabinet had passed by this same route on their way to Danville—and the supplies could have made it. But there was confusion in the War Department

A scene in ruined Richmond.

Century Magazine, June 1886

W. L. Sheppard's drawing of thirsty Confederates breaking ranks during the retreat.

as Richmond prepared for evacuation, and a request for clarification sent to Lee at Petersburg never reached him. The breakdown of the communications systems, not supply, had conspired against him. Where the fault lay, though, seemed immaterial. His men would have nothing to eat now but their daydreams of food, fantasies that could hardly fill empty bellies.

"No face wore a heavier shadow than that of General Lee," wrote an officer standing near him now. "The failure of the supply of rations completely paralyzed him. An anxious and haggard expression came to his face." There was nothing to do but send his wagons out into the countryside to forage for whatever they could find. At the same time, he issued a proclamation calling upon the people of Amelia County to give whatever they could to his quartermasters when they called. Meanwhile, he sent an urgent message off to Danville to ship him 200,000 rations from the stores collected at that place.

Hour after hour the famished regiments marched into Amelia Court House, only to find nothing to eat. Wilcox came in just after noon, followed sometime later by Heth. Gordon halted back about five miles to await Mahone, who was at Goode's Bridge holding it for Ewell, from whom nothing had been heard. Anderson and Fitzhugh Lee, who had been skirmishing much of the day with Sheridan and advance elements of the Federal V Corps, were not far away.

Finding their hopes of food destroyed had varying effects on the weary Confederates. Some, seeing nothing unusual in the situation, took it calmly. Others, already disheartened, began to melt away into the woods. They had given all but

Library of Congress

Indecision and confusion prevented Lieutenant General Richard S. Ewell from taking command at Sayler's Creek.

526

their last ounce of devotion to a cause which could not feed them. What little they had left might better be used to salvage some semblance of life from the war's wreckage. A few simply became delirious, lost their mental balance, and raved about or muttered quietly to themselves. For them the workings of the yet unexplored mysteries of the mind had mercifully ended their war.

But still the men could cheer, and they proved it by hurrahing Lee more than once. And late in the day heartening news did come. Finally word arrived from Ewell that he would shortly cross the Appomattox by a railroad bridge which was closer to his route of march than Goode's. By 9 p.m. his troops would almost all be over the river safely. This now meant that Mahone could destroy Goode's Bridge and march in to the main army.

Thus, by the next day Lee was assured of completing the concentration of his army. Unhappily, though, this also meant more hungry mouths to feed. His forage wagons would not be due back in his camps until the next morning. He had hoped to be on his way out of Amelia Court House within a few hours of his arrival. Now he could not expect to leave before late on the morning of April 5 at best. These were precious hours lost, hours when the Federal infantry was steadily catching up, closing the gap between themselves and the Confederates, cutting ever shorter Lee's chances of escape.

The night passed without giving rest. Light showers and winds whipped through and around the headquarters tents, where lights burned well into the morning. Lee tried to set his alternatives with the variables of his situation. If only he could get rations on the morrow, he could then march his army down the railroad toward Danville and the supplies known to be there. If, as he hoped, rations were going to be sent up the road to him from that place pursuant to his order, then they would reach him all the sooner. Well-fed and rested, he knew his army could outmarch the Federals to join Johnston, though all he now knew of the enemy was that Sheridan had broken off skirmishing at nightfall and that Meade's infantry was still several miles southeast of him. All through the night anxious ears listened amidst fitful sleep for the sound of a train coming from the south, a train bringing rations from Danville. It did not come. All they heard was the hollow patter of the rain on the tents.

For Mahone it had not been a difficult march. By midafternoon of April 3 his command had reached Chesterfield Court House, midway between Bermuda Hundred and Goode's Bridge. All along the way he encountered refugees, scattered and straggling soldiers, and a host of wagons of all description. Once at Chesterfield, he organized the wagons and stray soldiers. Soon after arriving, Mahone saw 2,000 sailors and Marines led by Commodore John R. Tucker marching in, having abandoned their naval batteries along the right bank of the James above Bermuda Hundred. They came, said Mahone, "armed with cutlass' and navy revolvers, every man over six feet and [the] picture of perfect physical development." Henceforward, Tucker's men would march with Mahone's, and that night they all set out again. By the evening of April 4 they had reached Goode's Bridge, where Mahone received Lee's order to come on to Amelia the next morning.

On the morning of April 5, amid a constant rainy drizzle, Mahone marched to Amelia Court House. What he found was depressing. The commissary wagons sent out the day before had come back. They brought almost nothing. The countryside had been giving bountifully to feed the army for four years. Now it had nothing more to give.

Passing through ranks of unhappy, grumbling, disheartened soldiers, Mahone made his way to report in person to Lee. He found the general seated with Longstreet at the edge of a barren oat field near the court house. Longstreet arose and gave Mahone his seat, then left. "The chat with Genl Lee was pleasant," Mahone recalled. As they talked, however, he noticed Lee was in his full dress uniform,

Often offensively egotistical, Major General William Mahone was still one of Lee's best fighting generals.

Commodore John R. Tucker led his seamen-turned-infantry out of Richmond to join Lee.

527

wearing his gold spurs and the famed "Maryland Sword" given him in better days by an anonymous Marylander. "He wore all his best clothes," wrote Mahone. "It impressed me that he anticipated some accident to himself and desired to be found in that dress."

If Lee had a premonition of death, he never spoke of it, but it required no prescience whatever to know what was in store for his army now. The day spent at Amelia Court House had been wasted and his precious lead over the Federals was all but vanished. He must move down the railroad quickly to meet the supplies hopefully coming from Danville. The men were ordered to form ranks. In order to allow the infantry to make the best time possible, the slow wagon train was ordered to move south toward Danville on a separate, parallel road. Mahone later wrote that while he and Lee were still talking, the other division commanders of the old Third Corps, Heth and Wilcox, came up and asked to whom they should now report. Almost as if he did not hear them, Lee pointed to their staff wagons, asked whose they were, and ordered that they be sent with the rest of the main wagon and artillery train. "Depend on your haversacks as I shall do," Lee told them. Then, almost as an afterthought, he told them to report to Longstreet, at the same time warning that he intended to reorganize the army to reduce the number of corps and division commanders. According to Mahone, even amid chaos, Lee was still thinking of efficiency in his command.

While everything that could not be taken with the army was put to the torch, Lee marched his columns off southwest along the Richmond & Danville tracks toward Jetersville. Longstreet took the advance, followed by Mahone, who accidentally got on the wrong road and ran into the wagon train after a mile or two. Retracing his steps, he found that the enemy cavalry stood between him and Longstreet, but he drove them away easily and united his column with Old Pete's. Behind Mahone came Anderson's corps and, later in the day, Ewell finally came up to the army with Custis Lee and Kershaw.

While the troops marched, Lee remained behind at the courthouse, gathering intelligence and generally overseeing the movement. Longstreet was there with him. Disturbing news came in that the wagon train had been attacked by enemy cavalry, and now they could hear the sounds of skirmishing as the gray columns moved toward Jetersville. Shortly after 1 p.m. Lee and Longstreet themselves rode south to find out the situation. They passed through Jetersville, eight miles from Amelia Court House, and then came upon Sheridan's dismounted cavalry behind earthworks placed squarely across their line of march. Enemy infantry was nearby and coming up quickly. Unless Lee could push his way through these Federals, there would be no rations and no escape to Johnston by this route.

Lee's immediate problem was whether or not to fight. On the one hand his men were tired, and worse, starving. There might not be enough fight in them. On the other hand, his only alternative was to go on fifteen miles west to Farmville, on the Appomattox. There he would rejoin the South Side Railroad, which ran back southeast to Burkeville, crossing the Danville line at Burke's Station. Unless the enemy cut off that route, too, he could then march south along the tracks, hoping that he could outdistance Grant and still join Johnston somewhere south of the Roanoke River.

While the men rested, Lee alone studied his maps and the enemy line. Curiously, he seems not to have consulted with Longstreet over the decision to be made, but instead called in Mahone—or so claimed "Little Billy." Perhaps it was not so curious after all, however, for Mahone's were the freshest troops in the command, and among the hardest fighters as well. Mahone's advice on what he could do in an attack now should be valuable. On the porch of a little farm house the two generals met, pouring over Lee's charts. By this time it was nearly sundown, and Mahone argued that it was too late for an attack. Besides, the army was not sufficiently

528

Major General Henry Heth, though cut off after Five Forks, rejoined the army as it marched toward Appomattox.

Major General Cadmus M. Wilcox

concentrated on this line to hit with full force. Move off to the right, advised Little Billy, concentrate the army, and then turn and hit the Federals in flank on the morrow.

When Lee ordered the army to move off toward Farmville, Mahone thought the commanding general had taken his advice in toto. In fact, Lee was taking the second of the alternatives that he had considered even before consulting Mahone. Risking a fight on the morrow without food, as Mahone suggested, would be even worse than risking it today. He must avoid battling with the enemy, at least until his men had eaten. He sent couriers to order supplies to be sent to Farmville from Lynchburg, forty miles west. He hoped they would be there when he arrived.

Alfred R. Waud's sketch of the brief fighting in the vicinity of Amelia Court House.

Having lost his lead over the Federals, Lee now had to push his men through every hour of daylight left and well into the night. Mahone and Field took the advance, then came the remnants of Heth's and Wilcox's divisions, behind them Anderson's tiny corps, then Ewell, and finally Gordon's rear guard. It was the worst march the Army of Northern Virginia ever suffered. Forced to go on the same road with the wagon and artillery train now, the men stumbled among the vehicles. Hundreds lost their grasp on reality, mumbled incoherently, wandered off into the woods to fall down in a stupor, or panicked at the slightest provocation.

Several times firing broke out as the men shot at shadows or, worse, each other. Many were killed, left where they fell by comrades who had not the strength or the time to bury them. The wounded had to do what they could for themselves. Men and officers who had held up under the greatest trials of the war now broke down. When Mahone came to Flat Creek he found that the bridge over it had collapsed. He let his men rest in ranks while his engineers repaired it. When the work was done, Colonel Charles Marshall of Lee's staff, one of the finest officers in the army, ordered Mahone's lead brigade under Brigadier General Nathaniel H. Harris to cross over and resume the march.

Under the strain, Marshall was drinking from a bottle of "pine top" whiskey—distilled from pine boughs in the absence of corn mash—and irresponsibly giving orders without consulting Mahone. As a result, Mahone's command was soon spread out along the road, its marching formation lost for the first time in the war. When the general, dining at a nearby farm house, discovered what had happened and why, he too gave way to the anguish and frustration of this terrible night and informed Lee in blunt terms that if Marshall ever again interfered with his command "Genl Lee would be short a staff officer." The strain was getting to them all, for what was at stake was their very existence. One of the soldiers in the ranks found time to note in his diary that "it is now a race for life or death."

In the end, this night march helped doom the army. Mahone, after re-forming his straggling division, continued on in good order behind the advance under Field. The rear led by Gordon was in equally good order. But in between the two the disorganized commands of Anderson and Ewell plodded wearily, straggling, struggling to keep up. The weakest point of the army now was at its very center. In this condition, once the sun appeared on April 6, the army would have to cross Sayler's Creek.

Confederates destroying the railroad from Appomattox toward Lynchburg, and artillerymen destroying gun-carriages, at nightfall, Saturday, April 8. From a sketch made at the time by William L. Sheppard.

The night marches were hard on the Federals, too, but their feet moved swiftly with the exhilarating assurance that these days of marching were numbered. Tomorrow, the next day, within a week, the war in Virginia would be over; the army that had so long kept them at bay would at last be vanquished. Following a day of little or no fighting on April 3, Sheridan rode hard on the fourth, sending the cavalry division of Brigadier General George Crook riding fast for Jetersville. "Our cavalry were untiring," wrote Crook. "We scarcely rested, but were going day and night. . . . We all felt that the end of the war was near at hand."

Crook reached Jetersville that same day, followed shortly by Sheridan himself, who set up a line somewhat south of the town. Elements of the V Corps under Brigadier General Charles Griffin, Warren's successor, marched in late in the afternoon. Sheridan entrenched the command across the road to Burkeville, hoping that Lee could be forced to surrender at Amelia Court House. The next afternoon Major General A. A. Humphreys' II Corps and Major General Horatio Wright's VI Corps arrived, and Sheridan placed them on either side of Griffin. Meade was present now as well but, feeling very ill, he asked Sheridan to direct the troops.

Grant, meanwhile, had stayed several miles in the rear, giving over-all direction to the pursuit. On the evening of April 5, however, he finally set out for the front after receiving a message from Sheridan which intimated that Meade might not press Lee hard enough, thus jeopardizing their chances of capturing the army. This could not be allowed to happen. The hard-luck Army of the Potomac had finally won a decisive victory at Petersburg. "That is all it ever wanted to make it as good an army as ever fought a battle," said Grant. Now it must follow that victory with a final triumph. His determination was enhanced by a captured letter which Sheridan sent to him. It had been written earlier that day by Colonel Walter H. Taylor of Lee's staff. "Dear Mamma," he wrote, "Our army is ruined, I fear."

Meade wanted to attack Amelia Court House with the full Army of the Potomac on the morning of April 6. Sheridan, however, argued that Lee would not be there then. Correctly reading Lee's intentions, he claimed on the basis of his intelligence that the Confederates were on their way west again. Still, Grant agreed to Meade's attack, but Sheridan's cavalry was not to be included in it. This would allow "Little Phil" to move toward Farmville to keep up with Lee if he was actually moving in that direction. "If we press on," Sheridan told Grant, "we will no doubt get the whole army."

Brigadier General Charles Griffin took over Warren's V Corps for the pursuit of Lee.

The cavalry division of Brigadier General George Crook was the first to cut the Richmond & Danville at Jetersville.

Leading his VI Corps in pursuit, Major General Horatio G. Wright helped cut off Lee's escape down the Richmond & Danville.

Major General A. A. Humphreys and his II Corps played a major part in the final entrapment of Lee.

531

On the morning of April 6 Meade advanced his army toward Amelia Court House, only to discover that Lee, indeed, was not there. Instead, part of the Confederate army could be seen off to the west. Meade turned his corps to the left to follow. For hours they pestered Lee's rear, Humphreys doing most of the work, while Sheridan's column paralleled Lee's line of march and harassed his flanks throughout the morning, in addition sending a detachment ahead to attack Lee's wagon trains. The fatal delay at Amelia Court House was now agonizingly evident. Lee must run for his life from a confident enemy whose relentless legions were within his very sight.

At 4 a.m., April 6, Lee ordered Gordon to destroy the Flat Creek bridge as soon as he crossed it. The rest of the army would soon pass through Deatonsville, taking the road to Rice's Station, about twelve miles away. From Rice's it would be only an hour or two to Farmville. Lee himself just now was at Amelia Springs, and he had good news. Commissary General Isaac M. St. John had come in to headquarters, having escaped from Richmond with a wagon train of rations which he had unsuccessfully tried to bring to Lee. Now, though he came empty handed, he did tell the general that 80,000 rations were waiting at Farmville. At last Lee's men would eat.

But they must get there first. As if the harrowing night march had not already strained them enough, now the Confederates felt the constant harassment of Sheridan and Humphreys. Time and again the men had to fall out of ranks to the left to form a line for meeting the Federal skirmishers. It was exhausting work to hungry men, especially to those in the center of the column under Anderson and Ewell. The command structure there had broken down almost completely, the officers exercising no control over the men at all. They straggled, stretching the line out even farther along the road, holding up Gordon in the rear.

Longstreet with the advance marched well, crossing Sayler's Creek and moving on to Rice's by shortly after noon. Mahone followed. There was word that Federal cavalry was ahead of them going toward Farmville. Longstreet sent part of Fitzhugh Lee's horsemen after them, while putting his own infantry in line facing south to meet an enemy infantry force reported a few miles below.

But by this time Lee was already worried about something much more serious. A gap had opened between Mahone and Anderson. What had happened was confusing but understandable considering the state of the men and officers by now. The wagons that were moving between Ewell and Gordon were being frequently attacked by Federal skirmishers. To protect them, and to keep the attacks on them from delaying Gordon, Ewell—senior officer with the center and rear of the army— ordered his own and Anderson's troops to halt to let the wagons move past them. He did so without consulting Lee or notifying him, with the result that as Mahone moved on unawares, a gap gradually opened. The wagons that passed Ewell moved on ahead into the gap, virtually unprotected as they crossed over Sayler's Creek.

Here was an opportunity that Sheridan would not pass by. Finding no openings to do real harm to the enemy trains when Gordon was guarding them, Sheridan had taken the bulk of his cavalry forward. He had just crossed the creek himself when he saw the unprotected wagons moving ahead of Ewell toward Rice's. At once he sent Crook and Merritt with their divisions to attack. The wagons never had a chance. Hundreds were captured and set ablaze, and with them he took sixteen pieces of artillery and several prisoners. But best of all, he now had two divisions astride the Confederate line of retreat, standing between Lee and Longstreet and the rest of their army.

532

Battles and Leaders of the Civil War

Major General Joseph B. Kershaw fought the remnant of his division to the last before being overwhelmed and captured.

Harper's New Monthly Magazine, April 1898

"Fighting Against Fate,"
Rufus Zogbaum's drawing of
Confederates vainly resisting
Grant's advance in the last
days of the war in Virginia.

When Anderson found what had happened in his front he tried to resume his march, only to discover Crook placed squarely across his path. As he halted, wondering what to do, a message came forward from Gordon saying that he was being attacked and urging that the advance continue. And now mistake followed hard upon mistake. Without orders, one of Anderson's brigades attacked Crook with some success but, since no one had ordered it, no arrangements had been made to send reinforcements to capitalize upon the initial advantage. The brigade fell back with the rest of the corps.

Meanwhile, to the rear, Ewell received news of what was happening in front and now took measures to save what remained of the wagon train behind him. The wagons were just then near a fork in the road. The lower fork, the one taken by the army, led on to Rice's. The upper fork paralleled the lower at a distance of about three miles. Ewell directed that the wagons take this upper fork to avoid the Yankee cavalry. It was a sound move. But just as no one had notified Mahone that Anderson was halting to let the wagons pass, now Ewell failed to send word to Gordon of the change in route. Since Gordon had been following these wagons for hours now, when they took the upper fork he naturally assumed that he was to follow. Thereby Anderson and Ewell effectively isolated themselves from any support for their front or rear. Lee and Longstreet could not reach them, and Gordon, who might have, was marching away from them.

Ewell and Anderson, leaders who had served competently in days gone by, stood bewildered, too tired to think clearly or to understand what had happened to them. For the moment, they debated whether to attack Crook and Merritt—now being joined by more divisions of Federal cavalry—and try to break out, or to move off to their right, to the north, in hope of striking the road that Gordon and the wagons were traveling. Ewell preferred the latter course, but could not make the decision, passing it to Anderson. That officer, too confused to see the wisdom of Ewell's choice, could think of nothing to do but to attack.

They were hardly in a good position for defense, much less offense. Both were on the south side of Little Sayler's Creek. To their front lay several hundred yards of timbered bottom land, on the other side of which ran another branch, Sayler's Creek. The ground was largely wooded, with clearings not more than two or three hundred yards wide spotted here and there. Behind them, north of Little Sayler's, a low ridge ran up past the Hillsman House and back to the fork in the road where Gordon had turned off. The Confederates had no artillery—it had all been sent ahead several miles for protection—and only about 7,000 men with whom to face Sheridan, whose troopers were well placed midway between the creeks.

Anderson directed the formation for the attack, but the men responded sluggishly, many only partially aware of what they were being asked to do. Meanwhile, Ewell began leading his command up the road to support Anderson when word came to him that Wright's VI Corps had come up behind him, where Gordon should have been, and was preparing to attack. They were facing the enemy now in front and rear.

Fighting back panic, Anderson sent Ewell around to hold off Wright while he attacked the cavalry in his front. But when he gave the order to advance, he found that his men acted "wholly broken down and disheartened." They made what he called a "feeble effort" and then broke up in confusion, falling back, surrendering, or simply dropping in exhaustion where they stood. One brigade, Brigadier General Henry Wise's, fought stubbornly, however, and managed to break its way out. Reaching the road on the other side of the enemy cavalry, they hurried on to join Lee at Rice's. Behind them lay men whose war would end before nightfall.

With the failure of his attack Anderson took position behind hasty breastworks and prepared to meet Sheridan's counterattack. Meanwhile, Ewell, facing Wright, had taken a position on the crest of a hill about 300 yards back from Little Sayler's Creek. He placed Custis Lee's little command on his left, and on Lee's right rear assigned Tucker's naval battalion. Kershaw's division of three brigades held the right of the line. They all faced across the creek, toward positions now occupied by two divisions of Wright's corps. Within a few minutes the Federals placed artillery near the Hillsman House and opened fire on the Confederates. In the bombardment that ensued, Ewell, lacking any artillery, could do nothing but crouch behind the crest of his hill and sit it out. As the cannonade went on, perhaps thinking that nothing was imminent on his front, the general rode back to Anderson's position. As he did so, Wright's divisions finally launched their assault, racing down their hill, splashing through the creek, and running on up the slope to the waiting Confederates. Confused though the gray line was, the men stood firm in their places. Tucker was shouting orders to his men in naval cant. "To the starboard, march," he cried. "Aye, aye," his web-footed "infantry" called back. Men were cut in two by the enemy's shells. One man, nearly severed by a shot, was thrown up in the air, his arms flailing and nearly slapping a comrade in the face as he flew past.

Brigadier General Henry Wise managed to lead his brigade out of the debacle at Sayler's Creek.

The last minutes of Ewell's command, surrendering at Sayler's Creek. Drawing by Alfred R. Waud.

Brigadier General Truman Seymour ensured the capture of Kershaw's division.

As the Federals closed to within yards, a strange silence was felt by many in the lines. They could see some of the Yankee officers holding white handkerchiefs, calling on them to surrender. Then a crushing volley from the gray line tore into the Federals and sent them reeling back. Lee's men and Tucker's battalion, not realizing that this was only a temporary repulse, leaped up and followed the Yankees to the creek, where the artillery fire began once more and cut them to pieces. "Quicker than I can tell it," wrote Confederate Major Robert Stiles, "the battle degenerated into a butchery and a confused melee of brutal personal conflicts." Bayonets and rifle butts crushed and pierced. Others who had lost their weapons used their teeth to bite noses and ears in the terrible scuffle. They were hopelessly outnumbered. Almost suddenly, the fight stopped for Lee and Tucker. Surrounded by much superior numbers, they surrendered or were captured in attempting to escape. "I was not sorry to end it thus, in red-hot battle," wrote Major Stiles.

Kershaw had kept better rein on his disciplined troops. He knew that when the first Federal advance was repulsed, another would come soon enough. And so it did. The right of Wright's line, the division of Brigadier General Truman Seymour, occupied itself with Lee and Tucker. Wright's left, Brigadier General Frank Wheaton's division—Wheaton was the son-in-law of the Confederacy's senior general, Samuel Cooper—faced Kershaw's front. Now to assist it, the cavalry brigade of Colonel Peter Stagg came up on Wheaton's left. As a result, in their advance the Federals faced Kershaw all along his front and overlapped his right flank.

Before Stagg came up, Wheaton advanced, and Kershaw fought like a tiger to hold him off. Word had come back from Anderson that he needed more time to break out, and Kershaw was determined to give it to him. As he frantically tried to hold off Wheaton, he suddenly saw Stagg's cavalry ride up and into his rear. In an instant Kershaw's right melted away in retreat, followed by the rest of his line. After futile attempts to bring some order out of this chaos, Kershaw allowed his men to try to save themselves as best they could. In minutes he and his entire command were surrounded and forced to surrender.

Kershaw did not then know that the remainder of Anderson's command, as well as Ewell, were prisoners by now, too. They never really recovered from the feeble attempt to attack, and a single advance by Sheridan's cavalrymen captured all but the brigade already escaped, and Anderson, Pickett, Bushrod Johnson, and a

Lieutenant General Richard H. Anderson, like Ewell, performed badly at Sayler's Creek, but managed to escape. Lee would barely speak to him.

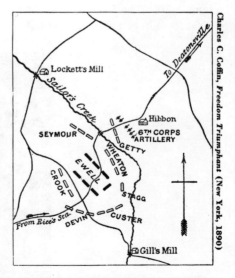

An elemental map of the fight at Sayler's Creek. The house shown as "Hibbon" is actually the Hillsman house.

535

handful of followers who managed to ride off toward Rice's Station. In all, nearly 6,000 Confederates and nine generals had been captured in the disaster along Sayler's Creek and Little Sayler's.

Meanwhile, to the north Humphreys' II Corps had come up to the rear of Gordon's corps and attacked him repeatedly. When Gordon himself tried to cross Sayler's Creek, the Federals hit again and cut off 1,700 men of his command before the rest got away. And up ahead at Rice's Station Ord's Army of the James was approaching while his cavalry, sent ahead earlier, threatened the Confederates' crossing points over the Appomattox at High Bridge and at Farmville a few miles away. Only spirited fighting preserved these structures for the retreating Army of Northern Virginia.

Lee, at Rice's Station, received little news of what was happening in his rear until word came that the wagon train had been captured. "Where is Ewell and where is Anderson?" he said to Mahone. "It is strange I cannot hear from them." He rode with Mahone's division back toward the scene of the fight until they topped a crest overlooking the battleground in the distance. "Here the scene beggars description," wrote Mahone. Lee, watching the debacle before him, straightened in his saddle, "looking more of the soldier if possible, then ever." Mahone heard him say, as if to himself, "My god has this army disolved?" At once Little Billy replied. "No Genl," he said, "here is a division ready to do its duty." "Yes Genl," said Lee, "there are some true men left." Lee asked him to keep "those people"—the Federals who had captured Ewell and the others—back. Mahone quickly went into line of battle, but by now dark was approaching and he knew the enemy would not press him.

Lee, meanwhile, was surrounded by the fleeing fugitives from Anderson's corps, and soon Anderson himself approached. Losing his equanimity for once, Lee refused even to look at Anderson, but only jerked his arm toward the rear disdainfully and told Anderson to take command of the stragglers and get them out of the way. Shortly afterwards Lee relieved Anderson, Pickett, and Johnson of command.

What to do now with only half an army left, and much of that disorganized, presented the greatest problem that Lee had yet faced since the evacuation of Petersburg. He had to get his command across the Appomattox above Farmville and burn the bridges behind him. Only then might he get some rest. He ordered Longstreet to proceed from Rice's on to Farmville to cross there, while Mahone and the remnants from the Sayler's Creek disaster would march north to High Bridge, where Gordon would be crossing that night.

536

Federal soldiers playfully gamble with Confederate bills captured in Mahone's personal baggage wagon.

Two views of the railroad span at High Bridge over the Appomattox, one taken from the east and the other from the west side of the river. Repairs to the burned portion are clearly evident.

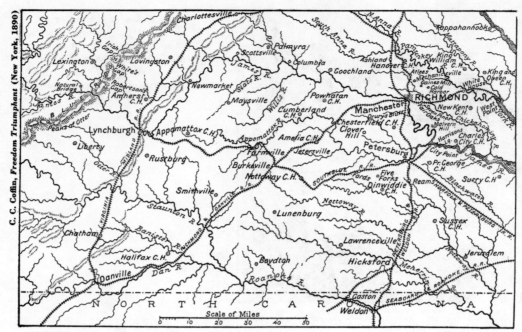

C. C. Coffin, Freedom Triumphant (New York, 1890)

For Longstreet the march was hard, but he made it to Farmville, crossing the river the next morning. And here, at last, his men found the rations St. John had promised, their first in five days. Gordon, meanwhile, crossed at High Bridge without difficulty, and Mahone followed. On the other side Mahone sought out Gordon, the slender, combative Georgian, and found him talking with Anderson. They were talking of surrender, and Mahone agreed with their views. It was decided that Anderson would approach Longstreet with the proposal, leaving it to Old Pete to take it up with Lee. Apparently, though, nothing was done. Mahone claimed that he left only after getting an assurance from Gordon that the latter would see to burning of the rail and wagon bridges at High Bridge before morning, a task which Gordon failed to do. The wagon bridge was left intact.

Dawn of April 7 brought a ray of hope for the Confederates as the rations were doled out to Longstreet's men. They began cooking their corn pone and what meat was to be had, only to learn that the Federals were crossing at High Bridge. Lee was furious—Mahone would always get the blame, though Gordon may deserve a share—and saw his hopes of gaining some time on the enemy dashed. Even before many of the regiments had received their longed-for rations, the rail cars had to be closed and sent off towards Lynchburg. Hopefully Lee could meet them somewhere down the line and finish feeding his men. For now, they started off once more. Longstreet marched north toward Cumberland Church, four miles away. Here Mahone and Gordon would rendezvous with him.

Before leaving Farmville, Lee closeted himself for discussions with Secretary of War Breckinridge, who himself led a narrow escape from Richmond and tried to bring a wagon train of supplies to Lee. When he emerged from the talk, Breckinridge sent President Davis a brief dispatch. "The situation," he said, "is not favorable."

At Cumberland Church a stiff rearguard action had to be fought against Humphreys while Lee turned west toward New Store, about ten miles distant. They would march on well into the morning of April 8 to reach it. Still Lee headed west, ever in the hope of reaching supplies from Lynchburg and of outrunning the enemy so that he might turn south toward Johnston, now near Smithfield, North Carolina.

It was not long after the Confederates left Farmville that Grant, accompanying Wright's corps, rode into the small but important railroad town. He sent Meade with Wright on north to join Humphreys in the pursuit of Lee, while ordering Major

Major General John Gibbon, Army of the James, helped Sheridan cut Lee's avenue of retreat and later served on the surrender commission.

538

General John Gibbon and Ord to move with Sheridan as he sought to outdistance Lee on the south. During the day Sheridan had learned that a trainload of rations was waiting for Lee at Appomattox Station, twenty-two miles west of Farmville, and now he meant to get them.

G rant, sitting on a porch in Farmville, reflected upon the military situation, and remarked to Gibbon, "I have a great mind to summon Lee to surrender." Taking pen and paper, he addressed a letter to the Confederate general:

Headquarters Armies of the United States
April 7, 1865—5 P.M.

General R. E. Lee,
    Commanding C.S. Army:
       General: The results of the last week must convince you of the hopelessness of further resistance on the part of the Army of Northern Virginia in this struggle. I feel that it is so, and regard it as my duty to shift from myself the responsibility of any further effusion of blood, by asking of you the surrender of that portion of the C.S. army known as the Army of Northern Virginia.
       Very respectfully, your obedient servant,

U. S. GRANT,
Lieutenant-General,
Commanding Armies of the United States.

At once Grant sent the letter off toward Lee by flag of truce, but it did not reach him until several hours later, when Lee and Longstreet were nearly ready to go to sleep as Mahone continued to hold at Cumberland Church. Lee read the note without any comment, then handed it to Longstreet. Old Pete's response was quick and to the point. "Not yet," he said emphatically. Lee agreed, but still there might be a chance in this overture from Grant to arrange for a peace on some basis short of surrender. Lee replied immediately. His situation was not so hopeless, he said, but he, too, wished to stop the bloodshed. What terms would Grant offer should he consider surrender?

Meanwhile, Lee's column moved steadily onward into the night. Since Longstreet's troops were still fairly fresh, he had them trade places with Gordon's much battered rear guard. And on they marched, past dawn, and on through the bright, warm sunshine of April 8. As on April 3 the presence of the enemy was little felt by the Confederates. They were allowed to march almost undisturbed. But still the knowledge of the ever-present enemy and the rumors in the command that notes

Major General George G. Meade, commanding the Army of the Potomac, operated largely under Grant's direction in pursuing Lee.

539

had been passed between Lee and Grant emboldened Lee's generals to make finally the entreaty that Gordon, Anderson, and Mahone had discussed two nights before. Major General William Pendleton, a man often mistaken for Lee himself, approached the general and suggested that it was time to capitulate. Lee would have none of it, and Pendleton went away considerably embarrassed.

By nightfall the advance under Gordon and Longstreet's rear guard had come to a halt about two miles from Appomattox Court House. Appomattox Station and the supplies that should be awaiting them there were only three miles beyond the little courthouse village. Word had come of Sheridan's advance toward that place, but as yet Lee had every reason to believe that he could reach the station first.

Appomattox Station, where Sheridan captured Lee's last long hoped-for supplies.

Now came another letter from Grant. His terms for surrender were simple. "Peace being my great desire," he said, his only condition was that the men surrendered take their parole and return to their homes, not to bear arms again until properly exchanged. Lee's response was that "I do not think the emergency has arisen to call for the surrender of this Army," but that, in a general way, he would be glad to discuss "the restoration of peace." What this implied was their coming to terms for all of the Confederate armies, in effect, the negotiation of a peace. This Grant was not empowered to do. Despite the fact that Lee had proposed that they meet between the picket lines on the following morning, Grant saw no choice but to decline the meeting.

Lee did not receive Grant's reply until the morning of April 9, but by that time something had happened to change his mind. About 9 p.m., April 8, he heard cannon off to the southwest. Not long afterward the dark skies in that direction turned a soft red on the horizon, reflecting the glow of thousands of campfires. Then reports came in. Sheridan had won the race. He stood squarely between the Confederates and Appomattox Station. Lee's last route of escape to North Carolina was closed, and behind him to the northeast Longstreet's rear guard faced two Federal infantry corps. He was trapped.

540

Major General George A. Custer.

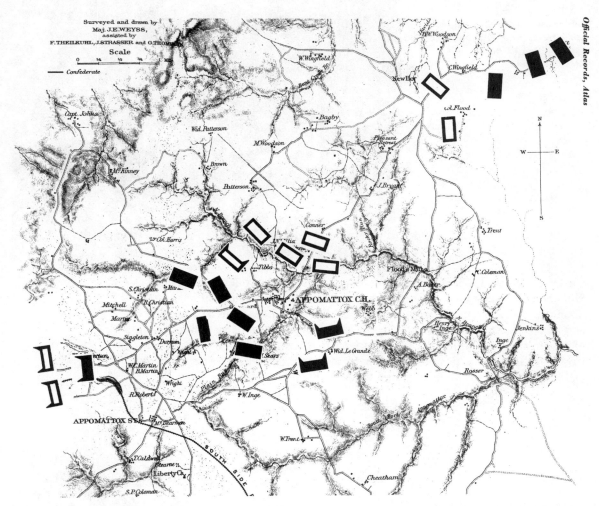

Official Records, Atlas

Surveyed and drawn by
Maj. J.E.WEYSS,
assisted by
F.THEILKUHL, J.STRASSER and G.THOMP...
Scale
0   ¼   ½   ¾   M...
——— Confederate

Sheridan had ridden hard that day, anxious to reach the Appomattox Station supplies before Lee did. And he knew something about those supplies that Lee did not. On April 4 Sheridan had captured one of Lee's couriers carrying orders for the supplies to be sent there from Lynchburg. Yet Sheridan himself directed that the message be carried through by one of his own scouts. He had far outdistanced his own supply trains, and could use those rations. He sent part of the division of brevet Major General George A. Custer around behind Appomattox Station to break up the track and prevent the trains from retreating, while the remainder of

A basic map showing the relative positions of Lee (hollow rectangles) and Grant (solid rectangles) at about 11 a.m., April 9. At the upper right Humphreys' corps is advancing against one division and scattered remnants led by Longstreet. Just above Appomattox Court House Gordon's corps and other remnants with W. H. F. Lee's cavalry division, face elements of Griffin's V Corps and Ord's Army of the James. Two of Sheridan's cavalry divisions close off any escape to the south, while another Federal horse division chases Fitzhugh Lee's fleeing cavalry toward the west. Obviously trapped, R. E. Lee has little choice but surrender.

The village of Appomattox Court House sketched at the time of the surrender. McLean's house stands at the right, the courthouse in the center.

Battles and Leaders of the Civil War

541

Lee confers with Gordon, Longstreet, and Fitzhugh Lee late April 8 to decide what must be done.

Custer's command rode into the depot and captured the supplies. Meanwhile, Sheridan also took much of the artillery which Lee had sent ahead of his army. Soon thereafter, the Confederate cavalry in advance of Lee's march came in sight and attacked, but Sheridan held. There was no sleep for him or his generals that night. He anxiously waited for Ord's infantry to arrive, and with it Griffin's V Corps. If they were in position with him by morning, Lee would be trapped, and "all knew that the rebellion would be ended on the morrow."

542

An unpublished photograph of Brigadier General William N. Pendleton, who looked much like Lee, and who dared to propose surrender.

An unpublished photograph of Major General Fitzhugh Lee, who commanded the cavalry of the Army of Northern Virginia and was reluctant to accept the verdict of war.

With the sound of those cannon at Appomattox Station, Lee knew it too. He called Fitzhugh Lee, Gordon, and Longstreet to him for what would be their last council of war. What should be done? Gordon and the younger Lee thought that the Federals had only cavalry at the station. If so, then they might attack and break through, out of the trap they were in between Sheridan on their front and Wright and Humphreys at their rear. But if Sheridan had infantry with him, then all was lost. Surrender would be the only alternative. It was agreed. Gordon and Lee would try the breakout, during the night if possible, by daylight for sure. Lee then retired to his tent and dressed himself yet again in his finest uniform. "I have probably to be General Grant's prisoner," he resignedly told Pendleton. "I must make my best appearance."

General Robert E. Lee astride his favorite mount, Traveller.

The attack was made shortly after 5 a.m., April 9, Palm Sunday. Gordon hit Sheridan first, who allowed himself to be pushed back slowly while Ord's infantry was taking position. When Gordon found that Ord was there and that Fitzhugh Lee's cavalry had been driven back on his right, he had no choice but to stop the attack. "I have fought my corps to a frazzle," he told the commanding general. Without support he could do nothing, but the only support was Longstreet, then engaged in holding back Meade and Humphreys. Hearing the report of Gordon's

543

Alfred R. Waud's drawing of the position of the Confederate army when the surrender was announced.

situation, Lee said sadly that, "then there is nothing left for me to do but to go and see General Grant, and I would rather die a thousand deaths." A little later, overwrought, Lee remarked that he was tempted to ride along his front line and expose himself to the enemy's bullets. "How easily I could be rid of this," he said. Then he regained control. "But it is our duty to live."

There was another conference with Longstreet and with Mahone as well. Both advised capitulation. "It is your duty to surrender," said Mahone. Longstreet would only say that "I agree with Mahone." By now it was 8:30 a.m., a clear, sunny, spring day. Lee mounted his horse Traveller. Accompanied by Marshall, Taylor, and Sergeant G. W. Tucker, he rode to the rear toward the meeting place he had proposed for the anticipated meeting with Grant at 10 o'clock. Strangely, he forgot to make any arrangements for a truce or temporary cease-fire in order to protect himself and Grant as they conferred.

At first the oversight seemed not to matter. Just as Lee reached the works of his rear guard, Lieutenant Colonel Charles Whittier rode up under a white flag and presented Lee with Grant's letter declining the proposed meeting. Now Lee had no choice but to ask for an interview to speak specifically of the surrender of his army. As he was writing, word came from Fitzhugh Lee that he had found a way out. Lee did not credit the report and ignored it, though in fact Fitzhugh Lee did break away with his cavalry.

An anxious three hours ensued. The sound of firing on Gordon's front reminded Lee that he had neglected to instruct his corps commanders to send out truce flags to halt the firing. The orders now went out. Then Whittier came back with a message from Humphreys saying that he had orders to attack Lee and could not find Grant to authorize a change in those orders. He had no choice but to advance. Lee was bitterly disappointed. He wanted no more lives lost, and now, as he read Humphreys' note, he tore it into tiny pieces and angrily stamped them into the ground. Soon the Federal line approached. Humphreys, wanting also to avert bloodshed, suggested that Longstreet withdraw slowly before him. Finally, with the Federals only 100 yards away, Lee mounted and rode back to safety to rejoin Longstreet. Then a note came from Meade agreeing to an hour's truce. Lee sent another copy of his last letter in the hope of its reaching Grant, and learned that Gordon had fallen back on Longstreet northeast of Appomattox Court House and that his army now was almost entirely surrounded. He was tired, fearful that Grant would exact humiliating terms. Longstreet, who had known Grant well in better days, assured Lee that such would not be the case. Lee lay down on a hastily made bed of blankets thrown over fence rails beneath an apple tree. For all the rest it afforded his tortured mind and heart, it might as well have been a bed of nails.

Custer receiving an improvised flag of truce at Appomattox. Sketch by Alfred R. Waud.

At a quarter past noon the reply from Grant finally came. He had only just received Lee's note sent by Whittier. He would meet Lee wherever he chose and was leaving immediately to come toward the front. The note came by Grant's aide Colonel Orville Babcock, and in company with him, Marshall, and Sergeant Tucker, Lee rode toward Appomattox Court House, between Sheridan's and Gordon's lines, the most likely place for the coming meeting. On the way he asked Colonel Marshall to go ahead of them to find a suitable place for the interview.

Into Appomattox Court House rode the bespectacled Marshall, accompanied by Tucker. It was a tiny hamlet, no more than a dozen houses, a store or two, and the courthouse of Appomattox County. A quiet village, untouched by war until now. "I rode forward and asked the first citizen I met to direct me to a house suitable for the purpose," wrote Marshall. As inscrutable chance would have it, the citizen that Marshall first met was Wilmer McLean.

Few stories of the war present more sad irony than that of this farmer-turned-businessman. At 47 too old to take arms at the war's outset, still McLean was an earnest, if not rabid, proponent of the Confederate cause. In 1861 he was living on a small plantation called "Yorkshire" near Manassas Junction, Virginia. There the peaceful life of the farmer was interrupted that summer by the first hostile movements of the same two armies that now were come to Appomattox. In June 1861 McLean helped General P. G. T. Beauregard inspect the area, and that same month a Confederate signal station was placed near the plantation home. In anticipation that there would be a battle soon, the Confederate army rented Yorkshire and its

The McLean house, with members of the family sitting on the porch, not long after the surrender.

The courthouse, left, and the McLean house at right appear much as they did in 1865 in this watercolor by George Frankenstein.

buildings to use as a hospital. The army occupied the buildings on July 17, McLean and his family already having departed for safer climes. The next day, at about noon, Beauregard was making his headquarters at McLean's house when a Federal battery 1,500 yards away came into sight and fired three shots. One plowed into the ground. Another struck a piece of farm machinery. The third tore into McLean's kitchen building. They were by all accounts the first hostile shots fired between the two major armies of the East.

Following the Battle of First Manassas, McLean returned to Yorkshire to work without compensation for the Confederate quartermaster. But slowly his support for the cause began fading into disillusionment. He saw inefficiency and incompetence in the Rebel supply system. While he was donating his time, being paid only for traveling expenses, he saw other businessmen gaining great profits from the war through speculation. Perhaps worst of all, he saw his beloved Yorkshire mistreated and abused by the soldiers. Eventually, McLean, too, began charging higher prices for the commodities he sold to the Confederates, hoping to recoup the losses suffered by his property. By March 1862 he would remain no longer.

Thereafter, McLean speculated with some success in the sugar market, traveling widely from Richmond to the Mississippi. By the fall of 1863, however, he was ready to find another home for his family. He found it at Appomattox, a quiet village in south central Virginia where, he said, he hoped he might never see another soldier. In fact, he bought a substantial dwelling there, the Charles Raine house, sometime in 1862, and the McLeans settled in. He did not take up farming again, though, for little land had come with the house. Instead, he continued his financial maneuvers in the sugar trade, probably working out of nearby Lynchburg. And here he was in April 1865, when fate once more brought the armies to his door.

McLean took Marshall to an empty brick house, unoccupied and unfurnished, but the Confederate complained, "Isn't there another place?" Giving in, McLean—remembering the ravages at Yorkshire—reluctantly took Marshall to his own home, just a few hundred feet from the courthouse. It was a comfortable house, well furnished, its lawn and outbuildings shaded by locust trees. Entering the house,

Wilmer McLean, who could not escape the warring armies.

547

Lieutenant General U. S. Grant beside his favorite warhorse, Cincinnati.

Marshall found the parlor on the left of the hallway to his liking and sent Tucker back to bring Lee and Babcock. When they arrived, Tucker took Traveller while the two officers joined Marshall inside. Lee walked to a small square-topped table and sat down beside it. Marshall and Babcock also took seats. For the next half hour, as they awaited the coming of Grant, the officers talked in what Marshall called "the most friendly and affable way." Exhausted, Lee may have dozed briefly. Then they heard hoofbeats on the road outside, followed by the pounding of Grant's boots upon McLean's porch.

Grant had awaked that morning with a terrible headache. One might have thought that the certain knowledge that Lee's days were almost done would have driven the pain from him, but it did not. At 4 a.m. Colonel Porter found the general pacing back and forth in the yard outside his quarters, his hands held to his head as if to pull out the pain. Coffee seemed to help some, and then he wrote to Lee, declining the proposed meeting and advising him that he could treat only with the surrender of the Army of Northern Virginia.

Riding to the front, Grant found Meade advancing against Longstreet with little difficulty. At once he decided to ride around the armies, to the south, to see how Sheridan was doing. After riding a few miles, he was approached by an officer bearing Lee's final request for an interview to discuss surrender. Grant's headache was still with him, "but the instant I saw the contents of the note," he wrote, "I was cured." He sent Babcock with his reply to Lee.

The ride to Appomattox Court House took Grant through Sheridan's lines and, just outside the village, he found Sheridan, Ord, and a number of other generals and staff officers. Sheridan was furious at the cease-fire. His were the instincts of a tiger. With the enemy mortally wounded, now was the time to pounce upon him for the glorious kill, not to talk terms. Grant would have none of it. "Is Lee over there," he asked, pointing to the village. "Yes," a disgruntled Sheridan replied, "he is in that brick house, waiting to surrender to you."

"Well, then," said Grant, "we'll go over."

Upon walking into the McLean parlor, Grant saw Lee arise. The two exchanged greetings, shook hands, and then Lee resumed his seat while Grant took a chair in the middle of the room and had a table moved over to him. Sheridan, Ord, and the others took seats or stood along the walls. Marshall stood beside Lee's chair.

"What General Lee's feelings were I do not know," Grant would recall, "but my own feelings, which had been quite jubilant on the receipt of his letter, were sad and depressed. I felt like anything rather than rejoicing at the downfall of a foe who had fought so long and valiantly, and had suffered so much." Grant, who had so often known humiliation in the years before the war, now felt embarrassed at the possible humiliation these proceedings might inflict upon Lee.

He hardly knew how to start. Reluctant to speak of the subject at hand, Grant mentioned that they had met once during the Mexican War, and that Grant remembered Lee well. Lee, too, recalled they had met. Glad to put off speaking of the surrender, Grant went on in this fashion for several minutes before Lee reminded him of why they were there. What were Grant's terms?

All he asked, said Grant, was that Lee lay down his arms and not pick them up again until and unless exchanged. All arms, ordnance, and supplies were to be surrendered. Lee assured Grant that he understood the terms as outlined, whereupon the Federal turned the conversation to other subjects once more, nearly as embarrassed by victory as Lee was by defeat.

Once again Lee brought them back to the subject. "Do I understand you to accept my terms?" asked Grant.

"I do," Lee replied, and then suggested that Grant write out the proposal formally in order that it might be put into effect. At once Grant took his order

This painting by Tom Lovell is considered the most accurate representation of the McLean house ceremony. From left to right: General Lee; Lieutenant Colonel Marshall; Major General Sheridan; Colonel Babcock; Lieutenant Colonel Porter; Major General Ord; General Grant; Major General Williams; Colonel Bowers; Colonel Parker; and Major General George A. Custer.

book from one of his staff, lit a cigar and puffed while trying to collect his thoughts, and then began to write with a pencil. Amid perfect silence, broken only by the scratching of the dull pencil across the rough paper, he spelled out the last of Lee's once magnificent army. Grant's mind moved faster than his fingers at the work, as he accidentally omitted words, hastily crossed out others, and wrote a verb in the wrong tense. When nearly finished, after providing for the surrender of the arms and artillery, he paused, glancing at Lee's beautiful Maryland sword. Once again he worried about humiliating this remarkably self-controlled man sitting before him. On he wrote: "This will not embrace the side arms of the officers, nor their private horses or baggage." Then a final sentence promising that the men would not be molested by the Federal Government so long as they observed their paroles, and Grant was done. He signed it "very respectfully."

Chair in which Grant sat.

Now it was Lee's turn to postpone the inevitable. Just as Grant had delayed by talking of other, better days, now, as he took the copy of the surrender terms, Lee performed a succession of studied, drawn-out motions. He set the order book carefully upon the marble-topped table beside him. From his vest pocket he withdrew his spectacles. From another pocket he took a handkerchief and wiped the lenses meticulously, perhaps seeing in every speck of dust on the glasses a moment more of life for his army before he agreed to its contract for death. He crossed his legs, deliberately placed his spectacles over his eyes, and picked up the book once more. He read as slowly as possible.

As he read, Lee, after asking Grant's permission, corrected one of Grant's errors, and then visibly showed his reaction when he read the part about the government not persecuting his men after the surrender. He had feared prison or even worse for them. "This will have a very happy effect on my army," he told Grant.

Table on which Grant wrote the Articles of Surrender.

Grant proposed that he have a copy made in ink for signing. Before this was done, though, Lee observed that in his army the artillerymen and cavalrymen owned their own horses. Might they take them with them? No, said Grant, the terms did not provide for that. Reading over the paper again, Lee said that "I see the terms do not allow it; that is clear."

Whether or not Lee meant his observation as a gentle hint he never said, but Grant read in it a wish that he was immediately prepared to fulfill. The Confederates would need their horses when they returned to their farms for the spring planting. He expected that this would be the last action of the war—he certainly hoped so—and he saw no reason why the men should not take their horses with them. He knew it would be a generous measure to start North and South on the long road to reconciliation. All those who claimed a horse would be allowed to take it. "This will have the best possible effect upon the men," Lee said with relief. "It will be very gratifying and will do much toward conciliating our people."

Table at which Lee sat.

Sometime either before or after the terms were discussed, Grant introduced Lee to the other officers in the room. Lee remarked that he had a number of Federal prisoners whom he could not feed and that, indeed, he could not feed his own troops. Grant asked if 25,000 rations would feed Lee's men. This would be ample, he replied, and Grant sent out immediate orders. Interestingly enough, many of the rations sent to Lee were from those same trains he had so desperately tried to reach at Appomattox Station.

Once the documents were completed, Grant signed the terms and gave them to Lee. Lee signed his letter of acceptance and gave it to Grant. The Army of Northern Virginia was officially surrendered.

Grant's mind was seemingly on other things. Still worried lest he embarrass Lee in the least, he now explained why he was dressed in a muddy field uniform and minus his sword. There had been no time to have his saber and dress uniform

Chair in which Lee sat.

Century Illustrated Monthly Magazine, October 1897

Century Illustrated Monthly Magazine, October 1897

This scene in McLean's parlor, by B. West Clinedinst, is somewhat inaccurately portrayed. Lee and Grant are placed more or less correctly, as is Marshall leaning against the mantel, but the Federal officers were actually either seated or standing along the wall, not hovering over Grant's shoulder.

Lieutenant Colonel Ely S. Parker, Seneca chief and Grant's military secretary, who transcribed the surrender terms for Lee's acceptance.

brought up from his baggage wagon some distance away. Lee understood. A little more conversation, more hand shaking, and sometime before 4 p.m. Lee and Marshall prepared to leave. The officers on the porch stood to attention when Lee stepped out. Deliberately he put on his hat, returned their salute, and then walked down into the yard, absent-mindedly smacking his gloved hands together several times. He seemed somewhere else at that moment, but quickly he returned to the present, called for his horse, and mounted. Just then Grant stepped out on the porch. Silently they raised their hats to each other. And then Lee rode back to tell his army that they were going home.

Harper's New Monthly Magazine, April 1898

Zogbaum's drawing of Lee, Marshall, and Sergeant Tucker riding away from the McLean house after the surrender negotiations were completed.

The ride back was agony for Lee. His soldiers had a fair idea of what had happened. "Are we surrendered?" they cried. "Blow, Gabriel, blow," shouted another, unwilling to outlive his army. They wept, they shouted. Officers drove their sabers into the ground and then broke the blades. Men bashed their rifles against trees. Proud, old banners that had gone through so many fights were torn to pieces that the men might have some memento to keep. Around Lee they gathered, uplifting their hands to touch him, to clasp his hands, to whisper or cry their assurances of devotion undimmed, their willingness to fight on to the death. Lee's eyes watered with tears, his iron self-control tested to the fullest to keep him from breaking down with the emotions he felt. When finally he dismounted with his staff, he could not stand still, but paced back and forth by himself. Later, when he rode back to his headquarters, it all happened again, and then he must stand in his tent and receive the throngs who came to make their farewells.

We, the undersigned Prisoners of War, belonging to the Army of Northern Virginia, having been this day surrendered by General Robert E. Lee, C. S. A., Commanding said Army, to Lieut. Genl. U. S. Grant, Commanding Armies of United States, do hereby give our solemn parole of honor that we will not hereafter serve in the armies of the Confederate States, or in any military capacity whatever, against the United States of America, or render aid to the enemies of the latter, until properly exchanged, in such manner as shall be mutually approved by the respective authorities.

Done at Appomattox Court
House, Va., this 9th day of
April, 1865.

The parole signed by Lee and his staff at Appomattox.

As for Grant, the depression he felt was almost as great as Lee's. As they watched the Confederate chieftain ride away from McLean's, one of Grant's staff members, Adam Badeau, commented that "this will live in history." Grant did not respond but only kept watching Lee. "I am sure the idea had not occurred to him until I uttered it," recalled Badeau. "The effect upon his fame, upon history, was not what he was considering." Then, in a final gesture to save the pride of his fallen foe, he sent members of his staff to the various commands to stop the firing of muskets and cannon which had begun when word of the surrender spread among the ranks. "The war is over," he told them. "The Rebels are our countrymen again."

As for poor Wilmer McLean, who had tried so desperately to escape the destruction of war at Manassas, the ravages of peace proved even worse. He was besieged by Federal officers wanting to buy this and that piece of furniture from the parlor. Ord bought one of the tables, Sheridan bought or took another. Men shoved money in McLean's hands despite his angry protestations that he was running no auction here. Soon his furnishings were simply looted, many of them broken into tiny bits as souvenirs. Even at Grant's headquarters, the officers bartered among themselves for mementoes of the surrender, while Grant himself sat down in his tent, surrounded by interested generals and staff who hoped to hear him tell the details of the meeting with Lee. Instead, as though nothing had happened, he began again to reminisce about the Mexican War.

Major General Edward O. C.
Ord and the marble top table
from the McLean house.

553

The working out of the actual details of the surrender was left to a commission to consist of three officers of each army. Lee appointed Longstreet, Gordon, and Pendleton; Grant sent Griffin, Merritt, and Gibbon, commanding the XXIV Corps of Ord's army. The next day, April 10, while Lee's men were enjoying the rations sent them by Grant the previous day, the commission met first in the Clover Hill Tavern, but found it cold and cheerless, and soon moved to the surrender room in McLean's house. As Longstreet came into the house to meet with the commission that morning, he passed a room that Grant was using as temporary headquarters. Grant looked up as Old Pete passed, "recognized me," said Longstreet, "rose, and with his old-time cheerful greeting gave me his hand." He also gave him a cigar.

While the commission deliberated over just which troops were included in the surrender—all those present? all within a twenty-mile radius? all those present when negotiations began on April 8? etc.—the officers of the two armies began to seek out old friends from before the war. Sheridan and two other generals asked Lee's permission to bring Wilcox, Longstreet, and Heth out to see Grant at his headquarters and asked Marshall to compose a farewell address to the army. Heth had served with him in Mexico. "We chatted for half an hour about old times, kissing the beautiful girls in the army, about Mexico," wrote Heth. They spoke not at all about the war which for them was ended, though the Confederates did express their gratitude for the generous surrender terms. Meanwhile, Meade went to Lee's headquarters to renew an old acquaintance. "What are you doing with all that gray in your beard?" asked Lee. Meade replied that "You have to answer for most of it!"

Appomattox Court House, taken during the Federal occupation that followed the surrender in the summer of 1865.

Clover Hill Tavern, where the surrender commission first met before going to the more comfortable McLean house. This building is now headquarters of the Appomattox Court House National Historical Park.

The Clover Hill Tavern as it appeared shortly after the war.

555

A rare, and imaginative, depiction of the surrender ceremonies made shortly afterward.

Now that the Army of Northern Virginia was surrendered, Grant and Lee did meet once more. Among other things they incidentally discussed the other armies of the Confederacy, but since the President and his fleeing government were still free, Lee did not feel that he could make any terms for Johnston and others without first consulting Davis. This ended the matter. Grant left for Washington that same day, unwilling to witness the final surrender ceremonies. Lee went back to his headquarters and asked Marshall to compose a farewell address to the army. Marshall, who usually acted as Lee's ghost writer when more than military prose was needed, presented him with a rough draft of General Order Number 9.

With their war done, Federal soldiers share their rations with starving Confederates. Drawing by Alfred R. Waud.

"The message of peace," Grant's hasty, belated telegram to Stanton.

Head-Quarters, *Appomattox C. H. Va,*

Apl. 9 1865, *4.30* o'clock, *P* M.

Hon. E. M. Stanton, Sec. of War Washington.
Gen Lee surrendered the Army
of Northern Va this afternoon on
terms proposed by myself. The
accompanying additional cor-
respondence will show the
conditions fully.

U. S. Grant
Lt. Gen.

By Command of

Following the meeting with Lee at Appomattox, and while riding back to his headquarters, Grant was reminded that he had forgotten to notify the War Department in Washington of Lee's surrender. Immediately he dismounted by the roadside and wrote out a hasty dispatch to the secretary of war. Drawing by Rufus Zogbaum.

557

As Lee read it, he found that Marshall had included a paragraph that showed his own bitterness, words not well calculated to heal the country's wounds. Lee struck it out. The rest was beautiful. "After four years of arduous service, marked by unsurpassed courage and fortitude, the Army of Northern Virginia has been compelled to yield to overwhelming numbers and resources." Lee had no choice, it said, but to surrender or else waste more of those lives that were more precious to him than his own. The terms were generous, and he prayed that "a Merciful God" would show them the same generosity in the days to come. "With an unceasing admiration of your constancy and devotion to your Country," it concluded, "and a grateful remembrance of your kind and generous consideration of myself, I bid you an affectionate farewell."

According to the agreement of the commissioners, that last farewell would take place on April 12. Actual paroling had begun two days before, but on this last day the Confederates were to go through the physical motions of surrender, stacking arms and turning over their flags. Brigadier General Joshua L. Chamberlain was given the honor of formally receiving the surrender. That morning he formed his command on either side of the Richmond-Lynchburg road, which led from the Confederate camps, across the North Branch of the Appomattox, and up a slope past the courthouse. "Great memories arose," he recalled, as they prepared to

The surrender of the Army of Northern Virginia at Appomattox, April 12, 1865. Painting by Ken Riley originally reproduced in *Life* magazine.

West Point Museum Collections

558

Brigadier General Joshua L. Chamberlain formally received the surrender.

receive "the last remnant of the arms and colors of that great army which ours had been created to confront for all that death can do for life."

The Confederates formed, too, silently, some sullenly. Lee would not take part in this, but stayed back in his tent. The other generals were here, though, Gordon's corps in the lead, followed by what remained of Anderson's men, then Heth's, and finally Longstreet's. Without drums or fifes they marched forward in the measured tread that had become a part of their souls. When they came in sight of the Federals, they presented a vision that made many gasp. With the ranks of most of the regiments thinned to the size of companies, the scores of battleflags that waved above them made it appear that "the whole column seemed crowned with red."

As Gordon approached, Chamberlain spoke to an aide and soon a bugle called the Federals to stiff attention, shifting them from "order arms" to "carry arms" as Gordon's men passed. It was, said Chamberlain, the marching salute. "Gordon at the head of the column, riding with heavy spirit and downcast face, catches the sound of shifting arms, looks up, and, taking the meaning, wheels superbly, making with himself and his horse one uplifted figure, with profound salutation as he drops the point of his sword to the boot toe; then facing to his own command, gives word for his successive brigades to pass us with the same position of the manual,—honor answering honor."

And so it went. Few eyes were dry on either side as the ragged yet proud Confederates passed, made their salutes, then dropped their rifles, bayonets, cartridge boxes, and flags in heaps beyond in a "triangle" formed just east of the courthouse by the main road and two private lanes. The sight woke "memories that bound us

W. L. Sheppard's drawing of a dejected Lee returning to his lines after surrendering to Grant.

together as no other bond. . . . What visions thronged as we looked into each other's eyes!" Finally they were all past, their actual number uncertain, but when all the stragglers had come in, and when all the wounded were found, 26,672 were paroled. In addition, Fitzhugh Lee and 1,559 cavalry finally surrendered in bits and pieces. But now no one thought of numbers, or of victory. "On our part," wrote Chamberlain of the ceremony, "not a sound of trumpet more, nor roll of drum; not a cheer, nor word nor whisper of vain-glorying, nor motion of man standing again at the order, but an awed stillness rather, and breath-holding, as if it were the passing of the dead!"

It was done. And now Lee and those who had followed him for so long must travel their separate roads to find what was left of the old life and make what they could of the new. Grant had generously given orders that the paroled soldiers should be allowed free passage on all government transportation in order to reach their homes. Many, accustomed to no other mode of travel but the march, walked.

Several days after the surrender, Colonel Robert McAllister, commanding a brigade in Humphreys' corps, was walking down the road between Burkeville and Farmville with a companion. They came upon a young paroled artilleryman resting under the shade of a tree. He had been captured by Sheridan the night before the surrender and took his parole with the rest. Now he joined McAllister, and as they walked he told the story of his and his army's last days. Barely 19, he showed a maturity brought by war, not by years. For a long time they walked and talked, the young man seeming reluctant to part with McAllister. He had known only the company and life of the soldier for years. Now, facing the uncertainties ahead, he clung to this last association with a man whose life and ways he understood, even if that man wore the blue. But finally he had to make his farewell and walk the road alone.

"Well, sir, where are you going?" McAllister had asked him.

"Home, sir," the boy replied.

"Home. . . ."

ABOVE: A view of the Peers house in 1865, from the road on which the Army of Northern Virginia made its last march. Watercolor by George Frankenstein.

LEFT: The Peers house in 1865, where the last Confederate shot was fired.

BELOW: The Peers house as it appears today. Lee's army marched up the road from beyond the tree at the left.

561

Lee, his son Custis at left, and his adjutant Lieutenant Colonel Walter Taylor, taken by Mathew Brady at Lee's home in Richmond shortly after the surrender.

Lee Parting With His Soldiers

By H. A. Ogden

(Ellis's History of the United States)

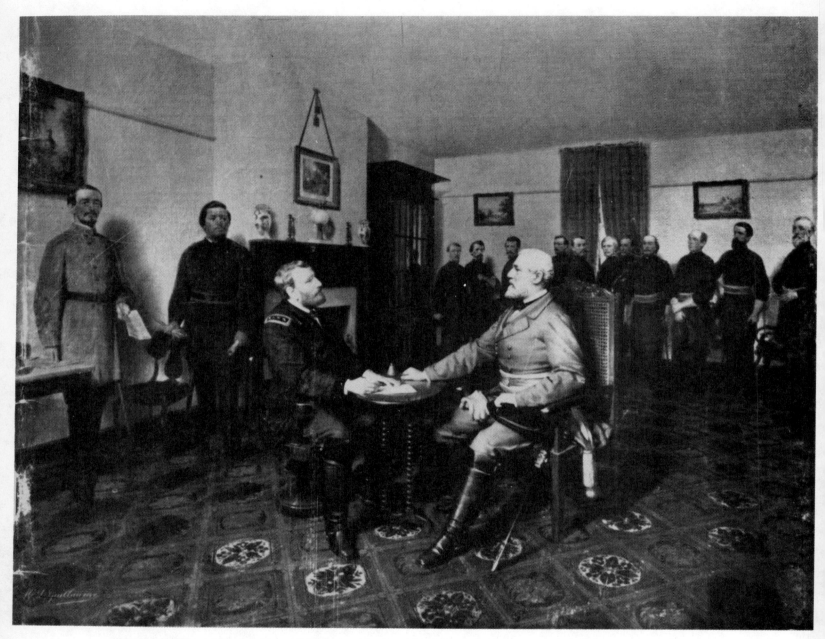

"The Surrender of Lee to Grant," by Louis Mathieu Guillaume (1816-1892). The painting is in error in placing Grant and Lee at the same table in the parlor of the McLean house; Lee sat at the table partially seen at the far left. Grant is shown wearing his officer's blouse; he was actually wearing a soldier's blouse with shoulder straps attached. Nor was the actual surrender witnessed by as many Federal officers as shown. Left to right are: Lieutenant Colonel Charles Marshall, aide-de-camp of General Lee, the only other Confederate officer present; Colonel Ely S. Parker, a full-blooded Seneca Indian and military secretary of General Grant. In the background the officers represented are believed to be: Lieutenant Colonels Adam Badeau, Theodore Bowers, Horace Porter, Orville E. Babcock; Major Generals Philip H. Sheridan and E.O.C. Ord; Brigadier General Frederick Tracy Dent; Major Generals Rufus Ingalls and Seth Williams; Brigadier General John Rawlins; and Major General John Barnard. This painting now hangs in the courthouse at

Appomattox Court House National Historical Park.

This 1867 representation of the surrender scene is highly inaccurate. It was designed and printed by Wilmer McLean in an attempt to recoup some of the financial damage that war, and peace, had done him. Interestingly, Lee refused to give McLean any assistance with it.

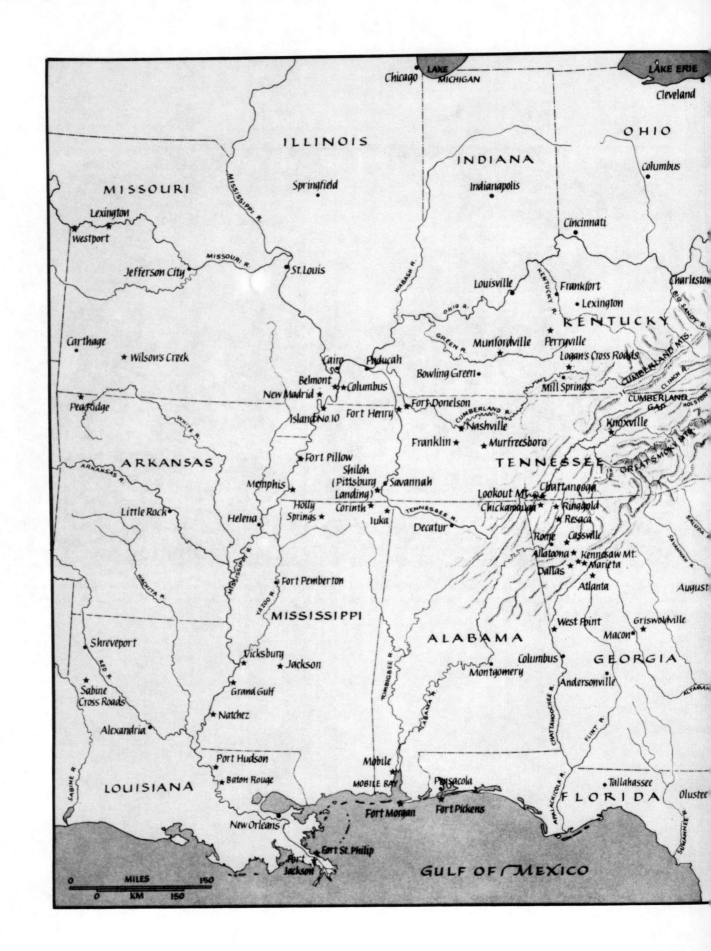

LAKE MICHIGAN
LAKE ERIE
Chicago
Cleveland

OHIO

ILLINOIS
INDIANA
Columbus

MISSOURI
Springfield
Indianapolis

Lexington
Cincinnati

Westport
Louisville
Frankfort
Charleston

Jefferson City
St. Louis
Lexington

KENTUCKY

Carthage
Munfordville
Perryville

Wilson's Creek
Cairo
Paducah
Logan's Cross Roads

Bowling Green
Mill Springs
CUMBERLAND MTS.

Belmont
Columbus
Fort Donelson
CUMBERLAND GAP

Pea Ridge
New Madrid
Fort Henry
Nashville
Knoxville

Island No. 10
Franklin
Murfreesboro

ARKANSAS
Fort Pillow
TENNESSEE
GREAT SMOKY MTS.

Shiloh
(Pittsburg
Landing)
Savannah

Memphis
Lookout Mt.
Chattanooga

Little Rock
Holly
Springs
Corinth
Chickamauga
Ringgold

Helena
Iuka
Resaca

Decatur
Rome
Cassville

Allatoona
Kennesaw Mt.

Dallas
Marietta

Fort Pemberton
Atlanta
Augusta

MISSISSIPPI
ALABAMA

West Point
Griswoldville

Shreveport
Columbus
Macon
GEORGIA

Vicksburg
Jackson
Montgomery
Andersonville

Grand Gulf

Sabine
Cross Roads
Natchez

Alexandria

Port Hudson

LOUISIANA
Baton Rouge
Mobile

MOBILE BAY
Pensacola
Tallahassee

FLORIDA
Olustee

Fort Morgan
Fort Pickens

New Orleans

Fort St. Philip

Fort
Jackson

GULF OF MEXICO

MILES
0
150

KM
0
150

566

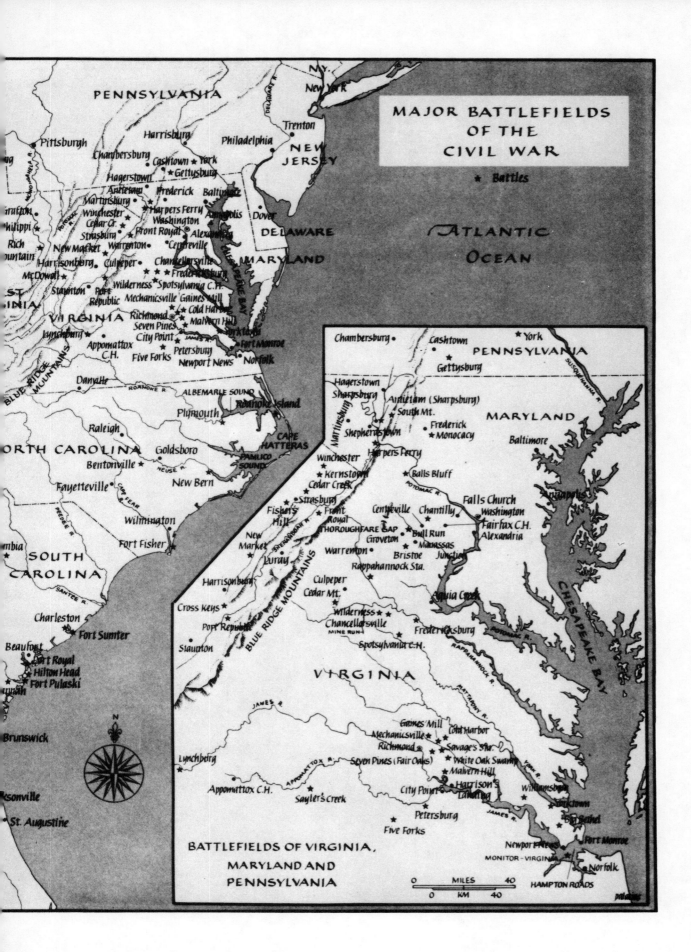

MAJOR BATTLEFIELDS
OF THE
CIVIL WAR

★ Battles

BATTLEFIELDS OF VIRGINIA,
MARYLAND AND
PENNSYLVANIA

567

A Chronology of the Great Battles of the Civil War

April 13, 1861: Battle of Fort Sumter

July 21, 1861: First Battle of Manassas (Bull Run)

April 6–7, 1861: Battle of Shiloh

February 13–16, 1862: Union siege of Fort Donelson

March 23–June 9, 1862: Stonewall Jackson's Shenandoah Campaign

August 29–30, 1862: Second Battle of Manassas (Bull Run)

September 17, 1862: Battle of Antietam

December 13, 1862: Battle of Fredericksburg

May 1–4, 1863: Battle of Chancellorsville

July 1–3, 1863: Battle of Gettysburg

November 2, 1862–July 4, 1863: Vicksburg Campaign

September 23–November 25, 1863: Confederate siege of Chattanooga

September 19–20, 1863: Battle of Chickamauga

May 5–6, 1864: The Wilderness Campaign

May 18–19, 1864: Battle of Spotsylvania

June 14, 1864–April 2, 1865: Petersburg Campaign

July 22, 1864: Battle of Atlanta

December 15–16, 1864: Battle of Nashville (Franklin and Nashville Campaign)

April 2–9, 1865: Appomattox Campaign

April 9, 1865: Lee's surrender at Appomattox

About the Authors

Albert Castel

Dr. Albert Castel, professor of history at Western Michigan University, Kalamazoo and author of this special issue, has to his credit three published works: *A Frontier State at War: Kansas, 1861-65* (1958), *William Clarke Quantrill: His Life and Times* (1962), and most recently *General Sterling Price and the Civil War in the West* (1968).

Joseph P. Cullen

Joseph P. Cullen, well known to "CWTI" readers through his brilliant texts for our specials on Chancellorsville and Petersburg, is a long-time student of the Virginia Campaign of 1864. For further reading on The Wilderness, he suggests: Edward Steere, *"The Wilderness Campaign"* (Harrisburg, Pa., 1960); Douglas S. Freeman, *"R. E. Lee"* (New York, 1934-35); Bruce Catton, *"Grant Takes Command"* (Boston, 1969); *U. S. Grant, "Memoirs"* (New York, 1885); *"Battles and Leaders,"* and the *"Official Records,"* Series I, Volume 36.

William C. Davis

William C. Davis, author of this special issue on Appomattox, is editor of CIVIL WAR TIMES *Illustrated* and the author of two books: *Breckinridge: Statesman, Soldier, Symbol* and *The Battle of New Market*. Among the many sources used in preparing this text which would provide good further reading, he suggests: Douglas S. Freeman, *Lee's Lieutenants* (New York, 1942-44), John B. Gordon, *Reminiscences* (New York, 1912), Joshua L. Chamberlain, *The Passing of the Armies* (New York, 1915), Burke Davis, *To Appomattox* (New York, 1959), Frank B. Cauble, *Biography of Wilmer McLean* (Washington, 1969), and Frank B. Cauble, *The Proceedings Connected with the Surrender of the Army of Northern Virginia, April 1865* (Washington, 1962).

Stanley F. Horn

Stanley F. Horn is a leading authority on the Confederate Army of Tennessee and the war in Tennessee. He is author of *"The Army of Tennessee,"* published by the University of Oklahoma Press, *"The Decisive Battle of Nashville,"* Louisiana State University Press, and other works on the Civil War. He is chairman of the Tennessee Civil War Centennial Commission and is a regular contributor to this magazine.

Dennis Kelly

Historian at Kennesaw Mountain National Battlefield, Georgia, Kelly is a regular contributor to *CWTI*. And he is certainly an authoritative source. A Philadelphia, Pennsylvania native, Kelly developed at an early age what might have seemed paradoxical to childhood friends—a keen affinity for Confederate military history. He later attended Temple University and earned a B.A. in history. While serving as a U.S. Army Paratrooper during the Dominican Republic Crisis (1964-67), he learned of soldiers' fear and the pervading sounds of battle. Kelly returned home to become a park technician at Manassas National Battlefield Park, and spent five years reliving Manassas history, one well-preserved in the artifacts, weaponry, and unchanging rolling terrain.

Edward J. Stackpole

Edward J. Stackpole, publisher of CIVIL WAR TIMES *Illustrated,* was the author of five books on the Civil War, one of which, *"They Met at Gettysburg,"* deals with the Gettysburg Campaign. A veteran of both World Wars, he was active in the Pennsylvania National Guard, which he headed as major general during its post-World War II reorganization. Elevated to lieutenant general on his retirement, he was active in publishing and allied fields in his native Harrisburg until his death in 1967.

Wiley Sword

Wiley Sword, a manufacturer's agent and lifetime student of the Civil War, is the author of this special issue. He is also the author of *Shiloh: Bloody April* (1974).

In preparing this issue, Mr. Sword consulted a large number of both primary and secondary sources. For further reading on Shiloh he recommends his own volume, James L. McDonough's *Shiloh: In Hell Before Night* (1977), and Otto Eisenchiml's *The Story of Shiloh* (1946).

Glenn Tucker

Glenn Tucker is a native of Indiana but long a resident of North Carolina. His articles have appeared frequently in the pages of this magazine. He has written a number of outstanding books about the Civil War, and on other phases of American history, particularly the early American Navy. He is looked on as one of the leading authorities on the Battle of Gettysburg.

He is a graduate of DePauw University and the Columbia University Graduate School of Journalism. He was correspondent for the old New York *World* at the White House during the late Wilson and the Harding and Coolidge administrations. He is the only three-time winner of the Mayflower Cup, awarded annually for the best nonfiction work by a North Carolina author, and the only two-time recipient of the Thomas Wolfe Memorial Award for "outstanding literary achievement" by a western North Carolinian.

His Civil War books are: *High Tide at Gettysburg; Lee and Longstreet at Gettysburg; Hancock the Superb; Chickamauga: Bloody Battle in the West; Front Rank; Zeb Vance: Champion of Personal Freedom.*

CIVIL WAR TIMES ILLUSTRATED has been the leading magazine in the nation covering the war between the states for the past twenty-five years. Once each year an entire issue has been devoted to a single major battle or campaign. These issues are now gathered for the first time in one volume in GREAT BATTLES OF THE CIVIL WAR. Some of the finest historians and writers of our time are represented in these pages.

Photo Credits

Sources of illustrations are listed on the side of the illustration. The following abbreviations are used:

BL: Battles and Leaders of the Civil War
HW: Harper's Weekly
FL: Frank Leslie's Illustrated Newspaper
KA: Kean Archives
LC: Library of Congress
NA: National Archives
S: The Soldier in Our Civil War